DATE DUE

FEB. 05.1999			
GAYLORD			PRINTED IN U.S.A.

AGING
AND
DEVELOPMENTAL
DISABILITIES

AGING
AND
DEVELOPMENTAL
DISABILITIES

Issues and Approaches

Edited by

MATTHEW P. JANICKI, PH.D.
*New York State Office of Mental Retardation
and Developmental Disabilities
Albany, New York
and*

HENRYK M. WISNIEWSKI, M.D., PH.D.
*New York State Office of Mental Retardation
and Developmental Disabilities
Institute for Basic Research
in Developmental Disabilities
Staten Island, New York*

·P A U L·H·
BROOKES
PUBLISHING C°

Baltimore • London

Paul H. Brookes Publishing Co.
Post Office Box 10624
Baltimore, MD 21204

Typeset by Brushwood Graphics, Baltimore, Maryland.
Manufactured in the United States of America by
The Maple Press Company, York, Pennsylvania.

Cover photograph by Pamela Parlapiano.

Library of Congress Cataloging in Publication Data
Main entry under title:

Aging and developmental disabilities.

Includes bibliographies and index.
1. Developmentally disabled aged—United States—Addresses, essays, lec-
tures. 2. Developmentally disabled aged—Government policy—United States—
Addresses, essays, lectures. 3. Mental health laws—United States—Addresses,
essays, lectures. 4. Developmentally disabled aged—Services for—United States
—Addresses, essays, lectures. 5. Aging—Addresses, essays, lectures.
6. Developmentally disabled aged—Care and treatment—United States—
Addresses, essays, lectures. I. Janicki, Matthew P., 1943–
II. Wisniewski, Henryk M., 1931–
[DNLM: 1. Aging. 2. Long Term Care—in old age. 3. Mental Retardation—in
old age. 4. Mental Retardation—rehabilitation. WM 308 A267]
HV3009.5.A35A35   1985   362.3′0880565   84-29304
ISBN 0-933716-46-X

Contents

Contributors

W. Ted Brown, M.D., Ph.D.
Chairman, Human Genetics Department
New York State Office of Mental Retardation and
    Developmental Disabilities
Institute for Basic Research in Developmental
    Disabilities
1050 Forest Hill Road
Staten Island, New York 10314

Robert H. Bruininks, Ph.D.
Department of Educational Psychology
University of Minnesota
Minneapolis, Minnesota 55455

Patricia M. Catapano, B.A.
Program Development Coordinator
Young Adult Institute and Workshop, Inc.
460 West 34th Street
New York, New York 10001

Nithiananda Chatterjie, Ph.D.
Head, Anticonvulsants Laboratory
Department of Neurochemistry
New York State Office of Mental Retardation and
    Developmental Disabilities
Institute for Basic Research in Developmental
    Disabilities
1050 Forest Hill Road
Staten Island, New York 10314

Mary Joan Delehanty, P.T., M.S.
Department of Physical Therapy
School of Allied Health Sciences
University of Vermont
Burlington, Vermont 05401

Rose Dobrof, D.S.W.
Brookdale Professor of Gerontology
and
Director, Brookdale Center on Aging
Hunter College of the City University of
    New York
425 E. 25th Street
New York, New York 10010

Jacob J. Feldman, Ph.D.
Associate Director for Analysis and
    Epidemiology
National Center for Health Statistics
3700 East-West Highway
Hyattsville, Maryland 20782

Eleanor R. Frenkel, M.S.
Jewish Community Council of Washington
    Heights-Inwood
121 Bennett Avenue
New York, New York 10033

Florence A. Hauber, Ph.D.
Department of Educational Psychology
University of Minnesota
Minneapolis, Minnesota 55455

Tamar Heller, Ph.D.
Coordinator of Applied Research and Evaluation
Institute for the Study of Developmental
    Disabilities
University of Illinois at Chicago
1640 West Roosevelt Road
Chicago, Illinois 60608

Stanley S. Herr, J.D., D.Phil.
University of Maryland
School of Law
510 West Baltimore Street
Baltimore, Maryland 21201

A. Lewis Hill, Ph.D.
Head, Clinical Psychology Division
Department of Clinical Psychology
New York State Office of Mental Retardation
    and Developmental Disabilities
Institute for Basic Research in Developmental
    Disabilities
1050 Forest Hill Road
Staten Island, New York 10314

Agnes M. Huber, Ph.D., R.D.
Professor of Nutrition
Simmons College
300 The Fenway
Boston, Massachusetts 02115

John W. Jacobson, M.S.
Associate Planner
New York State Office of Mental Retardation and
  Developmental Disabilities
44 Holland Avenue
Albany, New York 12229

Matthew P. Janicki, Ph.D.
Director of Research and Planning
New York State Office of Mental Retardation and
  Developmental Disabilities
44 Holland Avenue
Albany, New York 12229

Kent C. Jones, M.S.
Administrative Director
People, Inc./Services to the Developmentally
  Disabled Adult
320 Central Park Plaza
Buffalo, New York 14214

Dwight R. Kauppi, Ph.D.
Department of Counseling and Educational
  Psychology
State University of New York at Buffalo
Amherst, New York 14260

Barbara A. Kenefick, Ed.D.
New York State Office of Mental Retardation and
  Developmental Disabilities
44 Holland Avenue
Albany, New York 12229

Michele Kiely, M.P.H.
Research Scientist
Department of Epidemiology
New York State Office of Mental Retardation and
  Developmental Disabilities
Institute for Basic Research in Developmental
  Disabilities
1050 Forest Hill Road
Staten Island, New York 10314

Lewis A. Knox, Ph.D.
New York State Office of Mental Retardation and
  Developmental Disabilities
44 Holland Avenue
Albany, New York 12229

Joel M. Levy, CSW, FAAMD
Executive Director
Young Adult Institute and Workshop, Inc.
460 West 34th Street
New York, New York 10001

Philip H. Levy, Ph.D.
Associate Executive Director
Young Adult Institute and Workshop, Inc.
460 West 34th Street
New York, New York 10001

Leopold Lippman, Ph.D.
Developmental Disabilities Consultant
1162 East Laurelton Parkway
Teaneck, New Jersey 07666

David E. Loberg, Ph.D.
President
The Woods School
Langhorn, Pennsylvania 19047

Robert A. Lubin, Ph.D., M.P.H.
Chairman, Department of Epidemiology
New York State Office of Mental Retardation and
  Developmental Disabilities
Institute for Basic Research in Developmental
  Disabilities
1050 Forest Hill Road
Staten Island, New York 10314

Marsha Mailick Seltzer, Ph.D.
School of Social Work
Boston University
Boston, Massachusetts 02215

George S. Merz, Ph.D.
Head, Nerve Tissue Culture Laboratory
Department of Pathological Neurobiology
New York State Office of Mental Retardation and
  Developmental Disabilities
Institute for Basic Research in Developmental
  Disabilities
1050 Forest Hill Road
Staten Island, New York 10314

Robert Newcomer, Ph.D.
Aging Health Policy Center
University of California at San Francisco
San Francisco, California 94143

Evelyn S. Newman, M.L.S.
Ringel Institute of Gerontology
State University of New York at Albany
Albany, New York 12222

James P. Otis, Ph.D.
Director, Standards and Procedures Review Unit
New York State Office of Mental Retardation and
  Developmental Disabilities
44 Holland Avenue
Albany, New York 12229

Paul S. Puccio, M.P.A.
Director of Division of Policy Analysis and
  Planning
New York State Office of Mental Retardation and
  Developmental Disabilities
44 Holland Avenue
Albany, New York 12229

Judith H. Rettig, M.D.
Director of Health Services
New York State Office of Mental Retardation and
  Developmental Disabilities
44 Holland Avenue
Albany, New York 12229

Dorothy P. Rice, B.A., Sc.D.(Hon.)
Professor
Aging Health Policy Center/N-631
University of California at San Francisco
San Francisco, California 94143

Lisa L. Rotegard, M.A.
Department of Educational Psychology
University of Minnesota
Minneapolis, Minnesota 55455

Raul D. Rudelli, M.D., FCAP
Deputy Director
Consolidated Clinical Laboratories
New York State Office of Mental Retardation and
  Developmental Disabilities
Institute for Basic Research in Developmental
  Disabilities
1050 Forest Hill Road
Staten Island, New York 10314

Gary B. Seltzer, Ph.D.
Associate Professor
Human Behavior Sequence
School of Social Work
Boston University
Boston, Massachusetts 02215

Susan R. Sherman, Ph.D.
School of Social Welfare and
Ringel Institute of Gerontology
State University of New York at Albany
Albany, New York 12222

Robyn Stone, Ph.D.
Aging Health Policy Center
University of California at San Francisco
San Francisco, California 94143

Markley S. Sutton, Ph.D.
California Department of Developmental Services
Sonoma State Hospital and Developmental Center
Eldridge, California 95431

Julia Williams Robinson, A.I.A.
School of Architecture
University of Minnesota
Minneapolis, Minnesota 55455

Henryk M. Wisniewski, M.D., Ph.D.
Director
New York State Office of Mental Retardation and
  Developmental Disabilities
Institute for Basic Research in Developmental
  Disabilities
1050 Forest Hill Road
Staten Island, New York 10314

Krystyna Wisniewski, M.D., Ph.D.
Associate Director
Diagnostic Research Clinic
New York State Office of Mental Retardation and
  Developmental Disabilities
Institute for Basic Research in Developmental
  Disabilities
1050 Forest Hill Road
Staten Island, New York 10314

Wolf Wolfensberger, Ph.D.
Syracuse University
805 South Crouse Avenue
Syracuse, New York 13210

foreword

Thoughts on Aging among Persons with Disabilities

WHEN MENTAL RETARDATION was pushed into the limelight of public attention and governmental concern in the early 1950s by the strident protests emanating from the newly formed associations of parents and friends of mentally retarded children, there was hardly a mention of the problems to be faced as these children would grow into adulthood. As a matter of fact, a book that influenced many parents in those days was Pearl Buck's story of her own daughter published in 1950 under the title *The Child Who Never Grew* (Buck, 1950). Similarly, as enlightened an information source as the National Film Board of Canada issued in 1959 a well-received informational film on mental retardation entitled *Eternal Children*.

It was not until the 1960s that one can discern a growing awareness of the needs of adults with mental retardation, and much of this was due to the foresight of Mary Switzer, then Director of the United States Office of Vocational Rehabilitation, who recognized the need to be concerned with vocational training and work opportunities for that population. But the emphasis was on the adult and his or her training needs. Even in the first comprehensive text on the subject, *Focus on the Retarded Adult—Programs and Services* (Schulman, 1979), the words "aging" and "aged" are not to be found in the index. Yet, elderly persons with mental retardation did exist. Those living in the community were often protected from public view by their family, but anyone visiting mental retardation institutions could not help noticing the "old timers" who often enjoyed a somewhat privileged status and were free to roam the grounds.

One of them, Clint Tucker, gained a passing national prominence in 1972 as a plaintiff in a lawsuit charging the state of Tennessee with peonage. Clint Tucker, then 71, told the federal district court that for 22 years he rode the institution's garbage wagon 7 days a week, 12 hours a day, and later he worked a 40-hour week for 6 years, 3 years in the hospital, 2 years in the kitchen, 1 year in the laundry, and labored "on an assortment of other tasks over the years ranging from caring for poultry to cleaning buildings and working as a guard" (*Townsend v. Treadway*, 1973). At the time of the lawsuit, Clinton Tucker had just returned to the community where he was living with his wife, who had been a resident at Clover Bottom Hospital and School for 47 years and also was a plaintiff. But strangely, the fact that these two elderly, presumably mentally retarded people had married after their release from the institution and lived together at the Panorama Apartments in Nashville did not then attract further attention.

Today, in the mid-80s, there is not just an increasing awareness of the significance of aging in mental retardation and other developmental disabilities, but also increasing knowledge of how to deal with the needs of this population. This is demonstrated by the present volume, so ably edited by Matthew P. Janicki and Henryk M. Wisniewski. It encompasses a wide range of issues, from the epidemiological, sociological, and legal factors facing the administrator and policy-maker to the clinical and service approaches that will enable the practitioner to meet the needs of this new elderly clientele.

Taking into consideration the recent and long overdue program emphasis on early intervention, one might conclude that at long last the total lifespan of persons with mental retardation and other developmental disabilities has been explored and programmed. Unfortunately, this is not the case. An important omission, and one of particular significance to the subject matter of this book, is to be found in the lack of attention to the middle-aged lifespan, to the problems, needs, and desires of the 40- and 50-year-old group in this population. As a point of departure, one could think of Edgerton's work (Edgerton, Bollinger, & Herr, 1984) but it is limited by the fact that all members of his group were drawn from a sample of persons released from one large state institution. Still, their findings do not support the practice, encountered quite frequently, of setting the onset of aging for persons with mental retardation at 55 or even 50 years. Once the results of more planning and programming for this older middle-aged group are available, care providers will be in a better position to explore the process of their moving into that final life period that is dealt with in this present volume. Stanley Herr elaborates in his chapter (Chapter 5) on the right to dignified and age-appropriate programming. This goes against assigning 55-year-old men and women to an "aged" category, individual specific program needs to the contrary notwithstanding. However, to become a senior citizen at age 65 conveys a status (and privileges such as a senior citizen card that entitles the bearer to certain local benefits) that can have much meaning also for a person with a developmental disability.

Until now, the self-advocacy movement in this field has been largely carried by a younger group. As the policies and programs outlined in this volume will be put into practice, more and more will be heard from the elderly persons with developmental disabilities as they make known their feelings and desires, their likes and dislikes. Just as it was with the younger generation, the challenge will be: Are we ready to listen to what they are trying to communicate to us?

Gunnar Dybwad, Ph.D.
Professor Emeritus of Human Development
Florence Heller Graduate School
Brandeis University
Waltham, MA 02204

REFERENCES

Buck, P. (1950). *The child who never grew.* New York: The John Day Co.

Edgerton, R. B., Bollinger, M., & Herr, B. (1984). The cloak of competence: After two decades. *American Journal of Mental Deficiency, 88,* 345–351.

Schulman, E. D. (1979). *Focus on the retarded adult: Programs and services.* St. Louis: C. V. Mosby Co.

Townsend v. Treadway, Civil No. 6500, D. Tenn., 9-21-73.

Acknowledgments

The editors wish to acknowledge the contributions of Bruce Robinson, and in particular, Wanda Janicki, in aiding in the review and editing of the authors' contributions. Furthermore, the dedication and patience of all the contributors, many of whom agreed to write chapters because of a personal interest to explore this area, are especially appreciated. Lastly, the editors particularly wish to acknowledge the personal support offered by Paul Puccio, who provided the atmosphere for this book to be conceived and developed.

To Marc, Davin, and Bonnie
To Krystyna, Alex, and Thomas

AGING
AND
DEVELOPMENTAL
DISABILITIES

Some Comments on Growing Older and Being Developmentally Disabled

Matthew P. Janicki and Henryk M. Wisniewski

THAT MENTALLY RETARDED PERSONS age is neither a new phenomenon nor one unique to this population. However, two critical factors have converged to make the aging of mentally retarded and developmentally disabled people a growing concern. One factor is the shifting demographics of developed nations. The overall populations are "greying"; that is, the mean age of the population is increasing and large segments of these nations' populations are aging. The other factor is the result of progressive public policies that have over the past 20 years improved the quality of care for mentally retarded or otherwise developmentally disabled persons. These policies have resulted in improvements in rehabilitative and medical practices that have prolonged life and well-being among a significant segment of the disabled population. Coupled together—generations of disabled people who are growing older, and a population of older disabled persons who expect a greater life expectancy—these two factors have contributed to a recognition that society must plan and administer services to address the needs of the older developmentally disabled population.

This book is designed to offer workers in developmental disabilities and gerontology an opportunity to explore the significant issues that affect the lives of older mentally retarded

and developmentally disabled persons. Of obvious concern, as public policy begins to attend to the needs of this population, are ways to approach planning, administering, and delivering services for older developmentally disabled persons, and methods to obtain a better understanding of the aging process as it applies to individuals disabled throughout their lifespan. In designing this text we worked from the reality that little or no systematic material on the topic is readily available. When we began to explore what areas to include, we found that there were many questions, but few, if any, answers. Even now, we find that there are still many questions and few answers. The information we have assembled, however, should enable workers in gerontological developmental services to make more informed decisions.

We have organized the text into seven major sections, reflecting what we consider to be the major areas of concern related to aging among older mentally retarded and developmentally disabled persons. The first, "Issues in Aging and Disablement," addresses broad areas of public policy and the relationship between the elderly and the developmentally disabled populations. In the first chapter, Rice and Feldman offer a well-considered look at the future demographics of the population of the United States. The shifting demographics they observe obviously include a significant number of retarded and otherwise developmentally disabled persons. The trends presented suggest that the numbers of older developmentally disabled persons will increase over the next 50 years. Further, they offer a glimpse at future demands upon the health care and the long-term care systems. Their conclusions leave us with a sense of apprehension about what will happen if public administrators do not begin to plan for the future.

How our current public policies address the problems of elderly persons and what may have to be done in the future to address the needs of a shifting population are the focus of the following chapter by Stone and Newcomer. They examine the role of health care and public policy upon the nation's population and, in particular, upon the nation's dependent or chronically impaired population. The structure of developmental disabilities services must by nature be considered within the context of the nation's greater health services framework. The observations offered by the authors provide valuable insight into this framework. Lippman and Loberg place the developmentally disabled population in the context of current public policies and offer some questions reflecting the uncertainties prevalent in the field. They examine the circumstances of the development of specific legislation designed to address the needs of persons with developmental disabilities and comment on the structure and scope of the overall developmental disabilities system. Additionally, they raise some critical issues that vex the system and must be considered when attempting to address the needs of an aging developmental disabilities population.

The second section, "Philosophical and Legal Considerations," suggests how our ideological and legal bases can aid in structuring the services required by older mentally retarded and developmentally disabled persons, and how we can potentially respond to some of the inequities presented within our society. Wolfensberger offers some thoughts on how societal perceptions of deviancy and elder roles influence services and public commitment to services. The doubly devalued status of being

elderly and disabled has significant ramifications for older developmentally disabled persons. Wolfensberger offers some thoughts on practices to avoid in services as well as some fundamentals in service design that should be considered.

The legal status of persons with developmental disabilities has always been a concern. In the next chapter, Herr offers a commentary on the significant forces within the judicial process that have helped shape the current developmental disabilities system. Furthermore, he provides some observations on the legal aspects of care and protection of older persons who are mentally retarded that may clarify many of the concerns that arise in the course of providing for this population. Herr also offers comments on four of the legal issues that are of particular importance to developmentally disabled older persons: 1) the right to least restrictive residential programming, 2) the right to least restrictive day programming, 3) the right to nondiscriminatory access to generic services, and 4) the right of legal protection of interests.

The broad issues examined in the first two sections were selected in order to offer an overview of the critical concerns related to aging and persons with developmental disabilities. The field of developmental disabilities is relatively new, coming into its own with the recognition of a broader range of disabling conditions that affect normal growth and development among children and adolescents. Now with the original population of concern growing older, the developmental disabilities arena must be concerned with all aspects of lifespan development. This concern would include not only the transition from adolescence to adulthood but also the transition from adulthood to senescence. This phenomenon is not restricted to the United States; other western nations, as well, recognize the long-term effects of certain disabling conditions and have adopted public policies directed at prevention, amelioration, and rehabilitation. However, many significant issues remain unresolved. These include questions of population definition, program appropriateness and structure, and means of building a framework for services based upon research.

Section III, "The Older Developmentally Disabled Population," covers a broad range of information that aids us in better understanding the scope and structure of the population of older mentally retarded and developmentally disabled people. Lubin and Kiely note the factors that have contributed to the growth of this population; these include reductions in the incidence of birth defects, improvements in the capacity of health technology to reduce the risks of morbidity and mortality, and changes in societal practices. The epidemiological perspective presented by the authors offers a sound basis for understanding the parameters of the older mentally retarded and developmentally disabled population. The chapter by Jacobson, Sutton, and Janicki presents information regarding the demographics and characteristics of a population of older developmentally disabled people. Drawn from information available from the United States, England, and Australia, this chapter provides a valuable cross-cultural perspective of this population and its service environment. Using prevalence studies and service registry reports, the authors provide us with a valuable benchmark for estimating the scope of the older developmentally disabled population. Furthermore, the authors explore program utilization patterns and population characteristics.

To aid in planning for services to older mentally retarded and developmentally disabled people, Janicki, Knox, and Jacobson offer a perspective on the legislatively mandated planning requirements prevalent in the United States, and suggest a structure for approaching planning in a systemic manner. Social research of any significance in the area of aging and developmental disabilities is virtually nonexistent. Many of the specific questions raised by pioneers in this field remain unanswered. In her chapter, Seltzer examines the special methodological requirements particular to conducting research in this field and proposes a research agenda for the future that should serve to address many of these questions.

Lifespan development tells us much about how a person will behave as he or she ages. The fourth section, "Biological and Clinical Aspects of Aging," has seven chapters that approach aging from varying perspectives. First, Wisniewski and Merz present an overview of aging processes with particular emphasis on mental retardation. Aging can be seen as a complex process drawing from social experience, physiological processes, and behavioral change. The authors relate the specific aging experience influences of chronic mental handicap and the effects of Alzheimer's disease. Brown provides an overview of the current understanding of the genetic basis of the aging process. This is particularly important to our understanding of mental retardation and other developmental disabilities because many of these conditions have a strong genetic component. Alzheimer's disease, as a major source of impairment among the elderly, is now being expressed as a major public health issue. Its particular relationship to mental retardation and, in particular, to Down syndrome, is the topic addressed by Wisniewski and Hill. The authors present an overview of the clinical aspects of presenile dementia, and in particular Alzheimer's disease, and offer a suggested clinical assessment procedure. Next, Seltzer offers a review of the psychological aspects of aging as applied to the elderly in general and to retarded people in specific. He further explores grief reactions to death and dying related to retarded persons and provides some valuable insights into clinical approaches in working with this population.

The basis of aging is now being actively explored as a major basic research concern. In many ways, what happens to us as we age is programmed; our aging bodies react differently than they did when we were young. The remaining three chapters comprising this section begin to provide information on a number of aspects of aging as seen from a biological perspective. The process of aging within the musculoskeletal structure is the topic of the chapter by Rudelli, offering an understanding of the manner in which our body structures age. Since during aging, physiological changes occur in the body that affect nutrient requirements, it is of utmost importance for health and disease prevention to achieve optimum nutritional status. Huber offers a broad review of a range of nutritional issues and offers guidance to caregivers who have to plan and provide means for elderly persons. Finally, because aging produces changes in the body, and many elderly persons take prescription drugs, knowing the differential effects of medications upon the elderly is also critical. Chatterjie, in his review, offers valuable information on the medications in general use with elderly persons.

The area of service need and service provision has become a major concern to workers in gerontological developmental services. While there are both similarities and dissimilarities among nondisabled elders and older developmentally disabled persons, it is at the same time recognized that both groups require a range of health, social, psychological, and support services. How these service needs and approaches can be addressed is the focus of the next section, "Service Approaches." The chapter by Janicki, Otis, Puccio, Rettig, and Jacobson offers a general review of the major issues related to approaches to service delivery. These issues include the provision of adequate living arrangements, day services, health services, and support services. Day services, in particular, are the concern of Catapano, Levy, and Levy. One of the critical concerns of workers in this field is the transition from work to retirement. The authors explore a number of functional program models in the day services area and offer comments on the predominant means used for day programming. Aging has an effect on a number of factors generally related to activities of daily living, including vision, hearing, mobility, fine motor skills, and communication. Delehanty offers practical information, from an allied health professional's perspective, on some of these problems and presents some possible ways to address them.

Perhaps the most critical services area is the living arrangements domain; people must have somewhere to live. In many ways, where they live determines the type of services they re-

ceive. The chapters in the sixth section, "Residential Services," examine a number of factors related to the residential settings of older persons. Hauber, Rotegard, and Bruininks use the results of a national survey to offer a perspective on the types of residential settings that provide services to the nation's older developmentally disabled population. Furthermore, using these settings as a base, the authors provide an overview of the characteristics of the residents of these settings. Next, Kenefick offers an examination of a number of critical issues inherent in using congregate care settings as a residential option for older developmentally disabled persons. Her chapter also includes an overview of some of the models that have been used to provide housing to groups of older persons and defines the considerations faced by administrators and advocates. Certain models of residential care offer an environment that appears most conducive to life satisfaction and continued growth. Newman, Sherman, and Frenkel provide the results of their studies of one such environment—foster family care. They examine a number of factors related to this program model, including how it promotes the goal of community integration.

Movement among older people can be problematic. Heller examines the impact of residential relocation and movement upon older mentally retarded people and comments on the role of preparatory programs and social supports during periods of movement. The design of building spaces for older persons with developmental disabilities is the subject of the chapter by Robinson. Acknowledging that physical environments affect behavior on two levels, the symbolic and functional, the author examines the environments of a variety of settings used as housing for elderly developmentally disabled persons. She also offers information on ways to adapt housing to meet the needs of elderly disabled persons.

Section VII, "Roles and Perspectives," offers some commentary on service agency problems and general concerns related to serving older developmentally disabled persons. The chapter by Kauppi and Jones supports the concept that not only do populations undergo transition, but so do service agencies as their populations change. Dobrof offers some closing comments from the perspective of someone who has worked for many years in the field of aging. She examines a range of issues that demand continued thought and study. Clearly, what has been demonstrated is that we do not have unitary models of care for as diverse a population as are older, developmentally disabled persons. However, what all the authors have offered is a glimpse at the breadth of the needs of this elderly population as well as some service approaches. At this point, that may be sufficient to begin to shape both a responsive public policy and an effective service structure that is identified with gerontological developmental services.

section

I

ISSUES IN AGING AND DISABLEMENT

chapter

1

Living Longer in the United States
Demographic Changes and Health Needs of the Elderly

Dorothy P. Rice and Jacob J. Feldman

An in-depth study of the future demographics of the population of the United States shows that declining mortality and fertility rates have changed the age structure of the American population and resulted in a growing number of elderly persons. Declining mortality projections to the year 2040 for the five leading causes of death among the elderly are presented, followed by the resulting population projections that portray significant continued growth in the number and proportion of elderly persons. Current age-specific rates of activity limitation, utilization of, and expenditures for medical care services were applied to the projected populations to obtain estimates of the impact of the aging of the population on these factors. The assumptions used and the consequences of these demographic changes for our social and health institutions are discussed.

THE CHANGING AGE structure of the American population, with its growing number of elderly, has profound consequences for the nation's economic, social, and health institutions and services. Current discussions of the financing of Social Security and Medicare benefits for retired workers have highlighted the impact of the projected growth of the aged population. Statisticians, demographers, actuaries, epidemiologists, economists, physicians, biomedical researchers, geriatricians, policy makers, and others are heatedly debating the assumptions and concepts of morbidity and mortality, and various population projections are now available. We step into the arena with some trepidation, knowing full well that forecasting is open to immediate challenge, question, skepticism, and argument.

In this chapter, we focus on the demographic consequences of assumptions of declining mortality and slightly increasing fertility over the next 60 years and what these demographic changes may mean for the nation in terms of the health status, use of health services, and expenditures for health care. Although assumptions and projections may be questioned, the past trends are irrefutable. To grasp where we are heading, we must understand the historical

Copyright 1983 Milbank Memorial Fund and Massachusetts Institute of Technology. Reprinted from *Milbank Memorial Fund Quarterly*, Summer 1983, *61*(3), 362–396, by permission of MIT Press.

trends in morbidity, health status, and mortality, for it is the momentum of the recent past that will sweep us into the future.

Let us summarize the trends briefly:

Since 1960 the population aged 65 and over has grown more than twice as fast as the younger population. The elderly increased from 16.7 million in 1960 to 25.9 million in 1980—a 55% increase; for the population under age 65, the increase was only 24%. The elderly have also increased as a proportion of the population, from 9.1% in 1960 to 11.1% 20 years later. The number of the very elderly is growing even more rapidly. In the same time span, those aged 75 to 84 rose 65% while the 85 years and over group rose 174%.[1] Declining death rates from heart disease, cerebrovascular disease, influenza, and other causes of death contributed to the growth in the elderly population (National Center for Health Statistics, 1982a).

As more people live longer, chronic diseases, most commonly conditions of middle and old age, have emerged as major causes of death and disability. There are now many more persons suffering from conditions that are managed or controlled rather than cured. These conditions cause afflictions for decades, impairing ability to function and requiring much medical care. Because these conditions are often of long duration, they create burdens for the individual and for society. Approximately 32 million persons, 15% of the noninstitutionalized population, reported limitations of activity due to chronic diseases in 1979 (National Center for Health Statistics, 1981a). The number suffering limitation of activity increases with age, rising from 7.3% of the total under 45 years to 24.1% at ages 45 to 64 years, and 46% at age 65 and over.

Only a small proportion—5%—of the elderly

are in nursing homes, but 22% of the very old (85 years and over) are in nursing homes (National Center for Health Statistics, 1981b). As expected, nursing home residents are older and more dependent than the noninstitutional elderly. Nursing home residents' median age, in 1977, was 81 years, and 35% were 85 years and older. In general, elderly residents of nursing homes suffer from multiple chronic conditions and functional impairments. Almost one-third (32%) are senile, 35% have heart trouble, and 15% have diabetes. Orthopedic problems due to a variety of disease conditions are common; 37% are bedfast or chairfast and 26% are incontinent.

Medical care utilization patterns among the elderly reflect their poorer health status. They visit physicians, and use hospital and nursing homes considerably more frequently than the younger population, and the use rates rise significantly for the very old (Kovar, 1977). In 1981 the elderly comprised 11% of the noninstitutionalized population and consumed 29.8% of the hospital short-stay days of care (National Center for Health Statistics, 1982b).

Although the elderly comprised 10.9% of the population in 1978, 29.4% of the health care dollar was spent for their care. Persons aged 65 and over spent $2,026 per capita for health care—7 times the $286 per capita spending for persons under age 19, and 2½ times the $764 per capita expenditure for persons aged 19 to 64 (Fisher, 1980).

The aging of the population is a worldwide phenomenon among industrialized nations and the age structure of the population is a consequence of the demographic history of the country. In 1980, for example, 6.4% of East Germany's population was aged 75 and over due to its wartime losses, postwar population shifts, and low birthrates in sub-

---

[1]The 1980 population estimates used in this paper were prepared by the Social Security Administration (SSA) prior to the availability of the Bureau of the Census official 1980 counts. The SSA estimates are employed throughout this paper because they are the basis for the projections for the subsequent 60-year period. The official April 1, 1980, census count for the population aged 85 and over was 2,240,067. The July 1, 1980, census projection was approximately 2,265,000 or 12% lower than the SSA estimate. The increase in the population aged 85 and over between 1960 and 1980 according to the census estimate was about 140%. Because of differences in coverage, the official 1980 census percent of the population aged 65 and over was 11.3 rather than the 11.1 presented here.

sequent years; the proportion is estimated to decline to 5.8 by the year 2000 (Table 1). By comparison, 4.4% of the United States population was in this older age group in 1980 and the United Nations estimates an increase to 5.5% in 2000, a significantly lower proportion than projected in this chapter. The United Nations projection assumes that mortality rates in the older age groups will decline extremely slowly during the next two decades.

PROJECTIONS ASSUMPTIONS

Many other facts and figures could be presented that depict details relating to past trends of an aging population. How realistic is it to make projections based on past trends? One cannot be certain whether the momentum of the past will continue. Will death rates from diseases of the heart continue to decline? Will those for malignant neoplasms continue to increase for the next two decades? Will the onset of chronic illness be delayed as a result of changes in life-style, as has been suggested by

Table 1. Percentage of population age 75 and over, selected countries, 1980 and 2000

Country	1980	2000
Israel	2.5	3.1
Yugoslavia	3.0	4.1
Japan	3.0	5.0
Canada	3.1	4.0
Australia	3.2	4.3
Poland	3.3	4.2
Spain	3.9	5.5
Netherlands	4.4	5.7
United States	4.4[a]	5.5[a]
Italy	4.8	6.8
Switzerland	5.2	6.6
Federal Republic of Germany (West Germany)	5.5	6.0
United Kingdom	5.5	6.7
France	5.6	5.9
Sweden	6.2	8.0
German Democratic Republic (East Germany)	6.4	5.8

[a]The figures representing the older age groups in the United States in the most recent U.N. projections were in error. The 1980 U..S. Census figure appears in the present table for 1980 and an earlier U.N. projection is given for 2000. The projection for the U.S. appeared in United Nations, *World Population and its Age-Sex Composition by Country, 1950–2000* [U.N. Pub. ESA/P/WP.65] (New York, 1980).

Source: United Nations, *Demographic Indicators of Countries: Estimates and Projections as Assessed in 1980.* U.N. Pub. ST/ESA/SER.A/82. (New York, 1982).

Fries (1980)? Will new technologies and therapies reduce or increase medical care utilization by the aged? There is currently widespread disagreement regarding these issues among our foremost authorities.

We define in this section a future course of events derived from what we consider to be a heuristically useful set of assumptions. We are presenting projections, not forecasts, that will reveal the implications for the health care system of the continuation of recent trends in fertility, mortality, and morbidity.

By 1978 the accelerated downturn in the previous decade in the death rates from cardiovascular diseases were impressive and we made population projections based on the assumption that the rapid reductions in mortality from 1968 to 1978 across the age range would continue for 25 more years (Rice, 1978, 1979). More recently, the Social Security Administration (SSA) recognized the downturn by building into their population projections the assumption that mortality among the elderly would continue for the immediate future to decline at a relatively rapid rate. The SSA actuaries covered a range of alternative assumptions regarding the future course of fertility, mortality, and net immigration rates by publishing three sets of projections to the year 2080 (Faber & Wilkin, 1981). For our projections of health status, utilization, and expenditures, we are employing the intermediate set of projections that were based on the following assumptions:

Fertility Rates (Births per woman): The 1980 rate of 1.845 would rise to 2.100 by 2005, remaining at that rate annually thereafter.

Mortality Rates: Between 1980 and 2005 for each cause of death group, the rates of decline that characterized the 1968 to 1978 period would gradually be transformed into ultimate conservative annual rates of decline during the period 2005 to 2080.

Net Immigration (Excess of immigration over emigration): A constant annual rate of 400,000 persons would occur.

The Bureau of the Census also published three sets of projections to the year 2050 (Bureau of the Census, 1982) that are consistent with those prepared earlier by the SSA, except that the latter projections include certain small population groups not covered by the Bureau of the Census, including residents of Puerto Rico, the Virgin Islands, Guam, American Samoa, and federal civilian employees and their dependents overseas.

The accuracy of population projections, regardless of their source, may be questioned. In part, they reflect different beliefs about the future course of mortality, fertility, and net immigration. Stoto (1983) recently evaluated past population projections of the Bureau of the Census and the United Nations by taking into account the length of the projection period and the size of the projected population. He concluded that there is a very large confidence interval associated with the projections made in the past by the Bureau of the Census. In spite of these inherent inaccuracies of population projections, they are key elements in planning and policy studies. The SSA projections are used in this chapter to highlight the future impact of the aging of the population on health status, utilization, and expenditures. The precise numbers are less important than the need to recognize the problems facing the nation resulting from the aging population in the future.

MORTALITY PROJECTIONS

The improvements in mortality by cause of death postulated for the 2005 to 2080 period by the SSA actuaries were established by considering a variety of factors including:

Advances in research and the knowledge base regarding disease etiology
The development and application of new diagnostic and surgical techniques
The presence of environmental pollutants
The incidence of violence
Continued improvements in life-style such as exercise, improved nutrition, cessation of cigarette smoking, reduction of drug and alcohol abuse, as people assume increased responsibility for their own health

Employing the above assumptions and methods, the death rates projected by the SSA for the elderly populations in 5-year age groups to the year 2040 are shown in Table 2. The trend is downward for both men and women in these age groups. However, the rates for all causes are significantly higher for males than females and the downward trend is postulated to be somewhat slower for males. For example, in the 75–79 age group, the male death rates in 1968 for all causes was 57% higher than those for females. By 2040, death rates for males are projected to decline 34% compared with a 46% decline for females in this age group. Thus, by 2040 mortality rates for men are almost double those for women.

The greatest reductions from 1968 to 2040 in mortality rates in the age group 75–79 are for vascular diseases—69% for males and 74% for females. Mortality from diseases of the heart and from accidents, suicides, and homicides also is projected to decline significantly, by approximately one-half for men and three-fifths for women from both causes of death. Malignant neoplasm death rates, by contrast, are projected to rise about one-third for men and one-tenth for women in this age group. Smaller increases are projected for mortality from respiratory diseases—13% for men and 2% for women. Projected mortality rates for the other elderly age groups show similar trends.

POPULATION PROJECTIONS

What is the effect of declining mortality rates for vascular and heart diseases and accidents on the age structure of the population? The aging of the United States population is illustrated in Figure 1, which shows the population pyramids—the distribution of the population by 5-year age groups and by sex—in the 60 years ahead.

In 1980 the population totaled 233 million people—114 million men and 119 million women.[2] The postwar baby boom of the 1950s creates a bulge at ages 20 to 29, with the lower

---

[2]The official Bureau of the Census figure for April 1, 1980, is 226.5 million people. The SSA figure includes Puerto Rico and the outlying areas, an undercount adjustment, and a number of other adjustments. Throughout this chapter, we have presented the SSA estimates rather than the official census counts. This has been done for the sake of consistency with the projections.

Table 2. Number of deaths per 100,000 population by 5-year age group for selected causes by sex: United States, 1968–2040

Cause of death and age[a]	Males			Females		
	1968	2000	2040	1968	2000	2040
All causes						
65–69 years of age	4,224.8	2,706.1	2,368.0	2,145.5	1,367.6	1,184.3
70–74 years of age	6,128.2	4,202.4	3,664.8	3,327.3	2,115.8	1,810.1
75–79 years of age	8,836.2	6,738.2	5,856.2	5,610.8	3,571.0	3,013.5
80–84 years of age	12,755.8	9,465.0	8,209.1	9,278.7	5,388.3	4,483.8
85 years and over	21,732.0	12,997.3	11,190.0	18,425.0	8,691.9	7,142.4
Diseases of the heart						
65–69 years of age	1,883.0	941.5	738.0	870.6	369.5	289.6
70–74 years of age	2,747.8	1,488.7	1,166.9	1,467.5	679.2	532.3
75–79 years of age	4,000.1	2,443.9	1,915.9	2,583.4	1,333.5	1,045.0
80–84 years of age	5,854.8	3,542.8	2,777.3	4,396.1	2,255.3	1,767.5
85 years and over	10,078.0	5,256.6	4,120.5	8,850.1	4,105.7	3,217.6
Malignant neoplasms						
65–69 years of age	875.7	1,042.8	965.1	495.0	596.6	530.4
70–74 years of age	1,158.5	1,518.3	1,405.4	623.3	763.5	678.9
75–79 years of age	1,436.1	2,132.3	1,973.8	813.4	996.0	885.5
80–84 years of age	1,674.9	2,557.0	2,367.0	963.6	1,119.1	994.7
85 years and over	1,936.1	2,557.2	2,367.3	1,223.6	1,049.7	931.6
Vascular diseases						
65–69 years of age	533.7	180.4	130.4	341.9	103.8	75.1
70–74 years of age	948.8	348.1	251.6	630.1	208.2	150.5
75–79 years of age	1,622.7	692.3	500.5	1,250.2	444.0	320.9
80–84 years of age	2,752.5	1,095.3	791.9	2,388.1	849.1	613.7
85 years and over	5,443.9	1,770.3	1,279.8	5,261.5	1,649.4	1,192.2
Accidents, suicides, and homicides						
65–69 years of age	163.1	74.6	74.3	63.0	28.7	29.8
70–74 years of age	186.1	90.1	89.8	80.3	34.5	35.7
75–79 years of age	248.9	131.0	130.6	134.1	49.8	51.7
80–84 years of age	352.7	172.2	171.6	228.1	70.1	73.7
85 years and over	599.8	250.1	249.3	513.1	106.0	110.0
Respiratory diseases						
65–69 years of age	319.2	202.1	218.2	89.7	86.5	93.5
70–74 years of age	495.7	384.9	415.9	135.6	141.7	153.2
75–79 years of age	716.4	750.3	811.4	250.7	236.0	255.1
80–84 years of age	993.1	1,236.1	1,341.6	478.5	345.9	373.7
85 years and over	1,823.2	1,903.2	2,066.4	1,210.6	629.6	679.9

[a]The cause of death codes based on the International Classification of Diseases, 8th revision, follow: diseases of the heart (390–398, 402, 404, 410–429); malignant neoplasms (140–209); vascular diseases (400–401, 403, 430–458, 582–584); accidents, suicide, and homicide (E800–E989); diseases of the respiratory system (460–519).

Source: Social Security Administration, Office of the Actuary. Unpublished.

birthrates of the late 1960s and 1970s reflected in the narrow base. Persons aged 65 and over totaled 25.9 million and comprised 11.1% of the population in 1980 (Table 3). Forty years earlier, the elderly numbered about 9 million, over 6.8% of the total population. The aged population grew rapidly because of high birthrates during the early part of the twentieth century in combination with the long-term decline in mortality rates.

By the year 2000 the pyramid is quite distorted. A total of 274 million persons is projected—134 million men and 140 million women. The aged total 36.3 million and comprise 13.2% of the total population, and elderly women far outnumber the men—21.8 million women and 14.4 million men. The birth cohort of the 1990s is estimated at the replacement-level fertility rate—2.1 children for each woman.

The pyramid for the year 2020 is almost rectangular through age 69. The children born during the post–World War II era are now aged 60 to 69 and the elderly population constitutes 17.2% of the total. The birth cohort of the

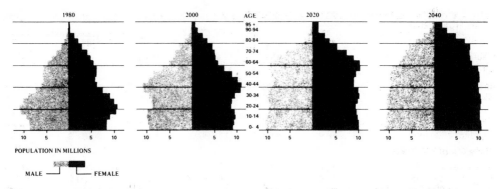

Figure 1.   Age structure of the U.S. population, population in millions. (*Source:* Social Security Administration.)

1950s is so large that the elderly will increase substantially between 2010 and 2020 regardless of whether fertility remains at its current low levels of 1.8 children per woman or takes an unexpected turn upward.

The pyramid for the year 2040 is almost rectangular rather than pyramidal. A child born in 1975 will be aged 65 in the year 2040. Of the 39 million children born between 1950 and 1960, 15 million are estimated to reach ages 80 to 89 in the year 2040. The aged population is at its peak at 67.3 million persons, or 20.5% of the total population. Aged women far outnumber the men—39.9 million women compared with 27.3 million men.

The projected changing age structure of the population is vividly seen in Figure 2. Between 1980 and 2040 the population as a whole is

Table 3.   Projected number of persons by age and sex: United States, 1960–2040[a]

Age and sex	1960	1980	2000	2020	2040
Total					
All ages	183,216	232,669	273,949	306,931	328,503
Under 20 years of age	70,828	74,045	77,001	80,376	84,234
20–44 years of age	59,216	87,145	98,261	97,345	102,160
45–64 years of age	36,466	45,587	62,435	76,557	74,853
65 years and over	16,706	25,892	36,252	52,653	67,256
65–74 years	11,094	15,627	18,334	30,093	29,425
75–84 years	4,671	7,688	12,496	14,909	24,565
85 and over	941	2,577	5,422	7,651	13,266
Male					
All ages	90,513	114,069	133,798	149,538	158,833
Under 20 years of age	35,957	37,807	39,334	41,067	43,045
20–44 years of age	29,126	43,754	49,424	49,063	51,513
45–64 years of age	17,852	22,086	30,592	37,616	36,935
65 years and over	7,578	10,422	14,448	21,792	27,340
65–74 years	5,168	6,819	8,250	13,779	13,559
75–84 years	2,043	2,838	4,741	5,907	9,895
85 and over	367	765	1,457	2,106	3,886
Female					
All ages	92,703	118,600	140,151	157,393	169,670
Under 20 years of age	34,871	36,238	37,667	39,309	41,189
20–44 years of age	30,090	43,391	48,837	48,282	50,647
45–64 years of age	18,614	23,501	31,843	38,941	37,918
65 years and over	9,128	15,470	21,804	30,861	39,916
65–74 years	5,926	8,808	10,084	16,314	15,866
75–84 years	2,628	4,850	7,755	9,002	14,670
85 and over	574	1,812	3,965	5,545	9,380

[a]Figures denote thousands.

Source: Social Security Administration, Office of the Actuary. *Actuarial Study No. 85,* July 1981.

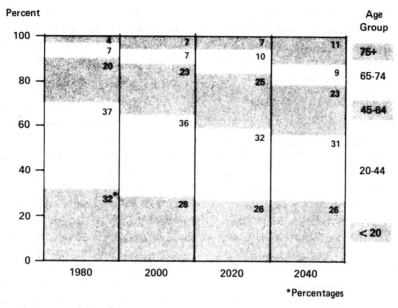

Figure 2. Age distribution of U.S population, selected years. (*Source:* Social Security Administration.)

projected to increase 41%. Of the younger population, those under age 45 will rise only 16% and decline in proportion to the total from 69% in 1980 to 57% in 2040. By contrast, persons aged 75 and over are projected to comprise 11% of the total in 2040, up from 4% in 1980. During this 60-year period, their numbers will almost quadruple from 3.6 million in 1980 to 13.8 million in 2040. It is important to note that the person reaching age 85 in 2040 was born in 1955 and is 30 years old today. A child born in 1985 will reach age 65 in the year 2050.

Returning briefly to Table 1 showing the proportion aged 75 and over in selected countries in the year 2000, it is noted that the United Nations projection for the United States is appreciably lower than that of the SSA actuaries—5.5% compared with 6.5% respectively. Up to the present, United Nations demographers have not taken into account the speed with which mortality rates have been declining in the United States. While mortality rates among the elderly have also been dropping rapidly in Japan, Australia, and in a few other countries, it is far from a universal phenomenon among all industrialized nations. The U.N. projections involve only a slow decline in

mortality rates at older age intervals, emphasizing how much difference the assumption of a rapid decline makes.

PROJECTIONS OF HEALTH STATUS, HEALTH SERVICES UTILIZATION, AND EXPENDITURES

What will these demographic changes mean for the nation in terms of health status, the use and cost of health care? We have not attempted to anticipate future trends in other factors that influence utilization of health services and expenditures for those services. Changes in levels of morbidity, in therapies and technologies, in the availability and cost of care, in social and economic conditions, will contribute to patterns and levels of utilization of medical care services, as will mortality rates and changes in the age structure of the population. Some of these factors may work to increase utilization while others may decrease it. Whatever else happens, however, the projected changes in the size and age distribution of the population would alone have a significant impact on utilization and, consequently, on expenditures. And since older people tend to have more health problems than younger people, the implications of the aging of the population on the demand for medical care and on public policy are significant.

To make these estimates, current age-specific rates of activity limitation and utilization patterns have been applied to the projected populations in future years as shown in Table 4. We realize full well that there is considerable conjecture and controversy regarding future morbidity patterns. Fries holds that the improved changes in life-style will result in a reduction in the prevalence of morbidity from chronic diseases and a compression of morbidity at the older ages (Fries, 1980; Fries & Crapo, 1981). He argues that there are biological constraints on human mortality. He foresees a continued decline in premature death and the emergence of a pattern of natural death at the end of a natural lifespan. He states that the "rectangularization of the survival curve may be followed by rectangularization of the morbidity curve and by compression of morbidity" (Fries, 1980, p. 135).

Ernest Gruenberg (1977) and Morton Kramer (1980), on the other hand, believe that chronic disease prevalence and disability will increase as life expectancy is increased, which will lead to a "pandemic" of mental disorders and chronic diseases. Thomas (1977) believes that the major diseases of human beings have become approachable biological puzzles, ultimately solvable. It follows from this that it is now possible to begin thinking about a human society relatively free of disease.

Manton (1982) elucidates the disagreement between the opposing viewpoints and points out that stability of morbidity and health status levels has characterized the aged population during the past decade. He views human aging and mortality as complex phenomena and as dynamic multidimensional processes in which chronic degenerative diseases play an essential role. His concept of "dynamic equilibrium" implies that the severity and rate of progression of chronic disease are directly related to mortality changes so that with mortality reductions there is a corresponding reduction in the rate of progression of aging of the vital organ systems of the body. He believes that the severity of chronic diseases will be reduced or its rate of

Table 4. Age-specific rates per 1,000 population used for projections, by sex

Age and sex	Percent with limitations in ADL[a]	Hospital days of care[b]	Physician visits[c]	Nursing home residents[d]
Male				
Total	1.3	1,053.4	4,048.0	3.6
Under 20	0.2	357.0	4,224.3	
20–44	0.4	608.4	3,231.0	0.9
45–64	1.9	1,587.9	4,388.0	
65 and over	6.8	4,243.9	5,925.8	30.7
65–74	4.4	3,370.0	5,539.5	12.7
75–84	9.7	5,476.4	6,799.3	47.4
85 and over	21.7	7,674.4	6,362.0	140.0
Female				
Total	1.9	1,355.0	5,413.0	8.4
Under 20	0.2	388.7	4,294.2	
20–44	0.5	1,070.0	5,739.1	1.0
45–64	1.8	1,604.0	5,679.7	
65 and over	10.4	3,999.8	6,763.5	59.7
65–74	5.1	2,977.3	7,018.7	15.9
75–84	15.0	5,009.0	6,524.8	80.6
85 and over	34.6	6,598.9	5,677.8	251.5

[a]Limitations in one or more activities of daily living (ADL): walking, bathing, using the toilet, dressing, eating, and getting in and out of bed. National Health Interview Survey, 1980 (Home Care Supplement).

[b]National Hospital Discharge Survey, 1980.

[c]National Health Interview Survey, 1980.

[d]National Nursing Home Survey, 1977.

progression slowed, resulting in reduced mortality rates and an increase in life expectancy. Other researchers have raised similar challenging and important issues (Hayflick, 1977; Keyfitz, 1978; Siegel, 1980).

An examination of past trends of health status indicators suggests little or no change in recent years. For example, there were 13.8 bed-disability days per person aged 65 and over in 1970 and in 1980 (National Center for Health Statistics, 1972, 1982b). Medicare and Medicaid, enacted in 1965, have resulted in varying rates of increases in the use of hospitals and nursing homes. From 1967 to 1979 the number of short-stay hospital discharges per 1,000 persons under age 65 increased 11%, for the elderly, it rose 35%. During this same period the average length of stay declined throughout the age range so that the number of days of care per 1,000 persons under age 65 declined 6% but increased 2% for the elderly (Lubitz & Deacon, 1982). Nursing home use rates, however, have increased significantly. In 1969 there were 37.1 residents per 1,000 persons aged 65 and over in nursing homes and personal care homes; by 1977 the rate had risen to 47.9, a 29% increase (National Center for Health Statistics, 1982c). For our projections of health status and health care utilization, we

are applying current, rather than increasing age-specific rates to the SSA population projections, which may well prove to be an underestimate.

An important measure of health status is the ability to perform the activities of daily living (ADL) such as walking, bathing, using the toilet, dressing, eating, and getting in and out of bed as reported in the National Center for Health Statistics' National Health Interview Survey (Figure 3 and Table 5). In 1980, 3.1 million noninstitutionalized persons were reported needing assistance in one or more of these activities. By 2040 the number is projected to more than double to a total of 7.9 million persons. The population will only increase during that period by two-fifths. The difference between the rates of growth in the population and in the number of persons with limitations in ADL is a reflection of the aging of the population. The impact of the aging of the population is shown clearly in the projected changing distribution by age. In 1980, 36% of the noninstitutionalized persons with limitations in ADL were aged 75 and over, by 2040 the proportion rises to 58%.

How will the aging of the population affect the use of health services? Projections are presented for physician visits, hospital and nurs-

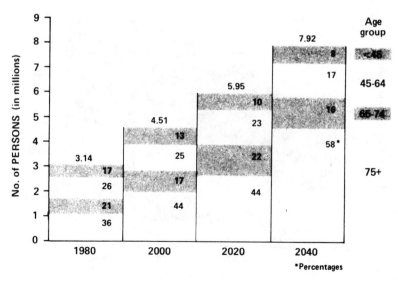

Figure 3. Number and distribution of persons with limitations, in activities of daily living. (*Source:* National Center for Health Statistics.)

Table 5. Projected number of persons with limitations in activities of daily living by age and sex: United States, 1980–2040[a]

Age and sex	1980	2000	2020	2040
Total				
All ages	3,141.7	4,509.1	5,951.3	7,922.4
Under 45 years of age	545.0	602.1	605.9	635.8
45–64 years of age	817.2	1,131.9	1,391.8	1,366.6
65–74 years of age	647.8	783.7	1,309.0	1,288.1
75 and over	1,131.7	1,991.3	2,644.7	4,631.9
Male				
All ages	1,411.6	1,996.7	2,629.3	3,393.6
Under 45 years of age	250.6	276.4	278.4	292.2
45–64 years of age	419.6	581.2	714.7	701.8
65–74 years of age	300.0	363.0	606.3	596.6
75 and over	441.3	776.1	1,030.0	1,803.1
Female				
All ages	1,730.1	2,512.5	3,322.0	4,528.8
Under 45 years of age	294.4	325.8	327.4	343.7
45–64 years of age	397.5	550.7	677.1	664.8
65–74 years of age	347.8	420.8	702.7	691.5
75 and over	690.4	1,215.3	1,614.8	2,828.9

[a]Figures denote thousands.

Source: National Center for Health Statistics, Office of Analysis and Epidemiology.

ing home care. The number of physician visits will increase in the future due to the aging of the population, but the increase will be less than for other measures of utilization because age-specific utilization rates do not vary as much for physician visits as, for example, for hospital care. Only 6% of the increase in visits from 1.1 billion in 1980 to 1.6 billion in 2040, an increase of 47%, results from the aging of the population. The distribution by age, however, will change (Figure 4). By 2040 persons aged 65 years and over will comprise 27% of the total visits compared with 15% in 1980.

The aging effect is quite different for hos-

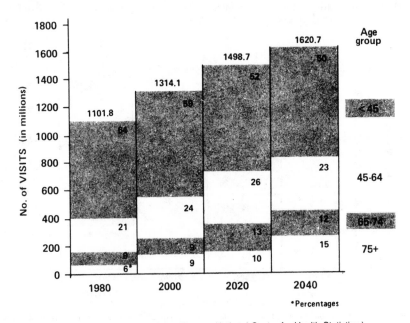

Figure 4. Number and distribution of physician visits. (*Source:* National Center for Health Statistics.)

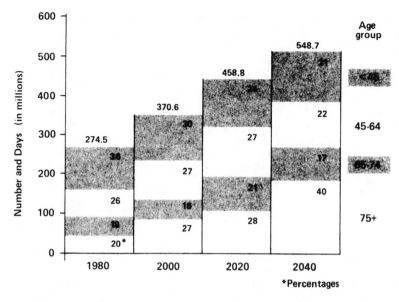

Figure 5. Number of distribution of short-stay hospital days by age. (*Source:* National Center for Health Statistics.)

pital and nursing home care. Total short-stay hospital days will double, increasing from 274 million in 1980 to 549 million in 2040, with more than half the increase due to the aging of the population. Forty percent of the days of care in 2040 are projected for those aged 75 and over; in 1980 only 20% were in that age group (Figure 5).

Again, assuming that current patterns of use prevail in the future, there will be very large increases in the number of nursing home residents. From 1.5 million in 1980, the number is projected to 5.2 million residents in 2040—a 3.5-fold increase (Figure 6 and Table 6). The increases are particularly large among residents 85 years of age and older where a 5-fold

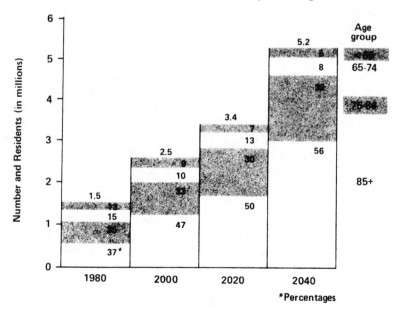

Figure 6. Number and distribution of nursing home residents. (*Source:* National Center for Health Statistics, projected from 1977 estimates.)

Table 6. Projected number of nursing home residents by age and sex: United States, 1980–2040[a]

Age and sex	1980	2000	2020	2040
Total				
All ages	1,511.3	2,541.8	3,370.8	5,227.1
Under 65 years of age	196.4	225.8	241.5	248.1
65 years and over	1,314.9	2,316.1	3,129.3	4,979.0
65–74 years of age	226.6	265.1	434.4	424.5
75–84 years of age	525.4	849.8	1,005.6	1,651.4
85 and over	562.8	1,201.2	1,689.4	2,903.1
Male				
All ages	421.5	640.9	864.8	1,303.6
Under 65 years of age	93.6	107.4	115.0	118.3
65 years and over	328.2	533.5	749.8	1,185.3
65–74 years of age	86.6	104.8	175.0	172.2
75–84 years of age	134.5	224.7	280.0	469.0
85 and over	107.1	204.0	294.8	544.0
Female				
All ages	1,089.8	1,900.9	2,506.1	3,923.5
Under 65 years of age	103.1	118.3	126.5	129.8
65 years and over	986.7	1,782.6	2,379.5	3,793.7
65–74 years of age	140.0	160.3	259.4	252.3
75–84 years of age	390.9	625.1	725.6	1,182.4
85 and over	455.7	997.2	1,394.6	2,359.1

[a]Figures denote thousands.
Source: National Center for Health Statistics, Office of Analysis and Epidemiology.

increase is projected in the number of residents. In 1980, 37% of the residents were aged 85 and over; by 2040 the proportion will be 56%. Adding the projected nursing residents aged 75 to 84, about 87% of the total residents will be aged 75 and over. It is evident that the aging of the population has a much greater impact on nursing home residents than on days of hospital care or physician visits.

Our final projections are expenditures for medical care. The Health Care Financing Administration annually estimates personal health care expenditures by type of expenditure, source of funds, and by age (Fisher, 1980). The latest available expenditure data for three age groups—under 19 years, 19 to 64 years, and 65 years and over—are for 1978. We have projected the age breakdown for 1980 and subsequent years by applying the population projections to obtain the impact of the aging of the population (Figure 7 and Table 7). We also made no attempt to forecast future inflation rates; thus, the expenditures are in constant 1980 dollars.

As with the use of medical care services, the proportional increase in expenditures is pro-

jected to rise at a significantly faster rate at the older ages. Of the total $219 billion spent in 1980 for personal health care, $64.5 billion or 29% was spent in behalf of the elderly population aged 65 and over. This amount would rise to $167.5 billion in 2040—an increase of 159%, due to the aging of the population during that 60-year period. By contrast, for the population under age 65, expenditures are projected to increase 30%.

Figure 8 and Table 7 enumerate the distribution of personal health care expenditures and populations by age for 1980 and 2040. In 1980, 11% of the population who were aged 65 and over consumed 29% of the expenditures; by 2040 the elderly are projected to comprise 21% of the population and almost half of the expenditures would be made in their behalf.

The projected growth in spending is greater for nursing home care. In 1980 about $21 billion was spent for nursing home care, comprising 9.4% of total personal health care spending. Assuming constant 1980 dollars, nursing home care spending would more than double by 2040, rising to $48.3 billion and comprising 13% of total personal health care expenditures.

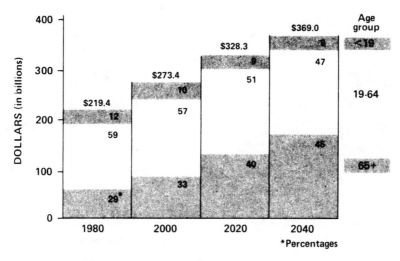

Figure 7. Personal health care expenditures by age, in constant 1980 dollars. (*Source:* Projected from Health Care Financing Administration estimates for 1978.)

For the elderly, nursing home expenditures are projected to constitute a quarter of total personal health care expenditures.

DISCUSSION

Underlying our projections are assumptions pertaining to three relatively distinct future trends in: birth and death rates; prevalence of ill-health and functional limitations; and the use of health care services. It is not until about 2050 that the assumptions regarding future birth rates influence the size of the population aged 65 and older. For 2040 and earlier, the population aged 65 or older has already been born. On the other hand, the projected population pyramids cover the entire age range and are highly sensitive to alternative assumptions regarding the birth rate. As indicated earlier, the projections presented here are based on an assumed upturn in the total fertility rate from the current 1.8 children per woman to 2.1 children per woman by the year 2005. Lower levels of fertility would result in fewer persons in the younger age groups.

The differential growth of the population by age can have important consequences for many of our social institutions, particularly in terms of dependency. Because the most slowly growing age group during the next half century will be those under 20 years, their proportionate share of the total population will diminish measurably.

Recent discussions of the financing of Social

Table 7. Projected personal health care and nursing home expenditures by age: United States, 1980–2040[a]

Age	1980	2000	2020	2040
Total expenditures				
All ages	$219.4	$273.4	$328.3	$369.0
Under 19 years of age	25.9	26.9	28.1	29.5
19–64 years of age	129.0	156.2	169.0	172.0
65 years and over	64.5	90.3	131.2	167.5
Nursing home expenditures				
All ages	$ 20.6	$ 28.0	$ 38.9	$ 48.3
Under 19 years of age	0.1	0.1	0.1	0.1
19–64 years of age	4.0	4.8	5.2	5.3
65 years and over	16.5	23.1	33.6	42.9

[a]Figures denote billions, in constant 1980 dollars.

Source: Projected from Health Care Financing Administration estimates for 1978.

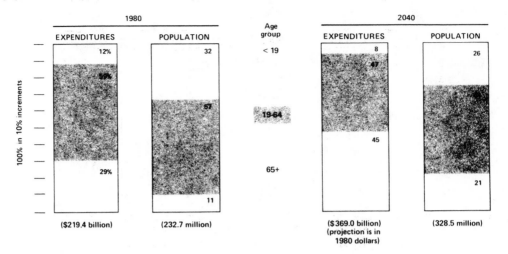

Figure 8. Percent distribution of personal health care expenditures and population by age and group and year. (*Source:* Projected from Health Care Financing Administration estimates for 1978.)

Security and Medicare benefits for retired workers and disabled persons have highlighted the long-run impact of the projected future demographic distribution of the population (Ball, 1982; Clark, Kreps, & Spengler, 1978; Federal Old-Age and Survivors Insurance and Disability Insurance Trust Funds, 1982; National Commission on Social Security Reform, 1983). Since the future financing of the system depends on the number of retirees in relation to workers, dependency ratios serve as useful indexes of the burden on society of the aging of the population. The "aged dependency ratio" is defined as the population aged 65 and over divided by the population aged 20 to 64. Under the previously stated assumptions regarding fertility and mortality trends, the SSA actuaries estimated this ratio would increase from 195 persons aged 65 or older for every 1,000 persons aged 20 to 64 in 1980 to 380 persons in 2040, almost doubling the aged dependency ratio (Table 8).

At the same time, low fertility rates will result in fewer younger persons and, thus, in a declining young dependency ratio, defined as the population under age 20 divided by the population aged 20 to 64. This ratio is projected to decrease 15% from 558 in 1980 to 476 young persons per 1,000 persons aged 20 to 64 in 2040.

The "total dependency ratio," the sum of the above ratios, is a crude index of the total burden on the working population of its support of both the old and young dependents. Adding the population under age 20 to the aged shows the projected rise of the total dependency ratio from 753 persons dependent on 1,000 persons of working ages in 1980 to 856 in 2040—an increase of 14%.

However, the relative costs of supporting the aged versus the young is a crucial consideration. One estimate is that "about three times as much public money is spent, on the average,

Table 8.   Dependency ratios, by age, 1960–2040

Year	Young[a]	Aged[b]	Total[c]
1960	.741	.174	.915
1970	.716	.184	.900
1980	.558	.195	.753
1990	.494	.215	.709
2000	.479	.226	.705
2010	.447	.236	.683
2020	.462	.303	.765
2030	.481	.378	.859
2040	.476	.380	.856

[a]Population under age 20 divided by the population aged 20–64.

[b]Population aged 65 and over divided by the population aged 20–64.

[c]Population under age 20 plus the population aged 65 and over divided by the population aged 20–64.

Source: Faber, F. and J. C. Wilkin, *Social Security Area Population Projections, 1981.* Social Security Administration, Actuarial Study No. 85. SSA Pub. No. 11–11532. (Washington, 1981).

per aged dependent than is spent on a younger one'' (Sheppard & Rix, 1977, p. 24). Since the aged will be the most rapidly growing age group and more costly, the burden on the working population to support young and old dependents is a major policy issue for Social Security and the hospital insurance program under Medicare, both financed by payroll taxes.

How closely the population projections presented here will correspond to actual demographic events depends largely on the relation between actual and projected future mortality and fertility trends. Although the mortality rate projections are by no means simple extrapolations of past trends, the current situation and the experience of the recent past do exert a great deal of influence. The method traditionally used in the United States has been termed ''population projection by reference to the informed guesses of experts'' (Preston, 1974, p. 728). The short-run portions of the projections are, of course, dampened extrapolations, but the longer run portions reflect expert opinion that is generally molded by the status quo and the events of the recent past. For example, mortality rates from vascular diseases have been declining very rapidly; it is assumed in the present projections that they will continue to decline very rapidly.

Should the mortality projections be treated as forecasts? Past experience suggests that great caution be exercised. After declining relatively steadily for many years, the mortality rates for males 15 to 54 years suddenly leveled off about 1955 and remained more or less level until the late 1960s. This change in trend came as a total surprise; it appeared to observers during the plateau period that earlier projections of male mortality reduction had been overly optimistic (Preston, 1974). In the early 1970s an unanticipated decline in mortality rates for older men began; it has made all earlier projections for men appear to be too pessimistic. Mortality trend projections for women have generally been far too pessimistic; for the older age groups, mortality rates are already well below the levels that had been projected for the year 2000. It is impossible to gauge the likelihood of another surprise change

in trend starting at some point in time during the next several decades. The SSA projected mortality trends still appear reasonable, but our understanding of the dynamics of mortality rates is, at best, rather poor. Since the causes of major trend reversals of the past, such as the mortality downturns for tuberculosis, stomach cancer, coronary heart disease, and stroke remain unclear, we cannot anticipate with any assurance, when the next alteration in course will take place (Stallones, 1979).

Similarly, projections of birth rates have corresponded quite well with reality when trends of the past have persisted into the future; changes in trend, however, have produced major discrepancies (Keyfitz, 1981; Stoto, 1983). Not many fertility projections accommodated the postwar baby boom; not many projections made in the midst of the boom accommodated its relatively abrupt end. Recent and anticipated advances in family planning sophistication suggest a closer correspondence in the future between actual and desired family size. The problem is, however, that we do not know how to foretell the fluctuations in desired family size that are going to be taking place (Lee, 1980).

Our crystal ball becomes much cloudier when we begin to project future trends in the prevalence of ill health and infirmity. As indicated earlier, forecasts range from those of Fries, who anticipates a compression of the period of morbidity prior to death, to those of Gruenberg and Kramer, who anticipate an appreciable lengthening of the duration of illness for at least certain segments of the population. It is, of course, quite possible that both phenomena will be taking place simultaneously; there may be an increasing proportion of individuals in quite good health up to the point of death and an increasing proportion with prolonged severe functional limitation, with a decline in the proportion with an only moderate degree of infirmity (Feldman, 1982). What effect this would have on the prevalence of morbidity would, of course, depend on the relative magnitudes of the various changes. Unfortunately, our current knowledge of the natural history of most conditions is rather meager and we have little systematic information about terminal illnesses.

Most of the current data derive from cross-sectional observations while longitudinal observations are required for epidemiologic analysis. Although there have been several notable studies that have followed cohorts of older people over considerable periods of time, they have rarely focused on the parameters of morbidity, functional capacity, and mortality required for useful modeling activities. Furthermore, the samples for most of these studies have been too small to delineate the pathways from good health to death, to estimate the frequency with which the different paths are followed, and to estimate the duration of time spent at each stage along the way. Epidemiological techniques need to be applied to the study of the natural history of disease and the process of dying.

Turning finally to assumptions regarding the future use of health services, we plunge even deeper into the great abyss. Two additional demographic considerations are important to consider: 1) the rate of childlessness may well be increasing for cohorts born since the mid-1930s or so. Elderly people without children may require more long-term care services than those with children; and 2) for at least the next few decades, the members of each cohort entering the elderly population will have had, on the average, more years of education than its predecessors. The more highly educated tend to live longer, be in better health, but, relative to their health condition, use more medical care than the less educated.

Of even greater consequence than such demographic factors are, of course, changes in our value structure. Medical advances may enable us to keep highly moribund individuals alive for long periods of time. What will our social norms prescribe that we do with that knowledge? Will the application of heroic measures be indicated under even the most dire of circumstances or will some minimal probability of recovery be required?

Our current public programs have great gaps in the types of services covered. Medicare tends to emphasize care for acute illnesses but does not provide for preventive care, extended nursing home care, or mental health services. Medicaid tends to emphasize nursing home care over inhome services and community alternatives. It is difficult to anticipate how the problems of long-term care will be handled in the future. Will alternative forms of long-term care replace long-term institutionalization for an appreciable proportion of the severely infirm?

We have begun to seek alternative solutions to institutionalization of the elderly and a variety have been developed—foster care homes, congregate housing and retirement communities, home care, personal care, homemaker and chore services, home delivered and congregate meals, and adult day care centers. The goal with many of these services is to enable the elderly to maintain their independence as long as possible. The development and availability of these services is uneven around the country, and public funds, where available, are inadequate. The issue of coverage of noninstitutional care and social services by public and private health insurance is an important one. Health insurance traditionally has emphasized and paid for hospital care, thereby discouraging the use of alternatives to high costs of hospital care. More attention is being focused on alternative approaches to long-term care in recent years (Congressional Budget Office, 1977; Estes, 1979; Institute of Medicine, 1977; Lee & Estes, 1979; Somers, 1980).

Given efforts at health promotion and higher educational attainment, it is possible that the elderly of the future may reach old age in better health status than the elderly of the past. The attractive concept set forth by Fries is that people in the future will have a longer disability-free life with a limit on the lifespan, perhaps reducing the pressure for long-term care services. As indicated earlier, Gruenberg and Kramer, on the other hand, believe that chronic disease prevalence and disability will increase as life expectancy is increased, which will lead to a pandemic of mental disorders and chronic diseases. In any event, if these trends in morbidity and mortality argue for a healthy population, they also argue for development of the range of supportive services that the very old need even in the best of health. At the same time, we must realize that the availability of alternative services will not necessarily reduce expenditures for long-term care. "Some have estimated that for every person residing in a nursing home, as many as two or three individuals who live in a community require an equivalent amount of care, which they are currently receiving, if at all, primarily from informal sources" (Health Care Financing Administration, 1981, p. 14). Alternative services may simply fill an, as yet, unmet need.

While it is certainly to be hoped that as time goes on we shall steadily become less dependent on halfway technologies, there may well be a relatively long transition period during which the armamentarium of moderately efficacious but extremely expensive procedures will grow and will be performed with increasing frequency. The assumption underlying our projections that age-specific utilization and expenditure levels will remain constant over time may well turn out to be overly optimistic.

In emphasizing the problematic character of a number of our assumptions, we may have left the impression that the future is totally indeterminate. Actually, the number of elderly will undoubtedly increase rapidly during the next half-century. As a consequence of such factors in our demographic history as past movements in birth and death rates and immigration, it is practically preordained that the number of elderly will grow rapidly. Even if there were not further declines in mortality rates, the number of individuals in the population aged 85 or older would approximately double during the next 25 years while the increase in the number of individuals in the 75 to 84 age bracket would be slightly slower. Younger age groups, however, are likely to be increasing at a far slower rate.

Since even the most optimistic predictions concerning changes in health practices and advances in medicine do not involve an immediate sharp decline in the incidence of illness or marked improvements in recovery rates, it is nearly certain that we shall be facing an increasing demand for medical services for at least the next several decades. Thus, while the projections presented here may possibly exaggerate the magnitude of the future changes, we can be certain that problems resulting from a rapid growth of the elderly population will be with us in the future.

REFERENCES

Ball, R. M. (1982, April). *The financial condition of the Social Security Study Group on the Social Security Program.* New York.

Bureau of the Census. (1982). *Projections of the Population of the United States: 1982–2050* (Advance Report). Current Population Reports, Population Estimates and Projections, Series P-25, No. 922. Washington, DC: U.S. Department of Commerce.

Clark, R., Kreps, J., & Spengler, J. (1978). Economics of aging: A survey. *Journal of Economic Literature, 16,* 919–962.

Congressional Budget Office. (1977). *Long term care for the elderly and the disabled.* Washington, DC: Author.

Estes, C. (1979). *The aging enterprise.* San Francisco: Jossey-Bass.

Faber, J. F., & Wilkin, J. C. (1981). *Social Security Area Population Projections, 1981.* Actuarial Study No. 85, Social Security Administration. (SSA Pub. No. 11-11532). Washington, DC.

Federal old-age and survivors insurance and disability insurance trust funds. (1982). *Annual Report.* Washington, DC.

Feldman, J. J. (1982). Work Availability of the Aged Under Conditions of Improving Mortality. Statement before the National Commission on Social Security Reform, June 21, 1982. Reprinted in *Milbank Memorial Fund Quarterly/Health and Society 61*(3), 1983.

Fisher, C. R. (1980). Differences by age groups in health care spending. *Health Care Financing Review 1*(4), 65–90. (HHS Publication No. 03045). Washington, DC.

Fries, J. F. (1980). Aging, natural death, and the compression of morbidity. *New England Journal of Medicine, 303,* 130–135.

Fries, J. F., & Crapo, L. M. (1981). *Vitality and aging: Implications of the rectangular curve.* San Francisco: W. H. Freeman.

Gruenberg, E. M. (1977). The failures of success. *Milbank Memorial Fund Quarterly/Health and Society, 55*(1), 3–24.

Hayflick, L. (1977). Perspectives on human longevity. In B. Neugarten & R. Havighurst (Eds.), *Extending the human life span: Social policy and social ethics* (pp. 1–12). Chicago: Committee on Human Development, University of Chicago.

Health Care Financing Administration. (1981). Long Term Care: Background and Future Directions. (HCFA 81-20047). 14. Discussion paper.

Institute of Medicine. (1977). *The elderly and functional dependency: A policy statement.* Washington, DC: National Academy of Sciences.

Keyfitz, N. (1978). Improving life expectancy: An uphill road ahead. *American Journal of Public Health, 68,* 954–956.

Keyfitz, N. (1981). The limits of population forecasting. *Population and Development Review, 7, 579–593.*

Kovar, M. G. (1977). Elderly people: The population 65 years and over. In *Health: United States: 1976–1977.* (DHHS Pub. No. HRA 77-1232). 3–25. Washington, DC.

Kramer, M. (1980). The rising pandemic of mental disorders and associated chronic diseases and disorders. In: Epidemiologic research as basis for the organization of extramural psychiatry. *Acta Psychiatrics Scandinavica, 62* (Supplement 285).

Lee, R. D. (1980). Aiming at a moving target: Period fertility and changing reproductive goals. *Population Studies, 34,* 205–226.

Lee, P. R., & Estes, C. L. (1979). Public policies, the aged, and long-term care. *Journal of Long-Term Care Administration, 7*(3), 1–15.

Lubitz, J., & Deacon, R. (1982). The rise in the incidence of hospitalizations for the aged, 1967 to 1979. *Health Care Financing Review, 3*(3), 21–40.

Manton, K. C. (1982). Changing concepts of morbidity and mortality in the elderly population. *Milbank Memorial Fund Quarterly/Health and Society, 60*(2), 183–244.

National Center for Health Statistics. (1972). *Current estimates from the national health interview survey: United States, 1970.* Vital and Health Statistics, Series 10, No. 72. (DHEW Pub. No. HSM 72-1054). Washington, DC.

National Center for Health Statistics. (1981a). *Health characteristics of persons with chronic activity limitation: United States, 1979.* Vital and Health Statistics, Series 10, No. 137. (DHHS Pub. No. PHS 82- 1565). Washington, DC.

National Center for Health Statistics. (1981b). *Characteristics of nursing home residents, health status, and care received: National nursing home survey, United States, May-December 1977,* by E. Hing. Vital and Health Statistics, Series 13, No. 51. Washington, DC.

National Center for Health Statistics. (1982a). Advance report on final mortality statistics, 1979. *NCHS Monthly Vital Statistics Report, 31*(6, Supplement). Washington, DC.

National Center for Health Statistics. (1982b). *Current estimates from the national health interview survey: United States, 1981,* by B. Bloom. Vital and Health Statistics, Series 10, No. 141. (DHHS Pub. No. PHS 82-1569). Washington, DC.

National Center for Health Statistics. (1982c). *Health, United States, 1982.* (DHHS Pub. No. PHS 83-1232). Washington, DC: Public Health Services.

National Commission on Social Security Reform. (1983). *Report of the National Commission on Social Security Reform.* Washington, DC.

Preston, S. H. (1974). An evaluation of postwar mortality projections in Australia, Canada, Japan, New Zealand and the United States. *World Health Statistics Report, 27,* 719–745.

Rice, D. P. (1978, October). *Projection and analysis of health status trends.* Paper presented at the 106th annual meeting of the American Public Health Association, Los Angeles.

Rice, D. P. (1979). Long life to you. *American Demographics, 1,* 9–15.

Sheppard, H. L., & Rix, S. E. (1977). *The graying of working america.* New York: Free Press.

Siegel, J. S. (1980). On the demography of aging. *Demography, 17,* 345–364.

Somers, A. (1980). Rethinking health policy for the elderly: A six-point program. *Inquiry, 17* (Spring), 3–17.

Stallones, R. A. (1979, October). *Unpublished remarks as discussant.* Paper presented at the 1979 annual meeting of the Institute of Medicine, National Academy of Sciences, Washington, DC.

Stoto, M. (1983). The accuracy of population projections. *Journal of the American Statistical Association, 78*(381), 13–20.

Thomas, L. (1977). Biomedical science and human health: The long-range prospect. *Daedalus.* Issued as *Proceedings of the American Academy of Arts and Sciences 106*(3).

chapter

2

Health and Social Services Policy and the Disabled Who Have Become Old

Robyn Stone and Robert Newcomer

This chapter describes the current financing and delivery system for health and social services for elderly persons, discusses a number of major problems in this system, and reviews the various reforms in this system that are being tested. The health and social services delivery system and the public and private financing of these services are largely oriented to acute-care hospital and physician services. Chronic long-term care for elderly and disabled persons is not extensively covered by private insurance. Public program coverage is limited to those with low incomes. Current public policy changes and service innovations are exploring means of reducing hospital costs and inappropriate nursing home placements. Expanded provision and financing of care for elderly and disabled persons in noninstitutional settings, however, continues to lag behind these efforts. Strikingly absent from these considerations are the unique needs and problems of disabled individuals who have become old.

THE CHANGING AGE STRUCTURE of the American population has profound implications for the nation's economic, social, and health institutions and services (Rice & Feldman, 1983). The elderly population is increasing at a faster rate than other segments of the population. It is estimated that the number of people aged 65 and over will grow from 27 million in 1983 to 67 million by 2040 when the elderly will account for one out of every five Americans. The number of those aged 75 and older is also increasing rapidly and is expected to account for 12% of the population by 2040 (Rice & Feldman, 1983). In addition, the convergence of such factors as research advances in disease etiology and management and the development and application of new diagnostic and surgical techniques is making it possible for increasing numbers of younger physically and mentally disabled individuals to reach old age.

People are living longer—but not necessarily better. In fact, many elderly and disabled persons are not receiving the kind of care they need; others have unmet needs for a variety of noninstitutional services, including home care and supportive living arrangements.

Accompanying the growth of the elderly population has been an increase in private and public expenditures to care for elderly and disabled persons. The escalation in nursing home expenditures has been particularly rapid, rising from

$5.6 billion in 1971 to more than $27 billion in 1982—an increase of 382% (compared to an increase of 12% in population and 182% in the gross national product) (Gibson, Waldo, & Levit, 1983). Long-term care costs now constitute the majority of health and social service expenditures for the elderly and threaten the solvency of federal and state programs.

In this chapter, we present a brief overview of the current system of policies and programs that provide health and social services for the elderly and a discussion of major problems within the existing structure. We also highlight selected state initiatives to reform the health and social services financing and delivery system. During the preparation of this chapter, we attempted to focus special attention on policies and programs that address the concerns of middle-age disabled individuals (e.g., mentally retarded, developmentally disabled, and/ or physically disabled) whose life expectancies are increasing to the point where they represent a substantial proportion of the "young old" elderly population. Since we found no evidence of programs or policies directed toward this emerging subpopulation, our discussion focuses on the health and social services financing and delivery structure targeted to the elderly population in general. The failure of the current system to recognize such demographic changes as the growth of a chronically disabled older population underscores the need for reforms to more effectively meet the needs of a diverse elderly constituency.

CURRENT FINANCING OF HEALTH AND SOCIAL SERVICES FOR THE ELDERLY

Current programs that benefit the elderly can be grouped into two types: those designed to serve all elderly and disabled individuals regardless of income; and those designed to benefit all age groups but with low income. Medicare and the Older Americans Act represent two important examples of the first category, and Medicaid and the Social Services Block Grant (SSBG) represent the second.

Medicare

The Medicare program was enacted in 1965 as Title XVIII of the Social Security Act (PL 89-97) in order to ensure adequate financial access to needed medical and hospital services for all persons aged 65 and over eligible for Social Security payments, and to younger disabled individuals who met special eligibility criteria. In 1982, 29.5 million persons, 90% of whom were 65 or over, received Medicare benefits and services amounting to $52.2 billion, averaging $2,700 per person (Gibson et al., 1983).

Medicare is a uniform, nationwide health insurance program consisting of two principal components. Medicare, Part A, the Hospital Insurance Program, is financed from Social Security trust funds from employer and employee contributions. Inpatient hospitalization and some skilled nursing home and home health care are among the services covered under this program. Beneficiaries must pay a deductible before Medicare will reimburse hospitals and nursing homes, and pay co-insurance for those services over the limit. Medicare, Part B, the Supplementary Medical Insurance Program, is financed through general federal revenues and deductibles. Those who opt for this coverage pay a $75 deductible and a 20% co-insurance for most services. Part B pays for necessary physician services, outpatient therapy, some medical equipment and supplies, rural health clinic services, and additional home health care visits (Commerce Clearing House, 1983).

Medicare is federally administered and is only indirectly linked with health programs administered by the states (e.g., Medicaid). Unlike Medicaid, Medicare is designed as a broad program for all elderly and disabled, rather than for all poor persons. Consequently, the Medicare program, with its broad eligibility and financing, is not specifically targeted for those who are the most needy. Because of its service limitations and co-payments, Medicare pays for only 44% of the health expenditures for the elderly. Medicaid, private payments, and insurance make up the remainder (Gibson et al., 1983).

Older Americans Act

The Older Americans Act (OAA), originally enacted in 1965 (PL 89-73), is the single federal social service statute designed specifically for the elderly. Initially funded at $6.5 million, the act established the Administration on Aging within the federal government, required states to establish state units on aging, and authorized state and community social service programs, as well as research, demonstration, and training projects. It also established a set of objectives aimed at improving the lives of older Americans in the areas of income, health, housing, employment, retirement, cultural and recreational opportunities, restorative services, community services, and gerontological research (U.S. Senate, 1982).

When the act was initially passed, it was implemented through small social service grants and research projects. The 1973 amendments significantly revised and expanded the scope of the Older Americans Act by creating area agencies on aging and explicitly delegating program priority setting and implementation decisions to state and substate areas. This change was significant for several reasons that went beyond the expanded, but still very limited, resources appropriated under the act ($253 million in 1973). First, decentralization created a focal point for aging within local communities. At this level of government, as at other levels, aging services traditionally had been accorded low priority, and providers and advocates associated with aging were accorded low status (Morris & Binstock, 1966). The new agency "focal points" were expected to be in a position to build a political constituency, legitimize themselves, and ultimately raise the visibility and viability of the elderly and services to aid them.

Subsequent amendments to the Older Americans Act have extended the authority for continued program operation and the basic strategy enunciated in 1973 (Coombs, Lambert, & Quirk, 1982). Area agencies are currently required to allocate "an adequate portion" of their social service funds to one or more of the national priority services. These include information and referral, transportation, inhome assistance, and legal services. In addition, there are separate authorizations for home-delivered and congregate meals, and a requirement that states operate a nursing home ombudsman program (U.S. Senate, 1982).

Appropriations under the Older Americans Act rose from a 1973 level of $253 million to $1,054 million in 1983. Although these appropriations grew substantially in the last decade, they nevertheless represent a relatively minor national social service expenditure when distributed among 57 states and territories and over 600 area agencies to serve more than 23 million older persons. Available funds are even more limited if actual funds for social services are considered separately. Funds for "area planning and social services" account for only about 26% of the total Older Americans Act appropriation. This compares with shares of 36% for the nutrition program and 29% for the community services employment program for older workers. Various other activities, including research and training, account for the remaining funds. In effect, the potential importance of the Older Americans Act arises not from the volume of funding for its social programs, but from its definition of national goals for the elderly and creation of a state and local network for planning, advocacy, and delivery (U.S. Senate, 1982).

Medicaid

Medicaid, Title XIX of the Social Security Act (PL 89-97), was enacted in 1965 to provide federal matching funds for state programs to pay for medical services to low-income individuals and families. All states except Arizona currently provide Medicaid benefits. (Arizona offers a Medicaid-like program under a U.S. Health Care Financing Administration demonstration program.) Individuals of families eligible for Supplementary Security Income (SSI) and Aid to Families with Dependent Children (AFDC) are automatically eligible for Medicaid. In addition, states can choose to cover several other categories of individuals. Included among these are the "medically needy.'' These are people whose large medical expenses have reduced their remaining income and assets to welfare levels. Thirty states had medically needy programs in 1982, and all states allow spend down to persons in institutions (Newcomer, Benjamin, & Sattler, 1985).

Federal regulations require that state Medicaid programs provide hospital inpatient care, physician services, skilled nursing facility care, laboratory and X-ray services, home health care, hospital outpatient care, family planning, rural health clinics, and early and periodic screening. In addition, states may provide up to 32 other optional services, including intermediate care, prescription drugs outside the hospital, dental services, and eyeglasses (Muse & Sawyer, 1982). The program is financed through a combination of federal and state (and, in some cases, local) funds. The federal government contributes between 50% and 77% of the Medicaid funds, based on a state per capita income formula (Muse & Sawyer, 1982).

Generally, Medicaid operates as a third-party insurance coverage program. The state, in other words, pays bills for services rendered to individuals eligible for the program. The services received are determined by the provider and patient rather than by Medicaid staff, thus creating a largely open-ended entitlement program. Once eligible for Medicaid, the beneficiary is entitled to receive state-covered service from any qualified provider. Providers participating in the program must accept the Medicaid reimbursement level as payment in full, with the exception that states may require co-payments on services. States assert fiscal control over the program mainly by changing program policies such as those on eligibility standards, scope or duration of services covered, utilization controls, and reimbursement rates.

Medicaid represents the primary public program for long-term care through its coverage of skilled and intermediate care facility costs. Although long-term care services essentially remain uncovered by Medicare and private insurance programs, Medicaid now covers about half of all costs for these services. Fed-eral and state Medicaid spending for nursing home care, totaling $13 billion in 1982, constituted 48% of total program costs, while inpatient hospital care represented 29%. The remaining 23% was accounted for by physician care, outpatient hospital services, drugs, home care, and other services (U.S. Health Care Financing Administration, 1982).

Social Services Block Grant

Since 1975, the primary source of federal social services funds has been Title XX of the Social Security Act (Social Services Amendments of 1974, PL 93-647). Title XX served as a block grant to states for providing an array of social services under the following program goals: economic self-support; personal self-sufficiency; protection from abuse, neglect, and exploitation; and arrangement for appropriate institutional care. Title XX widened the states' latitude in the provision of social services, yet was aimed at increasing the availability of services to vulnerable populations.

Under Title XX, Congress provided funds to states at the rate of 75% of federal funds to 25% in state funds. The states were required to prepare a state plan and report on service expenditures and recipients. States were allowed to determine their own services and eligibility requirements, within federal limits. States were required to spend 50% of their funds on low-income eligibles. Similarly, states were limited to providing services to individuals with incomes up to 115% of the state's median income. States could also declare specific population groups uniformly eligible for services. Services provided to elderly and disabled persons under Title XX included protective services, housing services, nutrition services, adult day care services, and homemaker/chore services.

The Omnibus Budget Reconciliation Act of 1981 (PL 97-35) renamed the Title XX program as the Social Services Block Grant (SSBG) and changed the social services program in several ways. The primary change was the reduction of federal funding from the requested $3.0 billion to $2.4 billion. In addition, states were no longer required to provide a 25% match, develop annual planning documents, report expenditure and recipient data, or utilize federal eligibility guidelines. The reduction of federal guidelines in the social service block grant increased state administrative discretion.

The role that the SSBG currently plays in providing services to elderly or disabled persons is difficult to ascertain because data on eligibility, services, expenditures, and providers are quite variable across states. Under Title XX, states had a great deal of flexibility in reporting numbers of clients served; the elimination of all reporting requirements under the SSBG makes efforts to track services to the elderly more difficult. Nevertheless, the Office of Management and Budget estimated that in FY 1981, approximately 21% of the total Title XX program dollars benefited elderly persons (U.S. Senate, 1982).

CURRENT ORGANIZATION AND DELIVERY OF SERVICES

The elderly require a wide variety of medical, health, and social services to meet their acute and long-term care needs. They are particularly vulnerable to functional disability frequently caused by chronic illness. An estimated 15% of the noninstitutionalized population has some degree of activity limitation. This becomes more prevalent as age increases (Rice & Feldman, 1983).

Table 1 illustrates the array of services provided in three types of settings: closed (institutionalized), open (community), and unorganized (informal/home). The boundaries between these environments are not static but mutable, subject to changing definitions, public policies, and funding patterns.

Services for elderly persons are designed to provide diagnostic, preventative, therapeutic, rehabilitative, supportive, and maintenance functions for individuals who have acute conditions or chronic physical and/or mental impairments, in both institutional and noninstitutional settings. They cover a multitude of medical and social programs as well as funding services. The method and means of financing

Table 1. The organization of care

Type of setting	Range of major services
Closed/ institutional	Acute care hospital
	Nursing homes
	Skilled nursing
	Intermediate care
	Psychiatric state hospital
	Hospice
	Respite
Open/ community	Health services
	Home health
	Adult day health care
	Community mental health
	Outpatient physician and clinic
	Social services
	Multipurpose senior center
	Congregate meals
	Meals on Wheels
	Transportation/escort
	Homemaker/chore
	Legal aid
	Adult day care
	Housing/residential care
	Domiciliary/adult foster care
	Residential group/hotel
	Life care communities
	Private residence
Unorganized/ informal	Variable degree of care provided by kin, friends, neighbors

Source: Adapted from Little (1982).

and the scope of services covered follow a complex pattern.

Despite this vast array of health and social services for persons age 65 and over, not all services are available at the time or place needed. Several barriers have impeded the full functional development of a continuum of care appropriate to the dynamic health and social services needs of the aged population.

Access to Care

Perhaps the most pervasive problem is access to the different levels of care. The wide variety of services and providers makes it difficult for individuals to determine what is available, needed, and appropriate as well as how to obtain reimbursement. Once individual needs are determined, access to services depends on either having private financial resources or qualifying for Medicare, Medicaid, or the other public programs that would finance the necessary care.

Different federal statutory requirements and state policies compound the problem as each has different definitions, coverage, and reimbursement methods. Medicare is an acute-care oriented program; thus, it pays for most hospital and physician services but excludes most long-term care expenses. This exclusion is particularly problematic for the noninstitutional population who are either bedridden or require assistance in the functions of daily living. Medicare covers short-term nursing home care following hospitalization and home health care but the latter is limited to medically oriented services, not personal or homemaking services. Medicaid is the primary payer of long-term care, representing about 90% of all public expenditures for long-term care for Medicaid eligibles only (U.S. Senate, 1982). Medicaid eligibility criteria and service coverage vary substantially from state to state, and restrictive eligibility criteria (especially for low-income families) in some states significantly impede access to care (Newcomer et al., 1985). Although Medicaid is less restrictive than Medicare, only 2% of the Medicaid budget supports noninstitutional home health care services. Moreover, these services are limited, in most states, to those covered by Medicare (U.S. Health Care Financing Administration, 1982). It is far easier to obtain Medicare and Medicaid benefits for hospital and nursing home care than for community-based or home care.

In 1981, the states were given greater flexibility to cover a wide range of home and community-based services through the waiver of Medicaid statutory requirements (Section 2176 of the Omnibus Budget Reconciliation Act of 1981). While most states have requested waivers for new programs in the last 3 years, these programs are small and generally limited in scope. States are cautious about developing new community-based programs because they fear that the increase in services will result in a general escalation of state program costs due to latent demand for this care (Greenberg & Lentz, 1983).

Another major barrier to access is the lack of alternatives to institutional care in most parts of the country. While a number of long-term care projects have been developed with demonstration grants (e.g., the Department of Health and Human Services National Long Term Care Channeling Demonstration Projects and the Social Health Maintenance Organization [S/HMO] Initiative), the supply of such programs statewide continues to be inadequate. Consequently, a large proportion of noninstitutionalized elderly people are cared for solely by families and friends because personal care, home health care, and housing needs cannot be met by community services. It is estimated that 60%–80% of the care for the impaired elderly is provided by relatives and friends who are uncompensated for their care (U.S. Health Care and Financing Administration, 1981).

Access to nursing home and residential care beds is another problem. Medicaid recipients and severely disabled individuals have particular difficulty in finding nursing home beds when Medicaid reimbursement rates are lower than the private pay rates (Scanlon, 1980). Homes select private paying and light-care patients in preference to public paying and "difficult" clients. As a result, some patients who should be in nursing homes are backlogged in acute-care hospitals at a higher cost to Medicaid and other third-party payers. Similarly, there is evidence that in states with low state supplements to the federal Supplemental Security Income (SSI) benefits, SSI recipients in need of residential care have found it difficult to obtain such services (Stone & Newcomer, 1985).

Costs

The financial burden of health care to individuals, government, and society has become intolerable in terms of the absolute cost, the rate of inflation, and in forecasts for the future. Among the factors contributing to these costs are that both Medicare and Medicaid are oriented toward expensive institutional services. Furthermore, many people are inappropriately placed or retained in institutions when their needs could be better met by community-based services. Estimates suggest that up to 50% of institutionalized patients could be cared for in less restrictive settings depending on the criteria of need that are used (U.S. Health Care Financing Administration, 1981).

Efforts to curb rapidly growing health care expenditures, especially in the Medicare program, have resulted in recent changes in reimbursement policies. During FY 1984, initiatives in prospective payment were implemented in the form of predetermined reimbursement rates for over 400 different diagnosis-related groups (DRGs). Under DRGs, hospitals are reimbursed based upon the diagnosis of the patient's illness, regardless of services provided or length of stay. The aim of this program is to force hospitals and attending physicians to consider the economic consequences of prescribed courses of treatment and, therefore, to cut hospital costs.

This program is expected to have significant consequences for other types of caregivers, particularly those serving the elderly. Nursing homes and home health agencies already are reporting an increase in the number of heavy-care patients. These changes are expected to have a ripple effect on the costs of long-term care and to necessitate relocating patients with lower care needs to less costly settings (e.g., residential or foster care). Thus, the development of an accessible continuum of long-term care will become even more critical as this and other constraints are placed on the hospital system.

Continuity of Care

The financial fragmentation of acute- and long-term care services contributes to a lack of continuity in the care of the elderly. Services are delivered by a variety of government-funded health and social services programs and by many different kinds of community and private organizations. Public agencies often purchase services from the voluntary and private sections. While the proliferation of voluntary agencies has increased the variety and flexibility of programs, it has further fragmented the delivery system and weakened accountability in the service network. The elderly face a complicated and confusing service system in which it is difficult to coordinate a comprehensive package of noninstitutional services (Harrington & Newcomer, 1982).

Another problem is the fragmentation of services among different population groups, particularly between the elderly and disabled. Some programs, such as those developed by the Administration on Aging and the state SSBG administrators, have targeted long-term care services to elderly persons; at the same time, services for disabled individuals have different funding sources. Medicare and Medicaid, in contrast, have integrated funding for the elderly and disabled. The separate delivery of services to the elderly and the disabled is particularly problematic for the increasing subpopulation of *aging disabled* persons, where the line between the two categories becomes indistinguishable. No strong rationale can be developed for separating long-term care service programs for different target groups since the range of service needs and access and continuity problems are similar. Perhaps as efforts are made to consolidate or integrate multiple funding sources at the point of service delivery or case management (as is occurring in many demonstration programs; see, for example, Hamm, Kickham, & Cutler, 1984), the dichotomy between the elderly and the disabled will become more recognized and resolved.

The dichotomy between programs based on the medical and social model represents another major obstacle to the continuity of care. For example, Medicare and Medicaid are designed as medical programs although some social services are included. Social services programs, such as those funded by the SSBG, have different types of managers, professionals, program criteria, and standards from those of health programs (e.g., home health aides versus homemaker/chore workers), even though the services may be identical. This sometimes artificial distinction between medical and social problems adds a further barrier to the continuity and comprehensiveness of services.

A related problem is the failure of the current system to recognize the interaction between acute illness, acute episodes of chronic conditions, and manageable impairments. This oversight has resulted in the separation of acute care into Medicare funding, long-term care (largely nursing home) into Medicaid financing, and community support services into social services funding (including OAA and SSBG resources). Needed is a financing and care management system capable of moving an individual from one level of care (not just services within one stratum of care) to another as needs or conditions warrant.

Finally, the current system complicates the potential for continuous case management. It lacks utilization in key areas of information and referral, coordination of service delivery, and allocation of scarce resources. The burden of these functions rests primarily with the patients and with their families. The result frequently is inappropriate placement, failure to obtain preventive care, and overall cost inefficiency.

ALTERNATIVES FOR REFORM OF THE HEALTH AND SOCIAL SERVICE SYSTEM[1]

A wide range of options are possible for reforming the current system of care for elderly individuals. They may be categorized as: regulatory and rate-setting reforms; alternative community-based service programs; coordination and management programs (e.g., case management); financial incentive programs; and alternative financing and delivery systems (e.g., S/HMOs) (Callahan & Wallack, 1981). These alternatives are not mutually exclusive and all are dependent upon: 1) the degree of federal, state, and local government involvement in the development of financing mechanisms and resources; 2) the existing financing structures; 3) the organization, management, and delivery of services; and 4) the amount of new resources required (Farrow, Joe, Meltzer, & Richman, 1981). While a number of federal and state demonstration projects have been funded to explore these options, the following discussion focuses on statewide initiatives to reform the system of care for the elderly. The examples are not meant to be definitive or all-inclusive; rather they reflect trends in the

current pattern of state initiatives and suggest the direction of future development in the area of health and social services system reform. (For a thorough discussion of the demonstration programs, see Hamm et al., 1984.)

Much of the current innovative state activity is concerned with changing who receives services, which services they receive, where they receive them, and how the system is organized and managed. Much less attention has been given to directly altering funding levels or methods of payment. In order to sort through the range of recent state approaches to long-term care, we can pose a series of policy questions to which these approaches are addressed.

Who gets into the long-term care services system and, more importantly, where in that system do they enter?

How can the utilization of present institutional resources be altered?

How can traditional modes of community care, including self-care and family care, be reinforced and supported?

Can statewide service systems, embracing institutional and community care, be created, developed, and managed?

How can present payment methods be altered to reduce the costs of both institutional care and community care?

How can the fragmentation among the various public funding streams that support long-term care services be reduced?

How can the level of resources available for community long-term care services be increased?

Preadmission Screening

Both the "remarkable" growth in Medicaid nursing home costs and the growing body of evidence that many nursing home residents either do not belong there or do not need the level of care they are receiving have persuaded at least 21 states to develop preadmission screening programs for Medicaid patients prior

[1]This section is based on a paper entitled, "State Government Perspectives on Financing Community Care for the Elderly" presented by A. E. Benjamin at a conference sponsored by the American Hospital Association in San Diego, CA, February, 1984.

to their entry into nursing homes. In a few states, preadmission screening has been extended to all persons considered for nursing home care, whatever the source of payment. In the context of long-term care, preadmission programs reflect the assumption that it is preferable to divert persons from entering nursing homes than to return nursing home residents to community settings (Knowlton, Clauser, & Fatula, 1982). While all states have been required to have utilization review programs for nursing homes, most evidence suggests that review takes place after admission and that at that point a return to the community is difficult or impossible.

A more specialized approach to controlling entrance to nursing homes has involved hospitals. Virtually any discussion with knowledgeable state officials responsible for long-term care turns eventually to the traditional role played by the hospital, and, specifically, hospital discharge planners, in channeling the elderly and others into nursing homes rather than community care. Increasingly, officials maintain that state efforts to do preadmission screening without specific, formal inclusion of hospital discharge planners are unlikely to be successful, since about one-third of nursing home residents go there directly from hospital stays. Some emphasis has been placed on establishing interagency agreements between county governments or other bodies responsible for screening, and all hospital discharge planning units. In at least two states, the first priority in nursing home/long-term care screening has been given to persons in hospitals.

Facility Construction

The major approach to controlling the supply of nursing homes, used everywhere, has been certificate-of-need regulation. A few states have even established moratoria on the construction of nursing home beds. An indirect method of controlling bed supply, also used widely, is a limit on Medicaid nursing home reimbursement rates. The net result of these three strategies has been that growth in nursing home bed supply has not kept pace with growth in the elderly population (Feder, 1983). As

increases in supply have slowed and efforts to screen admissions have increased, pressure apparently has grown to expand the use of hospital "backup" or "administrative" days under Medicaid. A number of states have responded to the liberalization of federal law and have authorized the establishment of "swing beds" in hospitals, particularly in rural areas, to deal with both low-occupancy rates in hospitals and with a shortage of long-term care beds.

Natural Supports

Natural supports, as used here, consist of efforts to reinforce existing family resources, individual financial capacity, and private insurance.

Direct Payments to Family Caregivers   In addition to controlling the supply and utilization of institutional services, many states are considering (and some are implementing) initiatives to reinforce traditional forms of support for the chronically ill. A number of states have some sort of family support programs, although most are limited in purpose and scope (e.g., many provide training and group support rather than more tangible resources). A few states pay family members or neighbors who provide care. Other states have begun to consider income tax deductions for family members who care for older persons.

Reverse-Equity Mortgage Plans   Reverse-equity mortgage plans are being considered in many states. Since more than two-thirds of the elderly own their own homes, this property provides the basis for a system of state financial support designed to improve the chances that older persons can afford to live at home longer, thus delaying the need for institutional care. One state has even considered a plan that establishes a state fund from which monthly support payments could be drawn. This fund would be replenished by "repayments" from the elderly or their estates when the homes are sold.

Private Health Insurance   Private health insurance is another potential resource for long-term care receiving public attention in a number of states. Two states have enacted statutes that mandate all health insurance policies providing coverage for inpatient hospital care also provide coverage for home health care benefits. State statutes have also required health insurance companies and health maintenance organizations to provide health care coverage of hospice services as an option to all policyholders.

Payment Methods

Payment methods in the long-term care area relate most directly to nursing home and home care, although a number of other financial waivers and integration plans have been the subject of experimentation.

Nursing Homes States have for years had the option of paying nursing homes on either a prospective or a retrospective basis. All but a handful of states now use some form of prospective payment. Most commonly, the rates may be individually negotiated with each facility or determined by the size of the facility or its geographic location. Case mix determined rates are beginning to receive attention and will likely become pervasive as the impact of hospital DRGs on nursing home patient case mix becomes more evident. Positive incentive payment systems for improving patient outcomes have been tried in a few states, but the difficulty of patient assessments has complicated the application of this approach.

Home Health Care The rapidly rising costs of home health care have become an issue at both the federal and state level although the absolute level of spending remains relatively small (i.e., around $500 million, or less than 2% of program costs in 1982). More than half the states have adopted methods other than traditional Medicare cost-based reimbursement for Medicaid home health benefits. Current data suggest that under Medicaid, states using Medicare cost-based methods have had greater rates of increase for home health expenditures than have states using modified cost-based methods or variants of prospective payment. Some would argue, however, that this difference results from Medicaid rates being too low to attract service providers. Recent provisions under federal law permit states to

substitute inexpensive homemaker services for more expensive home health services under Medicaid. It is likely that this will expand home care delivery while keeping per recipient costs down.

Funding and Service Coordination

Fragmentation of programs and funding sources has been among the more important problems plaguing the provision of community care services. Models of service have always begun with income status. This defined the funding category, which in turn determined the types of services "needed" (i.e., available through that category). With the increased Medicaid waiver flexibility available to the states to buy services once confined to other categorical programs (e.g., homemaker, personal care, and respite care), states are now able to contemplate a new model of service provision. This model begins by using assessment and screening procedures to determine which services are needed, and then considers several sources of payment available to pay for similar and related services. Twelve states have established statewide community care networks providing services with Medicaid, Social Service Block Grant, Older Americans Act, and general revenues under various state titles. The Oregon program (Project Independence) is particularly interesting because the case management/funding integration effort combines a nursing home deflection approach, with nursing home patient relocation efforts. Other states have integrated social services community care funding, but without directly tying these programs together with Medicaid.

New Resources

The level of resources available for community care remains very small due to a number of factors. First is the widespread fear among officials at all levels of government that the latent demand for community care is enormous. It is also widely believed that some portion of the estimated 80% of community care that is provided through natural support systems (i.e., family, friends, and others) would withdraw in the face of publicly provided services. Finally, the various economic and political constraints alluded to earlier impede the development of new resources. The Medicaid (Section 2176) waiver process does make available to states funds that were not before available to finance community care services; the actual amount of ''new money'' for community services remains a matter of conjecture. Still, in many states, waivers represent a significant increase in resources for community care. Not surprisingly, there is significant variation among the states in terms of their intended waiver efforts (Hamm et al., 1984).

In a period of budgetary caution, most states are more concerned with controlling the costs of public programs, particularly Medicaid, than with expanding commitments to community care. A few states, however, have appropriated relatively substantial amounts of new state funds under state titles to community care, although the levels are paltry when compared to nursing home expenditures. Three states, as an example, recently committed 20–30 million dollars in new state resources (annually) to community care programs, with an emphasis on inhome and related services. Seven or eight other states have appropriated much smaller sums (1–2 million dollars) under new state titles, again with the primary emphasis on home-based services. Various states also report some success in squeezing more resources out of the Community Services Block Grant and Older Americans Act programs for community care. These increases, however real, remain much too small—relative to the needs of the elderly, disabled, and others—to stir much excitement.

COMMON THEMES AND NEXT STEPS

States like Wisconsin, Connecticut, Oregon, Florida, Minnesota, and Massachusetts are establishing statewide networks of agencies responsible in various ways for managing or monitoring: 1) hospital discharge planning for the elderly and others that are chronically ill, 2) preadmission screening for nursing homes, 3) case management, and 4) the funding and coordination of community care services. A number of common themes and possible directions for the future emerge when community care programs in these six states are examined.

In each of these states, active community care strategies have been devised for gaining access to chronically ill individuals before they become poor enough to become Medicaid-eligible and before they are steered to terminal nursing home care. This effort to challenge categorical program funding and eligibility boundaries is accompanied by an effort to integrate health and social services in sensible and cost-conscious ways.

All of these states also have challenged the boundaries between acute and long-term care, although the intensity of this effort varies. At its simplest, this effort involves timely and informed discharged planning and the prescreening of anyone with the slightest chance of landing in a nursing home. It means selective short stays in nursing homes and hospital inpatient and outpatient care as needed, but with community care representing the core, or foundation, of required services. In Oregon, where there is an 18-day limit on hospital care under Medicaid, hospital discharge planners were reluctant to become involved in the community care process. But they learned quickly—even before DRGs—that ''planned'' timely discharge was probably to the advantage of patient and hospital alike.

Resistance by hospital planners to involvement in these community care networks is not unusual; hospitals are facing some new challenges to standard ways of doing business. In Wisconsin, for example, hospitals are part of the debate on a proposed long-term care block grant. Under this proposal, the state would determine the size of appropriations to each county for long-term care services, and the counties would decide how to allocate these funds. Hospitals and nursing homes alike are opposed to this, for at least two reasons. First, they do not want to deal with county govern-ments, especially where there are 72 with which to deal. Second, they do not want to compete with other providers for health care resources (e.g., in this scheme a hospital that wanted 12 swing beds would have to compete with home health agencies and other providers for the needed funds). If a proposed county long-term care block grant worries institutional providers in Wisconsin, the prospect of Medi-caid (Title XIX) capitation for both acute and long-term care in Minnesota certainly causes some alarm (whether appropriate or not) among hospitals in that state. In fact, state officials are convinced capitation can work for acute care, while they are nervous but hopeful regarding long-term care. The extent that cap-itation schemes encourage shifting of resources from acute to long-term care (or the reverse) remains unclear.

Another theme that emerges in all of the states with strong community care programs is the growing health care activism of aging inter-est groups. In states such as Minnesota and Wisconsin, independent groups of senior citi-zens are negotiating with hospitals to accept Medicare assignments. At hospitals in Min-neapolis and Milwaukee, contracts have been signed that ensure acceptance of assignment and coverage by the hospital of a portion of the Medicare deductible, in exchange for a guaran-teed enrollment by group members. Aging groups are also negotiating with physicians in those states; half the physicians in one county have agreed to accept the Medicare rate for individuals and couples under specified in-come levels. Some rural hospitals with low-occupancy rates in communities with many elderly citizens are planning to seek such agreements as a means to ensuring access to heavy users of medical care. Aging activism clearly has not been confined to community care issues. It is directed at the range of re-sources and services related to the health and social needs of older persons, whatever the setting of care.

CONCLUSION

One temptation in reviewing the accomplish-ments and shortcomings of health and social services policies is to express a panoply of criticisms and recommendations. It is clear that the health and social services system is a frag-mented collection of competing and comple-mentary services, with each element in this system having a vested interest in the con-tinuation of these patterns. It is also likely that any changes will have adverse consequences for at least some provider groups. In spite of this, there is a growing budget imperative. The costs of the present system have grown too rapidly and too large. But the central point to be made is as much philosophical as technical: there are no clearly identifiable and universally accepted solutions to these current problems.

In terms of the initial focus of this chapter—the disabled who grow old— the most critical issue is the fact that current policies do not recognize the extended longevity for an in-creasing number of physically and mentally disabled individuals and the implications this has for these individuals and society. The gen-eral concerns and specifications of this popu-lation have not been adequately addressed by the traditional system nor have they been ex-plicitly considered in the design of alternative strategies. Change and improvement will not occur unless questions are first asked. Many innovations and demonstrations have been de-signed to test various reforms in the current system. Some of these may have application for the disabled, some will not; perhaps other strategies will be needed. The first challenge is to reassess whether the categorical funding and segregated service delivery systems that sep-arate the disabled from the general population are really needed. Would more universal ser-vice entitlements and service coordination re-solve the problem? These and other related issues must be addressed if public policy is to meet the needs of disabled persons who be-come old.

REFERENCES

Benjamin, A. E., Jr. (1984, February). *State government perspectives on financing community care for the elderly*. Paper presented at the meeting of the American Hospital Association, San Diego, CA.

Callahan, J. J., & Wallack, S. S. (1981). *Reforming the long term care system*. Lexington, MA: D.C. Heath & Co.

Commerce Clearing House. (1983). *Medicare and Medicaid Guide*. Chicago: Author.

Coombs, S., Lambert, T., & Quirk, D. (Eds.). (1982). *An orientation to the Older Americans Act*. Washington, DC: National Association of State Units on Aging.

Farrow, F., Joe, T., Meltzer, J., & Richman, H. (1981). Introduction: The framework and directions for change. In J. Meltzer, F. Farrow, & H. Richman (Eds.), *Policy options in long-term care* (pp. 1–35). Chicago: University of Chicago Press.

Feder, J. (1983). Effects of changing federal health policies on the general public, the aged and disabled. *Bulletin of the New York Academy of Medicine, 59*(1), 41–49.

Gibson, R. M., Waldo, D. R., & Levit, K. R. (1983). National health expenditures, 1982. *Health Care Financing Review, 5*(1), 1–31.

Greenberg, J. N., & Lentz, W. N. (1983). *Financing long term care for the elderly: Building a base for long term solutions*. Unpublished manuscript, Brandeis University, University Health Policy Consortium, Waltham, MA.

Hamm, L. V., Kickham, T. M., & Cutler, D. A. (1984). Research, demonstrations and evaluations. In R. J. Vogel & H. C. Palmer (Eds.), *Long-term care: Perspectives from research and demonstrations* (pp. 167–253). Gaithersburg, MD: Aspen Systems.

Harrington, C., & Newcomer, R. J. (1982). United States: Coordinating services to the aged. In M. C. Hokenstad & R. Ritvo (Eds.), *Linking health and social services: International perspectives* (pp. 241–278). Beverly Hills: Sage Publications.

Knowlton, J., Clauser, S., & Fatula, J. (1982). Nursing home pre-admission screening: A review of state programs. *Health Care Financing Review, 3*, 75–88.

Little, V. (1982). *Open care for the aging*. New York: Springer.

Morris, R., & Binstock, R. H. (1966). *Feasible planning for social change*. New York: Columbia University Press.

Muse, D., & Sawyer, D. (1982). *The Medicare and Medicaid data book, 1981*. Baltimore: U.S. Health Care Financing Administration.

Newcomer, R. J., Benjamin, A. E., Jr., & Sattler, C. E. (1985). Equity and incentives in state Medicaid program eligibility. In C. Harrington, R. J. Newcomer, C. L. Estes, & Associates (Eds.), *Long term care of the elderly: Public policy issues*. Beverly Hills: Sage Publications.

Public Law 89-73. (1965). *The Older Americans Act of 1965 (as amended)*. Washington, DC: U.S. Government Printing Office.

Public Law 89-97. (1965). *Social Security Amendments of 1965*. Washington, DC: U.S. Government Printing Office.

Public Law 93-647. (1975). *Social Services Amendments of 1974*. Washington, DC: U.S. Government Printing Office.

Public Law 97-35. (1981). *Omnibus Budget Reconciliation Act of 1981*. Washington, DC: U.S. Government Printing Office.

Rice, D. P., & Feldman, J. J. (1983). Living longer in the United States: Demographic changes and health needs of the elderly. *Milbank Memorial Fund Quarterly/Health and Society. 16*(3), 362–396.

Scanlon, W. J. (1980). A theory of the nursing home market. *Inquiry, 17,* 25–41.

Stone, R., & Newcomer, R. J. (1985). Expanding the state role in board and care housing. In C. Harrington, R. J. Newcomer, C. L. Estes, & Associates (Eds.), *Long term care of the elderly: Public policy issues*. Beverly Hills: Sage Publications.

U.S. Health Care Financing Administration. (1981). *Long term care: Background and future directions*. Baltimore: Department of Health and Human Services.

U.S. Health Care Financing Administration. (1982). *Health care financing program statistics: The Medicare and Medicaid book, 1981*. Baltimore: U.S. Department of Health and Human Services.

U.S. Senate, Special Committee on Aging. (1982). *Developments in aging: 1981* (Report No. 97-314). Washington, DC: U.S. Government Printing Office.

chapter

3

An Overview of Developmental Disabilities

Leopold Lippman and David E. Loberg

The term "developmental disabilities" was first used to unite disabilities that are attributable to mental retardation, cerebral palsy, epilepsy, and other neurological conditions with etiologies that begin early in life or during the developmental period. The term first appeared in an enactment by Congress in 1970, and its meaning changed with every set of amendments during the next decade. This chapter examines the evolution of public concern for persons whose disabling conditions begin early in life. Before the rapid social change that occurred in the United States following World War II, the formation of nationwide organizations of parents, and the special public interest of a President of the United States, the options for parents of children with disabilities were few: institutionalization or lifetime care either paid for by families or, more often, provided by parents at home.

Today, as described in the following pages, there are numerous and varied programs, provided or sponsored by the states and financed in part by the federal government. Planning and coordination are the responsibility of the state developmental disabilities councils; advocacy, often leading to court suits, is the responsibility of state protection and advocacy agencies. Voluntary organizations of families, professional workers, and, increasingly, persons with developmental disabilities themselves constitute a growing source of strength and self-advocacy.

Persons with developmental disabilities only a generation ago had a short life expectancy. Today they are living longer, with the result that this population is changing, and so are the needs. Within the next 3 decades, new policy issues, especially those surrounding the aging of this population, will confront the planners and providers of services.

BEGINNINGS

UNTIL A RELATIVELY FEW years ago, parents of most handicapped children and adults, including even mildly mentally retarded individuals, were confronted with limited, and often painful, choices in meeting their children's needs for health care, therapy, education, and residential placement. As time passed and public schools began to offer special education classes, parents of adult sons or daughters whose handicaps limited their opportunities for employment and independent living were still offered few choices. Parents were essentially asked to choose between placement of their handicapped children in state-operated institutions that were almost always understaffed, overcrowded, and relatively inaccessible, or acceptance of the burden of providing care themselves either within the family or by paying for private, and generally expensive, care from their own resources for the indefinite future. In either case, the family viewed the long-term prospects for their handicapped offspring with anxiety made valid by the paucity of needed community services and the evident lack of the social commitment necessary to initiate and sustain them. The common advice given by family physicians and pediatricians was "try to find an institutional placement for such children so that parents could put them away and somehow hope to forget them."

This effort to "forget" was mirrored in the larger society as well. Individuals with mental retardation and cerebral palsy were routinely hidden by virtue of institutional placement along with, sometimes without distinction, mentally ill individuals. Families' sense of loss was attenuated by a sense of shame, guilt, or inadequacy. Concealment of the reality of having a mentally retarded child was common, sometimes by family members from one another.

In the middle of this century, conditions began to change for handicapped children and adults and their families. Some of these changes were the result of powerful forces that were set in motion by the global changes in the larger society that followed the conclusion of World War II. Others were initiated by the organizational work of parents and professionals that led to the establishment of, first, local associations and, later, networks of associations at the state and national level. Advocacy organizations such as the National Association for Retarded Children (now the Association for Retarded Citizens/United States), founded in 1950, and the United Cerebral Palsy Associations, founded the previous year, were effective in stirring public awareness of these disabilities not only as the problems of individuals and families but as social problems as well.

An important force for rapid social change in the late 1950s and 1960s was the militant assertion of civil rights by various groups: racial and ethnic minorities, especially blacks and, later, Hispanics, as well as youth, women, members of religious sects, senior citizens, homosexuals and, ultimately, various disability groups, including mentally ill and physically disabled individuals in the 1970s. Advocacy for the rights of individuals and groups

that had been traditionally left out of the mainstream of the society was a particularly relevant theme for advancing the needs of people with disabilities, and legislation and litigation on behalf of handicapped people began to appear as early as 1960.

It was also in 1960, at the sixth decennial White House Conference on Children and Youth, that the special problems of retarded children and their families were highlighted and the resulting discussions and decisions had the additional impact of encouraging Americans to recognize the problems of mental retardation as a shared responsibility.

There were also rising pressures on state legislatures and state governmental agencies with responsibility for the operation of public institutions for mentally retarded, cerebral palsied, and other disabled persons. Life expectancy of residents of institutions, which began to rise with improvements in health care (especially the advent of antibiotics), coupled with increasing postwar birthrates, produced increasingly extended waiting lists for admission to the state institutions in the 1950s. States were faced with the need for expensive institutional construction as well as the need to continually expand the numbers of institutions to meet the projected demand. Legislators were torn between the necessity for building costly new facilities and the dissatisfaction of parents with continuing institutional methods of service, especially when the needs of their handicapped children could be more appropriately met with community-based special education, therapies, specialized health care, and family support services. In this context, a variety of community-based services, especially increased use of outpatient mental health services, child guidance clinics, and family counseling, presented viable program models that offered the possibility of meeting the service needs of a fair portion of the severely handicapped population without relying on the traditional public institutions.

Another important development in the recognition of this population's special needs was the appointment by President John F. Kennedy, shortly after he took office in 1961, of the President's Panel on Mental Retardation, the first such national commission on the subject. President Kennedy instructed the panel to study existing services in the United States and elsewhere, and to, within a year, offer recommendations on what the federal government should do to improve services to mentally retarded individuals. The report, entitled: "A Proposed Program for National Action to Combat Mental Retardation," offered scores of recommendations under eight principal headings: research and scientific manpower; prevention; clinical and social services; education, vocational rehabilitation, and training; residential care; the law and the mentally retarded; public awareness; and organization of services—planning and coordination (President's Panel on Mental Retardation, 1962).

While many of the recommendations of the President's Panel were viewed as the responsibility of the U.S. Department of Health, Education and Welfare (now the Department of Health and Human Services), the report also proposed that states undertake comprehensive mental retardation planning at the state level as well.

President Kennedy also focused on the problems of mental disability when he gave his Special Message to the Congress on Mental Illness and Mental Retardation on February 5, 1963. He said, in part:

> mental illness and mental retardation are among our most critical health problems. They occur more frequently, affect more people, require more prolonged treatment, cause more suffering by the families of the afflicted, waste more of our human resources, and constitute more financial drain upon both the public treasury and the personal finances of the individual families than any other condition . . . The time has come for a bold new approach. (Public Papers of the Presidents, 1964, p. 126)

From the vantage point of the present it is possible to see how the problems faced by parents of handicapped children and adults began to be addressed and resolved. Within a few years of the founding of the National Association for Retarded Children and the United Cerebral Palsy Associations, these or-

ganizations, and others with a similar purpose, began to bring changes to the world of handicapped persons and their families: they created a vehicle through which parents of handicapped children could find each other and work together locally and nationally; they began to dispel families' feelings of shame, guilt, and isolation; they started to clear the way for public awareness of these disabilities as a social problem; and they launched the era of advocacy, which, in turn, resulted in the interest and support of political leaders such as President Kennedy and ultimately increased and expanded provisions for governmental funds and services for handicapped persons.

THE LEGISLATIVE HISTORY

In 1963, two significant pieces of federal legislation were passed by Congress. First, the Social Security Act was amended to authorize funds for maternal and infant care grants and for comprehensive mental retardation planning at the state level through Public Law 88-156 (Maternal and Child Health and Mental Retardation Planning Amendments). Second, a separate enactment in the same session of Congress provided funds for construction of mental retardation facilities and community mental health centers by the passage of Public Law 88-164 (Mental Retardation Facilities and Community Mental Health Centers Construction Act). Just 3 weeks before President Kennedy was killed, he signed this legislation.

In 1969, during the process of authorizing the continuation of the legislation of 1963, Congress was urged to broaden the focus of these programs beyond mental retardation since other neurologically handicapping conditions also presented needs for planning for services and treatment that were similar to the planning required for mental retardation. As a result, the expression "developmental disabilities" was substituted for "mental retardation," as used in the earlier law, and the following definition was enacted:

> The term "developmental disability" means a disability attributable to mental retardation, cere-

bral palsy, epilepsy, or other neurological condition of an individual found by the Secretary to be closely related to mental retardation or to require treatment similar to that required for mentally retarded individuals, which disability originates before such individual attains age eighteen, which has continued or can be expected to continue indefinitely, and which constitutes a substantial handicap to the individual. (Public Law 91-517, Developmental Disabilities Services and Facilities Construction Act, enacted October 30, 1970)

Thus, the "bold new approach" to mental illness and mental retardation, called for by President Kennedy in 1963, was expanded to include other disabling conditions by the 1970 enactment. In 1975, with additional amendments to the Developmental Disabilities Act (Public Law 94-103), the law was further broadened to include autism.

The conditions that are conventionally included within these categorical disabilities may vary in practice but the following descriptions and sources are representative:

Autism is generally described as being "characterized by a pervasive lack of responsiveness to other people, gross deficits in language and communication, bizarre responses to the environment, with onset most often prior to 30 months of age" (Grossman, 1983, p. 160).

Cerebral palsy is defined as a nonprogressive disorder that is characterized by "aberrations of motor function (paralysis, weakness, incoordination) and often other manifestations of organic brain damage, such as sensory disorders, seizures, mental retardation, learning difficulty and behavioral disorders" (Grossman, 1983, p. 163).

Epilepsy is clinically described as a convulsive disorder which, as a term, "subsumes a number of brain-centered nervous system disorders characterized as sudden seizures, muscle convulsions, and partial or total loss of consciousness due to abnormal patterns of discharges of brain cells" (Office of Mental Retardation and Developmental Disabilities, 1984, p. 137).

Mental retardation is characterized by "significantly subaverage general intellectual functioning existing concurrently with deficits in adaptive behavior and manifested during the developmental period." Levels of retardation are mild mental retardation (intelligence quotients of 50 or 55 to approximately 70), moderate mental retardation (intelligence quotients of 35 or 40 to 50 or 55), severe mental retardation (intelligence quotients of 20 or 25 to 35 or 40), and profound mental retardation (intelligence quotients below 20 or 25) (Grossman, 1983, p. 184).

In addition to expanding the category of eligible disabilities, the 1975 amendments to PL 94-103 directed the Secretary of Health, Education and Welfare to initiate a study to explore the suitability of the definition and to recommend a more effective approach.

A broadly representative task force was commissioned to study the issue, hold hearings, and make recommendations to the Secretary. In its report to the Secretary in 1977, the study group concluded that the term "developmental disabilities" should not be used to simply bring together a collection of existing labels or conditions. Rather, persons with developmental disabilities are individuals who are experiencing a chronic disability that substantially limits their functioning in a variety of areas of major life activity central to independent living (Thompson & O'Quinn, 1979). The study group advocated for the adoption of a generic or functional definition that would cut across specific categories or conditions and urged that a developmental disability be defined as a severe, chronic disability of a person that is attributable to a mental *or* physical impairment. This provision precipitated a public division within the task force and several of the members filed a minority report with the Secretary and the Congress. The minority report argued that the terms "mental or physical impairment" would produce confusion at the state administrative level, and it proposed retention of the most recently adopted categorical definition along with the addition of a series of specified disabling conditions. This difference between the two reports from the task force was carried into the Congressional deliberations, with the Senate adopting the recommendations of the task force majority and the House of Representatives adopting a bill that followed the recommendations of the task force minority. In the conference that followed the conflicting actions of the two houses of Congress, the Senate version, utilizing the "functional" rather than the "categorical" definition, was accepted and included as a part of the Rehabilitation, Comprehensive Services, and Developmental Disabilities Amendments of 1978 and, with the signature of President Carter on November 6, 1978, became the law (Public Law 95-602). The definition in this enactment, which is still embodied in Public Law 98-527, the Developmental Disabilities Act of 1984, is

A developmental disability is a severe, chronic disability of a person which—
1. is attributable to a mental or physical impairment or combination of mental and physical impairments;
2. is manifest before age 22;
3. is likely to continue indefinitely;
4. results in substantial functional limitations in three or more of the following areas of major life activity:
   a. self-care,
   b. receptive and expressive language,
   c. learning,
   d. mobility,
   e. self-direction,
   f. capacity for independent living, or
   g. economic self-sufficiency; and
5. reflects the need for a combination and sequence of special, interdisciplinary, or generic care, treatment, or other services which are
   a. of lifelong or extended duration and are
   b. individually planned and coordinated.

IMPLEMENTATION BY STATES

An important aspect of the legislation pertaining to developmental disabilities was the requirement that states, in order to qualify for federal Developmental Disabilities funds, must establish a state developmental disabilities planning council. This body, modeled in some ways on the President's Committee on Mental Retardation, was to be appointed by the governor, and was to include representatives of the various disabling conditions (e.g., persons with cerebral palsy, persons with epilepsy, parents of persons with mental retardation) along with other citizens and state officials whose agencies received or administered funds from the various federal sources that are used to serve people with developmental disabilities.

The primary responsibility of each state developmental disabilities planning council under federal law is to prepare, every 3 years, a comprehensive developmental disabilities plan, and to review it annually. The contents of the plan are to include a description of the population of developmentally disabled persons (by age and by county) a review of existing services, an assessment of the unmet need, and a prioritized set of recommendations for short-range and long-range development of additional needed services.

Federal law calls for each state council to designate two categories of services, at least one of which shall be selected from the following areas: case management services, child development services, alternative community living arrangement services, and employment related activities services. The council is required to allocate 65% of its basic allotment of federal funds for these specified services.

In addition to these mandated responsibilities, some state councils undertake to promote active cooperation and coordination among state government service agencies, and many embark on a variety of advocacy efforts. Just as they currently coordinate activities with state agencies such as public health, education, rehabilitation, social welfare, and recreation, it may be expected that, with the aging of the population with developmental disabilities, councils will work as well with state agencies serving older citizens.

In every state, there also exists a state department or a division of a larger agency that is specifically charged under state law with the responsibility for certain services to state residents with mental retardation and other developmental disabilities. Most of these state agencies existed long before the original enactment (1970) of federal legislation calling for developmental disabilities councils, and they continue to provide direct services and at many times administer one of the largest components of the state budget. In former years, these departments were known, in various states, by such names as "Institutions" or "Mental Hygiene." Today, they range from a Department of Developmental Services (California) to an Office of Mental Retardation and Developmental Disabilities (New York) or a Division of Mental Retardation in a Department of Human Services (New Jersey). (For a comprehensive list of the titles and addresses of state agencies with responsibility for serving individuals with developmental disabilities, see the Appendix at the end of this chapter.)

Whether a bureau, a division, or a full department, the state agency's responsibilities include operation of state residential facilities and either the direct provision or the funding under contract with counties or local agencies for the provision of community services. In many states, the same agency has responsibility for licensing and monitoring the services provided by voluntary and proprietary service organizations. In some states as well, the state developmental disabilities agency accepts responsibility for guardianship for those retarded or otherwise disabled individuals for whom no other guardian is available.

Under the federal Developmental Disabilities Act, each state must designate an administrative agency to carry out the implementing functions that follow from council policy decisions—for example, the disbursement and monitoring of grants for pilot demonstration projects under the council's service priorities. Often, though not always, the administrative responsibility is given to the same agency that provides direct services in the field.

The various legislative enactments pertaining to developmental disabilities also contained other important provisions. For example, to qualify for federal funds, states were required to establish or designate a Protection and Advocacy Agency for people with developmental disabilities who reside in the state. While most state councils clearly adopt an advocacy role in carrying out their planning and coordinative functions, the Protection and Advocacy Agency is expected to serve as the advocate for individuals by disseminating information concerning the rights of people with developmental disabilities and helping them (individually and by class action litigation) to obtain services from which they may have been discriminatorily excluded on the basis of disability or without due process. The Protection and Advocacy Agency may be a private, nonprofit entity or a unit of state government as, for example, the state consumer services agency, but it may not be a part of any state agency responsible for the provision of services specifically to people with developmental disabilities. The independence of protection and advocacy agencies is essential since they must be free to assist people with developmental disabilities in obtaining the services to which they are entitled, even when this assistance means contesting with other public agencies by advancing their claims through the courts.

A third component of the federal Developmental Disabilities Act is the provision for University Affiliated Programs (UAP). There are 51 such facilities throughout the United States, most of them operating under the auspices of medical schools. In addition to funding under PL 98-527 (Developmental Disabilities Act Amendments of 1984), most of them also receive federal funds under the Maternal and Child Health Program (MCH) as well as from other sources. Each university affiliated program is expected to provide training of professional and other workers in developmental disabilities and to conduct pertinent research, while some of them may also provide direct service as a model for state and community service providers. Under current law, the UAF has representation on the developmental disabilities council where it is located, but its responsibility is to the entire federal region in which it functions, rather than only to the state of its location.

It is generally acknowledged that states have expended and continue to expend considerable resources on behalf of their residents with developmental disabilities. The state agencies with responsibility for mental retardation services have relatively large budgets in comparison with other state programs. Comprehensive residential services for severely handicapped people are, for the most part, extremely labor intensive and the budgets of these agencies reflect the large expenditures that are required to house people in institutional living arrangements that meet even minimum standards of safety and sanitation.

It is important to recognize that this new approach to developmental disabilities was intended to assist states to make more effective use of resources that were already being disbursed. This new emphasis on planning was expected to be an appropriate remedy. To the extent that states could be assisted by the federal government to develop alternatives to institutional placements, the states could begin to achieve not only economies in their institutions, but also the possibility of an improved quality of life for people who were transferred to community-based living arrangements or diverted before placement in institutions to community-based living arrangements.

ISSUES OF STATE
LEVEL IMPLEMENTATION

In some respects, the value of this "new approach," especially the effectiveness of the use of planning as an explicit intervention to achieve nondisruptive reform and improvements in the delivery system of services for people with developmental disabilities, is still not fully realized. There is a growing consensus that states should realign their financial support, representing an impressively large share of general revenue expenditures in many states, away from the large institutions of the past and toward community-based services. At the same time, the states must wrestle with effecting this diversification—developing a full continuum of services—without sacrificing the continuity of services that is critically necessary for current recipients. The President's Committee on Mental Retardation from the beginning has urged that thousands of individuals be returned to their home communities from public institutions; however, the reality is that federal policy itself acts as a disincentive by continuing to

provide federal reimbursement more readily for institutional services than for community services.

During the past 20 years, in the face of often-intense resistance from families of institutionalized residents and public employees of institutions, the population of the large public institutions (i.e., over 100 residents) serving people with mental retardation has declined by nearly 70,000 residents, or 36% (Bruininks, Hauber, Hill, Lakin, McGuire, Rotegard, Scheerenberger, & White, 1983; Scheerenberger, 1976, 1982). More importantly, the growth in community-based services, including day programs and residential alternatives, has been dramatic. It is ironic that the policy positions of the federal and state governments seem almost to have been reversed in recent years. As recently as 15 years ago, most states were committed to congregate care in large, state-run institutions, and the federal government was beginning to articulate goals for large-scale deinstitutionalization (See President's Committee on Mental Retardation, 1969, 1970, 1971). Today, most states strive to refer disabled persons to placements other than institutions, but the relative volume of funds available and the regulatory requirements for participation in the Medicaid Program (Title XIX of the Social Security Act)—particularly for Intermediate Care Facilities for the Mentally Retarded (ICFs/MR)—have created incentives for continuing to rely on institutional services. Consider the following position statement of the National Association of State Mental Retardation Program Directors: "the central policy question which must be resolved is: how can we facilitate this process (providing a significant number of institutional residents with community-based services) through alterations in Federal policy. '. . [when]' existing Federal Medicaid policy offers the states powerful incentives to place and maintain disabled persons in large, multi-purpose long term care institutions . . .?" (National Association of State Mental Retardation Program Directors, 1984).

The success of the advocacy and legal services activities envisioned by the original developmental disabilities legislation is more easily demonstrated. The 16 years since 1969 have been filled with individual plaintiff and class action litigation directed often at state governments on behalf of people with developmental disabilities at every level of jurisdiction of the judicial system. While the various effects of this flood of advocacy and litigation, considering the neglected condition of the service systems of the states, in terms of cause, may not be directly associated to the federal developmental disabilities legislation alone, there is little question that litigation has had a significant impact on both the lives of individuals with developmental disabilities and the administrative practices of state service systems. In some cases the effect has been to stimulate legislation that was passed by state legislatures to correct the abuses that were first exposed through the courts. In other cases, administrative policy has been broadly changed in response to successful litigation, and, nearly everywhere, the attitudes of the public have changed in the direction of increasing acceptance of full citizenship and entitlement to publicly funded community services of people who are handicapped with developmental disabilities.

The examples are many: Public Law 94-142, the Education for All Handicapped Children Act of 1975, was stimulated directly by the success of the Pennsylvania Association for Retarded Children in its landmark case against the Commonwealth of Pennsylvania in which the Commonwealth accepted the "obligation to place each mentally retarded child in a free, public program of education and training appropriate to the child's capacity" (Lippman & Goldberg, 1973, p. 31). The *Wyatt* v. *Stickney* case in Alabama challenged, on the basis of a "right to treatment," the constitutionality of the services afforded the mentally ill and mentally retarded residents of Alabama's state hospitals. The Willowbrook Consent Decree successfully imposed on the state of New York the responsibility to afford the residents of Willowbrook a right to "protection from harm." Perhaps the most famous case, the Pennhurst suit, initiated by a parent of a resident of Pennsylvania's Pennhurst State School and

Hospital and supported by the Pennsylvania Association for Retarded Children, gave specificity to both the right to "protection from harm" and the principle of the right to be provided services in "the least restrictive alternative." These prominent cases are only the more visible symbols in an expanding volume of complaints and appeals with the result that it is now commonplace for courts to presume the validity of claims based on the right of people with disabilities to be free from discriminatory practices in receiving services in the same way that comparable protections are now presumptively recognized on the basis of race, sex, national origin, and religion.

THE ADVOCACY ORGANIZATIONS

A special, and in some ways unique, aspect of the evolving pattern of services for persons with developmental disabilities has been the prominence and impact of voluntary associations, organized principally by parents of disabled individuals, but often with the assistance of professionals.

The first two associations to achieve widespread organization, as alluded to earlier, were the National Association for Retarded Citizens (NARC, now the Association for Retarded Citizens/United States) and the United Cerebral Palsy Associations (UCPA). The first, NARC, consisted largely of parents of both children and adults, and its organizational pattern was largely from the bottom up; that is, the power and much of the activity were at the local unit level. UCPA, which has relied more substantially on professional workers and public relations and fund-raising specialists, was more centralized, operating at the national level. In the early years (the 1950s and early 60s), NARC sought to "obtain, not provide" services, while UCPA developed local direct service programs. Today, the local units of ARC/US provide services in most states and communities, in addition to maintaining their advocacy role, and UCPA engages in advocacy as well as the provision of services.

Other organizations that developed in subsequent years (some based on the model of NARC or UCPA, others with different styles)

include the Epilepsy Foundation of America (EFA), the National Society for Children and Adults with Autism (NSAC), and the Association for Children and Adults with Learning Disabilities (ACLD). There are also relatively new organizations that in some instances broke away from the broader organizations to provide more specialized services; among these are the National Down's Syndrome Congress and the Spina Bifida Association of America.

On the national level, most of these organizations conduct continuing efforts at public information. Their most significant and far-reaching impact is, perhaps, in the area of advocacy at the governmental level. Most of the organizations maintain offices in or near Washington, D.C., and stay in continual touch with Congressional committees and with key administrative officials in the executive branch. The shape of the Developmental Disabilities Act in 1970 was directly attributable in substantial part to the energetic efforts of two virtually full-time volunteers representing NARC and UCPA (Elizabeth M. Boggs and Elsie Helsel), who worked for many months on the national legislative scene to inform Congressional leaders and their staff. Today, EFA, NSAC, and some of the others maintain a continuing presence on Capitol Hill and in the offices of the Department of Health and Human Services, the Department of Education, and other key federal agencies.

These and other organizations are also active at the state level or within states when they have an affiliated chapter. Most of them also offer selected services, such as information and referral and parent assistance through local offices or by mail when local chapters are nonexistent. These organizations serve as forceful advocates for the disabled population, working both with state legislatures and public agencies. In this regard, they are often consulted concerning policy questions and asked to provide information on population prevalence estimates and service needs. Oftentimes, too, they are the source of members on state bodies such as the developmental disabilities planning councils or other planning or advisory bodies.

ESTIMATES OF THE DEVELOPMENTAL DISABILITIES POPULATION

As aptly noted by Lubin and Kiely in this volume (Chapter 6), reliable data on the incidence and prevalence of the full range of conditions representing developmental disabilities are difficult to obtain. For the purposes of public policy and administration in the developmental disabilities field, most estimates of the number of developmentally disabled people have not come from rigorous epidemiological studies, but from other means of estimating a population, such as the use of various national data sources (Barker & Kogan, 1983; Baroff, 1982; Boggs & Henney, 1979; Gollay, 1979; Summers, 1981). Consequently, for many of these studies, the differences in study methodology, clinical or program terminology, or even the criteria by which disabilities are defined call for caution in how these estimates are used.

For each of the categorical developmental disabilities, there are in use prevalent national estimates of the focal population. Each of the national advocacy organizations representing individual disability interests promotes prevalence figures for the disability for which it has a concern; these prevalence rates then in turn are used for national and regional population estimates. As an overall estimate of mental retardation, the Association for Retarded Citizens has historically used 3.0% of the population. Applying this rate against the total population of the United States would result in an estimate of some 6 million persons with mental retardation. The United Cerebral Palsy Associations uses a rate of 0.3% for estimating the number of Americans with cerebral palsy. Using this rate, this leads to an estimate of approximately 700,000 to 750,000 persons nationally with this disability. For estimating the number of persons in the United States with epilepsy, the Epilepsy Foundation of America uses 0.4%; this would lead to an estimate of some 1 million Americans with epilepsy. The National Society for Children and Adults with Autism estimates that there are about 80,000 children and adults in the United States who may be autistic.

State developmental disabilities plans are another source of gross estimation of the developmental disabilities population. Taking the aggregate of the population estimates in each of these plans results in an overall national estimate of some 3 million developmentally disabled persons in need of service in the United States (or a rate of 120/10,000). Correspondingly, the United States Department of Health and Human Service's Administration on Developmental Disabilities has estimated that there are about 3.9 million persons who can be characterized as developmentally disabled (Office of Human Development Services, 1984). However, this greater number is most probably used because of the federal government's "hold harmless" policy stemming from the change from the categorical to functional approach to defining developmental disabilities. Otherwise, a large number of mildly mentally retarded persons would be excluded from the current developmental disabilities program because of the restrictiveness of the substantial handicapped aspect of the functional definition.

There are a number of inherent difficulties in attempting to develop gross estimates of the number of individuals who may be developmentally disabled. Illustrative of this is the evolution of the definition of mental retardation. During the 1970s, as result of the work of a number of researchers such as Edgerton (1967), Mercer (1973, 1975), and others, the sociocultural perspective began to influence the manner in which mental retardation was defined and consequently what was meant by the data that evolved from a number of epidemiological studies. As a result, with the increasing emphasis on the need for a behavioral basis for defining mental retardation (rather than solely relying upon measures of intellectual performance), the American Association on Mental Deficiency (see Grossman, 1973) changed the threshold for the definition of significant subaverage intellectual functioning from an IQ of 85 to one of 70 (approximately 2 standard deviations below the mean) and required that there be a concurrent impairment in adaptive behavior. These changes and the influence of the work of Tarjan, Wright, Eyman, and Keeran (1973) and Mercer (1973) lead to 1% as the generally accepted revised estimate of mental retardation. In fact, Mercer's comprehensive survey of Riverside, California, was guided by her belief that some individuals who were potentially indentifiable as being mentally retarded by intelligence tests alone may be quite adept socially and need not become classified as mentally retarded.

Another factor that confounds attempts at estimating the number of persons with developmental disabilities is the confusion between the use of *incidence* and *prevalence* (Maloney & Ward, 1979). Incidence is the number of cases being identified at any particular time period. Prevalence is the total number of cases at any point in time. Confusion between these two measures often leads to differing estimates of a particular population; for example, the incidence of a condition may be 3% and the prevalence may be 1%.

Many national estimates of the total developmentally disabled population are confounded because rates for each of the individual disabilities are combined without regard to two factors: a) that there is overlap among the people ostensibly counted by this method— that is, one person may have more than one disability; and b) that only a portion of the overall number may have an impairment that renders them substantially disabled—thus meeting the definition of a developmental disability. For instance, if limiting cases to those with a substantial handicap had the effect of eliminating persons with mild mental retardation, then the consequent estimate for one portion of the developmentally disabled population would certainly be lower than previously estimated. Furthermore, if some 60%–80% of severely mentally retarded persons also have epilepsy, cerebral palsy, or autism (as some have estimated), then the overall population estimate would be reduced even further.

With the advent of the 1978 amendments to the Developmental Disabilities Act and the requirement of a functional rather than categorical approach to defining the developmentally disabled population, estimating this population has become even more difficult. The major attempt to project an estimate using the functional definition approach was that of Boggs and Henney (1979). Rather than a field investigation, they drew upon two sources: a) data that were available as a result of the Survey of Income and Education (SIE) that was conducted in 1976 by the United States Bureau of the Census (United States Bureau of the Census, 1976), and b) state developmental disabilities plans. Using these two sources, they concluded that there were some 3,350,000 persons with developmental disabilities in the United States (or approximately 1.57% of the overall population could be expected to meet the criteria inherent in the functional definition). However, these estimates cannot be accepted without certain reservations. First, the study used estimates for children age 2 and younger that were based upon the authors' hypothetical projections. Second, the SIE data excluded persons in institutions. Both these factors may have affected, in a variety of ways, the overall number that was obtained.

A more frequently used approach for estimation (sometimes referred to as treated prevalence) is simply to count the numbers of persons in service or in need of service. Such approaches usually add together the disabled persons receiving services from all sources with those on waiting lists. Although this method has its merits, it also has limitations. First, the same individual may be counted more than once when multiple providers are used, and second, it is difficult to estimate an unexpressed need for service. Many individuals may not be included in such counts because the disabled individual or his or her family may not be aware of the service system or, due to frustration with waiting lists, has dropped out of the demand population. Although local efforts have used this method and have produced estimates of both population and need, there are no national estimates of the overall population that have resulted from a treated prevalence approach.

As noted above, there are limitations to any developmental disabilities population estimation method that must be considered. For example, some are based upon theoretical projections from the normal distribution curve, rather than having an inductive data base. Data measures used in this method (other than with mental retardation) do not have the theoretical underpinnings of a normal distribution and a nationally promulgated threshold. Another limitation is that some figures include the milder levels of impairment of the various disabilities; consequently, these figures may not be consistent with generally accepted definitions of developmental disabilities (as used in law and accepted practice). Furthermore, some methods use straight addition that may yield misleadingly high figures, because many developmentally disabled persons, especially those most severely impaired, may have multiple conditions (Lubin, Jacobson, & Kiely, 1982). What this means is that although there are available general estimates of the overall developmentally disabled population, there remains great variability in the use and acceptance of any one particular estimate for the whole population. Epidemiological studies that focus on one disability or one specific cohort within a disability group offer more promise for developing a usable yet restrictive population figure; these are discussed in Chapter 6.

POLICY ISSUES: PRESENT AND FUTURE

There are numerous issues of public policy with regard to the status and treatment of persons with developmental disabilities who are aging through the middle years and into later life. Some of these issues are current; some are readily forecast for the coming decades and require early consideration. The questions that have dominated the dialogue of the past become even more difficult when we confront the fact that the population of people with development disabilities is, more than ever before, distributed across the length of the lifespan. While people with developmental disabilities are still significantly underrepresented among elderly persons in the United States, the proportion of people with developmental disabilities who, each year, reach the middle years and, for some, the "senior" period of life, is a

dynamic, new, social phenomenon. This overview is too limited to respond to the policy
questions; it is possible only to begin to *frame*
them. Some of the tentative answers are found
in the subsequent chapters of this book. The
other questions stand as continuing challenges
to professional workers, public officials, legislators, leaders in higher education, and researchers. What follows are some of the critical
issues that are certain to have an effect upon
persons with developmental disabilities.

*Will changing demographics affect the size
of the developmentally disabled population?* Demographic changes are predictable,
although of course not in every detail. It is safe
to anticipate that there will be increasing numbers of aging and elderly persons with developmental disabilities. It may also be expected, at
least for the short run, that infants with serious
damage will survive when formerly they would
have been stillborn or would have died in
infancy. It is not possible to predict the numerical size of these changes, but it is already clear
that families, the helping professions, and society will be confronted with a substantially new
population of persons in need.

*What will be the changes in the character of
the developmentally disabled population?*
Prevention and early intervention will also
affect long-term demographic trends. Advances
in technology and improvements in caregiving
will decrease the number of developmental
disabilities. Amniocentesis, with the possibility of termination of pregnancy, detection of
fetal anomalies *in utero* and prenatal corrective
action, infant stimulation and other early developmental services that may minimize the
seriousness of the disabling conditions, social
interventions to improve maternal and infant
nutrition, and reduction of the threat of lead
poisoning from the environment all may contribute to a reduced incidence of developmental
disabilities. On the other hand, the prevention
of the severe effects of phenylketonuria (PKU)
by mandatory testing of newborns and intervention through pharmaceutical diets may have
the secondary effect of enlarging the gene pool
of PKU women who, in the next generation,
may give birth to more children at risk (Hansen, 1975).

*What does aging among developmentally
disabled persons represent?* There are significant policy considerations that arise from
the impact of the aging process upon developmentally disabled persons. Perhaps more critical than attempting to pinpoint any specific
point in development that marks aging among
the developmentally disabled population is the
recognition that aging reflects a decreased reserve and there is a wide range of variability
among older developmentally disabled people
as to when age makes its initial impact. From
the perspective of public policy and clinical
services, chronological age should not be the
sole determinant of need; more important is
biological age. Furthermore, aging requires a
reformulation of the composition and character
of services that are offered to an older adult; it
also means that serious consideration must be
given to drawing upon new resources for comprising the set of services provided as part of an
older individual's program plan.

*What is the best way to handle residential
care for an aging population of people with
developmental disabilities?* Deinstitutionalization and its concomitant, community living,
remain important current issues. Increasingly,
there is social acceptance of the trend toward
the provision of services within the community
and in environments that represent the least
restrictive alternative. For children and young
adults, this is most often the treatment of choice;
and planners and budget-makers support it as
well. But what happens when disabled persons, as they age, develop new frailties and
experience additional needs for protection and
service? Is there a critical point at which they
may be at risk of being rehoused in congregate
care settings? If so, what kind of facilities will
these be: state-operated institutions? hospitals?
nursing homes? old age housing? After having
spent a significant portion of their lives in
community-based living arrangements, will
they be prepared for a more structured or different style of life in their later years?

*What will be the best means to offer legal
protection?* Increasingly frail and decreas-
ingly competent persons may require guardianship services in varying degrees. There may be
a need for different levels of guardianship and

protection responsive to the needs of dependent persons, not all of whom are totally incompetent by any means. The prototype legislation was developed in California in the 1960s (Kay, Farnham, Karren, Knakal, & Diamond, 1972), and today some 25 states have legal provisions for limiting the authority of guardians and conservators to those decisions that are demonstrably necessary on the basis of the needs of individuals with disabilities. Will these provisions for limited guardianship or conservatorship meet the special needs of aging persons with developmental disabilities?

What will the public attitudes be toward aging developmentally disabled persons? The attitudes of a generation ago that were so vigorously rejecting have begun to change. But, how soon—if ever—will persons with developmental disabilities be accepted fully in the public schools, in employment, in recreation, and as neighbors in residential communities? Will the problems of aging combined with those of developmental disability affect the progress that has been made in improving public recognition of the needs of developmental disabilities persons during the past 2 decades?

Will there be a commitment to fund needed services? The touchstone by which economists assess value and formulate policy issues is the concept of "scarce resources." More scarce or less scarce, there is no question that resources are finite, and the reality of this limitation poses important questions of public policy. In the current era, for a range of reasons, expansion of governmental support of human services has ceased. If there is not actual retrenchment, there is a decline in the rate of expansion of the resources for human services that represents a psychological swing of the pendulum away from reasonable levels of government support. There have always been competing claims for funding of human services. Now the competition is in a larger arena including the claims of the military at the national level, the crumbling infrastructure at the local level, and the resistance of taxpayers of the predominant middle class. All of these competing claims will mitigate against policies and programs that would have the effect of expanding the resources needed to care for increased numbers of aging developmentally disabled persons.

Who will provide services? A trend that has been developing for more than 2 decades is the changing balance and relationship between the public and voluntary sectors. There was a time when the two were easily distinguishable. On the one hand, governmental agencies dealt with economic disaster and its effects, and with disabled people deemed in need of institutional care. On the other hand, private social services were supported by philanthropy, making them more palliative but generally effective. Today—and more so in the years to come—the lines have become blurred. For instance, voluntary (nongovernmental) agencies provide services with public funding and governmental oversight. Public agencies operate in part through contracts with private agencies.

Will the voluntary agencies continue to change their roles? The role of organizations of disabled persons and their families has changed. In the 1950s, the National Association for Retarded Children set as one of its goals, "to obtain, not provide" the services children needed. Today, many of the local associations have moved into the role of service provider along with the role of advocate to obtain services. To what extent are these two activities compatible, and how long can the Association for Retarded Citizens, United Cerebral Palsy, and others continue to perform both functions?

Will self-help groups play a larger role in advocacy and service delivery? A fairly recent development has been the establishment by disabled individuals of self-help and self-advocacy organizations. Among these are People First, Disabled in Action, and the Centers for Independent Living. Their activity and impact have thus far been relatively small, but one may predict that they will grow in numbers and in influence. What changes will this phenomenon produce in the nature, pattern, and control of service programs? How, in turn, will the presence of increasing numbers of older people with developmental disabilities influence the agenda and the priorities of the self-advocacy organizations?

REFERENCES

Barker, L. T., & Kogan, D. (1983). Study of the federal definition of developmental disability, Final Report, done for the California Health and Welfare Agency, Berkeley, CA. Berkeley Planning Associates.

Baroff, G. S. (1982). Predicting the prevalence of mental retardation in individual catchment areas. *Mental Retardation, 20,* 133–135.

Boggs, E., & Henney, L. (1979). *A numerical and functional description of the developmentally disabled population in the United States by major life activities.* Philadelphia: EMC Institute.

Bruininks, R. H., Hauber, F. A., Hill, B. K., Lakin, K. C., McGuire, S. P., Rotegard, L. L., Scheerenberger, R. C., & White, C. C. (1983). *1982 National Census of Residential Facilities: Summary Report* (Brief #21), Minneapolis: University of Minnesota, Center for Residential and Community Services.

Edgerton, R. B. (1967). *The cloak of competence.* Berkeley: University of California Press.

Gollay, E. (1979). *The modified definition of developmental disabilities: An initial exploration.* Columbia, MD: Morgan Management Systems, Inc.

Grossman, H. J. (Ed.). (1973). *Manual on terminology and classification in mental retardation,* (1973 revision). Washington, DC: American Association on Mental Deficiency.

Grossman, H. J. (Ed.). (1983). *Classification in mental retardation.* Washington, DC: American Association on Mental Deficiency.

Hansen, H. (1975). Prevention of mental retardation due to PKU: Selected aspects of program validity. *Preventive Medicine, 4,* 310–321.

Kay, H. H., Farnham, L. J., Karren, B. D., Knakal, J., & Diamond, P. M. (1972). Legal planning for the mentally retarded: The California experience. *California Law Review, 60,* 438–529.

Lippman, L., & Goldberg, I. I. (1973). *Right to education: Anatomy of the Pennsylvania case and its implications for exceptional children.* New York: Teachers College Press.

Lubin, R., Jacobson, J. W., & Kiely, M. (1982). Projected impact of the functional definition of developmental disabilities: The categorically disabled population and service eligibility. *American Journal of Mental Deficiency, 87,* 73–79.

Maloney, M. P., & Ward, M. P. (1979). *Mental retardation and modern society.* New York: Oxford University Press.

Mercer, J. R. (1973). *Labeling the mentally retarded.* Berkeley: University of California Press.

Mercer, J. R. (1975). Sociocultural factors in educational labeling. In M. Begab & S. A. Richardson (Eds.), *The mentally retarded and society: A social science perspective* (pp. 141–157). Baltimore: University Park Press.

National Association of State Mental Retardation Program Directors. (1984). Position statement: Community and family living amendments of 1983 (S. 2053—Chafee), Alexandria, Virginia (mimeographed).

Office of Human Development Services. (1984, February). *Human Development News.* Washington, DC: United States Department of Health and Human Services.

Office of Mental Retardation and Developmental Disabilities, New York State. (1984). *The 1984–87 comprehensive plan for services to persons with mental retardation and developmental disabilities in New York state.* Albany: Author.

President's Committee on Mental Retardation. (1969). *Annual report: 1969.* Washington, DC: U.S. Government Printing Office.

President's Committee on Mental Retardation. (1970). *Annual report: 1970.* Washington, DC: U.S. Government Printing Office.

President's Committee on Mental Retardation. (1971). *Annual report: 1971.* Washington, DC: U.S. Government Printing Office.

President's Panel on Mental Retardation. (1962). *A proposed program for national action to combat mental retardation.* Washington, DC: U.S. Government Printing Office.

Public Law 88-156, Maternal and Child Health and Mental Retardation Planning Amendments of 1963.

Public Law 88-164, Mental Retardation Facilities and Community Mental Health Centers Construction Act of 1963.

Public Law 91-517, Developmental Disabilities Services and Facilities Construction Act of 1970, October 30, 1970.

Public Law 94-103, Developmentally Disabled Assistance and Bill of Rights Act of 1975, June 26, 1975.

Public Law 95-602, Rehabilitation, Comprehensive Services, and Developmental Disabilities Amendments of 1978, November 6, 1978.

Public Law 98-527, The Developmental Disabilities Act of 1984.

Public papers of the presidents—John F. Kennedy, 1963. (1964). Washington, DC: U.S. Government Printing Office.

Scheerenberger, R. C. (1976). *Public residential services for the mentally retarded.* National Association of Superintendents of Public Residential Facilities for the Mentally Retarded.

Scheerenberger, R. C. (1982). Public residential services, 1981: Status and trends. *Mental Retardation, 20,* 210–215.

Summers, J. A. (1981). The definition of developmental disabilities: A concept in transition. *Mental Retardation, 19,* 259–265.

Tarjan, G., Wright, S. W., Eyman, R. K., & Keeran, D. V. (1973). Natural history of mental retardation: Some aspects of epidemiology. *American Journal of Mental Deficiency, 77,* 369–379.

Thompson, R. J., Jr., & O'Quinn, A. N. (1979). *Developmental disabilities: Etiologies, manifestations, diagnoses, and treatments.* New York: Oxford University Press.

United States Bureau of the Census. (1976). *Survey of income and education.* Washington, DC: Author.

APPENDIX

State Agencies with Responsibility for Mental Retardation and Developmental Disabilities Services in the United States
1984

State	MR/DD State Unit	State Agency	Location
Alabama	Associate Commissioner for Mental Retardation	Department of Mental Health	Montgomery, Alabama
Alaska	Developmental Disabilities Section Division of Mental Health and Developmental Disabilities	Department of Health and Social Services	Juneau, Alaska
Arizona	Division of Developmental Disabilities	Department of Economic Security	Phoenix, Arizona
Arkansas	Developmental Disabilities Services	Department of Human Services	Little Rock, Arkansas
California	Department of Developmental Services	Health & Welfare Agency	Sacramento, California
Colorado	Division for Developmental Disabilities	Department of Institutions	Denver, Colorado
Connecticut	Department of Mental Retardation		West Hartford, Connecticut
Delaware	Division of Mental Retardation	Department of Health & Social Services	Dover, Delaware
District of Columbia	Mental Retardation/Developmental Disabilities Administration	Department of Human Services	Washington, D.C.
Florida	Developmental Services Program Office	Department of Health & Rehabilitative Services	Tallahassee, Florida
Georgia	Mental Retardation Services Division of Mental Health & Mental Retardation	Department of Human Resources	Atlanta, Georgia
Hawaii	Developmental Disabilities Planning and Advisory Council	Department of Health	Honolulu, Hawaii
Idaho	Bureau of Adult and Child Development Division of Community Rehabilitation	Department of Health and Welfare	Boise, Idaho

State	MR/DD State Unit	State Agency	Location
Illinois	Deputy Director for Developmental Disabilities	Department of Mental Health & Developmental Disabilities	Springfield, Illinois
Indiana	Assistant Commissioner for Mental Retardation and Developmental Disabilities	Department of Mental Health	Indianapolis, Indiana
Iowa	Division of Mental Health Resources	Department of Social Services	Des Moines, Iowa
Kansas	Director of Mental Retardation	Department of Social and Rehabilitative Services	Topeka, Kansas
Kentucky	Division of Community Services for Mental Retardation	Department of Health Services Cabinet for Human Services	Frankfort, Kentucky
Louisiana	Office of Mental Retardation	Department of Health and Human Resources	Baton Rouge, Louisiana
Maine	Bureau of Mental Retardation	Department of Mental Health & Mental Retardation	Augusta, Maine
Maryland	Mental Retardation and Developmental Disabilities Administration	Department of Health and Mental Hygiene	Baltimore, Maryland
Massachusetts	Commissioner for Mental Retardation	Department of Mental Health	Boston, Massachusetts
Michigan	Program Development and Support Systems	Department of Mental Health	Lansing, Michigan
Minnesota	Division of Retardation Services	Department of Public Welfare	St. Paul, Minnesota
Mississippi	Bureau of Mental Retardation	Department of Mental Health	Jackson, Mississippi
Missouri	Division of Mental Retardation and Developmental Disabilities	Department of Mental Health	Jefferson City, Missouri
Montana	Division of Developmental Disabilities	Department of Social and Rehabilitative Services	Helena, Montana
Nebraska	Office of Mental Retardation	Department of Public Institutions	Lincoln, Nebraska
Nevada	Division of Mental Health & Mental Retardation	Department of Human Resources	Carson City, Nevada

State	MR/DD State Unit	State Agency	Location
New Hampshire	Deputy of Director Developmental Disabilities Division of Mental Health & Developmental Disabilities	Department of Health & Welfare	Concord, New Hampshire
New Jersey	Division of Mental Retardation	Department of Human Services	Trenton, New Jersey
New Mexico	Behavioral Services Division	Department of Health and the Environment	Santa Fe, New Mexico
New York	Office of Mental Retardation and Developmental Disabilities		Albany, New York
North Carolina	Director for Mental Retardation Division of Mental Health/ Mental Retardation Services	Department of Human Services	Raleigh, North Carolina
North Dakota	Developmental Disabilities Division	Department of Human Services	Bismarck, North Dakota
Ohio	Department of Mental Retardation and Developmental Disabilities		Columbus, Ohio
Oklahoma	Developmental Disabilities and Mental Retardation Services	Department of Human Services	Oklahoma City, Oklahoma
Oregon	Program for Mental Retardation & Developmental Disabilities Division of Mental Health	Department of Human Resources	Salem, Oregon
Pennsylvania	Deputy Secretary for Mental Retardation	Department of Public Welfare	Harrisburg, Pennsylvania
Puerto Rico	Assistant Secretary for Family Services	Department of Social Services	Santurce, Puerto Rico
Rhode Island	Division of Retardation	Department of Mental Health, Mental Retardation & Hospitals	Cranston, Rhode Island
South Carolina	Department of Mental Retardation		Columbia, South Carolina
South Dakota	Office of Developmental Disabilities	Department of Social Services	Pierre, South Dakota
Tennessee	Assistant Commissioner for Mental Retardation	Department of Mental Health & Mental Retardation	Nashville, Tennessee

State	MR/DD State Unit	State Agency	Location
Texas	Deputy Commissioner for Mental Retardation Services	Department of Mental Health & Mental Retardation	Austin, Texas
Utah	Division of Services to the Handicapped	Department of Social Services	Salt Lake City, Utah
Vermont	Mental Retardation Programs	Department of Mental Health	Waterbury, Vermont
Virginia		Department of Mental Health & Mental Retardation	Richmond, Virginia
Virgin Islands	Mental Health, Alcoholism & Drug Dependency Services	Department of Health	St. Thomas, Virgin Islands
Washington	Division of Developmental Disabilities	Department of Social & Health Services	Olympia, Washington
West Virginia	Developmental Disabilities Services Division of Behavioral Health	Department of Health	Charleston, West Virginia
Wisconsin	Developmental Disabilities Office Bureau of Community Services	Department of Health & Social Services	Madison, Wisconsin
Wyoming	Institutions Coordinator	Board of Charities & Reform	Cheyenne, Wyoming

PHILOSOPHICAL AND LEGAL CONSIDERATIONS

Section

6

PHILOSOPHICAL AND
LEGAL CONSIDERATIONS

chapter

4

An Overview of Social Role Valorization and Some Reflections on Elderly Mentally Retarded Persons

Wolf Wolfensberger

"Social Role Valorization," the new term for what was formerly known as the principle of normalization in human services, has as its primary goal the establishment and protection of positively valued social roles for people who are devalued by society or at risk of devaluation. This includes people who are mentally retarded, those who are elderly, and therefore, those who are both. All the many implications of Social Role Valorization can be conceptualized as falling into seven themes, each of which is explained in detail.

Establishing what constitutes a social role valorizing service and life for elderly retarded persons is difficult, especially considering that what is typically available in society for nonretarded persons over age 65 is not an adaptive model for services to retarded elderly persons. Some thoughts are offered in this chapter on practices to avoid in services for such persons, as well as some potential features that should be incorporated.

THIS CHAPTER PRESENTS a brief review of "Social Role Valorization" (formerly called the principle of normalization), and of some major implications of this human services theory to the lives of, and services to, elderly retarded persons. The chapter addresses the theory, its derivations, its goals, and its major implications, and then offers a discussion on what all of this means to the situation of elderly retarded persons in society today.

DEFINING SOCIAL ROLE VALORIZATION

"Social Role Valorization" is the name that this author proposed in 1983 as a successor to the concept or term "principle of normalization." The reasons for this choice are given below, and are also explained at greater length in Wolfensberger (1983b). The adoption of the concept of Social Role Valorization is not meant to totally replace terms such as "normative," though "social role valorizing" is preferred to the old expression "normalizing." The most up-to-date detailed exposition of the quondam normalization principle is found in Wolfensberger and Thomas (1983).

Social Role Valorization implies, as much as possible, the use of culturally valued means in order to enable, establish, and/or maintain valued social roles for people. Though very brief, this definition has a vast number of implications for human services, ranging from the most global to the most minute. The definition reflects the almost paradigm-breaking assumption that the single highest secular goal of human services is social role enhancement or role defense of the people served.

Obviously, this definition also incorporates the recognition that if a person's social role were a societally valued one, then other desirable things would be accorded to that person within the resources and norms of his or her society. Indeed, so powerful is a valued social role that those attributes of a person that would otherwise be viewed negatively by society may be viewed positively, or at least tolerated, if the person's role is a valued one. For example, an inventive, industrious, and wealthy man can have all sorts of peculiar behaviors (such as Howard Hughes did), but as long as the person fills a valued role as a wealthy and productive worker, these behaviors will be tolerated or pardoned as "eccentricities." On the other hand, for exhibiting the same behaviors, a poor, unemployed man who may even be defined as unemployable because he lacks certain skills, and who therefore does not fill socially valued roles, would be called mentally disordered and placed in an institution. Similarly, an elderly woman who is valued in society and travels to exotic places, engages in liaisons with younger men, and gives away freely of her possessions may be called a blithe spirit and may even be touted as a model of how carefree old age should be. On the other hand, for exhibiting the very same behaviors, a woman who lacks a valued social role would be judged to be foolish, promiscuous, incapable of managing her affairs, and incompetent.

Dynamics of Deviancy-Making

In order to perceive the crucial function of role enhancement, it is necessary to understand the dynamics of deviancy-making. Persons can be considered "deviant" or devalued when a significant characteristic (a "difference") of theirs is negatively valued by the segment of society that constitutes the majority or that holds dominating power. While numerous differences do exist among individuals, it must be clearly kept in mind that differentness by itself does not cast a person into deviant status unless/until it becomes sufficiently negatively value-charged in the minds of observers. Thus, deviancy is in the eyes of the beholder, which is to say that it is culturally relative, as illustrated by the following examples.

A person who has hallucinations that would render the person devalued in some cultures might be respected and admired in other cultures for being favored by God, as has reportedly been the case in certain American Indian tribes or in the Arab world. Similarly, until recently, a very wealthy person in the Far East might have had his or her hands rendered useless by growing exceedingly long fingernails, so that what would be considered a serious functional impairment in American society would there have been a sign of the person's high status, and others would be made clearly aware that the person was having all necessary functions performed for him- or herself by servants and retainers.

Although different cultures define different types of human characteristics or conditions as deviant, in all cultures it is human differences in one or more of three broad categories that usually become defined as devalued: a) congenital or adventitious physical differences of people, perhaps associated with disease, age, bodily impairments, and so forth; b) overt and covert behaviors (the latter include religious, political, and other beliefs); and c) people's descent, nationality, the ethnic group from which they derive, the language they speak, or their attributed identity such as caste.

As indicated above, it is only recently that this author began using the term "Social Role Valorization" in preference to "normalization," and the reason for this change has been explained at greater length elsewhere (Wolfensberger, 1983b). Briefly, shortly after realizing that the enhancement or defense of the social roles of (devalued) people was really the ultimate goal of the principle of normalization, the author also discovered that French-speaking human services circles had begun to use the phrase *valorisation sociale* to connote roughly the opposite of social devaluation. In English, valorization has also existed as a somewhat arcane word meaning the attachment of value to something. Thus, the author proposes the term "Social Role Valorization" as superior to the word "normalization" in that it is not only a more accurate descriptor of what the theory of normalization has been all about, but just as importantly, the phrase can serve as a very instructive consciousness-raiser to those who hear and use it.

There are nine major negative social roles into which devalued individuals are universally cast. These roles are depicted in Table 1. In North America, the people who fall into one or more of these devalued social role categories add up to an astonishing one-third of the population, and they currently include both elderly as well as mentally retarded persons, and therefore also elderly retarded ones.

Implications of Devaluation

Obviously, how a person is perceived affects how that person will be treated. This implies three things (among others). First, devalued persons will be badly treated. Others will usually accord less esteem and status to them than to nondevalued citizens. Devalued people are apt to be rejected, even persecuted, and treated in ways that tend to diminish their dignity, adjustment, growth, competence, health, wealth, and lifespan. Generally, societal responses to people who are devalued will fall into only two universal categories: a) "distantiating" the devalued people, that is, placing some sort of physical or social distance between them and the valued society, by either physical segregation, social degradation, or brutalization and outright destruction (e.g., genocide); or b) efforts at reversal or prevention of deviancy, which may include attempts to change the devalued person, and/or to change society.

Second, the (bad) treatment accorded to devalued people takes on forms that express the way members of a society conceptualize the roles of various devalued persons or groups. For instance, if a group of children are (unconsciously) viewed as animals, then they may be segregated in a special class that is given an animal name—often even the name of an animal that is seen as expressive of the devalued people's identity. Thus, a class for retarded children may be called "The Turtles." Relatedly, the animal kingdom may be seen as an analogue, or source of service measures, for that group of people, perhaps in the belief that the devalued people served will benefit more

Table 1. Some societally devalued groups and the common historical deviancy roles into which they are most apt to be cast

People who are devalued due to:	Common deviancy roles								
	Pity	Charity	Menace	Sick	Sub-human	Ridicule	Dread	Childlike	Holy innocent
Mental disorder	X	X	X	X	X	X	X	X	X
Mental retardation	X	X	X	X	X	X		X	X
Old age	X	X		X	X	X		X	
Alcohol habituation	X	X	X	X		X			
Poverty	X	X	X		X		X		
Racial minority membership			X		X	X	X	X	
Epilepsy	X	X		X			X		
Drug addiction	X	X	X	X					
Criminal offenses			X	X	X		X		
Physical handicap	X	X					X		
Deafness/hearing impairment	X	X							
Blindness/visual impairment	X	X							
Illiteracy	X	X							
Political dissidence			X						

from animals than they would from interactions with other people. Thus, monkeys may be trained to serve devalued people, research may be conducted on chimpanzee language in order to improve the language development of a group of devalued people, and various "pet therapies" may be implemented. Things like these are becoming increasingly widespread in services to rejected and abandoned elderly people, as is exemplified by the recruitment of animal mascots, "dog visitors," and "pet companions" for nursing home residents—practices that numerous nursing homes and other services for the elderly are everywhere pursuing.

Similarly, if adults are perceived in the role of eternal or second childhood, then they may be called (even when they are elderly) "children," "kids," "boys," and "girls"; be encouraged to play children's games and to follow children's and school schedules rather than adult and work schedules; be dressed in children's clothing styles; be served in children's settings or in settings decorated for children; have their services funded by departments charged with serving children; and be served in adult day programs with names such as "day care center."

Also, it is very common in the area of habilitation for a perception of people as being in the sick role to be played out vis-à-vis clients who certainly are no sicker than most of the population and who really need a developmental approach, adult education, industrial apprenticeship training, and the like. For example, clients may be interpreted as sick by association with medically trained and named staff; by names such as "hospital" or "clinic" for the places where they live, go to school, and work; and by having every conceivable activity of their lives interpreted as a form of "therapy" ("work therapy," "reading therapy," "religion therapy," "garden therapy," "recreation therapy," "pet therapy," etc.). While the imposition of the sick role is often promoted as being positive—at least, more positive than certain other roles, such as that of menace—when applied to devalued people, it actually plays largely the function of differentiating them from staff and society, and of imaging them as diseased (sometimes even death-bound), contagious, impaired, incompetent, and passive (e.g., "patient").

The above three deviancy roles are strongly imposed on elderly persons, and especially retarded elderly persons, who are very apt to be perceived and interpreted as animalistic, childlike, sick and dying.

Third, how a person is perceived and treated by others will in turn strongly determine how that person subsequently behaves. Therefore, the more consistently people are perceived and treated as filling devalued social roles, the more likely it is that they will conform to that expectation and demonstrate the kinds of behavior that are socially expected—namely, behaviors that are not valued by society. It is, therefore, no surprise that many mentally retarded persons act very childlike and incompetent; that mentally disordered people act sick or menacing; that elderly people act like children or become prematurely sick and even die earlier than would be expected. Likewise, the more social value is accorded to people, the more they will usually be encouraged to assume roles and behaviors that are appropriate and desirable, the more will be expected of them, and the more they are apt to achieve.

PREVENTING, MINIMIZING, OR REVERSING SOCIETAL DEVALUATION THROUGH SOCIAL ROLE VALORIZATION

The fact that deviancy is culturally defined and therefore relative points to a two-pronged strategy for enabling devalued persons to attain (more) valued roles in society by: a) reducing or preventing the differentness or stigmata that may cause a person to become devalued in the eyes of observers, and b) changing other people's perceptions and values in regard to a particular characteristic or condition, so that people with a given characteristic are no longer seen as devalued.

As mentioned, social role enhancement is the ultimate goal of human services, but both stigma reduction/prevention as well as societal attitude change can be pursued through two major subgoals: a) the enhancement of the social image of a person or group, and b) the enhancement of the competencies of the person or group, including such things as bodily, sensory, and intellectual performance; the practice of valued skills and habits; and positive relationships with others.

Image enhancement and competency enhancement are clearly reciprocally reinforcing, both positively and negatively. That is, a person who is competency impaired is highly at risk of becoming seen and interpreted as of low value, and thus of suffering image impairment; a person who is impaired in image and social value is apt to be responded to in ways that reduce his or her competency. Both processes work equally in the reverse direction.

Social Role Valorization places emphasis on "the use of culturally valued means" to enhance a devalued person's social status. Service structures, programs, methods/technologies, tools, and so forth, are all means toward role enhancement, and their value in the eyes of society is largely determined by the degree to which these means are used in the larger culture with and for *valued* persons of the same age and sex. For example, the daily, weekly, and yearly schedules in a school for nonhandicapped children would usually constitute the culturally valued practices (i.e., analogue) to be adopted/imitated in an education program for handicapped children of the same age. Culturally valued practices to be emulated by vocational programs for young adults might include apprenticeship, vocational school, night classes in vocational subjects, on-the-job training, and adult education. Not suitable would be "job therapy," simulated work (valued people who perform fake work are highly at risk of getting devalued), or playing games.

There are at least four reasons why culturally valued means are so important:

1. Images transfer to things, concepts, and people with which they are associated, as the world of advertising and public relations knows only too well. Therefore, the value message that is contained in any aspect of a human service is highly apt to become attached to the people whom the program serves. If the materials given to elderly persons to exercise their arthritic hands are children's toys and puzzles, then the people are apt to be seen as childlike. Relatedly, if a program utilizes means that deviate widely from cultural standards and norms, the devalued persons whom the program serves are apt to be seen as different from other citizens—and *not* in a valued sense. As a result, the already devalued status of devalued people will be accentuated rather than minimized. In the end, the means that a service program uses will have a powerful long-term effect on public attitudes toward (devalued) people. If one goal is to increase the level of public acceptance of people who are seen as negatively different, the message sent by what a program does is as important as the changes it tries to achieve in its clients—and sometimes even more so.

2. If the means by which a service is delivered are positively valued and positively familiar to clients, then clients are apt to relate much better to such services, both in terms of attitudes and competencies.

3. The skills, habits, and relationships that are prerequisites for a meaningful life in open society are difficult to acquire in settings that are culture-alien, lack culturally familiar cues, reduce opportunity, impose or suggest alien or devalued roles, and so on.

4. The public (to some degree also families and staff) is less likely to support, and relate positively to, a human services program that is unfamiliar, culture-alien, and perceived as "outlandish."

It is possible to schematize Social Role Valorization in a number of ways that can help one to understand it better, and to formulate a variety of specific action measures. One way is to classify the implications into the various social system levels where they can be applied, as follows:

1. Actions on the level of the (devalued) person concerned, usually a client
2. Actions on the level of the person's relevant *primary* social systems (e.g., the family)
3. Actions on the level of the person's *secondary* social systems (e.g., neighborhood, community, service agency)
4. Actions on the level of society as a whole (i.e., actions that shape society's values, language usage, laws, customs, etc.)

Thus, combining the second and third levels, all action implications could be represented by the schema in Table 2.

THE SEVEN CORE THEMES OF SOCIAL ROLE VALORIZATION

A second way to conceptualize Social Role Valorization is to break it into seven major strategies or strategy-related dynamics that are called *core themes*. Most people understand Social Role Valorization best by reviewing these themes that capture and express most of the relevant goals and processes. These seven core themes, each explained further below, are: a) the role and importance of (un)consciousness in human services; b) the relevance of role expectancy and role circularity to deviancy-making and deviancy-unmaking; c) the "conservatism corollary" to Social Role Valorization, with its implications of positive compensation for people's devalued or at-risk status; d) the developmental model and personal competency enhancement; e) the power of imitation; f) the dynamics and relevance of social imagery; and g) the importance of personal societal integration and valued social participation.

The Role of (Un)consciousness in Human Services

It is well known that for a variety of reasons, human beings function with a remarkably restricted range of consciousness, and, therefore, also with a high degree of unconsciousness. A major portion of perception, memory, and motivation takes place at or below the consciousness threshold. Largely unconscious dynamics control, or at least influence, many of our routine acts and habits, such as what and how we eat, what we wear and buy, how we spend our money, where we live, what kind of work we do, whom we select as friends and mates, how we interact with other people, how we raise our children, and so forth. Furthermore, there may be even yet greater unconsciousness about complex social behaviors, especially on the large systems level.

It is, therefore, fully to be expected that the phenomenon of unconsciousness that is so prevalent in every aspect of human existence would also be prevalent in human services. Service

Table 2.   Implications of the two major goals of social role valorization on three levels of social organization

Levels of action	Major action goals	
	Enhancement of personal competencies	Enhancement of social images
The individual	Eliciting, shaping, and maintaining useful bodily, mental, and social competencies in persons by means of direct physical and social interactions with them	Presenting, managing, addressing, labeling, and interpreting persons in a manner that creates positive roles for them and that emphasizes their similarities to, rather than their differences from, other (valued) persons
Primary and secondary social systems	Eliciting, shaping, and maintaining useful bodily, mental, and social competencies in persons by adaptive shaping of such primary and secondary social systems as family, classroom, school, work setting, service agency, and neighborhood.	Presenting, managing, labeling, and interpreting the primary and secondary social systems that surround a person or that consist of persons at risk so that these systems, as well as the persons in them, are perceived in a valued fashion
Societal systems	Eliciting, shaping, and maintaining useful bodily, mental, and social competencies in persons by appropriate shaping of such societal systems and structures as entire school systems, laws, and government	Shaping cultural values, attitudes, and stereotypes so as to elicit maximum feasible acceptance of individual differences

planners, administrators, workers, leaders, trainers, and clients are all trapped in individual and collective unconscious patterns. For instance, most people in human services are not conscious of: a) the real functions of these services, b) the reality, extent, and dynamics of social devaluation of large numbers of people *by* large numbers of people, and c) the nature of the plight of people who are handicapped, devalued, oppressed, poor, needy, or wounded. One dynamic that contributes heavily to this high degree of unconsciousness, and that is so relevant to any effort at deviancy-unmaking, is the fact that the ideologies that control much of what goes on in human services are very negative, in that they enact society's real but destructive intentions, and/or address needs other than those of the clients. Unpleasant realities such as this one are apt to be denied and repressed into unconsciousness, the more so that they stand in contrast to the higher values and ideals that people profess on the conscious level. Such denial and repression can take place as much or even more on a systemic (e.g., organizational and societal) level as on a personal/individual one. Thus, entire systems, such as service agencies, service professions, service sectors (e.g, mental health, gerontology), even entire societies, can be totally unconscious of some of the most important things they are doing.

Social Role Valorization is concerned with identification of the unconscious, and usually negative, dynamics within people and human services that contribute to the devaluation and oppression of devalued groups in a society, and with providing conscious strategies for remediating the devalued social status of such people. Furthermore, service evaluation instruments such as Program Analysis of Service Systems (PASS) (Wolfensberger & Glenn, 1973a, b, 1975a, b) and especially Program Analysis of Service Systems' Implementation of Normalization Goals (PASSING) (Wolfensberger & Thomas, 1980, 1983) that are explicitly tied to Social Role Valorization theory have been deliberately structured so as to reward consciousness of important human services issues on the part of personnel of a human service.

The Relevance of Role Expectancy and Role Circularity to Deviancy-Making and Deviancy-Unmaking

The social roles that people adopt or impose on each other are among the most powerful social influence and control methods known. As with unconsciousness, the dynamics of role expectancies and role circularities are ever present. A person or group holding certain expectancies about the behavior or potential for growth and development of another person or group will create conditions and circumstances that have a high likelihood of eliciting the expected behavior. There are at least five major powerful media through which role expectancies can be conveyed. These include the way in which the physical environment is structured; the activities that are offered to, provided for, or demanded of people; the language that is used with and about them; the way people are grouped and juxtaposed; and miscellaneous other ways of attaching images and symbolisms to them. All of these factors are powerful in eliciting from a person who is the object of the role expectancies an inclination or commitment to act in the expected manner. When a person then acts as anticipated, the expectancies held by observers are reinforced, thus further strengthening both their expectancies and the expressions of these expectancies, and so on, until the expected and the emitted behaviors have become very powerfully ingrained.

In the case of socially devalued people, the role expectancies that are imposed upon them are commonly the negative ones noted in Table 1. These role circularities are very effective in that devalued people often live up to them. Role expectancy creation is pervasive in human services, but most often carries out the (usually unconscious) societal function of creating and maintaining people in devalued status and roles.

In contrast to these traditional negative practices, Social Role Valorization theory implies that contributive, positive social roles should be identified for people at risk, and that corresponding positive role expectancies such as those of pupil, worker, teacher, owner, guide, tenant, neighbor, friend, spouse, and citizen should be extended to them. In order for these role expectancies to be conveyed to people at risk, it is important to promote: a) normatively attractive, comfortable, and challenging physical (including service) settings for them; b) age-appropriate and challenging (program) activities; c) age-appropriate and culturally valued personal appearance of clients; d) image-enhancing matches between the needs of the devalued people being served, the nature of their program, and staff identities; and e) status-enhancing labels and forms of address for the people at risk. Indeed, desired benefits, including both competency and image enhancement in virtually all areas of people's identities, will flow forth automatically if people at risk occupy valued social roles, because once a person fills a valued social role, society will tend to bestow upon the person, or at least make available to the person, a plethora of the things that that society values. As mentioned, society will tolerate, overlook, or even interpret positively the oddities (i.e., the negative differences) that a valued person may have.

Thus, it is important that human services for devalued people, and other parties as well, do everything within their power to break the negative roles into which devalued people have been cast, and to establish such persons in as many positive social roles as possible.

The "Conservatism Corollary" to Social Role Valorization

Many people have negatively valued characteristics, but these are usually so few or minor that a person is not cast into a deviant role or hindered in functioning as a result. Unlike other citizens, however, the identity of devalued people is so negatively valued that they exist in a state of heightened vulnerability to further devaluations and negative experiences. Consequently, the more vulnerable a person is to societal devaluation and its consequences, the greater the impact in terms of the person's perceived social worth that can be achieved by: a) reduction/prevention of any such vulnerabilities, and/or b) compensating for such vulnerabilities with positively valued manifestations

or compensations. For example, if an elderly man has a speech impediment, acts nearsightedly, and has an odd hairstyle and a few odd mannerisms, these realities will interact more multiplicatively than additively in eliciting negative reactions from most people. If the person also limps and wears shabby, ill-fitting clothes, then even a casual passerby who had never seen the individual before would probably conclude on sight that there is something very wrong with this person, perhaps evoking judgments of "deinstitutionalized mental patient," "village idiot," "senile," or "ought to be locked up." Thus, people can be stereotyped on sight—often correctly so.

A devalued person is also put at heightened risk of devaluation and rejection as a result of the number and appearance of other stigmatized persons with whom she or he is grouped. Six individuals walking about separately in an ordinary street crowd would make little impact on an observer if one of those people were very old, one limped, one had an odd hairstyle, or another was garbed in odd clothing. People with such minor oddities are seen on the street all the time. But when a significant proportion of people in one discrete or compact group have one or more such oddities, then the whole group, including its nonstigmatized members, is apt to be negatively stereotyped. In fact, it takes only one glance out of the corner of one's eye—less than 1 second—for an observer to conclude that a group of people must be from some nearby group home or institution, or that they are "street people."

Therefore, the conservatism corollary posits that the greater the number, severity, and/or variety of deviancies or stigmata of an individual, *or* the greater the number of deviant stigmatized persons there are in a group or setting, the greater is the positive impact of: a) diminishing one or a few of the individual stigmata, b) reducing the number of deviant people in the group, or c) balancing (compensating for) the stigmata, deviancies, or number of devalued persons by the presence or addition of positively valued manifestations and/or people in the group.

A further implication is that people who are

cast into socially devalued status need to not only experience life conditions that are relatively typical, common, and prevalent for nondevalued citizens, but optimally to even experience conditions that are highly valued by the culture, because such conditions, being more valued, have more power to compensate for the negatively valued condition of devalued status. In other words, what is "normal" for the members of a society may not be what is most enhancing for a person who is devalued or at risk of devaluation—and may, in fact, even be deviancy-making or deviancy-enlarging at times. Thus, it is not enough to be merely neutral in neither diminishing nor enhancing the status of devalued persons in the eyes of others; instead, one ordinarily must seek to effect the most positive status possible for devalued people. For instance, on occasions where either a suit-and-tie or a sports jacket, casual slacks, and sport shirt are equally appropriate attire, an elderly man at value-risk in society would fare better wearing the suit-and-tie.

The Developmental Model
and Personal Competency Enhancement

Often, people with physical, mental, or emotional impairments also have functional impairment(s) that render them less competent than nonimpaired persons. Because of such handicaps, such a person may be unable to obtain or hold a job, to relate adaptively or maturely with other people, to take care of his or her person, to learn easily, and so forth. Even devalued people who are not handicapped may be severely limited in competence because they have been subjected to low (or outright negative) role expectancies, denied opportunities and experiences that contribute to growth and development, segregated with people who present negative role models, and served by human services workers of low competence. Enhancement of the roles of devalued people or people at risk of devaluation requires that their personal competencies be enhanced, for a variety of reasons. One is the fact that even the *appearance* of competency in a person tends to elicit positive feedback from observ-

ers. Second, society will be more accepting of any devalued traits or behaviors of people who have valued skills and competencies. In addition, a lack of competencies may inhibit devalued persons in many areas of functioning, a crucial one being social interactions, especially with valued persons.

The seven core themes of Social Role Valorization have different levels of importance for various devalued groups. The theme of personal competency enhancement sketched here is particularly relevant to those groups whose social devaluation is related to their low competence, that is, people who are mentally retarded, senile, untrained, physically impaired, socially maladaptive, and the like.

The Power of Imitation

Imitation is one of the most powerful learning mechanisms known. People's personalities, their ways of interacting with others and with their environment, their dress and language habits—indeed, just about every aspect of human behavior—is strongly affected by this dynamic.

The models that are available for devalued people to imitate are often negative ones. Devalued people typically are: a) segregated from valued society and models, b) grouped with other devalued people who very frequently have socially devalued characteristics and exhibit socially devalued behaviors, and c) often served by less competent personnel than are valued people. For instance, handicapped children typically have been denied socialization with adaptive, nonhandicapped peers, and have instead been served with each other or with handicapped adults who model handicapped behaviors; mildly impaired persons are often grouped with a larger number of severely impaired people who engage in many more inappropriate behaviors; and elderly people are typically segregated with people who are failing in health, lack vigor and energy, and are inactive and unproductive. Social Role Valorization requires that the dynamic of imitation be capitalized upon in a positive way so that the role models provided to devalued persons are people who function routinely in an appropriate and valued fashion. Relatedly, it is important to increase the sense of identification of devalued people with valued models, because people are much more apt to imitate those people with whom they identify.

The Dynamics and Relevance of Social Imagery

Like role expectancies and imitation, the use of image association is another effective learning and behavioral control mechanism. Historically, devalued people have been attached to and surrounded by symbols and imagery that overwhelmingly represent culturally negatively valued qualities. While these image associations often occur unconsciously, they strongly influence the role expectancies for, and the social valuation of, the persons so imaged.

Values that are associated with various images transfer to the persons, settings, or objects to which these images are connected and juxtaposed. If images that convey negative values are tied to a person or group, then that person or group is apt to be negatively, or at least less positively, perceived by an observer. Especially if the people to whom these images are associated have already been identified or suspected as deviant, these images then tend to elicit in observers the expectation, and even confirmation, that those persons are indeed negatively valued, will act deviantly, and should be treated differently.

Conversely, if the images associated with societally devalued people were highly valued ones, then at least some of the positive value contained in this imagery would likely transfer to such devalued people, who would then be more apt to be seen in a positive light. Thus, as much as possible, any features of a human service that can convey image messages about clients who are devalued or at value-risk should be positive. The incorporation of the dynamic of image transfer has implications for every aspect of a human service, such as the physical setting in which the service is rendered (e.g., its location, cleanliness, beauty, what it is near), the name of the service and its administrative body, the agency logo, the source of funds, how clients are grouped, what kinds of programming are provided, the appearance that is projected by the clients, what they are called, and what the service activities are and are called.

A human service for devalued clients will enhance its clients' image if it is in a physical location that is positively valued, and if it groups its clients with other people who are highly valued and in age configurations that match those in culturally valued analogues. Furthermore, clients will be more highly valued if staff have an appropriate (positively imaged) identity for the type of service being rendered (e.g., medically imaged staff only in a truly medical service to people who have significant medical needs), and if the activities and schedules for the program are highly valued and consistent with what would be expected for valued people of the same age. Services should be named in ways that are consistent with culturally valued analogues, and should elicit positive associations in an observer. Funding must come from age-appropriate sources and must avoid pity/charity and other negative imagery; a service should support a positive and age-appropriate personal appearance for its clients and refer to them in image-enhancing ways.

The Importance of Personal Social Integration and Valued Social Participation

Humans have a universal tendency to respond to the presence of a disfigured or disliked person or object by trying to place some distance between themselves and the unpleasant stimulus. Since societally devalued people are experienced by many other people as unpleasant, they tend to be rejected and segregated, which has a vast number of negative effects upon the segregated persons. For example, their segregated existence denies them normative, typical experiences that valued members of the culture take for granted, and since they are not exposed to normative growth experiences, their competencies are often diminished. Segregation also negatively interprets the segregated groups as "needing" to be kept apart because they are so different, so helpless, so in need of management and services that are profoundly different from those needed by valued people. Especially when handicapped people are segregated together (i.e., congregated), members of the group commonly present negative, inappropriate, and socially devalued behavior models to each other, thus increasing the socially devalued characteristics of the segregated individuals. Similarly, segregation of a societally devalued group has negative effects on society. For one thing, it tends to reduce the society's level of tolerance for diversity, and induces collective unconsciousness of its own practices. Also, because segregation tends to make people more devalued and more dependent, society pays a high price for it in many complex and deeply hidden ways.

Social Role Valorization requires that, as much as possible, a devalued person or group has the opportunity to be personally integrated into the valued social life of society. This means devalued people would be enabled to live in normative housing within the valued community, and with valued people; to be educated with their nondevalued peers; to work in the same facilities as other people; and to be involved in a positive fashion in worship, recreation, shopping, and all the other activities in which members of a society engage. Various supports can make significant or even decisive contributions to whether valued personal social integration will be truly successful in the life of a devalued person. These include: a) the presence of ideological and administrative support, b) positive perceptions of the persons to be integrated, c) people who can competently transact the integration, d) sufficient backup service options in case one level of integrative effort is unsuccessful, e) supports that will enable the person to remain integrated in the first place from childhood on, and f) a comprehensive continuum of service options.

It must be emphasized that the type of integration implied by Social Role Valorization theory is very specific: *personal* social integration and *valued* social participation. "Physical integration," which consists merely of the physical presence of devalued people and of services to them in the community, is only a potential *facilitator* of actual valued social participation by individuals. Also, social integration is not the same as what is called "mainstreaming" and "deinstitutionalization"; these terms have confused meanings, and what is done under them is often not truly integrative.

The Interrelationship among the Seven Core Themes

Although each of the seven themes can be described separately, in actual service practice, they are interrelated. For instance, people's unconscious devaluations are characteristically expressed in the negative images that they attach to devalued persons, and these images often serve to promote devalued role behavior in their victims. Furthermore, the implications of the seven themes can sometimes conflict with each other. For instance, it is not always possible to simultaneously optimize both the image-enhancing and the competency-enhancing features of a service, as described in more detail elsewhere (e.g., Wolfensberger, 1980b, 1983a). At present, human services workers and others have a low awareness of the relative importance of various implications, and may resolve conflicts on the basis of incoherent, unconscious, or single criteria. For these reasons, instruments designed to help people become cognizant of such conflicts, such as PASS (Wolfensberger & Glenn, 1973a, b, 1975a, b) and PASSING (Wolfensberger & Thomas, 1980, 1983), have been developed and may be helpful in weighing the value of conflicting criteria in a given instance.

ADDITIONAL PERSPECTIVES ON SOCIAL ROLE VALORIZATION

One can say that the goal of Social Role Valorization has been achieved if a person is accorded valued roles, life conditions, experiences, valued participations, autonomy, and choices that are available to at least the majority of other people of the same age and sex, *and* if these things have been accorded because the person is seen as valuable. Because these things are not attainable in full for every person, it is important to keep in mind the qualifying phrase "as much as possible" in the social role valorization definition. Relevant strategies take into account the particular individual concerned, the limits of current know-how, and the individual's capacity to make his or her own choice of personal goals and means. Low expectations, inappropriate pessimism, and stereotyped roles can have a very destructive effect on the person involved. Consequently, an adaptive human management approach is to maintain a healthy skepticism when confronted with the assertion that a specific social role valorizing human service measure or interpretation is unattainable or unrealistic.

The erstwhile normalization principle has sometimes been criticized as imposing cultural uniformity. (A detailed analysis of various critiques of the quondam normalization principle can be found in Wolfensberger, 1980b, c.) In truth, it: a) promotes social tolerance and bridge-building, b) opens up an enormous range of valued options that are commonly denied to the almost one-third of the population who is devalued, and c) enables (not coerces) many people who have been devalued and excluded *against their will* to participate more fully. Only a few people or groups can be said to truly and deliberately choose social marginalization and devaluation of their own free will. Even when they say they do, they often do so only reactively, that is, in response to *prior* rejection *by* society. For example, there never existed a self-segregatory movement among elderly people until relatively recently, when aging became a human state that received strongly patterned societal rejection and discrimination.

This discussion has provided a limited introduction to Social Role Valorization and its many implications. More substantial explanations can be found in Wolfensberger (1972, 1980b, c), Wolfensberger and Glenn (1975b), and Wolfensberger and Thomas (1983). The implications of Social Role Valorization for architecture and the physical environment of services can be found in Wolfensberger (1977 or 1978).[1]

SOME REFLECTIONS ON THE SITUATION OF ELDERLY MENTALLY RETARDED PERSONS

Within the context of this brief explanation of Social Role Valorization and its major implications, the following addresses the application of the principle and its corollaries to mentally retarded persons who are elderly. An increasing number of people are becoming concerned about such individuals and the services to them, and have been asking questions about how to structure services to elderly retarded persons within the context of a Social Role Valorization perspective.

Until the late 1960s, services specifically for mentally retarded individuals consisted primarily of special education, and secondarily institutionalization. Everything else was quantitatively negligible. If retarded people lived long enough to become elderly, they almost invariably ended up in an institution for retarded persons, because in those days there were few nursing homes, and few of those nursing homes accepted retarded clients in any numbers. Today, we are faced with the need to provide for elderly retarded persons who have either lived at home and attended day programs, or who have been living in community residences, or who have been released or "dumped" from institutions, or who are living in institutions but could live in more normative or at least smaller settings.

However, in considering the needs of aging retarded persons from a Social Role Valorization perspective, one must first recognize the social status of elderly *non*retarded persons in society. Unfortunately, at this time in our culture, youth is idolized and aging in general is

[1]The Training Institute for Human Service Planning, Leadership and Change Agentry (805 South Crouse Avenue, Syracuse, New York, 13210, USA; telephone 315/423-4264) has compiled a number of relevant resources, and a list of current resources and publications is available free on request. Short training workshops on social role valorization, and on evaluating human services in relation to social role valorization criteria, take place reasonably often in many locales in North America; the Training Institute can also provide information on these.

viewed increasingly as a very undesirable process that is to be avoided and postponed as much as possible, and ended quickly. Because our culture also wants very much to avoid anything perceived as unpleasant, elderly persons are increasingly segregated from the rest of society and congregated in locations or contexts in which they have significantly lowered visibility. Similarly, the unpleasantness of aging is increasingly being interpreted and treated as: a) a sick role that calls for medicalization of elderly persons and administration of related services, and b) a "socialization into death" under the guise of humanism and good medical care. Thus, images of disease and death are increasingly projected onto elderly persons.

Implications of the Contemporary Attitudes toward Aging for Service Strategies for Elderly Mentally Retarded Persons

The developments reviewed above in regard to the decreasing societal respect for elderly people in general have several major implications for strategies toward elderly mentally retarded persons in particular.

Problems in Using Generic Services for the Elderly Usually, Social Role Valorization calls for the utilization of generic services and resources because these are typically role valorizing to devalued persons. However, in regard to elderly persons, it is now the case that services and resources specifically for them are no longer either truly generic or valued; that is, the services have become segregated and, to a significant degree, devalued. For example, while a general hospital is a generic service that can be used by anyone, a nursing home is so much aimed at special and devalued groups (such as elderly, severely retarded, or severely physically handicapped persons) that it no longer can be viewed as a generic resource. Thus, to suggest that an elderly retarded person in our culture receives the same services as an elderly nonretarded person runs contrary to Social Role Valorization, because the chances have become so high that services aimed at nonretarded elderly individuals will be segregatory, demeaning, image- and competency-di-

minishing, and quite possibly even socially and physically destructive.

An additional problem with such services is that the elderly nonretarded persons who use them may be adamant that they do not want to share the service with retarded persons. For this, there may be at least two reasons. First, people who are elderly today grew up at a time when individuals with mental retardation were much more severely devalued than they are today. At least for a few more decades, elderly people can be expected to continue to have more negative attitudes toward retarded people than the younger generations. Second, the elderly clients may fear (consciously or unconsciously) that their already poor social image is likely to suffer even more harm if they are juxtaposed with elderly handicapped persons whose social image is even worse than their own. This fear is valid, and the juxtaposition of retarded and nonretarded elderly people can do little to enhance the image of the retarded ones, but could do much to impair the image of nonretarded ones.

Additionally, service workers in programs for elderly people sometimes do not perceive their mission as being one to all elderly persons, but as service only to elderly people whom they see as being, or as once having been, "normal." That this is a difficult enough task for them already is manifested by the fact that the satisfaction of workers in services to the elderly is commonly found to be very low and that annual turnover rates of up to 70% have sometimes been reported across entire domains of such services (e.g., for nursing home systems of entire states). Thus, even if it were desirable for elderly mentally retarded people to use "generic" services for elderly persons, they might receive poor treatment there at the hands of both other clients and staff.

Necessity to Safeguard the Lives of Elderly Mentally Retarded Persons in Medical Settings Furthermore, even as there has been a distinct and documented improvement in attitudes toward mentally retarded persons in general, there has also been a deterioration in society in regard to the definition of human life and the value of the lives of certain types of people. Rapidly, support has been growing for the legitimization and legalization of "euthanasia," especially where elderly persons, severely handicapped persons, and handicapped newborn infants are involved (Duff & Campbell, 1973; Horan & Delahoyde, 1982; Mansson, 1972; Ostheimer, 1980; Quay, 1977; Todres, Krane, Howell, & Shannon, 1977; Wolfensberger, 1980a, 1981, in preparation). The shift from a qualitative to quantitative definition of life, which has both been expressed in and brought about by the legalization and wide acceptance of abortion, is also causing an increasing proportion of citizens to question the value of the lives of severely impaired individuals. In fact, despite gains in attitudes toward mental retardation in general, attitudes toward *severely* retarded persons have deteriorated in some quarters to such a degree that a severely retarded individual is no longer assured of adequate medical service where major medical efforts and procedures are involved (e.g., Action Coalition of Elders, 1975; Duff & Campbell, 1973; Horan & Mall, 1980; Todres et al., 1977; Wolfensberger, in preparation; readers are also referred to *Lex Vitae,* a journal entirely devoted to such incidents and issues). This phenomenon is compounded when the severely retarded person also happens to be elderly. At this point in time, an elderly severely mentally retarded person is literally no longer safe in many general hospitals but is highly at risk of having rather basic life support systems withheld or withdrawn, quite possibly without the significant persons in his or her life being informed or consulted. Several times this author has become aware that people who follow Social Role Valorization in pursuing medical care in general hospitals for severely retarded and especially elderly retarded persons have found it necessary to station a companion, perhaps even a registered nurse, around the clock by the bedside of such a retarded individual in order to protect that individual's life from the physicians and nurses who view ending that life as a service to society and even to the individual himself or herself. Again, the unfortunate consequence of this reality is that use of genuinely generic services may require careful safeguards, and may even have to be sacrificed in order to procure "safe" services, even if segregated ones, for an elderly retarded person. In fact, as objectionable as residential institutions are, it is conceivable that not long hence, they may constitute one of the safer places for severely retarded and elderly retarded persons.

Problems in Applying to Retarded Elderly People the Practices of Larger Society toward Elderly People in General An issue that comes up very commonly in regard to retarded persons who are 65 or older is the one of retirement. It is culturally normative in society for people to retire sometime in their mid 60s. However, while such retirement may be statistically normative, to a significant degree it has been forced upon an often reluctant elderly population by legislation that ultimately was designed not so much as a socially protective measure for elderly people, but as an economic protective measure for young and middle-age workers. Indeed, so unprotective of the elderly is retirement that it forces them out of the labor market and often into poverty and poor health. Thus, once more it becomes necessary to take a hard and skeptical look at the appropriateness of applying normative practices for non-retarded elderly persons to retarded ones. Additionally, we know that retirement is very apt to be followed by loss of function and competencies, and often to have a life-terminating impact upon nonretarded individuals. To subject a retarded person to the same process of function-stripping and physical and mental deterioration that accompanies termination of working life among nonretarded elderly people can hardly be viewed as consistent with Social Role Valorization.

Furthermore, to talk about "retirement" is ludicrous for the vast majority of mentally retarded people whose adult lives may have been spent in utter inactivity, or at best in very poorly challenging programs that make low demands and operate short hours. In fact, in a "retirement program" for elderly retarded persons, the clients may experience the same or worse life-wasting activities as they did earlier (i.e., doing nothing much of the time, watching television, listening to music, wandering around, sleeping too much, eating too much, playing games), only now under a new title that gives such disgraceful practices legitimacy. Instead, such persons are desperately in need of activity, enhancement of their skills, and a positive image both in their own eyes and in the view of others that comes with being a productive, contributive worker.

Thus, programs for elderly mentally retarded persons do not follow a very adaptive course when they emulate the "day activities" programs that have been set up to occupy the time of nonhandicapped elderly persons in our culture. Programs such as senior citizen centers, "day care" centers for the elderly, nutrition centers, and similar such services generally do very poorly in terms of protecting and enhancing the competencies and image of their elderly clients, and, therefore, have a negative effect on the social roles of elderly persons. The adoption of such programs as analogues for service to elderly persons who are also mentally handicapped can only harm their social image and competencies in the same ways this happens to ordinary elderly persons.

Some Conceivable Service Strategies that Are Consistent with Social Role Valorization

A painful consequence of the above realities for persons committed to mentally retarded people is that a social advocacy stance on behalf of elderly retarded persons demands pursuit of life-styles and services for them that are *even better* than those unsatisfactory life conditions and services available to so many elderly nonretarded persons. Indeed, if we look to the domain of aging at all for suitable service analogues, then perhaps the only relevant ones might be those in which we find extremely valued elderly people! Such persons commonly: a) continue in their earlier valued roles, b) work if they are able to and as much as they are able, c) are supported by valets, maids, servants, private nurses, and so on, d) receive meticulous body care, e) are well dressed and groomed, and f) maintain their previous rela-

tionships and involvements as long as possible. Unfortunately, such supports will only be available to mentally retarded people who are wealthy and who have concerned advocates.

However, there are still some other implications. One route would be to provide maximal work and activity involvement for the elderly retarded person, much as many nonretarded elderly citizens in society today still find it possible to maintain a work role to the very end of their lives. The feasible option here would probably be the continued inclusion of elderly retarded persons in sheltered work settings among nonelderly workers so as to avoid the low expectancies and disease/death role that so commonly are attached to elderly persons—especially when they are grouped with their age peers.

Another suitable service model would be the inclusion of an elderly retarded person as a valued member of a valued (residential) communal group, such as a family or other communal body. In such contexts, what wealthy retarded people get done for themselves by paying for it (e.g., body care, household help) will often be voluntarily rendered, at least in part, by members of the communality. This option does not rule out the additional use of paid individual assistance, such as a personal attendant, for at least part of the time.

There are yet other viable—sometimes even gratifying—options that are one or more steps removed from the ideal. An example would be a maximally social role valorizing community group residence in which elderly retarded persons can play a valued role. This might be accomplished by having some special small community group homes specifically under the jurisdiction of a body that is as positively as possible identified with mental retardation, in which the retarded and elderly residents may require considerable support. Another option might be to include within specific selected community group residences for retarded adults a *small* proportion of elderly retarded residents.

Here, considerably more experience needs to be accumulated as to what the feasible options are and what problems are posed by different circumstances. For instance, what type of day program would an elderly retarded person attend outside the home, if any? Do such programs exist, or must they be created? How can such an elderly person be served in either a day program or residence without diminishing the competencies and image of the younger retarded persons in the residence, or of the other handicapped persons in the day program? If the elderly person does not attend day programs outside the home, what would be the implications for inhouse activities and/or staff support needs? It seems that these and related questions simply have not been explored in adequate detail to permit us to take a strong stance.

The above observations on role-valorizing and role-defending options are offered on a tentative basis, and it is hoped that readers would reflect upon their own views and experiences and share these, so that a more systematic position consistent with Social Role Valorization theory can be evolved.

REFERENCES

Action Coalition of Elders. (1975). *Kane Hospital: A place to die*. Ithaca, NY: Glad Day Press.

Duff, R. S., & Campbell, A. G. M. (1973). Moral and ethical dilemmas in the special care nursery. *New England Journal of Medicine, 289*, 890–894.

Horan, D. J., & Delahoyde, M. (Eds.). (1982). *Infanticide and the handicapped newborn*. Provo, UT: Brigham Young University Press.

Horan, D. J., & Mall, D. (Eds.). (1980). *Death, dying, and euthanasia*. Frederick, MD: University Publications of America (Aletheia Books Division).

Mansson, H. H. (1972). Justifying the final solution. *Omega, 3*, 79–87.

Ostheimer, J. (1980). The polls: Changing attitudes toward euthanasia. *Public Opinion Quarterly, 44*(1), 123–128.

Quay, E. A. (1977). *And now infanticide*. Thaxton, VA: Sun Life.

Todres, I. D., Krane, D., Howell, M. C., & Shannon, D. C. (1977). Pediatricians' attitudes affecting decision-making in defective newborns. *Pediatrics, 60*, 197–201.

Wolfensberger, W. (1972). *The principle of normalization in human services*. Toronto: National Institute on Mental Retardation.

Wolfensberger, W. (1977). The normalization principle, and some major implications to architectural-environmental design. In M. J. Bednar (Ed.), *Barrier-free environments* (pp. 135–169). Stroudsburg, PA: Dowden, Hutchinson, & Ross.

Wolfensberger, W. (1978). *The normalization principle, and some major implications to architectural-environmental design*. Atlanta: Georgia Association for Retarded Citizens.

Wolfensberger, W. (1980a). A call to wake up to the beginning of a new wave of "euthanasia" of severely impaired people (Editorial). *Education & Training of the Mentally Retarded, 15*, 171–173.

Wolfensberger, W. (1980b). Research, empiricism, and the principle of normalization. In R. J. Flynn & K. E. Nitsch (Eds.), *Normalization, social integration, and community services* (pp. 117–129). Baltimore: University Park Press.

Wolfensberger, W. (1980c). The definition of normalization: Update, problems, disagreements, and misunderstandings. In R. J. Flynn & K. E. Nitsch (Eds.), *Nor-*

malization, social integration, and community services (pp. 71–115). Baltimore: University Park Press.

Wolfensberger, W. (1981). The extermination of handicapped people in World War II Germany. *Mental Retardation, 19*(1), 1–7.

Wolfensberger, W. (1983a). *Guidelines for evaluators during a PASS, PASSING, or similar assessment of human service quality*. Toronto: National Institute on Mental Retardation.

Wolfensberger, W. (1983b). Social role valorization: A proposed new term for the principle of normalization. *Mental Retardation, 21*,234–239.

Wolfensberger, W. (in preparation). *The new genocide of handicapped and afflicted people*. Unpublished manuscript, Syracuse University, New York.

Wolfensberger, W., & Glenn, L. (1973a). *PASS (Program analysis of service systems): A method for the quantitative evaluation of human services. Rationales and structure* (2nd ed.). Toronto: National Institute on Mental Retardation.

Wolfensberger, W., & Glenn, L. (1973b). *PASS (Program analysis of service systems): A method for the quantitative evaluation of human services. Field manual* (2nd ed.). Toronto: National Institute on Mental Health.

Wolfensberger, W., & Glenn, L. (1975a; reprinted 1978). *PASS (Program analysis of service systems): A method for the quantitative evaluation of human services. Handbook*. (3rd ed.). Toronto: National Institute on Mental Retardation.

Wolfensberger, W., & Glenn, L. (1975b; reprinted 1978). *PASS (Program analysis of service systems): A method for the quantitative evaluation of human services. Field Manual*. (3rd ed.) Toronto: National Institute on Mental Retardation.

Wolfensberger, W., & Thomas, S. (1980). *PASSING (Program analysis of service systems' implementation of normalization goals)* (Experimental ed.). Syracuse, NY: Training Institute for Human Service Planning, Leadership and Change Agentry.

Wolfensberger, W., & Thomas, S. (1983). *PASSING (Program analysis of service systems' implementation of normalization goals) Normalization criteria and ratings manual* (2nd ed.). Toronto: National Institute on Mental Retardation.

chapter

5

Legal Processes and the Least Restrictive Alternative

Stanley S. Herr

Older persons with developmental disabilities have a wide variety of legal problems that have so far received little scholarly or activist attention. In comparison to other older people and other developmentally disabled people, this population has relatively limited access to the legal system. Although there are many statutes that pertain to disabled children and young persons, federal statutes that provide financial assistance to states, such as the Developmentally Disabled Assistance and Bill of Rights Act (PL 94-103, as amended) and the Rehabilitation Act (PL 93-112, as amended), do not contain old age–specific provisions. Four legal issues are of special importance to developmentally disabled elders: the right to least restrictive residential programming, the right to dignified least restrictive day programming, the right to nondiscriminatory access to generic services, and planning to ensure a qualified spokesperson and advocate for the person unable to protect his or her own interests. Securing these rights and services will require action on local, state/provincial, and national levels by family members, program providers, policy makers, lawyers, and other advocates.

HARRY S., a 55-year-old severely retarded man, was institutionalized at the Rosewood Center when his mother died and his 81-year-old father could no longer care for him on his own. Harry had lived his entire life at home, and had always taken part in family and community events. Now he was suddenly faced with life in a noisy institutional cottage populated by much younger men who were sometimes disruptive and assaultive. In the first months at Rosewood, Harry suffered from depression and several physical injuries, including a broken clavicle. Lawyers sought a less drastic residential alternative for him, but state workers claimed that they had none available. After months of intensive advocacy, Harry was placed in a community residence.

Asserting the legal rights of aging persons with developmental disabilities represents a frontier area of civil rights activity. There is a voluminous literature on the legal rights of

older persons (Brown, Allo, Freeman, & Netzorg, 1979; Krauskopf, 1983; Weiss, 1977). There is a fast-growing literature on rights and advocacy for developmentally disabled persons (Herr, 1983; Symposium Stanford Law Review, 1979; Vitello & Soskin, 1985). But at the intersection of these two fields, practitioners and scholars will find only passing references (Dybwad, 1962). This chapter identifies some of the legal issues of special significance to this group of aging and elderly disabled persons. It also identifies some of the reasons for the comparative neglect of their legal problems. As the case of Harry S. reveals, to be both developmentally disabled and elderly is to face a form of double jeopardy—a compounding of stigma and risk of isolation.

Such double jeopardy is reflected by this

population's severely limited access to the legal system. Studies document that elderly mentally disabled persons are even more underrepresented than other mentally disabled persons (Herr, 1979; Human Services Research Institute, 1982). This may be due to a variety of factors: poverty, social isolation, unavailability of legal services, communication barriers, social stigma, and conscious as well as unconscious priority settings by advocates that emphasize the needs of younger developmentally disabled persons. Planners of advocacy services seldom target the legal needs of such elderly persons for special attention.

The elderly disabled population has a wide variety of legal problems. These entail rights to income (including Social Security benefits), social services, freedom from age and handicap discrimination, health care, protective services, as well as transactions that arise from guardianship, wills, estates, and control of assets. Rather than a cursory examination of all these concerns, this chapter examines four legal issues that are of special importance to developmentally disabled elders. The right to least restrictive residential programming has great importance to a population already in facilities or at risk of institutionalization. The right to dignified, least restrictive day programming can lead to opportunities for enjoyable activity with others and alone. The right to nondiscriminatory access to generic services can promise entry to medical, social, and recreational services for elderly persons with developmental disabilities on terms similar to elderly persons without such disabilities. Another critical issue involves legal planning by family members and their professional advisers to ensure that the property and personal interests of the disabled person will be protected in old age.

THE RIGHT TO LEAST RESTRICTIVE RESIDENTIAL PROGRAMMING

The invisible elderly population is residing in large institutions, nursing homes, board-and-care homes, and other congregate care facilities. Their numbers are known, but seldom are

their names. Occasionally, a journalist, lawyer, or social scientist has investigated and reported the life story of an aging or elderly developmentally disabled person sequestered away or deinstitutionalized after long decades of confinement (Edgerton, Bollinger, & Herr, 1984; Panitch, 1983; Rodricks, 1983; Skidmore, 1982; Sweeney & Wilson, 1979). But for the most part, there has been little systematic study of their aspirations, abilities, and desires for less restrictive, community-based forms of living. Being under the "double jeopardy" of age and disability, they tend to remain where they are. In too many cases, it is the place where they have been since childhood.

The laws that mandate least restrictive alternatives for developmentally disabled persons do not distinguish between young and old, or between aging and elderly individuals. The Developmentally Disabled Assistance and Bill of Rights Act of 1975 (PL 94-103, as amended) requires that treatment, services, and habilitation should be provided in "the setting that is least restrictive of the person's personal liberty" (42 U.S.C. §6010(2)). The statutory definition of developmental disability requires a severe, chronic disability that is not only manifest before the person attains age 22 but is likely to continue indefinitely and to require lifelong services. Although the U.S. Supreme Court has ruled that the Act's bill of rights provisions express policy preferences and not judicially enforceable rights, the Act imposes some contractual assurances of human rights that may be enforceable (*Pennhurst State School and Hospital* v. *Halderman*, 1981). The Rehabilitation Act of 1973 (PL 93-112, as amended) prohibits federally assisted programs from excluding, denying benefits to, or discriminating against an "otherwise qualified handicapped individual . . . solely by reason of his handicap." This particular provision, known as Section 504, has far-reaching applications (see pages 83–84). Under regulations of the U.S. Department of Health and Human Services, affected programs must assure such handicapped persons "equal opportunity to obtain the same result, to gain the same benefit [as nonhandicapped persons] in the most integrated setting appropriate to the person's needs'' (U.S. Department of Health and Human Services, 1981). The potential of these statutes as well as federal constitutional law to require nondiscriminatory habilitation in community settings has yet to be fully tested (*Pennhurst State School and Hospital* v. *Halderman*, 1984). Unlike the many state and federal statutes that define the rights of disabled children and young persons, these federal statutes providing financial assistance to state programs lack age-specific provisions that would benefit elderly persons in particular.

Complex regulatory and ethical issues are sometimes presented by individuals who could be called the ''pensioner residents.'' Pensioner residents are persons who should not have been confined in their youth, and now lack the supports or options to leave. What approach should care providers and regulators take for residents of state institutions who have been institutionalized for 30, 40, or even 60 years or more? As in the case of Charles Turner, the pensioner resident may not be retarded at all, but may be habituated to the patterns, routines, and associations of institutional life (Rodricks, 1983). On humanitarian, client autonomy, and legal grounds, care providers should honor the refusal by such a resident to be placed into an unfamiliar community setting. Such considered refusals should not, however, be confused with refusals based on lack of information or poor counseling. Even the oldest residents of institutions can sometimes desire and succeed in community placements (Cohen & Dickerson, 1983; Panitch, 1983).

The courts have seldom dealt specifically with the deficiencies of residential care for older persons with developmental disabilities. This may, in part, reflect the absence of geriatric facilities catering exclusively to developmentally disabled persons. But courts are not roving commissions of inquiry, and their lack of specific attention to the legal problems of these elders reflects the types of claims raised by attorneys. The few relevant legal precedents are the by-products of actions undertaken for wider groups (such as all residents of an institution, or recipients of a service program or benefit). For example, a recent class action on behalf of psychiatric patients receive professionally recognized, psychological, and recreational programming, and that mentally retarded patients who no longer have psychiatric diagnosis be placed in the least restrictive settings appropriate to their needs (*R. A. J.* v. *Miller,* 1984).

Class action lawsuits seeking systemic reform have helped to shift the continuum of services toward a community-based model. Cases in Maine, Massachusetts, Michigan, New York, Pennsylvania, and elsewhere have led to the creation of small community residences and the phasing out of central institutions (Herr, 1983). Ironically, the pioneering case of *Wyatt* v. *Stickney* (1972) began as an action on behalf of patients in a hospital for the mentally ill and expanded to the residents of an institution for mentally retarded persons as a result of the investigation of the Partlow State School as a potential transfer site for the hundreds of geriatric patients that burdened the state mental hospital. The proposal to cast those elderly persons in one catch-all facility was dropped when lawyers for the plaintiffs and amici visited Partlow and observed its intolerable living conditions. Instead, the lawyers amended their complaint, ultimately established a constitutional right to adequate habilitation, and began a decade-long struggle to enforce a right to least restrictive conditions of habilitation.

Interventions for individuals present other frustrations. The precedent-setting case of *Lake* v. *Cameron* (1966) illustrates the tension between declarations of rights and pledges of unfulfilled paternalism. Catherine Lake, 60 years old and somewhat senile, sometimes wandered the streets of Washington, D.C., and had a poor memory. She was involuntarily committed to St. Elizabeth Hospital after a doctor and a judge decided that she needed protection and was incapable of self-care. Although the U.S. Court of Appeals for the District of Columbia Circuit held that, under a statute authorizing exploration of less restrictive alternatives, Mrs. Lake could not be compelled to stay in a mental hospital if some less drastic form of protection would suffice, on remand the lower court found that no alternatives were available. As a result, Mrs. Lake, a peaceful woman who suffered from poverty and cerebral arteriosclerosis, remained in the hospital. She died there after 9 years of confinement. Despite this unhappy outcome for the litigant, the *Lake* decision became the cornerstone for more effective law reforms that created new alternatives—group homes, foster care, halfway houses—for people with disabilities.

Securing residential placements that are truly less restrictive can be a complex task. Parents and other family members should investigate alternatives for long-term and respite care before an emergency arises, bringing the needs of their handicapped member to the attention of public and private agencies and making appropriate use of waiting lists for community-based residential services. Through homemaker services, collective action by several families, and other imaginative private arrangements, some individuals can continue to live in their family homes even after the death of a parent. Clinicians and administrators have a professional obligation to be familiar with the principle of the least restrictive alternative and to take actions in preparing individual service plans, budgets, and policy proposals that make the principle attainable in practice (Turnbull, Ellis, Boggs, Brooks, & Biklin, 1981). To protect the rights of their clients to live in the least restrictive individually appropriate environment, professionals must sometimes engage in job action, administrative, legislative, and/or judicial action (American Association on Mental Deficiency, 1975). Advocates, too, have professional responsibilities to make use of this full range of forums, to build coalitions for community-based care, and to satisfy client aspirations. One vivid illustration is the attempt in a federal district court to block the reinstitutionalization of 233 former residents of Massachusetts's Belchertown State School who currently live in nursing homes (*Ricci* v. *Okin,* 1984). There the Center for Public Representation defends elderly residents of nursing homes who like their homes, refuse to return to Belchertown, and want legal help to live where they choose. In addition to local and state actions, consumers, advocates, clinicians, and administrators should become involved with the Congressional debate on the extent to which Medicaid monies should support small living facilities (S. 2053, 1983). In 1985, new legislation will be offered that would shift financial incentives from institutional to community-based care. Thus, on many levels, elderly disabled persons will be affected by the issues of identifying, creating, and maintaining less restrictive residential options.

THE RIGHT TO LEAST RESTRICTIVE DAY PROGRAMMING

Adults in general, and older adults in particular, have a paucity of day care programs from which to choose. This problem begins as early as age 21 with the so-called "aging-out" crisis. Under United States statutes, handicapped young adults are no longer eligible for free educational services after age 21, and alternative structured activities are in short supply. Although the problem is nationwide, only a few states, such as New York, have any legal procedures for identifying individuals whose care will otherwise be terminated at age 21, and for initiating a planning process to determine if, and what type of, adult services are needed (New York Mental Hygiene Law). This law does not, however, mandate the provision of such services. And unlike the "right to services" model law proposed by the American Bar Association's Developmental Disabilities State Legislative Project, there are few, if any, entitlements to day services for older developmentally disabled persons (Sales, Powell, Van Duizend, & Associates, 1982).

All too often, legal mandates for day activity programs are tied to institutionalization in one form or another. The *Willowbrook* case, for example, required a minimum of 6 scheduled hours of programming per weekday for residents or ex-residents of that state developmental center (*New York State Association for Retarded Children* v. *Carey,* 1975). These prescriptions, however, should be individualized to take into account the possibility of declining vigor or the desire for less activity that an older person may express (*R. A. J. v. Miller*, 1984). Although family care payments for natural parents of deinstitutionalized persons have sometimes been granted in New York, an appellate court rejected equal protection claims raised by natural parents for similar payments for retarded persons who were never institutionalized (*Sundheimer v. Blum*, 1980). Legislators and commentators have called for greater emphasis on deinstitutionalizing elderly developmentally disabled persons and implementing programs of institutional diversion at the preadmission stage (Developmentally Disabled Assistance and Bill of Rights Act, 1975; Janicki & MacEachron, 1984).

At present, the absence of well-considered diversion planning and the dearth of community-based recreational, vocational, and habilitative day activity programs for older developmentally disabled persons results in a curious administrative strategy. Many such persons are being routed through restrictive institutions in order to be *deinstitutionalized* and thereby gain a higher priority for scarce day and residential services in the community. Yet sometimes residents get stranded midway through the circuit. This almost occurred in the case of Harry S., the Rosewood resident mentioned at the beginning of this chapter. Administrators have now located a community placement for Harry but only after vigorous legal advocacy contesting the long-term commitment on constitutional and statutory grounds, negotiations with staff, stipulations between the superintendent and counsel detailing the required community-based services, and an order from the hearing officer specifically denying commitment on the basis that the state had not demonstrated that a less restrictive alternative was unavailable. Although this legal action will require the state of Maryland to provide a package of community-based day activities and a residence in a small supervised apartment unit, such advocacy is no substitute for the systemic planning that should have yielded the same result without Harry's 9-month stay at Rosewood and the stress and costs of protracted advocacy. Case-by-case advocacy can be cumbersome and frustrating, but, gradually, prece-

dents on state law issues can uphold duties to provide care for mentally retarded persons in the least restrictive environment (*In re Joseph Schmidt*, 1981).

Administrators generally endorse the analogous principle of normalization, including the disabled individual's opportunities for "age-appropriate routines" (Maryland State Planning Council, 1983, p. 30). But what routine is age-appropriate for aging and elderly developmentally disabled persons given the diversity of images, roles, energy levels, and individual abilities that aging and elderly persons in the general population display? Clearly, these decisions must be individualized to reflect the choices of clients to the greatest extent possible, and the choices of their legal representatives, if any, regarding a variety of service needs. For elderly retarded individuals, those priority needs include access to health-related services, fulfillment of social and emotional needs, housing, vocational services, recreational and leisure time activities, transportation, financial assistance, advocacy and protective services, and support for families caring for elderly members, such as day care, counseling, and respite care (Segal, 1977). Planning to meet these needs on an individual and statewide basis takes on a special urgency when one considers that many deinstitutionalized persons have experienced physical and mental deterioration as a result of their institutional experiences (DiGiovanni, 1978). Furthermore, 50%–60% of known elderly developmentally disabled persons reside in institutional settings, even though a significant number could reside in less restrictive and less costly alternative living arrangement care settings (Janicki & McEachron, 1984). For example, Pennhurst in 1978 housed 1,154 persons, aged 9 to 82, and 5 years later, under the impetus of litigation, it housed 628 persons (Temple University & Human Services Research Institute, 1983). Over 425 people of all ages had moved to community living arrangements, receiving an average of over 10 hours of service per day.

Lawyers have not yet adequately explored legal theories of compensation that might assist a current older generation deprived of education and other civil rights during its youth. A few court cases have required compensatory education plans for children and young adults previously denied public education (*Mills* v. *Board of Education of the District of Columbia,* 1972; *Pennsylvania Association for Retarded Children (PARC)* v. *Commonwealth of Pennsylvania,* 1972). But such plans have not been extended to aging, developmentally disabled people whose educations were cut short in the past, but who could benefit from specialized adult education. Similarly, some residents of public facilities have been required to perform institution-maintaining labor without any pay (*Townsend* v. *Clover Bottom Hospital and School,* 1978). Their productivity may even have delayed their release to community care, as staff were sometimes reluctant to see these more able residents leave. Yet only rarely, as in the case of Charles Turner, have those residents made claims for money or "pensions" for decades of uncompensated labor, for lives needlessly stunted, or for the devaluation of their productive efforts (Rodricks, 1983). Now they face "retirements" without the benefits of Social Security because their work was not "covered employment" or because their employers did not meet reporting requirements and did not pay Social Security taxes for them. Thus, they are not only denied a secure income, but also the comforts and self-esteem that those payments could bring.

International documents recognize that mentally handicapped persons have rights to learning opportunities and self-determination to the full extent of their abilities and situations. These rights and needs do not terminate with old age. Thus, the United Nations Declaration on the Rights of Disabled Persons states that such persons have the "same fundamental rights as their fellow-citizens of the same age, which implies first and foremost the right to enjoy a decent life, as normal and full as possible" (United Nations, 1975, Art. 3). The earlier Declaration on the Rights of Mentally Retarded Persons embodied a similar principle; on grounds of mental retardation alone, no person should be denied the fundamental rights that fellow citizens of similar age enjoy (United Nations, 1971). Yet on a practical level, fam-

ilies need support from the community to protect those rights, to maximize the handicapped person's skills and independence, and to provide a comprehensive range of secure and stable homes for elderly mentally handicapped people (Thomas & Fryers, 1982). International statements of this type can spark reforms in policy, law, and human services delivery at local and national levels (Dybwad, 1984; Herr, 1980). For example, the benefits accorded senior citizens—from concession cards and low-cost travel to a fair share of services for elderly individuals—should be allocated to these senior citizens, too.

To summarize, older developmentally disabled persons, like other older people with low or poverty incomes, suffer from an acute paucity of effective social services and day care facilities (Browne & Olson, 1983). Given current federal policy, advocates are likely to encounter stiff resistance to increased government spending on age-based social services and income entitlements. Advocates for developmentally disabled elders can, however, make a convincing case that their clients are a segment of the elderly population facing the greatest need and receiving little or no targeted assistance under the Older Americans Act and Title XX of the Social Security Act. Thus, they are in a position to capitalize on the need-based eligibility approaches that may emerge in a leaner political environment (Brodsky, 1983). To some extent, this will mean a re-allocation of resources from the more well-off elderly to the disadvantaged elderly. But cost consciousness and equity concerns should also lead to inhome support and respite services for families who have so far avoided institutionalization of their disabled members. With the greying of both the general and the developmentally disabled population, this policy and legal agenda should attract increasing attention.

THE RIGHT TO NONDISCRIMINATORY ACCESS TO GENERIC SERVICES

Although use of generic service systems is a major goal of developmental disabilities service planners, the older person with developmental disabilities is seldom welcomed in a network of agencies serving other older persons. Even when programs have claimed to serve elderly and disabled individuals, developmentally disabled persons have seldom been a targeted client group. For example, a Wisconsin experiment in delivering inhome services as alternatives to nursing home services reported that the presence of developmentally disabled clients in their home-care caseload "came as a surprise." The new clientele was the result of the freezing of the budget of a mental health center, the primary provider of developmentally disabled services in that county (Seidl, Applebaum, Austin, & Mahoney, 1983, p. 82). Although some professionals and agency personnel contend that no special concern or attention is required to meet the needs of mentally retarded persons age 65 or older because their needs are similar to the "normal" older population (Sweeney & Wilson, 1979), this approach may foster benign neglect rather than social integration. Because of their historic exclusion from generic services and special needs for long-term supportive services, habilitation, and increased medical services, older developmentally disabled persons in some situations require different service responses (Janicki, Otis, Puccio, Rettig, & Jacobson, Chapter 17, this volume).

The older disabled person sometimes confronts outright rejection when he or she tries to use recreational facilities generally available to others. For example, the author represented a 60-year-old Greek American, Penny, who attempted to enroll in an adult education course in the Greek language at a local YMCA. After two sessions, the instructor excluded her from further attendance on the grounds that other students were "disturbed" by the unusual appearance of this physically disabled, but mentally alert resident of Fernald State School in Massachusetts. Following vigorous advocacy (including letter writing and negotiations) by members of the Harvard Law School Clinical Program and a Fernald staff member, the instructor relented and agreed to readmit Penny and to foster a more accepting atmosphere in his classroom. A developmentally disabled

person, lacking such social supports, might not have tried to use generic community services, might not have protested a refusal of service, might not have had access to the services of trained advocates, and might not have had obtained an effective remedy. Furthermore, it is tragic that many members of a generation that experienced discrimination in institutions now often face discrimination in community settings.

Yet, antidiscrimination laws may cover many of these situations. Can a federally assisted senior citizens center categorically refuse to serve senior citizens who are developmentally disabled? Under Section 504 of the Rehabilitation Act of 1973, no otherwise qualified handicapped individual can be excluded from participation in any program receiving federal financial assistance solely by reason of his or her handicap. Although there is no case law directly on this point, a senior citizens center presumably could be required to make reasonable accommodations for age- and income-eligible clients who could be served without undue financial hardship and without extensive modification of the program (*Southeastern Community College* v. *Davis,* 1979; *Lynch* v. *Maher,* 1981). Furthermore, rehabilitation programs open to specific populations may not exclude otherwise qualified elderly disabled individuals, as demonstrated by a federal court decision that found it unlawful under Section 504 to bar a 77-year-old man from a prison vocational program on the basis of his mental disability (*Sites* v. *McKenzie,* 1976).

Can a place of public accommodation, such as a restaurant or a motion picture theater, close its doors to developmentally disabled elders? The majority of state antidiscrimination laws make it unlawful for such establishments to deny those facilities to any person on discriminatory grounds that include age, or physical or mental handicap (Sales et al., 1982). These laws do, however, contain exceptions. For example, Maryland proprietors and their employees would not commit a prohibited act if they denied service to "any person for failure to conform to the usual and regular requirements, standards and regulations for the establishment so long as the denial is not based upon discrimination'' on categorical grounds (Md. Code Ann. Art. 49B, 1984). Thus, a restaurant owner could refuse to serve rowdy patrons who happen to be disabled, but could not lawfully refuse to serve disabled persons simply because their presence is unwelcome or esthetically offensive to other patrons. Although instances of discrimination abound, actual cases on behalf of developmentally disabled individuals are seldom brought to the attention of public officials, equal opportunity agencies, commissions, or courts.

Section 504 regulations have had a well-publicized impact on decision-making about medical care for congenitally handicapped infants, but not about such care for congenitally handicapped elders. The death of Baby Doe of Bloomington, Indiana, resulting from a lack of nutrition and failure to overcome parental opposition to surgery for the repair of an esophageal defect, provoked court cases and federal rule-making (*In re Infant Doe,* 1983; *United States* v. *University Hospital,* 1983; U.S. Department of Health & Human Services, 1984a). The Child Abuse Amendments of 1984 (P.L. 98-457) have now superseded Section 504–based rules. Proposed rules clarify the states' obligations to respond to reports of medical neglect: the withholding of medically indicated treatment from a disabled infant with a life-threatening condition. Whether these rules and guidelines, with their emphasis on state law remedies, access to medically beneficial treatment, ethics committees, and legal and multidisciplinary advice to health care providers, will set a precedent for determining what constitutes nondiscriminatory care and medical treatment for disabled patients of other ages remains to be seen (U.S. Department of Health & Human Services, 1984b, 1984c). At present, there are few sources of guidance in these sensitive matters when the lives of elderly, disabled citizens are at stake.

For example, a Massachusetts case on withholding chemotherapy from an elderly profoundly retarded man provides broad principles for such nondiscriminatory decisions. Joseph Saikewicz suffered from an incurable illness (acute leukemia). He was found to be unable to comprehend the adverse side effects and immediate suffering that would result from chemotherapy, or even to understand the other traumatic costs of prolonging his life, such as removal to strange surroundings, physical restraints, and other forms of discomfort and disorientation. The guardian appointed by the probate court, therefore, recommended that chemotherapy not be administered. After weighing the considerations for and against such treatment, the court ordered that no treatment for leukemia be given, but that all reasonable and necessary steps be taken to safeguard the well-being of Saikewicz and to reduce his discomfort. Four months later Saikewicz died at the Belchertown State School infirmary, apparently without pain. Distinguishing between lifesaving and life-prolonging treatments, the Supreme Judicial Court of Massachusetts ruled that a patient incompetent to make decisions to refuse medical treatment in appropriate circumstances has the same right to refuse treatment as does any other patient (*Superintendent of Belchertown State School* v. *Saikewicz,* 1977). It based this right on the constitutional right to privacy, from which flows the individual's right to free choice and self-determination. For the incompetent person, this right can be exercised by a guardian who satisfies a probate court that nontreatment meets the substituted judgment test. That test calls on the participants in such guardianship proceedings to first establish that the individual is incompetent to choose, and to then determine ''with as much accuracy as possible the wants and needs of the individual involved.'' Although some states have instead opted for the somewhat more objective *best interests standard* and left such decisions to the individual's guardian, family, attending physician, and hospital ethics committee, Massachusetts leaves the ultimate decision to a court. Until legislatures offer more definitive guidance, these controversies at the twilight of life will continue to surface in the judicial process.

There is much to be done to remedy patterns and instances of discrimination, neglect, and abuse. Public and professional education to increase awareness of prohibited practices is clearly a first step. Professional and consumer organizations can also contribute to the search for an ethical consensus on treatment principles for handicapped elders as they did for handicapped infants (American Association on Mental Deficiency, 1983). Legislative revisions of state law can strengthen reporting and other protective service provisions affecting adult disabled persons. In some states, this may require new laws or amendments to provide clearer operational definitions, coverage of individuals in institutional as well as community settings, reporter immunity from liability, emergency intervention services, and other model law features (Kerness, 1984). In addition, human rights committees, now mandated by accreditation standards, Medicaid regulations, and state laws, have important monitoring responsibilities in identifying and remedying abuse and discrimination (Herr, 1984). Depending on the nature of the violations established, suitable legal remedies can include negotiated settlements, mediation, and referral to official administrative agencies with oversight duties (such as commissions dealing with human rights, civil rights, or human relations), and funding terminations by administrative agencies. In narrowly defined circumstances, abuse or willful withholding of essential medical treatment from a disabled adult can result in judicial actions for damages, injunctive relief, or criminal liability. Protection and advocacy agencies, operating in every state, territory, and the District of Columbia under the federal developmental disabilities law, can offer concerned individuals advice as to appropriate remedies when serious neglect or discrimination is suspected. (See Appendix A.)

THE RIGHT TO PROTECTION OF PROPERTY AND INTERESTS IN OLD AGE

One of the most worrisome problems that confronts the parents of a developmentally disabled adult is who will safeguard the interests of their son or daughter after the death or disablement of the parents. As longevity for persons with developmental disabilities increases, these disabled elders may not only survive their parents, but some of their siblings, other relatives, and trusted family friends. Permanent institutional care in a large state facility was once viewed as the answer, but this approach, now discredited on humane and programmatic grounds, is less and less available. Moreover, there are real practical, ethical, and legal constraints on a facility's superintendent acting *in loco parentis*. Similarly, conflicts of interest may disqualify care-providing staff from serving as personal representatives of individual residents (International League of Societies for the Mentally Handicapped, 1969). For most families whose developmentally disabled members live at home, there are other concerns, including a well-documented need for more home-care services, crisis intervention, and personal advocacy services, particularly as age or infirmity impairs the ability of parents to be vigilant protectors of their adult child. The Academy Award–winning documentary film, *Best Boy,* vividly portrays the human dimensions of this need for continuity of care and emotional support when a parent is no longer available (Wohl, 1980). Can parents make legal provisions to fill the role of parent advocate when death or permanent disablement removes them from the scene?

The legal process has developed three traditional solutions to this question. In drafting a will, a parent can name an *executor* or *co-executors* to carry out his or her testamentary wishes and can make testamentary provision for a child with a disability. Typically, these provisions include arrangements for someone to exercise a continuing personal interest as a friend or advocate for the disabled person after the death of the surviving parent; and for creation of a fund to care for the child's needs without disqualifying the child from Supplemental Security Income (SSI), Medicaid benefits, and state entitlement programs.

Estate planners frequently advise families to establish a testamentary trust fund for the life of a disabled beneficiary, giving the *trustees* absolute discretion to disburse funds in order to provide the beneficiary with a higher quality of life than would otherwise be available to him or her under public entitlement programs, and at the same time preserve the funds from seizure by the state for the costs of public care (Davis, 1983; MICPEL, 1983; Moore, 1981). These trusts are referred to as luxury trusts or discretionary trusts since they give the trustee discretion as to whether and how income should be distributed. Lawyers caution against putting assets directly in the name of the child in order to prevent possible disqualifications from public benefits. On the other extreme, disinheriting the child can have injurious consequences in view of the subsistence nature of most government benefits and uncertainties in predicting the child's future needs.

Under guardianship laws, courts may appoint *conservators* or *guardians* to protect the property or person of an adult who is proved incapable of managing himself or herself and/ or his or her affairs due to mental disability or age. Because of the cost, inflexibility, and restrictions on personal liberty arising from an incompetency determination and the requirement that the appointment of a guardian be the least restrictive method of safeguarding the individual's interest, guardianship is generally not recommended unless there is clear evidence of a compelling legal need for it. Although some health care providers may insist on a guardian's consent for serious medical procedures, most will recognize the validity of next-of-kin authorization and all should recognize that there are many developmentally disabled persons capable of authorizing medical treatment for themselves. Limited guardianships may also offer an alternative means of meeting the needs of those unable to give informed consent. Family members should not, however, be pressured or cajoled into becoming limited guardians for the sake of an agency's convenience when the resulting expense and restriction is not warranted. Given the complexity of these topics and variations in state laws, interested persons should consult local advocacy groups, state protection and advocacy systems, or consumer organizations

for descriptions of locally available surrogate arrangements and for referrals to legal specialists sensitive to the problems associated with mental retardation and other developmental disabilities.

Joint trusts represent an important and increasingly popular innovation in this field of protective services. They can combine personalized visiting arrangements for disabled persons with an organization that can pool resources and can act as an informed monitor of services for enrolled members. This concept of a community trust offers a number of advantages: in contrast to public guardianship agencies, the organization can adopt a more intimate style of operation; individuals with small estates can join an established trust and avoid the greater expense of creating and maintaining their own individual trusts; staff and volunteers providing the monitoring can be better trained and supervised; and the trust organization can become a repository of expertise and a pressure group for its enrolled beneficiaries. Although some of these trust programs are still in early stages of operations, they deserve close study and encouragement as a promising response to a widely felt advocacy need. There are some 15 programs of this type in the United States (Davis, 1983), as well as similar programs in England and New Zealand. Typically, they are nonprofit corporations, affiliated with established advocacy groups such as associations for mentally retarded citizens, and provide case management, planning assistance, and other advocacy services on an enrollment fee basis.

The Trust for Intellectually Handicapped People (Inc.), a registered charitable trust in New Zealand, offers a relatively sophisticated model that others might follow. In a country of only 3 million inhabitants, the Trust has enrolled over 600 beneficiaries and accumulated more than NZ$425,000 from fees, trust income, and donations. The trust board, composed of a physician, high court judge, chartered accountant, company director, and a parent of a person with a mental handicap, provides a management group of recognized expertise and integrity. For a one-time enrollment fee of NZ$1,500, the trust undertakes to appoint a personal visitor for the intellectually handicapped person and to "watch over the happiness, welfare and rights" of that person for the rest of his or her life. Active monitoring of the individual's welfare begins on the death or permanent disablement of parents. As of July, 1983, personal visitors had been appointed for 49 persons who were receiving this "full support" (Trust for Intellectually Handicapped People, 1983). In addition, the trust has conducted staff seminars on effective monitoring techniques, published attractive promotional literature, and participated in efforts to reform guardianship legislation so as to protect the rights of mentally handicapped adults when their rights cannot be ensured in any other way.

The monitoring and advocacy role of the personal visitor is central to the trust's mission. The personal visitor is expected to act as a friend, practical guide, and advocate, not as a guardian or entertainer. Visitors are expected to visit the enrollee on at least a monthly basis and are reimbursed for expenses and paid on an hourly basis. As tutors and advisers, they can contribute to the enrollee's social communications, personal appearance, and development of relationships with others of his or her age group. The appointed visitor's most important role, however, is to act as a spokesperson for the handicapped person in protecting that person from abuse, and in asserting his or her rights as one would assert one's own rights. To prepare for this role, the visitor receives checklists on residential routines, recreational activities, and personal preferences of clients as well as information on broad areas of human and legal rights. If the visitor feels that the enrollee's rights are being violated, he or she is advised to observe circumstances carefully, to resolve the problem on the spot when possible, and to inform the district adviser if further action may be warranted. By reporting to the trust, next of kin, and any estate managers, the visitor increases communication about the needs and well-being of the person with a mental handicap.

Community leaders in the United States are developing parallel, but independently conceived, trust arrangements. For instance, the Maryland Trust for Retarded Citizens (MTRC), an affiliate of the Maryland Association for Retarded Citizens, offers a variety of personal advocacy and case coordination services. For an enrollment fee of $1,200, MRTC will establish a case file to record family data (child's needs and wishes; sponsor's desires for enrollee's future), and will provide a minimum base level of services to active clients. These services include regular visitation by a staff social worker or volunteer, and such additional advocacy and case-following services as warranted by the client's needs and the trust's resources.

For an additional negotiated fee based on MRTC's actual operating costs, the trust has proposed a Family Supplemental Services Plan that would assist both during and after the lifetime of the sponsor in such matters as:

Representation at hearings affecting a client's placement and program

Investigation of services that would be appropriate and available to the client

Assistance in obtaining and evaluating quality and continuity of services from public or private agencies

Advice concerning legal issues such as entitlements, estate planning, and eligibility for services

Other forms of assistance in advocacy, companionship, and fiduciary matters for the handicapped client

Although the trust did not become fully operational until it enrolled 200 members, it achieved this minimum goal in October, 1984. At present, it provides active services to the five currently eligible members—clients whose parents have died or become disabled.

Active services can take a variety of forms. For example, MRTC helped to ensure a prompt and appropriate community group home residential placement for a middle-age man whose father had died. In another case, its representatives met with a bank trust officer and nursing home officials in order to prevent the funds of a

58-year-old client from being needlessly exhausted and to investigate day care programming for him at a nearby ARC center. These types of interventions are illustrative of the promise and potential of permanent community trust organizations.

Providing adequate legal and social protection for older adults requires diligence, creativity, and long-term planning by families and their professional advisers. Various advocacy, trust, or guardianship arrangements can be tailored to assure that someone speaks for the elderly developmentally disabled person. A legal representative may be empowered to determine the organization affecting the individual's personal environment, and to protect the individual's privacy, possessions, and basic right. For example, families should engage in estate planning to ensure that an inheritance to a handicapped individual will not disqualify him or her from federal and state entitlement programs and to make sure that the inheritance is kept from the reach of governmental agencies providing services to that individual (Moore, 1981). In sum, arrangements for visiting and advocacy on a lifelong basis are critically needed aspects of estate planning for the developmentally disabled beneficiary.

REFLECTIONS

Legal and political processes can make problems of elderly persons with developmental disabilities more visible. As one director of a senior citizens center put it, that group now occupies a bureaucratic "no man's land." They fall outside the conventional services offered the elderly. They receive very little care or attention from rehabilitation or developmental disabilities programs that have long focused on the needs of the young and the nonelderly adult. And, most important, with the deaths or disablements of their parents, those individuals lose vital sources of support, protection, guidance, and advocacy. It will take enormous amounts of lobbying, profes-

sional planning, and advocacy on individual and class levels before these difficult problems are addressed systematically.

The concept of the least restrictive alternative has many potential applications in the resolution of those problems. For individuals who are only mildly handicapped, it must be determined whether generic services for the elderly can and will be made more accessible to them. This will surely require adjustments for some senior centers in terms of hiring adequately trained staff members, or for overcoming the social barriers that prevent current clients from accepting their developmentally disabled age peers. Nonetheless, a few centers have begun to work together with associations for retarded citizens and other disability care providers to mainstream those newcomers. And for individuals who are institutionalized, we must ask whether that is really the solution that is in their best interests. For individuals who live at home or in home substitutes, it must be determined whether there are sufficient recreational and other out-of-home day programs to prevent homes from becoming confining experiences that result in regression and social isolation. As society plans to close institutions like Willowbrook and Pennhurst, it must open new pathways to help elderly developmentally disabled persons to live in the midst of society.

These possibilities will remain largely untested until family members, advocates, planners, program providers, and public officials make a conscious priority of mitigating this double jeopardy—old age coupled with developmental disability. On the level of the individual, this will mean balancing concerns for stability with stimulation, for safety with sensible risk, and for continuity with change. For society, it will mean designing and funding a network of services that can replace the dead-end shelters of the past. Law and legal processes are inevitably connected with these projects. The legal profession may not have a large role in this, but surely it has a role to play, one it can neither shirk nor avoid.

REFERENCES

American Association on Mental Deficiency. (1975). *Position papers: Rights of mentally retarded persons.* Washington, DC: Author.

American Association on Mental Deficiency. (1983). *Principles of treatment of disabled infants.* Washington, DC: Author.

Brodsky, D. (1983). Future policy directions. In W. P. Browne & L. K. Olson (Eds.), *Aging and public policy* (pp. 221–238). Westport, CT: Greenwood Press.

Brown, R. N., Allo, C. D., Freeman, A. D., & Netzorg, G. W. (1979). *The rights of older persons* (An American Civil Liberties Union Handbook). New York: Avon Books.

Browne, W. P., & Olson, L. K. (1983). An introduction to public policy and aging. In W. P. Browne & L. K. Olson (Eds.), *Aging and public policy* (pp. 3–18). Westport, CT: Greenwood Press.

Cohen, J., & Dickerson, M. (Eds.). (1983). *Hey, we're getting old: A monograph on aging and mental retardation.* Downsview, Ontario: National Institute on Mental Retardation.

Davis, C. (1983). Financial and estate planning for parents of a child with handicaps. *Western New England Law Review, 3,* 495–535.

Developmentally Disabled Assistance and Bill of Rights Act, 42 U.S.C. §§6000–6081 (1983).

DiGiovanni, L. (1978). The elderly retarded: A little-known group. *The Gerontologist, 18,* 262–266.

Dybwad, G. (1962). Administrative and legislative problems in the care of the adult and aged mental retardate. *American Journal of Mental Deficiency, 66,* 716–722.

Dybwad, G. (1984). Aging and mental retardation: An international perspective. In C. M. Gaitz & T. Samorejski (Eds.), *Aging 2000: Our health care destiny* (Vol. 1). New York: Springer Verlag.

Edgerton, R. B., Bollinger, M., & Herr, B. (1984). The cloak of competence: After two decades. *American Journal of Mental Deficiency, 88,* 345–351.

Herr, S. S. (1979). *The new clients: Legal services for mentally retarded persons.* Washington, DC: National Legal Services Corporation.

Herr, S. S. (1980). Rights of disabled persons: International principles and American experiences. *Columbia Human Rights Law Review, 12,* 1–55.

Herr, S. S. (1983). *Rights and advocacy for retarded people.* Lexington, MA: D. C. Heath & Co.

Herr, S. S. (1984). *Issues in human rights.* New York: Young Adult Institute and Workshop.

Human Services Research Institute. (1982). *Further exploration of advocacy models for the mentally disabled.* Boston: Author.

In re Infant Doe, No. GU 8204-00 (Cir. Ct., Monroe Co., Ind., Apr. 12, 1982), *writ of mandamus dismissed sub nom.* State ex rel. Infant Doe v. Baker, No. 482 S140 (Ind. Sup. Ct., May 27, 1982 (case mooted by child's death), *cert. denied,* 52 U.S. Law Week (U.S. Sup. Ct. Nov. 7, 1983).

In re Joseph Schmidt, 494 Pa. 86, 429 A.2d 631 (1981).

International League of Societies for the Mentally Handi-capped. (1969). *Symposium on guardianship of the mentally retarded.* Brussels, Belgium: Author.

Janicki, M. P., & MacEachron, A. E. (1984). Residential, health and social services needs of elderly developmentally disabled persons. *The Gerontologist, 24,* 128–137.

Kerness, J. (1984). *Preventing abuse and neglect: An analysis of state law and proposed model legislation* (Research Project). Miami Shores, FL: Barry University School of Social Work, Abuse and Neglect Prevention.

Krauskopf, J. M. (1983). *Advocacy for the aging.* St. Paul, MN: West Publishing Co.

Lake v. Cameron, 364 F.2d 657 (D.C. Cir. 1966).

Lynch v. Maher, 507 F. Supp. 1268 (D. Conn. 1981).

Maryland Code Ann. Art 49B §5 (1984 Cum. Supp.).

Maryland Institute for Continuing Professional Education of Lawyers (MICPEL). (1983). *Estate planning for families with handicapped dependents.* Baltimore: Author.

Maryland State Planning Council on Developmental Disabilities. (1983). *Maryland state plan for developmental disabilities—fiscal years 1984, 1985, 1986.* Baltimore: Author.

Mills v. Board of Education of the District of Columbia, 348 F. Supp. 866, 879 (D.D.C. 1972).

Moore, R. J. (1981). *Handbook on estate planning for families of developmentally disabled persons in Maryland, the District of Columbia, and Virginia.* Baltimore: Maryland State Planning Council on Developmental Disabilities.

New York Mental Hygiene Law §7.37 (1984 Supp.).

New York State Association for Retarded Children v. Carey, 393 F. Supp. 715 (E.D.N.Y. 1975).

Panitch, M. (1983). Mental retardation and aging. *Canada's Mental Health, 31*(3), 6–10.

Pennhurst State School and Hospital v. Halderman, 451 U.S. 1 (1981).

Pennhurst State School and Hospital v. Halderman, No. 81-2101, 52 U.S.L.W. 4155 (U.S. Sup. Ct. Jan. 23, 1984).

Pennsylvania Association for Retarded Children v. Commonwealth of Pennsylvania, 343 F.Supp. 279, 314 (E.D. Pa. 1972).

R. A. J. v. Miller, 590 F. Supp. 1310, 1312, 1317 (N. D. Texas 1984).

Rehabilitation Act of 1973, 29 U.S.C. §794 (1981).

Ricci v. Okin, C.A. 72-469-T, Community classmembers' opposition to plaintiffs' motion to require the return of classmembers to the Belchertown State School who presently reside in nursing homes (D. Mass., filed Feb. 17, 1984).

Rodricks, D. (1983, December 21). Charlie only asks his debt from society. *The (Baltimore) Evening Sun,* p. A1.

S. 2053, 98th Cong., 1st Sess. (1983). A bill to promote the full participation of severely disabled individuals in community and family life.

Sales, B. D., Powell, D. M., Van Duizend, R., & Associates. (1982). *Disabled persons and the law.* New York: Plenum Press.

Segal, R. (1977). Trends in services for the aged mentally retarded. *Mental Retardation, 15*(2), 25–27.

Seidl, F. W., Applebaum, R., Austin, C., & Mahoney, R. (1983). *Delivering 'In-Home' services to the aged and disabled: The Wisconsin experiment.* Lexington, MA: D.C. Heath & Co.

Sites v. McKenzie, 423 F. Supp. 1190, 1197 (N.D. W.Va. 1976).

Skidmore, B. (1982, December 30). An old man dies who barely lived. *Independent Record* (Helena, Montana), p. A1.

Southeastern Community College v. Davis, 442 U.S. 397 (1979).

Sundheimer v. Blum, 79 A.D.2d 512, 433 N.Y.S.2d 456 (1980).

Superintendent of Belchertown State School v. Saikewicz, 373 Mass. 728, 370 N.E.2d 417 (1977).

Sweeney, D. P., & Wilson, T. Y. (1979). *Double jeopardy: The plight of aging and aged developmentally disabled persons in Mid-America.* Ann Arbor, MI: Institute for the Study of Mental Retardation and Related Disabilities.

Symposium Stanford Law Review. (1979). Mentally retarded people and the law. *Stanford Law Review, 31,* 541–829.

Temple University & Human Services Research Institute. (1983). *Pennhurst longitudinal study, 1979 to 1983, fourth year summary.* Philadelphia and Boston: Authors.

Thomae, I., & Fryers, T. (1982). *Aging and mental handicap: A position paper.* Brussels, Belgium: International League of Societies for Persons with Mental Handicap.

Townsend v. Clover Bottom Hospital and School (Tenn. Sup. Ct. 560 S.W. 2d 623, 1978).

Trust for Intellectually Handicapped People. (1983, July). *Newsletter.* Wellington, New Zealand: Author.

Turnbull, H. R., III. (1979). Law and the mentally retarded citizen: American responses to the declarations of rights of the United Nations and International League of Societies for the Mentally Handicapped—Where we have been, are, and are headed. *Syracuse Law Review, 30,* 1093–1143.

Turnbull, H. R., III, Ellis, J., Boggs, E., Brooks, P., & Biklin, D. (1981). *The least restrictive alternative: Principles and practices.* Washington, DC: American Association on Mental Deficiency.

United Nations. *Declaration on the rights of disabled persons.* G.A. Res. 3447, 30 U.N. GAOR, Supp. (No. 34) 92, U.N.Doc. A/10034 (1975).

United Nations. *Declaration on the rights of mentally retarded persons.* G.A. Res. 2856, 26 U.N. GAOR, Supp. (No. 29) 99, U.N.Doc. A/8429 (1971).

United States v. University Hospital, State University of New York at Stony Brook, 575 F. Supp. 607 (E.D.N.Y. 1983), aff'd 729 F. 2d 144 (2d Cir. 1984).

U.S. Department of Health and Human Services. (1981). *Nondiscrimination on the basis of handicap in programs and activities receiving benefits from federal financial assistance.* 45 C.F.R. Part 84.

U.S. Department of Health and Human Services (1984a, Jan. 12). Final rules on nondiscrimination on the basis of handicap: Procedures and guidelines relating to health care for handicapped infants. *Federal Register, 49,* 1622–1654.

U.S. Department of Health & Human Services. (1984b, Dec. 10). Interim model guidelines for health care providers to establish infant care review committees. *Federal Register, 49,* 48170–48173.

U.S. Department of Health & Human Services. (1984c, Dec. 10). Proposed rules on child abuse and neglect prevention and treatment program. *Federal Register, 49,* 48160–48169.

Vitello, S., & Soskin, R. (1985). *Mental retardation: Its social and legal context.* New York: McGraw-Hill Book Co.

Weiss, J. A. (Ed.). (1977). *Law of the elderly.* New York: Practicing Law Institute.

Wohl, I. (1980). *Best boy* [documentary film]. New York: Documentary Films Co.

Wyatt v. Stickney, 344 F. Supp. 373, 344 F. Supp. 387 (M.D. Ala. 1972).

APPENDIX A

Information Resources

The best sources of information on the precise nature of the rights and legal processes affecting older developmentally disabled persons are the advocacy organizations that specialize in this field.

Each state, territory, and the District of Columbia has an established "protection and advocacy system" for persons with developmental disabilities. A list of the names, addresses, and phone numbers of those agencies can be obtained by writing the Administration on Developmental Disabilities, U.S. Department of Health and Human Services, Humphrey Building, 300 Independence Avenue, S.W., Washington, D.C. 20201, or telephoning (202) 245-2897.

There are several directories that identify advocacy organizations on a state-by-state basis. The National Legal Aid and Defender Association (NLADA) publishes an annual directory of legal aid and defender offices in the United States. This lists offices that provide civil legal assistance to persons unable to retain private counsel, and civil and defender offices that provide programs for the special needs of developmentally disabled persons, senior citizens, and other handicapped persons. NLADA's address is 1625 K Street, N.W., Washington, D.C. 20006. The American Bar Association Commission on the Mentally Disabled (1800 M Street, N.W., Washington, D.C. 20036) publishes *Mental Disability: A General Listing*. In addition to national and local legal aid groups, their pamphlet includes private attorneys, state-agency advocates, and bar association referral sources. In 1982, the Human Interaction Research Institute (10889 Wilshire Boulevard, Suite 1120, Los Angeles, CA 90024) published an extensive survey of advocacy groups titled *National Directory of Mental Health Advocacy Programs*. For senior citizens, the American Bar Association Commission on Legal Problems of the Elderly compiled *The Law and Aging Resource Guide* (December, 1981), a list of advocacy projects funded by the Administration on Aging and the Legal Services Corporation.

Centers for legal advice and referral exist in a number of countries. In Canada, the National Legal Resources Service of the National Institute of Mental Retardation provides training, technical assistance, and various advocacy services. Its address is 4700 Keele Street, Downsview, Ontario M3J 1P3. In England, there are three principal sources of information: the Advocacy Alliance, the National Society for Mentally Handicapped Children, and the Campaign for Mentally Handicapped People (12A Maddox Street, London, W1R 9PL, England). New Zealand, as previously discussed, has created the Trust for the Intellectually Handicapped, a charitable trust with close links to the New Zealand Institute for Mental Retardation. Any correspondence to the Trust should be addressed to P.O. Box 335, Wellington, New Zealand.

APPENDIX B

General Readings

Crystal, S. (1982). *America's old age crisis: Public policy and the two worlds of aging*. New York: Basic Books.

Friedman, P. R. (1976). *The rights of mentally retarded persons*. New York: Avon Books.

Hayes, S. C., & Hayes, R. (1982). *Mental retardation: Law, policy and administration*. Sydney, Australia: The Law Book Company.

Herr, S. S. (1983). *Rights and advocacy for retarded people*. Lexington, MA: D. C. Heath & Co.

International League of Societies for Persons with Mental Handicap. (1976). *Step by step: Some analytical guidelines for national societies*. Brussels, Belgium: Author.

Kindred, M., Cohen, J., Penrod, D., & Shaffer, T. (Eds.). (1976). *The mentally retarded citizen and the law*. New York: The Free Press.

Regan, J. J. (1972). Protective services for the elderly: Commitment, guardianship, and alternatives. *William and Mary Law Review, 13,* 569–622.

section

III

THE OLDER DEVELOPMENTALLY DISABLED POPULATION

chapter

6

Epidemiology of Aging in Developmental Disabilities

Robert A. Lubin and Michele Kiely

Reductions in the incidence of birth defects, improvements in the capacity of health technology to reduce the risks of morbidity and mortality, and enlightenment in societal practices toward the delivery of educational and social services have led to changes in the life expectancy and quality of life for persons who would have been or are developmentally disabled. Furthermore, these factors have influenced the overall number, age distribution, and characteristics of the population of persons considered to be developmentally disabled. This chapter considers these issues from an epidemiological perspective, and presents information on definitions of aging and developmental disabilities, age-specific prevalence, and trends in morbidity and mortality. Special attention is given to the epidemiology of aging in mental retardation, as it is the most common form of developmental disability. The epidemiology of aging in mental retardation is considered in terms of diagnostic etiology, especially the unique morbidity and mortality patterns associated with Down syndrome.

THE PAST DECADES have witnessed dramatic changes in the risks of manifesting birth defects and in the consequences of being developmentally disabled. There have been reductions in the incidence of certain birth defects, improvements in the capacity of health technology to reduce the risks of morbidity and mortality, and an enlightenment in societal practices toward the delivery of educational and social services for developmentally disabled children and adults. All of these factors, both individually and in concert, have led to changes in life expectancy and quality of life for persons who would have been or are developmentally disabled. Furthermore, these factors have influenced the overall characteristics of the population of persons considered to be developmentally disabled, in terms of age,

level of disability, and health status. This chapter considers these issues from an epidemiological perspective, and presents information on the age-specific prevalence of mental retardation. Additionally, the chapter focuses on the patterns of morbidity and mortality that can be expected in the future. Finally, the chapter considers the extent to which morbidity and mortality patterns of developmentally disabled persons differ from the population at large.

ISSUES OF DEFINITION

A primary goal of epidemiological research on the subject of aging and mental retardation/developmental disabilities is to establish age-specific prevalence patterns and to examine how these patterns have changed over time.

95

However, in order to reach this goal it is necessary to obtain agreement on the definitions of both "aging" and "developmental disabilities." Unfortunately, there is no consensus on either of these definitions (see discussion by Marsha Seltzer, Chapter 9, this volume). This is especially a problem in terms of establishing the parameters of a definition of mental retardation or developmental disabilities (e.g., Kiely & Lubin, 1983; Lubin, Jacobson, & Kiely, 1982). Definitions of developmental disabilities have been based on etiology (i.e., cause), functional limitations, or categorical conditions (e.g., autism, cerebral palsy, epilepsy, mental retardation). Each of these definitional approaches identifies somewhat different populations, thus complicating agreement on the establishment of age-specific prevalence.

The controversy concerning the definition of mental retardation is neither new nor likely to be resolved in the upcoming years. Educators, clinicians, and health/social services administrators each bring their unique philosophical perspective to the issue of definitions, and it is unlikely that consensus can be expected. Yet from an epidemiological perspective, this situation complicates attempts to determine (or even estimate) prevalence and to assess age-specific and longitudinal prevalence trends. A description of the predominant definitional approaches is beyond the scope of this chapter. Interested readers are referred to Grossman (1983) for the most recent description of the definitional issues and recommended categories. Other relevant references include the *Diagnostic and Statistical Manual of Mental Disorders* (DSM-III) of the American Psychiatric Association (1980), the *International Classification of Diseases, Ninth Revision, Clinical Modification* (Commission on Professional and Hospital Activities, 1978), and the *International Classification of Impairments, Disabilities, and Handicaps* (World Health Organization, 1980).

There are also differences in the definitions used by professionals in efforts to characterize the concept of "aging." From a biological perspective, aging can be considered as a developmental process that occurs across one's lifetime, beginning with birth and ending with death. However, such a definition is difficult to utilize in conducting epidemiological analyses. From another perspective, a socioeconomic definition of aging would reflect contemporary social values and characteristics and the age distribution of a population. For example, governmental attention to so-called "aging persons" would be influenced by the extent to which increased life expectancy allows an "aged" cohort to comprise an increasingly large proportion of the population and utilize available social resources. Specifically, these social values and characteristics would be based on such quantifiable factors as: 1) relative life expectancy, 2) legislative guidelines, 3) economic productivity, and 4) proportion of total population (Blake, 1981; Siegel, 1980). While these factors are also important in the context of epidemiological research, they are considered only in interpreting, as opposed to analyzing, research data. For example, these factors are used to interpret trends in terms of regional, economic, gender, ethnic, or secular differences.

The primary factor for defining aging in the context of epidemiological research is simply chronological age, whether expressed in terms of absolute age, categories of age (e.g., 5- or 10-year categories), or on some occasions, year of birth. The patterns associated with year of birth are especially useful in examining how specific factors may have affected given birth cohort(s). For example, improvements in health practices have had selective effects depending upon the age at which a person was able to benefit from the availability of a new technology. This is well illustrated by the relatively recent improvements in reducing the sequelae of childhood diseases through immunization programs. Childhood morbidity and mortality patterns are markedly different for birth cohorts born before and after the availability of immunizations.

PREVALENCE OF MENTAL RETARDATION

As with any other categorical developmental disability, mental retardation is difficult to define with a high degree of certainty. There are numerous etiological factors contributing to the categorical disability of mental retardation, as well as a number of ways to define the disorder. Mental retardation can be defined in terms of IQ, neurological functioning, social adaptability, behavioral competence, or any combination of these. As the prevalence of any condition varies with the definition of the disorder, it is not surprising that there are wide variations in the reported prevalence of mental retardation.

The most widely accepted classification schema for mental retardation has been based upon the severity of the associated symptomatology. According to this definition, "mental retardation refers to significantly subaverage general intellectual functioning existing concurrently with deficits in adaptive behavior, and manifested during the developmental period" (American Association on Mental Deficiency, 1977). This classification schema includes four categories of mental retardation (i.e, mild, moderate, severe, and profound) and is based upon the statistical distribution of IQ scores. However, most epidemiological studies on the prevalence of mental retardation do not utilize measures of adaptive behavior and only report two categories of IQ. As a result of this dichotomy, the use of the term "severe mental retardation" is actually inclusive of the categories of moderate, severe, and profound mental retardation. In these studies, "severely" retarded persons are defined on the basis of an IQ below 50 or 55, while "mildly" retarded persons are defined on the basis of an IQ between normal and 50 to 55.

Table 1 presents the sampling strategies and age-specific prevalence from previously reported epidemiological studies of the prevalence of mental retardation. The age-specific rates are presented in order to show the marked variations in prevalence rates as a function of age. More information is presented on the age-specific prevalence of children than of adults, as children are more frequently the focus of epidemiological investigations. The trends in the prevalence of mild mental retardation and severe mental retardation are described separately. The first column on the left side of the page presents author(s) name and year of publication. The next column presents the site(s) at which the study was conducted. The third column on the left-hand page presents a capsule description of the characteristics of the group and/or the method of case identification. This information is provided because it is important to consider the case-finding strategy when evaluating prevalence rates. Different case-finding strategies may yield different rates even when used on the same population. The last column on the left page presents the "denominator data." This is the population in which the cases were found. When considered with the number of cases (i.e., the numerator), the size of the population (i.e., the denominator) allows for the calculation of prevalence rates.

The right-hand side of the table presents information on the reported prevalence rates. In most situations, the information is presented in the form of age-specific prevalence rates. Age-specific rates are those that are limited to a specific age or age ranges. When such rates are given, the age restriction applies to both the numerator and the denominator. The information on age-specific rates is provided because prevalence varies with age. When the information was available, the reported overall prevalence rates are included under the heading "Total." In some studies, the age distribution is not presented in the same manner in which the table is organized. In those studies, the data are presented and labeled as reported by the author(s).

Severe Mental Retardation

In most studies that evaluate the prevalence of mental retardation across several age ranges, it has been found that there is a steady increase through late adolescence, usually until the age ranges of 10 to 14 or of 15 to 19 years. If the study also includes adults, then a relatively consistent decline in prevalence is noted as a function of increasing age after late adolescence.

There are four studies (Bernsen, 1976; Brask, 1972; Goodman & Tizard, 1962; Lewis, 1929) that report a peak in prevalence in the 10- to 14-year age range rather than the 15- to 19-year age group. There are several possible explana-

Table 1. Prevalence of mental retardation

Author, year	Location	Numerator data/Case-finding method	Denominator data
Lewis, 1929	England & Wales	Sampling from six urban and six rural areas, each with a population of approximately 100,000. 1) Review of educational, community, and agency records. 2) Group screening of 7- to 14-year-olds in school. 3) Medical assessment by principal investigator.	1921 census data
Lemkau, Tietze, and Cooper, 1941, 1942a,b, 1943	Baltimore, MD	Eastern Health District examination of all community, school, and state agency records (including hospitals, social agencies, and law courts)	Population count conducted by the National Health Survey
New York State Department of Mental Hygiene, 1955	Onondaga County, NY	Mentally retarded citizens <18 years identified by schools, physicians, public, and private agencies.	Estimated population
Bienenstock and Cox, 1956	New York	1) Questionnaires sent to school districts. 2) Information from state institutions and New York City psychiatric clinics. 3) School exemption records.	1955 school census
Kushlick, 1961	Salford, England	Register of mentally retarded persons maintained by the Mental Health Service	1951 census data
Goodman and Tizard, 1962	London and Middlesex, England	Register of all mentally retarded persons. 1) Ascertained prevalence: in London an 8.3% sample of the register and in Middlesex a list of all mentally retarded children and all severely mentally retarded adults. 2) "True" prevalence: includes only Middlesex. All severely mentally retarded children (<16 years old) were re-examined and if necessary reclassified.	Estimates from Registrar General
Levinson, 1962	Maine	Mailed questionnaire to all schools and "child-serving" residential institutions	Census data and other sources
Oregon State Board of Health, 1962	Oregon	32% stratified sample of the state's population	1960 federal census, adjusted
Scally and Mackay, 1964	North Ireland	Mentally retarded persons known to the special care services	1961 census

a Calculated by Kushlick and Blunden (1975)

b Calculated by Penrose (1972).

c Age groups are 0–4, 5–9, 10–14, 15–19, 20–24, 25–34, 35–44, 45–54, 55–64, 65+.

d Recalculated from Table 15 (p. 88).

e Includes children 15–17 years.

f Includes persons 15 and over.

g Age range is 15–20 years.

	Age-specific prevalence rates/1,000 population									
	0–4	5–9	10–14	15–19	20–29	30–39	40–49	50–59	60+	Total
Severe mental retardation	0.69	3.09	4.35	2.84	2.07	1.49	1.22	0.90	0.48	1.87
Mild mental retardation[a]	0.51	11.41	21.25	7.96	6.33	4.21	4.18	4.00	2.42	6.73
Severe and mild mental retardation[b]	1.20	15.50	25.60	10.80	8.40	5.70	5.40	2.42	2.90	8.60

	0–4	5–9	10–14	15–19	20–29	30–39	40–49	50–59	60+	Total
Severe mental retardation			3.3							
Severe and mild mental retardation[c]	0.7	11.8	43.6	30.2	7.2	8.1	8.3	6.4 2.6	1.9	12.2

	0–4	5–9	10–14	15–19						Total
Severe and mild mental retardation[d]	4.52	39.27	77.28	44.67[e]						35.2

Severe mental retardation	5–6 years	7–15.9 years
	1.94	3.32

	0–4	5–9	10–14	15–19	20–29	30–39	40–49	50–59	60+	Total
Severe mental retardation	0.87	1.47	2.66	3.89	2.90	3.15	2.33	1.78	0.55	2.13
Mild mental retardation	0.15	0.33	0.31	9.23	3.50	1.53	2.42	1.09	0.63	1.96
Severe and mild mental retardation	1.09	1.80	2.97	13.11	6.44	4.68	4.74	2.96	1.18	4.16
London ascertained severe mental retardation	0.89	1.86	2.81	1.07[f]						1.29
Middlesex ascertained severe mental retardation	0.91	2.69	2.83	0.94[g]						
"true" severe mental retardation	0.98	3.02	3.61							2.53

	0–4	5–9	10–14	15–19						Total
Severe mental retardation	—	2.87	3.88	4.08[g]						3.71
Mild mental retardation	—	16.69	33.73	16.39[g]						
Severe and mild mental retardation	—	19.56	37.60	20.99[g]						

Severe and mild mental retardation	0–5 years	6–8 years	9–14 years							
	7.32	18.28	27.78	25.10						

	0–4	5–9	10–14	15–19	20–29	30–39	40–49	50–59	60+	Total
Severe mental retardation	1.1	3.4	3.7	4.0	3.9	1.9	1.7	1.3	0.6	2.3

(continued)

Table 1.   Prevalence of mental retardation (*continued*)

Author, year	Location	Numerator data/Case-finding method	Denominator data
Richardson and Higgins, 1965	Almance County, North Carolina	1) Review of health agency registers. 2) A household survey. 3) A diagnostic, clinical examination of "presumed" handicapped children.	Adjustment to census data
Drillien, Jameson, and Wilkinson, 1966	Edinburgh, Scotland	Included children 7½–14½ years old. Review of public health department and school medical service registers, voluntary day centers for handicapped children, residential institutions, voluntary and state schools for mentally and physically handicapped	Population estimated
Kushlick and Cox, 1967	Wessex, England	Mental retardation registers, hospitals for retarded persons, general hospitals, and hospitals for the chronically ill	1961 census
Innes, Kidd, and Ross, 1968	Northeast Scotland	Mental retardation registers of the North Eastern Regional Hospital Board or local authority services. Preschool age children were identified from the diagnostic index of the Royal Aberdeen Hospital for Sick Children	1961 census[i]
Birch, Richardson, Baird, Horobin, & Illsley, 1970	Aberdeen, Scotland	Included children 8–10 years old. Health and education records of children in special classes, group test results, and individual psychological assessment for all children identified as "subnormal"	Census of 8- to 10-year-olds residing in Aberdeen
Rutter, Tizard, and Whitmore, 1970	Isle of Wight	Group screening of the total population in three age groups. If findings suggested they might have a disabling condition, they were given individual examinations by physicians, psychologists, and social scientists. Reports were obtained from parents, schools, hospitals, other agencies.	Census of all children residing on the Isle of Wight
Wing, 1971	Camberwell, England	Mental retardation register	1966 10% sample census
Brask, 1972	Aarhus, Denmark	Case records from the mental retardation service	Mean between the 1960 and the 1965 census

[h]In cases where IQ was unknown or level of severity was approximated, the term "presumptive retardation" was used.
[i]From Abramowicz and Richardson (1975).
[j] The prevalence rate of 25.28/1000 is based on IQ standardized to the Isle of Wight norms. The prevalence rate of 14.57/1000 is based on figures given in the WISC manual.

	Age-specific prevalence rates/1,000 population									
	0–4	5–9	10–14	15–19	20–29	30–39	40–49	50–59	60+	Total
Agency data	0–20 years									
presumptive[h]	14									
severe mental retardation	2									
mild mental retardation	12									
Household										
severe and mild mental retardation	48	81	97	89						
Clinical examination	0–20 years									
presumptive[h]	8									
severe mental retardation	11									
mild mental retardation	70									
	7½–14½ years									
Severe mental retardation	4.99									
Mild mental retardation	6.30									
Severe and mild mental retardation	11.29									
Severe mental retardation	0.53	2.41	2.57	3.42	2.82	2.13	1.82	1.23	0.51	
Mild mental retardation	0.18	0.57	0.48	2.97	2.90	1.78	1.71	1.34	0.56	
Severe and mild mental retardation	0.73	3.03	3.07	6.41	5.73	3.93	3.56	2.59	1.09	
Severe mental retardation	0.80	3.5	2.3	3.7	3.2	2.1	2.0	1.8	1.3	2.1
Severe and mild mental retardation	3.06	9.57	9.59	13.18	8.82	4.75	4.50	3.57	2.62	6.02
	8–10 years									
Severe mental retardation	3.7									
Mild mental retardation	23.7									
Severe and mild mental retardation	27.4									
	5–14 years									
Severe mental retardation	3.40									
Severe and mild mental retardation[i]	25.28									
	14.57									
Severe mental retardation	3.12	4.09	3.66							
Severe mental retardation	1.13	2.81	3.69							
Mild mental retardation	0.23	2.03	4.71							
Severe and mild mental retardation	1.36	4.84	8.40							

(continued)

Table 1.   Prevalence of mental retardation (*continued*)

Author, year	Location	Numerator data/Case-finding method	Denominator data
McDonald, 1973	Quebec, Canada	Information requested from hospitals, institutions, schools and homes for retarded children, clinics for evaluation of mental retardation, social and welfare agencies, school boards and associations for mentally retarded children. Children examined by investigator.	1958 birth cohort studied at ages 8–12 years[i]
Bernsen, 1976	Aarhus, Denmark	Children aged 0–14 years. Main source was the register maintained by the Danish National Mental Retardation Service. Additional medical and social agencies were contacted.	Population description given, but no indication of how it was obtained.
Stein, Susser, and Saenger, 1976 a, b	Netherlands	Records of four annual cohorts of men, born 1944–1947, examined at age 19 years for military induction.	Same as numerator data.

tions for this phenomenon. In the Lewis study (1929), the 7- to 14-year olds were more thoroughly studied by group-screening examinations. Both Brask (1972) and Bernsen (1976) evaluated children only up to age 14. Had they included 15- to 19-year-olds in their studies, the peak prevalence might have been in the older age group. In the presentation of their results, Goodman and Tizard (1962) may have masked a potential peak in prevalence in the 15- to 19-year age range by grouping everyone over 15 years of age, including adults.

It should be recognized that the pattern of age-specific increases in reported prevalence of mental retardation is not necessarily reflecting the "true" prevalence rates. As most severe mental retardation is present at birth or from an early age, it is unlikely that the increasing age-specific prevalence rates are due to a higher incidence (i.e., new cases) of mental retardation in later childhood. Rather, the increasing age-specific prevalence is more likely a reflection of the manner in which developmentally disabled children become known to service providers. In many circumstances, younger children may not have a need for specialty services, or the services simply may not be available. Thus, in those studies that use

agencies to identify "cases," the prevalence rates for young children may be an underestimate of the true prevalence rates.

In summary, the prevalence of severe mental retardation is consistently found to be between 3 and 5 per 1,000. This pattern has been found since the early study by Lewis (1929), and in both industrial and developing countries (Narayanan, 1981).

Mild Mental Retardation

In those studies that separately report the prevalence of mild and severe mental retardation, there is a considerably higher proportion of mild mental retardation relative to severe mental retardation. This marked difference is primarily observed in the age ranges of adolescence and young adulthood. However, there are exceptions to this pattern. For example, Kushlick (1961) and Kushlick and Cox (1967) also found a higher proportion of mildly mentally retarded persons, but the extent of the difference was considerably smaller than reported by others.

In a study conducted in England, Kushlick (1961) identified relatively few mildly mentally retarded persons who were below the age of 15. The numbers of mildly mentally retarded

	Age-specific prevalence rates/1,000 population									
	0–4	5–9	10–14	15–19	20–29	30–39	40–49	50–59	60+	Total
Severe mental retardation	8–12 years									
	3.84									

	0–4	5–9	10–14							
Severe mental retardation	2.45	3.45	4.50							

				15–19						
Severe mental retardation				19 years						
				3.73						
Mild mental retardation										
based on special school attendance				30.5						
based on low IQ score				57.6						
based on clinical diagnosis				61.4						

persons who were identified did increase rapidly during the age range of 15 to 19. The prevalence rate reached a peak of 9.2 persons per 1,000 population in this age group, and declined sharply between the ages of 20 and 29 and more gradually after the age of 29. In another study conducted by Kushlick and Cox (1967), the peak prevalence of mild mental retardation was also found in the 15 to 19 age group, but only reached a level of 2.97 persons per 1,000 population. As with the previous study, the prevalence of mild mental retardation appeared to decline after age 19. The most plausible explanation for this relatively lower prevalence rate than has been reported in other studies is that the participating health authorities were focusing their attention on persons with the most serious disabilities.

An interesting finding concerning the relationship between age-specific prevalence and level of mental retardation was reported by Krupinski, Stoller, MacMillan, and Polke (1966). In a study of children (birth to age 16) in Victoria, Australia, Krupinski et al. noted that the only dramatic increase in the age-specific prevalence of mental retardation occurred among mildly retarded children. There were no notable age-specific increases in the

prevalence of moderate, severe, and profound mental retardation. In part, this finding lends support to the hypothesis that the prevalence of mild mental retardation is dependent on social factors, while the prevalence of severe mental retardation is dependent on organic factors. If the cause(s) of mental retardation were due to organic factors present at birth, then it would be expected that the prevalence of mental retardation would remain relatively stable across all age groups. As this pattern is not observed for mild mental retardation, it can be hypothesized that its causes are different from the causes of more severe mental retardation. Rather, it may be reasonable to hypothesize that social factors contribute to the observed pattern of increasing prevalence of mild mental retardation with increasing age (e.g., societal demands increase with age).

The relatively wide variations in the reported rates of mild mental retardation can be attributed, in part, to the method of case ascertainment and the criteria for defining mental retardation. With regard to case ascertainment, it has been shown that surveys that use service providers to identify persons with mild mental retardation will have lower rates than studies based upon a comprehensive survey of a population. With regard to the definition of mental retardation, Stein, Susser, and Saenger (1976b) have shown that varying the criteria of mental retardation causes substantial differences in prevalence rates. In their study of 19-year-old Dutch men, three criteria were employed and varying prevalence rates were obtained: 1) educational criteria (i.e., "special classes for the backward" or "schools for the illiterate") resulted in a prevalence of 30.5/1,000; 2) psychometric criteria (i.e., failure to complete or a score in the lowest 5 percentiles on the Raven Progressive Matrices, after excluding individuals with severe retardation) resulted in a prevalence of 57.6/1,000; and 3) diagnostic criteria (based upon the 1948 International Classification of Diseases) resulted in a prevalence of 61.4/1,000.

Reliability of Prevalence Rates

The reliability of the data in studies of the prevalence of mental retardation can be assessed on the basis of an evaluation of methods used for both case finding and denominator enumeration (i.e., the population at risk). In theory, the studies considered to have data of the highest reliability are those that use a standard evaluation methodology to survey an entire population. Four studies can be considered to fall into this category: Birch, Richardson, Baird, Horobin, and Illsley (1970), Lewis (1929), Rutter, Tizard, and Whitmore (1970), and Stein, Susser, and Saenger (1976a,b). Data from several other studies are judged to be highly reliable (Drillien, Jameson, & Wilkinson, 1966; Wing, 1971). Although the case-finding in the later studies was based upon agency registries, the derived rates may be considered good estimates of the "true" prevalence. As the participating agencies represented an extensive and highly organized system of mental retardation services within a well-defined area, it is likely that the case-finding was relatively comprehensive. The data from the two studies from Aarhus, Denmark (Bernsen, 1976; Brask, 1972) may also be considered highly reliable estimates of ascertained prevalence. The Danish system of

socialized medicine facilitates service provision, and an accurate description of the population is obtainable from the National Person Registraton Office.

The data reported by Kushlick (1961) and Kushlick and Cox (1967) are considered highly reliable in regard to their estimates of severe mental retardation because severe disability was the primary focus of their study. Goodman and Tizard (1962) provide estimates of prevalence for Middlesex and London. In Middlesex, all children less than 16 years old, considered severely retarded, were examined further. Thus, the prevalence rates for children in Middlesex with severe mental retardation are considered highly reliable because of the intensive follow-up examination of all suspected cases. The prevalence estimates for mentally retarded children in London and persons over 16 years of age in Middlesex are considered somewhat less reliable because no individual follow-up examinations were conducted. Five studies are considered to provide reliable estimates of ascertained prevalence: Lemkau, Tietze, and Cooper (1941, 1942a, 1942b, 1943), Oregon State Board of Health (1962), Innes, Kidd, and Ross (1968), McDonald (1973), and Scally and Mackay (1964). All of these studies were based upon relatively thorough reviews of agency records, but did not use supplementary information or follow-up examinations.

Four studies included in the table provide relatively less reliable prevalence estimates (Bienenstock & Cox, 1956; Levinson, 1962; New York State Department of Mental Hygiene, 1955; Richardson & Higgins, 1965). This assessment of relatively less reliable prevalence estimates is based on several factors: 1) insufficient information concerning the record-abstracting process (all four studies); 2) no children examined (Bienenstock & Cox, 1956; Levinson, 1962; New York State Department of Mental Hygiene, 1955); 3) only limited attempts to identify mentally retarded individuals (Bienenstock & Cox, 1956; Levinson, 1962); 4) inclusion of children who were only suspected of being mentally retarded (New York State Department of Mental Hygiene,

1955); and 5) authors' judgment concerning the relative incompleteness of the main source of identification (Richardson & Higgins, 1965).

PREVALENCE OF OTHER DEVELOPMENTAL DISABILITIES

Considerably less information is available on the age-specific prevalence of the categorical developmental disability of autism than on the prevalence of mental retardation. Epidemiological studies of persons with autism have been limited to persons age 19 or below (Janicki, Lubin, & Friedman, 1983), and range from 0.21 autistic persons per 1,000 (Csapo, 1979) to 0.48 autistic persons per 1,000 (Wing, Yeates, Brierley, & Gould, 1976). Relatively more information is available on the age-specific prevalence of cerebral palsy and epilepsy. The interested reader is referred to Kiely, Lubin, & Kiely (1984) for a comprehensive review of the age-specific prevalence of cerebral palsy. In brief, the expected prevalence is approximately 2–3/1,000 in children between the ages of 5 and 14. After this age, the prevalence rates generally decline with increasing age.

The age-specific prevalence of epilepsy has been found to vary widely (e.g., Hauser & Kurland, 1975; Kurland, 1959; Ross, Peckham, West, & Butler, 1980; Stanhope, Brody, & Brink, 1972), but the variations are generally attributed to differences in the definition of epilepsy and the extensiveness of case-finding efforts. Accordingly, it is difficult to identify consistent patterns for the age-specific prevalence of epilepsy.

LIFE EXPECTANCY

There is substantial evidence that life expectancy for the population at large, as well as for the developmentally disabled population, has increased significantly over the past decades. The increase in life expectancy is primarily attributable to changes at the very early, rather than during the later, years of life (Siegel, 1976, 1980). Among other factors, advances in health care practices and the availability of

health resources have, in an actuarial perspective, been credited with the decreased risk of mortality at all ages. However, the predominant effects on life expectancy have been observed in the youngest cohorts, since the neonatal and infant mortality rates have shown the steepest decline over time of all age cohorts (Blake, 1981). For example, the mortality rate in New York in 1910 for infants below 1 year of age was in excess of 110 per 1,000 live births (New York State, 1980), but declined dramatically in later decades. The infant mortality rate decreased to approximately 37/1,000 live births by 1940, and to less than 14/1,000 live births by 1980. In other words, there has been an almost eight-fold decrease between 1910 and 1980 in the probability of an infant not surviving the first year of life.

The relative decrease in mortality risks for newborns and infants, as compared to older persons, is also reflected in terms of life expectancy. For example, a 65-year-old man in 1910 could expect to live an additional 11 years to age 76. However, life expectancy has only increased marginally in the intervening years. A man who was 65 years old in 1940 could only expect to survive an additional 11.3 years to 76 years of age. A man who was 65 years old in 1978 could expect to survive an additional 14.1 years to 79 years of age (New York State, 1980). Thus, the increased life expectancy for a man who was 65 years old in 1978 or 1940, relative to a 65-year-old man in 1910, was less than 1% and 4%, respectively. On the other hand, the life expectancy of a male newborn in either 1940 or 1978 was 26% or 46% longer, respectively, than a male newborn in 1910.

The primary purpose of the above examples is to emphasize that mortality rates and life expectancy in the population at large have changed most dramatically in the youngest cohorts. The following describes how comparable trends have occurred among the developmentally disabled population. This is not to suggest that mortality rates and life expectancy in disabled and nondisabled persons are similar. Developmentally disabled persons, in general, have considerably higher age-specific mortality rates than the population at large. Nevertheless, the extent of differences between these groups has diminished over the past decades.

The relatively higher mortality rates among mentally retarded persons as compared to the population at large has been discussed elsewhere (e.g., Balakrishnan & Wolf, 1976; Deaton, 1973; McCurley, Mackay, & Scally, 1972; Miller & Eyman, 1978; O'Connor, Justice, & Warren, 1970; Richards, 1975; Richards & Sylvester, 1969). Information about the mortality patterns among persons with other types of developmental disabilities, such as cerebral palsy and epilepsy, is less available.

It is important to recognize that mortality rates among developmentally disabled persons are strongly related to degree of intellectual functioning or handicap, associated health problems, and a variety of other personal and demographic factors (e.g., Richards, 1975). The latter factors would include gender, history of institutional placement, etiology, availability of early intervention programs, and birth cohort, among others.

Etiological Diagnosis

It does appear that mortality rates among persons with various other types of developmental disabilities are also in excess of the population at large, with the extent of excess being related to the relative severity of the disability. For example, during the 15-year period *after* adolescence, survival rates in cerebral palsy seem to be above 90% (Ingram, 1964; Kudrjavcev, Schoenberg, & Kurland, 1982) and are comparable to those found in severe mental retardation. With childhood-onset epilepsy, the chances of survival to adulthood appear to be very high when seizures arise in the absence of any definite evidence of structural damage to the brain. More than 98% of persons with such conditions have been found to survive for at least 30 years (Hauser, Annegers, & Elveback, 1980; Hauser & Kurland, 1975). Unfortunately, there are no studies of the epidemiology of epilepsy or cerebral palsy that examine survival beyond the age of 50.

There has been more interest in mortality trends among persons with Down syndrome than for any other form of developmental disability. This interest is probably attributable to three distinct characteristics of persons with Down syndrome. First, Down syndrome represents the most common known cause of mental retardation associated with a genetic anomaly. Second, there is considerable recent evidence of the beneficial effects of early biomedical interventions on the life expectancy and health status of children with Down syndrome. Third, persons with Down syndrome appear to have unique age-specific mortality and morbidity patterns, suggesting a possible genetic link to the aging process.

As previously mentioned, the life expectancy in all forms of mental retardation is less than the population at large, and persons with Down syndrome appear to be particularly at risk. For example, life expectancy for Down syndrome children was reported to be approximately 9 years in 1929 (Penrose, 1949), approximately 12–15 years by 1947 (Penrose, 1949), and 18.3 years in 1961 (Collman & Stoller, 1963b). These relatively low estimates of life expectancy relative to the general population are primarily attributable to the first years of life (Collman & Stoller, 1963a; Forssman & Akesson, 1965; Oster, Mikkelsen, & Nielsen, 1964; Record & Smith, 1954; Thase, 1982). For example, Record and Smith (1954) developed the first life-table for Down syndrome and showed that less than half of 250 Down syndrome children survived the first year, and only 40% were alive by 5 years of age. The results of a life-table constructed by Carter (1958) were strikingly similar to the results of Record and Smith. Of 725 children with Down syndrome, less than half were alive after 1 year, and less than 40% survived to the age of 5. A review by Thase (1982) stated that the mortality rate in Down syndrome has been reported as being between 28% and 54% in the first year of life. However, this did not include a recent report by Mulcahy (1979) that provided evidence that at least 25% of infants born with Down syndrome do not survive the first few years of life.

While it is important to note that mortality rates in Down syndrome are exceptionally high relative to all children below age 5, the mortality rates have declined dramatically over recent years. Subsequently published life-tables support the observations that the life expectancy in Down syndrome is increasing. Fabia and Drolette (1970) developed a life-table for a population of 2,421 people with Down syndrome born to residents of Massachusetts from 1950 through 1966. Twenty percent of these persons died within the first year of age as compared to the approximately 50% in the earlier studies (i.e., Carter, 1958; Record & Smith, 1954). In a similar improvement in life expectancy, Fabia and Drolette (1970) found that only 32% of the cases died prior to age 5 as compared to the earlier 60% mortality rate in this age group. Gallagher and Lowry (1975) studied 927 people with Down syndrome who were born in British Columbia between 1952 and 1971 inclusive. They found that approximately 10% died within the first year of life and 16% by age 5.

On the basis of the above and other studies (e.g., Fabia & Drolette, 1970; Gallagher & Lowry, 1975; Mulcahy, 1979; Oster et al., 1964), Thase (1982) concluded that mortality rates were reduced 50%–80% in the 20-year period beginning in 1960 relative to the period beginning in 1940. Thase further suggests that the overall secular decline in mortality rates in Down syndrome is primarily attributable to a decline in the risk of mortality in the first year of life.

Forssman and Akesson (1965) have indicated that the excess mortality rates in adults with Down syndrome is limited to adults over age 40. This observation was primarily based on a follow-up of Down syndrome persons with a history of institutionalization. Nevertheless, the observation of the excess mortality rate in older persons is noteworthy in light of other evidence of unique aging patterns in older Down syndrome persons. Jervis (1948) first described a pattern of premature senility in Down syndrome, and subsequent studies have reported relatively early manifestation of neurofibrillary degeneration, senile plaques, cor-

tical atrophy, and Alzheimer-type dementia (Malamud, 1964; Neumann, 1967; Olson & Shaw, 1969; Solitaire & La Marche, 1966). In fact, it has been reported that nearly all individuals with Down syndrome over age 40 have the neuropathological changes consistent with Alzheimer-type dementia. Detailed descriptions of the characteristics and distribution of Alzheimer's disease can be found in Wisniewski and Hill, Chapter 12, this volume.

Alzheimer's disease (presenile dementia) can be characterized clinically by the presence of progressive dementia and dysphasia. These characteristics, as well as their clinical identification, are described by Wisniewski and Hill (Chapter 12, this volume). Although the etiology of Alzheimer's disease is unknown, there are a number of specific criteria that allow accurate pathological identification. The microscopic changes of the brain are somewhat similar to those that occur with senility (Wisniewski & Terry, 1973). There is a diffuse loss of cells in all layers of the affected cortex, secondary gliosis, neuritic and amyloid plaques, and neurofibrillary changes (Wisniewski & Merz, 1983).

Although Alzheimer's disease is very rare in normal populations, it is quite common in cases of older individuals wth Down syndrome. In general, studies that examine the incidence of Down syndrome show that the disease is usually absent prior to age 35, but appears with increasing frequency after that age (Wisniewski, Wisniewski, & Wen, in press). Liss, Shim, Thase, Smeltzer, Maloone, and Couri (1980) also claimed a strong association between age and dementia in Down syndrome. They reported that all persons in their study with Down syndrome over age 30 had developed Alzheimer's disease.

The largest and most notable study linking Alzheimer's disease and Down syndrome was undertaken by Malamud (1964). Malamud examined 347 individuals with Down syndrome and attempted to correlate the incidence of Alzheimer-type changes with age. No Alzheimer changes were observed from birth to 10 years of age. Similarly, only two of 85 people with Down syndrome between the ages of 11 and 30 demonstrated even minimal pathological abnormalities. However, these changes were observed in three of 10 cases between the ages of 31 and 40 and in all 35 cases between the ages of 41 and 70. A similar age-associated increase in Alzheimer-type changes was noted in a neuropathological postmortem study of 100 brains of individuals with Down syndrome (Wisniewski et al., in press). No Alzheimer-type changes were noted in the brains of 20 children below age 10; a few plaques and tangles were noted among four of 20 brains of children who died between 10 and 20 years of age. Some plaques and tangles were found in four of 11 brains of persons between age 21 and 30, but the density was still relatively low. Among 49 Down syndrome persons who died after age 30, all the brains were found to have plaques and tangles and the density appeared to increase with progressing age. These incidence patterns are not observed either in other forms of mental retardation or in normal individuals with such a high frequency or at such an early age.

According to Jervis (1948), the few Down syndrome persons

> who reach the fourth or fifth decade of life undergo remarkable personality changes, resulting from intellectual and emotional deterioration. In these patients, the underlying brain lesions are those of a pathological senility. The term early senile dementia seems appropriate to characterize this reaction which shows the clinico-pathological features of senile dementia, but develops at a considerably earlier age than the commoner type. (p. 102)

Olson and Shaw (1969) appear less likely to accept the existence of a behavioral or psychological deterioration in cases of older Down syndrome. They claim that the distribution, severity, and behavioral concomitants of Alzheimer's disease are inconsistent. However, only 15% (four of 26) of the people examined by Olson and Shaw were over the age of 40. In retrospective clinicopathological studies, Wisniewski, Wisniewski, and Wen (1983) described the clinical signs of Alzheimer's disease in 27% (13 of 49) of persons with Down syndrome who died after age 30. Dalton and

Crapper (1984) found measurable clinical changes of Alzheimer's disease in 24% (12 of 49) of persons with Down syndrome over age 40. Solitaire and La Marche (1966) described the existence of defects in perception and comprehension, the presence of seizures, and neurological deficits that lead to incapacitation and death within 4 years of diagnosis of Alzheimer's disease.

CAUSES OF DEATH

The overall trends in the causes of death in the mentally retarded population are distinct from the trends in the population at large (Carter & Jancar, 1983; Forssman & Akesson, 1965; McCurley et al., 1972; Polednak, 1975; Primrose, 1966; Richards, 1976; Richards & Sylvester, 1969). These differences are attributable to both the unique health problems of mentally retarded persons and the overall differences in life expectancy. This latter factor is especially important, as persons are at risk for certain conditions only if they achieve a sufficiently old age at which a condition becomes manifest. Thus, in order to assess differences, it is necessary to consider carefully age-specific trends in morbidity and causes of death.

Richards and Sylvester (1969) showed that the primary cause of death in the periods of 1929 to 1938 and 1960 to 1967 among mentally retarded persons was respiratory disease, accounting for approximately 37% of all deaths in these time periods. In fact, Richards (1976) argued that respiratory infections attributable to cerebral palsy, epilepsy and reduced efficiency in coughing, feeding, breathing, and so on, are the major factors contributing to the excess mortality in mentally retarded populations. Only about 5%–7% of all deaths in the population at large are attributable to respiratory disease.

McCurley et al. (1972) showed that the primary causes of death in institutionalized mentally retarded populations (i.e., cardiovascular, cerebrovascular, and respiratory infection) were associated with level of intellectual functioning. Persons who were considered to be severely and profoundly retarded were more likely to have died as a result of respiratory infections. Conversely, persons who were mildly retarded were more likely to have a cardiovascular or cerebrovascular cause of death.

A recent survey of causes of death at an institution in England is further illustrative of the differences between mentally retarded populations and the population at large (Carter & Jancar, 1983). While persons who are institutionalized are not representative of mentally retarded people in general, they are more reflective of the more seriously disabled groups in the population. Notwithstanding such methodological problems, it can be seen that the major causes of death among the mentally retarded population are unique. Carter and Jancar reported that approximately 50% and 24% of all deaths between 1976 and 1980 were due to respiratory tract infections and tuberculosis, respectively. These rates are greatly in excess of the 1978 rates in the United States for the population at large (National Center for Health Statistics, 1980). In combination, influenza, pneumonia, bronchitis, emphysema, and asthma were listed as the causes for approximately 4% of the deaths in the population at large. Tuberculosis accounted for only 0.1% of all deaths. Carcinomas and cardiac failure accounted for approximately 15% of all deaths reported by Carter and Jancar (1983), as opposed to over 30% for carcinomas and 50% for cardiac failures in the 1978 United States population at large.

In part, the lower rates of deaths from carcinomas and cardiac failures are probably attributable to differences in the age distribution between the two groups. Carcinomas and cardiac failures are predominantly causes of death among older persons, and the life expectancy of mentally retarded persons is considerably lower than for the population at large. The mean age of death for the mentally retarded population described by Carter and Jancar (1983) was 59 years of age in the time period 1976–1980. The expectation of life for the United States general population in 1978 was 73.3 years of age.

The trends in the specific proportions of all deaths in the mentally retarded population pro-vide further evidence that causes of death are related to life expectancy. The proportions of death attributable to carcinomas or cardiac failure reported by Carter and Jancar (1983) showed a generally increasing trend from 10% in the period 1936–1940, 7% in 1946–1950, 16% in 1956–1960, 23% in 1966–1970, to 19% in 1976–1980. In the same time period, the mean age of death rose from 21 in 1936–1940, 26 in 1946–1950, 39 in 1956–1960, 44 in 1966–1970, to 59 in 1976–1980. While there assuredly were changes in such factors as admissions policies, health services, and so on, the association between causes of death and life expectancy emphasizes the importance of considering age-specific data rather than overall data.

A recent report by Herbst and Baird (1984) also described the patterns of mortality and causes of death among a group of mentally retarded persons in British Columbia. However, the authors focused only on individuals whose retardation was not due to a specific cause. This case-finding approach led to a data base that excluded individuals whose mental retardation was attributable to: 1) infections or intoxications; 2) trauma or physical agents; 3) disorders of metabolism, growth, or nutrition; 4) gross brain disease; 5) chromosomal abnormalities; or 6) neural tube defects. As the authors do not describe how the "excluded" group compares to individuals included in the analyses, it is difficult to either draw comparisons with earlier studies or generalize from the findings.

HISTORY OF INSTITUTIONALIZATION

It has been reported frequently that mortality rates among developmentally disabled persons vary as a function of placement history (Balakrishnan & Wolf, 1976; Carter & Jancar, 1983; McCurley et al., 1972; Miller & Eyman, 1978; Nelson & Crocker, 1978; Richards, 1975; Richards & Siddiqui, 1980; Richards & Sylvester, 1969; Thase, 1982). Specifically, it has been found that the mortality rate among persons who have been institutionalized is higher than among persons who have remained at home with their families. The basis for such differences is uncertain. Differences between these groups may not be attributable to placement per se, but instead to variables associated with placement. These include severity of disability, gender, ethnicity, associated handicaps, and availability of services. Differences between the characteristics of institutionalized and noninstitutionalized persons have been even further complicated by recent changes in both admissions and deinstitutionalization policies. Younger children are now less likely to be admitted to institutional settings.

Given the complex interaction of the above variables with placement and health status, it is difficult to isolate the relative contribution of each factor. For example, it would be expected that children with more severe physical or medical handicaps are more likely to be institutionalized, as their parents would have more difficulty caring for them at home. As these children would also have higher morbidity and mortality risks than children with no or few handicaps, a selective placement pattern would contribute to a higher mortality rate in institutions.

The strong association between placement and mortality risks serves to highlight significant problems in estimating patterns of morbidity and life expectancy. The data for many epidemiological studies in mental retardation are based upon well-circumscribed and accessible institutional populations. However, these populations are not likely to be representative of developmentally disabled persons, and may lead to severely biased findings. Thus, it is important to consider the extent of biases in case-finding when evaluating morbidity and mortality reports.

A recent study by Carter and Jancar (1983) has shown that the mortality trends among mentally handicapped patients in hospitals has both improved over a 50-year period and is more closely reflected by the mortality patterns of the population at large. Carter and Jancar showed a consistent increase in the average age of death from the period 1931–1935 to the period 1976–1980. Across this period, the mean age of death of all patients increased over

three-fold from 18.5 years to 59.1 years. A more dramatic five-fold increase was shown for persons with Down syndrome. The mean age of death increased from 11.0 years in 1931–1935 to 54 years of age in 1976–1980. It is important to recognize that these increases are attributable, in part, to changes in admissions policies. However, improved health practices were assuredly a major cause of the increased life expectancy, as is evident in dramatic decreases for certain specific causes of death (e.g., tuberculosis, status epilepticus). While the mortality rate among this population is still in excess of the population at large, the extent of the difference has markedly diminished, especially in Down syndrome.

CONCLUSION

Epidemiological studies appear to indicate that the overall prevalence of developmental disabilities is increasing. This increase is attributed to a number of factors, including increases in the incidence of certain disorders previously associated with neonatal death, increases in life expectancy among disabled children and adults, and improvements in health care and social service programs leading to the prevention of morbidity and mortality. The current and expected future changes in the characteristics and age-specific distribution of developmentally disabled persons has made it necessary to introduce new resources and re-allocate existing economic and social resources. As developmentally disabled persons age, more resources will be needed to maintain their quality of life. Additionally, resources will also be needed to provide for the necessary improvements in institutional and community-based services for the increasing numbers of younger developmentally disabled persons entering the service system.

Increases in the life expectancy and age-specific prevalence of older persons with Down syndrome have introduced a unique concern, as there is apparently a high incidence of Alzheimer's disease among older individuals with Down syndrome. In addition to studies of the aging patterns associated with Down syndrome, further areas of needed epidemiological research relate to studies of the unique health and social service needs of older developmentally disabled persons, the short- and long-term consequences of changes in the incidence of various forms of birth defects and developmental disabilities, and the extent to which improvements in health and social practices will continue to affect the life expectancy and health status of older developmentally disabled persons.

REFERENCES

Abramowicz, H. K., & Richardson, S. (1975). Epidemiology of severe mental retardation in children: Community studies. *American Journal of Mental Deficiency, 80,* 18–39.

American Association on Mental Deficiency. (1977). *Manual on terminology and classification in mental retardation.* Washington, DC: Author.

American Psychiatric Association. (1980). *Diagnostic and statistical manual of mental disorders* (3rd ed.). Washington, DC: Author.

Balakrishnan, T. R., & Wolf, L. C. (1976). Life expectancy of mentally retarded persons in Canadian institutions. *American Journal of Mental Deficiency, 80,* 650–662.

Bernsen, A. H. (1976). Severe mental retardation in the county of Aarhus, Denmark: A community study on prevalence and provision of service. *Acta Psychiatrica Scandinavica, 54,* 43–66.

Bienenstock, T., & Cox, W. W. (1956). Census of severely retarded children in New York State. Albany: Interdepartmental Health Resources Board, State of New York.

Birch, H. G., Richardson, S. A., Baird, D., Horobin, G., & Illsley, R. (1970). *Mental subnormality in the community: A clinical and epidemiologic study.* Baltimore: Williams & Wilkins Co.

Blake, R. (1981). Disabled older persons: A demographic analysis. *Journal of Rehabilitation, 48,* 19–27.

Brask, B. H. (1972). Prevalence of mental retardation among children in the county of Aarhus, Denmark. *Acta Psychiatrica Scandinavica, 48,* 480–500.

Burger, P. C., & Vogel, S. (1973). The development of the pathologic changes of Alzheimer's Disease and senile dementia in patients with Down's Syndrome. *American Journal of Pathology, 73,* 457–468.

Carter, C. O. (1958). A life-table for mongols with the causes of death. *Journal of Mental Deficiency Research, 2,* 64–74.

Carter, G., & Jancar, J. (1983). Mortality in the mentally handicapped: A 50 year survey at the State Park Group of Hospitals (1930–1980). *Journal of Mental Deficiency Research, 27,* 143–156.

Collman, R. D., & Stoller, A. (1963a). Data on mongolism in Victoria, Australia: Prevalence and life expectation. *Journal of Mental Deficiency Research, 7,* 60–68.

Collman, R. D., & Stoller, A. (1963b). A life-table for mongols in Victoria, Australia. *Journal of Mental Deficiency Research, 7,* 53–59.

Commission on Professional and Hospital Activities. (1978). *International classification of diseases, Ninth revision, Clinical modification.* Ann Arbor, MI: Edwards Brothers, Inc.

Csapo, M. (1979). Prevalence and needs assessment study of autistic children in British Columbia. *British Columbia Journal of Special Education, 3,* 159–161.

Dalton, A. J., & Crapper, D. R. (1984). Incidence of memory deterioration in aging persons with Down syndrome. In J. M. Berg (Ed.), *Perspectives and progress in mental retardation. Vol. 2: Biomedical aspects* (pp. 55–62). Baltimore: University Park Press.

Deaton, J. G. (1973). The mortality rate and cause of death among institutionalized mongols in Texas. *Journal of Mental Deficiency Research, 17,* 117–122.

Drillien, C. M., Jameson, S., & Wilkinson, E. M. (1966). Studies in mental handicaps: Part 1. Prevalence and distribution by clinical type and severity of defect. *Archives of Diseases in Childhood, 41,* 528–538.

Fabia, J., & Drolette, M. (1970). Life tables up to age 10 for mongols with and without congenital heart defect. *Journal of Mental Deficiency Research, 14,* 235–242.

Forssman, H., & Akesson, H. O. (1965). Mortality in patients with Down's syndrome. *Journal of Mental Deficiency Research, 9,* 146–149.

Gallagher, R. R., & Lowry, R. B. (1975). Longevity in Down's syndrome in British Columbia. *Journal of Mental Deficiency Research, 19,* 157–164.

Goodman, N., & Tizard, J. (1962). Prevalence of imbecility and idiocy among children. *British Medical Journal, 1,* 216–219.

Grossman, H. J. (1983). *Classification in mental retardation* (rev. ed.). Washington, DC: American Association on Mental Deficiency.

Hauser, W. A., Annegers, J. F., & Elveback, L. R. (1980). Mortality in patients with epilepsy. *Epilepsia, 21,* 399–412.

Hauser, W. A., & Kurland, L. T. (1975). The epidemiology of epilepsy in Rochester, Minnesota, 1935 through 1967. *Epilepsia, 16,* 1–66.

Herbst, D. S., & Baird, P. A. (1984). Survival rates and causes of death among persons with nonspecific mental retardation. In J. M. Berg (Ed.), *Perspectives and progress in mental retardation, Vol. 2: Biomedical aspects* (pp. 3–15). Baltimore: University Park Press.

Ingram, T. T. S. (1964). *Paediatric aspects of cerebral palsy.* Edinburgh: E&S Livingston.

Innes, G., Kidd, C., & Ross, H. S. (1968). Mental subnormality in Northeast Scotland. *British Journal of Psychiatry, 114,* 35–41.

Janicki, M. P., Lubin, R. A., & Friedman, E. (1983). Variations in characteristics and service needs of persons with autism. *Journal of Autism and Developmental Disabilities, 13,* 73–85.

Jervis, G. A. (1948). Early senile dementia in mongoloid idiocy. *American Journal of Psychiatry, 105,* 102–106.

Kiely, M., & Lubin, R. (1983). Epidemiological research

methods in mental retardation. In J. Matson & J. Mulick (Eds.), *Comprehensive handbook of mental retardation* (pp. 541–566). New York: Pergamon Press.

Kiely, M., Lubin, R., & Kiely, J. (1984). Descriptive epidemiology of cerebral palsy. *Public Health Reviews, 12*, 79–101.

Krupinski, J., Stoller, A., MacMillan, C. H., & Polke, P. (1966). Survey of mental retardation amongst Victorian children. *Journal of Mental Deficiency Research, 10*, 33–45.

Kudrjavcev, T., Schoenberg, B. S., & Kurland, L. T. (1982). Cerebral palsy—Distribution and survival rates by clinical subtype: Rochester, Minnesota, 1950–1976 (Abstract). *Neurology, 32*, A186.

Kurland, L. T. (1959). The incidence and prevalence of convulsive disorders in a small urban community. *Epilepsia, 1*, 143–161.

Kushlick, A. (1961). Subnormality in Salford. In M. W. Susser & A. Kushlick (Eds)., *A report on the mental health services of the city of Salford for the year 1960*. Salford: England Health Department.

Kushlick, A., & Blunden, R. (1975). The epidemiology of mental subnormality. In A. M. Clarke & A. D. B. Clarke (Eds.), *Mental deficiency, the changing outlook*. New York: The Free Press.

Kushlick, A. A., & Cox, G. (1967). The ascertained prevalence of mental subnormality in the Wessex Region on 1st July, 1963, Montpellier, France. *Proceeding of the First Congress of the International Association for the Scientific Study of Mental Deficiency*.

Lemkau, P., Tietze, C., & Cooper, M. (1941). Mental hygience problems in an urban district: First paper. *Mental Hygiene, 25*, 624–646.

Lemkau, P., Tietze, C., & Cooper, M. (1942a). Mental hygiene problems in an urban district: Second paper. *Mental Hygiene, 26*, 100–119.

Lemkau, P., Tietze, C., & Cooper, M. (1942b). Mental hygiene problems in an urban district: Third paper. *Mental Hygiene, 26*, 275–288.

Lemkau, P., Tietze, C., & Cooper, M. (1943). Mental hygiene problems in an urban district: Fourth paper. *Mental Hygiene, 27*, 279–295.

Levinson, E. (1962). *Retarded children in Maine*. Orono: University of Maine Press.

Lewis, E. O. (1929). *Report of the mental deficiency committee, being a joint committee of the board of education and board of control, parts I, II, III, IV*. London, England: H. M. Stationery Office.

Liss, L., Shim, C., Thase, M., Smeltzer, D., Maloone, J., & Couri, D. (1980). The relationship between Down's syndrome and dementia Alzheimer's type. *Journal of Neuropathology and Experimental Neurology, 39*, 371.

Lubin, R., Jacobson, J., & Kiely, M. (1982). Projected impact of the functional definition of developmental disabilities: The categorically disabled population and service eligibility. *American Journal of Mental Deficiency, 87*, 73–79.

Malamud, N. (1964). Neuropathology. In H. A. Stevens & R. Heber (Eds.), *Mental retardation*. Chicago: University of Chicago Press.

McCurley, R., Mackay, D. N., & Scally, B. G. (1972). The life expectation of the mentally subnormal under community and hospital care. *Journal of Mental Deficiency Research, 16*, 57–66.

McDonald, A. D. (1973). Severely retarded children in

Quebec: Prevalence, causes, and care. *American Journal of Mental Deficiency, 78*, 205–215.

Miller, C., & Eyman, R. (1978). Hospital and community mortality rates among the retarded. *Journal of Mental Deficiency Research, 22*, 137–145.

Mulcahy, M. T. (1979). Down's syndrome in Western Australia: Mortality and survival. *Clinical Genetics, 16*, 103–108.

Narayanan, H. S. (1981). A study of the prevalence of mental retardation in Southern India. *International Journal of Mental Health, 10*, 28–36.

National Center for Health Statistics. (1980). *Monthly Vital Statistics Report, Advance Report, Final Mortality Statistics, 1980* (DHHS Publication No. PHS 80-1120, 29(6) Supplement 2). Washington, DC: U.S. Government Printing Office.

Nelson, R. P., & Crocker, A. C. (1978). The medical care of mentally retarded persons in public residential facilities. *New England Journal of Medicine, 299*, 1039–1044.

Neumann, M. A. (1967). Langdon Down syndrome and Alzheimer's disease. *Journal of Neuropathology and Experimental Neurology, 26*, 149–150.

New York State Department of Mental Hygiene, Mental Health Research Unit. (1955). A special census of suspected referred mental retardation, Onondaga County, New York. In *Technical report of the mental health research unit*. Syracuse: Syracuse University Press.

New York State (1980). *Vital statistics of New York State*. New York: State Department of Health.

O'Connor, G., Justice, R. S., & Warren, N. (1970). The aged mentally retarded: Institution or community care? *American Journal of Mental Deficiency, 75*, 354–360.

Olson, M. I., & Shaw, C. M. (1969). Presenile dementia and Alzheimer's disease in mongolism. *Brain, 92*, 147–156.

Oregon State Board of Health. (1962). *Mental retardation prevalence in Oregon*. Oregon: Oregon State Board of Health.

Oster, J., Mikkelsen, M., & Nielsen, A. (1964). The mortality and causes of death in patients with Down's syndrome (Mongolism). *Proceedings of the International Copenhagen Congress for the Scientific Study of Mental Retardation, 1*, 231–234.

Penrose, L. S. (1949). The incidence of mongolism in the general population. *Journal of Mental Science, 95*, 685–688.

Penrose, L. S. (1972). *The biology of mental defect (4th ed.)*. London: Sidgwick & Jackson.

Polednak, A. P. (1975). Respiratory disease mortality in an institutionalized mentally retarded population. *Journal of Mental Deficiency Research, 19*, 165–172.

Primrose, D. A. (1966). Natural history of mental deficiency in a hospital group and in the community it serves. *Journal of Mental Deficiency Research, 10*, 159–189.

Record, R. G., & Smith, A. (1954). The incidence, mortality, and sex distributions of mongoloid defectives. *British Journal of Preventative Social Medicine, 9*, 10–15.

Richards, B. W. (1969). Age trends in mental deficiency institutions. *Journal of Mental Deficiency Research, 13*, 171–183.

Richards, B. W. (1975). Mental retardation. In J. G.

Howells (Ed.), *Modern perspectives in the psychiatry of old age*. New York: Brunner/Mazel.

Richards, B. W. (1976). Health and longevity. In J. Wortis (Ed.), *Mental retardation and developmental disabilities: An annual review, Vol. 13* (pp. 168–186). New York: Brunner/Mazel.

Richards, B. W., & Siddiqui, A. Q. (1980). Age and mortality trends in residents of an institution for the mentally handicapped. *Journal of Mental Deficiency Research, 24*, 99–105.

Richards, B. W., & Sylvester, P. E. (1969). Mortality trends in mental deficiency institutions. *Journal of Mental Deficiency Research, 13*, 276–292.

Richardson, W. P., & Higgins, A. C. (1965). *The handicapped children of Alamance County, North Carolina*. Wilmington, DE: Nemours Foundation.

Ross, E. M., Peckham, C., West, P. B., & Butler, N. R. (1980). Epilepsy in childhood: Findings from the National Child Development Study. *British Medical Journal, 1*, 207–210.

Rutter, M., Tizard, J., & Whitmore, K. (1970). *Education, health, and behaviour*. London: Longman Group Limited.

Scally, B. G., & Mackay, D. N. (1964). Mental subnormality and its prevalence in Northern Ireland. *Acta Psychiatrica Scandinavica, 40*, 203–211.

Siegel, J. S. (1976). *Demographic aspects and the older population in the United States*. Washington, DC: Department of Commerce, Bureau of Census.

Siegel, J. S. (1980). On the demography of aging. *Demography, 17*, 345–364.

Solitaire, G. B., & La Marche, J. B. (1966). Alzheimer's disease and senile dementia as seen in mongoloids: Neuropathological observations. *American Journal of Mental Deficiency, 70*, 840–848.

Stanhope, J. M., Brody, J. A., & Brink, E. (1972). Convulsions among the Chamorro people of Guam, Mariana Islands: I. Seizure disorders. *American Journal of Epidemiology, 95*, 292–298.

Stein, Z. A., Susser, M. W., & Saenger, G. (1976a). Mental retardation in a national population of young men in the Netherlands: I. Prevalence of severe mental retardation. *American Journal of Epidemiology, 103*, 477–485.

Stein, Z. A., Susser, M., & Saenger, G. (1976b). Mental retardation in a national population of young men in the Netherlands: II. Prevalence of mild mental retardation. *American Journal of Epidemiology, 104*, 159–169.

Thase, M. E. (1982). Longevity and mortality in Down's syndrome. *Journal of Mental Deficiency Research, 26*, 177–192.

Wing, L. (1971). Severely retarded children in a London area: Prevalence and provision of services. *Psychological Medicine, 1*, 405–415.

Wing, L., Yeates, S., Brierley, H., & Gould, J. (1976). The prevalence of early childhood autism: Comparisons of administrative and epidemiological studies. *Psychological Medicine, 6*, 89–100.

Wisniewski, H. M., & Merz, G. S. (1983). Neuritic and amyloid plaques in senile dementia of Alzheimer type. Bayberry Report 15: *Biological Aspect of Alzheimer Disease*. Cold Spring Harbor Laboratory.

Wisniewski; H. M., & Terry, R. D. (1973). Reexamination of the pathogenesis of the senile plaque. In H. M. Zimmer (Ed.), *Progress in neuropathology, Vol. 2* (pp. 1–26). New York: Grune & Stratton.

Wisniewski, K. E., Wisniewski, H. M., & Wen, G. Y. (1983). Plaques, tangles, and dementia in Down syndrome. *Journal of Neuropathology and Experimental Neurology, 42*, 340.

Wisniewski, K. E., Wisniewski, H. M., & Wen, G. Y. (in press). Occurrence of Alzheimer's neuropathology and dementia in Down syndrome. *Annals of Neurology*.

World Health Organization. (1980). *International classification of impairments, disabilities, and handicaps*. A manual of classification relating to the consequences of disease. Geneva: Author.

chapter

7

Demography and Characteristics of Aging and Aged Mentally Retarded Persons

John W. Jacobson, Markley S. Sutton, and Matthew P. Janicki

This chapter presents information regarding the demographics and characteristics of persons with mental retardation age 55 years or older, with special emphasis on morbidity, mortality, and residential trends (program utilization patterns). Information drawn from the mental retardation literature and registries in the United States, Australia, and England and Wales suggests that aging and elderly persons with mental retardation represent a growing population that will place exceedingly varying demands upon care systems in coming decades. A review of this information shows that life expectancies and mortality rates parallel those of the general population, greatly increasing the number of aging and elderly mentally retarded persons requiring services. In particular, information from registries suggests that a range of residential options should be available for this population and that these options should correspond to the diverse abilities and needs evident among older persons with mental retardation, because patterns of intellectual and adaptive skills for aging and elderly persons are related to the restrictiveness of the program settings in which they reside.

THE POPULATIONS OF industrialized nations are growing progressively older as life expectancy increases (Grundy, 1983). Substantial increases in the proportion of populations over age 55 in Australia, Canada, Czechoslovakia, England, Wales, Finland, Japan, Poland, and the United States have been reported; these increases often exceed several times the growth of general population (Acheson, 1982; Anonymous, 1982; Blake, 1981; Ikegumi, 1982; Panitch, 1983; Renker, 1982; Siegal & Taeuber, 1982; Wasylenki, 1982). About 11% of the population of the United States is age 65 years or older (Siegal & Taeuber, 1982). This proportion is expected to triple by the early 2000s (Blake, 1981). Similarly, the proportion of persons age 65 or older in Australia increased to 9.4% during the 1970s, and has grown at a rate 1.7 times as great as the size of the general population. In England and Wales, persons age 65 or older constitute 15.1% of the general population; the rate of growth in this group is 7.3 times greater than that for the total population size.

Marked increases in the size of aging and elderly populations present potential crises of care for human services systems. Although only 5% of persons age 65 or older in the United States, or about 1,280,000 people, live in institutional settings (Blake, 1981), many others receive public income or medical care assistance. Furthermore, a disproportionately large amount of public medical care expenditures is currently directed to elderly individuals (Blake, 1981). There is evidence that the community is the primary locus of health care for elderly individuals in other countries as well; for example, in Japan and Canada, only 6.5% and 9%, respectively, of the elderly population reside in institutions (Ikegumi, 1982; Wasylenki, 1982). Nevertheless, increases in the absolute size of the elderly population may necessitate substantial increase in the capacity of institutional health care and health-related facilities in industrialized nations. Initiatives that minimize long-term needs for institutional services and emphasize potentially less costly community care systems will be necessary to contain health care expenditures over the next several decades.

Within the aging and elderly populations, individuals with chronic, pre-existing mental and physical handicaps represent a particular concern. Historically, these individuals have been largely retained in institutional settings. However, during the past 2 decades, changes in treatment philosophy and habilitative technology in many Western nations have promoted the use of smaller community-based programs as the preferred residential and service locus. Aging and elderly persons with mental retardation represent a population especially vulnerable to institutional admission or readmission due to the impact of functional impairments that may increase in prevalence with progressing age.

A combination of social circumstances indicate that there will be an increase in demand for services among aging and elderly mentally retarded persons, at least in the United States. This group, as with other population subgroups, will experience increased longevity as a result of the advances in health care and improved standards of living that have taken place over the course of recent decades (Eyman, 1983). Furthermore, the dimunition of extended family networks, coupled with trends toward two-income families, decreases the extent to which siblings of elderly and aging

disabled persons can be relied upon to defray needs for out-of-home care.

A necessary step toward the development of a responsive system of specialized services involves the definition of the service population and an assessment of its needs. Such needs assessment should provide a description of characteristics of the population, services needed, service patterns, and discrepancies between service needs and patterns (Janicki, Castellani, & Norris, 1983; Robins, 1982). Although a number of reports have presented anecdotal or small group data on characteristics and service needs of the general elderly population, few reports have presented contemporary data on the demography, morbidity, and residential situations of aging or elderly mentally retarded persons (cf. Janicki & MacEachron, 1984; Seltzer, Seltzer, & Sherwood, 1982; Willer & Intagliata, 1984).

This chapter presents an overview of available information regarding the demography of aging and elderly mentally retarded persons, and their characteristics and distribution within residential environments. Sources of data include published reports and registry data on characteristics of aging and elderly persons drawn from studies conducted in Australia (Cocks & Ng, 1983) and England and Wales (Department of Health and Social Security, 1972; D. Felce, personal communication, 1983). Similar data on the United States were acquired by the authors from registries employed by state mental retardation agencies in California, Masssachusetts, and New York.

DEFINING THE AGING/ELDERLY MENTALLY RETARDED POPULATION

The process of aging encompasses biological, sociological, and psychological components that reflect progressive changes that individuals undergo as they move from a state of full physical maturity through the adult phases of the life cycle toward old age and death (Thomas, Acker, & Cohen, 1979; Wisniewski & Merz, Chapter 10, this volume). These three components interact and impact differentially upon older persons, and will affect demographic and disability level characterizations.

The chronological age criterion at which a person is deemed to be aging or elderly will vary with the purpose, issue, or concern to be addressed. However, any criterion age must bear correspondence to the biological aspects of lifespan development, and the tenets of the society in which it is to be applied. Problems similar to those found in seeking a unitary definition of aging, aged, or elderly for the general population are encountered when one attempts to define aging and elderly mentally retarded persons.

For the purpose of this chapter, aging and elderly mentally retarded persons will be defined as follows:

Aging mentally retarded persons: individuals within the larger mentally retarded population who are age 55 to 64 years

Elderly mentally retarded persons: individuals within the larger mentally retarded population who are age 65 years or older

These chronological age breakouts will be used to compare data across registries, and whenever possible, to summarize data from previous studies. These breakouts were employed: a) to obtain consistency with the use of age 65 as a benchmark of the later years of life, and b) to limit the population of aging individuals to persons who have survived to a comparatively advanced age and who have the greatest probability of evidencing impairments of aging (i.e., persons age 55 and over). However, findings and data are not uniformly available within these guidelines and, consequently, exceptions to this rule will be noted throughout the chapter.

ESTIMATING THE SIZE OF THE AGING/ELDERLY MENTALLY RETARDED POPULATION

Kushlick and Cox (1973) reviewed age-specific prevalence rates for mental retardation reported in 12 studies in England, Wales, Ireland, Scotland, Sweden, and the United States between 1926 and 1968. Prevalence rates for persons age 60 and older ranged from 3.7/10,000 to 5.1/10,000 for moderately, severely, and profoundly retarded individuals (i.e., IQ less than or equal to 50), and from 4.3/10,000 to 24.2/10,000 for mildly retarded individuals. Similarly, prevalence rates of 23/10,000 and 12/10,000 were found for persons with mental retardation who were ages 60 to 69 and 70 or older, respectively, in Sweden in 1973 (Sterner, 1976). Rates of 16.7 (male) and 15.9 (female) per 10,000 individuals for mentally retarded persons age 55 to 64, and of 12.2 (male) and 10.5 (female) per 10,000 individuals for mentally retarded persons age 65 or older have been reported in England and Wales (Department of Health and Social Security, 1972). Similar findings have been reported for Northern Ireland by MacKay (1971).

As noted by DiGiovanni (1978) and Seltzer and Seltzer (1984), considerable disagreement exists as to the probable size of the aging and elderly mentally retarded population. Using a 1% general population prevalence rate for mental retardation, DiGiovanni (1978) developed estimates of the aging and elderly group from other studies ranging from 50,000 to 315,000 to a maximum of 382,000 individuals in the United States. In contrast, Seltzer and Seltzer (1984), using a 3% general population prevalence rate, derived estimates of from 1,100,000 to 1,380,000 aging and elderly mentally retarded persons in the United States. Variations in population estimates of this magnitude are to be expected, not only because of different base rates, but also because studies that may be employed to develop population estimates are typically conducted within a circumscribed geographic area or within a specific category of program. The estimation process is further complicated by discrepancies in age cohort definitions among studies.

The availability of information about the individuals who currently participate in, or are registered with, service systems may be more useful for policy and program development purposes. Table 1 summarizes the findings of large area studies conducted within recent years, and shows the total identified mentally retarded population, together with the number

Table 1. Known aging and elderly mentally retarded individuals reported in the literature

Survey/study	Area	N Total	N Aging/elderly	% Aging/elderly
Sweeney & Wilson (1979) Agency survey/age 35+ only	Illinois, Indiana, Michigan, Minnesota, Ohio, Wisconsin (USA)	8,320	1,485/3,578	17.8/43.0
Lindberg (1976) Prevalence	West Virginia (USA)	7,485	449/120*	6/1.6
Lindberg & Putnam (1979) Prevalence/noninstitutional only	West Virginia (USA)	405	16[a]	4
Bruininks, Hill, & Thorsheim (1982) Facility resident survey	USA (national)	219,368	46,651/9,309[b]	21.3/4.2
Sutton (1983) Service population	California (USA)	66,899	2,046/1,015[c]	4.6/1.5
Scheerenberger (1981) Survey of institutional residents	USA (national)	101,193	18,948/6,327[d]	18.7/6.3
Renker (1982) Report on prevalence of disability worldwide	Ireland	12,540	1,070[e]	8.5
Hill & Bruininks (1981) Sample of community and institutional residential settings	USA (national)	1,961	158/93[f]	8.1/4.7
Cocks & Ng (1984) Analysis of service population	Victoria (Australia)	10,378	1,199/321[g]	11.6/3.0
Janicki & MacEachron (1984) Analysis of service population	New York (USA)	49,954	3,927/3,896[c]	7.9/7.8
Miller & Eyman (1978) Mortality study	California (USA)	3,817	255[h]	6.7
Department of Health & Social Security (1972) Mental deficiency hospital survey	England and Wales	64,173	9,552/7,096	14.9/11.1

*Estimated   [c]Age 53–62/63+   [e]Age 55+   [g]Age 41–60/61+
[a]Age 59+   [d]Age 40–59/60+   [f]Age 57–61/62+   [h]Age 50+
[b]Age 40–62/63+

and percentage of individuals who were identified as aging or elderly within the survey data reports. These studies all vary in their limitations for the purposes of projecting population size. One study (Sweeney & Wilson, 1979) included data solely on adults age 35 years or older; others (Bruininks, Hill, & Thorsheim, 1982; Hill & Bruininks, 1981; Scheerenberger, 1981) reviewed only those individuals residing in mental retardation facilities. Three surveys, in California (Sutton, 1983), New York (Janicki & MacEachron, 1984), and Victoria, Australia (Cocks & Ng, 1983), employed a rate in treatment approach to describe the characteristics of the service populations in these areas.

Each of the studies shown in Table 1 provides information that may be valuable in anticipating the level of demand for developmental services to aging and elderly individuals. The findings reported in Sweeney and Wilson (1979), for example, provide a basis for expecting that aging and elderly mentally retarded persons constitute a relatively important adult subpopulation. Findings by Lindberg (1976) and Lindberg and Putnam (1979), on the other hand, suggest that, within the overall mentally retarded population, aging and elderly individuals represent between 4% and 7.6%. Even in the context of differing age cohorts, these rates contrast with the 2.4% of the mentally retarded population age 60+ proposed by O'Connor, Justice, and Warren (1970). Furthermore, the findings by Bruininks et al. (1982) and Scheerenberger (1981) that 6.3% of mental retardation institutional residents were over age 59 and 4.3% were over age 62 (not shown in Table 1) suggest a changing age structure within the institutional population over the period since the O'Connor et al. study. Similarly, over one-quarter of mental handicap (i.e., mental retardation) hospital residents in England and Wales are over age 55, and comparison with historical information suggests that similar change (i.e., a "graying") is taking place in the United Kingdom as well (Department of Health and Social Security, 1972; Richards & Siddiqui, 1980).

In the three large area studies, rates of aging/ elderly mentally retarded individuals range from 6.1% (Sutton, 1983) to 15.7% (Janicki & MacEachron, 1984) of the service population with mental retardation. If the typical proportion of elderly/aging individuals within any single state's system lies within this range, the number of aging/elderly persons in adult care service population will be sufficient to justify the development of specialized programs. Applying 12.13%, the mean proportion of the service population found to be aging or elderly in these three studies, to the 1.0% of the 1982 United States adult population projected to be mentally retarded by Baroff (1982), approximately 196,000 individuals nationally, or 0.396% of the United States general population age 55 or older, can be projected to be within the aging and elderly mentally retarded population. These same projections would indicate

a population of some 150,000 developmentally disabled individuals age 60 or older.

Alternatively, an estimate of the number of persons known to service systems who are age 55 years or older can be developed using age-specific prevalence rates, as shown in Table 2. These rates, developed by combining 1980 U.S. Census data with the number of known cases in the registries, provide an estimate of 47,000 individuals nationally age 55 or older (with a range of from 24,000 to 74,000). The individuals encompassed in these three data bases $(N = 9,960)$, therefore, represent nationally from 13% to 42% of service system participants age 55 or older. In contrast, the general populations age 55 years or older of California, Massachusetts, and New York together represent 21% of the comparable national population.

Summary

Applying data from prevalence and program studies, the following estimates may be provided:

The aging and elderly mentally retarded population (based on the 1980 census and adjusted for 1982) encompasses as many as 195,680 persons age 55 and older and 150,000 persons age 60 and older in the United States, and perhaps one-quarter of these persons receive services from the mental retardation system.

Probable (age-specific) prevalence of such individuals in industrialized nations lies within the range of 18 to 20 per 10,000 persons in the general population.

Table 2.   Prevalence rates and population estimates

Age	Age-specific prevalence[a]		Number of cases		×	Factor[b]	=	National estimate		
	55–64	65+	55–64	65+		55–64	65+	55–64	65+	55+
California (CA)	7.85	2.78	1,724	672		9.88	10.58	17,083	7,110	24,143
Massachusetts (MA)	14.43	6.57	849	478		36.88	35.16	31,311	16,806	48,117
New York (NY)	19.18	12.71	3,490	2,746		11.92	11.82	41,601	32,458	74,059
CA/MA/NY (combined)	13.17	7.35	6,063	3,896		4.72	4.82	28,617	18,779	47,396
CA/MA/NY[c] (mean)	13.82	7.35	—	—		—	—	29,989	18,731	47,330

[a]Per 10,000 general population in age group (1980 U.S. Census).
[b]National population in age group/state or multistate population in age group.
[c]Mean of observed state-specific rates; national estimate derived by multiplying rate by age-specific population.

Probable representation of such individuals within service systems approaches 10% of known service system participants, although statistics suggest that the majority of aging and elderly persons are not represented within the service systems.

It is possible that many aging or elderly individuals are not participating in service systems because community services were undeveloped for the greater portion of their lives and a large number may reside in generic health care facilities. Many persons in these facilities may be known by staff to be mentally retarded, but not reported as such in information systems.

REGISTRIES

In the United States, a number of states have initiated comprehensive needs assessment/ information system projects to gather detailed data regarding the mental retardation service population. Such systems have a common limitation; outreach activities to identify unserved individuals with mental retardation are typically limited. The value of information lies in its characterization of the service population rather than of the needs of individuals not yet encountered by the service system. Extrapolation of registry population characteristics to unserved individuals is usually unwarranted. There is a reasonable expectation that, in a system that encompasses a range of community and institutional settings, the group of persons served will, in general, be more severely impaired than the group of persons who are unserved. DiGiovanni (1978), in his discussion of the characteristics and service needs of aging and elderly mentally retarded individuals, has noted reasons why these persons may not be detected by the service system. These include the adequacy of support systems (e.g., family, spouse) until advanced years are reached, and difficulties determining the presence of mental retardation. Given awareness of these limitations and biases, the use of registries, nevertheless, can constitute a valuable resource for demographic analysis and consideration of ser-

vice practices (Goldberg, Gelfand, & Levy, 1980).

The registries in California, Massachusetts, and New York provide summaries of demographic, functional, and residential program use characteristics of the mental retardation system's service populations in each state. Each of these states operates a comprehensive system of residential and habilitative care that includes institutions, group homes, foster family care, and intermediate care facilities for mentally retarded individuals as care alternatives. Data from registries were obtained through the cooperation of the respective mental retardation agencies in each state. Detailed information regarding these registry systems is presented in the appendix at the end of this chapter.

MORTALITY

Trends

Given stable birth rates and migratory patterns, decreases in mortality rates can be expected to result in an increase in the proportion of older persons in a population. Two studies widely separated in time (Balakrishnan & Wolf, 1976; Dayton, Doering, Hilferty, Maher, & Dolan, 1932) have considered the life expectancies of persons with mental retardation. Comparison of these studies indicates that survival rates have improved during the time between these investigations. Twenty-eight percent of those in the earlier study who were alive at age 10 years survived to reach age 60, whereas in the more recent study, 46% survived. It seems reasonable, therefore, to estimate that 40% or more of those persons who are mentally retarded survive to the age of 60. This estimate is further supported by the 0.396% rate for mental retardation among older persons, derived earlier, as contrasted with a 1.0% rate for mental retardation among adults in general.

A number of recent studies have reviewed mortality trends in mental retardation institutions and community programs, and have found that life expectancy appears to be increasing for persons with mental retardation, although it remains lower than for the general population (Carter & Jancar, 1983; Forssman & Akesson, 1965; Lubin & Kiely, Chapter 6, this volume; Miller & Eyman, 1978; Richards & Siddiqui, 1980; Richards & Sylvester, 1975; Tait, 1983). Furthermore, within the mentally retarded population, life expectancies are greater for women, ambulant persons, persons not affected by Down syndrome, less severely impaired persons, and persons who have never lived in an institution. Nevertheless, improved life expectancy has been demonstrated even among persons who have Down syndrome (cf. Richards & Siddiqui, 1980). A number of reports have commented upon high mortality among the youngest age groups and have noted that individuals who survive their early years are likely to survive to old age and to differ little from the general population in resistance to disease (Balakrishnan & Wolf, 1976; Richards & Sylvester, 1975; Tait, 1983).

Although mortality trends have an impact upon the age structure of a population, there is some evidence that the mortality differential between persons with mild/moderate and severe/profound mental retardation may not markedly affect the characteristics of the aging and elderly institutional population until a very advanced age. Scheerenberger's (1981) report on public residential facility residents shows an average of 947 persons in each single year cohort within the range of 40 to 59 years of age, but only 299 persons in the single year cohorts within the range of 60 to 79 years. However,

the intellectual distributions of these age groups demonstrate only modest shifts between these cohorts, with around one-quarter of both the 40 to 59 and the 60 to 79 age groups functioning within the mild/moderate ranges of mental retardation. A slightly more pronounced trend is apparent when persons with profound mental retardation are considered separately; they represent nearly half of the 40 to 59 age group, but less than two-fifths of the 60 to 79 age group. Notably, among persons age 80 years or older, over one-third of the individuals are classified as mildly/moderately mentally retarded; individuals with profound mental retardation account for only one-quarter of these groups. It is possible that these differences reflect admission of elderly, severely impaired individuals to public facilities at rates lower than the mortality levels of severely impaired residents.

Registry Data

Table 3 shows 10-year age cohort data for California's and New York's aging and elderly groups with mental retardation (age group cutoffs reflect data availability). Although age group cohorts cannot be assumed to be identical in their original sizes, it will be noted that the number of persons age 53–62 equate to a substantial proportion of persons age 43–52, making it possible to estimate that from 60% to 80% of persons age 43–52 may survive to age 53–62; this forms a basis for projecting future

Table 3. Age cohort size and intellectual level patterns in California and New York

| Age | California | | New York | |
	N/%	% Next younger group	N/%	% Next younger group
43–52	3,312/52.0	—	3,964/37.6	—
53–62	2,046/32.1	61.8	3,440/32.7	86.8
63–72	800/12.6	39.1	2,024/19.2	58.8
73–82	186/2.9	23.3	899/8.5	44.4
83+	29/0.7	15.6	205/2.0	22.8
Total	6,373/100.0		10,532/100.0	

Age	Mild/moderate MR	Severe/profound[a] MR	Mild/moderate MR	Severe/profound MR
53–62 N	1106	794	1600	1840
Row %	(58.2)	(41.8)	(46.5)	(53.5)
63–72 N	449	305	977	1047
Row %	(59.5)	(40.5)	(48.3)	(51.7)
73+ N	104	92	507	592
Row %	(53.1)	(46.9)	(45.9)	(54.1)

[a]Persons with known intellectual level only.

demands for aging services. Similarly, it may be noted that of persons age 53 or older, persons age 53–62 years constitute from 50% to 67% of cases.

Noteworthy, however, is that, when intellectual level is considered, the California population tends to evidence intellectual skills in the mild and moderate ranges of mental retardation, while severe and profound levels predominate in the New York findings. However, if data on persons within the borderline range are included (see Figure 1), a shift of intellectual level composition in the direction of less marked impairment is seen in comparison of aging and elderly individuals in Massachusetts and New York. Similarly, as shown in Figure 2, a gender reversal is seen to take place between the two age groups, with males predominating among persons 55 to 64 years and females predominating among persons 65 years or older.

When the New York data alone are considered in 5-year age cohorts (see Table 4), age group size as a percentage of the next younger group is seen to decrease at about age 63 to 67, and to decrease once again at about age 78 to 82, suggesting disproportionate mortality during these age periods or those immediately preceding these periods. Moreover, these data show that the proportion of individuals with severe or profound mental retardation rises with advancing age. This finding, largely inconsistent with mortality trends already noted, underscores the need to develop demographic data for administrative applications on aging populations that are specific to a geographic area.

Summary

Review of mortality studies within aging and elderly mentally retarded populations supports the perspective that:

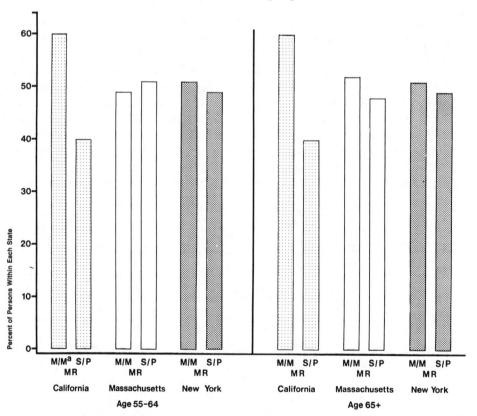

Figure 1.   Intellectual level distribution of age groups drawn from three state registries. (M/M = mild/moderate mental retardation; S/P = severe/profound mental retardation; M/Mª =   mild/moderate includes borderline.)

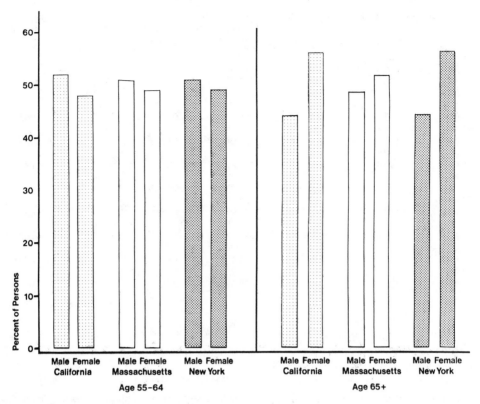

Figure 2.   Gender distribution of age groups drawn from three state registries.

Life expectancies are lower, and mortality rates are higher, at earlier and later ages, in the mentally retarded population than in the general population.

Life expectancies are increasing and a larger proportion of mentally retarded adults now in their middle years should be expected to survive to older age, compared to earlier generational groups.

By the year 2000, increases in the number of aging and elderly mentally retarded persons requiring services will occur at a rate that exceeds those expected from improved life expectancy alone, as persons born during the post–World War II "baby boom" enter the 55+ age group. Within future generational cohorts, however, this increase may be mediated by decreases in the incidence of mental retardation possible through sustained programs of preventive services.

When life expectancies and mortality rates for individuals with Down syndrome are dis-counted, life expectancies and mortality rates parallel those found in the general population.

Higher mortality rates have typically been found among males, persons with more marked mental retardation, nonambulatory persons, and institution residents.

If continuing benefits are realized from corrective medical procedures applied to both children and adults, life expectancies for many retarded individuals should more closely approximate those in the general population.

MORBIDITY

Decline of physiological functioning and reserve capacity, greater susceptibility to infections, and greater probability of chronic impairment with advancing age serve to define the focus of rehabilitative activity for many aging and elderly individuals with mental retardation. As noted by Cape (1983), an illness or injury will typically have a more marked effect

Table 4. Age cohort size and intellectual level patterns in New York

Age	Mild/ moderate MR	% Next younger group	Severe/ profound MR	% Next younger group	Total MR	% Next younger group
43–47 N	907		1,130		2,037	
(%)	(44.5)	—	(55.5)	—		—
48–52 N	866		1,061		1,927	
(%)	(44.9)	95.5	(55.1)	93.9		94.5
53–57 N	837		1,014		1,851	
(%)	(45.2)	96.7	(54.8)	95.6		96.0
58–62 N	763		826		1,589	
(%)	(48.0)	91.1	(52.0)	81.5		85.8
63–67 N	584		598		1,182	
(%)	(49.4)	76.5	(50.6)	72.4		74.4
68–72 N	393		449		842	
(%)	(46.7)	67.3	(53.3)	75.1		71.2
73–77 N	274		299		573	
(%)	(47.8)	69.7	(52.2)	66.6		68.1
78–82 N	152		174		326	
(%)	(46.6)	55.5	(53.4)	58.2		56.9
83–87 N	61		89		150	
(%)	(40.7)	40.1	(59.3)	51.1		46.0
88–92 N	20		35		55	
(%)	(36.4)	32.7	(63.6)	39.3		36.7

on an elderly individual and consume much more time for recovery. The prevention of major, additional handicap through timely attention to minor disablements may be a major service consideration (Jernigan, 1981).

During the early years, and into the years of adult life, individuals in the general population vary in their functional abilities; this variation slowly increases during the later years of life. After maturity there is a general tendency for biological capability and performance to decrease over the entire age span (Cape, 1983; Zarit, 1980). Shifts in biological capability signal a decline in key aspects of general functioning, potential rapidity of adaptation to situational demands, and the absolute magnitude of performance capability. In essence, these shifts represent decrements in physical resilience or flexibility and the extent to which reserves may be drawn upon. It should be noted, however, that while these trends are general, individual exceptions abound and considerable individual variations are present in the timing and occurrence of age-related changes in function. Furthermore, the rate of change varies with the type of performance. Performance of complex activities, involving the use and integration of several body systems, generally deteriorates more rapidly than the performance of simpler activities (Cape, 1983; Zarit, 1980).

Early Aging

Although cross-sectional studies have suggested that declines in intellectual skills accompany the aging process, longitudinal studies have generally shown stability of intelligence scores from maturity through the later years of life (Zarit, 1980). For example, Goodman (1976) investigated patterns of IQ change with advancing age among 402 institutionalized individuals with mental retardation and found that IQ did not decline with age; rather, slight increments were noted in some areas of functioning.

Notwithstanding evidence of intellectual growth continuing through the later years of life, a substantial body of literature shows that some individuals who are mentally retarded, particularly persons with Down syndrome, experience increased age-related debilitation at an atypically early chronological age (Lott & Lai, 1982; Tait, 1983). This anomalous aging process is termed "dementia," or "senile dementia," and reflects neurological changes that result in progressive erosion of basic mental abilities and attributes that is most clearly seen in diminished social interest, language use, and activities of daily living (Lott & Lai, 1982). Many conditions can result in presenile (early onset) dementia with the most common one identified as Alzheimer's disease. Reid and Aungle (1974) have proposed dementia rates of 71/1,000 among aging individuals with mental retardation who are age 45 to 64 and 136/1,000 among aged individuals with mental retardation who are age 65 + . Current research suggests that mentally retarded persons with Down syndrome are particularly prone to Alzheimer's, with perhaps one-fifth to one-third of persons who reach age 40 developing the syndrome (Wisniewski & Merz, Chapter 10, this volume). In comparison, the rate at which chronic (irreversible) organic brain syndromes (inclusive of Alzheimer's) occurs within the general aging population is estimated at only 7% of all individuals (Levenson, 1983).

Health Status

Limited information is available regarding the health status of aging/elderly individuals with mental retardation. Anglin (1981) has reported on physician reviews of 28 mentally retarded individuals age 50 years and older. The health status of these persons was similar to that of other elderly persons. Individuals with mental retardation were more likely to have seizure disorders and hearing problems, but less likely to have cardiac or cardiovascular problems. Similarly, Seltzer, Seltzer, and Sherwood (1982) noted seizure disorders, Parkinson's disease, multiple sclerosis, and respiratory conditions as special health problems among aging individuals with mental retardation. Janicki and Jacobson (1982), in a review of New York's population with mental retardation and other developmental disabilities, noted that the rate of cerebral palsy was lower by 50% among persons age 60 years or older compared to those age 22 to 59 years. Similarly, the rate of persons with epilepsy declined by 35%.

However, it should be noted that the great majority of elderly people in the general population retain completely independent life-styles throughout their later years, and many individuals with chronic health impairments are represented within this group (Cape, 1983; Coe, 1983). Given that among persons with mental retardation, persons with serious physiological anomalies will evidence high mortality, it may be expected that persons who survive to old age will have a health status similar to that of other older individuals. In comparing health status information for the older mentally retarded and general populations (cf. Blake, 1981), it appears that discrepancies are due largely to chronic physical conditions that predate aging for the population with mental retardation.

Registry Data

Table 5 shows the percentage of persons with a variety of reported categorical disabilities, functional limitations, and medication requirements in California, Massachusetts, and New York. In comparing the prevalence of impairments among the two age groups, cerebral palsy and epilepsy are seen to occur at lower rates with advancing age (except in Massachu-

Table 5. Percentage of persons with reported conditions and impairments in three state registries

Condition/impairment	Percentage of persons with conditions					
	Age 55–64			Age 65 +		
	CA	MA	NY	CA	MA	NY
Cerebral palsy present	13	5	6	11	3	4
Epilepsy present	21	18	17	15	20	12
Hearing impairment present	19	24	14	29	32	26
Vision impairment present	22	23	16	27	29	21
Mobility limitation present	—	16	16	—	21	23
Displays problem behaviors	—	48	57	—	49	48
Receives medication						
Psychotropic	—	17	27	—	18	19
Diabetic	—	2	4	—	4	6
Anticonvulsive	—	21	17	—	21	12
Cardiac	—	6	5	—	9	10
Other	—	42	17	—	49	18

setts where a modest increase in the rate of epilepsy may be noted). Conversely, rates of hearing impairment, vision impairment, and mobility limitations are higher among older persons, with each affecting about 25% of all older individuals (similar to rates reported for the general older population for hearing and vision impairments by Blake, 1981). However, behavior management needs, as described by the rate of reported problem behaviors, are seen to be lower among older persons in New York and to be similar for the two age groups in Massachusetts. Furthermore, data on medication administration practices suggest modest differences in needs for psychotropic and anticonvulsive medications, but increased need for diabetic, cardiac, and other specific-usage medications within the older age group.

Table 6 shows the prevalence of chronic physical conditions as a function of age group and affected body system (Commission on Professional and Hospital Activities, 1978). As in the general population, sensory (special sense), musculo/skeletal, and cardiovascular systems are prominently affected. The incidence of neurological problems is also quite high, but may reflect lifelong impairment rather than aging. In general, the prevalence of physical problems is seen to be either similar for the two age groups, or greater among older persons. By inference, with some exceptions for treatment of neurological and to a lesser

degree endocrine problems, the health care needs of this population should be comparable to those of the general aging and elderly population. Readers are cautioned that some of the observed trends in functional and body system impairments may represent birth cohort differences for the two age groups, because these data are not longitudinal.

Summary

Review of the limited literature on morbidity within the aging and elderly mentally retarded and general populations suggests that:

Vision, hearing, musculo/skeletal, and cardiovascular problems are common in both groups.

A key difference among population groups is that, among aging and elderly mentally retarded individuals, vision, hearing, and musculo/skeletal problems may more often predate their entry to the aging/elderly lifespan segment.

Although early onset of aging (as well as Alzheimer's disease) has been estimated to affect individuals with Down syndrome, such impact has not been observed among other subpopulations of persons with mental retardation.

Among non–mentally retarded elderly individuals placed out-of-home, dementia appears to occur at a higher rate than among mentally retarded elderly individuals (most

Table 6. Percentage of persons with physical/medical conditions reported in two state registries

Body system	Percentage of persons			
	Age 55–64		Age 65 +	
	MA	NY	MA	NY
Growth impairment	(−)[a]	1	(−)	2
Musculo/skeletal	5	11	6	15
Special sense	(−)	17	(−)	21
Respiratory	6	2	6	4
Cardiovascular	18	14	23	25
Digestive	6	4	6	3
Genito/urinary	4	2	6	2
Hemic/lymphatic	1	0	2	0
Skin	4	2	3	4
Endocrine	5	5	8	7
Neurological	18	25	21	19
Neoplastic	1	2	1	3
Nonspecified	34	(−)	42	(−)

[a](−) = not specified as specific option in data reports.

of whom are also placed out-of-home). However, this may reflect differential availability of diagnostic services or problems in establishing an accurate diagnosis for disabled persons who already lack communication and self-care skills.

In general, at least in terms of chronic conditions, the health care needs of the aging/elderly mentally retarded population appear similar to those of nondisabled age peers.

By inference, many aging/aged mentally retarded persons will need out-of-home care because of limited social support networks, but few of these individuals will *require* congregate care or special health care if appropriate acute care services are available to complement community settings.

PROGRAM UTILIZATION PATTERNS

As already noted, a small proportion of the general population of the United States age 65 or older resides in institutional or alternative care settings. Of such individuals, over two-thirds are age 75 or older (Cape, 1983). However, elderly individuals do make extensive use of acute care medical facilities, principally hospitals and personal physicians. In fact, over the course of a year, more than one-fifth of all elderly individuals will be admitted to an acute-care hospital, and one-fourth of this group will be admitted more than once (Brody, 1983). Not only do elderly individuals account for nearly two-fifths of patient days in hospitals, but they also use physicians' services half again more frequently than do younger persons (Brody, 1983). This service utilization pattern is driven, however, in large part by public policy. The Medicare program in the United States stresses acute care in its reimbursement practices, and limits the financial accessibility of certain out-of-home options and home-care services (Webb, 1981). The acute-care utilization pattern among elderly individuals contrasts sharply with the provision of lower cost, and cost-containing, services for elderly individuals. It has been estimated that less than 6% of those in need are receiving any quantity of

home health services from the formal health care system (Brody, 1983; Rossman, 1983).

Similarly, public policy and administrative practice will have an impact upon program utilization by aging and elderly mentally retarded populations. The impact of policy and practice may be, in addition, even more pronounced for this population, since this population does not possess the personal, social, and financial resources needed to secure preferential treatment or accommodation. For the better part of the twentieth century, the principal public response to out-of-home care needs of disabled persons has been institutional care. While this stance has shifted to a more articulated system that provides a variety of care options, there is reason to believe that aging and elderly individuals have not fully realized the benefits of deinstitutionalization.

Administrative practices, which focus deinstitutionalization efforts on children, young adults, and generally intact and capable individuals, may account in part for the "graying" of the institutional population. There is also reason to believe that, apart from chronological age, intellectual ability, or adaptive skills, physical frailty by virtue of chronic impairment or impairments of aging may limit opportunities for movement from an institution. These factors would also promote movement from a natural family to an institutional setting in the absence of appropriate community settings. Such trends cannot, however, be interpreted to reflect inherent needs for intensive residential care among aging and elderly mentally retarded persons, but must be understood within the context of policies and practices that are more responsive to children and young adults. Nevertheless, it should be expected that many, if not the majority, of the oldest aging mentally retarded persons still reside in institutions. As community services continue to be developed, as appropriate alternative care models that address individual impairments of aging are articulated, and as the diversity in ability levels and physical capabilities within this population are increasingly recognized, a shift toward community care for this population becomes more feasible.

In one of the earliest reports to consider issues of care for older mentally retarded individuals, Dybwad (1962) commented both on distinct and apparent increases in the lifespans of mentally retarded institutional residents, and on issues of community care. Talkington and Chiovaro (1969) presented one of the first published reports that described a service program designed to address the needs of older mentally retarded institutional residents. Their model, intended to decrease observed regression trends, emphasized rehabilitative programming and involvement in constructive personal activities, and probably represented the state-of-the-art and typical program setting for older persons with mental retardation in the later 1960s.

O'Connor et al. (1970) provided an early description of aging and elderly persons with mental retardation in 19 western institutions in 1968. Of the 463 persons found in these facilities (a total of 2.4% of the institutional population), 52.5% were female, and 76.4% were age 60 to 69 years, 19.9% were age 70 to 79, and 3.7% were age 80 or older. Forty-six percent (46%) were severely or profoundly mentally retarded (11.9% were classified borderline mentally retarded or unknown). Fully 59% of these individuals were considered by facility staff to be eligible for placement into a community setting, but placement was hampered by a lack of effective community programs. Similarly, Ballinger (1978) compared elderly individuals (age 65+) in a mental handicap hospital with those in a psychiatric hospital. Elderly individuals constituted 6% and 61% of these populations, respectively. Of the mentally retarded group, 72% were female, and 14% were severely/profoundly mentally retarded. Although 39% of the group with mental retardation showed signs of psychiatric impairment, 42% did not appear in need of hospital care to address health problems.

Substantial evidence has been presented that a variety of residential settings are now employed to accommodate the out-of-home placement needs of aging and elderly mentally retarded persons. Institutional settings do not constitute the sole alternative available to these persons. In their 1974 national survey of group homes for individuals with mental retardation, Baker, Seltzer, and Seltzer (1974) found that 38 of the 381 sites in their sample exclusively served persons age 50 or older. Willer and Intagliata (1984) noted that domiciliary care facilities (including board-and-care homes and health care facilities) were also used as residences for aging and elderly mentally retarded persons. Of a sample of 464 persons deinstitutionalized, they found 12.5% placed into board-and-care homes and 5% into health related facilities. The median age of those persons placed in board-and-care homes was 63; the median age of those persons placed in health-related facilities was 69. Information reported by Bruininks et al. (1982) further supports the perspective that differential use is made of a variety of living situations for this population. In their 1977 national survey of residential programs for mentally retarded persons, Bruininks et al. found that 31.2% of foster care, 19.9% of community residential facility (CRF), and 21.5% of public residential facility (PRF) occupants were age 40 to 62 years. Similarly, 11.8% of foster care, 3.5% of CRF, and 4.3% of PRF residents were age 63 or older. Considered from another standpoint, however, it should be noted that 70.0% of persons age 40 to 62 years and 70.2% of persons age 63 years or older resided in PRFs.

England and Wales

Reports by the Department of Health and Social Security (1972) regarding mental handicap services in England and Wales in 1969 show that over 90% of adults receiving residential services were living in mental handicap or other hospitals. As noted in Table 7, of the 64,173 persons in residence in all types of hospitals at the end of 1970, approximately 26% were age 55 or older. Comparison of individuals age 55 to 64 to those age 65 or older shows higher proportions of males, individuals with moderate, severe, or profound mental retardation (IQ LTE 50), and persons receiving services or employed, in the younger group. Conversely, mobility impairments were more prevalent within the older group. Compared to

Table 7.   Characteristics of aging/elderly residents of mental handicap and other hospital units in England and Wales—1970

Characteristic	% Age 55–64	55+	% Age 65+	% All ages
Proportion hospital population	15		11	100
Male	49		42	54
IQ LTE 50	64		55	74
Mobility impairment	10		13	22
Incontinent	10		11	30
Needs assistance in self-care	12		12	42
Severe behavior problem present	6		5	32
Receiving education or training, or employed	81		71	74
Percent of persons visited at hospital during				
3-month period	35		25	49
Male (1954)		38		53
(1963)		43		54
Proportion hospital population (1954)		9		100
(1963)		19		100

Adapted from Department of Health and Social Security (1972).

hospital residents of all ages, aging/elderly individuals evidence lower proportions of males; moderate, severe, or profound retardation; mobility impairments; incontinence; needs for assistance in self-care; and behavior problems. Comparative census data available from 1954 and 1963 suggest that aging and elderly individuals have increased as a percentage of the hospital population, and that males have increased as a percentage of the aging/elderly hospital population.

More recent information regarding characteristics of aging and elderly mentally retarded persons in England is available through the Wessex Mental Handicap Register (WMHR) (D. Felce, personal communication, 1983; Kushlick, Blunden, & Cox, 1973; May, Hallett, & Crowhurst, 1982). The WMHR is a registry and service planning system used within the Wessex region of England, a five-county area with a general population of about 2.7 million persons. A total of 1,007 persons with mental retardation, age 55 years or older, are currently reported to live within this region (for an overall rate of 3.73/10,000 in the general population of all ages) (D. Felce, personal communication, 1983). Table 8 summarizes data on these individuals in terms of age and intellectual level.

Several trends are apparent in Table 8. Older individuals tend to be female, to reside in mental handicap institutions, and to be slightly more capable in regard to social and physical capabilities compared to younger persons. In particular, it is noteworthy that nearly 20% of younger persons with greater intellectual skills reside at home. Furthermore, although it is not readily apparent from this table, 39% of persons age 55 or older, 45% of persons age 55 to 64, and 31% of persons age 65 or older reside in noninstitutional settings. In addition, 46% of the individuals age 55 or older living in institutions have an IQ of 50 to 70, compared to 59% of persons in noninstitutional settings. These patterns are consistent with differential program utilization as a function of individual characteristics and suggest a shift toward community care in the past decade.

Victoria, Australia

Table 9 shows the age and intellectual level distributions by residential setting for aging and elderly individuals registered with the Mental Retardation Division, Health Commission of Victoria, Australia (Cocks & Ng, 1983). Several trends are apparent:

Within the defined aging and elderly population with mental retardation, the proportion of persons represented in the group 61 years or older is highest in institutions and lowest living with their families.

Persons age 41 to 60 years are more than twice as likely to live with their families than are persons age 61 or older.

Table 8.   Characteristics of aging and elderly mentally retarded persons in the Wessex region, England in 1983

	Intellectual level							
	IQ 50–70		IQ LT 50		Intellectual level undetermined		All intellectual levels	
Age	% 55–64	% 65 +	% 55–64	% 65 +	% 55–64	% 65 +	% 55–64	% 65 +
Sex								
Male	61	45	47	50	53	40	54	46
Female	39	55	53	50	47	60	46	54
Program participation								
National health service								
residence[a]	42	58	67	83	51	64	55	69
Other residence	27	22	18	12	24	24	23	18
Training center	9	2	9	1	16	6	10	2
Home care	21	17	6	4	9	8	12	11
Social/physical abilities								
Nonambulatory	6	6	8	5	2	6	6	5
Severely behavior dis-								
ordered	2	1	7	4	4	0	4	2
Severely incontinent	1	3	3	2	4	0	2	2
Severe self-care deficits[b]	5	5	16	16	0	4	10	10
Mild self-care deficits[c]	68	75	62	67	20	20	61	66
Undetermined	18	10	4	6	71	71	17	15
Number of cases	235	220	250	200	51	51	536	471

[a]Primarily mental handicap institutions.
[b]Continent, ambulatory, no behavior disorder, but cannot feed, wash, or dress self.
[c]Continent, ambulatory, no behavior disorder, and can feed, wash, or dress self.

Within both age groups, a greater proportion of persons living in institutions are severely or profoundly mentally retarded compared to those in other settings.

The majority of individuals in both age and intellectual level groups live in institutions.

Nearly one-third of individuals age 41 to 60 years with mild/moderate mental retardation live with their families compared to one-seventh of persons of the same age with severe/profound mental retardation.

Over 80% of aging and elderly persons with mild/moderate mental retardation and 90% of aging and elderly persons with severe/profound mental retardation live in institutions.

These patterns contrast sharply with those found within the entire Victoria survey population. For example, 31.3% of the registered group resides in institutions, 60.0% with their families, and 8.3% in community residential programs.

California, Massachusetts, and New York

Figures 3 and 4 illustrate program utilization practices for persons in California, Massachu-

setts, and New York as a function of age and residential setting. In these figures a variety of living situations are listed. These settings are defined in Table 10.

Patterns of residential program utilization may be expected to vary from state to state depending upon the character of available options, specific placement practices, and service system histories. Figure 3 shows the percentage of individuals in California, Massachusetts, and New York who live in each of a variety of residential settings. Patterns are quite divergent across states and age groups. In comparison to aging individuals, in each state a lower proportion of elderly individuals live with their families and a higher proportion live in state mental retardation institutions. In California and New York, elderly individuals are more strongly represented in health care and foster family facilities than are aging individuals; the converse is observed in Massachusetts. In Massachusetts and New York, a lower proportion of elderly individuals lives in group homes or ICFs/MR when compared to aging individuals; in California a higher proportion lives in such settings. Despite these specific variations, the age group patterns show a ten-

Table 9. Characteristics of aging and elderly disabled persons in Victoria, Australia—1982

		Live with kin	Community settings	MR/DD institution	All settings
Age[a]					
41–60	N	387	120	646	1,153
	Col %	89.5	80.5	73.5	79.0
	Row %	33.6	10.4	56.0	100.0
61+	N	45	29	233	308
	Col %	10.5	19.5	26.5	21.0
	Row %	14.6	9.4	76.0	100.0
Degree of MR (col %)					
Age 41–60					
Mild/moderate		87.6	83.5	71.8	77.2
Severe/profound		12.4	16.5	28.2	22.8
Age 61+					
Mild/moderate		87.1	100.0	82.7	82.7
Severe/profound		12.9	0.0	19.0	17.3
Degree of MR (row %)					
Age 41–60					
Mild/moderate		31.0	9.8	59.2	100.0
Severe/profound		14.9	6.6	78.5	100.0
Age 61+					
Mild/moderate		11.6	7.7	80.7	100.0
Severe/profound		8.2	0.0	91.8	100.0
Total N		432	149	879	1,460
	Row %	29.6	10.2	60.2	100.0

Adapted from Cocks and Ng (1983).
[a]Excludes persons with unspecified intellectual level (approximately 13% of population).

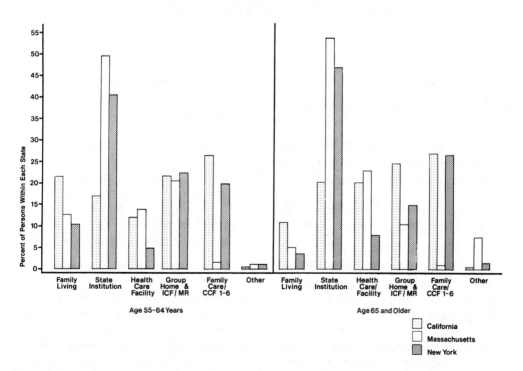

Figure 3. Percent of aging/elderly persons within each of three states residing in various residential settings. (CCF 1-6, community-integrated residential program in California certified to care for from one to six persons.)

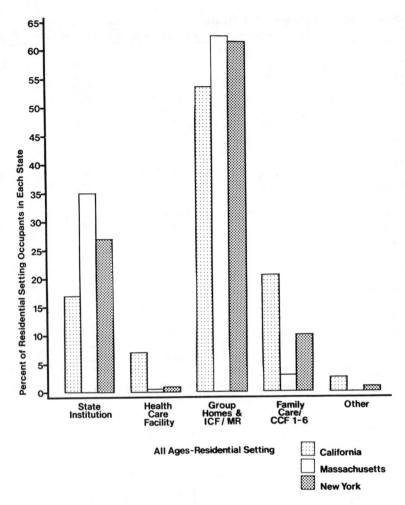

Figure 4. Percent of MR/DD individuals within each state residing in various residential settings. (CCF 1-6, community-integrated residential program in California certified to care for from one to six persons.)

dency to accommodate the residential needs of older individuals through a mixture of foster family care and the most restrictive care settings.

Each state's overall residential care pattern differs from the others as well:

California versus New York: California shows a higher utilization of natural families, health care facilities, group homes, and foster care settings and a lower utilization of state mental retardation institutions.

Massachusetts versus New York: Massachusetts shows a greater utilization of natural families, state mental retardation institutions, and health care facilities and a lower

utilization of group homes and foster family settings.

California versus Massachusetts: California shows a greater utilization of natural families, group homes, and foster family care and a lower utilization of state mental retardation institutions and health care facilities.

It is also useful to consider the manner in which residential program patterns differ between aging and elderly individuals compared to other disabled individuals within each state. Figure 4 shows each state's specialized residential program utilization patterns for mentally retarded persons of all ages. This figure was developed by combining community resi-

Table 10.   Definitions of living situations

Family living	—residing with one's natural family
State institution	—publicly operated congregate care facility or institution serving mentally retarded and developmentally disabled individuals; typically providing comprehensive treatment services and a residential environment for several hundred persons
Health care facility	—publicly and privately operated facilities licensed to provide skilled nursing and medical care; includes skilled nursing facilities, health-related facilities, nursing homes, convalescent care homes
Group homes/ICFs/MR	—publicly and privately operated community programs that typically serve from 4 to 12 individuals; these are typically staffed settings; group homes (community residences, board and care homes) rely upon a cooperative socialization model for adaptive growth; ICFs/MR or Intermediate Care Facilities for the Mentally Retarded are similar to group homes, but also provide comprehensive treatment services
Family care	—a surrogate family living situation wherein foster parents own or lease a home; most sites serve from 1 to 6 individuals
Other	—includes any other type of setting, (i.e., general hospital, rehabilitative facility, psychiatric facility) not encompassed by the other categories

dential facilities survey data collected by R. H. Bruininks, F. A. Hauber, B. K. Hill, K. C. Lakin, L. Rotegard, and C. White (personal communication, October 3, 1983) and institutional survey data collected by Epple and Jacobson (1983), both for 1982. Some differences found among residential service patterns for aging and elderly persons are mirrored in systemic variations among the states. Nevertheless, inspection of Figures 3 and 4 shows that, in comparison to persons of all ages, higher proportions of aging and elderly persons in each state reside in state mental retardation institutions or health care facilities and lower proportions in group homes. Furthermore, in California and New York, higher utilization levels are apparent for foster family care settings among aging and elderly individuals in comparison to the all ages groups in these states.

Patterns of residential program utilization should reflect variations in resident characteristics (i.e., more severely impaired persons should typically be served in more intensive or restrictive settings). Figure 5 shows the intellectual level characteristics of each residential program group as a function of state and age. The following observations apply:

Intellectual patterns for residents in each setting are similar for the two age groups.

There is a lower representation of older persons functioning within the severe or profound ranges of mental retardation in each setting. With the exception of health care facilities, the intellectual level patterns of residents are similar for each setting across states; health care facilities in California appear to serve a more severely impaired group than do similar settings in the other two states.

By age 55, 35% or less of persons still living with kin are classified as severely or profoundly mentally retarded.

The intellectual patterns of residents both within and across states suggest an association between intellectual level and the intensity of services and supervision; more severely impaired individuals tend to be served in more intensive care settings.

The applicability of behavior assessment or rating scales to the evaluation of both geriatric and developmentally disabled groups has been aptly demonstrated in a number of studies (Bock & Joiner, 1982; Bock, Roberts, & Bakkenist, 1977; Meyers, Nihira, & Zetlin, 1979; Patterson, Eberly, & Harrell, 1983; Schnelle & Traughber, 1983). Patterns of longitudinal, lifespan development of adaptive skills among persons with mental retardation were investigated by Meyers, Nihira, and Zetlin (1979), who reported their findings in terms of Adaptive Behavior Scale factor scores (Nihira, Foster, Shellhaas, & Leland, 1974). As in the nondisabled population, different skills and abilities were found to vary in development and decrement. Furthermore, patterns of development varied among intellectual groups.

In comparing adaptive development between persons age 30 to 49 years and persons

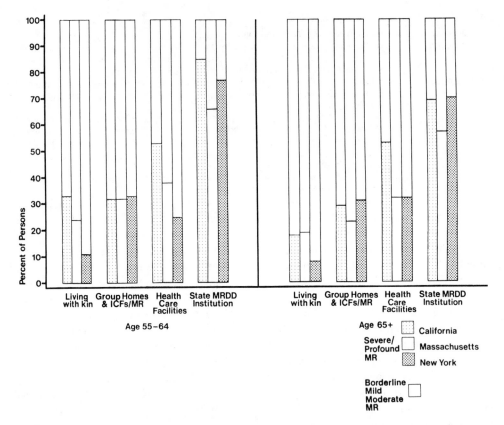

Figure 5. Intellectual level characteristics of known aging/elderly persons residing in various residential settings in three states.

age 50 to 69 years, decreases in personal self-sufficiency scores were found for each intellectual group except persons with profound mental retardation, whose skills increased. Decreases in community self-sufficiency scores were noted for persons with borderline, mild, or moderate mental retardation, while increases were found for persons with severe and profound mental retardation. In contrast, a decrease in personal-social responsibility scores was found only for persons with borderline mental retardation; persons with more severe impairments evidenced increases. These patterns, although not necessarily applicable to individuals in their 70's or 80's, underscore the selective impact of impairments of aging. They also suggest that adaptive maintenance and gains may be realized through habilitative services for aging/elderly individuals with mental retardation.

As in the instance of intellectual levels, it can be expected that adaptive skills should vary among persons living in different residential settings if different settings are being used to accommodate persons whose adaptive status is best addressed through specific program models. Figures 6, 7, and 8 show means of scores within behavior scale domains for aging and elderly mentally retarded individuals in California, New York, and Massachusetts (see the appendix at the end of this chapter for a description of the scales).

Inspection of Figure 6 discloses that, in general, among different residential settings, more limited adaptive skill levels are associated with a greater range of abilities across domains. More capable individuals show general high skill development in a number of domains while less able individuals evidence a wider range of ability levels depending on the

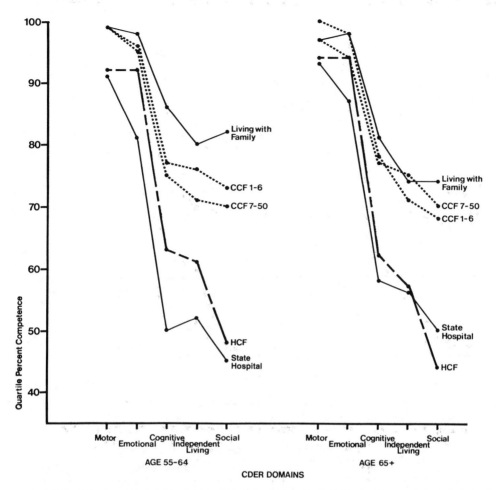

Figure 6.   Adaptive behavior measure profiles for aging/elderly disabled persons in California. (CDER domains, Client Development Evaluation Report [see Appendix]; state hospital, state-operated residential facility [congregate care]; HCF, health care facility; CCF 1-6, community residential facility serving from one to six persons; CCF 7-50, community residential facility serving from 7 to 50 persons.)

domain. Furthermore, greater variation is seen among social, independent living, and cognitive scores than among motor and emotional scores within the setting groups. This pattern suggests that degree of adaptive development in social, independent living, and cognitive ability may be more important than motor and emotional functioning in placement decision-making for aging/elderly individuals. Alternatively, small variations in motor and emotional functioning may have a disproportionate impact upon placement compared to other considerations.

As might be expected in light of intellectual level patterns, persons living with kin are more capable in terms of adaptive skills, while persons living in institutions (state mental retardation facilities or health care facilities) are least capable. There is also a clear differentiation in the abilities of persons living with their families or in community care settings, compared with the abilities of persons living in institutions. In most important aspects, the ability profiles of residential setting groups are similar for the two age cohorts. However, with advancing age, a slight diminution of ability can be noted for persons living with family and, in contrast, a slight increase in ability can be noted for persons living in health care facilities.

Inspection of Figure 7 shows that, despite

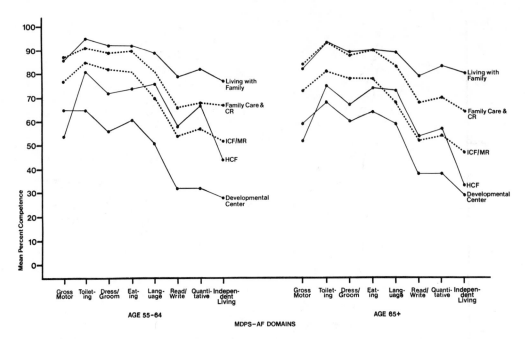

Figure 7. Adaptive behavior measure profiles for aging/elderly disabled persons in New York. (MDPS—AF, Minnesota Developmental Programming System Behavior Scales—Abbreviated Form [see Appendix].)

selected differences in specific program models, ability profiles of New York's residents are similar to those of California's residents in that:

Among residential settings, more limited adaptive skill levels are associated with a wider range of abilities across domains.

Greater differentiation is seen within some domains than others (i.e., language, read/write, quantitative, and independent living versus gross motor, toileting, dress/groom, and eating).

Persons living with family or in foster family care homes or group homes are most capable; persons living in institutions are least capable; and differentiation between these groups is again clear.

One additional pattern shown by the New York profiles is noteworthy: the apparent role of the ICF/MR as an intermediate level of community care between institutions and other alternative care settings. The ability levels of ICF/MR residents overlap with those for HCF residents, with differences seen primarily in abilities relating to gross motor function, dressing/grooming, and independent living, aspects

of functioning in which more marked deficits are observed among health care facility occupants. However, although the typical ability level of ICF/MR residents is lower than that of family care and group home residents, the profiles are essentially parallel across domains. Overlap of the ability curves for persons living in health care facilities with those for persons living in each of the other settings also suggests that individual patterns of ability in combination with special health care needs, rather than general adaptive capability, may differentiate health care facility residents from persons in other settings.

Figure 8 shows the ability profiles of Massachusetts registrants. Although differences among residential program profiles do not appear as marked as those shown for California and New York, nevertheless some commonalities are apparent:

Persons who live with their families are most capable.

Persons who live in group homes or health care facilities are similar in their ability profiles, but slightly less capable in overall ability compared to persons living with family.

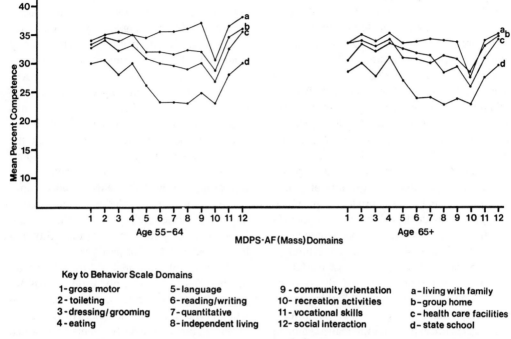

Key to Behavior Scale Domains

1- gross motor	5- language	9 - community orientation	a- living with family
2- toileting	6- reading/writing	10- recreation activities	b- group home
3- dressing/grooming	7- quantitative	11- vocational skills	c- health care facilities
4- eating	8- independent living	12- social interaction	d- state school

Figure 8. Adaptive behavior measure profiles for aging/elderly disabled persons in Massachusetts. (MDPS—AF [Mass], Massachusetts version of the Minnesota Developmental Programming System Behavior Scales—Abbreviated Form [see Appendix].)

Persons living in state hospitals or schools (institutions) are less capable of performing a wide variety of activities than are persons in other settings.

Summary

Review of registry data from England and Wales, Australia, California, Massachusetts, and New York suggests that the following generalizations can be made about residential accommodation practices for the aging and elderly mentally retarded population:

These individuals typically reside in sheltered care settings; in particular, they are less likely to be maintained in their natural family (or extended family) setting than are younger adults.

Public mental retardation institutions constitute the primary sheltered care setting for these individuals.

Foster family care settings tend to be used in preference to group settings for those individuals not placed in institutions.

Patterns of intellectual and adaptive skills for aging and elderly individuals bear correspondence to the restrictiveness of the program settings in which they reside.

Future Demographics

Although it has been noted earlier in this chapter that older individuals constitute an ever-growing percentage of the general population, the implications of this trend are most apparent when the number of persons is considered. Using projections reported by Rice and Feldman (Chapter 1, this volume), it may be expected that the size of the general population cohort age 55 years or older will increase over 1980 levels by 39% by the beginning of the twenty-first century, and by 87% by the year 2020. Assuming that improvements in life expectancy during these periods for mentally retarded individuals will parallel those for the general population, the use of DiGiovanni's (1978) estimates of the number of aging and elderly mentally retarded individuals would imply a population range of from 20,000 to 438,000 such persons in the United States in the year 2000, and from 94,000 to 589,000 such persons in the year 2020. Based on national service utilization trends of current service system participants (as presented in this chapter), the number of aging and elderly mentally retarded persons (age 55 and older) within the nation's service system would increase substantially by the year 2000. Because aging and elderly individuals are disproportionately represented within residential care populations, it is possible that the rate at which increased needs for residential care are noted for aging individuals will exceed the growth rate in this population. This phenomenon, in turn, would necessitate increased efforts to develop and implement lower cost models of care that are responsive to the diversity of abilities and needs evident within this population. Furthermore, to the extent that significant advances in life expectancy are realized among the most severely disabled persons, it can be anticipated that such individuals will become more strongly represented within service populations. This shift will lead to increased needs for intensive services within the population of aging and elderly mentally retarded persons as a whole.

CONCLUSIONS

The aging and elderly mentally retarded population currently represents a substantial number of individuals, 196,000 in the United States alone, with an estimated age-specific prevalence rate of 18–20/10,000 internationally. All indications are that this population will increase in the coming years.

Currently, aging and elderly persons with mental retardation constitute about 10% of the known service system participants. Since these individuals are typically served in sheltered care settings and public institutions, increasing demands on the service system are bound to be experienced. In order to prepare for this eventuality, we have attempted to outline the information available in this little examined area.

Although there are numerous stereotypes regarding the mentally retarded population, in general, and the aging/elderly mentally retarded population in specific, it has been rarely examined. The authors have attempted as thorough a review as possible in this brief space, including a review of mortality, morbidity, and living circumstances. In general, their findings suggest that aging and elderly mentally retarded persons have much in common with the general aging or mentally retarded populations. It is certain that life expectancy is increasing and mortality rates are decreasing. Although mentally retarded individuals generally have a shorter life expectancy, those reaching middle age have a greater probability of a longer life now than in past years.

The available information, though mostly demographic, can certainly yield a basis for preparing for the service needs of this population in the future. Residential circumstances of the aging and elderly mentally retarded population appear to be changing as the requirements of the individuals and philosophies of care continue to change. Greater numbers of alternatives and opportunities are found and utilized as states and nations adapt their service systems to the needs of this population and other identifiable subpopulations. New alternatives and service models, or the increased use of existing models of home care and intensive home care, within both natural family and alternative care settings, will be required if the program needs of this population are to be fully and progressively addressed.

Mentally retarded persons constitute only one of a number of populations of disabled individuals who will be competing for scarce residential resources. During the next several decades, competiton for residential services will increase as demand is driven by changing general population demographics. Today, loss of natural family supports is likely to precipitate institutionalization of elderly mentally retarded persons. The survival of what appears to be the most physically intact mentally retarded individuals into the later years of life, however, suggests that institutional placement often results from the absence of appropriate alternative care and health care services in the community, rather than assessed need for congregate care. Long-term commitments to costly institutional environments may be re-emphasized in the face of demands by the general aging population and the convenience of recycling vacant public residential facility space. If retrogression in care systems is to be prevented, public policy must be responsive to the reality of older individuals' care needs instead of stereotypes. Solutions to the care needs of chronically disabled populations will not be found in historical precedents, but in a recognition of the shortcomings of past approaches and an appreciation of innovation and diversity.

REFERENCES

Acheson, E. D. (1982). The impending crisis of old age: A challenge to ingenuity. *Lancet, 2-8298,* 592–594.

Adams, M. (1975). Foster family care for the intellectually disadvantaged child: The current state of practice and some research perspectives. In M. J. Begab & S. A. Richardson (Eds.), *The mentally retarded and society: A social science perspective.* Baltimore, MD: University Park Press.

Anglin, B. (1981). *They never asked for help: A study of needs of elderly retarded people in Metro Toronto.* Maple, Ontario: Belsten Publishing.

Anonymous. (1982). Aging and people with mental handicaps. *Canadian Journal on Mental Retardation, 32,* 28–30.

Baker, B. L., Seltzer, G. B., & Seltzer, M. M. (1974). *As close as possible: Community residences for retarded adults.* Boston: Little, Brown & Co.

Balakrishnan, T. R., & Wolf, L. C. (1976). Life expectancy of mentally retarded persons in Canadian institutions. *American Journal of Mental Deficiency, 80,* 650–662.

Ballinger, B. R. (1978). The elderly in a mental subnormality hospital: A comparison with the elderly psychiatric patient. *Social Psychiatry, 13,* 37–40.

Baroff, G. (1982). Predicting the prevalence of mental retardation in individual catchment areas. *Mental Retardation, 20,* 133–135.

Blake, R. (1981). Disabled older persons: A demographic analysis. *Journal of Rehabilitation, 47*(4), 19–27.

Bock and Associates. (1979). *Massachusetts service coordination battery (MSCB).* St. Paul, MN: Author.

Bock, W. H., Hawkins, C., Jayachandran, P., Tapper, H., & Weatherman, R. F. (1975). *Minnesota Developmental Programming System—Behavior Scales.* St. Paul: University of Minnesota.

Bock, W. H., & Joiner, L. M. (1982). From institution to community residence: Behavioral competence for admission and discharge. *Mental Retardation, 20,* 153–158.

Bock, W. H., Roberts, K., & Bakkenist, K. (1977). The Minnesota developmental programming system: Its history and application in ICFs/MR and SNFs. *Journal of Medicaid Management, 1,* 17–26.

Bock, W. H., Weatherman, R. F., Joiner, L. M., & Krantz, G. C. (1978). *Assessment of behavioral competence of developmentally disabled persons: The MDPS.* Minneapolis: University of Minnesota.

Brody, S. J. (1983). Formal long-term support system for the elderly. In R. D. T. Cape, R. M. Coe, & I. Rossman (Eds.), *Fundamentals of geriatric medicine.* New York: Raven Press.

Bruininks, R. H., Hill, B. K., & Thorsheim, M. J. (1982). Deinstitutionalization and foster care for mentally retarded people. *Health and Social Work, 7,* 198–205.

Cape, R. D. T. (1983). The geriatric patient. In R. D. T. Cape, R. M. Coe, & I. Rossman (Eds.), *Fundamentals of geriatric medicine* (pp. 9–16). New York: Raven Press.

Cape, R. D. T., Coe, R. M., & Rossman, I. (Eds.). (1983). *Fundamentals of geriatric medicine.* New York: Raven Press.

Carter, G., & Jancar, J. (1983). Mortality in the mentally handicapped: A 50 year survey at the Stoke Park group of hospitals. *Journal of Mental Deficiency Research, 27,* 143–156.

Cocks, E., & Ng, C. P. (1983). Characteristics of those persons registered with the Mental Retardation Division. *Australia and New Zealand Journal of Developmental Disabilities, 9,* 117–127.

Coe, R. M. (1983). Comprehensive care of the elderly. In R. D. T. Cape, R. M. Coe, & I. Rossman (Eds.), *Fundamentals of geriatric medicine* (pp. 3–8). New York: Raven Press.

Commission on Professional and Hospital Activities. (1978). *International classification of diseases, clinical modification: ICD-9-CM* (9th ed.). Ann Arbor, MI: Edwards Brothers.

Cotten, P. D., Sison, G. F. P., & Starr, S. (1981). Comparing elderly mentally retarded and non-mentally retarded individuals: Who are they? What are their needs? *The Gerontologist, 21,* 359–365.

Dayton, N. A., Doering, C. R., Hilferty, M. M., Maher, H. C., & Dolan, H. H. (1932). Mentality and life expectation in mental deficiency in Massachusetts: Analysis of the fourteen year period 1917–1930. *New England Journal of Medicine, 206,* 555–570, 616–631.

Department of Developmental Services. (1978). *Client development evaluation report (CDER).* Sacramento: California Department of Developmental Services.

Department of Health and Social Security. (1972). *Census of mentally handicapped patients in hospital in England and Wales at the end of 1970.* London: Her Majesty's Stationery Office.

DiGiovanni, L. (1978). The elderly retarded: A little-known group. *The Gerontologist, 18,* 262–266.

Dybwad, G. (1962). Administrative and legislative problems in the care of the adult and aged mentally retarded. *American Journal of Mental Deficiency, 66*, 716–722.

Epple, W. A., & Jacobson, J. W. (1983). *Staffing in residential programs: A report on staffing ratios in large state-operated residential facilities for mentally retarded persons in the United States*. Albany: New York State Office of Mental Retardation and Developmental Disabilities.

Eyman, R. K. (1983). On the survival and development of the mentally retarded. *Psychology in Mental Retardation, 9*, 1–2.

Forssman, H., & Akesson, H. O. (1965). Mortality in patients with Down's syndrome. *Journal of Mental Deficiency Research, 9*, 146.

Goldberg, J., Gelfand, H. M., & Levy, P. S. (1980). Registry evaluation methods: A review and case study. *Epidemiologic Reviews, 2*, 210–220.

Goodman, J. F. (1976). Aging and IQ change in institutionalized mentally retarded. *Psychological Reports, 39*, 999–1006.

Grundy, E. (1983). Demography and old age. *Journal of the American Geriatrics Society, 31*, 325–332.

Hill, B. K., & Bruininks, R. H. (1981). *Physical and behavioral characteristics and maladaptive behavior of mentally retarded people in residential facilities*. Minneapolis: Center for Residential and Community Services, Department of Psychoeducational Studies, University of Minnesota.

Ikegumi, N. (1982). Institutionalized and the non-institutionalized elderly. *Social Science and Medicine, 16*, 2001–2008.

Jacobson, J. W., & Janicki, M. P. (1983). Observed prevalence of multiple developmental disabilities. *Mental Retardation, 21*, 87–94.

Janicki, M. P., Castellani, P. J., & Norris, R. G. (1983). Organization and administration of service delivery systems. In J. L. Matson & J. A. Mulick (Eds.), *Handbook of mental retardation* (pp. 3–23). New York: Pergamon Press.

Janicki, M. P., & Jacobson, J. W. (1979). *New York's needs assessment and developmental disabilities: Preliminary report* (Tech. mono. 79-10). Albany: New York State Office of Mental Retardation and Developmental Disabilities.

Janicki, M. P., & Jacobson, J. W. (1982). The character of developmental disabilities in New York State: Preliminary observations. *International Journal of Rehabilitation Research, 5*, 191–202.

Janicki, M. P., & MacEachron, A. E. (1984). Residential, health, and social service needs of elderly developmentally disabled persons. *The Gerontologist, 24*, 128–137.

Jernigan, J. A. (1981). Loss of physical function and disability: Health problems of older people. *Journal of Rehabilitation, 47*(4), 34–37.

Kriger, S. (1975). *Lifestyles of aging retardates living in community settings in Ohio*. Columbus, OH: Psychologia Metrika.

Kushlick, A., Blunden, R., & Cox, G. R. (1973). A method of rating behavior characteristics for use in large scale surveys of mental handicap. *Psychological Medicine, 3*, 466–472.

Kushlick, A., & Cox, G. R. (1973). The epidemiology of mental handicap. *Developmental Medicine and Child Neurology, 15*, 748–759.

Levenson, A. J. (1983). Organic brain syndromes, other non-functional disorders, and pseudodementia. In R. D. T. Cape, R. M. Coe, & I. Rossman (Eds.), *Fundamentals of geriatric medicine* (pp. 139–150). New York: Raven Press.

Lindberg, D. (1976). *Prevalence of developmental disabilities in West Virginia*. Elkins, WV: Davis & Elkins College.

Lindberg, D., & Putnam, J. (1979). *The developmentally disabled of West Virginia: A profile of the substantially handicapped who are not in institutions*. Elkins, WV: Davis & Elkins College.

Lott, I. T., & Lai, F. (1982). Dementia in Down's syndrome: Observations from a neurology clinic. *Applied Research in Mental Retardation, 3*, 233–239.

Lubin, R. A., Jacobson, J. W., & Kiely, M. (1982). Projected impact of the functional defintion of developmental disabilities: The categorically disabled population and service eligibility. *American Journal of Mental Deficiency, 87*, 73–79.

MacKay, D. N. (1971). Mental subnormality in northern Ireland. *Journal of Mental Deficiency Research, 15*, 12–19.

May, A. E., Hallett, W., & Crowhurst, S. (1982). The inter-rater reliability of the Wessex Mental Handicap Register. *Journal of Mental Deficiency Research, 26*, 121–122.

Meyers, C. E., Nihira, K., & Zetlin, A. (1979). The measurement of adaptive behavior. In N.R. Ellis (Ed.), *Handbook of mental deficiency, psychological theory and research* (2nd ed.) (pp. 431–481). Hillsdale, NJ: Lawrence Erlbaum Associates.

Miller, C., & Eyman, R. K. (1978). Hospital and community mortality rates among the retarded. *Journal of Mental Deficiency Research, 22*, 137–145.

Newman, E. S., & Sherman, S. R. (1979). Foster-family care for the elderly: Surrogate family or mini-institution? *International Journal of Aging and Human Development, 10*, 165–176.

Nihira, K., Foster, R., Shellhaas, M., & Leland, H. (1974). *AAMD Adaptive Behavior Scale, 1974 Revision*. Washington, DC: American Association on Mental Deficiency.

O'Connor, G., Justice, R. S., & Warren, D. (1970). The aged mentally retarded: Institution or community care. *American Journal of Mental Deficiency, 75*, 354–360.

Oktay, J. S., & Volland, P. J. (1982, November). Community foster care homes for the frail elderly: A program evaluation. Presentation at the Annual Meeting of the Gerontological Society of America, Boston, MA.

Panitch, M. (1983). Mental retardation and aging. *Canada's Mental Health, 31*, 6–7.

Patterson, R. L., Eberly, D. A., & Harrell, T. L. (1983). Behavioral assessment of intellectual competence, communication skills and personal hygiene skills of elderly persons. *Behavioral Assessment, 5*, 207–218.

Reid, A. H., & Aungle, P. G. (1974). Dementia in aging mental defectives: A clinical psychiatric study. *Journal of Mental Deficiency Research, 18*, 15–23.

Renker, K. (1982). World statistics on disabled persons. *International Journal of Rehabilitation Research, 5*, 196–197.

Richards, B. W., & Siddiqui, A. Q. (1980). Age and mortality trends in residents of an institution for the mentally handicapped. *Journal of Mental Deficiency Research, 24*, 99–105.

Richards, B. W., & Sylvester, P. E. (1975). Mortality trends in mental deficiency institutions. *American Journal of Mental Deficiency, 80,* 276–292.

Robins, B. J. (1982). Local response to planning mandates: The prevalence and utilization of needs assessment by human services agencies. *Evaluation and Program Planning, 5,* 199–208.

Rossman, I. (1983). Physician as geriatrician. In R. D. T. Cape, R. M. Coe, & I. Rossman (Eds.), *Fundamentals of geriatric medicine* (pp. 17–24). New York: Raven Press.

Scheerenberger, R. C. (1981). *Public residential services for the mentally retarded.* Minneapolis: Center for Community and Residential Services, Department of Psychoeducational Studies, University of Minnesota.

Schnelle, J. F., & Traughber, B. (1983). A behavioral assessment system applicable to generic nursing facility residents. *Behavioral Assessment, 5,* 231–243.

Segal, R. (1977). Trends in services for the aged mentally retarded. *Mental Retardation, 15,* 25–27.

Seltzer, M. M., & Seltzer, G. B. (1984). The elderly mentally retarded: A group in need of service. In G. Getzel & J. Mellor (Eds.), *Gerontological social work practice in the community.* New York: Haworth Press.

Seltzer, M. M., Seltzer, G. B., & Sherwood, C. C. (1982). Comparison of community adjustment of older vs. younger mentally retarded adults. *American Journal of Mental Deficiency, 87,* 9–13.

Sherman, S. R., & Newman, E. S. (1977). Foster-family care for the elderly in New York State. *The Gerontologist, 17,* 513–520.

Shock, N. W. (1983). Aging of regulatory mechanisms. In R. D. T. Cape, R. M. Coe, & I. Rossman (Eds.), *Fundamentals of geriatric medicine.* New York: Raven Press.

Siegal, J. S., & Taeuber, C. M. (1982). The 1980 census and the elderly: New data available to planners and practitioners. *The Gerontologist, 22,* 144–150.

Steinhauer, M. B. (1982). Geriatric foster care: A prototype design and implementation issues. *The Gerontologist, 22,* 293–300.

Sterner, R. (1976). *Social and economic conditions of the mentally retarded in selected countries.* Brussels, Belgium: International League of Societies for the Mentally Handicapped.

Sutton, M. S. (1983, August). *Treatment issues and the elderly institutionalized developmentally disabled individual.* Paper presented at the annual convention of the American Psychological Association, Anaheim, CA.

Sweeney, D. P. (1978). Denied, ignored or forgotten?: An assessment of community services for older/aged developmentally disabled persons within HEW Region V. In D. P. Sweeney & T. Y. Wilson (Eds.), *Double jeopardy: The plight of aging and aged developmentally disabled persons in mid-America* (research monograph) (pp. 54–88). Ann Arbor, MI: University of Michigan, Institute for the Study of Mental Retardation and Related Disabilities.

Sweeney, D. P., & Wilson, T. Y. (Eds.). (1979). *Double jeopardy: The plight of aging and aged developmentally disabled persons in mid-America* (research monograph). Ann Arbor, MI: Institute for the Study of Mental Retardation and Related Disabilities.

Tait, D. (1983). Mortality and dementia among aging defectives. *Journal of Mental Deficiency Research, 27,* 133–142.

Talkington, L. W., & Chiovaro, S. J. (1969). An approach to programming for aged MR. *Mental Retardation, 7,* 29–30.

Tarjan, G., Wright, S. W., Eyman, R. K., & Keeran, C. V. (1973). Natural history of mental retardation: Some aspects of epidemiology. *American Journal of Mental Deficiency, 77,* 369–379.

Thomas, N., Acker, P., & Cohen, J. (1979). Defining a service population. In D. P. Sweeney & T. Y. Wilson (Eds.), *Double jeopardy: The plight of aging and aged developmentally disabled persons in mid-America* (research monograph) (pp. 36–53). Ann Arbor, MI: Institute for the Study of Mental Retardation and Related Disabilities.

Wasylenki, D. (1982). The psychogeriatric problem. *Canada's Mental Health, 30*(3), 16–19.

Webb, A. (1981). The view from the states. In R. Morris (Ed.), *Allocating health resources to the elderly and disabled.* New York: Heath & Co.

Willer, B., & Intagliata, J. (1984). *Promises and realities for mentally retarded citizens: Life in the community.* Baltimore: University Park Press.

Zarit, S. H. (1980). *Aging and mental disorders: Psychological approaches to assessment and treatment.* New York: The Free Press.

APPENDIX

Three State Registries

CALIFORNIA

Every individual determined to be in need of services due to mental retardation is registered with one of 23 regional centers in California; a regional center is a nonprofit, independent corporation that contracts with the California State Department of Developmental Services (DDS). A Client Developmental Evaluation Report (CDER) (Department of Developmental Services, 1978) protocol is completed annually for every client of a regional center. The CDER provides demographic data for every client as well as an assessment and evaluation of his or her skill levels. The CDER is completed by the staff who are most familiar with the client. In the case of clients living in a state hospital, the state hospital staff complete the CDER. These data are entered into a state-wide data base maintained by the Department of Developmental Services.

One component of the CDER is used to record client demographic, disability, and adaptive skill characteristics. Adaptive skill data are recorded within a five-domain instrument addressing motor, emotional, cognitive, independent living, and social skills. Clients are rated as to performance quality for each item within each domain and a summary score is computed for each domain. In this chapter, CDER domain data are presented as quartile percent competence scores. In order to define these competence values, quartiles were computed for each domain and the number of individuals with scores falling within each quartile were determined. A mean quartile score was then derived for each group and converted from a range of 1.00 to 4.00 to one of 1 to 100 for presentation purposes. CDER data on aging/elderly individuals are reported in varying numbers in this report depending upon age ranges used, and represent from 3.6% to 11.8% of the 67,000 cases reported in the CDER data base. Data on 3.6% of the cases were complete in regard to all pertinent client characteristics and were used in interstate comparisons.

MASSACHUSETTS

The comprehensive registry/client information system document used by the Department of Mental Health and Mental Retardation's (DMHMR) Division of Mental Retardation is the Massachusetts Service Coordination Battery (MSCB) (Bock and Associates, 1979). This protocol, implemented in 1980, summarizes data on the demographic, diagnostic, functional, service receipt, and adaptive skill characteristics of persons who receive services

funded or provided by DMHMR. It is completed annually. Forms are completed by professional and paraprofessional staff, usually area service coordinators, who are familiar with the client and the services he or she receives. Many items in the MSCB share format and response alternatives with the comparable New York data system. MSCB data elements include formal measures of adaptive skills; a 12-domain form of the Minnesota Developmental Programming System Behavior Scales (MDPS) (Bock, Hawkins, Jayachandran, Tapper, & Weatherman, 1975; Bock, Weatherman, Joiner, & Krantz, 1978). Data reported in interstate comparisons represent 7.8% of the 17,000 cases reported in the MSCB data base.

NEW YORK

The Office of Mental Retardation and Developmental Disabilities (OMRDD) in New York maintains a client information system termed the Developmental Disabilities Information System (DDIS) (Janicki & Jacobson, 1979, 1982). The DDIS was implemented in 1978 and summarizes data on demographic, diagnostic, functional, service receipt, and adaptive skills characteristics of persons receiving developmental disabilities services funded or provided by OMRDD. Limited outreach surveys using the DDIS have been conducted to obtain information on unserved and prospective service populations. DDIS protocols are completed once for each person, with annual updates completed thereafter using an abbreviated version of the initial protocol. Forms are completed by professional and paraprofessional staff, often case managers, who are familiar with the client. The DDIS includes the abbreviated eight-domain, 80-item version of the MDPS Behavior Scales (Bock et al., 1975, 1978) developed originally for use in this information system. The eight 10-item domains summarize skill levels in regard to gross motor, toileting, dressing/grooming, eating, language, reading/writing, quantitative, and independent living skills. Items are endorsed to reflect performance incidence (four-point scale of 0 to 3 points, from "always as appropriate" to "never as appropriate"), with a possible total of 30 points per domain. Thirty points converts to a score of 100 "percent competence" and a score of 0 converts to 0 "percent competence" (Janicki & Jacobson, 1982). Cases reported in interstate comparisons represent from 10.9% to 13.7% of the 57,000 cases in the data base, depending upon the specific analysis.

8

Planning for an Older Developmentally Disabled Population

Matthew P. Janicki, Lewis A. Knox, and John W. Jacobson

This chapter addresses planning requirements inherent in three federal acts: the Developmental Disabilities Assistance and Bill of Rights Act, the Older Americans Act, and the National Health Planning and Resources Development Act. In addition, this chapter examines issues related to planning for an older developmentally disabled population. In order to reflect the demands of the population, services must anticipate and respond to the needs of a variety of individuals with disabilities and different levels of impairment. A foundation for planning such comprehensive services for an older developmentally disabled population is offered; this includes a discussion of the definition of the population, an assessment of needs, the definition of the services system and its gaps, and strategies designed to address the system gaps.

THE NATURE OF developmental services encourages a comprehensive approach to planning—comprehensive in that all levels of need will be met by a coherent system of services and founded on a principle of human management that espouses both the integration of disabled persons within society and the primacy of individual needs. Usually lifelong in application, developmental services ideally are community-based, with most services close to the home of the disabled person. The promotion and/or advancement of strong linkages among all the components of the developmental disabilities system is critical to developmental services planning. A system of comprehensive services must encompass all the resources required to provide assistance to developmentally disabled people. To ensure comprehensiveness, a service system must

meet the needs of all age groups, cope with the problems of all degrees of disability, compensate for groups of different socioeconomic and cultural backgrounds, and be available when and where needed by an individual and/ or his or her family (Janicki, Castellani, & Norris, 1983). Planning activities are undertaken with the intent of realizing these ends through anticipation of future trends and system stresses.

Historically, the focus of community service system design for persons with developmental disabilities has been on families of children and adolescents, as well as on adults living with their families, living independently, or residing in a variety of sheltered care settings (Braddock, 1981; Bradley, 1978). The design of, and planning for, these systems has taken into account a variety of service needs, including

143

residential, vocational, educational, clinical, health, mental health, and social aspects. Local services have been predominantly concerned with those individuals at the beginning or middle phases of their lifespan. As a growing population of older and aging developmentally disabled persons becomes identified, planning for this population should become a salient concern.

In the United States and Canada, systems planning for developmental disabilities services has not been a focus at the federal level. At the state and provincial level in these countries, however, population-specific planning for both the developmentally disabled and elderly populations has been much more prominent; in the United States this primarily resulted from two different federal laws, the Mental Retardation Facilities and Community Mental Health Centers Construction Act of 1963 (PL 88-164) (now the Developmental Disabilities Assistance and Bill of Rights Act [PL 98-527]) and the Older Americans Act (PL 89-73, as amended). Additionally, in a number of states, state agencies dedicated to mental retardation and/or developmental disabilities conduct planning for this population either in response to state statute or because of administrative considerations. Furthermore, in some states, both elderly and mentally retarded/developmentally disabled populations are included in the framework of the state's state health plan, area health system agencies' plans, and annual implementation plans required under provisions of the National Health Planning and Resources Development Act (PL 93-641, as amended).

The purpose of this chapter is to review these legislatively mandated planning requirements as well as to examine some of the issues related to planning for an older developmentally disabled population.

PLANNING UNDER PROVISIONS OF THE DEVELOPMENTAL DISABILITIES ACT

The Developmental Disabilities Assistance and Bill of Rights Act of 1984 (PL 98-527) requires that each state have in force a 3-year developmental disabilities state plan issued jointly by the state's developmental disabilities planning council and the governor. Receipt of the state's allocation of federal funds under the Act's formula grant program is contingent upon the development of such a plan (see Lippman & Loberg, Chapter 3, this volume). These plans, pursuant to law, must:

1. Set out the specific objectives to be achieved under the plan and list programs and resources available or to be made available to meet such objectives.
2. Describe the extent and scope of services being provided, or to be provided, to persons with developmental disabilities under other state plans for federally assisted state programs, including:

    Education for the handicapped
    Vocational rehabilitation
    Public assistance
    Medical assistance
    Social services
    Maternal and child health
    Crippled children's services
    Comprehensive health and mental health
    Other programs as required
3. Describe how funds allotted to the state will be used.
4. Assess and describe the extent and scope of priority services.
5. Establish methods for the periodic evaluation of the plan's effectiveness in meeting its objectives.

Persons included within state developmental disabilities plans are those whose disabilities correspond to the functional definition of a developmental disability (see Lippman & Loberg, Chapter 3, this volume). In general, federal guidelines suggest that state plans include estimates of the state's developmentally disabled population, as well as demographic information on the developmental disabilities population, both by age and geography, and an analysis of the issues and concerns that influence the lives of and services for persons with developmental disabilities. The plans must include goals and objectives for the state as well as strategies for the coordination of the diverse services available under a variety of federally mandated or enabled state programs. The plans also must include assurances that the states will comply with various provisions of the Developmental Disabilities Act.

PLANNING UNDER PROVISIONS OF THE OLDER AMERICANS ACT

The provisions of the Older Americans Act of 1965 (PL 89-73, as amended) call for each state unit on aging to have in force a state plan on aging in order to qualify for federal funds for state and community programs authorized under the act. States may choose to use a 2-, 3-, or 4-year plan format, with possible annual revisions. Plans are developed by the state's agency on aging in cooperation with the state's Older Americans Act advisory committee, and are based upon the state's area agencies on aging plans. Generally such state plans, consistent with federal guidelines issued by the federal Administration on Aging, include assurances of state compliance with the requirements of Title III of the Act, specific program objectives, and objectives linked to the coordination of the activities of the state's area agencies on aging as well as of the other state agencies serving older individuals.

Under the Act, the substantive plans are those developed and maintained by each area agency on aging. The Act requires that each area agency have in force, and have approved by the state aging agency, an area plan that addresses how the area agency will: 1) provide for, through a comprehensive and coordinated approach, supportive services, nutrition services, and a system of other community-based services; 2) ensure that support services associated with access to services, such as transportation, outreach, and information and referral are available; 3) provide for inhome services (such as homemaker and home health aide, visiting and telephone reassurance, and chore maintenance); and 4) provide for legal services.

Eligibility for services under the Act is generally limited to persons age 60 and older. Exceptions are made for younger spouses or individuals living with persons 60 or older in certain residential settings. Specifically, the Act enables states to provide for a range of services, including residential, inhome supports, transportation, legal aid, and nutrition services; serve as an ombudsman in matters related to long-term care; and provide for centers where services for older persons can be co-located and more effectively coordinated.

PLANNING UNDER PROVISIONS OF THE NATIONAL HEALTH PLANNING ACT

Under the National Health Planning and Resources Development Act of 1974 (PL 93-641, as amended), the state's health planning and development agency (SHPDA) is responsible for conducting health planning activities in the state. It is aided in its work by the state's statewide health coordinating council (SHCC), a body of citizens appointed by the state's governor. The Act authorizes the establishment of regional health systems agencies whose purposes, among others, are to improve the health of the residents of their service areas, to increase the availability, accessibility, acceptability, continuity, quality, and cost-effectiveness of the health services in their areas, and, at least triennially, to issue a health systems plan (with its attendant annual implementation plans), which is a detailed statement of goals describing a "healthful environment" and responsive to the needs and resources of its area. Furthermore, each state's SHPDA is charged to prepare, at least triennially, a state health plan that reflects the health systems plans of its state and is subject to approval by the governor. The plan is to be a synthesis of strategies that would promote a comprehensive approach to the delivery and promotion of health care and maintenance services.

In most states, state health plans and health systems plans address critical health promotion and health systems actions designed to bring about a healthier population. Increments of improvement in health systems, of course, are easier to substantiate than immediate improvements in the population's health status.

Although the Act specifically refers to the

coverage of mental health, alcoholism, and substance abuse concerns, inclusion of mentally retarded and/or developmentally disabled populations in these health-oriented plans (as has been done in several states) is usually the result of administrative decisions at the executive or state agency level, or recommendation by the SHCC. Since PL 93-641 does not specifically include references to mental retardation or developmental disabilities as a population of concern (in contrast to mental health, alcoholism, and substance abuse), inclusion of concerns related to developmental disabilities is discretionary. As long as it is clear that health promotion implies more than simply medical concerns, inclusion of developmental disabilities in state health plans can be a constructive example of interagency cooperation.

Most states now recognize elderly individuals as a population to be included within the health planning structure, since the SHPDA must concern itself with both utilization of acute and long-term care services and related institutional programs. The inclusion of the older developmentally disabled population within such plans is a natural consequence, particularly because these individuals represent a population group that consumes an inordinate proportion of acute and long-term care services (see Jacobson, Sutton, & Janicki, Chapter 7, this volume).

PLANNING FOUNDATIONS

Services, to be fully comprehensive, must be organized and administered in a manner that will anticipate and meet the needs of a variety of individuals with disabilities of differing levels of impairment. Planning is fundamental to the forging of a reasonable and responsive system of services. One of the outcomes of planning is the development and issuance of a working document, or plan, that delineates how the system will respond to the needs of its constituency. An adequate and purposive plan must answer the following questions:

Who is to be served?
How many are there of those to be served?

What are their needs?
Are there sufficient existing services to meet their needs?
What and where are the gaps in services?
What should be done to best meet their needs?

These questions lead to several general planning process steps. These include: 1) the definition of the population to be served, 2) the assessment of the needs of the population and the resources available or needed to meet those needs, 3) the definition of the service system and an identification of the gaps in the system in relation to the needs of the constituency, and 4) the determination of how to best address service gaps.

Defining the Population

There are no set planning guidelines on the definition of the older developmentally disabled population. Marsha Seltzer (Chapter 9) and Janicki, Otis, Pucchio, Rettig, and Jacobson (Chapter 17) note that a variety of age delineations have been used, most defining the older developmentally disabled population as those individuals in their sixth decade of life and older. Furthermore, as Table 1 shows, a large percentage of state developmental disabilities plans designate aging/elderly developmentally disabled persons as those who are age 65 or older. Since age 60 is the initial age for eligibility for programs under the Older Americans Act, state councils should use this age point for beginning to designate the older developmentally disabled population. In fact, when publishing population estimates, state plans should consider using either the following age categories: age 50–59, 60–74, and 75 and older, or 55+ and 60+. The one area where age-related definitional problems may be particularly troublesome is with mentally retarded persons with Down syndrome; for this group, biological aging can be apparent much earlier, often during an individual's late 30s or early 40s. In these instances and in instances where Alzheimer's disease, progeria, or similar conditions are present, special provisions must be made to include persons with premature aging in the definition of the older or aging/elderly developmentally disabled population.

Table 1. Results of survey of state developmental disabilities councils and state aging agencies relative to planning for older developmental disabilities populations

Planning/coordination issue	State DD plans (N = 46)	State aging plans (N = 45)
Percentage of states:		
—having specific reference to elderly developmentally dis- abled population in the developmental disabilities state plan	48%	NA
—having specific reference to elderly developmentally dis- abled population in the state aging plan	NA	9%
—defining older developmentally disabled persons as 65 and older	41%	NA
—defining older developmentally disabled persons as 62 and older	4%	NA
—defining older developmentally disabled persons as 55 and older	6%	NA
—having a working definition of older developmentally dis- abled population	6%	4%
—with any type of state level interagency agreement related to older developmentally disabled population	26%	43%
—having specific estimate of the size of their older develop- mentally disabled population	50%	24%
—using federal act grant process to fund special projects for older developmentally disabled persons	15%	11%
—indicating that consideration will be given to older developmentally disabled population in future plan updates	39%	52%

Adapted from Janicki, Ackerman, and Jacobson (1984).

Defining the older developmentally disabled population also includes estimating the numbers of individuals encompassed within the definition for each jurisdiction under consideration. In these instances, data readily available from the United States Census should be of assistance. Table 2 provides the 1982 United States population figures for persons age 55 +, 60 +, and 65 + by state. Table 3 provides the percentage of each state's older persons in these age groups. Figure 1 illustrates the variability of the number of older persons across the states.

Table 4 offers suggested estimates of the number and relative percentages (in relation to the estimated overall number of such individuals in the nation) of the older developmentally disabled population for each state. These were derived from the older developmentally disabled population numbers offered by Jacobson, Sutton, and Janicki (Chapter 7, this volume) and adjusted for the proportion of older persons in the state. Since in most instances, no definitive data are available on the specific numbers of older developmentally disabled persons by state, these estimates may prove

helpful. However, care should be taken in using these estimates. Planners should note that state age-specific rates will vary depending upon extent of generational cohorts, in-state population distributions, and the state's in-migration and out-migration patterns, particularly in those states that have significant populations of individuals who have settled there following retirement.

Currently, no uniform mental retardation/ developmental disabilities data systems exist in the United States that would offer comprehensive population-based national information on the older developmentally disabled population (Rowitz, 1984). However, through the state agency responsible for mental retardation and/ or developmental disabilities services, a number of states do maintain computerized registry-type data bases that can be used by planners to derive treated prevalence estimates. The information available from these registries offers the best available source of data that could be used by planners at either the state or local level. For example, Tables 5, 6, 7, and 8 illustrate the character, respectively, of New York's and California's older developmentally

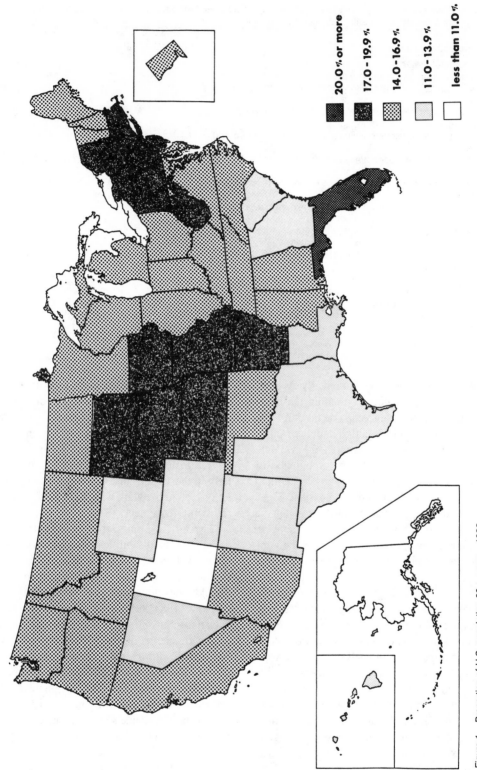

Figure 1. Proportion of U.S. population 60 + years—1982.

Legend:
20.0% or more
17.0 - 19.9%
14.0 - 16.9%
11.0 - 13.9%
less than 11.0%

148

Table 2.   Select age groups of older U.S. population by state[a]

State	All ages	55+ years	60+ years	65+ years
1. Alabama	3,943	825	635	461
2. Alaska	438	36	23	13
3. Arizona	2,860	606	473	340
4. Arkansas	2,291	543	433	323
5. California	24,724	4,843	3,640	2,553
6. Colorado	3,045	503	376	264
7. Connecticut	3,153	725	550	387
8. Delaware	602	122	91	63
9. District of Columbia	631	135	103	73
10. Florida	10,416	3,008	2,428	1,808
11. Georgia	5,639	1,023	775	549
12. Hawaii	994	175	126	85
13. Idaho	965	180	140	101
14. Illinois	11,448	2,406	1,829	1,313
15. Indiana	5,471	1,123	854	614
16. Iowa	2,905	676	535	401
17. Kansas	2,408	545	426	316
18. Kentucky	3,667	757	584	426
19. Louisiana	4,362	785	591	419
20. Maine	1,133	255	199	147
21. Maryland	4,265	830	612	420
22. Massachusetts	5,781	1,341	1,036	751
23. Michigan	9,109	1,809	1,358	964
24. Minnesota	4,137	860	674	502
25. Mississippi	2,551	517	404	299
26. Missouri	4,951	1,144	895	666
27. Montana	801	161	125	90
28. Nebraska	1,586	355	280	212
29. Nevada	881	162	117	77
30. New Hampshire	951	196	151	109
31. New Jersey	7,438	1,709	1,286	900
32. New Mexico	1,359	238	179	126
33. New York	17,659	4,043	3,074	2,198
34. North Carolina	6,019	1,214	917	648
35. North Dakota	670	142	112	84
36. Ohio	10,791	2,293	1,727	1,224
37. Oklahoma	3,177	685	532	390
38. Oregon	2,649	566	443	325
39. Pennsylvania	11,865	2,943	2,251	1,604
40. Rhode Island	958	239	184	132
41. South Carolina	3,203	593	446	310
42. South Dakota	691	159	126	94
43. Tennessee	4,651	977	750	542
44. Texas	15,280	2,715	2,037	1,442
45. Utah	1,554	222	167	118
46. Vermont	516	104	82	60
47. Virginia	5,491	1,041	775	537
48. Washington	4,245	842	649	464
49. West Virginia	1,948	445	341	247
50. Wisconsin	4,765	1,027	800	592
51. Wyoming	502	77	57	39
TOTALS	231,534	48,918	37,397	26,824

Source: U.S. Bureau of the Census, Current Population Reports, Series P-25, No. 930, "Estimates of the Population of States, by Age: July 1, 1981, and 1982" and unpublished tabulations.

[a]Numbers in thousands.

Table 3.   Select age groups of older U.S. population as percentage of total state population

State	55+ years	60+ years	65+ years
1. Alabama	20.9	16.1	11.7
2. Alaska	8.3	5.2	3.1
3. Arizona	21.2	16.6	11.9
4. Arkansas	23.7	18.9	14.1
5. California	19.6	14.7	10.3
6. Colorado	16.5	12.3	8.7
7. Connecticut	23.0	17.4	12.3
8. Delaware	20.3	15.1	10.4
9. District of Columbia	21.4	16.3	11.6
10. Florida	28.9	23.3	17.4
11. Georgia	18.1	13.7	9.7
12. Hawaii	17.6	12.7	8.5
13. Idaho	18.6	14.5	10.5
14. Illinois	21.0	16.0	11.5
15. Indiana	20.5	15.6	11.2
16. Iowa	23.3	18.4	13.8
17. Kansas	22.6	17.7	13.1
18. Kentucky	20.6	15.9	11.6
19. Louisiana	18.0	13.6	9.6
20. Maine	22.5	17.5	12.9
21. Maryland	19.5	14.4	9.9
22. Massachusetts	23.2	17.9	13.0
23. Michigan	19.9	14.9	10.6
24. Minnesota	20.8	16.3	12.1
25. Mississippi	20.3	15.8	11.7
26. Missouri	23.1	18.1	13.5
27. Montana	20.1	15.6	11.3
28. Nebraska	22.4	17.7	13.3
29. Nevada	18.3	13.3	8.7
30. New Hampshire	20.6	15.8	11.5
31. New Jersey	23.0	17.3	12.1
32. New Mexico	17.5	13.2	9.3
33. New York	22.9	17.4	12.4
34. North Carolina	20.2	15.2	10.8
35. North Dakota	21.2	16.8	12.5
36. Ohio	21.3	16.0	11.3
37. Oklahoma	21.6	16.7	12.3
38. Oregon	21.4	16.7	12.3
39. Pennsylvania	24.8	19.0	13.5
40. Rhode Island	24.9	19.2	13.8
41. South Carolina	18.5	13.9	9.7
42. South Dakota	23.0	18.2	13.7
43. Tennessee	21.0	16.1	11.6
44. Texas	17.8	13.3	9.4
45. Utah	14.3	10.8	7.6
46. Vermont	20.2	15.8	11.7
47. Virginia	19.0	14.1	9.8
48. Washington	19.8	15.3	10.9
49. West Virginia	22.8	17.5	12.7
50. Wisconsin	21.6	16.8	12.4
51. Wyoming	15.3	11.3	7.9
TOTALS	21.1	16.2	11.6

Source: U.S. Bureau of the Census, *Current Population Reports,* Series P-25, No. 930, "Estimates of the Population of States, by Age: July 1, 1981, and 1982" and unpublished tabulations.

Table 4. Estimates of number of older developmentally disabled persons (age 55+ and 60+) by state and percent of state older developmentally disabled population relative to total in nation[a][b]

State	Developmentally disabled population age 55+		Developmentally disabled population age 60+	
	Estimated state population N	State population relative to national %	Estimated state population N	State population relative to national %
1. Alabama	3,300	1.68	2,540	1.70
2. Alaska	144	0.01	92	0.01
3. Arizona	2,424	1.24	1,892	1.26
4. Arkansas	2,172	1.11	1,732	1.16
5. California	19,372	9.90	14,560	9.77
6. Colorado	2,012	1.03	1,504	1.01
7. Connecticut	2,900	1.48	2,200	1.48
8. Delaware	488	0.25	364	0.24
9. District of Columbia	540	0.28	412	0.27
10. Florida	12,032	6.15	9,712	6.52
11. Georgia	4,092	2.09	3,100	2.08
12. Hawaii	700	0.36	504	0.34
13. Idaho	720	0.37	560	0.38
14. Illinois	9,624	4.92	7,316	4.91
15. Indiana	4,492	2.30	3,416	2.30
16. Iowa	2,704	1.38	2,140	1.44
17. Kansas	2,180	1.11	1,704	1.14
18. Kentucky	3,028	1.55	2,336	1.57
19. Louisiana	3,140	1.60	2,364	1.59
20. Maine	1,020	0.52	796	0.53
21. Maryland	3,320	1.70	2,448	1.64
22. Massachusetts	5,364	2.74	4,144	2.78
23. Michigan	7,236	3.70	5,432	3.64
24. Minnesota	3,440	1.76	2,696	1.81
25. Mississippi	2,068	1.06	1,616	1.08
26. Missouri	4,576	2.34	3,580	2.40
27. Montana	644	0.33	500	0.33
28. Nebraska	1,420	0.73	1,120	0.75
29. Nevada	648	0.33	468	0.31
30. New Hampshire	784	0.40	604	0.40
31. New Jersey	6,836	3.49	5,144	3.45
32. New Mexico	952	0.49	716	0.48
33. New York	16,172	8.26	12,296	8.25
34. North Carolina	4,856	2.48	3,668	2.46
35. North Dakota	568	0.29	448	0.30
36. Ohio	9,172	4.69	6,908	4.63
37. Oklahoma	2,740	1.40	2,128	1.43
38. Oregon	2,264	1.16	1,772	1.19
39. Pennsylvania	11,772	6.01	9,004	6.04
40. Rhode Island	956	0.49	736	0.49
41. South Carolina	2,372	1.21	1,784	1.20
42. South Dakota	636	0.34	504	0.34
43. Tennessee	3,908	2.00	3,000	2.01
44. Texas	10,860	5.55	8,148	5.47
45. Utah	888	0.45	668	0.46
46. Vermont	416	0.21	328	0.22
47. Virginia	4,164	2.18	3,100	2.08
48. Washington	3,368	1.72	2,596	1.74
49. West Virginia	1,780	0.91	1,364	0.92
50. Wisconsin	4,108	2.10	3,200	2.15
51. Wyoming	308	0.16	228	0.15
TOTALS	195,680	100.00	149,592	100.00

[a]Population estimates based upon an older developmentally disabled population projection of 0.396% of the same age general population (*Source:* Jacobson, Sutton, & Janicki, Chapter 7, this volume).

[b]1982 U.S. population projections.

Table 5.   Distribution of the general and developmentally disabled populations in New York[a]

Age group[b] (years)	% New York population	% NY population Males	% NY population Females	% DD population[c]	% NY DD population Males	% NY DD population Females
0–12	13.2	51	49	11.7	61	39
13–22	17.1	50	50	18.6	61	39
23–32	16.8	48	52	27.2	57	43
33–42	14.0	47	53	16.9	54	46
43–52	10.5	47	53	9.2	54	46
53–62	11.3	46	54	8.0	52	48
63–72	8.9	44	56	5.0	49	51
73–82	5.6	38	62	2.2	41	59
83+	2.6	32	68	.6	32	68
Total N	17,557,228	8,339,422	9,217,806	49,954	28,071	21,883

[a]Adapted from Janicki and MacEachron (1984).

[b]Age groups reflect 10-year interval cohorts (e.g., 73–82 age group was born between 1900 and 1909).

[c]Registered on New York's Office of Mental Retardation and Developmental Disabilities' Developmental Disabilities Information System (DDIS).

disabled populations. Although it is assumed that other states' older developmentally disabled populations will differ in some respects, these tables offer an example of how population information could be used to help an area delineate its older developmentally disabled population.

In summary, the definition of an older developmentally disabled population should include: 1) agreement on the age group to be

Table 6.   Comparisons of demographic, disability, and basic skill characteristics among elderly developmentally disabled persons in New York by age group

	Age group		
	Ages 53–62 (N = 3,927) %	Ages 63–72 (N = 2,476) %	Ages 73–99 (N = 1,420) %
Sex			
Female	48	51	61
Male	52	49	39
Race			
White	90	96	95
Nonwhite	10	4	5
Developmental disability			
Cerebral palsy	8	5	3
Epilepsy	20	14	12
Mental retardation	94	95	94
Mild/moderate	41	42	38
Severe/profound	51	48	50
Independent in			
Mobility	80	79	67
Toileting	71	72	64
Eating	68	69	67
Dressing/grooming	47	49	43
Medication use	61	63	69
Special diet use	43	47	70
Physical disabilities	(n = 1,924)	(n = 1,436)	(n = 1,008)
Musculoskeletal	25	28	35
Special sense	29	32	45
Respiratory	3	4	7
Cardiovascular	19	32	57
Neurological	40	34	30
Digestive	8	9	11

Adapted from Janicki and MacEachron (1984).

Table 7.   Distribution of general and developmentally disabled populations in California[a]

Age group (years)	% California population	% California population Males	% California population Females	% DD population[b]	% CA DD population Males	% CA DD population Females
0–2	4.45	2.28	2.17	5.53	2.96	2.57
3–12	14.28	7.92	6.98	21.63	12.47	9.15
13–22	18.00	9.24	8.76	25.27	14.29	10.98
23–32	18.78	9.51	9.27	25.81	14.44	11.37
33–42	13.02	6.52	6.50	12.25	6.78	5.47
43–52	9.96	4.93	5.04	4.95	2.59	2.36
53–62	9.73	4.63	5.10	3.06	1.57	1.48
63–72	6.82	3.07	3.75	1.20	0.56	0.64
73–82	3.63	1.42	2.21	0.28	0.11	0.17
83+	1.32	0.40	0.92	0.04	0.02	0.03
TOTAL	23,667,902	11,666,485	12,001,417	66,899	37,323	29,576

[a]Adapted from Sutton (1983).

[b]Registered on California's Department of Developmental Services' Client Developmental Evaluation Report (CDER).

Table 8.   Comparisons of demographic, disability, and basic skill characteristics among elderly developmentally disabled persons in California by age group[a]

Characteristic	Ages 53–62 (N = 3,046) %	Ages 63–72 (N = 800) %	Ages 73–99 (N = 215) %
Sex			
Male	51.47	46.50	40.46
Female	48.53	53.50	59.54
Ethnicity			
Other	18.38	17.50	9.30
White	81.62	82.50	90.70
Cerebral palsy			
No	85.78	87.88	88.37
Yes	14.22	12.13	11.63
Epilepsy			
No	74.73	82.13	80.47
Yes	25.27	17.88	19.54
MR level			
Mild/moderate	54.06	56.13	48.37
Severe/profound	38.81	38.13	42.79
Other	7.14	5.75	8.84
Other skill areas[b]			
Mobility			
No	15.45	17.88	31.16
Yes	84.56	82.13	68.84
Toileting			
No	6.55	7.00	7.91
Yes	93.45	93.00	92.09
Eating			
No	4.99	5.88	5.58
Yes	95.01	94.12	94.42
Dressing			
No	15.15	17.38	19.07
Yes	84.85	82.62	80.93

[a]Adapted from Sutton (1983).

[b]"Other skill areas" indicates areas of competence; that is, if the response is "no," the client is reported to have deficiencies in the area, and if "yes," the client does not have reported deficiencies in the area.

included, 2) agreement on the types of individuals to be included, and 3) an estimate of the scope of the population.

Needs Assessments

Needs assessments are generally designed to determine the characteristics and service needs, and service utilization patterns of a particular population (Milord, 1976; Warheit, Bell, & Schwab, 1977). A needs assessment can have two primary targets: 1) the population of an area, and 2) the service providers within that area. Determining the number of developmentally disabled individuals in a geographic area aids in defining their met and unmet service needs. Identifying the providers in an area and what services they provide aids in determining the extent of available services and the corresponding gaps. Such information facilitates the projection of the number of individuals needing specialized services within a geographic area, taking into account individual characteristics such as severity of disability, age, and residential living arrangement. It also aids in determining goals for service development and the potential capability of service providers to accommodate unmet needs.

Large-Scale Needs Assessments Needs assessment approaches can vary, particularly in terms of the focus of the assessment. Large-scale needs assessment efforts approach the assessment on a population basis. Targeted needs assessments focus on a segment of an issue and offer partial, yet helpful, information that can further aid in planning. Large-scale needs assessments can be done in conjunction with a client-find effort or registry-development approach. Such approaches have been carried out in a number of areas (for example, in the Lower Mainland region of British Columbia in Canada, the state of Victoria in Australia, the Wessex region of the United Kingdom, and the states of California, Massachusetts, Minnesota, New York, and Oregon in the United States) (Blenner-Hassett, 1984; Cocks & Ng, 1983; D. Felch, personal communication, 1983; J. Ratcliffe, personal communication, 1984). These efforts generally use standardized computer-compatible survey forms

that are developed and distributed by the area's public mental retardation or mental handicap authority. The results of the surveys are collected, tabulated, and then used for a number of purposes. Most of these surveys include items related to client demographics, disability characteristics, basic competency skills, physical and health status, residential status and needs, and day program and clinical service status and needs. These broad client-find efforts have produced useful treated prevalence indicators that permit the estimation and description of an area's developmentally disabled population; such efforts also obviously aid in defining the scope and character of the area's older developmentally disabled population. However, these data have their limitations. Most efforts of this sort inevitably are biased; that is, they pick up on persons in service rather than from all population segments. Therefore, unless very extensive, they are primarily useful in targeting service improvements and secondarily useful in developing comprehensive population descriptions.

Targeted Needs Assessments Although not as broad in scope, targeted needs assessments are conducted with a specific focus. A good example is the assessment of needs of metropolitan Toronto's older mentally retarded population that was conducted by Ontario's Metropolitan Toronto Association for the Mentally Retarded (Anglin, 1981). Using two short questionnaires, the Association's staff surveyed a number of older mentally retarded individuals and their families. The surveys covered the following areas: personal/family data, present home, previous placements, self-sufficiency abilities, health, work, recreation, friends, advocacy, and guardianship. The Association used the results of their survey to identify a number of unmet needs among their clientele. They also developed a number of recommendations for services that were used by the Association in setting up new programs. Targeted assessments of this type can be very useful when conducted by local or area authorities as well as by service agencies concerned with new service demands.

Often, local conditions will dictate whether

local assessments should be carried out, or whether more general national information sources will suffice in assessing service gaps. Needs assessments, in general, have been found to be useful tools. Robins (1982) noted that most agencies take such efforts seriously and tend to alter their policies based upon the findings of such efforts. Assessments designed and implemented by users also tend to be more valued than those done by outsiders (even though those done by outsiders are usually more methodologically sound). Robins also noted that needs assessments are most valuable when they are integrated into an organization's planning process.

System Definition and Gaps Analysis

Two important assumptions to system definition are that services are parts of an overall system and that legal or regulatory structures aid in shaping it. A service system is a network of specialized and generic services linked for a common purpose. These services, from a planning perspective, can be organized into subsystems or components. Terminology defining these components can vary, but the essential character of these parts will not. Generally, the types of services that older developmentally disabled persons need can be clustered within four major service categories: 1) support services, 2) living arrangements, 3) activity services, and 4) health care. These four domains are, for the most part, mutually exclusive and account for the major service need areas of any older individual's life.

In planning for an older developmentally disabled population, provisions must be made to accommodate each of these domains. Each of these domains can also have aspects of a continuum. For example, living arrangements represent a variety of settings, ranging from the most restrictive (such as nursing homes or public institutions) to the least restrictive (such as the individual's own home or a shared, unsupervised apartment). Alternatives in each domain must be present within, or accessible to, the local services system to accommodate the diverse needs of the locality's older developmentally disabled population.

Once these parameters of the system are delineated and the elements of the components more fully defined, examination can be made regarding whether the system offers what the population needs. The assessment of the gaps is where planning is most potent; follow-up is reflected by the recommendations or actions that address domain-centered system gaps and needs of the target population.

Assessing the system's ability to be responsive and identifying unmet needs of older developmentally disabled persons also involve examining a number of system structural aspects. One such aspect is the state's or province's statutes and regulatory environment. For example, it may be determined that regulatory barriers prevent the successful adaptation of existing programs for an older developmentally disabled clientele. This may happen in instances where a state's regulations governing retardation/developmental services programs pose unnecessary barriers to flexible programming or shifting to more age-appropriate activities for older persons. Furthermore, statutes may not specifically encourage access to the particular generic programs or services that would prove especially beneficial to older developmentally disabled persons. In the absence of enabling legislation, or when regulatory barriers are identified, planning may provide the primary vehicle for the development of agency policies or interagency agreements to enhance change and improve accessibility.

Another aspect of planning is an assessment of the system's support structures, in particular, informal supports such as parental capacities (and conversely the need for parental supports). In regard to parental supports, the problems are acute. Many adult developmentally disabled persons beyond middle age have parents who are in their 70s or older, and who are experiencing diminished capacities due to their own aging. Assessments and planning must consider how to address the problems posed by older developmentally disabled persons living at home with elderly parents. Service need projections must consider a broader clientele than just the disabled individual. Furthermore, research has indicated that supports in the form of services are preferable to other forms of assistance, such as financial aid (e.g., Horowitz & Shindelman, 1984). Consequently, planning must anticipate a greater potential demand upon support services.

Finally, changing demands for care, both in residential settings and at day program sites, may pose different demands upon staffing patterns, staff capability, and the site's physical environment. Assessment of system gaps and planning must consider these aspects of the service system and anticipate where shifts of the older developmentally disabled population will create significant demands and require changes in patterns of care. Furthermore, planning should also address how workers in the developmental disabilities services arena will be exposed to geriatric and gerontology inservice programs. Another area is examining the extent of physical barriers that serve as impediments to the point of service. Planning, in particular capital planning, must take into account requirements to change buildings and make service areas physically accessible.

In summary, planning must include a process that allows for system definition and an assessment of service gaps. These aspects are particularly important in planning services for a population (such as older developmentally disabled people) that historically has not had a natural provider system upon which to rely.

Addressing System Gaps

Planning to address the needs of a population as diverse as older developmentally disabled people must involve an acknowledgment of all the components of a geographic area's services structure. Table 9 offers a listing of a variety of public agencies and the associated services that may affect planning for an older developmentally disabled population. All these facets of public service structure must be taken into account when addressing system gaps. Illustrative of this would be a plan that accommodates the diversity of needs of its target population, including: health-oriented residential care, sheltered housing, and inhome supports to accommodate residential care needs; socialization, vocational, day care, and recreation services to accommodate day program needs; counseling, guardianship, placement/permanency planning, pastoral supports, and attendant care services to accommodate family and support service needs; and medical, physical rehabilitation, nutrition, and nursing care to accommodate health care needs. Such a plan would have to acknowledge available local resources, financial supports, and access and referral mechanisms existing within a range of public and private agencies. Furthermore, population and utilization pattern estimates would need to be linked to the various sources of these ser-

Table 9. Services related to older developmentally disabled persons and primary governmental agency

Agency type	Services
Social services, public welfare, human resources, and so forth	Adult protective, advocacy, homemaker, counseling, crisis intervention, legal, information and referral, transportation, case management, sheltered care, food supplementation, financial supports
Housing	Public housing, sheltered housing, retirement communities, senior citizen housing, rent control, home energy assistance, rental subsidies
Health, public health	Health care, hospitalization, skilled nursing care, nutrition, health maintenance
Aging, elder affairs	Nutrition, senior centers, legal assistance, advocacy, social activities, transportation, housing assistance, employment
Mental health, mental hygiene	Psychiatric care, counseling, family supports
Mental retardation, developmental disabilities, mental handicap, and so forth	Vocational, habilitative, and socialization activities, residential care, case management, family services, employment, recreation and leisure activities

vices, and potential and actual gaps identified. The plan would consequently indicate to the participating agencies where demand will fall and what resources need to be redirected to accommodate shifts in the identified demand.

At the same time, plans and the planning process serve several other functions. The area's key agencies, funding sources, legislators, public officials, and others responsible for older people with developmental disabilities have, in such planning documents, statements of both the status of the service system and the goals and objectives that serve to help shape policies and operations. Such statements form the basis for implementation or action plans that would move from general goals and objectives to very specific activities, actions, or initiatives that involve identified actors, time lines for stages of completion, and required resources.

Aside from the direct effects on system development, planning for an older developmentally disabled population should begin with a set of conceptual fundamentals that permit analyses of, and response to, the complexity of problems facing older developmentally disabled people. For example, a categorical approach to clustering service domains was proposed earlier in this chapter; such a clustering approach can facilitate plan activities that focus on specific plan sections. The first domain, support services, can be promoted through both the formal and informal networks of services. Process issues include how the formal system can provide transportation, recreation, respite, and other support services that bolster, rather than replace, those services provided by the informal system. Furthermore, plan activities should indicate how these services are to be funded, and to what extent the generic care system should be involved.

The second domain, living arrangements, includes process issues such as how to provide for as much independent living as possible, recognizing diminishing family supports as parents die or become frail, the compounding effects on behavior of both aging and a developmental disability, the degree of structured care required, and a policy commitment that promotes integration into the generic care system and society in general. Planning must consider the demand for out-of-home care, particularly in health-related or skilled nursing facilities, as older developmentally disabled persons develop conditions that require more medically oriented care. Activities in this domain must account for the means to address the residential care needs of older developmentally disabled persons with age-related diminished capacities. Additionally considered must be the system capacities that will address current and future residential needs.

The activity services domain, including such program services as sheltered workshops and day training and developmental activities, is another process issue area where it is particularly appropriate to implement tailor-made programs for older developmentally disabled persons. On the one hand, custodial care without programming should not be an option; on the other hand, highly intense programming, as provided for younger developmentally disabled persons, may not be wholly appropriate for a population that is experiencing diminishing function and is at the stage of life where disengagement and retirement are considered typical. Planning activities related to addressing service needs within this domain must be sensitive to this balance of demands and anticipate changes in needs for involvement in day services. Cooperative planning between developmental services and aging agencies would aid in promoting responsive day services.

The primary process issue raised within the health services domain is how to best provide for increasing health services needs across the continua of care. However, confounding this is the broader issue of serving a proportionately greater number of elderly people and an increasing elderly developmentally disabled population in the face of shrinking resources and more competition for these resources among human services providers. Then there are the problems associated with the accessibility and appropriateness of health care services. As deinstitutionalization has progressed, one of the side effects has been less attention to the medical services provided in institutional settings. Since institutions now typically serve a more physically disabled and older population, planning must consider how to bolster, where necessary, medical services. When structured care is provided in the community, it is necessary to ensure accessibility to health care services. Part of this can be addressed by activities related to medical staff training and retraining in the exigencies of aging and developmental disabilities. Moreover, in less restrictive settings, older people with developmental disabilities must be provided with access to a generic health care system that will serve them without prejudice and with an appreciation of their functional needs. Consequently, in addressing health services domain issues, determinations of system capacities should lead to the identification of strategies that would increase availability and improve accessibility of health services. In this regard, the coordination of developmental disabilities planning with the state's health planning process would be both advisable and beneficial.

In summary, service domain-based strategies related to promoting greater responsibility of the specialized and generic systems have their foundations in basic planning principles. Coupled with legislation or administrative direction calling for planning, the definition of the population, needs assessment, system definitions and gaps analyses, and methods of addressing population needs are critical factors in defining and addressing the needs of an older and aging developmentally disabled population.

COMMENTARY

Older developmentally disabled persons are, in one respect, a new population of concern. Little or no planning has been attendant with this population. Recently, a limited number of studies have noted the presence and characteristics of older developmentally disabled individuals and have underscored the necessity to anticipate changing needs from adulthood through the later years of life. Some have suggested approaches for the provision of services. Unfortunately, these approaches do not provide sufficient guidance, in and of themselves, toward general administrative and specific planning initiatives.

Planning for an older developmentally disabled population should reflect both systemic realities and the demands of this population. Certain considerations are evident. First, population statistics should be used that consider at least those individuals age 60 and older; second, individuals who age prematurely must be included; third, emphases within service domains should be shifted to reflect greater needs for support and health care and a decreased demand for vocational services; fourth, strategies for integration of older developmentally disabled persons within generic aging services (related to the Older Americans Act) should be considered; fifth, how services will be financed must be considered; and sixth, planning efforts must address the basic questions raised earlier in this chapter.

At present, planning efforts in the areas of aging and disablement are plagued by uncertainties about the size of the population, the needs of the population, and the manner in which these persons are to be served. Initial analyses (see Jacobson, Sutton, & Janicki, Chapter 7, this volume) suggest that although the older population is continuing to grow in numbers, many older disabled persons are not now receiving services from the specialized developmental disabilities system. While other types of state and local agencies are undoubtedly providing some services to this population, experience suggests that these services will not fully address all care needs, nor will they be based in a philosophy of care that is fully responsive to the nature of developmental disablement. Further evaluation of the overall population is needed if a substantive basis for deliberate service development is to be established. Population-based studies on the following aspects are critical:

Demographic studies to assess the scope of the population of those developmentally disabled persons age 60 and above and those persons in their middle-age years (age 40 and above)

Longitudinal research on mortality to more adequately assess contemporary trends, especially for the large proportion of disabled persons who have never been institutionalized

Applications of information that exists in state data systems, both to assess program placement practices and to permit the estimation of probable difficulties in service availability and accessibility

Research on program models that can most effectively accommodate the changing health and habilitative care needs of aging and elderly disabled persons without recourse to inherently limited and debilitating institutional alternatives

Clinical studies, especially those that encompass a sufficient number of persons to justify generalization rather than a case study approach, that are needed to assess the magnitude of changes in care needs that take place, to identify those individuals who evidence premature or more substantive physical and behavioral declines and the extent to

which they constitute an important (or simply notable) segment of the aging disabled population, and to identify the clinical strategies that are most effective in promoting the maintenance of skills and positive life quality for older disabled persons

Initiatives at both the federal and state levels could effectively direct attention to the present and certainly to the future importance of the aging developmentally disabled population as both a social and fiscal phenomenon. Essentially, however, it will be the state planners and administrators who will be responsible for assessing population characteristics, elaborating on program models, supporting the development of a comprehensive service response for this population, and advocating for the financial resources needed to bring this response to actuality. It is the carefully designed and integrated use of the various statutory planning structures available within the states that will offer the vehicle for developing services for the older developmentally disabled population.

REFERENCES

Anglin, B. (1981). *They never asked for help: A study on the needs of elderly retarded people in Metro Toronto.* Maple, Ontario: Belsten Publishing Co.

Blenner-Hassett, M. (1984). *Incidence/prevalence of mental retardation in British Columbia.* Unpublished report, Woodlands Center, New Westminster, BC.

Braddock, D. (1981). Deinstitutionalization of the retarded: Trends in public policy. *Hospital and Community Psychiatry, 32,* 607–615.

Bradley, V. J. (1978). *Deinstitutionalization of developmentally disabled persons: A conceptual analysis and guide.* Baltimore: University Park Press.

Cocks, E., & Ng, C. P. (1983). Characteristics of those persons with mental retardation registered with the mental retardation division. *Australia and New Zealand Journal of Developmental Disabilities, 9,* 117–127.

Horowitz, A., & Shindelman, L. W. (1984). Social and economic incentives for family caregivers. *Health Care Financing Review, 5*(2), 25–33.

Janicki, M. P., Ackerman, L., & Jacobson, J. W. (1984). *Survey of state developmental disabilities and aging plans relative to the state's older developmentally disabled population.* Albany: New York State Office of Mental Retardation and Developmental Disabilities.

Janicki, M. P., Castellani, P. J., & Norris, R. G. (1983). Organization and administration of service delivery sys-

tems. In J. Matson & J. Mulick (Eds.), *Handbook of mental retardation* (pp. 3–23). New York: Pergamon Press.

Janicki, M. P., & MacEachron, A. E. (1984). Residential, health and social service needs of elderly developmentally disabled persons. *The Gerontologist, 24,* 128–137.

Milord, J. T. (1976). Human service needs assessment: Three non-epidemiological approaches. *Canadian Psychological Review, 17,* 260–269.

Robins, B. J. (1982). Local response to planning mandates: The prevalence and utilization of needs assessment by human service agencies. *Evaluation and Program Planning, 5,* 199–208.

Rowitz, L. (1984). The need for uniform data reporting in mental retardation. *Mental Retardation, 22,* 1–3.

Sutton, M. (1983, August). *Treatment issues and the elderly institutionalized developmentally disabled individual.* Paper presented as part of symposium, "Service issues in growth and aging among retarded persons," at the annual convention of the American Psychological Association, Anaheim, CA.

Warheit, G. J., Bell, R. A., & Schwab, J. J. (1977). *Needs assessment approaches: Concepts and methods.* Washington, DC: Alcohol, Drug Abuse, and Mental Health Administration.

chapter

9

Research in Social
Aspects of Aging
and Developmental Disabilities

Marsha Mailick Seltzer

This chapter addresses the special methodological challenges that are encountered in the course of research on the aging process and on the aging developmentally disabled individual. Drawing primarily from the field of gerontology, which has developed a considerable literature in this area, this chapter examines three components in the research process—sampling, research design, and measurement. Regarding sampling, complexities involved in defining "old age" in a developmentally disabled population are considered. In addition, problems in obtaining representative samples are reviewed. Regarding design, the relative advantages of cross-sectional and longitudinal designs are discussed in light of threats to internal validity. Regarding measurement, instruments developed by the field of gerontology are reviewed and their transferability to research on developmentally disabled persons are considered. Finally, an agenda for future research on aging and developmental disabilities is offered, consisting of five areas currently in need of study, including: 1) basic demographic epidemiological descriptive data, 2) the identification of predictors of longevity and successful aging, 3) identification of unique features of the aging developmentally disabled group as distinct from nondevelopmentally disabled elderly and younger developmentally disabled adults, 4) the need for program evaluation, and 5) the assessment of the informal support systems of aging developmentally disabled persons.

THIS CHAPTER PRESENTS an overview of special methodological challenges that are encountered in the course of research on the aging process and on the aging individual. The discussion draws almost exclusively from publications from the field of gerontology and attempts to identify research methodological issues that are most applicable to the study of aging in developmentally disabled persons. It should be noted, however, that the applicability of major gerontological concepts and techniques to research on aging developmentally disabled persons remains unknown because so little research has been conducted to date on this population.

During the past several decades, a substantial literature has been assembled on special gerontological research methods. Research on

The author wishes to gratefully acknowledge the contributions of Dr. Marty Wyngaarden Krauss and Dr. Gary B. Seltzer, who commented on an earlier version of this chapter.

aging was defined by Birren (1959) as "the systematic inquiry into the regularities in the structures and functions of living organisms as they move forward in time in the latter part of the life span" (p. 5). In large part, the special methodological issues pertinent to research on aging are a function of this focus on the assessment of change in individuals over time. Many research questions on the aging process require longitudinal studies that involve repeated measurement of the same dependent variable in the same individuals over long periods of time. This type of research has the potential to be fraught with sampling, design, and measurement problems that could place substantial limitations on the validity of the generated findings. Gerontologists have developed strategies for use in the design and conduct of longitudinal research that minimize methodological problems such as those noted above. Gerontological methodologists have also addressed the problems inherent in cross-sectional designs that attempt to compare groups of individuals of different ages in order to make inferences about the aging process. Both types of designs are discussed below.

Although the field of gerontology has made great progress in the development of special methodological strategies, work in this area is by no means complete. Gerontology is a comparatively young field, and, as Maddox and Wiley (1976) have noted:

> recognition of aging as a social problem is recent; recognition of aging as a social scientific problem is more recent still. The social scientific study of aging needs but currently lacks widely shared paradigms which would provide common conceptualization of issues, standard measurements, and clearly defined agenda for the systematic testing of hypotheses derived from theory. (p. 4.)

This assessment is even more accurately descriptive of the current state of research on aging developmentally disabled persons. Thus, although gerontologists recognize the limitations in the progress made by their field in the study of aging as a social scientific (and be-

havioral) problem, much is to be gained in the field of developmental disabilities by becoming familiar with gerontologists' work in the area of research methodology.

The remainder of this chapter considers three major components in the research process—sampling, research design, and measurement—and for each identifies the special methodological issues that need to be addressed in research on the developmentally disabled aging population. The chapter concludes with the formulation of a research agenda in the area of aging and developmental disabilities.

SAMPLING

The first step in sample selection is defining the population. In the study of the aging developmentally disabled population, definitions of both "aging" and "developmental disabilities" are required. The current definition of a developmental disability, adopted in 1978 (PL 95-602: Rehabilitation, Comprehensive Services, and Developmental Disabilities Amendments of 1978), is as follows:

> The term developmental disability means a severe chronic disability of a person which
> (A) is attributable to a mental or physical impairment or combination of mental and physical impairments;
> (B) is manifested before the person attains age 22;
> (C) is likely to continue indefinitely;
> (D) results in substantial functional limitations in three or more of the following areas of major life activity: (i) self-care, (ii) receptive and expressive language, (iii) learning, (iv) mobility, (v) self-direction, (vi) capacity for independent living, and (vii) economic sufficiency; and
> (E) reflects the person's need for a combination and sequence of special, interdisciplinary, or generic care, treatment, or other services which are of lifelong or extended duration and are individually planned and coordinated.

For a full discussion of the various approaches to the definition and classification of developmental disabilities in general and mental retardation in specific, see G. Seltzer (1983).[1]

---

[1]Mentally retarded persons form the largest subgroup of the developmentally disabled population. Therefore, in this chapter, some points are illustrated with examples about mentally retarded persons in specific rather than developmentally disabled persons in general.

The definitions of "aging" and "elderly" are far more complicated. Demographically, age is defined in years. Common ages used to demarcate the onset of old age include 60, 62, 65, and 72 (Siegel, 1980). Some gerontologists (e.g., Streib, 1983) differentiate the "young old" (ages 65–74) and the "old-old" (ages 75 +), although other interval limits have also been used to divide the elderly into two age groups.

Several gerontologists have proposed alternative models for the definition of aging and old age. For example, Siegel (1980) suggested that old age could be defined as the period of life beginning at an arbitrarily chosen fixed number of years before the expected time of death for a particular subgroup of the population. For example, if the average life expectancy for men is 72 years and for women 78, and if the last 10 years of life are considered to be "old age," old age for men would begin at age 62 and for women at age 68. There are also functionally based definitions of old age. For example, Eisdorfer (1983) identified four stages in life: 1) children and youth in whom society invests resources in anticipation of future benefit, 2) adult workers (paid and unpaid) who generate the goods and services used by the entire society, 3) healthy persons who have retired from paid employment but who are not functionally dependent upon others, and 4) frail individuals who cannot function independently. Many moderately and severely developmentally disabled adults below the age of 55 would fall within Eisdorfer's categories 3 or 4 even though they are closer in chronological age to those in category 2. The absence of a high correlation between chronological age and functional abilities has long been recognized as a defining characteristic of the developmentally disabled.

Yet another approach to the definition of aging was summarized by Birren (1959), who conceptualized three components of aging: 1) biological aging, which is an individual's capacity for survival; 2) psychological aging, which is a function of changes in a person's "adaptive capacities," and 3) social aging, which is the extent to which an individual

fulfills the expected social and cultural roles. Both psychological and social age as defined by Birren contain elements of the American Association on Mental Deficiency's definition of adaptive behavior (Grossman, 1983), one of the three criteria used to define mental retardation. A serious lack of conceptual clarity would exist if in a study the same criteria were used in the definition of aging and mental retardation.

In research on developmentally disabled populations, the term "elderly" generally has been defined demographically (age in years). No studies have been conducted that employ more complex functional, psychological, or social definitions of aging. In the literature, various ages have been used as the lower limit of old age, including age 50 (Baker, Seltzer, & Seltzer, 1977; Talkington & Chiovaro, 1969), age 55 (Neuman, 1981; Segal, 1977; Seltzer, Seltzer, & Sherwood, 1982), and age 60 (O'Connor, Justice, & Warren, 1970).

Once a definition of the elderly developmentally disabled population has been chosen, the selection of a sample from this population can proceed. Depending upon the research question, the sample will include the elderly segment of the developmentally disabled population exclusively, or both elderly persons and younger adults. However, when only the elderly are studied, there is the possibility that correlations that in fact exist between age and variables of interest (e.g., health measures) will not be detected in the analysis because of restriction in the range of the age variable in the sample. That is, if in the total population, declining health is associated with advancing age, this inverse relationship might not be detected in the sample if only elderly persons are studied, since there will not be any younger, more healthy individuals with whom to compare the elderly, less healthy individuals. The problem of restriction in range will be less severe in the study of factors that are highly variable within the elderly developmentally disabled population. That is, if functional abilities decline markedly with age, it may be possible to detect this relationship in a sample made up only of individuals over the age of 55. However, when dimensions are studied that are more subtly related to age (e.g., life satisfaction), the exclusion of a younger adult comparison group could result in the incorrect conclusion that life satisfaction is not related to age.

Next, a strategy must be developed for selecting a sample that is as representative of the population as possible. General sampling theory and methods are, of course, applicable here. In addition, a few points specifically pertinent to the selection of representative samples among aging populations should be noted. First, a sample of adults selected at any point in the aging process will not be representative of the birth cohort of the sampled individuals. Among the general population of elderly persons, those who survive are systematically and substantially different from those who do not. The nonrepresentativeness of surviving cohorts is probably even more marked among the elderly developmentally disabled population due to the relatively higher incidence among the developmentally disabled population of genetic, metabolic, and physical disorders, birth traumas, and other disabilities that are associated with a shorter lifespan. Thus, generalizing from the surviving members of the cohort to the original birth cohort is ordinarily not warranted.

A second point regarding the representativeness of samples in research on aging pertains in particular to longitudinal studies. Even if samples are representative only of the surviving population at the time that they are selected, they generally lose their representativeness over time, as an increasing number of the sample members drop out at each time of data collection due to death, increasing frailty, geographical migration, or unwillingness to continue to participate in the study. Thus, over time, samples in longitudinal studies tend to become less representative than they were when they were first selected. This is one instance in which cross-sectional designs are superior to longitudinal designs.

Another limitation in the representativeness of a sample is introduced by the process of obtaining informed consent. Some research has been conducted on the general elderly population in order to identify characteristics that distinguish those who are likely to participate in research from those who refuse to participate. Strain and Chappell (1982) noted that elderly service users are more likely than nonusers to give consent, even when procedures followed for attempting to obtain consent are similar. In Mercer and Butler's (1967) study, those potential sample members who refused to participate were older and were more likely never to have had children than those who gave consent. Atchley (1969), in a study of retired women, found that those who refused to be interviewed differed from those who agreed in that the former were in poorer health, had less contact with friends, felt that they did not have enough money, but had high self-esteem. The limited evidence thus suggests that persons who are older, more isolated interpersonally, and not service recipients may be inclined to refuse to participate in research; their relatively high self-esteem may give them the courage to voice their reluctance to participate. How these findings generalize to developmentally disabled individuals, for whom obtaining informed consent is also a complex matter, is not yet known.

In sum, the key considerations in selecting a sample from the elderly developmentally disabled population are:

1. Defining the population
2. Deciding whether to include younger adults as well as elderly persons in the sample
3. Maximizing the representativeness of the sample in light of the problems of obtaining informed consent initially and loss of subjects during longitudinal studies

DESIGN

One of the most important research design issues in the study of aging populations is encountered in studies that attempt to identify age-related differences between younger and older groups of individuals. Two major explanations have been advanced in the gerontological literature to account for age-related differences: the maturation hypothesis and the generation hypothesis.

The maturation hypothesis postulates that as individuals age, certain predictable and developmental changes occur in their physical, psychological, and social capacities. Siegler, Nowlin, and Blumenthal (1980) explain that some of these "time-related changes [are] intrinsic to the organism" (p. 602), known as primary aging, while other changes are due to the impact of disease and other environmental influences, known as secondary aging. Thus, if there are differences between younger adults and elderly persons, the maturation hypothesis would seek to explain these differences on the basis of gradual changes that occur within persons as they age, due either to primary or to secondary aging.

The generation hypothesis postulates that differences between younger adults and elderly persons exist at least in part because each generation (or cohort) is exposed to somewhat unique environmental and social influences that make them different to some degree from other generations. For these purposes, a cohort is defined as a group of individuals born within a defined period of time. Maddox and Wiley (1976) explain that "human characteristics which stabilize in early life, but which are nevertheless subject to environmental influence during the period of most rapid growth, fall within the class of processes that could generate cohort effects" (p. 22). For example, the cohort of mentally retarded persons for whom special education classes were only minimally available may very well be different from later-born cohorts who attended school in greater numbers. The generation hypothesis would explain differences between mentally retarded persons of different age groups on the basis of different early life experiences, in this case different educational opportunities.

Both the maturation hypothesis and the generation hypothesis are true to varying degrees with respect to specific age-related differences. Some age-related differences are due to intra-individual aging (maturation) while others are due to intergroup experiential differences (generation). The theoretical and methodological challenge facing researchers is to select an appropriate research design so as to avoid attributing the incorrect explanation to specific age-related differences.

The two most commonly used research designs in the study of age-related differences are cross-sectional designs and longitudinal designs. In cross-sectional designs, two or more age groups (cohorts) are compared with respect to one or more dependent variables at a single point in time. If the goal of a cross-sectional study is to allow for valid inferences to be drawn about the effects of aging by means of between-group comparisons, then two assumptions must be true. First, it must be true that at some time in the future the younger group will be similar to the older group. Second, it must be true that in the past the older group was similar to the younger group. If either of these two assumptions is not true, then any between-group differences that are found must be due at least in part to factors other than the aging process. As Siegler et al. (1980) point out, there will always be some degree of non-comparability between younger and older cohorts because the younger cohort contains persons who will die before they reach the age of the older cohort.

Longitudinal designs, in which a single group of persons is followed over time, are not subject to the same problems characteristic of cross-sectional designs. However, there are three factors that limit researchers' ability to infer aging effects from longitudinal studies, namely, current environmental influences, testing effects, and drop-out effects. Current environmental influences, such as changes in eligibility for benefits, could have an influence on sample members and could be mistakenly interpreted to be aging effects. In Campbell and Stanley's (1963) terminology, this is the threat to internal validity of history.

Testing effects are also potentially problematic in longitudinal designs. Campbell and Stanley (1963) defined testing as "the effects of taking a test upon the scores of the second testing" (p. 5). Because longitudinal designs involve the repeated measurement of the same group of subjects, they may be particularly vulnerable to testing effects. A solution identified by Baltes (1968) based on Campbell and

Stanley's (1963) work involves an adaptation of the Solomon four-group design, in which subjects are randomly assigned to a series of groups that differ only in the number of times they are tested. For example, if the research design calls for measures to be taken at four points in time, three control groups would be created, as depicted in Figure 1. Each control group provides an estimate of how similar individuals would have scored in the absence of one set of measures. Group 4 is most like the general (untested) population. If there are no differences among the four groups with respect to the measures taken at the fourth observation, then the possibility of testing effects can be ruled out. If between-group differences are found, then the magnitude of the differences provides an indication of the magnitude of the testing effects. The greater the number of observation times planned, the greater the number of control groups and the larger the number of subjects needed for this type of design, which in turn limits its feasibility.

The third potentially confounding effect in longitudinal designs is the drop-out effect (the threat to internal validity of experimental mortality). As noted earlier, some proportion of the original sample is likely to be lost over time due to death or debilitation, geographical migration, or refusal to continue to participate in the study. There are few effective strategies that prevent drop-out effects because most of the factors resulting in dropping out are outside of the researcher's control.

Baltes (1968) pointed out the complexity of attempting to understand what seem to be age-related differences in longitudinal studies. In any one study, history, testing, and drop-out

effects could occur. However, "the effects need not occur in the same direction in the same degree in the different measurement variables" (Baltes, 1968, p. 153), making inferences about "pure" age effects very difficult to draw. An additional limitation of longitudinal studies is that by studying one group of subjects who are usually relatively homogeneous in age, it may be invalid to generalize findings to other generations who may differ from the study group in ways discussed above in relation to cross-sectional designs.

Thus, neither cross-sectional nor longitudinal designs alone are adequate to make inferences about the effects of aging. An alternative approach, termed the general developmental model, was proposed by Schaie (1965) and Baltes (1968). They asserted that the minimum design needed to make valid inferences about age-related differences includes at least two age cohorts, each assessed longitudinally for at least two sets of measures. Here, the essential elements of both cross-sectional and longitudinal designs are included. According to Baltes (1968), this methodological approach

> permits the separation of the . . . effects of age and cohort. . . . It is possible to examine the extent to which (a) the observed behavioral characteristic is affected significantly by age, (b) the observed behavioral characteristic is affected significantly by cohort, and (c) the extent to which the effect of age is different when age is combined with different levels of cohort. (pp. 159–160)

For the bifactorial developmental model to protect against testing effects, control groups would have to be added for each time of measurement. Thus, with two cohorts each measured at two points in time (the simplest expres-

Group						
1	R	O_1	O_2	O_3	O_4	(study group)
2	R		O_2	O_3	O_4	(control group 1)
3	R			O_3	O_4	(control group 2)
4	R				O_4	(control group 3)

Figure 1.   The application of the Solomon four-group design to longitudinal studies of aging. (R, random assignment; O, observation).

sion of the bifactorial developmental model), four groups would be needed, as shown in Figure 2.

An example of the application of this model in research on mentally retarded persons can be found in Goodman (1976), who first divided the subjects into cohorts on the basis of their age at the first IQ test on record. The subjects were then followed up with repeated administrations of the IQ test. Fisher and Zeaman (1970) also presented a useful discussion of the application technique of this method to research in mental retardation.

In sum, a minimally adequate research design in a study attempting to distinguish the effects of aging from early generational environmental influences must involve at least two age cohorts each assessed at least two times. In addition, attention should be paid to minimizing the threats to internal validity of maturation, history, and experimental mortality.

MEASUREMENT

The field of gerontology has developed a large number of useful measures that assess a variety of characteristics of elderly persons. Care has been taken to establish adequate levels of reliability and validity for many of the commonly used measures. It is important to note that there has been a receptivity on the part of different gerontological investigators to use each others' measures, facilitating comparisons from study to study. Kane and Kane (1981), in a volume devoted entirely to the description of methods helpful in conducting assessments of elderly

persons, identified the domains in need of measurement in order to obtain a comprehensive, multifaceted assessment of an aging individual. These include:

1. Physical functioning
2. Performance of activities of daily living (ADL)
3. Performance of instrumental activities of daily living (IADL)
4. Cognitive functioning
5. Affective functioning
6. Social functioning
7. Social supports
8. Economic resources

Table 1 presents some commonly used measures for each of these eight domains. Two of the most adequately developed domains are activities of daily living (#2) and affective functioning (#5), possibly because these two sets of characteristics are major determinants of the quality of life of older persons. While the field of developmental disabilities does not suffer from a lack of measures of ADL, it is much less advanced in the assessment of affective functioning than the gerontology field. Conducting reliable and valid assessments of affective functioning is certainly more difficult with developmentally disabled persons than with cognitively intact elderly persons, which is one reason for the limited emphasis placed by developmental disabilities professionals on this domain. It is also possible that the affective domain, which includes satisfaction, morale, subjective well-being, and happiness, has not been considered to be as important as the functional domains (including performance of ADL and IADL skills) by professionals and policymakers in developmental disabilities (see O'Connor, 1983 for discussion of this issue). Larson's (1978) review of 30 years of gerontological research on the measurement of subjective well-being has much to offer to conceptual models and research designs.

Gerontologists have developed a number of multidimensional measures of aging. The most well-conceptualized and commonly used of these is the OARS (Older Americans' Resources and Services) Multidimensional Functional

Group	Cohort		Observations	
1	1	R	O_1 O_2	
2	1	R		O_2
3	2	R	O_1 O_2	
4	2	R		O_2

Figure 2. The bifactorial development model with control groups for testing effects. (R, random assignment; O, observation).

Table 1. Commonly used instruments in 8 domains for use with elderly persons

Domain	Instruments
1. Physical functioning (health)	• Cornell Medical Index (Brodman, Erdmann, Lorge, & Wolff, 1951) • Health Index (Rosencranz & Pihlblad, 1970) • Sickness Impact Profile (Carter, Bobbitt, Bergner, & Gilson, 1976)
2. Activities of daily living (ADL)	• Katz Index of ADL (Katz, Ford, Moscowitz, Jackson, & Jaffee, 1963) • Barthel Index (Mahoney & Barthel, 1965) • OARS: Physical ADL (Duke University Center for the Study of Aging and Human Development, 1978)
3. Instrumental activities of daily living (IADL)	• PGC Instrumental Role Maintenance Scale (Lawton, 1972) • PACE II (U.S. Department of Health, Education, & Welfare, 1978) • OARS: Instrumental ADL (Duke University, 1978)
4. Cognitive functioning	• VIRO Orientation Scale (Kastenbaum & Sherwood, 1972) • Short Portable Mental Status Questionnaire—OARS (Duke University, 1978) • Mini-Mental State (Folstein, Folstein, & McHugh, 1975)
5. Affective functioning	• PGC Morale Scale (Lawton, 1975) • Beck Depression Index (Beck, Ward, Mendelson, Mock, & Erbaugh, 1961)
6. Social functioning	• Social Behavior Assessment Schedule (Platt, Weyman, Hirsch, & Hewett, 1980) • HRCA Social Interaction Inventory (Sherwood, Morris, Mor, & Gutkin, 1977)
7. Social supports	• HRCA Social Interaction Inventory (Sherwood, Morris, Mor, & Gutkin, 1977) • Social Isolation Index of the Care (Gurland et al., 1977) • OARS Economic Resources Scale (Duke University, 1978)
8. Economic resources	• OARS Economic Resources Scale (Duke University, 1978)

Assessment Questionnaire (OMFAQ), which was developed at the Center for the Study of Aging and Human Development at Duke University (Duke University, 1978). The OMFAQ assesses individual functioning in the following five dimensions: social, economic, mental health, physical health, and self-care capacity (corresponding with domains 6, 8, 5, 1, and 2 of Table 1, respectively). A judgment is made by an interviewer of the elderly person's functioning in each of the dimensions using a 6-point scale (ranging from excellent to totally impaired). The OMFAQ takes about 45 minutes to administer. For a discussion of the reliability and validity of this instrument and a more detailed description of its contents, see Fillenbaum and Smyer (1981).

Clearly, there would be substantial benefits if research on aging developmentally disabled persons incorporated measures developed and standardized on the general aging population. By including such measures in research on aging developmentally disabled samples, it would be possible to make direct comparisons between two populations. Such comparisons would yield data useful in evaluating the appropriateness and feasibility of integrating developmentally disabled aging persons into generic senior citizens' programs. Such data collected longitudinally would also facilitate the comparison of the two populations with respect to their rates of deterioration in various life domains. The findings would be an important contribution because it is currently not known whether aging developmentally disabled persons decline at a rate similar to, faster than, or slower than nonaging developmentally disabled persons.

However, two obstacles will be encountered when gerontological measures are used with aging developmentally disabled persons. First, many of the measures listed in Table 1 depend on self-report data provided by the elderly person. A large proportion of developmentally disabled persons are incapable of providing such information with an acceptable degree of reliability and validity. Thus, different data collection strategies will have to be developed. See M. M. Seltzer (1983) for a discussion of the relative advantages and disadvantages of the uses of various data collection strategies when studying a mentally retarded population. The work of Sigelman and her colleagues (Sigelman et al., 1983) has clarified how best to interview mentally retarded persons.

The second obstacle concerns the degree of precision needed in conducting a reliable and valid assessment of a developmentally disabled individual. The Katz ADL Index (Katz, Ford, Moscowitz, Jackson, & Jaffee, 1963), for example, consists of six items that have been shown to reliably and validly assess ADL performance among elderly persons. Scales assessing performance in this domain developed for use with a developmentally disabled population are generally much more lengthy. For example, the Adaptive Behavior Scale (Nihira, Foster, Shellhaas, & Leland, 1975) contains 21 items that fall within the ADL domain. One reason for this difference is that there may be a greater degree of within-person variability in performance among mentally retarded persons than among the elderly. That is, whereas it would be possible to, in a very few items, assess the dressing abilities of an elderly person (the Katz Index devotes one item to dressing), with a developmentally disabled person, as many test items as articles of clothing would perhaps be needed. This difference between

population groups may be due to the fact that all (or nearly all) elderly persons once were independent in dressing skills; deterioration in their functioning occurred later in life as a result of either increased fraility, injury, or illness. In contrast, for many moderately and severely developmentally disabled persons, the skills needed to independently put on or remove each article of clothing must be taught separately and an individual not given training in a particular skill (e.g., tying shoes) might never acquire mastery of it. Thus, less consistency of performance can be assumed for a developmentally disabled person than for an elderly person. For this reason, and for those discussed above, instruments designed for use with an elderly population may require modification prior to use with a developmentally disabled population.

In sum, research on the elderly developmentally disabled population will be enriched by the utilization of measures developed by gerontologists and standardized on a general aging population. However, these instruments should be modified for use with the aging developmentally disabled population to avoid the reliance on self-report data and to increase the precision of the measures.

RESEARCH AGENDA

There are at least five major areas currently in need of research in the field of aging and developmental disabilities. Some of the questions resulting from a lack of research are drawn directly from the field of gerontology while others address the interface of the two fields of gerontology and developmental disabilities.

The first and most basic area in need of research at the present time concerns the collection of *basic demographic and epidemiological descriptive data* about the aging developmentally disabled population. Questions such as the following need to be addressed:

How many developmentally disabled persons over the age of 55 can be identified in the United States, and what is the age distribution of this group?

Can the size of the aging developmentally disabled population be expected to change substantially during the next 20 years? How many developmentally disabled persons are between the ages of 35 and 55?

What is the average life expectancy for developmentally disabled persons? How is life expectancy related to severity of disability?

What are the major causes of morbidity and mortality among aging developmentally disabled persons?

What is the distribution of the aging and developmentally disabled population with respect to male/female ratio, severity of disability, and type of residential setting?

National baseline data are needed for service planning purposes and for future research efforts. The field of demography has much to contribute to the design of studies addressing questions such as those outlined above with respect to sampling, data collection, procedures, and data analytic methods, and with respect to providing a population context for research on the aging developmentally disabled subgroup. Siegel's (1980) paper *On the Demography of Aging* may prove to be a valuable resource in this regard.

A second area of research needed to increase knowledge about aging developmentally disabled persons involves the *identification of predictors of longevity and of successful aging* in this group. If variables predictive of a longer and higher quality life can be identified, it may be possible to modify existing services and programs so as to promote these desired outcomes.

Gerontologists have had a major interest in the prediction of longevity and successful aging. The Duke Longitudinal Studies on Aging were begun in the middle 1950s in order to identify physical, social, and mental predictors of longevity. Palmore (1982) presented the results of a 25-year follow-up of sample members from the Duke Longitudinal Study in which predictors were identified that accounted for a difference in longevity of 16 years for men and 23 years for women. In a related analysis, Palmore (1979) identified the predictors of "successful aging," defined as survival to age 75, good health, and happiness. The methodological approach and the variables that were found to predict long life and successful aging that were used in these studies can serve as a guide to research on the prediction of these outcomes in the aging developmentally disabled population.

A third area of needed research involves the *identification of similarities and differences between aging developmentally disabled persons, and two comparison groups: a) younger adult developmentally disabled persons, and b) aging nondevelopmentally disabled persons.* Research on age-related differences within the developmentally disabled population is needed for at least two reasons. First, this type of information would be extremely useful for future planning. If, in 20 years, the 40-year-olds of today will be like the 60-year-olds of today (consistent with the maturation hypothesis), then today's 60-year-olds must be studied in order to plan programs for the aging developmentally disabled population of the future. If, on the other hand, it is found that today's 40-year-olds will not, in 20 years, be like today's 60-year-olds (consistent with the generation hypothesis), then current planning efforts will be limited. Another reason that knowledge of age-related differences within the adult/aging developmentally disabled population is needed pertains to the issue of age-generic versus age-specific programs for developmentally disabled persons. If it is found that age-related differences are minimal, special programs for the aging developmentally disabled populations, as distinct from younger adult developmentally disabled persons, may not be needed in most cases. Conversely, if large age-related differences are found, age-generic programs might not be appropriate or successful.

Some preliminary work has begun in which aging developmentally disabled persons were compared with younger developmentally disabled adults (Bell & Zubek, 1960; Janicki & MacEachron, 1984; Krauss & Seltzer, 1984;

Seltzer et al., 1982). These studies, using cross-sectional methodologies, attempted to identify behavioral, functional, and social correlates of aging. Whether the differences between the age groups that were revealed by these studies signify changes brought on by the aging process (maturation hypothesis) or are reflective of differences between different cohorts of individuals (generation hypothesis) cannot be firmly determined from the cross-sectional designs. A few longitudinal studies of age-related changes in the developmentally disabled population have been conducted (e.g., Fisher & Zeaman, 1970; Goodman, 1976). However, as was discussed earlier, longitudinal designs are also limited in the extent to which they allow for a valid inference to be made about the effects of aging.

Comparisons are needed between aging developmentally disabled persons and aging non-developmentally disabled persons to identify similarities and differences between these two groups. As noted, similarities will argue for the inclusion of aging developmentally disabled persons in generic programs and services for the elderly. Large differences will argue in favor of the need for specialized programs. Studies that have been conducted to assess the degree of difference between aging developmentally disabled and aging nondevelopmentally disabled persons include Callison et al. (1971), Cotton, Sison, and Starr (1981), Kirby, Nettlebeck, and Goodenough (1978–79), and Sherwood and Morris (1983).

A fourth area in need of research concerns the *evaluation of programs* (age-generic or age-specialized) that are intended to meet the needs of aging developmentally disabled persons. A few program descriptions are available in the literature (e.g., Talkington & Chiovaro, 1969), but in general the field lacks both descriptive research about programs for the aging developmentally disabled population and evaluation research about the effects of such programs. An exception is the Sherwood and Morris (1983) study in which the differential effectiveness of a domiciliary care program for elderly, mentally ill, and mentally retarded

persons was assessed. A full discussion of strategies useful in conducting evaluation research about programs for aging persons can be found in Estes and Freeman (1976).

A fifth area in need of research attention at the present time involves an *assessment of the informal support system* of aging developmentally disabled persons. Informal supports are services provided by family and friends. There is much evidence from the gerontological literature that informal supports enhance the ability of an elderly person to live in noninstitutional settings even after he or she has difficulty managing independently (Branch & Jette, 1982; Brody, Poulshock, & Masciocchi, 1978; Greenberg & Ginn, 1979; Lowy, 1983; Palmore, 1976). The informal support system appears to be a potentially important resource for the aging developmentally disabled population. There is an extremely high rate of institutionalization among the elderly developmentally disabled population receiving state-supported services; it is reported to be over 50% (Janicki & MacEachron, 1984; Krauss & Seltzer, 1984). The rates of institutionalization among retarded persons of all ages and among the general elderly population have never exceeded 5%, but elderly developmentally disabled individuals appear to be at a much higher risk of continued institutional placement. Whether siblings, nieces, and nephews can be mobilized as informal supports for aging developmentally disabled persons when their parents die is not known, nor is it known whether the involvement of such relatives would have an impact on the rate of institutionalization in this group. However, in light of the positive impact of informal supports on the risk of institutionalization of the nondevelopmentally disabled elderly population, this appears to be an important area for research.

In conclusion, the five areas in need of study constitute a research agenda that warrants attention at the present time. The lack of knowledge about elderly developmentally disabled persons will continue to be an obstacle in efforts to plan and provide high quality services for them. By addressing the five general areas discussed here, along with additional issues identified in other chapters of this book, the field will be able to better conceptualize and develop services appropriate to this newly identified client group. The utility of the findings of any body of research depends in large part on the adequacy of the research methods used. The quality of studies of the aging developmentally disabled population can be improved by incorporating the relevant wisdom and techniques of gerontological researchers along with this field's own methodological tradition.

REFERENCES

Atchley, R. C. (1969). Respondents vs. refusers in an interview study of retired women: An analysis of selected characteristics. *Journal of Gerontology, 24,* 42–47.

Baltes, P. B. (1968). Longitudinal and cross-sectional sequences in the study of age and generation effects. *Human Development, 11,* 145–171.

Baker, B. L., Seltzer, G. B., & Seltzer, M. M. (1977). *As close as possible: Community residences for retarded adults.* Boston: Little, Brown & Co.

Beck, A. T., Ward, C. H., Mendelson, M., Mock, J., & Erbaugh, J. (1961). An inventory for measuring depression. *Archives of General Psychiatry, 4,* 53–63.

Bell, A., & Zubek, J. P. (1960). The effect of age in the intellectual performance of mental defectives. *Journal of Gerontology, 15,* 285–295.

Birren, J. E. (1959). Principles of research on aging. In J. E. Birren (Ed.), *Handbook of aging in the individual,* (pp. 3–42). Chicago: The University of Chicago Press.

Branch, L. G., & Jette, A. M. (1982). A prospective study of long-term care institutionalization among the aged. *American Journal of Public Health, 72,* 1373–1379.

Brodman, K., Erdmann, A. J., Lorge, I., & Wolff, H. G. (1951). The Cornell Medical Index—Health Questionnaire: II. As a diagnostic instrument. *Journal of the American Medical Association, 145,* 152–157.

Brody, S., Poulshock, S., & Masciocchi, C. (1978). The family caring unit: A major consideration in the long-term support system. *The Gerontologist, 18,* 556–561.

Callison, D. A., Armstrong, H. R., Elam, L., Cannon, R. L., Paisley, C. M., & Himwich, H. (1971). The effects of aging on schizophrenic and mentally defective patients: Visual, auditory, and grip strength measurements. *Journal of Gerontology, 26,* 137–145.

Campbell, D. T., & Stanley, J. C. (1963). *Experimental and quasi-experimental designs for research.* Chicago: Rand McNally & Co.

Carter, W. B., Bobbitt, R. A., Bergner, M., & Gilson, B. S. (1976). Validation of an interval scaling: The Sickness Impact Profile. *Health Services Research, 11,* 516–528.

Cotton, P. D., Sison, G. F. P., & Starr, S. (1981). Comparing elderly mentally retarded and non-mentally retarded individuals: Who are they? What are their needs? *The Gerontologist, 21,* 359–365.

Duke University Center for the Study of Aging and Human Development. (1978). *Multidimensional Functional Assessment: The OARS Methodology.* Durham, NC: Duke University.

Eisdorfer, C. (1983). Conceptual models of aging: The challenge of a new frontier. *American Psychologist, 38,* 197–202.

Estes, C. L., & Freeman, H. E. (1976). Strategies of design and research for intervention. In R. H. Binstock & E. Shanas (Eds.), *Handbook of aging and the social sciences,* (pp. 536–560). New York: Van Nostrand Reinhold Co.

Fillenbaum, G. G., & Smyer, M. A. (1981). The development, validity, and reliability of the OARS Multidimensional Functional Assessment Questionnaire. *Journal of Gerontology, 36,* 428–434.

Fisher, M. A., & Zeaman, D. (1970). Growth and decline of retardate intelligence. In N. R. Ellis (Ed.), *International review of research in mental retardation* (Vol. 4) (pp. 151–191). New York: Academic Press.

Folstein, M. F., Folstein, S., & McHugh, P. R. (1975). Mini-Mental State: A practical method for grading the cognitive state of patients for the clinician. *Journal of Psychiatric Research, 12,* 189–198.

Goodman, J. F. (1976). Aging and IQ change in institutionalized mentally retarded. *Psychological Reports, 39,* 999–1006.

Greenberg, J., & Ginn, A. (1979). A multivariate analysis of the predictors of long-term care placement. *Home Health Care Services Quarterly, 1,* 75–99.

Grossman, H. (Ed.). (1983). *Manual on terminology and classification in mental retardation.* Washington, DC: American Association on Mental Deficiency.

Gurland, B., Kuriansky, J., Sharpe, L., Simon, R., Stiller, P., & Birkett, P. (1977). The Comprehensive Assessment and Referral Evaluation (CARE)— Rationale, development, and reliability: Part II. A factor analysis. *International Journal of Aging and Human Development, 8,* 9–42.

Janicki, M. P., & MacEachron, M. P. (1984). Residential, health, and social service needs of elderly developmentally disabled persons. *The Gerontologist, 24,* 128–137.

Kane, R. A., & Kane, R. L. (1981). *Assessing the elderly: A practical guide to measurement.* Lexington, MA: Lexington Books.

Kastenbaum, R., & Sherwood, S. (1972). VIRO: A scale for assessing the interview behavior of elderly persons. In D. P. Kent, R. Kastenbaum, & S. Sherwood (Eds.), *Research, planning, and action for the elderly* (pp. 166–200). New York: Behavioral Publications, Inc.

Katz, S., Ford, A. B., Moscowitz, R. W., Jackson, B. A., & Jaffee, M. W. (1963). Studies of illness in the aged. The Index of ADL: A standardized measure of biological and psychosocial function. *Journal of the American Medical Association, 185,* 94.

Kirby, N. H., Nettlebeck, T., & Goodenough, S. (1978–79). Cognitive rigidity in the aged and the mentally retarded. *International Journal of Aging and Human Development, 9,* 263–272.

Krauss, M. W., & Seltzer, M. M. (1984, May). *Age-*

related differences in functional ability and residential status in mentally retarded adults. Paper presented at the 108th annual meeting of the American Association on Mental Deficiency, Minneapolis, MN.

Larson, R. (1978). Thirty years of research on the subjective well-being of older Americans. *Journal of Gerontology, 33,* 109–125.

Lawton, M. P. (1972). Assessing the competence of older people. In D. Kent, R. Kastenbaum, & S. Sherwood (Eds.), *Research, planning, and action for the elderly* (pp. 122–143). New York: Behavioral Publications, Inc.

Lawton, M. P. (1975). The Philadelphia Geriatric Morale Scale: A revision. *Journal of Gerontology, 30,* 85–89.

Lowy, L. (1983). Social policies and programs for the elderly as mechanisms of prevention. *Aging and Prevention, 3,* 7–21.

Maddox, G. L., & Wiley, J. (1976). Scope, concepts, and methods in the study of aging. In R. H. Binstock & E. Shanas (Eds.), *Handbook of aging and the social sciences* (pp. 3–34). New York: Van Nostrand Reinhold Co.

Mahoney, F. I., & Barthel, D. W. (1965). Functional evaluation: The Barthel Index. *Rehabilitation, 14,* 61–65.

Mercer, J. R., & Butler, E. W. (1967). Disengagement of the aged population and response differentials in survey research. *Social Forces, 46,* 89–96.

Neuman, F. (1981, May). *Ready, set, go—The institutionalized aging and aged developmentally disabled client: A new look at an old topic.* Paper presented at the 105th annual meeting of the American Association on Mental Deficiency, Detroit, MI.

Nihira, K., Foster, B., Shellhaas, M., & Leland, H. (1975). *AAMD Adaptive Behavior Scale.* Washington, DC: American Association on Mental Deficiency.

O'Connor, G. (1983). Social support of mentally retarded persons. *Mental Retardation, 21,* 187–196.

O'Connor, G., Justice, R. S., & Warren, N. (1970). The aged mentally retarded: Institution or community care? *American Journal of Mental Deficiency, 75,* 354–360.

Palmore, E. B. (1976). Total chance of institutionalization among the aged. *The Gerontologist, 16,* 504–507.

Palmore, E. B. (1979). Predictors of successful aging. *The Gerontologist, 19,* 427–431.

Palmore, E. B. (1982). Predictors of the longevity difference: A 25-year follow-up. *The Gerontologist, 22,* 513–518.

Platt, S., Weyman, A., Hirsch, S., & Hewett, S. (1980). The Social Behavior Assessment Schedule (SBAS): Rationale, contents, scoring, and reliability of a new interview schedule. *Social Psychiatry, 15,* 43–55.

PL 95-602. (1978). *Rehabilitation, Comprehensive Services, and Developmental Disabilities Amendments of 1978.*

Rosencranz, H. A., & Pihlblad, C. T. (1970). Measuring the health of the elderly. *Journal of Gerontology, 25,* 129–133.

Schaie, K. W. (1965). A general model for the study of developmental problems. *Psychological Bulletin, 64,* 92–107.

Segal, R. (1977). Trends in services for the aged mentally retarded. *Mental Retardation, 15,* 24–27.

Seltzer, G. (1983). Systems of classification. In J. L. Matson & J. A. Mulick (Eds.), *Handbook of mental retardation* (pp. 143–156). New York: Pergamon Press.

Seltzer, M. M. (1983). Non-experimental field research methods. In J. L. Matson & J. A. Mulick (Eds.), *Handbook of mental retardation* (pp. 557–570). New York: Pergamon Press.

Seltzer, M. M., Seltzer, G. B., & Sherwood, C. C. (1982). Comparison of community adjustment of older vs. younger mentally retarded adults. *American Journal of Mental Deficiency, 84,* 9–13.

Sherwood, S., & Morris, J. N. (1983). The Pennsylvania Domiciliary Care Experiment: I. Impact on quality of life. *American Journal of Public Health, 73,* 646–653.

Sherwood, S. J., Morris, J., Mor, V., & Gutkin, C. (1977). *Compendium of measures for describing and assessing long-term care populations.* Boston: Hebrew Rehabilitation Center for Aged (mimeographed).

Siegel, J. S. (1980). On the demography of aging. *Demography, 17,* 245–364.

Siegler, I. C., Nowlin, J. B., & Blumenthal, J. A. (1980). Health and behavior: Methodological considerations for adult development and aging. In L. W. Poon (Ed.), *Aging in the 1980s: Psychological issues* (pp. 599–612). Washington, DC: American Psychological Association.

Sigelman, C. K., Schoenrock, C. J., Budd, L. C., Winer, J. L., Spanhel, C. L., Martin, P. W., Hromas, S., & Bensberg, G. J. (1983). *Communicating with mentally retarded persons: Asking questions and getting answers.* Lubbock: Research & Training Center in Mental Retardation, Texas Tech University.

Strain, L. A., & Chappell, N. L. (1982). Problems and strategies: Ethical concerns in survey research with the elderly. *The Gerontologist, 22,* 526–531.

Streib, G. (1983). The frail elderly: Research dilemmas and research opportunities. *The Gerontologist, 23,* 40–44.

Talkington, L. W., & Chiovaro, S. J. (1969). An approach to programming for aged MR. *Mental Retardation, 7,* 29–30.

U.S. Department of Health, Education, & Welfare (DHEW). (1978). *Working document on patient care management.* Washington, DC: U.S. Government Printing Office.

section

IV

BIOLOGICAL AND CLINICAL ASPECTS OF AGING

chapter

10

Aging, Alzheimer's Disease, and Developmental Disabilities

Henryk M. Wisniewski and George S. Merz

An important aspect of meeting the needs of the increasing number of elderly mentally retarded and developmentally disabled persons is an understanding of the consequence of aging in the central nervous system (CNS). Conceptually, aging in general can be viewed as the erosion of functional reserve with the passage of time. The major consequence of this erosion is an increased susceptibility to diseases. In the central nervous system the erosion is seen clinically as "benign forgetfulness." Anatomically, these changes are loosely associated with neuronal loss, decreased interneuronal connections, and formation of abnormal structures such as neurofibrillary tangles and neuritic and amyloid plaques. Of much greater significance than these relatively benign changes is the occurrence of age-associated CNS disease. In the general population the most prevalent is senile dementia of the Alzheimer type. Its incidence and clinical course among mentally retarded and developmentally disabled individuals is not known. An exception to this is Down syndrome where there is both an unusually high frequency (20%–30% of those reaching age 40) and an unusually early age of onset (35–40). The cause and high frequency of senile dementia of the Alzheimer type in Down syndrome is not known. Current thinking suggests that the condition is caused when a genetically susceptible individual is infected by one of a class of unusual infectious agents similar to those causing Creutzfeldt-Jakob disease in man and scrapie disease in sheep and goats.

OVER THE PAST SEVERAL decades there has been an increase in both the length and the quality of life for developmentally disabled individuals. This is due in large measure to the improvement in methods of management, diagnosis, and therapy. As a consequence of these method improvements, the number of disabled individuals reaching old age is increasing. With this increase has come a need to tailor programs and policies to provide appropriate care for the elderly client. At this point one finds oneself in terra incognita since very little is known about how aging affects developmentally disabled persons. There is a particular need to understand the biology of aging as it occurs among developmentally disabled individuals. A particularly important question is whether the aging process is modulated by the existence of an underlying disability. What might be the nature of such modulations? For example, should one expect an accelerated and/or accentuated aging? This issue is particularly important with respect to the aging of the central nervous system (CNS) since this is the area most commonly affected by developmental disabilities.

AGING AS A LOSS OF RESERVE

In its most general way, aging is best thought of as a loss of reserve with the passage of time. As it is used here, reserve has a very specific physiological meaning. All higher organisms are composed of a collection of tissues and organs each of which is dedicated to a particular specialized function that is necessary for the survival of the individual. However, built into each organ's architecture is an inherent, limited functional capacity (e.g., the surface area used for blood-oxygen exchange). In normal, healthy young individuals, this functional capacity greatly exceeds the amount of functional effort required for bare survival. Reserve, then, is the amount of functional capacity that the cell, organ, or organism can lose before there are signs and symptoms indicative of a level of functioning that is suboptimal.

From this point of view, the aging process can be thought of as the continual erosion of structural and functional reserve with the passage of time. This loss is perceived by the individual as a decrease in resistance to disease and other environmental insults as well as a more and more circumscribed repertoire of activities.

A very important feature of this erosion is that it does not occur at a uniform rate either from organ to organ or from individual to individual. This lack of uniformity is plainly evident in the apparent disparity between the chronological and biological age of a particular individual.

In trying to define the causes of the loss of reserve, one can distinguish between those that are imposed by the environment—the ''wear and tear'' processes (e.g., wearing down of teeth), and those that are inherent in genetic makeup. These latter, which are the fundamental, primary aging processes that lead to loss of functional capacity, operate directly on the fundamental biological unit, the cell. Among the most prominent mechanisms of cellular aging are spontaneous mutation, developmentally programmed cell death, and specific aging genes.

Spontaneous Mutation

With time, the genetic information in a cell accumulates errors. These errors may be the direct result of environmental effects on the cell's genes such as cosmic radiation, virus infection, or mutagenic chemicals. They also arise from chance mistakes made during the replication or repair of cellular DNA. Such mistakes then become part and parcel of the cell's genetic makeup. Changes such as these accumulate continually over time. Eventually they occur among genes that are responsible in some way for the cell's special functions and thereby lead to an impaired function.

Developmentally Programmed Cell Death

At certain stages of normal embryological development, more cells are produced than are needed in the mature adult. For example, in the dorsal root ganglia of the spinal cord, approximately 40% more motor neurons are produced than are found at maturity. This excess is removed by normal developmental processes that deliberately destroy the extra cells as a part of the normal developmental sequence. Although this programmed cell death is usually thought to operate only at specific stages of development, it has been postulated that part of the cell losses associated with aging may be a consequence of an incomplete shutting down of this process after development is completed. It has been assumed that this process leads to the progressive loss of nerve cells, which begins approximately at the age of 20. The number of cells disappearing daily has been calculated to be approximately 100,000. If a person could live long enough (about 410 years), his or her brain might become completely devoid of nerve cells (Olszewski, 1968).

Specific Aging Genes

Certain genes in an individual's genetic makeup appear to have direct control on the rate of aging. For example, alteration in a single specific gene gives rise to a condition called progeria. Affected individuals develop many signs of old age such as wrinkled skin, arteriosclerosis, and so on, before they reach their teens.

The fact that alteration of a single gene can lead to such dramatic precocious aging suggests that the rate at which people age may, at least in part, be inherited and under direct genetic control. Another example is Down syndrome. This most prevalent of developmental disabilities is remarkable because this condition exhibits more signs and symptoms of precocious aging than any of the other developmental disabilities. Once again, it appears that altered genetic makeup, in this case the presence of extra copies of genes on chromosome 21, leads to signs of premature aging. (For a more detailed discussion of these genes and how they exert their effects, see Brown, Chapter 11, this volume.)

Regardless of the exact nature of these processes, their net effect is the same. The cell in question is either killed outright or it survives in such a way that its ability to perform its specialized function is impaired. The consequence of this is a "cascade effect" in which the total functional capacity of the organ in which the cell resides is now correspondingly diminished. As more cells become functionally disabled, the organ's capacity to function is reduced. Eventually this diminished capacity of organ function will affect the integrated functioning of the organism and be manifest as a decreased range of activities or behaviors, or more importantly an increased incidence of environmental insults such as infectious disease.

AGING AND DISEASE

An important question in aging research is that of the relationship between aging processes and disease conditions. This problem arises because most of the changes that are found in aged organs including the brain are also found in pathological conditions occurring in young and middle-age individuals. In many cases the only difference between the two age groups is a quantitative one because the same changes are found in large numbers in the disease state but only in low numbers in elderly but otherwise normal individuals. This raises several questions. Are the morphological changes in organs of elderly but clinically normal individuals pathological? How different is the aging process from pathological processes seen in various diseases? Are aging and disease separate entities or is aging a "subclinical" disease?

Any consideration of aging requires the recognition of the fact that all measurable and visible deviations from the state where function is optimal are, by definition, pathological. If by reason of their number and location, these pathological changes elicit a clinical expression, then there is disease.

This perspective also suggests that there is a continuum of change that leads from the normal elderly state to the diseased state such that "normal aging" is simply that stage of pathology that has not *yet* led to any clinical expression. Thus, the pathological changes found in the elderly individual cannot be considered to be solely a consequence of senescence. However, genetically programmed, time-dependent changes in the cell (such as those described above), with or without exposure to environmental insults, may open the way to an increased incidence of pathological alterations. Therefore, one might say the aged cell, organ, or organism is an environment in which certain pathological changes can more readily develop.

AGING AND THE CENTRAL NERVOUS SYSTEM

Consideration of how the CNS ages must take into account the high degree of structural and functional specialization that is built into the brain. In almost every other organ in the body, there is a very direct relationship between structure and function (e.g., muscle mass and strength). There is a basic cell or group of cells that serves as the fundamental functional unit. The total functional capacity of the organ is basically a matter of how many of these units there are. While it is true that the neuron is the basic functional unit of the nervous system, the mosaic of behaviors and capacities embodied in the nervous system cannot be accounted for on a simple additive basis. In this regard the nervous system is quite different and is best conceptualized as a "multiorgan organ." This is a consequence of the unique architecture of the nervous system. Unlike most other organs, the brain is responsible for carrying out the integrated expression of many different functions. This is accomplished in several ways. Many of the functions are separated anatomically in different regions of the brain (e.g., cognition in the frontal-parietal-temporal cortex or vision in the retina and occipital cortex). However, even this regional specialization is not sufficient to account for all of the varieties of brain activity. In some cases, a given function is defined by the interaction of signals arriving from several different parts of the brain. In other words, CNS functioning is also determined by how different groups of different neurons in different regions interact with each other.

Current understanding of CNS aging is based on neuropathological and biochemical changes in brain tissue seem to accumulate with advancing age and the documentation of age-associated changes in an individual's behavior, cognition, and affect. It would be ideal to relate these two phenomena such that one could identify which changes or combination of changes is responsible for alterations in an individual's behavior and cognitive functions. Unfortunately, this synthesis has yet to be realized.

The list of age-associated changes in the CNS is quite long. The most prominent are loss of brain weight, loss of neurons, loss of functional connections between neurons, decreased amount of neurotransmitters, deposition of degradation products such as lipofuscin granules, the vacuolation of cells and their processes, and the formation of unusual fibrous structures such as the neurofibrillary tangle and the neuritic and amyloid plaques. Curiously, some of the changes (neurofibrillary changes) seen in the human brain of elderly persons are also seen in a variety of CNS diseases in children or adults (Wisniewski, Jervis, Moretz, & Wisniewski, 1979).

SENILE DEMENTIA

One very dramatic age-associated behavioral change is senile dementia. This is by far the most dramatic CNS change associated with old age. The condition is characterized by a progressive deterioration of memory and cognition that culminates in a state akin to profound mental retardation in which the individual becomes bedridden and devoid of much of what is regarded as uniquely human. In the general United States population, the number of individuals at risk with respect to senile dementia (i.e., those over age 65) is about 25 million. Of these, about 10% or 2.5 million have some degree of cognitive impairment. Of these, about 50% or 1.3 million are so severely demented as to require institutional care. Current demographic projections indicate that in the absence of intervention, one can expect that the number of individuals at risk (i.e., those over age 65) will double over the next 40 years.

One of the remarkable features of senile dementia is that 90% of the cases are caused by only two conditions, Alzheimer's disease and multi-infarct pathology (Table 1). Of these two, Alzheimer's disease is involved in 70% of the cases making it the single most important cause of senile dementia.

ALZHEIMER'S DISEASE AND SENILE DEMENTIA OF THE ALZHEIMER TYPE

The name Alzheimer is taken from the neuropathologist who in 1907 reported a case of profound dementia in a 51-year-old woman. Because of her age, the condition was regarded as presenile dementia. Microscopic examination of the brain revealed many neurons filled with fibrous material and neuropil lesions called senile or neuritic plaques. Only later was it

Table 1. Major causes of senile dementia and their frequencies

Senile dementia of the Alzheimer type (SDAT)	55%
Multi-infarct dementia (MID)	22%
SDAT + MID	15%
Other dementias (virus, trauma, alcoholism, etc.)	8%

found that the same type of changes were present in cases of senile dementia as well as in healthy old people (in much lower numbers) (Tomlinson, Blessed, & Roth, 1970). Because slow progressive intellectual deterioration and memory loss are the most characteristic clinical features of this disease, the question of an identity between the presenile condition, Alzheimer's disease, and the senile dementia arose. Today, cases with an age of onset under 65 are called Alzheimer's disease (AD) and those over age 65 are called senile dementia of the Alzheimer type (SDAT). It should be emphasized that the distinction is somewhat artificial in that, in spite of some clinical differences, the two conditions appear to be manifestations of the same disease. For this reason, the acronym AD/SDAT will be used to denote the disease for the rest of this chapter.

Neurofibrillary Tangles and Neuritic Plaques

The most characteristic changes in the brains of AD/SDAT patients are the neurofibrillary tangles and neuritic and amyloid plaques. Their prominence is such that the final diagnosis of AD/SDAT is only made when large numbers of them are found in the brain when biopsy is done or at autopsy. Comparison of the severity of the dementia with the number of plaques and tangles found at autopsy reveals a strong, positive correlation between the number of plaques and tangles in the brain and degree of dementia (Tomlinson et al., 1970). While such a correlation does not necessarily establish a cause-and-effect relationship between the lesions and the dementia, it does imply that the process of lesion formation is closely tied to the process that causes the dementia.

Neurofibrillary Tangles The Alzheimer type tangles are found in a wide variety of human CNS diseases including subacute sclerosing panencephalitis, Guam-Parkinson dementia complex, postencephalitic Parkinson's disease, dementia pugilistica, and Hallerworden-Spatz disease (Wisniewski et al., 1979). The lesion is also found, in much lower numbers in the aged but otherwise normal human

brain. Thus, neurofibrillary tangles are not limited to Alzheimer's disease but rather appear to be one of the limited responses of the human nervous system to insults from different causes. Virtually nothing is known of how they are formed or how they might interfere with the normal functioning of a neuron.

Neuritic and Amyloid Plaques These lesions are composed of extracellular deposits of another abnormal filamentous structure called amyloid fibers. Intermingled with the amyloid fibers are degenerating and regenerating nerve cell process and reactive cells (microglia, pericytes, and astrocytes). Unlike the neurofibrillary tangles, the plaques are not limited to the human CNS. Plaques have been reported in monkeys, dogs, mice, and sheep (Beck & Daniel, 1965; Bruce, Dickinson, & Fraser, 1976; Wisniewski, Ghetti, & Terry, 1973; Wisniewski, Johnson, Raine, Kay, & Terry, 1970). It is worth emphasizing that the plaques are associated with only three conditions: the aged CNS, AD/SDAT, and certain unconventional virus diseases known as the transmissible encephalopathies (e.g., scrapie, kuru, Creutzfeldt-Jakob disease, Gerstmann-Straussler syndrome) (Wisniewski, Merz, & Carp, 1984).

SDAT AND ITS RELATION TO THE AGING CNS

Although SDAT is not thought to be the direct expression of CNS aging, it is nonetheless still closely related to the aged CNS since: 1) the majority of cases occur after age 65; 2) both of the lesions that define the disease neuropathologically (neurofibrillary tangles and neuritic plaques) are found, in low numbers, in the aged but otherwise normal brain; and 3) there is a high incidence (20%–30%) of SDAT among older individuals (age 35 or older) with Down syndrome, a condition with many features indicative of premature aging (Martin, 1977). Thus, AD/SDAT is of great interest to neuropathologists and gerontologists alike since an understanding of the pathogenesis and etiology of the disease should also provide important clues to the nature of the CNS aging process.

The concept that there is a continuum of change (see above) that leads from the normal elderly state to the diseased state is very much in evidence in AD/SDAT. In addition to the plaques and tangles mentioned above, there are some other features of AD/SDAT that are consistent with this idea. Acetylcholine is a neurotransmitter whose activity is closely tied to memory and cognition. The amount of the substance present in the brains of AD/SDAT patients is reduced to about 5%–10% of normal. It is also thought to be somewhat reduced in the normal aged brain (Dziedzic, Iqbal, & Wisniewski, 1980). Similarly, while neurons are lost as part of the aging process, it has been shown that in AD/SDAT the number of some classes of neurons in the cerebral cortex are 40%–50% lower than the numbers found in normal aged brain (Terry & Katzman, 1983). The fact that the difference between these changes as they occur in SDAT and the aged brain is only quantitative suggests that they are formed by the same pathogenic process and they only differ in the rate and intensity at which they progress. These observations raise several fundamental questions. Is the "cause" of aging the same as the cause of AD/SDAT? What event or entity is responsible for accelerating the rate of pathological change?

While there is no definitive answer to these questions, the authors would like to offer the following hypothesis: AD/SDAT is caused by infection of genetically susceptible individuals with one of the agents causing the transmissible encephalopathies. Implicit in this hypothesis is the assumption that the ubiquity of the agents is responsible for the neuritic and amyloid plaques seen in the aged normal brain. This notion is not without precedent. Studies with scrapie disease in mice have shown quite clearly that certain combinations of agent and host lead to infections with incubation periods that exceed the lifespan of the host (Dickinson, Bruce, & Scott, 1983). In these cases, it is possible to isolate the infective agent from spleens and brains of inoculated mice that show little or no clinical or neuropathological signs of disease.

The fact that not all individuals develop SDAT is, according to the authors' hypothesis, explained by the existence of a gene(s) that determines susceptibility to the disease. Such genes might well be responsible for the autosomal patterns of inheritance seen in familial SDAT. Again this idea has precedents among the slow infections where both Creutzfeldt-Jakob disease and Gerstmann-Straussler syndrome also occur in pedigrees consistent with an autosomal dominant inheritance (Brown, Cathala, Sadowsky, & Gajdusek, 1979; Brown, Salazar, Gibbs, & Gajdusek, 1982). Although the function of these putative "susceptibility genes" is not known, it is tempting to equate them to genes thought to contribute to the expression of normal aging. It has been postulated (Cutler, 1982) that these genes and their products are responsible for self-maintenance and repair. Such genes could lead to increased susceptibility to scrapie-like agents by: 1) age-associated accumulation of damage in elderly individuals leading to SDAT, 2) unbalanced expression in Down syndrome leading to a high incidence of Alzheimer-type dementia among people with trisomy 21, and 3) inherited defects leading to the presenile form of Alzheimer's disease.

In summary, based on all of the foregoing, the authors would suggest that there is a continuum between the pathology of "normal" aging and SDAT and that the clinical signs and symptoms of Alzheimer-type dementia develop in genetically susceptible individuals. However, whether the pathological changes such as neurofibrillary tangles and neuritic and amyloid plaques are the result of a metabolic, age-associated alteration or, as the authors believe, a response to infection by one of the agents of the transmissible encephalopathies remains to be determined.

AD/SDAT AND DEVELOPMENTALLY DISABLED PERSONS

In general, there is little information on the overall incidence of AD/SDAT among mentally retarded and developmentally disabled individuals. This is largely a consequence of the fact that it is only relatively recently that 1) AD/SDAT has come to be regarded as a disease (and in principle, is amenable to intervention), and 2) disabled individuals are reaching an age to be at risk.

An exception to this are individuals with Down syndrome where the condition occurs with an unusually high frequency. Between 20% and 30% of individuals with Down syndrome that reach age 30 will develop clinical signs and symptoms of Alzheimer's disease. In addition, almost 100% of these individuals over age 30 will have neurofibrillary tangles and neuritic and amyloid plaques in numbers equivalent to what is found in Alzheimer's disease in non–Down syndrome cases (Wisniewski, Wisniewski, & Wen, in press). The reason for this high incidence of Alzheimer pathology in Down syndrome is not known. As already stated, it is the authors' hypothesis that Alzheimer's disease is the result of infection of genetically susceptible individuals. Of all of the developmental disabilities, Down syndrome has the highest number of features indicative of premature aging (see Brown, Chapter 11, this volume). If, as the authors suggest

above, the genes responsible for Alzheimer's disease are part of an individual's collection of aging genes, then one need only postulate that they reside on chromosome 21 to explain the association of high frequency of Alzheimer's disease and premature aging seen in Down syndrome. Under these circumstances, the chromosome 21 trisomy that causes Down syndrome could be of great importance to the study of the molecular biology of the aging process in man.

In summary, from the foregoing it should be evident that there is much that is not known about how the CNS ages particularly among mentally retarded and developmentally disabled individuals. What is clear is that by their very makeup, these disabling conditions impose a decreased functional reserve on the affected individuals. This in turn sets the stage for an early manifestation of CNS aging that may take the form of an early age of onset of age-associated disease such as the high incidence and precocious age of onset for senile dementia of the Alzheimer type in Down syndrome. It also seems likely that other examples of accelerated or accentuated manifestations of aging will emerge as research on disabled elderly individuals continues.

REFERENCES

Beck, E., & Daniel, P. M. (1965). Kuru and scrapie compared: Are they examples of system degeneration. In D. C. Gajdusek, C. J. Gibbs, & M. Alpers (Eds.), *Slow, latent and temperate virus infections* (pp. 85–93). (NINDB Monograph #2, Public Health Service Publication No. 1378).

Brown, P., Cathala, F., Sadowsky, D., & Gajdusek, D. C. (1979). Creutzfeldt-Jakob disease in France. II. Clinical characteristics of 124 consecutive verified cases during the decade 1968–1977. *Annals of Neurology, 6,* 430–437.

Brown, P., Salazar, A. M., Gibbs, C. J., Jr., & Gajdusek, D. C. (1982). Alzheimer's disease and transmissible virus dementia (Creutzfeldt-Jakob disease). *Annals of the New York Academy of Science, 396,* 131–143.

Bruce, M. E., Dickinson, A. G., & Fraser, H. (1976). Cerebral amyloidosis in scrapie in the mouse: Effect of agent strain and mouse genotype. *Neuropathology and Applied Neurobiology, 2,* 471–478.

Cutler, R. G. (1982). The dysdifferentiative hypothesis of mammalian aging and longevity. In E. Giacobini (Ed.), *The aging brain: Cellular and molecular mechanisms of aging in the nervous system* (pp. 1–19). New York: Raven Press.

Dickinson, A. G., Bruce, M. E., & Scott, J. R. (1983). The relevance of scrapie as an experimental model for Alzheimer's disease. In R. Katzman (Ed.), Banbury Report 15, *Biological aspects of Alzheimer's disease* (pp. 387–398). New York: Cold Spring Harbor Laboratory.

Dziedzic, J. D., Iqbal, K., & Wisniewski, H. M. (1980). Central cholinergic activity in Alzheimer dementia. *Journal of Neuropathology and Experiments in Neurology, 39,* 351.

Martin, G. M. (1977). Genetic syndromes in man with potential relevance to the pathology of aging. In E. L. Schneider (Ed.), *Genetic effects of aging.* Washington, DC: National Foundation, March of Dimes.

Olszewski, J. (1968). Introduction to degenerative disease. In J. Minckler (Ed.), *Pathology of the nervous system* (Vol. 1, pp. 1109–1112). New York: McGraw-Hill Book Co.

Terry, R. D., & Katzman, R. (1983). Senile dementia of the Alzheimer type. *Annals of Neurology, 14,* 493–506.

Tomlinson, B. E., Blessed, G., & Roth, M. (1970). Observations on the brains of demented old people. *Journal of Neurological Science, 11,* 205–242.

Wisniewski, H. M., Ghetti, B., & Terry, R. D. (1973).

Neuritic (senile) plaques and filamentous changes in aged rhesus monkeys. *Journal of Neuropathology and Experiments in Neurology, 32,* 566–584.

Wisniewski, H. M., Johnson, A. B., Raine, C. S., Kay, W. J., & Terry, R. D. (1970). Senile plaques and cerebral amyloidosis in aged dogs. *Laboratory Investigations, 23,* 287–296.

Wisniewski, H. M., Merz, G. S., & Carp, R. I. (1984). Senile dementia of the Alzheimer type: Possibility of an infectious etiology in genetically susceptible individuals. *Acta Neurologica Scandinavica, Supplementum 99, 69,* 91–97.

Wisniewski, K., Jervis, G. A., Moretz, R. C., & Wisniewski, H. M. (1979). Alzheimer neurofibrillary tangles in diseases other than senile and presenile dementia. *Annals of Neurology, 5,* 288–294.

Wisniewski, K., Wisniewski, H. M., & Wen, G. Y. (in press). Occurrence of Alzheimer's neuropathology and dementia in Down syndrome. *Annals of Neurology.*

chapter

11

Genetics of Aging

W. Ted Brown

This chapter presents an overview of current understanding of the genetic basis of the aging process. This is particularly relevant to the understanding of mental retardation and developmental disability, since these conditions have a strong genetic component. About 40% of the cases of severe mental retardation are due to genetic defects including single gene mutations and chromosomal abnormalities, and 20% more have a significant genetic susceptibility component such as spina bifida and seizures.

A consideration of the evolution of longevity suggests that a few genes, perhaps 10 to 20, may play a key role in determining the rate of aging and the species-specific maximal lifespan potential. Current information suggests that these genes may encode enzymatic systems that play a self-protective role in maintaining the integrity of the genetic material itself and in regulating the timing of development. Twin and parent-child longevity correlation studies suggest that single genes do not increase longevity. Rather, longevity is likely to be multifactorial and due to the action of a number of genes. Some human genetic diseases shorten lifespan. Several of these, such as Down syndrome, Werner's syndrome, Cockayne's syndrome, and progeria, produce a picture of apparent accelerated aging. They are considered model diseases for the study of genetic aspects of the aging process. Understanding the basic defects involved in these diseases may lead to insights into how specific genes control the aging process as well as developmental disability.

AGING IS ENCODED in the genes. This is reflected by the wide range of maximal lifespan potential (MLP) that animal species possess. The MLP in different animal species has over a 50,000-fold range and varies from about 1 day (*Ephemera sp.*, imago form) to over 150 years (*Tedudo summeri*) (Lints, 1978). Among mammals, a 100-fold range exists from about 1 year in the smokey shrew (*Sorex fumeus*) (Hamilton, 1940) to 118 years in man (McWhirter, 1984). This 100- to 50,000-fold variation reflects the fact that there are underlying differences in the genetic constitution of species that control the rate of aging.

It appears likely that the genetic basis of aging involves two types of species-specific

differences. The first type of difference is in rates of maturation and programmed timings of developmental stages. The second type relates to biochemical systems involving self-maintenance. Evidence suggests that the most common type of evolutionary genetic change is due to changes in the regulated levels of expression of genes rather than changes in the specific activity of enzymes (Brown, 1979). Regulatory changes in gene expression may have major influences on morphological development, increased brain size, and increased longevity.

Some key enzymatic systems show species-specific levels of expression that are genetically determined. These include DNA repair processes and systems involved in protection from internal and external insults to the genetic machinery. The regulation of expression of these systems appears to have evolved coordinately with increased MLP. Specific examples of these include an ultraviolet (UV) DNA repair system that allows for increased ability to repair DNA (Hart & Setlow, 1974), an arylhydrocarbon hydroxylase system that produces reactive intermediates that could lead to carcinogenic mutations (Schwartz, 1975), and increased levels of certain anti-oxidant enzymes such as superoxide dismutase (Cutler, 1980) that protect against the damaging effects of an oxidizing environment. Other enzymes and factors may also have evolved species-specific levels of expression designed to protect longer lived species against an oxidizing environment and free radical intermediates including alpha tocopherol, Beta carotene, glutathione, ascorbic acid (Harman, 1981), and uric acid (Ames, Cathcart, Schwiers, & Hochstein, 1981). Changes in gene regulation and expressed levels of self-protective enzyme systems are examples of the types of defined evolutionary genetic changes that appear to encode the process of aging.

THE GENETIC COMPLEXITY UNDERLYING AGING

Although more than 3,000 specific human genetic conditions are known (McKusick, 1982), no single mutation appears to lead to a significantly longer lifespan. This suggests that the evolution of increased longevity may be the result of the modification of a number of genes. To attempt to bracket the number of genes that may underly the evolution of human longevity, Cutler (1975, 1976, 1980), Sacher (1975, 1976, 1980), and Sacher and Staffeldt (1974) analyzed the genetic complexity underlying this process. Based on the apparent rapid increase in human brain size and corresponding lifespan in the period 200,000 to 100,000 years before the present, and assuming known rates of amino acid substitution, they estimated that from 70 to 240 genes may have received one adaptive substitution. Since most amino acid substitutions have a minimal effect on enzyme activity, it seems likely that only a small percentage of these, perhaps 10%, might have had a significant bearing on increasing lifespan and brain size.

If lifespan had a simple genetic basis, one might predict that parental and offspring lifespan would be strongly correlated. Based on multiple longitudinal studies, it appears that this is only a weak correlation at best (Murphy, 1978). Although there is an almost uniform familial component to length of life, expressed as a number, this adds only about 1 year of expected life to the offspring for every 10 extra years of parental lifespan beyond the expected mean. This increase is as likely to be due to social or environmental factors as to genetic factors. Familial patterns of exercise, smoking, and drinking appear to be of greater importance than parental longevity in determining average life expectancy.

A long-term study comparing lifespans of identical and fraternal twins has shown that identical twins generally have had a smaller difference in their lifespans (Jarvik, Falek, Kallman, & Lorge, 1960). However, this difference was statistically significant ($p < .05$) only for female monozygotic twins. When one female twin died in the age range 60–69 years, there was a mean difference of 6 years 9 months of lifespan for monozygotes compared to a mean difference of 14 years 5 months for dizygotes. The differences were found to be not significant for female twins at other ages or for male twins. The simplest interpretation of this study is that single gene differences may tend to shorten lifespan because of detrimental effects rather than lengthen it due to beneficial effects. People are apt to show increasing homogeneity in their physical characteristics as they approach the upper limits of their natural lifespan potential since they have been selected for superior health and any detrimental genes have been eliminated. Therefore, the basis for the inheritance of longevity seems unlikely to be simple from a genetic point of view but rather to reflect the interaction of a number of genes and to be multifactorial in its origin.

There are rare autosomal dominant genetic conditions of serum lipids (hypo β-lipoproteinemia and hyper α-lipoproteinemia) that decrease susceptibility to atherosclerosis and resultant coronary disease (Glueck, Gartside, Fallat, Sieski, & Steiner, 1976). However, they appear to increase the average life expectancy without affecting the expected maximal lifespan. It seems likely that the human maximal lifespan is approximately 118 years (McWhirter, 1984). In the absence of acceptable documentation, reports of extreme longevity must be viewed with scepticism. As summarized by Medvedev (1974), the supposed longevity of individuals in the Russian Caucasus seems unfounded and without scientific basis.

LIFE-SHORTENING GENETIC DISEASES

Although no specific genes have been identified that appear specifically to increase maximal lifespan, there are many life-shortening diseases that may involve specific genes. About 20% of the population suffers from diseases that have a genetic component and lead to a reduced life expectancy. These diseases include: diabetes, arthritis, HLA-associated life-shortening diseases (histocompatability locus antigen), hyperlipidemia, α-1-antitrypsin deficiency, and cystic fibrosis. Furthermore, it is estimated that about 40% of infant mortality is a result of genetically determined conditions. In some families, cancer proneness may have a genetic component such as in familial colon cancer.

Senile dementia of the Alzheimer type (SDAT) is an important life-shortening age-associated disease that may affect 5%–10% of the population over 65 (Wisniewski & Iqbal, 1980). SDAT has been suggested to have a genetic component; a number of pedigrees have been described with a pattern of SDAT inheritance that is consistent with an autosomal dominant mode (Heston & White, 1978). Occurrences of Creutzfeldt-Jakob disease (CJD), a rapidly progressing dementia, and the Gerst-mann-Straussler syndrome (GSS) of spino-cerebellar ataxia with dementia and neuritic and amyloid plaque formations have shown apparent autosomal dominant inheritance (Masters, Gajdusek, & Gibbs, 1981a,b). It may be that what is inherited is a genetic susceptibility to an infectious agent such as may be involved in CJD, GSS, and scrapie (Wisniewski, Merz, & Carp, 1984). A genetic component to SDAT is also suggested by mouse models. Certain strains of mice inocculated intracerebrally with particular strains of scrapie agent will develop amyloid and neuritic plaques indistinguishable from that seen in humans with SDAT (Wisniewski et al., 1984). Walford and Hodge (1980) have reported that unrelated patients with SDAT show a high frequency of certain unrelated HLA antigens, suggesting that genetic susceptibility to dementia may be based on inheritance of immune response genes. Weitkamp, Nee, Keats, Polinsky, and Guttormsen (1983) confirmed this immune susceptibility in part by finding an association with HLA loci and the inheritance of SDAT in a large familial SDAT pedigree in which 257 individuals were tested.

Most developmental disabilities that have a genetic basis are associated with a decreased life expectancy. These include a variety of neurodegenerative and storage diseases, as well as chromosomal abnormalities such as Down syndrome. The most common Mendelian inherited form of mental retardation appears to be the fragile-X syndrome (Brown & Jenkins, 1984). It is inherited in an X-linked manner and has an estimated prevalence in the general population of 1 per 2,000 people. Individuals with this syndrome usually are fairly normal in appearance but are moderately to severely retarded. The syndrome is diagnosed by finding an abnormal fragile site at the end of the X chromosome when blood cells are grown in a low folic acid environment. Sufficient data are not yet available to determine whether this condition is associated with a reduced life expectancy. Only one autopsy has been performed on an adult male known to have the fragile-X chromosome. He died at the early age of 58 of complications resulting from a chronic form of leukemia (Rudelli et al., 1985).

PREMATURE AGING SYNDROMES

McKusick's (1982) catalog of recognized human genetic conditions inherited in a Mendelian fashion lists over 3,000 autosomal dominant, recessive, and X-linked conditions. Martin (1977) reviewed the 1975 edition of the Mc-Kusick catalog that listed 2,400 genetic conditions along with the three common chromosomal conditions—Down syndrome (trisomy 21), Turner's syndrome (XO), and Klinefelter's syndrome (XYY)—to select those with the highest number of phenotypic features he judged to be associated with senescence. The features he included were intrinsic mutagenesis, chromosomal abnormalities, associated neoplasms, defective stem cells, premature loss of or grey hair, senility, slow virus susceptibility, amyloid deposition, lipofuscin deposition, diabetes mellitus, disturbed lipid metabolism, hypogonadism, autoimmunity, hypertension, degenerative vascular disease, osteoporosis, cataracts, mitochondrial abnormalities, fibrosis, abnormal fat distribution, and a single group of other associated features of aging. Ten genetic diseases were identified that had the highest number of these senescent features. They were ranked in the following order: Down syndrome, Werner syndrome, Cockayne syndrome, progeria (Hutchinson-Gilford syndrome), ataxia telangectasia, Seip syndrome, cervical lipodysplasia, Klinefelter syndrome, Turner syndrome, and myotonic dystrophy. It is noteworthy that selected for inclusion in this list of genetic syndromes with the highest number of premature aging features were the three chromosomal syndromes. This suggests that regulatory abnormalities such as reflected in the quantitative type of gene dosage differences seen in chromosomal syndromes play an important role in producing the senescent phenotype.

The following section includes analyses of the clinical features and summaries of research being done on the four genetic diseases with the highest number of features of premature aging.

DOWN SYNDROME

Down syndrome (DS) may have the greatest number of features associated with the senescent phenotype and may be the highest ranking candidate as a "segmental progeroid syndrome" according to Martin's (1977) analysis. Patients with DS show premature greying of hair and hair loss, increased tissue lipofuscin, increased neoplasms and leukemia, variations in the distribution of adipose tissue, amyloidosis, increased autoimmunity, hypogonadism, degenerative vascular disease, and cataracts. The life expectancy of patients with DS is markedly reduced (Smith & Berg, 1976). Most neuropathological studies have reported findings indistinguishable from senile dementia of Alzheimer type (SDAT) in many DS patients over the age of 40 (Burger & Vogel, 1973; Wisniewski, Wisniewski, & Wen, in press). Progressive neurological and psychiatric abnormalities in older DS patients have been reported indicating the neuropathological changes are reflected as precocious aging and dementia (Wisniewski, Howe, Williams, & Wisniewski, 1978). In Table 1, the features for and against DS as a model of aging are summarized.

In DS, a specific qualitative gene defect such as underlies progeria and Werner's syndrome is not present. Rather, DS is most commonly due to an extra chromosome 21 (trisomy 21). This leads to disturbances in gene dosage and to quantitative differences in expression of genes located on the 21st chromosome. However, it is also possible that the extra genetic material may cause effects on the expression of genes on other chromosomes as well.

Although the majority of cases of DS are due to the presence of an extra chromosome 21, about 4% are due to mosaicism, where the individual is composed of a mixture of both normal diploid and abnormal trisomic cells. Another 4% of cases are due to translocations, mostly of the Robertsonian type, with nearly the whole of chromosome 21 translocated to another chromosome. In addition, a small number of cases of partial trisomy 21 have been

Table 1.   Down syndrome as a model of aging

Pathological changes related to aging	Pathological changes unrelated to aging
1. Premature greying and hair loss 2. Increased tissue lipofuscin 3. Increased incidence of leukemia 4. Amyloid deposition 5. Increased autoimmunity 6. Hypogonadism 7. Adipose tissue redistribution 8. Degenerative vascular changes 9. Cataracts 10. Senile dementia of Alzheimer type 11. Calcification in the basal ganglia 12. Chromosome abnomalities 13. Possible DNA repair defects	1. Generalized developmental delays 2. Mental retardation 3. Developmental reduction in neuronal population and synaptic aborizations 4. Cardiac and other organ malformations

reported with translocations of part of 21 to other chromosomes (Jenkins et al., 1983).

The specific pathogenesis of DS and other aneuploidies is unknown. Current research efforts are underway to apply the powerful methods of DNA recombinant technology to understand just what genes are involved in DS. A unique gene segment that was located by *in situ* hybridization was recently isolated and identified to be only on chromosome 21 (Devine et al., 1984). Studies of gene segments such as these, employing the recombinant DNA technological approaches, promise to yield insights into how abnormalities in gene dosage can produce the features of accelerated aging as well as developmental disabilities.

WERNER'S SYNDROME

Werner's syndrome (WS), also called progeria of the adult (Brown, 1983; Epstein, Martin, Schultz, & Motulsky, 1966), has a number of features that resemble premature aging, but also a number of features that do not, as summarized in Table 2. WS patients generally appear normal during childhood but cease growth during their early teenage years. Premature greying and whitening of hair occurs. Striking features include early cataract formation, skin that appears aged with a sclerodermatous appearance, a high pitched voice, peripheral musculature atrophy, poor wound healing, chronic leg and ankle ulcers, hypogonadism, widespread atherosclerosis, soft tissue calcification, osteoporosis, and a high prevalence

of diabetes mellitus. About 10% of patients develop neoplasm with a particularly high frequency of sarcomas and meningiomas. The diagnosis of WS is usually made in the third decade. Patients commonly die of complications of atherosclerosis in the fourth decade.

The mode of inheritance of WS is clearly autosomal recessive. There are less than six known living patients in the United States. In Japan where there is a higher consanguinity rate, a large number of cases have recently been reported (Goto, Horiuchi, Tanimoto, Ishii, & Nakashima, 1978; Goto, Tanimoto, Horiuchi, & Sasazuji, 1981; Murata & Nakashima, 1982).

A basic enzymatic or metabolic abnormality has not yet been established for WS. However, a number of investigations have suggested tantilizing clues as to the nature of the underlying defect. WS is clearly inherited as an autosomal recessive; by analogy with other recessive diseases in which the basic defect is known, WS may be due to the absence of a single specific enzyme.

Cultured fibroblasts from WS patients uniformly show a greatly reduced *in vitro* lifespan potential. While some 40–80 generations *in vitro* are typical for normal cells, WS fibroblasts show a lifespan of only 5–20 generations (Martin, Sprague, & Epstein, 1970; Salk, 1982). Thus, WS cells show rapid aging in culture, which appears to mimic the apparent rapid aging of WS patients. WS fibroblasts and lymphocytes have been found to have chromosome abnormalities. Examination of chromosomes

Table 2. Werner's syndrome as a model of aging

Pathological changes related to aging	Pathological changes unrelated to aging
1. Generalized atherosclerosis	1. Unusual calcifications in skin
2. Greying and loss of hair	2. Ankle ulcerations
3. Aged and pigmented skin changes	3. Chromosome translocation mosaicism
4. Osteroporosis	4. Elevated urinary hyaluronic acid
5. Hypogonadism	
6. Frequent diabetes	
7. Cataracts	
8. Cortical atrophy without senile dementia or accelerated plaque and tangle formation	
9. Frequent neoplasms	

in cultured fibroblasts has shown that a wide variety of translocations occur spontaneously (Salk, 1982).

People normally excrete a small amount of glycosaminoglycans (GAG) in the urine. Patients with metabolic storage diseases, such as mucopolysaccharidoses, may excrete large amounts of GAGs. Normally, less than 1% of the GAGs are in the form of hyaluronic acid (HA). WS patients appear to have elevated levels of urinary HA but normal total GAG levels. HA levels of 10%–20% of GAGs are usually seen (Goto & Murata, 1978; Kieras, Brown, Houck, & Zebrower, 1984; Murata, 1982; Tokunaga, Futami, Wakamatsu, Endo, & Yosizawa, 1975). This elevation of HA is distinctly abnormal, and with the exception of progeria (discussed below), has not been recognized for any other genetic disease. Thus, an elevated urinary level of HA appears to be a metabolic marker for WS. The elevated hyaluronic acid may play a role as an inhibitory growth factor of angiogenesis (Kieras et al., 1984). Whether it relates to the abnormalities of cell growth and chromosomes seen in WS has yet to be determined. However, by inhibiting angiogenesis it may explain the premature aging phenotype.

COCKAYNE'S SYNDROME

Cockayne's syndrome (CS) is a rare recessive disease associated with the appearance of premature senescence. It is usually also associated with mental retardation (Cockayne, 1936). Patients generally have a normal appearance in infancy. They develop growth retardation with a variable age of onset. Their eyes are sunken and microcephaly is usually present. Their skin frequently shows marked photosensitivity. They lose subcutaneous fat. Their ears are usually prominent. Patients have long limbs and large hands and usually develop progressive joint deformities. Hypogonadism develops, but people may develop secondary sexual characteristics. They are usually not bald, but optic atrophy, deafness, and progressive ataxia develop. A striking feature is progressive intracranial calcification, which can be detected by CAT scan or skull X ray. Although the degree of neurological deterioration can be quite variable, death usually is a result of progressive neurodegeneration in late childhood or early adolescence.

CS fibroblast cultures exhibit increased sensitivity to ultraviolet (UV) irradiation (Schmickel, Chu, Trosko, & Chang, 1977). Growth of cells as assayed by colony-forming ability following UV irradiation is much reduced as compared to normal. This abnormal sensitivity to UV has been used to allow prenatal diagnosis of the syndrome (Sugita et al., 1982). No known defect in excision or DNA repair has yet been defined. It has been suggested that UV irradiation produces a chromatin alteration that inhibits replicon initiation (Cleaver, 1982). Three complimentation groups have been defined based upon RNA synthesis following somatic fusion and UV irradiation (Lehmann, 1982), which suggests that heterogeneity is present in the syndrome. This disease illustrates that abnormal sensitivity to irradiation can be associated with a premature aging phenotype.

PROGERIA (HUTCHINSON-GILFORD PROGERIA SYNDROME)

Progeria is a rare genetic disease with striking clinical features that look like premature aging (DeBusk, 1972). Patients with this condition generally appear normal at birth, but severe growth retardation is usually seen by about 1 year of age. Balding occurs, and loss of eyebrows and eyelashes is common in the first few years of life. Widespread loss of subcutaneous tissue occurs, and as a result the veins over the scalp become particularly prominent. The skin appears aged and pigmented age spots develop. The patients are very short, averaging about 40 inches in height, and usually weigh no more than 25 to 30 pounds even as teenagers. Their weight to height ratio is thus very low. Voice is thin and high pitched. Sexual maturation usually does not occur. They have a characteristic facial appearance with prominent eyes, a beaked nose, a ''plucked bird'' facial appearance and a facial disporportion, with a small jaw and a large cranium. The large head, balding, and small face give them an extremely elderly appearance. The bones show distinctive changes with frequent resorption of the collar bones and replacement by fibrous tissue. Resorption of the terminal finger bones, stiffening of finger joints, and a peculiar horse-riding stance are all seen. Aseptic necrosis of the head of the femur and hip dislocation are common. The patients have normal to above normal intelligence. The mean age of death is 13 years of age. Over 80% of deaths are due to heart attacks or congestive heart failure. Widespread atherosclerosis with interstitial fibrosis of the heart is seen at postmortem examination. Occasionally marked enlargement of the thymus gland is noted. However, some features associated with normal aging are not present, including increased frequency of cancer, cataracts, diabetes mellitus, and amyloid deposition. Thus, progeria represents a model disease for studies of aging as summarized in Table 3.

The genetic mode of inheritance of progeria has not been definitely established, but is most likely to be sporadic dominant with each case representing a fresh mutation. A consideration of the mode of inheritance, whether dominant or recessive, is important in progeria since this may suggest the type of underlying biochemical abnormality associated with the disease and, therefore, with the senescent phenotype. Recessive diseases frequently are due to the homozygous deficiency of an enzyme leading to a metabolic disturbance, as, for example, phenylketonuria. However, the underlying molecular basis of most dominant diseases is usually unknown, although abnormalities involving structural proteins have been found in a few dominant diseases. Examples of these include collagen in Marfan's syndrome and receptor deficiencies in familial hypercholesterolemia. Although progeria had been considered to be a recessive condition, it is more likely a sporadic autosomal dominant mutation because of several observations including: 1) a lower frequency of consanguinity than expected, 2) a paternal age effect, and 3) low frequency of reoccurrence in families (Brown, 1979; Brown & Darlington, 1980; Brown, Darlington, Fotino, & Arnold, 1980). The reported incidence is about one in 8 million live births. For such a rare recessive, consanguinity would be expected to be present in 50%–80% of cases. It appears to be present in less than 6% of cases. A paternal age effect is present, which is also a common feature of other new dominant mutations. There have been several kindreds re-

Table 3. Progeria as a model of aging

Pathological changes related to aging	Pathological changes unrelated to aging
1. Generalized atherosclerosis	1. Unusual degenerative bone changes
2. Balding	2. Elevated hyaluronic acid
3. Hypogonadism	
4. Osteroporosis	
5. Loss of subcutaneous fat	
6. Pigmented skin changes	
7. Variable elevated tissue	

ported in which more than one case was apparently present, but this may reflect somatic mosaicism with a stem cell mutation in testes or ovary. The vast majority of cases occur with no siblings affected even in large pedigrees. Therefore, it seems most appropriate to regard progeria as a sporadic dominant-type mutation.

A progeria registry of all known cases has been established at the New York State Institute for Basic Research in Developmental Disabilities. By 1984, about one dozen living cases in the United States and six overseas cases had been identified. The National Institute of Aging supports a cell repository where cultured progeria cells are stored and supplied to scientists interested in research in progeria (Aging Cell Repository, Institute for Medical Research, Camden, New Jersey 08103).

Basic studies of progeria have involved a search for a genetic marker in an attempt to help define the underlying defect. Research has been conducted regarding investigating growth of progeria cells in culture, altered proteins, abnormalities of immune function, and defective DNA repair processes. Evidence for a distinctive marker in progeria is inconclusive (Brown & Wisniewski, 1983). However, one Japanese case was reported in which an abnormally high level of HA was found in the urine similar to that seen in WS (Tokunaga et al., 1978). The authors have recently confirmed this finding in three additional progeria cases (Kieras et al., 1985). This unusual biochemical finding may help to develop an understanding of how abnormal gene functioning can produce the features of accelerated aging. Any breakthrough in the understanding of this remarkable experiment of nature may provide insight into the nature of genetic factors that may underlie the aging process.

SUMMARY

A consideration of the evolution of longevity indicates that a few genes, perhaps 10 to 20, may play a key role in determining the rate of aging and the species-specific maximal lifespan potential. Current information suggests that these genes may encode for enzymatic systems that play a self-protective role in maintenance of the integrity of the genetic material itself and regulate the timing of development. Twin and parent-child longevity correlation studies suggest that single genes do not increase longevity. Rather, longevity is likely to be multifactorial and due to the action of a number of genes. Some human genetic diseases shorten lifespan. Several of these, such as Down syndrome, Werner's syndrome, Cockayne's syndrome, and progeria, produce a picture of apparent accelerated aging. They are considered model diseases for the study of genetic aspects of the aging process. Understanding the basic defects involved in these diseases may lead to insights into how specific genes control the aging process as well as produce developmental disability.

REFERENCES

Ames, B. N., Cathcart, R., Schwiers, E., & Hochstein, P. (1981). Uric acid provides an antioxidant defense in humans against oxidant- and radical-caused aging and cancer: A hypothesis. *Proceedings National Academy of Science, U.S.A., 78,* 6858–6862.

Brown, W. T. (1979). Human mutations affecting aging—a review. *Mechanisms Aging Development, 9,* 325–336.

Brown, W. T. (1983). Werner's syndrome. In J. German (Ed.), *Chromosome mutation and neoplasia* (pp. 85–93). New York: Alan R. Liss, Inc.

Brown, W. T., & Darlington G. J. (1980). Thermolabile enzymes in progeria and Werner syndrome: Evidence contrary to the protein error hypothesis. *American Journal of Human Genetics, 32,* 614–619.

Brown, W. T., Darlington, G. J., Fotino, M., & Arnold,

A. (1980). Detection of antigens on cultured progeria fibroblasts. *Clinical Genetics, 17,* 213–219.

Brown, W. T., & Jenkins E. C. (1984). The fragile X syndrome. In J. M. Berg (Ed.), *Perspectives and progress in mental retardation: Biomedical aspects* (Vol. 2, pp. 211–217). Baltimore: University Park Press.

Brown, W. T., & Wisniewski, H. M. (1983). Genetics of human aging. *Review of Biological Research in Aging, 1,* 81–99.

Burger, P. C., & Vogel S. (1973). The development of the pathologic changes of Alzheimer's Disease and senile dementia in patients with Down's Syndrome. *American Journal of Pathology, 73,* 457–468.

Cleaver, J. E. (1982). Normal reconstruction of DNA supercoiling and chromatin structure in Cockayne syndrome cells during repair of damage from ultraviolet light. *American Journal of Human Genetics, 34,* 566–575.

Cockayne, E. A. (1936). Dwarfism with retinal atrophy and deafness. *Archives of Disease in Childhood, 11,* 1–5.

Cutler, R. G. (1975). Evolution of human longevity and the genetic complexity governing aging rate. *Proceedings National Academy of Science, U.S.A., 72,* 4664–4668.

Cutler, R. G. (1976). Nature of aging and life maintenance processes. In R. G. Cutler (Ed.), *Interdisciplinary topics of gerontology.* (Vol. 9, pp. 83–133). Basel: Karger.

Cutler, R. G. (1980). Evolution of human longevity. *Advances in Pathology, 7,* 43–49.

DeBusk, F. L. (1972). The Hutchinson-Gilford progeria syndrome. *Journal of Pediatrics, 80,* 697–724.

Devine, E. A., Nolin, S. L., Houck, G. E., Jenkins, E. C., Miller, D. L., & Brown, W. T. (1984). Isolation and regional localization by *in situ* hybridization of a unique gene segment to chromosome 21. *Biochemical and Biophysical Research Communications, 121,* 380–385.

Epstein, C. J., Martin, G. M., Schultz, A. L., & Motulsky (1966). Werner's syndrome: A review of its symptomatology, natural history, pathologic features, genetics and relationship to the natural aging process. *Medicine, 45,* 177–221.

Glueck, C. J., Gartside, P., Fallat, R. W., Sieski, J., & Steiner, P. M. (1976). Longevity syndromes: Familia hypobeta and familial hyper-alpha lipoproteinemia. *Journal of Laboratory Clinical Medicine, 88,* 941–957.

Goto, M., Horiuchi, Y., Tanimoto, K., Ishii, T., & Nakashima, H. (1978). Werner's syndrome: Analysis of 15 cases with a review of the Japanese literature. *Journal of American Geriatrics Society, 26,* 341–347.

Goto, M., & Murata, K. (1978). Urinary excretion of macromolecular acidic glycosaminoglycans in Werner's syndrome. *Clinica Chimica Acta, 85,* 101–106.

Goto, M., Tanimoto, K., Horiuchi, Y., & Sasazuji, T., (1981). Family analysis of Werner's syndrome: A survey of 42 Japanese families with a review of the literature. *Clinical Genetics, 19,* 8–15.

Hamilton, W. J. (1940). The biology of the smokey shrew (*Sorex fumeus fumeus* Miller). *Zoologica (New York), 23,* 473.

Harman, D. (1981). The aging process. *Proceedings National Academy of Science, U.S.A., 78,* 7124–7128.

Hart, R. W., & Setlow, R. B., (1974). Correlation between deoxyribonucleic acid excision repair and life span in a number of mammalian species. *Proceedings National Academy of Science, U.S.A., 71,* 2169–2173.

Heston, L. L., & White, J. (1978). Pedigrees of 30 families with Alzheimer disease: Associations with defective organization of microfilaments and microtubules. *Behavioral Genetics, 8,* 315–331.

Jarvik, L. F., Falek, Kallman, F. J., & Lorge, I. (1960). Survival trends in a senescent twin population. *American Journal of Human Genetics, 12,* 170–179.

Jenkins, E. C., Duncan, C. J., Wright, C. E., Giordano, F. M., Wilbur, L., Wisniewski, K. W., Sklower, S. O., French, J. H., Jones, C., & Brown, W. T. (1983). Atypical Down syndrome and partial trisomy 21. *Clinical Genetics, 24,* 97–102.

Kieras, F. J., Brown, W. T., Houck, G. E., & Zebrower, M. (1985). *Elevation of urinary hyaluronic acid in Werner syndrome and progeria.* Manuscript submitted for publication.

Lehmann, A. R. (1982). Three complementation groups in Cockayne syndrome. *Mutation Research, 106,* 347–356.

Lints, F. A. (1978). Genetics and ageing. In H. P. von Hahn (Ed.), *Interdisciplinary topics in gerontology* (Vol. 14, pp. 1–31). Basel: Karger.

McKusick, V. A. (1982). Mendelian inheritance in man. *Catalogues of automsomal dominant, autosomal recessive and X-linked phenotypes* (6th ed.). Baltimore: Johns Hopkins University Press.

McWhirter, N. (1984). *Guinness book of world records.* (pp. 15–19). New York: Bantam Books.

Martin, G. M., Sprague, C. A., & Epstein, C. J. (1970). Replicative life-span of cultivated human cells: Effects of donor's age, tissue and genotype. *Laboratory Investigations, 23,* 86–92.

Martin, G. M. (1977). Genetic syndromes in man with potential relevance to the pathobiology of aging. *Birth Defects Original Article Series, Genetics of Ageing, 14,* 5–39.

Masters, C. L., Gajdusek, D. C., & Gibbs, C. J. (1981a). Creutzfeld-Jakob Disease virus isolations from the Gerstmann-Straussler syndrome with an analysis of the various forms of amyloid plaque deposition in the virus-induced spongiform encephalopathies. *Brain, 104,* 559–588.

Masters, C. L., Gajdusek, D. C., & Gibbs, C. J., (1981b). The familial occurence of Creutzfeld-Jakob Disease and Alzheimer's Disease. *Brain, 104,* 535–558.

Medvedev, Z. A. (1974). Causasas and Altay longevity: A biological or social problem. *The Gerontologist, 14,* 381–387.

Murata, K. (1982). Urinary acidic glycosamınoglycans in Werner's syndrome. *Experientia, 38,* 313–314.

Murata, K., & Nakashima, H. (1982). Werner's syndrome: Twenty-four cases with a review of the Japanese medical literature. *Journal of American Geriatrics Society, 30,* 303–308.

Murphy, E. A. (1978). Genetics of longevity in man. In E. L. Schneider (Ed.), *The genetics of ageing* (pp. 261–302). New York: Plenum Press.

Rudelli, R. D., Brown, W. T., Wisniewski, K., Wisniewski, H. M., Jenkins, E. C., & Montas, J. C. (1985). *Fragile X autopsy. Pathological features of adult fragile X syndrome.* Manuscript submitted for publication.

Sacher, G. A. (1975). Maturation and longevity and relation to the cranial capacity in huminid evolution. In R. Tuttle (Ed.), *Antecedents of man and after. I. Primates: functional morphology and evolution* (pp. 417–441). The Hague: Montox.

Sacher, G. A. (1976). Evaluation of the ectrophy and information terms governing mammalian longevity. In R. G. Cutler (Ed.), *Interdisciplinary topics of gerontology* (Vol. 9, pp. 69–82). Basel: Karger.

Sacher, G. A. (1980). Mammalian life histories: Their evolution and molecular-genetic mechanism. *Advances in Pathobiology, 7,* 21–42.

Sacher, G. A., & Staffeldt, E. F. (1974). Relationship of gestation time to brain weight for placental mammals: Implications for the theory of vertebrate growth. *American Natural, 108,* 593–615.

Salk, D. (1982). Werner syndrome: A review of recent research with an analysis of connective tissue metabolism, growth control of cultured cells, and chromosomal aberrations. *Human Genetics, 62,* 1–20.

Schmickle, R. D., Chu, E. H. Y., Trosko, J. E., & Chang, C. C. (1977). Cockayne syndrome: A cellular sensitivity to ultraviolet light. *Pediatrics, 60,* 135–139.

Schwartz, A. G. (1975). Correlation between species lifespan and capacity to activate 7, 12-dimethyl-benz[*a*]anthracene to form a mutogenic to a mammalian cell. *Experimental Cell Research, 94,* 445–447.

Smith, G. F., & Berg, J. M. (1976). *Down's anomaly* (pp. 239–245). New York: Churchill Livingston.

Sugita, T., Ikenaga, M., Suehara, N., Kozuka, T., Furuyama, J., & Yabuchi, H. (1982). *Clinical Genetics, 22,* 137–142.

Tokunaga, M., Futami, T., Wakamatsu, E., Endo M., & Yosizawa, Z. (1975). Werner's syndrome as "hyaluronuria." *Clinica Chimica Acta, 62,* 89–96.

Tokunaga, M., Wakamatsu, E., Sato, K., Satake, S., Aoyama, K., Saito, K., Sugawara, M., & Yosizawa, Z. (1978). Hyaluronuria in a case of progeria (Hutchinson-Gilford Syndrome). *Journal of American Geriatrics Society, 26,* 296–302.

Tolmasoff, J. M., Ono, T., & Cutler, R. G. (1980). Superoxide dismutase: Correlation with lifespan and specific metabolic rates in primate species. *Proceedings National Academy of Science, 77,* 2777–2781.

Walford, R. L., & Hodgem S. E. (1980). HLA distribution in Alzheimer's disease. Joint report, eight international workshops. In P. I. Terasaki (Ed.), *Histocompatibility testing nineteen eighty* (Vol. 1, pp. 727–729). Los Angeles: UCLA Tissue Typing Laboratory.

Weitkamp, L. R., Nee, L., Keats, B., Polinsky, R. J., & Guttormsen, S. (1983). Alzheimer disease: Evidence for susceptibility loci on chromosomes 6 and 14. *American Journal of Human Genetics, 35,* 443–453.

Wisniewski, H., & Iqbal, K. (1980). Ageing of the brain and dementia. *Trends in Neurosciences, 3,* 226–228.

Wisniewski, H., Merz, G. S., & Carp, R. (1984). Senile dementia of the Alzheimer type: Possiblity of infectious etiology in genetically susceptible individuals. *Acta Neurologica Scandinavia, 69,* 91–97.

Wisniewski, K., Howe, J., Williams, D. G., & Wisniewski, H. M. (1978). Precocious ageing and dementia in patients with down's syndrome. *Biological Psychiatry, 13,* 619–627.

Wisniewski, K., Wisniewski, H. M., & Wen, G. Y. (in press). Occurrence of Alzheimer's neuropathy and dementia in Down syndrome. *Annuals of Neurology.*

12

Clinical Aspects of Dementia in Mental Retardation and Developmental Disabilities

Krystyna Wisniewski and A. Lewis Hill

Individuals with developmental disabilities may be at a higher risk for dementia. Cognitive and behavioral as well as other signs of progressive neurological diseases may occur at any stage of life. This chapter discusses the causes of dementia and the clinical aspects of neurological and neuropsychological assessments. Particular emphasis is placed on the relationships among Alzheimer's disease, developmental disabilities, and the diagnostic evaluation. The differential diagnosis of the etiology of the dementia is especially important because many of the causes are treatable, with a subsequent return to a higher functioning level.

A mental status evaluation, specifically aimed at developmentally disabled clients, is presented. In addition, new techniques based on experimental research and designed to examine early indications of the dementia process are discussed.

IN MODERN WESTERN SOCIETY, the problems of elderly persons with or without mental retardation or other developmental disabilities have become more important as the number of older people increases. The normal aging process is often characterized by a gradual decline in psychomotor functioning, cognitive capacities, initiative, and creative imagination, as well as a narrowing of interests and an increase in egocentricity. These may lead to personality changes (e.g., paranoid ideations, generalized anxiety, depression, or a feeling of insecurity and inadequacy). It is not unusual for some elderly individuals to become irritable and stubborn, and to display enhanced symptoms of unresolved intra- and interpersonal problems.

Within the developmentally disabled population, there are five major categories of disabilities. These disabililties are defined by different clinical signs and symptoms, called symptomatological diagnoses, that is, 1) mental retardation, 2) cerebral palsy, 3) autism, 4) seizure disorders, and 5) other neurological impairments. Some persons with one of these diagnoses may also have more than one of these disabilities. Within each disability, some of the individuals are mildly affected, others moderately, while others are severely or profoundly affected. There are thousands of different etiological factors that may cause individuals to become developmentally disabled. These etiological factors may also be subgrouped into those that are static in their effects on the central nervous system (CNS) processes (e.g., status post trauma, infection, anoxia) and those that have progressive CNS effects (e.g., inborn errors of metabolism, some neurodegenerative processes).

Static CNS conditions are more commonly due to nongenetic factors in which dementia is sometimes demonstrated in the later stages of life. The progressive CNS processes are more commonly due to genetic factors. Here dementia may occur at any stage of life, even in early infancy, childhood, or adolescence (Dyken & Krawiecki, 1983). In many of the neurodegenerative conditions (about 600 are known at the present time), the biochemical defect or genetic marker is still unknown.

DEFINITION OF DEMENTIA

Dementia is a symptomatological diagnosis in which there is a loss of intellectual functioning severe enough to interfere with occupational or social functioning (American Psychiatric Association, 1980). Dementia is a statement of current functioning lower than previous functioning levels. It may be consistently progressive, with a slow or rapid time course, variable with periods of stable functioning, or remitting (distinct from past usage implying only a progressive disorder).

Katzman (1981) suggests that there are about 50 different causes of dementia in nonretarded adults that, in the authors' opinion, may also occur within individuals with retardation. He has classified these causes into primary degenerative, vascular, and secondary dementias. Some of the etiological classification of these dementias is summarized in Table 1.

For developmentally disabled individuals who have a lower level of cognitive, occupational, and social functioning, the diagnosis of

Table 1. Some examples of diseases associated with dementia and their etiology

I. Diffuse parenchymatous diseases of the central nervous system	Organic compounds
	Carbon monoxide
Presenile dementias (below 65 years)	Drugs
Alzheimer's disease	Wernicke-Korsakoff syndrome
Pick's disease	Pellagra
Creutzfeldt-Jakob disease	Marchiafava-Bignami disease
Parkinson-dementia complex	Vitamin B_{12} deficiency
Huntington's chorea	VI. Brain tumors
Senile dementia of Alzheimer's type (above 65 years)	VII. Trauma
	Open and closed head injuries
II. Metabolic diseases	Subdural hematoma
Inborn errors of metabolism (i.e., amino acidopathies, mucopolysachandis, glycogen, lipid storage disease)	Heat stroke
	VIII. Infections
Disorders of the thyroid and parathyroid glands	Subacute infectious panencephalitis
Wilson's disease	Brain abcess
Liver encephalopathies	Bacterial meningitis
Seizure encephalopathies	Fungal meningitis
Hypoglycemia	Encephalitis
Remote effects of carcinoma	Progressive multifocal leukoencephalopathy
Cushing's syndrome	Behçet's syndrome
Uremic encephalopathy	Kuru
	Lues
III. Vascular disorders	IX. Other degenerative diseases
Multi-infarct dementia	Hallervorden-Spatz disease
Inflammatory disease of blood vessels	Spinocerebellar degenerations
Aortic arch syndrome	Progressive myoclonus
Binswanger disease	Epilepsy
Arteriovenous malformations	Progressive supranuclear palsy
Lacunar state dementia	Parkinson's disease
IV. Normal pressure hydrocephalus	Other heredodegenerative diseases
	Multiple sclerosis
V. Toxins, drugs, vitamins	Muscular dystrophies
Metals	Whipple's disease

dementia is particularly difficult. Dementia is a multifaceted disorder involving a variety of higher order functions (e.g., memory, abstract thought, attention, praxis, judgment, etc.). Personality and behavioral changes may also occur, as well as impairment of activities of daily living. In the early stages of dementia, a neurological examination usually will reveal no focal, sensory, or coordination deficits, except, perhaps, frontal release signs and/or impairment of fine motor coordination. In later stages, the individual may be affected with extrapyramidal signs, seizures, and urinary incontinence. For instance, Table 2 presents a summary of abnormal responses on neurological examination in 50 Down syndrome individuals (24 above, 26 below age 35) suggesting precocious aging (Wisniewski, Howe, Williams, & Wisniewski, 1978).

ASSESSMENT OF DEMENTIA

Any aspect of clinical dementia must be assessed within the context of the background functioning (i.e., other aspects of the individual), the individual history of premorbid functioning, and expectations based on the usual course of aging. Thus, a drop in functioning on a standardized test, such as an intelligence test, does not per se suggest dementia. One must take into account the degree of lowered functioning as well as the areas in which the functioning level has decreased.

Most intellectual decline among nonretarded persons is seen within four areas of intellectual activity. The first of these, memory of recent past, or short-term memory, is also one of the most pronounced clinical features of dementia (Eysenck, 1945; Lezak, 1976). Allison (1961) has categorized the main memory deficits into four types: 1) an inability to remember proper names and names of objects when the object or person is not present; 2) time disorientation, which may be seen in altered sequencing of remembered events; 3) topographical deficits in which spatial relationships are not remembered; and 4) "amnestic indifference" in which memory is not used to aid orientation or thinking.

The second area of intellectual decline among nonretarded persons is the loss of the ability for abstract thinking. This has been reported to be a very sensitive measure; some investigators feel it may be the earliest indicator of dementia (Bilash & Zubeck, 1960; Clark, 1960). Among mentally retarded persons, this occurs only among individuals who are considered to be higher functioning (e.g., mildly retarded).

Williams (1970) has reported a third area, mental inflexibility. Mental inflexibility is demonstrated by an inability to change mental sets and by difficulties adapting to new situations or solving novel problems (Goldstein & Shelly, 1975; Reitan, 1967). The fourth area is a general slowing of activity, which can be easily seen in both nonretarded and retarded populations. This behavioral slowing affects perceptual, cognitive, and psychomotor tasks (Birren, 1963; Jarvik, 1975).

Table 2. Abnormal responses of neurological examination in 50 Down syndrome cohorts

Item description	CA < 35[a]		CA ≥ 35[b]	
	N	%	N	%
Snout reflex	2	7.7	17	70.8
Sucking reflex	0	0	8	33.3
Palmomental signs	7	26.9	17	70.8
Hoffman's signs	0	0	5	20.8
Decreased muscle tone	7	26.9	0	0.
Increased muscle tone	7	26.9	12	50.0
Hyperreflexia	8	30.8	19	79.2
Babinski	1	3.9	5	20.8
Absence of Mayer's	13	50.0	19	79.2
Facial muscle hyperreflexia	8	30.8	17	70.8

[a]26 patients below age 35 years.

[b]24 patients age 35 years and above.

THE USE OF PSYCHOMETRICS
AND MENTAL STATUS
EVALUATION TO ASSESS DEMENTIA

Psychological testing for dementia among individuals with mental retardation generally begins with an IQ test. The choice of the particular instrument depends on the estimated level of functioning as well as the history of previous testing. For learning disabled and mildly mentally retarded individuals, almost all of the usual psychometric batteries can be employed to assess current functioning levels and the major memory deficit can be easily identified. Difficulties occur when lower functioning individuals are tested. For instance, the Leiter International Performance Scale may be more appropriate for lower functioning as well as deaf or some physically impaired individuals. While the Slosson Intelligence Test for Children and Adults and the Stanford-Binet Intelligence Scale can be used to assess very low functioning individuals, they rely heavily on verbal skills and, therefore, may be less appropriate than other tests (such as the Cattell Infant Intelligence Scales) for individuals at the severe and profound levels.

For many individuals (depending on program requirements or regulation), recent evaluations may be available. There are two potentially beneficial effects to using an assessment instrument that was previously used with an individual: 1) it provides a direct comparison with previous performances, and 2) it helps establish rapport with the person. However, the examiner should also be aware that having had the test before may agitate the individual who realizes that he or she is not doing as well as he or she had done the last time the test was given. Furthermore, "testing limits" and certain Halstead-Reitan subtests also are prominent causes of agitation.

In addition to establishing and comparing IQ scores, specific measures of attention, memory, language, gross and fine motor coordination, constructional abilities, social functioning, and personality should be taken. While a great number of tests exist in these areas, many are inappropriate for individuals with mental retardation, particularly at the lower levels of functioning. For instance, reaction-time tasks are often employed as measures of speed of cognitive functioning among nonretarded persons. Such measures are not particularly meaningful with lower functioning mentally retarded individuals who have difficulty with instructions to do a task "as quickly as you can."

Tests for such abilities as attention and concentration are particularly difficult with this population, and it may be necessary to interview "significant others" to obtain information. Informant scales, such as the Vineland Adaptive Behavior Scales, The Minnesota Developmental Programming System's Behavior Scales, or the American Association on Mental Deficiency's Adaptive Behavior Scales, can be particularly useful in determining social and behavioral functioning. This is particularly true if the results of the present testing can be compared to previous testings. If not, they will serve as a baseline for retesting.

Traditional measures or indices of brain injury, such as the deterioration quotient or deterioration index, which compare subtests of the Wechsler Adult Intelligence Scale (WAIS) (Wechsler, 1955), are not particularly useful with persons with mental retardation. For instance, one of the categories (concrete thinking or the absence of abstract attitude) is measured by the use of proverbs presented in the Comprehension subtest. This category may be useful among nonretarded individuals, but these questions generally are not even asked when using the Wechsler Adult Intelligence Scale–Revised because most retarded individuals have failed items in this section before the proverbs are presented. In addition, Wechsler norms for individual subtests among retarded individuals are not necessarily those that would be expected.

Wechsler Adult Intelligence Scale norms for higher functioning institutionalized mentally retarded individuals have been presented by Hill (1978) (Table 3). The scaled scores on Comprehension, Picture Completion, and Object Assembly were among the highest subtests, while Arithmetic, Digit Symbol, and

Table 3. Mean subtest scaled scores on the WAIS

Subtest	Mean
Information	3.9
Comprehension	4.3
Arithmetic	2.9
Similarities	3.3
Digit Span	3.3
Vocabulary	3.5
Digit Symbol	2.9
Picture Completion	4.1
Block Design	3.4
Picture Arrangement	3.2
Object Assembly	4.5
N	1,107

Adapted from Hill (1978).

Picture Arrangement were among the lowest. However, some inconsistencies were found between the five populations reported in this study. One of the samples (originally reported by Barclay, Giray, & Altkin, 1977, and not reported in Table 3) did not correlate with any of the other four samples. In addition, tests of homogeneity of variance between the samples indicated increased variability within this sample as compared to the other samples and to a higher functioning group in general. It could be that the pattern of functioning is related to overall intelligence and that different norms will be needed for each functioning level. While further research needs to be performed to test this hypothesis, Hill (1978) performed one analysis of 111 institutionalized mentally retarded individuals whose full-scale IQ scores fell within five ranges (i.e., 11–21, 22–32, 33–43, 44–54, above 54) and found similar patterns among the groups, suggesting that the pattern of WAIS subtest scores does not change appreciably with IQ for mentally retarded and developmentally disabled individuals.

While standardized psychometric evaluations provide important information, they are not fully satisfactory for all mentally retarded individuals and do not measure all areas of cognitive functioning. To supplement these tests, new tasks, derived from experimental research, and a mental status evaluation are needed. Each of these must be adjusted to the overall functioning level of the individual.

One example of a new test for dementia based on experimental research, appropriate to

mentally retarded persons, is that developed by Dalton (Dalton & Crapper, 1977; Dalton & Crapper McLachlan, 1984; Dalton, Crapper, & Schlotterer, 1974). Employing a two-choice, matching-to-sample, and delayed matching-to-sample task among severely and profoundly mentally retarded institutionalized residents, Dalton and his colleagues have been able to provide early identification and follow-up of dementing Down syndrome individuals. This paradigm has been extended to include a more complicated three-choice, delayed matching-to-sample task using a computer in order to test higher functioning, noninstitutionalized mentally retarded persons employed by sheltered workshops. This population is the subject of a 5-year follow-along period. In conjunction with this study, mental status evaluation for this population is being standardized (see Appendix A). This evaluation has more detail than that used before by Thase, Liss, Smeltzer, and Maloon (1982) and Wisniewski et al. (1978). In addition, annual standardized psychometric evaluations and neurological examinations are employed.

The mental status evaluation, as employed here, is a relatively informal, open-ended measure of specific functioning areas (orientation to person, place, and time; color naming; concentration; motor and amnestic apraxia, and memory; and anomia). It allows for informal observations (e.g., ability to attend to a conversation), as well as structured tasks (e.g., color naming). Each of the questions is initially phrased so as to elicit a response in which the individual recalls the information. Items that are failed are repeated in the form of a recognition test in which the individual has a choice of three responses (e.g., "Is today Sunday, Tuesday, or Friday?"). To assess orientation, three areas are tested: person, place, and time. Items that are recognized but not recalled are given half credit.

Color naming is assessed through the following process. Four colored objects (red, blue, green, and yellow) are presented and the individual is requested to name the colors. The task is repeated and a total score of correct naming is obtained. Incorrect substitutions, if closely related (e.g., calling a yellow object "orange") and used consistently, are considered correct. Recognition trials are given by asking the individual to point to the object that has a particular color. Correct recognition responses are counted as half credit.

To assess concentration, the individual is requested to recite the alphabet, to count forward to 30 and backward from 20. Omissions are scored and the subject may be prompted within each of the tasks if it appears that he or she is searching for the next item.

To assess for motor and amnestic apraxia, the individual is required first to write his or her name and print the alphabet. Verbal prompts are allowed if the individual omits letters in the alphabet; written examples are not allowed. He or she is also asked to draw figures from memory. Examples of each figure failed are presented and the individual is asked to copy each making his or her drawing the same size as the original. During the presentation, each figure is named. After all figures have been copied, the individual is asked to draw each figure on command (e.g., "draw a circle"). Amnestic apraxia would be suggested by an inability to draw all the figures on command. Scoring is based on qualitative judgments of the individual's ability to draw horizontal, vertical, oblique, and curved lines rather than the figure itself. Mild impairments are indicated by wavy lines, corners failing to meet, hand shakiness, obvious compensating mechanisms (e.g., making the productions very small), and a comparison of the letter writing to any previous examples that may be in the individual's records.

To assess anomia, the individual is asked to name five objects. Full credit is obtained if the whole name is given or if a differentiation can be made between the object (e.g., heel) and the expected confusion (e.g., shoe). Further questioning is allowed (e.g., "Yes, but what do we call this part of the shoe?").

DIFFERENTIAL DIAGNOSES

Once dementia has been documented, the etiology of the decline in functioning must be established (a differential diagnosis among three types of dementia is presented in Table 4). The differential diagnosis is conducted to define

Table 4. Differentiating depression, Alzheimer's, and multi-infarct dementia

	Depression	Alzheimer's	Multi-infarct
Onset	Relatively rapid changes in mood and behavior	Insidious, ill-defined	Abrupt, step-wise
Mood and behavior	Stable, depressed or agitated	Labile, may be depressed	Variable with periods of recovery
Mental competence	Unaffected except for attention, concentration, and interests	Increasingly defective	Defective with recovery; step-wise losses
Complaints	Memory concentration and self-image, overconcern with symptoms, loss of interest	Other's complaints about him or her, denial of symptoms	Memory and behavioral losses appropriate to area of infarct
Somatic symptoms	Anxiety, sleep, eating, fatigue	Sleep disorders, anxiety	Anxiety, focal, neurological
Prognosis	Generally self-limited; 20%–35% of cases are chronic	Chronic and progressive	Progressive unless treatable
Past history	Depression episodes	None specifically related	Hypertension
CT scan	Normal	Generalized atrophy	Focal evidence of stroke
EEG	Normal	Generalized slowing	Focal abnormalities

multi-infarct dementia (see Table 4). These conditions depress cognitive functioning and psychomotor activity. Part of the difficulty in the differential diagnosis lies in the fact that depression often accompanies dementia of other types. The individual may recognize that he or she can no longer perform as well as before and becomes depressed by this fact. On the other hand, the decrease in cognitive functioning may be a result of depression. Often the differential diagnosis is made as a result of the clinical history, time factor, and the response to antidepressants.

Historical information is particularly important in the differential diagnoses between different causes of dementia. Dementia of the Alzheimer's type is relatively progressive and of variable duration. Often there are periods in which the cognitive level remains at a static level before continuing its progressive decline. Depression and multi-infarct dementias (MID) tend to have a relatively rapid onset and to fluctuate in the severity of cognitive losses exhibited by the individuals. Depression is usually a reversible condition, while MID may be partially or completely reversible in some cases only with time and appropriate treatment.

It is also important to interview the individual to discover how he or she feels about his or her condition. For instance, depressed people tend to complain about their lives and to exaggerate their failures, whereas individuals with Alzheimer's disease tend to externalize their complaints and to cover up their symptoms. In addition, depressed individuals tend to have a history of depression and respond well to medications. Individuals with Alzheimer's disease typically do not have such a history. While these people may respond to antidepressants, cognitive symptoms reappear relatively soon. Additional evidence that may help in the differential diagnosis can be obtained from interviewing relatives or significant others who know the person. These people tend to complain more about the memory of depressed persons and about the more generalized disabilities of persons with Alzheimer's disease (Gurland & Toner, 1983). It must be pointed out, however, that memory loss is the most frequent consistent finding in dementia of the Alzheimer's type. Sim and Sussman (1962) reported that memory loss was the first symptom in 22 of their 33 cases. In addition it has been present in almost all of the histories of individuals whose dementia has been confirmed by neurological reports (e.g., Coblentz et al., 1973; Goodman, 1953; Ziegler, 1954). No other symptom was so frequently encountered upon first presentation or within the first year. Recent memory loss as an early indication of dementia also occurs among persons with mental retardation (Dalton & Crapper McLachlan, 1984).

In practice, when attempting differential diagnosis, one should consider the overlap of symptoms as well as the possibility of mixed etiology (e.g., a diagnosis of Alzheimer's disease does not rule out the possibility of co-occurrence of MID). This overlap makes the diagnoses particularly difficult (see Liston & La Rue, 1983, for a review of some of the problems).

In summary, the diagnosis of Alzheimer's dementia is made on the basis of clinical history, psychological and neurological examination repeated annually, additional lab tests (e.g., electrophysiological, electroencephalogram [EEG], brain stem auditory evoked response [BAERs], neuroradiological, computerized transaxial tomography [CTT] scan), and, if indicated, biochemical data (e.g., B_{12}, folic acid, thyroid, parathyroid levels, SMA 12, CBC) to determine the cause or causes of dementia.

DEMENTIA IN DOWN SYNDROME

In addition to the importance of the problem of
aging and dementia among mentally retarded
persons in general, one subpopulation, persons
with Down syndrome (DS), are of particular
interest. Several investigators have reported
decreases in intellectual and developmental
quotients with advancing age in persons with
Down syndrome (Carr, 1975; Dameron, 1963;
Griffiths, 1976; Koch, 1973).

Clinical Evidence of Alzheimer's Disease

Clinical histories of neurological regression
including personality aberrations in the form of
apathy, sudden affective changes, deterioration of personal hygiene, loss of vocabulary,
and increasingly abnormal neurological signs
have been reported (Dalton & Crapper, 1977;
Dalton & Crapper McLachlan, 1984; Dalton et
al., 1974; Loesch-Mdzewska, 1968; Owens,
Dawson, & Losin, 1971; Thase et al., 1982;
Wisniewski, Dalton, Crapper McLachlan, Wen,
& Wisniewski, in press; Wisniewski et al.,
1982, 1978; Wisniewski & Wisniewski, 1983).
Dalton and Crapper McLachlan (1984) have
reported that recent memory loss as measured
by a delayed matching-to-sample task was consistently among the first indicators of dementia
within an institutionalized population of severely and profoundly mentally retarded individuals with Down syndrome. According to
their results, 24% of the Down syndrome individuals over the age of 40 showed signs of
memory impairment. None of the elderly,
matched, mentally retarded controls, nor
younger mentally retarded controls, with or
without Down syndrome, failed the task. In a
prospective clinical-pathological study, seven
individuals with clinically suggestive Alzheimer's disease and Down syndrome have
been followed for up to 12 years beyond the
first clinical indications (Wisniewski et al., in
press). Retrospective clinical-pathological
studies of 49 Down syndrome cases above the
age of 30 indicated dementia of the Alzheimer's type occurred in up to 30% of the
cases (Wisniewski & Wisniewski, 1983; Wisniewski et al., in press). An example of de-

mentia of the Alzheimer type is that of a
60-year-old Down syndrome individual who
was moderately retarded, has regressed, and is
now profoundly demented. She was at home all
her life, cleaning the house, helping to cook
and shop, playing with children, and had developed good self-care skills until the age of 48
years. She also enjoyed watching television
programs. Academically she was functioning
at about a 6- or 7-year level, but socially she
was minimally dependent in her daily activities
and was oriented to time, place, and person.
Progressively, she lost all these abilities within
6 to 8 years. Now, at 60 years, she is completely dependent in daily life activities, dis-
oriented to time and place, and exhibits no
speech or comprehension. Overall she is currently functioning at a 1-year level. At the age
of 57 she developed urinary incontinence and
severe sleep difficulties. The CTT scan suggested low pressure hydrocephalus. At 58
years of age, a ventriculo-peritoneal shunt was
performed. She obtained transient urinary control but her mental status did not change. She
recently developed grand mal type seizures
that, with Dilantin treatment, are well controlled. She looks older than her age (see Figure 1), and the neurological examination also
demonstrated frontal release signs, hyperreflexia, apraxia, and poor fine motor coordination. The CTT scan showed brain atrophy
(Figure 2), and an EEG showed slow background activity (Figure 3).

Neuropathological
Evidence of Alzheimer's Disease

Neuropathological changes in the form of neurofibrillary tangles and senile plaques, identical to Alzheimer's disease, have been described in persons with Down syndrome who
died after the age of 35 years by Jervis (1948)
and Struwe (1929), and more recently by Crapper, Dalton, Skopitz, Scott, and Hachinski
(1974), Malamud (1964, 1972), Olson and
Shaw (1969), Ropper and Williams (1980),
Wisniewski et al. (in press), Wisniewski, Jervis,
Moretz, and Wisniewski (1979), and Wisniewski, Wisniewski, and Wen (1983). Occasionally, these changes can be seen in some brains

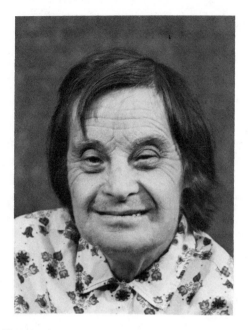

Figure 1. A 56-year-old Down syndrome person. Note wrinkled skin and sparse, fine hair. She has Alzheimer's disease.

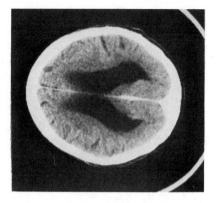

Figure 2. Computerized transaxial tomography scan shows brain atrophy.

of younger persons with Down syndrome, even in the second decade (Malamud, 1964, 1972; Wisniewski et al., 1983, in press). Detailed descriptions of neuropathological changes in Alzheimer's disease can be found in Wisniewski et al. (1984).

Extensive studies (Dalton & Crapper, 1977; Dalton & Crapper McLachlan, 1984; Thase et al., 1982; Wisniewski et al., 1983, in press) have demonstrated that dementia in Down syndrome does not occur in all individuals, contrary to what might be expected from the neuropathological observations reported in the literature. Dalton and Crapper McLachlan (1984) reported evidence of progressive dementia in only 24% of their severely and profoundly retarded Down syndrome subjects. Wisniewski et al. (1983, in press) obtained evidence that dementia occurred in 30%, while Thase et al. (1982) reported that 45% of Down syndrome individuals showed signs of clinical dementia. The Down syndrome population in these studies was mostly institutionalized and functioned at the severe and profound levels of mental retardation.

Wisniewski et al. (1978) studied 50 institutionalized individuals with Down syndrome to determine the clinical course of precocious aging, as well as mental and neurological deterioration. This study established statistically significant differences in neurological and psychological abnormalities (mental deterioration) between individuals younger and older than 35 years of age, pointing to the possibility of progressive Alzheimer's type changes in the central nervous system. A higher incidence of memory loss, impairment of short-term visual retention, frontal release signs, hypertonia, hyperreflexia, long-tract signs, and psychiatric problems, as well as the presence of external features of precocious aging, were found in the older group (see Table 2). Although the only comparisons made were on the basis of age groups (under and over 35 years old), such signs of clinical regression corresponded with subsequently reported acceleration of age-associated changes in the brain (Wisniewski et al., 1982, 1983).

Using CTT scan in 30 Down syndrome individuals, Wisniewski et al. (1982) reported that 26.6% of the cases showed basal ganglia calcification and 85% showed different degrees of brain atrophy. Also, seven individuals had clinical evidence of regression and a history of seizures (one during the second decade, three during the third, and three during the fourth decade of life). In this group, calcium homeostasis was investigated in 12 Down syndrome

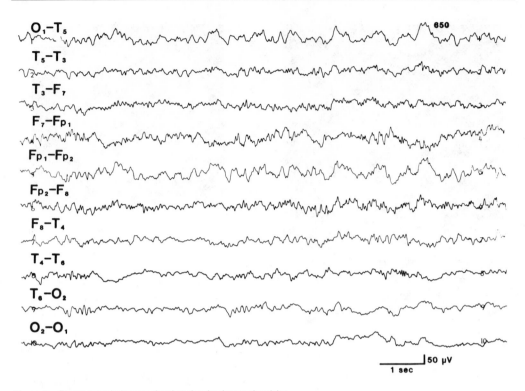

Figure 3. Electroencephalogram showing slow background activity.

subjects (total serum and ionized calcium, 25 OHD [25-hydroxy calciferol] and PTH [para-thormone]). None of these studies showed abnormalities.

Absence of evidence of a generalized calcium metabolic disturbance in association with a higher incidence of basal ganglia calcification (BGC) among Down syndrome individuals suggests that local brain factors may be causative and may be associated with an acceleration of aging in the nervous system of individuals with Down syndrome. Wisniewski et al. (1982) also studied the frequency and intensity of histologically detected BGC in 100 Down syndrome brains. The BGC was demonstrated in all 100 brains. This strengthens the hypothesis that BGC may be a characteristic of Down syndrome and is a manifestation of premature aging in this disorder. BGC in non-Down syndrome persons is usually not apparent until beyond the fifth decade; in the Down syndrome postmortem study, it was seen much earlier (Wisniewski et al., 1982).

A third study (Wisniewski et al., 1983) reported on the conditions of the brains of Down syndrome individuals who died in institutions. There were 51 individuals below and 49 above the age of 30 years. A history of regression (loss of intererst in work and surroundings; loss of cognitive, motor function, and personal hygiene skills) was documented from the medical records in two cases (3.8%) below and 13 (28%) above the age of 30. It was found that seven of the 51 individuals below 30 (13.7%) and all (100%) of the 49 above age 30 had neuritic plaques with or without neurofibrillary tangles. The numbers of plaques and tangles correlated well with the history of regression, with the duration of regression, and with the age of the individuals. However, there were some brains of Down syndrome individuals who were over the age of 35 in which the number of plaques and tangles was very small. Based on these clinico-pathological findings, it seems reasonable to conclude that about 30% of Down syndrome individuals over the age of

30 have clinical signs and symptoms of dementia with corresponding pathological changes compatible with senile dementia of the Alzheimer's type (SDAT). These data also suggest that not all Down syndrome individuals will develop clinical SDAT. However SDAT may develop much earlier in Down syndrome and is about 3–5 times more prevalent than in the general population. Thus, Down syndrome appears to be of great importance to the study of the etiology and pathogenesis of Alzheimer's disease.

RECOMMENDATIONS

With advances in medicine and the continued life expectancies of persons who are mentally retarded, dementia among this population will continue to pose problems for meeting the needs of elderly mentally retarded persons. Added to this is the fact that more and more individuals with mental retardation are now living within the community rather than in institutions. Increasing numbers of independent practitioners will see mentally retarded individuals among their clientele. Thus, there is a greater need for clinicians to be aware of the needs and patterns of behaviors of this population.

Mentally retarded individuals, particularly those over the age of 30 or 40, should have annual evaluations not only of their physical status, but also of their mental status (see Appendices A and B). If individuals are found to have early indications of dementia, they should be referred for more detailed examinations by a psychologist and a neurologist and, if indicated, laboratory investigation should be conducted to properly differentiate and define etiology. Special attention needs to be paid to indications of personality changes, occurrence of seizures, and urinary incontinence.

In addition to these annual evaluations, formalized psychometric evaluations should be conducted at least every 2–3 years to obtain early indications of any loss of functioning and to serve as a baseline for further evaluations when and if they become necessary. These biannual or triannual evaluations should also include a formalized neurological examination to look for minor and major neurological signs.

If dementia occurs and is associated with a genetic deterioration process, genetic counseling may be recommended for the relatives of the individual who is dementing (e.g., if dementia is due to familial Alzheimer's disease, Huntington's chorea, etc.). In addition to the differential diagnosis to define the etiology of the dementia, it is necessary to obtain appropriate treatment. (For more detail on treatment, see Chatterjie, Chapter 16, this volume.)

REFERENCES

Allison, R. S. (1961). Chronic amnesic syndromes in the elderly. *Proceedings of the Royal Society of Medicine, 54,* 961–965.

American Psychiatric Association. (1980). *Diagnostic and statistical manual of mental disorders III.* Washington, DC: Author.

Barclay, A. G., Giray, E. F., & Altkin, W. M. (1977). WAIS subtest score distributions of institutionalized retardates. *Perceptual and Motor Skills, 44,* 488–490.

Bilash, I., & Zubek, J. P. (1960). The effects of age on factorially "pure" mental abilities. *Journal of Gerontology, 15,* 175–182.

Birren, J. E. (1963). Research on the psychologic aspects of aging. *Geriatrics, 18,* 393–403.

Carr, J. (1975). *Young children with Down's syndrome.* London: Butterworths.

Clark, J. W. (1960). The aging dimension: A factorial analysis of individual differences with age on psychological and physiological measurements. *Journal of Gerontology, 15,* 183–187.

Coblentz, J. M., Mattis, S., Zingesser, L. H., Kasoff, S. S., Wisniewski, H. M., & Kutzman, R. (1973). Presenile dementia: Clinical aspects and evaluation of cerebrospinal fluid dynamics. *Archives of Neurology, 29,* 299–308.

Crapper, D. R., Dalton, A. J., Skopitz, M., Scott, J. W., & Hachinski, V. C. (1974). Alzheimer degeneration in Down syndrome. Electrophysiologic alterations and histopathologic findings. *Archives of Neurology, 32,* 618–623.

Dalton, A. J., & Crapper, D. R. (1977). Down's syndrome and aging of the brain. In P. Mittler (Ed.), *Research to practice in mental retardation: Biomedical Aspects* (Vol. 3, pp. 391–400). Baltimore: University Park Press.

Dalton, A. J., & Crapper McLachlan, D. R. (1984). Incidence of memory deterioration in aging persons with Down's Syndrome. In J. M. Berg (Ed.), *Perspectives and progress in mental retardation: Biomedical Aspects* (Vol. 2, pp. 55–62). Baltimore: University Park Press.

Dalton, A. J., Crapper, D. R., & Schlotterer, G. R.

(1974). Alzheimer's disease in Down's syndrome: Visual retention deficits. *Cortex, 10,* 366–377.

Dameron, L. E. (1963). Development of intelligence of infants with mongolism. *Childhood Development, 34,* 733–738.

Dyken, P., & Krawiecki, N. (1983). Neurodegenerative diseases of infancy and childhood. *Annals of Neurology, 13,* 351–364.

Eysenck, M. D. (1945). An exploratory study of mental organization in senility. *Journal of Neurology, Neurosurgery, and Psychiatry, 8,* 15–21.

Goldstein, G., & Shelly, C. H. (1975). Similarities and differences between psychological deficit in aging and brain damage. *Journal of Gerontology, 30,* 448–455.

Goodman, L. (1953). Alzheimer's disease: A clinico-pathologic analysis of 23 cases with a theory on pathogenesis. *Journal of Nervous and Mental Disease, 118,* 97–130.

Griffiths, M. I. (1976). Development of children with Down's syndrome. *Physiotherapy, 62,* 11–15.

Gurland, B., & Toner, J. (1983). Differentiating dementia from nondementing conditions. *Advances in Neurology, 38,* 1–17.

Hill, A. L. (1978). WAIS subtest score characteristics of institutionalized mentally retarded samples. *Perceptual and Motor Skills, 47,* 131–134.

Jarvik, L. F. (1975). Thoughts on the psychobiology of aging. *American Psychologist, 30,* 576–583.

Jervis, G. A. (1948). Early senile dementia in mongolid idiocy. *American Journal of Psychiatry, 105,* 102–106.

Katzman, R. (1981). Early detection of senile dementia. *Hospital Practice, 16,* 61–76.

Koch, G. (1973). *Down-syndrome; mongolismus.* Erlangen, in Kommission bei. Palm & Enke.

Lezak, M. D. (1976). *Neuropsychological assessment.* New York: Oxford University Press.

Liss, L., Shim, C., Thase, M., Smeltzer, D., Maloon, J., & Couri, D. (1980). Relationship between Down syndrome (DS) and dementia Alzheimer type (DAT). (Abstract) *Journal of Neuropathology and Experimental Neurology, 39,* 371.

Liston, E. H., & La Rue, A. (1983). Clinical differentiation of primary degenerative and multi-infarct dementia: A critical review of the evidence. Part 1: Clinical studies. *Biological Psychiatry, 18,* 1451–1465.

Loesch-Mdzewska, D. (1968). Some aspects of the neurology of Down's syndrome. *Journal of Mental Deficiency Research, 12,* 237–246.

Malamud, N. (1964). Neuropathology. In H. A. Stevens & R. Heber (Eds.), *Mental retardation: A review of research* (pp. 429–452). Chicago: The University of Chicago Press.

Malamud, N. (1972). Neuropathology of organic brain syndromes associated with aging. In C. M. Gaitz (Ed.), *Aging and the brain* (pp. 63–87). New York: Plenum Press.

Olson, M. I., & Shaw, C. M. (1969). Presenile dementia and Alzheimer's disease in monogolism. *Brain, 92,* 147–156.

Owens, D., Dawson, J. C., & Losin, S. (1971). Alzheimer's disease in Down's syndrome. *American Journal of Mental Deficiency, 75,* 606–612.

Reitan, R. M. (1967). Psychological changes associated with aging and with cerebral damage. *Mayo Clinic Proceedings, 42,* 653–673.

Ropper, A. H., & Williams, R. S. (1980). Relationship between plaques, tangles, and dementia in Down syndrome. *Neurology, 30,* 639–644.

Sim, M., & Sussman, I. (1962). Alzheimer's disease: Its natural history and differential diagnosis. *Journal of Nervous and Mental Disease, 135,* 489–499.

Struwe, F. (1929). Histopathologisch untersuchungen uber Entstehung und Wesen der senilen plaques. *Zeitschrift Fuer Die Gesamte Neurologie und Psychiatrie, 122,* 291–307.

Thase, M. E., Liss, L., Smeltzer, D., & Maloon, J. (1982). Clinical evaluation of dementia in Down's Syndrome: A preliminary report. *Journal of Mental Deficiency Research, 26,* 239–244.

Wechsler, D. (1955). *Manual for the Wechsler Adult Intelligence Scale.* New York: Psychological Corp.

Williams, M. (1970). Geriatric patients. In P. Mittler (Ed.), *The psychological assessment of mental and physical handicaps* (pp. 319–339). London: Methuen.

Wisniewski, K. E., Dalton, A. J., Crapper McLachlan, D. R., Wen, G. Y., & Wisniewski, H. M. (in press). Alzheimer disease in Down syndrome: Clinico-pathological studies. *Neurology 1984.*

Wisniewski, K. E., French, J. H., Rosen, J. F., Kozlowski, P. B., Tenner, M., & Wisniewski, H. M. (1982). Basal ganglia calcification (BGC) in Down's syndrome (DS)—another manifestation of premature aging. *Annals of the N.Y. Academy of Sciences, 396,* 179–189.

Wisniewski, K., Howe, J., Williams, D. G., & Wisniewski, H. M. (1978). Precocious aging and dementia in patients with Down's syndrome. *Biological Psychiatry, 13,* 619–627.

Wisniewski, K., Jervis, G. A., Moretz, R. C., & Wisniewski, H. M. (1979). Alzheimer neurofibrillary tangles in diseases other than senile and presenile dementia. *Annals of Neurology, 5,* 288–294.

Wisniewski, K. E., & Wisniewski, H. M. (1983). Age associated changes and dementia in Down's syndrome. In B. Reisberg (Ed.), *Alzheimer's disease* (pp. 319–326). New York: The Free Press.

Wisniewski, K., Wisniewski, H. M., & Wen, G. Y. (1983). Plaques, tangles and dementia in Down Syndrome. (Abstract) *Journal of Neuropathology and Experimental Neurology, 42,* 340.

Wisniewski, K. E., Wisniewski, H. M., & Wen, G. Y. (in press). Plaques, tangles and dementia in 100 DS brains with retrospective clinico-pathological study. *Annals of Neurology.*

Ziegler, D. K. (1954). Cerebral atrophy in psychiatric patients. *American Journal of Psychiatry, 111,* 454–458.

General Instructions for Evaluation of Mental Status

This is a test of mental status. We are interested in four areas of functioning:

1. Orientation (Numbers 1–15)
2. Anomia (Numbers 16–29)
3. Concentration (Numbers 30–32)
4. Coordination (Numbers 33–37)

Questions in each area are organized to investigate the client's ability to recall information, or if the client is unable to recall the information, he or she is given three choices for recognition.

In addition, examples of handwriting and drawings are requested.

If the client is unable to draw the figures on command, the examiner should draw the figure and ask the client to copy it. All figures produced by the examiner should be clearly labeled as such.

The questionnaire is designed to assist in the client's annual evaluation, and comparisons between evaluations should be made in order to objectively assess possible deterioration of functioning capacity.

Questionnaire for IBR Evaluation of Mental Status

(Put answers on score sheet)

1. What is your name? Is it _____, _____, or _____?
2. How old are you? Are you _____, _____, or _____?
3. When is your birthday? Is it _____, _____, or _____?
4. Who do you live with? (If living independently "Who are your neighbors"?)
   Do you live with _____, _____, or _____?
5. What is the name of your supervisor? Is it _____, _____, or _____?
6. What is the name of the street where you live? Is it _____, _____, or _____?
7. What is the name of this city (town)? Is it _____, _____, or _____?
8. In what state do you live? Is it _____, _____, or _____?
9. Where do you eat lunch? Is it _____, _____, or _____?
10. Where are we now? Are we _____, _____, or _____?
11. What day is today? Is it _____, _____, or _____?
12. What year is it? Is it _____, _____, or _____?
13. What time is it? Is it _____, _____, or _____?
14. What do we call this season? Is it _____, _____, or _____?
15. What month is it now? Is it _____, _____, or _____?
16. What color is this? Which is the red one?
17. What color is this? Which is the blue one?
18. What color is this? Which is the yellow one?
19. What color is this? Which is the green one?
20. What is this? (finger) Is it _____, _____, or _____?
21. What is this? (nail) Is it _____, _____, or _____?
22. What is this? (belt) Is it _____, _____, or _____?
23. What is this? (buckle) Is it _____, _____, or _____?
24. What is this? (button) Is it _____, _____, or _____?
25. What is this? (hole) Is it _____, _____, or _____?
26. What is this? (shoe) Is it _____, _____, or _____?
27. What is this? (heel) Is it _____, _____, or _____?
28. What is this? (watch) Is it _____, _____, or _____?
29. What is this? (band) Is it _____, _____, or _____?
30. Name the letters in the alphabet: A B C D E F G H I J K L M N O P Q R S T U V W X Y Z
31. Count from 1 to 30. _____
32. Count backwards from 20 to 1. _____

33.   Print the alphabet (A–E) here (on the score sheet).
34.   Numbers 1 to 5 here (on the score sheet).
35.   Draw a circle here (on the score sheet).   Copy.
36.   Draw a square here (on the score sheet).   Copy.
37.   Draw a diamond here (on the score sheet).   Copy.

Score Sheet for IBR Evaluation of Mental Status

Name or I.D. no. _____

Date of birth: _____

Diagnosis: _____

Last IQ score: _____ Date given: _____ Test given: _____

Date of examination: _____

For each of the following items, indicate X for yes, recall or good recognition, or O for no, no recall or no recognition.

	Recall	Recognition
Person		
1. Name	_____	_____
2. Age	_____	_____
3. Birthday	_____	_____
4. Living	_____	_____
5. Supervisor	_____	_____

33. Handwriting—Letters A to E

Place		
6. Street	_____	_____
7. City (town)	_____	_____
8. State	_____	_____
9. Lunch	_____	_____

34. Numbers one to five

Time		
10. Now	_____	_____
11. Day	_____	_____
12. Year	_____	_____
13. Time	_____	_____
14. Season	_____	_____
15. Month	_____	_____

35. Circles

Color		
16. Red	_____	_____
17. Blue	_____	_____
18. Yellow	_____	_____
19. Green	_____	_____

36. Squares

Anomia		
20. Finger	_____	_____
21. Nail	_____	_____
22. Belt	_____	_____
23. Buckle	_____	_____
24. Button	_____	_____
25. Hole	_____	_____
26. Shoe	_____	_____
27. Heel	_____	_____
28. Watch	_____	_____
29. Band	_____	_____

37. Diamonds

30. Reciting alphabet	List omissions _____	Prompts _____
31. Counting (1 to 30)	List omissions _____	Prompts _____
32. Counting (20 to 1)	List omissions _____	Prompts _____

Examiner comments: _____

_____

In comparison to previous assessment: *(Circle one)*

Much better   Better   The same   Worse   Much worse

chapter

13

Selected Psychological Processes and Aging among Older Developmentally Disabled Persons

Gary B. Seltzer

There exists a paucity of knowledge related to the psychological domains of cognitive, behavioral, and affective processes as experienced by elderly developmentally disabled persons. Drawing from the gerontological and mental retardation literature, this chapter describes selected aspects from within each of these psychological domains. In the cognitive domain, memory and intellectual functioning are reviewed, and it is concluded that elderly developmentally disabled persons need to be exposed to social reinforcement in order to maintain their level of mental functioning. Behavioral and affective implications are drawn from prevailing psychosocial theories of aging. Also discussed is the role of activities, as well as life satisfaction, environmental opportunities, and individual competence as variables that are relevant to theories of psychological functioning of elderly developmentally disabled persons. The chapter concludes with a discussion about grief, death, and dying—life cycle tasks that have important psychological meaning for elderly developmentally disabled individuals. This chapter also offers a number of implications for the provision of services to developmentally disabled persons age 65 and older. The chapter points to the importance of attending to the psychological needs and strengths of an aging developmentally disabled person in addition to responding to the more commonly recognized need for residential and health care services.

ONLY RECENTLY HAS there been a recognition in the research literature that disabled persons reach old age and that, as a part of this aging process, they experience developmental transitions at times similar to and in other cases different from their non–developmentally disabled aging counterparts (Cotton, Sison, & Starr, 1981; DiGiovanni, 1978; Tymchuk, 1979). The placement of older develop-

mentally disabled individuals into a variety of community settings has been described (Bruininks, Hill, & Thorsheim, 1982; Janicki & MacEachron, 1984; O'Connor, Justice, & Warren, 1970). These studies examined demographic, service, and individual characteristics of this increasingly visible group of people. Other studies made comparisons between cohorts of younger and older develop-

The author wishes to thank Dr. Marsha M. Seltzer for her comments on earlier drafts and Marge Drugovich for her technical assistance. Also, appreciation is extended to Leslie Peterson for her aid in preparing the manuscript and to Suzanne Benson for sharing her insights about this client group.

mentally disabled persons with respect to type and prevalence of psychiatric and behavior problems (Jacobson, 1982a, b) and community adjustment (Seltzer, Seltzer, & Sherwood, 1982). Only a few studies have presented descriptions of quality of life of aging developmentally disabled persons (Baker, Seltzer, & Seltzer, 1977; Edgerton, Bollinger, & Herr, 1984). No studies were found that specifically examined the elderly developmentally disabled person's experience in coping with the developmental tasks of aging such as death and dying, and cognitive and physical losses.

The relative dearth of descriptive accounts, theoretical papers, and research investigations limits the understanding of the range of affective and behavioral processes experienced by the elderly developmentally disabled person. Little is known about the variability in this group regarding how they spend their days and even less about what meaning they attribute to their activities or inactivity. However, on the basis of known characteristics described in the burgeoning gerontological literature and some of the mental retardation literature, it is possible to extrapolate characteristics of elderly developmentally disabled persons. Some of the common life cycle problems that occur for older persons in general can prove meaningful when applied to older developmentally disabled individuals.

There are some risks in using this body of literature that are related to the methodological problems of translation from one population group to another (see M. Seltzer, Chapter 9, this volume), particularly as the literature relates to those developmentally disabled persons who cognitively, socially, or emotionally are most impaired. Busse (1980) notes that as humans age, they accumulate a large array of different life experiences, becoming increasingly divergent rather than similar. He also observes, though, that "perhaps this divergence phenomenon reverses in extreme old age, as very old people show considerable similarity in certain characteristics" (p. 523). That is, as able-bodied persons become older and experience increasing difficulties in functioning, they may become impaired and their quality of life may be similar to that of the lifelong disabled person. From this perspective, the elderly developmentally disabled person might be most similar to frail, elderly individuals, usually "old old" persons over age 75, as distinguished from "young old" persons, age 65–75 (Kane, Solomon, Beck, Keeler, & Kane, 1981). For the elderly developmentally disabled person, functional limitations in the biological, social, or psychological spheres might supersede chronological age as a cause of frailty.

It seems both pragmatic and theoretically justifiable for the purposes of this chapter to assume that as people age, disabled or not, they confront many similar developmental tasks, although the timing of the life experience might differ as might the problem-solving approach utilized and subsequent meaning derived from the experiences. Furthermore, the perspective presented herein is that the process of becoming older per se may not independently change one's psychological status. Rather, the passage through life experiences toward challenges of accepting cognitive, biological, and functional limitations; reorienting one's priorities from work to other meaningful activities; coping with losses of primary relationships; and accepting death and mortality and other developmental tasks in this phase of the life cycle influences behavior, thought patterns, and life satisfaction.

The paragraphs that follow are devoted to a description of the psychological processes experienced by elderly persons in general and by elderly developmentally disabled persons. A broad array of topics was chosen for study, albeit from an even larger arena of untapped possibilities. Omitted from this chapter is a review of psychopathology and aging. The topics chosen—mental status; psychological implications derived from theories of aging; and grief, death, and dying—were selected on the basis of availability of literature and according to the author's judgment of their relevance.

MENTAL STATUS

Siegler (1980) notes the broad range of topics included within the psychology of aging and suggests organizing these topics into psychology as a natural science and psychology as a social science. The latter grouping includes topics covered in this chapter such as bereavement, grief and dying, and the psychological processes and theories of aging. This section on mental status falls within the natural science category. Reviewed selectively and briefly herein are the laboratory-based research studies on intelligence and memory. Once again, most of the research cited has been conducted on non–developmentally disabled persons; however, implications are drawn for elderly developmentally disabled persons.

Methodologically, the study of mental status in the general elderly population poses assessment and, often, research design problems that commonly exist in the study of mental status among developmentally disabled persons as well. These methodological problems occur because of the increased prevalence of chronic illnesses in older persons. For example, older persons with arthritis or Parkinson's disease are likely to do poorly on timed tasks because of their disability and not necessarily because of an impaired ability to reason. In addition, older people are more likely to be research and laboratory "shy" than younger subjects because of minimal exposure to new technology and probably, even more importantly, because of the fear of failure. Certainly, the latter dynamic of fear of failure prevails among persons with developmental disabilities. Furthermore, cohort or generational differences, such as differential educational achievements and economic status, are problematic when conducting studies on aging and cognitive process. Since cross-sectional studies that compare younger and older persons' performance on laboratory tasks comprise a large amount of the research in the area, it is important to weed out the above-mentioned type of external factors (chronic illness, fear of failure) from those that might truly be attributable to age.

Although physical health plays a major mediating role in the study of mental status and aging (Abrahams & Birren, 1973; Avorn, 1982), it is too broad a topic to discuss here. Health and its relationship to mental status, particularly as it relates to dementia, is an important issue among elderly developmentally disabled persons, and many investigators are studying this problem (e.g., Eisner, 1983; Lott & Lai, 1982; Tait, 1983). Nevertheless, for the purposes of this chapter, accelerated neurological aging due to particular syndromes (e.g., Down syndrome) or other illnesses is not presented. Also, the relationship between psychopathology and mental status, although quite prevalent among elderly developmentally disabled persons, is beyond the scope of this section. However, emotional responses and their relationship to cognitive processes are discussed.

Intelligence

Of the cognitive functions described in this section, intelligence is the broadest and perhaps most controversial. The history of mental retardation in this century is replete with examples of abuse and misuse of this construct and associated measurement instruments (Robinson & Robinson, 1976; Rosen, Clark, & Kivitz, 1976). Nevertheless, in the field of developmental disabilities, intelligence remains a key construct used to explain etiological factors related to substantial functional limitations in areas of major life activities, particularly those of learning, language ability, and self-direction. In the aging field, too, the domain of intellectual abilities has been one target of dispute, rhetoric, and investigative pursuits (Baltes & Schaie, 1974; Botwinick, 1967). Few gerontologists would disagree with the statement that, as a rule, intelligence declines with age; however, after some 60 years of extensive study of age differences in adult intelligence, there still remain questions about when the decline begins, which functions are involved, and, importantly, which declines are related to decrements in the performance of daily living activities.

Thorough reviews of the literature pertaining to intellectual decline and aging are available (e.g., Botwinick, 1977; Eisdorfer & Wilkie, 1973; Siegler, 1980). Botwinick (1977) examines the methodological problems posed by both the cohort effect in cross-sectional research and the selective subject loss in the longitudinal research, and argues that the knowledge accrued via each method is more compatible than not and concludes with the following findings.

There appears to be some consistency in intellectual performance throughout the fifth and sixth decade with decline increasing thereafter in older age.

There is some evidence to suggest that certain changes in test performance levels relate to distance from death. (This is often referred to as "the terminal drop hypothesis" [see Siegler, 1975].)

Although intellectual performance in younger years corresponds closely to performance in later years, the performance level when young does not seem to predict the rate or extent of decline in old age.

There does seem to be a greater decline in performance-based intellectual tasks (e.g., those requiring speed of response, perceptual motor skills) than on verbal items as age increases. This testing pattern, as gleaned from the verbal versus performance test scores of the Wechsler Adult Intelligence Scale (WAIS), has been referred as the "classic aging pattern" (Botwinick, 1977, p. 584).

Interestingly, two studies examining the relationship between age and IQ suggest that as mentally retarded persons age, their intellectual functioning does not remain constant. Goodman (1976) examined Wechsler test scores for some 402 persons ages 11 to 44. Over the two tests administered, Goodman found that Full Scale IQ scores did not decrease with age and, in fact, slight increments were found in Performance IQ scores. Bell and Zubek (1960) studied four age groupings (20, 30, 40, and 50 years of age) of retarded persons ($N = 100$). They administered Wechsler-Bellevue Intelligence Scales twice over a 5-year period and found that Verbal Scale gains were in evidence at the older age levels while Full Scale and Performance Scale scores diminished with age, a pattern similar to the "classic aging pattern."

A note of caution is appropriate, though, when examining relationships among age, developmental disabilities, and intelligence. Intellectual capacity, at most ages and for most individuals, is an emotion-laden term. All too often, inferences are drawn about a person's worth and/or abilities from the assumed knowledge of how smart he or she is. Skinner (1953) has described the logical fallacy made when "we begin with intelligent behavior, pass to behavior which shares intelligence, and then to behavior which is the effect of intelligence" (p. 202). Throughout their lifetime, many developmentally disabled persons have probably heard their behavioral limitations explained away by their intellectual limitations. Alternative explanations such as unavailable or inappropriate environmental support, physical limitations, economic limitations, and the like are ignored. Ultimately, the use of intelligence as an explanation of behavior diminishes one's control and responsibility for his or her behavior as well as deeming support or environmental intervention unlikely. Some recent work examines how such environmental messages may be interpreted as loss of control or incompetence and suggests that these messages might in fact affect performance on cognitive tasks (Avorn & Langer, 1982; Rodin & Langer, 1980). Given the propensity of some developmentally disabled persons to be outerdirected, it seems important to be aware of the degree to which inferences are made about the behavior of elderly developmentally disabled persons in relation to intelligence, especially since so little empirical evidence is presently available on the topic.

Memory

Conceptual and empirical data on memory and aging are complicated as are the theoretical frameworks and research paradigms applied in this area of experimental work. Two recently edited books provide an excellent review of the theoretical positions and research findings in this area (Craik & Trehub, 1982; Poon, Fozard, Cermak, Arenberg, & Thompson, 1980). In this section only a brief summary of the concepts and findings related to memory and aging is presented. Once again, references are drawn to elderly developmentally disabled persons, although data directly related to this client group seem unavailable.

Craik (1977) refers to two models that are used in the study of memory performance: the process model of memory, and the three-stage model. The latter, more traditional model of information-processing posits a sequential stage organization of memory into three components: sensory memory, primary memory, and secondary memory. The former, the process model, seeks to explain memory function as encoding of information rather than splitting memory into more or less discrete stages of stored information. A review of the research on level of memory processing and aging is presented by Craik and Simon (1980). Craik and Lockhart (1972) suggest that memory is related to the durability of the memory trace that in turn is determined by the level of processing of information during acquisition. Shallow levels of processing are related to sensory and physical types of stimuli. Deeper processing is concerned with semantic, abstract, and associative processes. In general, several studies have found that older subjects are less able to engage in shallow processing when new material is to be learned or retrieved (Craik & Tulving, 1975; Eysenck & Eysenck, 1979; Mistler-Lachman, 1977; Simon, 1979). An implication of this finding is that acquisition and/or retrieval of unfamiliar or nonverbal material in older subjects is impaired. However, Perlmutter (1978) has shown that by appropriate structuring of processing at input and retrieval, production deficits in older subjects can be reduced. For elderly developmentally disabled persons who might already have language and other cognitive deficits, attention to the method of presentation of material to be encoded is underscored by these findings. New and complicated material is unlikely to be retained spontaneously and, therefore, careful instructions and environmental aids may be helpful external strategies to use in order to maximize this client group's memory performance.

Additional findings relevant to elderly developmentally disabled persons can be gleaned from an examination of literature related to the three-stage model of memory functions. The first component, sensory memory, is hypothesized to be extremely time limited ($\frac{1}{4}$ to 2 seconds). Input into sensory memory is mainly from the visual and auditory systems. Siegler (1980) suggests that poor processing at this early stage may be related to poor recall because information was never fully processed. She suggests that attention deficits are highly associated with decreased performance in this secondary stage and that older persons have been found to perform more poorly than younger subjects in the presence of competing environmental stimuli.

Information moves from the sensory memory to primary memory where information is thought to be coded, organized, and then transferred for storage to secondary memory. Except for a decrease of retrieval speed from primary memory (Thomas, Waugh, & Fozard, 1978), few age differences are evidenced in primary memory (Craik, 1977). Short-term forgetting is thus thought to be a function of interfering stimuli rather than a loss of information due to decay.

In the major storage area of secondary or long-term memory, there are some findings that suggest differences in memory performance between older and younger subjects. For the most part, it is within the stage of secondary memory that shallow and/or deeper processing deficits referred to earlier occur. Overall, the studies reviewed by Craik (1977) suggest that older subjects have difficulty in both acquisition into and retrieval from secondary memory. Retrieval failures associated with poor recall are more in evidence in elderly individuals than are recognition problems that require subjects to generate a minimum of retrieval cues. Acquisition difficulties in older persons are associated with less spontaneous use of elaborate encoding procedures resulting in shallower acquisition of material than is found in younger subjects.

There are a myriad of implications that might be drawn from these findings and applied to elderly developmentally disabled individuals. First and quite importantly, there is a need to conduct research in and out of the laboratory with elderly developmentally disabled persons to learn how memory and aging affect the performance of structured tasks and the demands of daily living. How do the above-discussed memory deficits translate into choices people make about activities they perform and even where they might be living? It seems reasonable to assume that among elderly developmentally disabled persons, changes in memory are associated with considerable anxiety. When such fear is present, it is likely to affect one's general sense of psychological well-being, behavior, and even memory performance itself. Included within the rubric of psychological well-being is self-concept. It is likely that many developmentally disabled persons have regularly and perhaps intensely defended themselves against assaults on their memory or developed strategies to accommodate to their deficits. Change in memory status might evoke or rekindle considerable feelings about self-worth. In turn, these feelings might be associated with behavioral changes such as a withdrawal or a greater dependency on significant others to help them ''pass'' or deny their perceived limitations.

Although many more implications may be generated from this as yet unexplored area of psychological study, the last one presented here relates to the role that memory plays adaptively or maladaptively in the later years. A common misconception about memory and aging is that older people are better able to remember past events than present happenings. Although the evidence does not support this observation, older people do seem to engage in reminiscence more than younger persons. Butler (1963) viewed this process as adaptive and labeled it as life review. He conceived of it as a means to consolidate one's life, perhaps leading toward the psychosocial stage of integrity versus despair described by Erikson (1963). For the elderly developmentally disabled person as for any older person, the ability to use one's memory as a tool toward further development might have important implications for later life adjustment.

However, Cautela (1972) warns that the lack of sensory stimulation associated with a decline in cognitive status, social contacts, and pleasurable activities might lead to a spiral of maladaptive behavior.

> If the stimulation is not supplied from outside, the person tends to supply his own stimulation in terms of thoughts, fantasies and imagery. The aged individual's constant preoccupation with past events can be explained in this manner. The past experiences act as a source of stimulation and stimulus variability. . . . This leads to further inattention to the environment which of course leads to more isolation and stimulus consistency. (p. 69)

Many elderly developmentally disabled individuals are quite dependent upon environmental stimuli and, as such, may be particularly sensitive to the loss of social reinforcement as they age. The resultant condition might lead, as Cautela suggests, to reduced interactions with the environment and assumed cognitive losses that might then be diagnosed as dementia. Consequently, it seems important for elderly developmentally disabled persons to be exposed to social reinforcement in order to maintain their level of mental functioning. The role of activities in the lives of elderly developmentally disabled persons is discussed next in the section on psychological processes and theories of aging.

PSYCHOLOGICAL PROCESSES AND THEORIES OF AGING

Gerontologists have generated a number of theories of aging to help understand and predict behavior. The intent of developing these theories or models of aging is to integrate behavioral observations into logically consistent explanations of human behavior. For the most part, though, these theories have been poorly developed and investigated. When subjected to empirical verification, many have been found lacking. Baltes and Willis (1977) suggest that these limitations are not peculiar to psychological theories of aging. In fact, they note that in the entire field of psychology, there exists no pressure to develop a unifying theory to explain how, over time, behavior is organized. However, even though ''all existing theories are of the prototheoretical kind and are incomplete or insufficient in precision, scope and deployability'' (p. 148), theories of aging can inform us of key behavioral, social, and environmental elements related to psychological processes in aging. They are attempts at explanation and description of individual and group differences in aging behavior.

The most pervasive and perhaps controversial theory of aging is the disengagement theory (Cumming & Henry, 1961). It posits a gradual and psychologically positive withdrawal from activities (e.g., social, occupational, etc.) on the part of both the elderly individual and society. Life satisfaction is thought to be enhanced by the reduction in the number of roles performed and expected of the individual. Separation occurs between society and individuals—the process of disengagement is mutually beneficial to each party. Many gerontologists have vociferously criticized the disengagement theory, claiming, for example, that it is too simplistic (Crandall, 1980), unsupported empirically (Roman & Taietz, 1967), contrary to clinical observation of behavior (Hussian, 1981), and explainable by alternative formulations (Maddox, 1964).

A theory of aging antithetical to the disengagement theory is the activity theory. It posits that the more active an older individual is, the happier he or she will be. Successful aging requires replacement of relationships and roles when they diminish in order to maintain a satisfactory level of life satisfaction. Basically, this aging theory suggests a positive correlation between activity level and life satisfaction— the higher the activity level the greater life satisfaction and vice versa. In contrast, disengagement theory is formulated upon an inverse relationship between activity and life satisfaction—the higher the activity level maintained and strived for the lower the life satisfaction obtained in older age. Proponents of activity theory acknowledge that it is simple and probably unable to explain all behavior of elderly individuals (Maddox & Eisdorfer, 1962). There is some evidence in support of the activity theory (e.g., Tobin & Neugarten, 1961). A few studies examine alternative explanations for the assumed relationship between activity and

life satisfaction in this theory (e.g., Lemon, Bengtson & Peterson, 1972; Lowenthal & Haven, 1968). These studies found that having a trusting, stable relationship with at least one confidant was a determinant of high life satisfaction rather than the person's involvement in a large number of roles or activities.

Neugarten and her associates (Neugarten, 1971; Neugarten, Havighurst, & Tobin, 1968) offered another variable to consider as part of a theory on aging—personality. As a part of their longitudinal research on the Kansas City Study of Adult Life, these investigators examined a subsample of men and women between the ages of 70 and 79. Their intent in this study was to describe patterns of aging, using three elements: personality type, extent of social role activity, and degree of life satisfaction. They derived four major personality types and examined patterns of adjustment related to role activity and life satisfaction among these personality types. Presented in order of positive personality type, the classification includes: integrated, defended, passive-dependent, and disintegrated. Of particular importance to this discussion was their finding that within the integrated personality type, all patterns delineated were high on life satisfaction but differed among themselves with regard to role activity and patterns of aging. Thus, in this formulation, adapting to older age and maintaining a reasonable life satisfaction is not dependent solely on level of activity, but seems to also be related to personality styles, those patterns thought to emerge from innate human needs and forces that direct thought and behavior in interaction with the physical and social environment.

The Neugarten formulation used an ego psychological formulation as its psychological theory base. A behavioral theory of aging is presented by Hussian (1981). This model, relatively new, is known as the compensatory model. It suggests that the repertoire of behavior in later life is dependent both upon endogenous changes and the resources available to compensate for these changes. It notes that although for most earlier life stages, the best predictor of future behavior was past performance, this may be less true in old age because the biological process of aging causes the older person to generate different and substantially less consistent responses than prior to the occurrence of endogenous change. Furthermore, it suggests that

> increasing incentives for more flexible responding and the teaching of successful coping strategies and skills may eliminate the commonly observed negative (non-constructive) behavior. In this model, the elderly person is seen as trying to adapt to changes in function of a physical nature as well as to changes in the social environment, decreases in social reinforcement, and differences in the responsiveness to stress by the autonomic nervous system. (p. 21)

As formulated in this model of aging, the environment needs to be modified to stimulate the performance of as much adaptive behavior as possible in order to compensate for physiological, behavioral, social, and psychological decrements. Unless new coping strategies are developed and the environment modified, the elderly person is likely to take few risks, reduce social contact, and do less for himself or herself in personal and community-oriented activities.

Common to all the theories of aging discussed above is activity level and type of activities performed. The basic question of what tasks people need or want to perform on a daily basis in order to at least survive in the community or at best achieve a satisfactory quality of life transverses the field of aging and developmental disabilities (Kane & Kane, 1981; Seltzer, Granger, & Wineberg, 1982). That maintenance of functional ability is critical to an understanding of developmental disabilities is clearly underscored by the fact that the definition of a developmental disability delineated within the Rehabilitation, Comprehensive Services, and Developmental Disabilities Amendments of 1978 (PL 95-602, as amended) requires the presence of substantial functional limitations in three or more major areas of life activity such as self-care, mobility, self-direction, or communication among others (Lubin, Jacobson, & Kiely, 1982; Seltzer, 1983).

The performance of adaptive behavior as noted in the compensatory model and as implied in the activity theory is as key a variable in understanding psychological issues for elderly developmentally disabled individuals as it is for understanding psychological processes in younger persons who are developmentally disabled. What constitutes adaptive behavior for elderly persons versus the younger person and the meaning derived from the performance of these life activities probably varies with age as might the type of environmental supports and expectations. For example, training for occupational proficiency is probably less adaptive in the older group than is exposure and teaching of leisure time activities.

Lawton and his associates (Lawton, 1972, 1977; Lawton & Nahemow, 1973) have helped establish a theoretical framework that organizes activities (adaptive behavior) and their relationship to psychological functioning. Using the construct of competence, Lawton (1972) organized behaviors into a number of domains—activities of daily living (ADL), instrumental activities of daily living (IADL), and mobility. Within and across the domains, he ordered the behaviors into increasing levels of complexity, the sum total of which equals one's functional competence. Katz (1983) noted that the IADL behaviors (e.g., shopping, cooking, money management) grouped by Lawton are similar to those described by others as social competency and are more complex in their organization than the continuum from simple to complex found in ADL activities.

Lawton and Nahemow (1973) used an ecological framework to establish a model that discusses the complex relationship among the domains of adaptive behavior, aging, and psychological functioning. Their ecological theory of adaptive behavior and aging is quite relevant to elderly developmentally disabled persons and is, therefore, described in some detail. In the following discussion the terms used by Lawton and Nahemow are sometimes modified to fit developmentally disabled persons.

As a prelude to their model, these authors caution that

> [t]he great missing link in psychological knowledge about the ecology of aging is knowledge of

the conditions under which continuing states of homeostasis, as contrasted with activation, (a) are sought by the aged individual, (b) are facilitated by the contemporary environment of the aged person, and (c) lead to adaptive behavior and internal states of well being. (pp. 658–659)

The missing link that is referred to also applies to the aforementioned theories of aging, particularly the activity and disengagement theories. In particular, these theories do not address the interaction between the environment and the individual's needs, drives, and other motivational systems, or how this interaction produces, maintains, or impedes adaptive behavior proficiency and quality of life satisfactions.

To help resolve this problem of a missing link in psychological knowledge, Lawton and Nahemow (1973) suggest that psychological functioning is best understood by examining the ecological interplay (i.e., the environment-behavior transactions) among the domains of degree of individual competence, environmental press, adaptive behavior, affective responses, and adaptation level. The latter domain, adaptation level, refers to the cognitive, affective, and perceptual level of experiences, and is mediated by the former four domains. Individual competence is defined by the collection of abilities such as physical health, cognitive abilities (IQ), and psychological adjustment. Environmental press refers to the forces in the environment that evoke a response. Adaptive behavior is the observable performance of behaviors that, when aggregated, group into the previously defined ADL, IADL, and mobility functional domains. Lastly, affective response represents the internal emotional component assumed to be related to one's life satisfaction within one's environment.

In order to analyze the relationships among the above components, Lawton and Nahemow (1973) refer to the environmental docility hypothesis developed earlier by Lawton and Simon (1968). Basically, this hypothesis suggests that as the individual's competence decreases, "the proportion of behavior attributable to environment, as contrasted with personal characteristics increases" (p. 658). The similarities between this hypothesis and the role of environmental support described earlier in the compensatory model are striking. Once again, the assumption underlying both is that as an individual's competence wanes, and the individual becomes more vulnerable, he or she is more apt to be controlled by environmental stimuli, a circumstance that is often associated with the cognitive and behavioral styles of field dependence, external locus of control, and outerdirectedness.

Given this relationship between environment and individual competence, Lawton and Nahemow's (1973) model suggests that the behavioral and affective outcomes of the person-environment transaction can be understood in relation to the fit between level of competence and degree of environmental press. The authors theorize that an adaptation level zone exists wherein positive affect and adaptive behavior occur as a function of a reasonable fit between an elderly person's competence level and environmental press. Maladaptive behaviors and negative affect are hypothesized to occur under conditions, for example, where environmental press is too strong for the competence level of the person or vice versa, or where the person is too competent to be functioning within a weak environment press.

The components of this theory and the relationships among them are quite consonant with prevailing theories of community adjustment for adults who are developmentally disabled (Reynolds, 1981; Seltzer, 1981; Seltzer & Seltzer, 1984). For example, Seltzer (1981) studied the relationships among environment, performance (adaptive behavior), and satisfaction (affective component) and found that while the number of skills an individual had correlated with individual characteristics such as IQ, the percentage of adaptive behaviors performed regularly and independently was more highly related to attributes of the residential environment (e.g., training provided and responsibilities given to residents) than to individual characteristics. Furthermore, affectively, there appeared to be a relationship between subjects' level of satisfaction with their environments and specific environmental features (e.g., the availability of skill training was related to satisfaction with in-house responsibilities). Thus, in this study, as in the Lawton and Nahemow (1973) model, adjustment and satisfaction were strongly related to the person-environment transactions.

Figure 1 is presented as a summary of ideas related to the above described theories of aging with specific application to elderly developmentally disabled persons. The model is presented as a heuristic device to depict some of the key biopsychosocial components to consider in the study of psychological processes among aging developmentally disabled persons. It is offered with the knowledge of its limitations in dealing with the broad scope of the content, the uncertainty about the relationships among and within the domains, and the lack of empirical verification. Still, as a schematic representation of content, it might spark theory building, empirical studies, and clinical interventions.

Antecedent Conditions

Antecedent conditions are viewed in the model as influencing the experience and perhaps completion of developmental tasks that are common during the senescent life period. Antecedent conditions were selected that represent a range of domains that are likely to affect a developmentally disabled person's ability to cope with the developmental challenges of older age.

Brain-Behavior Mediators The extent to which these antecedent conditions influence developmental tasks is pictured as being mediated by a number of cognitive and physiological processes, termed *brain-behavior mediators*. The elements are placed within a single box because these are physiologically interdependent. They are represented separately from the antecedent condition element of physical condition because the latter is assumed to be more related to lifelong limitations (e.g., cerebral palsy) whereas these processes are ones in flux in older age. Decrements in function in any one of these processes can alter the coping balance for an elderly developmentally

disabled person. Any one or combinations of mediators are likely to affect one or more of the developmental tasks.

Developmental Tasks

Developmental tasks are life adjustments that are likely to occur in older age. Some tasks are more closely related to biological changes, while others involve social expectations or psychological conflicts. Overall, though, each task involves some psychological, sociological, and biological elements. In contrast to stage theories such as Erickson's (1963) and Piaget's (1950), these tasks are not meant to represent an invariant or irreversible order, nor are they arranged in a hierarchical manner. However, the dotted lines are drawn to suggest the potential overlap among the tasks. For example, learning to cope with reduced physical capacity often involves a restructuring of roles and an adjustment to some losses such as moderating social contacts and perhaps loss of income. Acceptance of one's mortality, is, for some, the ultimate adjustment to loss.

The psychological meaning of these tasks is intertwined with the position one holds in a number of networks—one's family, friends, community, and the larger society. Behavioral norms and expectations are established within and across these networks and the related age-appropriate behavior that is expected affects one's self-image. Kastenbaum (1972) notes that aging is often assumed to be a monolithic concept of "inevitable (develomental) regression" (p. 47). The developmental task of coping with societal prejudices is included here because being both developmentally disabled and elderly may make these individuals particularly vulnerable to negative expectations, the consequences of which may be regression and reduced quality of life.

Outcomes The *outcomes* associated with adjusting to, moving through, resolving, or being in conflict with these developmental tasks are represented by behavioral, cognitive, and intrapersonal elements. How one thinks, feels, and acts is primarily affected by one's participation in developmental tasks (straight lines) and in turn this affects (dotted lines)

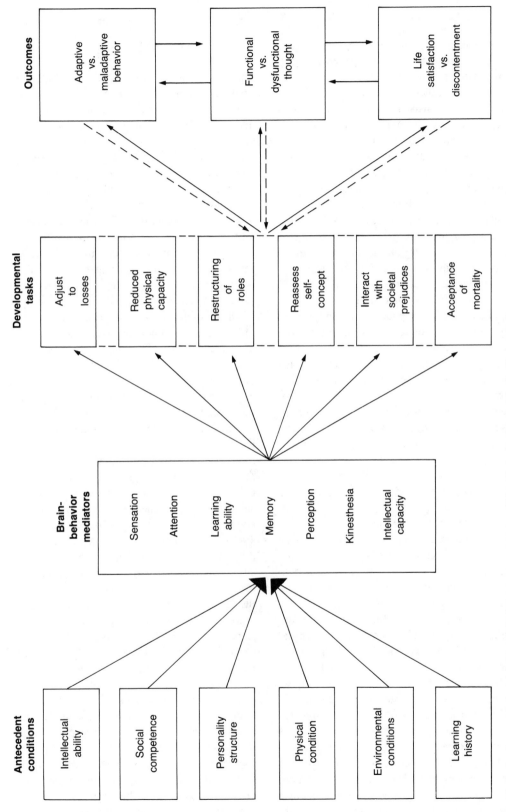

Figure 1. A conceptual model of psychological processes experienced by elderly developmentally disabled persons.

221

one's coping strategy with developmental tasks. Thus, the two domains are depicted as interacting with one another.

In summary, there appear to be a number of variables that consistently emerge in theories on aging that are relevant to the understanding of the psychological functioning of elderly developmentally disabled persons. These are activities (numbers and type), life satisfaction, environmental opportunities, and individual competence. By definition, elderly developmentally disabled persons have some known or unknown organic and/or functional problems that influence their individual competence. Also by definition, this compromise in individual competence affects their performance of major life activities. Interestingly then, life as an elderly developmentally disabled person may not be very discrepant structurally from that of a younger developmentally disabled person. That is, having matured to older age with a disability, a person probably has confronted, many times, psychological issues related to independence-dependence, self-image disparities, and physical limitations. For sure, these psychological processes emerge and re-emerge and are handled with a different perspective at different developmental periods. Having coped with and survived these life stresses already, though, elderly developmentally disabled individuals might experience the difficult life tasks of senesence from a stronger experiential base than nondisabled individuals. For example, having learned to depend on prosthetic devices, environmental aids, or interpersonal relationships to compensate for functional limitations, the developmentally disabled person may have developed syntonic mechanisms to help him or her cope with additional, age-related decreases in functional abilities. At the same time, however, resources might be less available and even small increments of loss in the physical, psychological, social, or economic spheres might be experienced by the aging developmentally disabled person as quite profound circumstances to which to adjust, yet again. The next section examines in some detail a frequent type of loss in older age—grief, death, and dying.

GRIEF, DEATH, AND DYING

The last section of this chapter is fittingly the final developmental task experienced by most elderly developmentally disabled persons—understanding and coping with one's own mortality and that of significant others. Although the probability of experiencing grief and one's own death is more common and imminent in older age, many developmentally disabled persons may have had exposure to this life event or related experiences, such as abrupt separations that occur in both institutionalization and community placements (e.g., relocation and stress; see Heller, Chapter 23, this volume). The death of a parent, caregiver, friend, or lover certainly touches the lives of this client group. It is a part of the human experience and yet very little is known about the psychological processes related to death, dying, and grief among developmentally disabled persons—young or old.

The absence of literature on this topic is remarkable and might relate to a variety of founded or unfounded concerns about the ability of elderly developmentally disabled persons to process the experience. Many prominent thanatologists have expounded upon the difficulty, fear, and taboo nature with which this subject is approached for most individuals (Becker, 1973; Kalish, 1976; Kubler-Ross, 1969). Many social systems such as families, religious organizations, and health delivery systems conspire, deny, repress, or protect their members, acting *in loco parentis* against the overt expression of this inevitable and omnipresent phenomenon. Since acting *in loco parentis,* necessarily or not, is more commonly exhibited toward developmentally disabled persons than in general, the neglect or avoidance of this topic is not surprising.

On the other hand, death is a difficult and complex phenomenon to comprehend. The degree to which one understands aspects of death and dying is related to cognitive development (Koocher, 1973). The extent to which some developmentally disabled persons are impaired cognitively will affect their comprehension of the topic. Thus, the overview presented below not only borrows again from the gerontological literature but also relies on material from the study of child and cognitive development. The breath of the topic delimits the depth to which material can be covered. Averill and Wisocki (1981) and Kalish (1976) have written outstanding reviews of the literature related to aging, death, dying, and grief, albeit without specific reference to the elderly developmentally disabled population.

Two classic child studies describing the developmental progression involved in understanding the meaning of death are helpful indicators of the range of understanding of death among some elderly developmentally disabled persons. Anthony (1940) reported a developmental, chronological sequence of understanding from ignorance to personal reference. Nagy (1948) found a similar progression, noting that children under the age of 9 tended not to comprehend death as irreversible, inevitable, and universal. Although more recent reviews about children's perceptions of death have been critical of this research for its methodological and conceptual flaws (Kastenbaum & Costa, 1977; Koocher, 1983), this research seems to coincide with the more sophisticated Piagetian framework that elaborates upon the meaning of death by levels of progressive cognitive development (i.e., preoperational thought to formal operational reasoning). In an important study with 65 mentally retarded adults (mean age of 37, range 17–70 years of age), Lipe-Goodson and Goebel (1983) found that age and, to a lesser extent, IQ were related to understanding the concept of death. That is, as mentally retarded adults with higher cognitive capacities age, they appear to have a better concept of death than their younger counterparts. The investigators note that "perhaps chronological age serves as an index of experience in both mentally retarded and nonmentally retarded populations" (p. 72).

A related finding from the gerontological literature is that there is a seemingly greater acceptance and lowered fear of death in elderly than among younger persons. Kalish (1976) suggests that as people age, a socialization process to death occurs. As friends, relatives, caregivers, or others die in substantial numbers, an older person is confronted repeatedly

with the experience of death and may even begin to evaluate and plan for his or her own death. A behavioral repertoire related to cultural, ethnic, and religious rituals surrounding death and funerals is learned. As suggested by Lipe-Goodson and Goebel's (1983) findings, the index of experience or practice effect might enhance the elderly developmentally disabled person's ability to understand the meaning of death.

The assumption underlying the above-described adaptive response toward death is that one has coped with or has the capacity to cope with the processes of bereavement. Bereavement refers to the complex process individuals experience following the death of a significant other. Lindemann's (1944) classic study of grief set the conceptual stage for the study of the sequelae of bereavement. Parkes (1970) delineated the following four stages of bereavement: 1) shock or numbness; 2) protest and yearning; 3) disorganization and despair; and 4) detachment and reorganization of behavior. Averill and Wisocki (1981) note that although there are difficulties in conceptualizing grief in foreordained stages, "grief is not a grab bag of individual symptoms without internal coherence. Grief is a process, a progression, a way of coming to terms with a new reality" (p. 129). Furthermore, these authors emphasize the point that bereavement is not a pathological response but rather an adaptive syndrome, the etiology of which is traceable to the biological, psychological, and sociocultural history of the individual and the species.

As is true of most normal psychological processes, there may be antecedent or mediating circumstances that inhibit or disrupt the adaptive outcomes related to the bereavement process. For example, Epstein, Weitz, Roback, and McKee (1975) among others, reviewed the bereavement literature related to conjugal morbidity and mortality and found contradictory conclusions, partially explained by mediating variables such as age, premorbid health, length of illness, sex of survivor, and life-style changes. Seltzer and Seltzer (in press) note that the death of parents or other family members presents particular problems for elderly mentally retarded individuals. An aging family system might result in a loss of emotional, advocacy, and other support resources. Furthermore, the bereavement process might be inhibited by the strong interdependent relationship between the deceased family member and older retarded person which, when severed, initiates issues in separation that have no adaptive learning history behind them.

There is a paucity of documentation on the topic of elderly developmentally disabled persons and grief, death, and dying. Nevertheless, it seems probable that the meaning of death and the process of bereavement is mediated by cognitive development factors as well as by life and, in particular, family circumstances. The vista is wide open for exploration of the topic by a variety of disciplines. Cognitive psychologists might collaborate with anthropologists to explore the relationships among stages of cognitive development, thought patterns, and accompanying feelings that occur during bereavement. Service providers and planners might team up with researchers to explore and evaluate program options related to funeral and estate planning. The generation of ideas is not a problem; the commitment to the topic will, it is hoped, maintain or grow so that future chapters on psychological processes of older developmentally disabled persons can review literature that had particularly targeted for study the elderly developmentally disabled population.

SUMMARY

In order to examine selected cognitive, behavioral, and affective processes, this chapter has liberally integrated other bodies of literature together with that which is peculiar to elderly developmentally disabled individuals. As noted earlier, there are few quantitative or qualitative descriptions available that describe how developmentally disabled persons spend their days —how they think and feel about what they are or are not doing with their lives. In the presence of this void, the tendency might be to overgeneralize from what limited data are available. Consequently, throughout this chapter, caution

has been exercised to minimize overgeneralizations by highlighting the formative nature of the information presented and by noting that the implications drawn have been derived most often from populations other than the elderly developmentally disabled population.

Given the paucity of literature in this area, there is a clear need to conduct exploratory and experimental research. From among all of the psychological processes examined, the level and type of activities in which elderly developmentally disabled persons engage consistently emerge as an investigative area for research. While the data and theories of aging presented in this chapter suggest that, in general, the type and level of activities participated in by this group have important psychological implications, very little specific knowledge exists regarding which types of activities are healthy, adaptive, or related to a higher quality of life. Similarly, it is not known whether there is an optimal *level* of activity for a developmentally disabled person during older age. It is possible, for example, that the relationship between level of activity and quality of life is curvilinear with too little or too much activity not as adaptive as a moderate level. Implicit in this formulation, of course, is the expected variability in individual characteristics attributable to such factors as memory, intellect, and other cognitive functions as well as environmental opportunities and physical endowments. These individual characteristics make it likely that many adaptive patterns will emerge for elderly developmentally disabled persons. Thus, when investigating adaptive quality of life patterns, studies might be designed to determine the specific individual characteristics that interact with different types and levels of activities. That is, given the substantial degree of heterogeneity within this population, it is necessary to determine what types of persons (as defined by their abilities and disabilities) evidence declining capacities, behaviorally and affectively, and at what stages and under what conditions do these changes occur. Moreover, such research should examine how declines in function are experienced by the person and how these changes in function relate to the performance of developmental tasks of older age.

In addition to suggesting future research directions, the material presented in this chapter offers a number of implications for the provision of services to aging developmentally disabled persons. Given the salience of activity level to psychological functioning, it is important to ensure that environmental opportunities are available that enable an elderly developmentally disabled person to remain active. The challenge, of course, is to create social and leisure type options, and thereby, help people retire, when appropriate, from the more traditional sheltered and other work activities. Another type of psychological service suggested by the death and dying section of this chapter is counseling and support to assist elderly developmentally disabled persons in maintaining relationships with their loved ones and close friends and to minimize unnecessary separations and losses. When losses are unavoidable, due to the deterioration or death of a significant other, there is often a need to provide services tailored to the person's cognitive abilities and/or life circumstance to help him or her with the bereavement process. Lastly, this chapter points to the importance of attending to the psychological needs and strengths of an aging developmentally disabled person in addition to responding to the more commonly recognized need for residential and health care services.

REFERENCES

Abrahams, J. P., & Birren, J. E. (1973). Reaction time as a function of age and behavioral predisposition to coronary heart disease. *Journal of Gerontology, 28,* 471–478.

Anthony, S. (1940). *The child's discovery of death.* New York: Harcourt, Brace.

Averill, J. R., & Wisocki, P. A. (1981). Some observations on behavioral approaches to the treatment of grief among the elderly. In H. J. Sobel (Ed.), *Behavior therapy in terminal care: A humanistic approach* (pp. 125–150). Cambridge, MA: Ballinger Publishing.

Avorn, J. (1982). Studying cognitive performance in the elderly: A biopsychosocial approach. In F. I. M. Craik & S. Trehub (Eds.), *Aging and cognitive processes* (pp. 317–329). New York: Plenum Publishing Corp.

Avorn, J., & Langer, E. (1982). Induced disability in nursing home patients; A controlled trial. *Journal of The American Geriatrics Society, 30,* 397–400.

Baker, B. L., Seltzer, G. B., & Seltzer, M. M. (1977). *As close as possible: Community residences for retarded adults.* Boston: Little, Brown & Co.

Baltes, P. P., & Schaie, K. W. (1974). Aging and IQ: The myth of the twilight years. *Psychology Today, 7,* 35–40.

Baltes, P. B., & Willis, S. L. (1977). Toward psychological theories of aging and development. In J. E. Birren & K. W. Schaie (Eds.), *Handbook of the psychology of aging* (pp. 128–154). New York: Van Nostrand Reinhold Co.

Becker, E. (1973). *The denial of death.* New York: The Free Press.

Bell, A., & Zubek, J. P. (1960). The effect of age on the intellectual performance of mental defectives. *Journal of Gerontology, 15,* 285–295.

Botwinick, J. (1967). *Cognitive processes in maturity and old age.* New York: Springer Publishing Co.

Botwinick, J. (1977). Intellectual abilities. In J. E. Birren & K. W. Schaie (Eds.), *Handbook of the psychology of aging* (pp. 580–605). New York: Van Nostrand Reinhold Co.

Bruininks, R. H., Hill, B. K., & Thorsheim, M. J. (1982). Deinstitutionalization and foster care for mentally retarded people. *Health and Social Work, 7,* 198–205.

Busse, E. W. (1980). Old age. In S. I. Greenspan & G. H. Pollock (Eds.), *The course of life: Psychoanalytic contributions toward understanding personality development. Vol III: Adulthood and the aging process* (pp. 519–543). Rockville, MD: National Institute of Mental Health.

Butler, R. M. (1963). The life review: An interpretation of reminiscence in the aged. *Psychiatry, 26,* 65–76.

Cautela, J. R. (1972). Manipulation of the psychosocial environment of the geriatric patient. In D. Kent, R. Kastenbaum, & S. Sherwood (Eds.), *Research, planning and action for the elderly* (pp. 61–69). New York: Behavioral Publications.

Cotton, P. D., Sison, G. F. P., & Starr, S. (1981). Comparing elderly mentally retarded and non-mentally retarded individuals: Who are they? What are their needs? *The Gerontologist, 21,* 359–365.

Craik, F. I. M. (1977). Age differences in human memory. In J. E. Birren & K. W. Schaie (Eds.), *Handbook of the psychology of aging* (pp. 384–420). New York: Van Nostrand Reinhold Co.

Craik, F. I. M., & Lockhart, R. S. (1972). Levels of processing: A framework for memory research. *Journal of Verbal Learning and Verbal Behavior, 11,* 671–684.

Craik, F. I. M., & Simon, E. (1980). Age differences in memory: The role of attention and depth of processing. In L. W. Poon, J. L. Fozard, L. S. Cermak, D. Avenberg, & L. W. Thompson (Eds.), *New directions in memory and aging: Proceedings of the George A. Tallard memorial conference* (pp. 95–112). Hillsdale, NJ: Lawrence Erlbaum Associates.

Craik, F. I. M., & Trehub, S. (Eds.). (1982). *Aging and cognitive processes*. New York: Plenum Publishing Corp.

Craik, F. I. M., & Tulving, E. (1975). Depth of processing and the retention of words in episodic memory. *Journal of Experimental Psychology: General, 104,* 268–294.

Crandall, R. C. (1980). *Gerontology: A behavioral science approach*. Reading MA: Addison-Wesley Publishing Co.

Cummings, E., & Henry, W. E. (1961). *Growing old*. New York: Basic Books.

DiGiovanni, L. (1978). The elderly retarded: A little-known group. *The Gerontologist, 18,* 262–266.

Edgerton, R. B., Bollinger, M., & Herr, B. (1984). The cloak of competence: After two decades. *American Journal of Mental Deficiency, 88,* 345–351.

Eisdorfer, C., & Wilkie, F. (1973). Intellectual changes with advancing age. In L. F. Jarvik, C. Eisdorfer, & J. E. Blum (Eds.), *Intellectual functioning in adults* (pp. 21–29). New York: Springer Publishing Co.

Eisner, D. (1983). Down's Syndrome and aging: Is senile dementia inevitable? *Psychological Reports, 52,* 119–124.

Epstein, G., Weitz, L., Roback, H., & McKee, E. (1975). Research on bereavement: A selective and critical review. *Comprehensive Psychiatry, 16,* 537–546.

Erikson, E. H. (1963). *Childhood and society* (2nd ed.). New York: W. W. Norton & Co.

Eysenck, M. W., & Eysenck, M. C. (1979). Processing depth, elaboration of encoding, memory stores, and expanded processing capacity. *Journal of Experimental Psychology: Human Learning and Memory, 5,* 472–484.

Goodman, J. F. (1976). Aging and IQ change in institutionalized mentally retarded. *Psychological Reports, 39,* 999–1006.

Hussian, R. A. (1981). *Geriatric psychology: A behavioral perspective*. New York: Van Nostrand Reinhold Co.

Jacobson, J. W. (1982a). Problem behavior and psychiatric impairment within a developmentally disabled population: I. Behaviors and frequency. *Applied Research in Mental Retardation, 3,* 121–139.

Jacobson, J. W. (1982b). Problem behavior and psychiatric impairment within a developmentally disabled population: II. Behavioral severity. *Applied Research in Mental Retardation, 3,* 369–381.

Janicki, M. P., & MacEachron, A. E. (1984). Residential, health, and social service needs of elderly developmentally disabled persons. *The Gerontologist, 24,* 128–137.

Kalish, R. A. (1976). Death and dying in a social context. In R. H. Binstock & E. Shanas (Eds.), *Handbook of aging and the social sciences* (pp. 483–507). New York: Van Nostrand Reinhold Co.

Kane, R. A., & Kane, R. L. (1981). *Assessing the elderly: A practical guide to measurement*. Lexington, MA: Lexington Books.

Kane, R. L., Solomon, D. H., Beck, J. C., Keeler, E. B., & Kane R. A. (1981). *Geriatrics in The United States: Manpower projections and training considerations*. Lexington, MA: Lexington Books.

Kastenbaum, R. (1972). A developmental-field approach to aging and its implications for practice. In D. Kent, R. Kastenbaum, & S. Sherwood (Eds.), *Research, planning and action for the elderly* (pp. 37–49). New York: Behavioral Publications.

Kastenbaum, R., & Costa, P. T. (1977). Psychological perspectives on death. *Annual Review of Psychology, 28,* 225–249.

Katz, S. (1983). Assessing self maintenance: Activities of daily living, mobility, and instrumental activities of daily living. *Journal of The American Geriatrics Society, 31,* 721–727.

Koocher, G. P. (1973). Childhood, death, and cognitive development. *Developmental Psychology, 9,* 369–347.

Koocher, G. P. (1983). Grief and loss in childhood. In C. E. Walker & M. C. Roberts (Eds.), *Handbook of clinical child psychology* (pp. 1273–1284). New York: John Wiley & Sons.

Kubler-Ross, E. (1969). *On death and dying*. New York: MacMillan Publishing Co.

Lawton, M. P. (1972). The dimensions of morale. In D. Kent, R. Kastenbaum, & S. Sherwood (Eds.), *Research, planning and action for the elderly* (pp. 144–165). New York: Behavioral Publications.

Lawton, M. P. (1977). The impact of environment of aging and behavior. In J. E. Birren & K. W. Schaie (Eds.), *Handbook of the psychology of aging* (pp. 276–301). New York: Van Nostrand Reinhold Co.

Lawton, M. P. & Nahemow, L. (1973). Ecology and the aging process. In C. Eisdorfer & M. P. Lawton (Eds.), *Psychology of adult development and aging* (pp. 619–674). Washington, DC: American Psychological Association.

Lawton, M. P., & Simon, B. B. (1968). The ecology of social relationships in housing for the elderly. *The Gerontologist, 8,* 108–115.

Lemon, B. W., Bengtson, V. L., & Peterson, J. A. (1972). An exploration of the activity of aging: Activity types and life satisfaction among inmovers to a retirement community. *Journal of Gerontology, 27,* 511–523.

Lindemann, E. (1944). Symptomatology and management of acute grief. *American Journal of Psychiatry, 101,* 141–148.

Lipe-Goodson, & Goebel, B. L. (1983). Perception of age and death in mentally retarded adults. *Mental Retardation, 21,* 68–75.

Lott, I. T., & Lai, F. (1982). Dementia in Down Syndrome: Observations from a neurology clinic. *Applied Research in Mental Retardation, 3,* 233–239.

Lowenthal, M. F., & Haven, C. (1968). Interaction and adaption: Intimacy as a critical variable. In B. L. Neugarten (Ed.), *Middle age and aging: A reader in social psychology*. Chicago: University of Chicago Press.

Lubin, R., Jacobson, J. W., & Kiely, M. (1982). Projected impact of the functional definition of developmental disabilities: The categorically disabled population and service eligibility. *American Journal of Mental Deficiency, 87,* 73–79.

Maddox, G. L. (1964). Disengagement theory: A critical evaluation. *The Gerontologist, 4,* 80–82.

Maddox, G. L., & Eisdorfer, C. (1962). Some correlates of activity and morale among the elderly. *Social Forces, 40,* 254–260.

Mistler-Lachman, J. L. (1977). Spontaneous shift in encoding dimensions among elderly subjects. *Journal of Gerontology, 32,* 68–72.

Nagy, M. (1948). The child's theories concerning death. *Journal of Genetic Psychology, 73,* 3–27.

Neugarten, B. L. (1971). Grow old with me: The best is yet to be. *Psychology Today, 5,* 45–48, 79–81.

Neugarten, B. L., Havighurst, R. J., & Tobin, S. S.

(1968). Personality and patterns of aging. In B. L. Neugarten (Ed.), *Middle age and aging: A reader in social psychology* (pp. 173–178). Chicago: The University of Chicago Press.

O'Connor, G., Justice, R. S., & Warren, N. (1970). The aged mentally retarded: Institutions or community care? *American Journal of Mental Deficiency, 75,* 354–360.

Parkes, C. M. (1970). "Seeking" and "finding" a lost object. *Social Science and Medicine, 4,* 187–201.

Perlmutter, M. (1978). What is memory aging the aging of? *Developmental Psychology, 14,* 330–345.

Piaget, J. (1950). *Psychology of intelligence.* New York: Harcourt and Brace.

Poon, L. W. Fozard, J. L., Cermak, L. S., Arenberg, D., & Thompson, L. W. (Eds.). (1980). *New directions in memory and aging: Proceedings of the George A. Tallard memorial conference.* Hillsdale, NJ: Lawrence Erlbaum Associates.

Reynolds, W. M. (1981). Measurement of personal competence of mentally retarded individuals. *American Journal of Mental Deficiency, 85,* 368–376.

Robinson, N. M., & Robinson, H. B. (1976). *The mentally retarded child.* New York: McGraw-Hill Book Co.

Rodin, J., & Langer, E. (1980). Aging labels: The decline of control and the fall of self-esteem. *Journal of Social Issues, 36,* 12–29.

Roman, P., & Taietz, P. (1967). Organizational structure and disengagement: The emeritus professor. *The Gerontologist, 7,* 147–152.

Rosen, M., Clark, G. R., & Kivitz, M. S. (Eds.). (1976). *The history of mental retardation: Collected papers* (Vols. 1–2). Baltimore: University Park Press.

Seltzer, G. B. (1981). Community residential adjustment: The relationship among environment, performance, and satisfaction. *American Journal of Mental Deficiency, 85,* 624–630.

Seltzer, G. (1983). Systems of classification. In J. L. Matson & J. A. Mulick (Eds.), *Handbook of mental retardation* (pp. 143–156). New York: Pergamon Press.

Seltzer, G. B., Granger, C. V., & Wineberg, D. E. (1982).

Functional assessment: Bridge between family and rehabilitation medicine within an ambulatory practice. *Archives of Physical Medicine and Rehabilitation, 63,* 453–457.

Seltzer, M. M., & Seltzer, G. B. (1984). Functional assessment of persons with mental retardation. In C. V. Granger & G. E. Gresham (Eds.), *Functional assessment in rehabilitation medicine* (pp. 273–287). Baltimore: William & Wilkins Co.

Seltzer, M. M., & Seltzer, G. B. (in press). The elderly mentally retarded: A group in need of service. *Journal of Gerontological Social Work.*

Seltzer, M. M., Seltzer, G. B., & Sherwood, C. C. (1982). Comparison of community adjustment of older vs younger mentally retarded adults. *American Journal of Mental Deficiency, 87,* 9–13.

Siegler, I. C. (1975). The terminal drop hypothesis: Fact or artifact? *Experimental Aging Research, 1,* 169–185.

Siegler, I. C. (1980). The psychology of adult development and aging. In E. W. Busse & D. G. Blazer (Eds.), *Handbook of geriatric psychiatry* (pp. 169–221). New York: Van Nostrand Reinhold Co.

Simon, E. (1979). Depth and elaboration of processing in relation to age. *Journal of Experimental Psychology: Human Learning and Memory, 5,* 115–124.

Skinner, B. F. (1953). *Science and human behavior.* New York: The Free Press.

Tait, D. (1983). Mortality and dementia among aging defectives. *Journal of Mental Deficiency Research, 27,* 133–142.

Thomas, J. C., Waugh, N. C., & Fozard, J. L. (1978). Age and familiarity in memory scanning. *Journal of Gerontology, 33,* 528–533.

Tobin, S. S., & Neugarten, B. L. (1961). Life satisfaction and social interaction in aging. *Journal of Gerontology, 16,* 344–346.

Tymchuk, A. J. (1979). The mentally retarded in late life. In O. Kaplan (Ed.), *Psychopathology of aging* (pp. 197–209). New York: Academic Press.

chapter

14

The Syndrome of Musculoskeletal Aging

Raul D. Rudelli

Musculoskeletal tissues undergo interrelated modifications during their aging. This chapter discusses certain mechanisms that, acting simultaneously or successively, bring about the changes that we designate as the syndrome of musculoskeletal aging.

The syndrome manifests in a particularly premature and severe fashion in developmentally disabled persons. Aside from those features, musculoskeletal aging in this group does not differ from that of other individuals. Aging muscle fiber loss parallels mass and strength declines. Oxidative reconfiguration of remaining motor units correlates with increase in endurance despite decreases in strength and speed of contraction. Sarcoplasmic enzymatic systems, including those that intervene in protein synthesis and catabolism, show declines in activity. Denervational, disuse, and ischemic mechanisms are major agents for the above changes. Decreased muscle strain, disuse, ischemia, inadequate diet, abnormal vitamin metabolism, and, most importantly, hypogonadism, affect in turn compact and trabecular bone compartments, resulting in aging bone fragility (osteoporosis). Genetic factors are significant in determining the age of onset, rate of progression, and the severity of the latter process, rare in elderly black individuals. Aging osteopenia shows rich biochemical and morphological heterogeneity in contrast to aging myopathy. While osteoarthrosis and osteoporosis may be mutually exclusive from a mechanical point of view, aging arthropathy, by further reducing or impeding motor activity, accelerates muscle and bone wasting. Factors leading to cartilage aging are largely unknown but abnormal collagen/glycoprotein synthesis and catabolism may be of importance. Exercise schedules may improve the general cardiorespiratory function of elderly individuals and slow musculoskeletal wasting, but will not revert muscle fiber or trabecular bone losses. Training may bring about an improvement of muscle oxidative and glycolytic capacities with increases in muscle strength and strain on bone with subsequent compact and trabecular bone density increase. Additional measures, such as adequate diet, hormonal, vitamin and mineral supplements, may help bring about a reduction in fracture/immobility complication rates, a realistic long-term goal.

MUSCULOSKELETAL DISORDERS constitute not only the *third* most frequent reason for medical office visits by elderly individuals (D'Elia & Folse, 1978; Kovar, 1977), but also the *third* leading cause of incapacity in this group. Recognition of the particular changes that the musculoskeletal structures undergo during the aging process, as well as their etiopathogenetic mechanisms, should assist in the adoption of adequate diagnostic baselines and early therapeutic interventions. A progressive musculoskeletal disability syndrome that leads to weakness, motion restriction, deformity, and chronic pain can be identified in about 50% of individuals over the age of 70. This syndrome is characterized by muscular atrophy (aging myopathy), osteoporosis (aging osteopenia), and degenerative joint disease (aging arthropathy). Although their age of presentation is different in an elderly individual, osteoporosis and large joint osteoarthrosis represent the opposite ends of this musculoskeletal spectrum, which also includes chondrocalcinosis and spondylosis. Aging arthropathy generally presents about a decade after the onset of osteoporosis. In about 1% of the individuals, osteoporosis and osteoarthrosis may begin simultaneously. Osteoporotic and osteoarthritic changes may coexist in the elderly vertebral column. However, studies of the simultaneous prevalence of both processes are limited and additional data are required (Foss & Byers, 1972; Roh, Dequeker, & Mulier, 1974; Solomon, Schnitzler, & Browett, 1982).

The syndrome of muscular atrophy, osteoporosis, and degenerative joint disease is the major source of disability in daily living activities of elderly individuals (Aniansson, Grimby, Rundgren, Svanborg, & Orlander, 1980). Multiple interdependent factors, known and unknown, participate in the pathogenesis of this heterogeneous disorder, including endocrine, neural, vascular, and metabolic processes. Reduced motor performance, with secondary bone and muscle disuse, is a common result of the syndrome, and is also the major cause of its self-perpetuation.

Individuals presenting with hypotonia and mental retardation related or unrelated to chromosomal or metabolic disorders show no specific differentiating morphological features in their musculoskeletal aging with the exception of the *early onset* of the syndrome. Certain chromosomal disorders that are characterized by marked postnatal motor disability, including contractures, abnormal posture, and reduced mobilization of certain muscle groups may also show more severe incapacity in aging. The presence of abnormal muscle groups (e.g., unusual insertion of extensor digitorum and extensor digiti minimi, abnormality or absence of the palmaris longus and brevis, plantaris and peroneus tertius, and supernumerary muscles) is one of the particular anatomical features of trisomic disorders (13, 18, and 21) conducive to abnormal mobilization (Bersu, 1980; Pettersen, Koltis, & White, 1979; Ramirez-Castro & Bersu, 1978). Although muscle fiber maturational delay (reduced size or number) has been observed postnatally in mentally disabled persons, these changes have not been seen to persist beyond childhood (Curless, Nelson, & Brimmer, 1978; Fenichel, 1967). Reduced motor performance in mentally retarded individuals is characterized by reduced activity (disuse), poor coordination, and diminished strength. Differences in maximum strength may range about 25% between young adult probands and controls (Dobbins, Garron, & Ravick, 1981). *Disuse* leads to early loss of both muscle and bone mass.

Moderate to severe osteoporosis complicates several developmental disability metabolic syndromes including Lowe syndrome, osteogenesis imperfecta, Type I, acrodysostosis, and Albright hereditary osteodystrophy. Osteoporosis and osteoarthritis could both become symptomatic at an early age in homocystinuria. Metabolic disorders with premature and severe aging osteoarthritis include mucopolysaccharidosis, Wilson's disease, alcaptonuria, and Gaucher disease. In the mucopolysaccharidosis, particularly in Hunter disease, joint incongruity may be an important factor leading to premature spinal and epiphysial osteoarthrosis. Articular cartilage becomes brittle and undergoes calcification in alcaptonuria. Although generalized articular changes are present, the spinal compromise is particularly severe.

The subchondral bone is abnormal in Gaucher disease. Osteoarticular involvement is severe in both chronic non-neuronopathic (Type I, adult) and subacute neuronopathic (Type III, juvenile) forms, leading to abnormal gait and restriction of activity. Aseptic bone necrosis of the hip joint may mimic Legg-Calvé-Perthes disease. Apart from the hip joint, vertebral bodies are commonly involved, which may result in vertebral collapse and subsequent nerve root compression. Chondrocalcinosis is present in Wilson's disease, often associated with severe bone involvement (Feller & Schumacher, 1972). Progressive flexion contractures with joint fixation, deformity, and disuse osteopenia are features of the X-linked (Becker type), myotonic, and limb girdle dystrophies that may accelerate musculoskeletal aging.

Awareness of the prematurity and severity of osteoarticular aging in developmentally disabled individuals will assist in delineating adequate and timely therapeutic approaches.

AGING MYOPATHY

Generalized loss of skeletal muscle bulk is a known feature of advanced age. Proximal and distal muscles are affected, although the distal compromise is visually more striking. As noted by Adams, Denny-Brown, and Pearson (1962), "the hands become thin and bony, and the interosseous spaces may be so prominent as to suggest progressive muscular atrophy . . . the arm and leg muscles tend to be thin and flabby." This decrease in skeletal muscle mass has been estimated to begin in the third decade and to amount to about 0.6% to 1.5% per year, based upon the changes in body cell mass, determined by creatinine excretion (Tzankoff & Norris, 1977) and whole-body counting of potassium (^{10}K) (Allen, Anderson, & Langham, 1960; Grimby, Danneskiold-Samsoe, Hvid, & Saltin, 1982; Steen, Bruce, Isaksson, Lewin, & Svanborg, 1977).

Overshadowing the overall occurrence and prevalence of neurogenic and distrophic atrophies, *age-related atrophy* constitutes the *most frequent form* of muscular atrophy observed in clinical practice. Despite its frequency, it is one of the least understood because of its pathogenesis and effects upon functional performance.

Functional Characteristics

Muscle function can be assessed through the determination of maximum isometric and isokinetic (knee extension) strengths, speed of contraction (speed of movement), and endurance capacity. By evaluation of such parameters, aging muscle exhibits peculiar functional characteristics that clearly differentiate its performance from that of young muscle.

Strength A 30%–50% decline in the major parameters of muscular strength occurs between the ages of 30 and 80. This decrease parallels a similar reduction in the size of individual muscles, as measured by ultrasonography and computed tomography (Borkan, Hults, Gerzof, Robbins, & Silbert, 1983; Imamura, Ashida, Ishikawa, & Fujii, 1983; Young, Stokes, & Crowe, 1981). The decrement is not generalized or synchronous and involves certain strength modalities and muscle groups earlier on and in a more severe degree than others.

Accelerated maximum dynamic and isometric strength losses usually begin during the sixth decade (Larsson, Grimby, & Karlsson, 1979) or later (Aniansson, Grimby, Hedberg, Rundgren, & Sperling, 1978; Aniansson, Grimby, & Rundgren, 1980) in both males and females, although the onset may occur earlier in females. This decline has been observed in both occupationally active and retired cohorts. Female values (for peak isokinetic and isometric torques) range between 50% and 70% of the male levels (Aniansson, Grimby, Hedberg, & Krotkiewski, 1981; Aniansson, Grimby, & Rundgren, 1980; Grimby, Aniansson, Danneskiold-Samsoe, & Saltin, 1980). Decrement of isometric strength of knee extensors (40% decrease) begins earlier and is more significant than that of upper extremities or trunk muscle groups (10%–30% decrease) (Montoye & Lamphier, 1977; Sperling, 1980). Isokinetic torques tend to be affected at high angular velocities in both sexes (Grimby et al., 1980). The overall strength decline is more pronounced in the isokinetic (50% loss) than in the isometric strength (40% loss) (Larsson et al., 1979).

Speed of Contraction While the maximum speed of contraction (MSC) decreases nearly 10% between 30 and 70 years, the major reduction, about 7%, occurs from 50 to 70 years of age (Larsson et al., 1979). Type II relative area and percentage correlate significantly with peak isokinetic strength and faster contraction velocities in young adults

(Coyle, Costill, & Lesmes, 1979; Gollnick, Armstrong, Saubert, Piehl, & Saltin, 1972; Thorstensson, Grimby, & Karlsson, 1976). In elderly individuals, decline of peak isokinetic torques and MSC does not significantly correlate with aging reconfiguration of fiber-type areas and distribution patterns, that is, with the approximate 15% reduction of Type IIB (fast twitch) fiber area and proportion. Better correlation is noted with overall fiber loss (Aniansson et al., 1981; Larsson et al., 1979). When compared to young control subjects, fast maximal voluntary contraction in elderly subjects has been found to obtain 19% higher strength than slow contraction (Clarkson, Kroll, & Melchionda, 1981), suggesting that methodological limitations may tend to overestimate strength loss on certain modalities with aging.

Endurance Endurance has been defined as either the maximum period of time 40%–50% of maximum (isometric) tension can be sustained, or as the capability to maintain an isokinetic tension level during repeated contractions. Strength-corrected isometric and dynamic endurances do not decline and even tend to increase with age (Larsson & Karlsson, 1978; Petrofsky & Lind, 1975), indicating improved exercise and working capacity under endurance conditions. This may compensate for the declines in strength. The modification of the muscle composition (increased percentage of Type I) is believed to correlate with such findings, although endurance varies with the muscle group studied and corresponding maximum isometric torques (Gregor, Edgerton, Perrine, Campion, & DeBus, 1979; Hulten, Thorstensson, Sjodin, & Karlsson, 1975; Kroll, Clarkson, Melchionda, & Wilcox, 1981; Thorstensson & Karlsson, 1976).

The voluntary nature of testing protocols, differences in subject cooperation and psychological motivation, and the in-test training cause variations in the results. These factors limit their accuracy as absolute indicators of strength loss. However, data obtained through a protocol of muscle tensions generated by electrically evoked contractions of triceps surae, recently reported as an unbiased method to assess elderly muscle function, did not differ significantly from voluntary protocols (Davies & White, 1983a,b). A series of parameters were found to be abnormal in the subjects that Davies and White used (mean age 69.6 ± 1.3 years), including increased time to development of the peak tension (slower contracting muscles), prolonged half relaxation times, and decreased maximal tetanic tensions (increased fatigability). No significant differences were observed in maximal tensions and endurance. These results confirmed the findings of voluntary contraction protocols. They also were consistent with a muscle fiber-type redeployment and suggested a possible participation of ischemic events in aging because of noted increased fatigability.

Morphological Characteristics

Total fiber loss and changes in fiber-type composition and distribution constitute the major histopathological features of aging myopathy (Bucciante & Luria, 1934; Tomlinson, Walton, & Rebeiz, 1969). Fiber loss averages between 30% and 40% of total fiber both in human and experimental animals (Caccia, Harris, & Johnson, 1979; Gutmann & Hanzlikova, 1966; Hooper & Shiel, 1978; Lexell, Henriksson-Larsen, Winblad, & Sjostrom, 1983; Rowe, 1969). In aging, both Type I and Type II populations decrease very slowly in parallel patterns at a rate that may not be detected by routine morphological studies (Jennekens, Tomlinson, & Walton, 1971; Lindboe & Torvik, 1982). Reduction of muscle mass and muscle strength is the primary result of fiber loss. Length of muscle fibers decreases also with age, due to a reduction in the number of their sarcomeres (Hooper, 1981). This reduction in fiber length may also result in diminished joint mobility.

Changes in Fiber-Type Composition and Distribution In normal adult muscle, two major types of fibers could be identified: Type I, which constitutes about 35% of the total number, and Type II, which accounts for the remaining 65%. Type I fibers have high oxidative and low glycolytic (phosphorylase) enzyme content. Their myofibrillar (adenosine triphosphate) ATPase level is low in comparison to Type II fibers that are conversely low oxidative and high glycolytic. Type I fibers have slow twitch speed and are fatigue resistant. Three Type II fibers could be differentiated on the basis of their histochemical characteristics: IIA, IIB, and IIC. Type IIA are also known as fast twitch fatigue resistant, oxidative, and glycolytic fibers. They show inhibition of ATPase staining at incubations below pH 4.6. Type IIB fibers are oxidatively and glycolytically different from Type IIA fibers (e.g., lactic dehydrogenase activity is higher in IIB and, conversely, levels of citrate synthase activity are lower). Thus, these fast twitch fibers are less oxidative than IIA (Brooke & Kaiser, 1970; Essen & Henriksson, 1980).

Studies of healthy elderly subjects in the eighth decade show an increase in size variability and a 15%–33% reduction of Type II fiber area (size), especially Type IIB (Table 1). This decrease in Type II relative area accelerates between the seventh and eighth decades. The percentage of Type IIA and IIB fibers also declines between the third and eighth decades from about 65% to 40% while Type I proportion increases. Type IIB area decreases in 78-year-old individuals to $2.3 \pm 05 \ \mu m^2 \times 10^3$ from the $4.8 \pm 0.4 \ \mu m^2 \times 10^3$ of the 61-year-old group (Aniansson, Grimby, & Rundgren, 1980; Aniansson, Grimby, Rundgren, Svanborg, & Orlander, 1980; Grimby et al., 1982; Larsson & Karlsson, 1978), resulting in a Type IIA relative predominance. Type IIB replacement by Type I and IIA fibers indicates a shift to more oxidatively efficient fibers. This correlates with the improved endurance of elderly individuals. Type I relative area remains practically unchanged; thus, by the eighth decade it exceeds Type II total area, clearly reversing the young adult pattern (Aniansson et al., 1981; Brooke & Engel, 1969). The Type II/Type I ratio (fast twitch/slow twitch ratio) tends to decrease with age from about 1.30 to 0.95 (in males) and to 0.76 (in females).

The size of the sample and the muscle selected for biopsy are significant in the evaluation of the histological findings. Increased intramuscular variation of fiber-type clusters in elderly persons (Nygaard & Sanchez, 1982) makes needle biopsy of vastus lateralis an inaccurate indicator of morphological changes. Also, selection of a lower extremity (gastrocnemius, vastus lateralis) versus upper extremity (deltoid) muscle group is important. Aging changes occur first in muscles of the lower extremities, in particular gastrocnemius and quadriceps. Trunk and superior extremities are affected later on and to a lesser degree.

Ultrastructural Findings Diverse and contradictory changes have been reported both in human and animal aging muscle. They include alterations of the configuration and number of tubular-membranous systems, myofibrils, mitochondria, myonuclei, satellite cells, and synapses, as well as the presence of lipofuscin inclusions (Table 2). These changes are largely nonspecific, as they have been noted to occur in disuse atrophy and other myogenic, neurogenic, and ischemic muscle disorders (Mair & Tome, 1972). Thus, they fail to provide any distinct clues toward the etiopathogenesis of muscle aging. Lipofuscin accumulation seems not to be a specific change as it has been seen also in disuse atrophy. Accumulation of this pigment may be linked to T-system or to Golgi apparatus function (Shafiq, Lewis, Dimino, & Shutta, 1978).

Biochemical Characteristics

Resting and postexertion levels of the major energy-rich phosphogens (ATP, ADP, AMP, and phosphocreatine) are diminished in aging muscle. The decrease of ATP, in particular, becomes significant only after exertion, which indicates a reduced rate of ATP resynthesis (Aniansson et al., 1981; Dudley & Fleck, 1983; Ermini, 1976; Ermini, Szelenyi, Moser, & Verzan, 1971; Moller, Bergstrom, Furst, & Hellstrom, 1980). In contrast, myosin ATPase activities of both resting and exercised muscle are unaffected or only slightly reduced (Larsson & Karlsson, 1978; Matsuki, Tadeda, & Tonomura, 1966; Rockstein & Brandt, 1961).

The abnormal postexertion recovery of energy-rich phosphogens is not linked to any local significant decrease in aerobic energy capacity of the aged muscle. Local muscle

Table 1. Histochemical findings in humans

Author	Sex/Age	Muscle(s)/ Technique	Type II fiber	Type I fiber	Type grouping
Jennekens, Tomlinson, and Walton (1971)	NR[a]	BB[b], RF[c], G[d], EDB[e]/ Surgical	Size decrease	Size decrease	Present Type I
Tomonaga (1977)	Both sexes/ 60–90	Various/ Surgical	Area-size decrease	NSC[f]	Present
Larsson and Karlsson (1978); Larsson, Grimby, and Karlsson (1979); Larsson (1982)	Male/ 22–65	VL[g]/ Needle	33% area decrease IIC unchanged	11% increase Area unchanged	NR[a]
Aniansson, Grimby, and Rundgren (1980); Aniansson, Grimby, Hedberg, and Krotkiewski (1981)	Both sexes/ 61–76	VL[g]	Area-size decrease	NSC[f]	Present
Scelsi, Marchetti, and Poggi (1980)	Both sexes/ 65–89	VL[g]/ Surgical	Area-size decrease	Predominance	Present
Grimby, Danneskiold-Samsoe, Hvid, and Saltin (1982)	78–81	VL[g]/ Needle	15% IIB, IIA area decrease	Slight area increase	Present Type I 30% cases
Nygaard and Sanchez (1982)	Male/ 72–88	VL[g], BB[b]/ Autopsy	Area-size NSC[f]	NSC[f]	Present NSC[f]
Lexell, Henriksson-Larsen, Winblad, and Sjostrom (1983)	Male/ 72 ± 1 year	VL[g]/ Autopsy	60% number decrease	NSC[f]	Present

[a]NR = Not reported.   [c]RF = Rectus femoris.   [e]EDB = Extensor digitii brevis.   [g]VL = Vastus lateralis.
[b]BB = Brachial biceps.   [d]G = Gastrocnemius.   [f]NSC = No significant changes.

oxidative metabolism is somewhat preserved in contrast to the generalized decrease in oxygen uptake capacity. The increased proportion of Type I fibers parallels the status of several oxidative parameters: increased B oxidation of fatty acids, unchanged cytochrome oxidase activity, reduction in the volume but not number of mitochondria, abnormal mitochondrial ATP/ADP exchange, and decreased lactate dehydrogenase and hexokinase activities

Table 2. Summary of ultrastructural findings in aging myopathy in human and experimental animals

	Reference[a]	Major changes	Age-species
Inclusions	5, 7, 8, 10	Curvilinear bodies Lipofuscin accumulation	60–90 years[b] 88–735 days[c]
Internal membranes	1, 2, 3, 6, 8, 10	SR proliferation, dilation T-system disorganization, proliferation SR and T-system volume and surface reductions	60–90 years[b] 88–735 days[c]
Mitochondria	2, 4, 5, 7, 10	Increased/decreased/unchanged number and volume (mean and total) Paracrystalline inclusions (subsarcolemmal) Focal aggregates	60–90 years[b] 88 days–27 months[c]
Myofibrils	2, 3, 5, 8, 10	Splitting condensation (Homogenization) Disorganization, disintegration Whorled arrangements (lamellar figures) Smudging of filaments	60–90 years[b] 88 days–27 months[c]
Myonuclei	2, 9, 10, 11	Deformation, indentation Increased heterochromatin Aggregation, size reduction Constant nucleocytoplasmic ratio and size	60–90 years[b] 88–735 days[c]
Satellite cells	9, 10	Degenerated, dense appearance of nuclei Lipofuscin accumulation	60–90 years[b]
Synapses	3, 9	Decreased, thickened subsynaptic folds Increased vesicles	69–90 years[b] NS[c]
Z discs	2, 5, 8	Focal streaming (nonatrophic fibers) "Dislocation" Nemaline rods	60–90 years[b] 88 days–27 months[c]

[a]1. DeCoster, DeRenck, Sieben, & Van Der Eecken, 1981; 2. Fujisawa, 1975; 3. Gutmann & Hanzlikova, 1976; 4. Kiessling, Pilstrom, Karlsson, & Piehl, 1973; Kiessling, Pilstrom, Bylund, Saltin, & Piehl, 1974; 5. Ludatscher, Silbermann, Gershon, & Reznick, 1983; 6. McCarter, 1978; 7. Orlander, Kiessling, Larsson, Karlsson, & Aniansson, 1978; 8. Shafiq, Lewis, Dimino, & Shutta, 1978; 9. Snow, 1977; 10. Tomonaga, 1977; 11. Vassilopoulos, Lumb, & Emery, 1977.

[b]Human.

[c]Rodent.

SR = sarcoplasmic reticulum; NS = not specified.

(Bass, Gutmann, & Hanzlikova, 1975; Farrar, Martin, & Murray-Ardies, 1981; Fitts, Booth, Winder, & Holloszy, 1975; Larsson & Karlsson, 1978; Nohl, 1982; Orlander, Kiessling, Larsson, Karlsson, & Aniansson, 1978). Reductions of muscle oxidative capacity described by certain authors may be only reflecting reductions in peak muscle functional blood flow.

Several stages of protein synthesis are affected in experimental models. Although muscle mRNA content has not been measured, the rate of total RNA synthesis is decreased. Protein and ribosome incorporation of labeled amino acid precursors and several translational steps are overall decreased in rate (Britton & Sherman, 1975). This decrease is nonlinear; it is present both in cardiac and skeletal preparations and may reach 85% over the control values (Blazejowski & Webster, 1983). Increased leucine incorporation in human muscle has only been reported by Lundholm and Schersten (1975) and has not been confirmed by others. A similar but nonspecific decrease in muscle protein synthesis accompanied by increased protein catabolism has been observed in aging, disuse, and denervation myopathies (Goldspink, 1977). In aged animals, muscle aldolase and phosphoglycerate kinase enzymes have shown between 40% and 60% reduction of their specific activities (Chetsanga & Liskiwskyi, 1977; Orlovska, Demchenko, & Veselovska, 1980). This is due to altered polypeptide conformation and not to covalent changes. Protein-altered conformations may not only be the result of abnormal synthesis but also of unknown postsynthetic modifications. Partial denaturation of the enzymes will result in decrease of their specific activity, alteration of their ultraviolet (UV) absorption ranges, thermolability, and immunogenicity (Gafni, 1981; Gershow, 1979; Hansford & Castro, 1982; Roch Norlund & Borrebaek, 1978; Sharma, Prasanna, & Rothstein, 1980).

A reduction in the protein degradation rate similar to that of ischemic muscle is noted with an increase in age (Mayer, Amin, & Shafrir, 1980, 1981; Millward, 1978; Salminen & Vihko, 1981; Shannon, Adams, & Courtice, 1974). The increase in the half-life of proteins may lead to their structural alteration rendering them less susceptible to degrading mechanisms. Short-term exercise causes an increase of aldolase and creatine kinase activities in young but not in old mice (Reznick, Steinhagen-Thiessen, Gellersen, & Gershon, 1983; Steinhagen-Thiessen & Hilz, 1976). This indicates not only a reduced adaptive capacity but

also irreversibility of these enzymatic changes. However, *long-term* training may prevent reductions in enzyme activity. Extracellular water, serum sodium, and chlorides increase in aged muscle; other electrolytes and amino acids remain basically unchanged (Moller, Alvestrand, Bergstrom, Furst, & Hellstrom, 1983).

Pathogenesis: Role of Disuse, Denervation, and Ischemia

As shown in Table 3, disuse, denervation, and chronic ischemia share numerous features in common with aging myopathy, suggesting a complex interaction and overlap between all of these mechanisms. Furthermore, a peculiar muscle-aging pathology results from all these mechanisms, with the denervational features predominating. Disuse could manifest itself by preferential reductions in the fiber proportion and size of either Type II (Type IIB) (Brooke & Kaiser, 1970; Bundschu, Suchenwirth, & D'Avis, 1973; Edstrom, 1970; Patel, Razzak,

Table 3. The role of disuse, denervation, and ischemia in relation to the aging process[a]

	Disuse	Denervation	Chronic ischemia	Aging
Muscle groups affected:	Proximal-Distal	Distal	Proximal-Distal	Distal
Histochemistry				
a. Fiber-type(s) affected	II↓ I↓ II↓ only I↓ only	II↓	II↓	II I II only
b. Fiber-type grouping	+	+++	+	++
Ultrastructure				
a. Myofibrillar disorganization/ augmentation	+	++	++	++
b. T-system proliferation	+−	++	++	++
c. Lipofuscin	+	+	−	+
d. Endplate degeneration	+−	++	+−	−
Neuromuscular junction				
a. Terminal sprouting	+	+++	NR	++
b. Extrajunctional acetylcholine (ACh) sensitivity	+	+++	NR	++
c. Acetylcholinesterase (AChE) decrease	+	+++	NR	++
d. Transmitter synthesis	↓ or N	↓	N	
e. Resting membrane potential	↓	↓	NR	NR
Biochemistry				
Muscle protein synthesis	↓	↓	↓	↓
Muscle protein breakdown	↑	↑	↑−	↓
Electromyography				
Denervational activity	0	+++	+	++

[a]See text for references.

+ = mild; ∓ = minimal; − = absent; ++ = moderate; +++ = severe; NR = not reported; N = normal; ↑ = increased; ↓ = decreased.

& Dastur, 1969; Sargeant, Davies, Edwards, Maunder, & Young, 1977; Sirca & Susec-Michieli, 1980), Type I, or both fiber types (Herbison, Jaweed, & DiTunno, 1979; Jaffe, Terry, & Spiro, 1978; Lindboe & Platou, 1982). Fiber-type grouping may also occur (Dastur, Gagrat, & Manghani, 1979).

It is likely that this variability in the morphological picture of disuse depicts different responses to immobilization or reduction of activity by different muscle groups that are affected in different positions and degree. For example, in osteoarthritis of the hip, motility is not completely abolished, but is both simultaneously modified and reduced. This abnormal activity may have generated the particular quadriceps pattern with Type II fiber atrophy and loss that was observed in one study (almost 30% reduction in both parameters), although superimposed denervation may have played a role (Sirca & Susec-Michieli, 1980). Meanwhile, tenotomy and immobilization in increased degree of stretch may provoke a preferential Type I atrophy in the gastrocnemius (Edstrom, 1970; Engel, Brooke, & Nelson, 1966; Sargeant et al., 1977).

Type II fibers are sensitive to ischemia. Individuals with mild chronic ischemia, with or without claudication, show selective atrophy of these fibers in occasions accompanied by an increase of Type I relative number and area. Type I fiber grouping has also been observed in ischemia (Makitie & Teravainen, 1977; Sjostrom, Angquist, & Rais, 1980; Sjostrom, Neglen, Friden, & Eklof, 1982). The role of circulatory disturbances in aging myopathy is poorly understood; however, a significant decrease in muscle blood flow in experimental aged animals has been observed (Frolkis, Martynenko, & Zamostyan, 1976).

Fiber-type grouping (more than 15 fibers) with enclosed fibers is present in needle biopsies of 30% of the individuals 80 years of age and older. Together with fiber-type redistribution, it provides evidence of denervation loss and secondary reinervation of fast twitch units. The progressive loss of functioning motor units, with simultaneous reorganization of motor units noted after the fifth decade of life, is also electrically accompanied by an increase in *motor unit potential size* (amplitude and complexity), *fiber variability* (jitter), and a *prolongation of the contraction and relaxation of isometric twitches,* as shown by routine, single-fiber and macro electromyograms (EMGs) (Brown, 1972; Campbell, McComas, & Petito, 1973; Carlsson, Alston, & Feldman, 1964; Sica, Sanz, & Colombi, 1976; Stalberg & Fawcett, 1982). Reduction of the maximum conduction velocities occurs in major motor and sensory nerves with age, although the decrease is more severe in sensory velocities. After age 55, the decrease for median nerve ranges about 2 m per second per decade and for the ulnar nerve 3 m per second per decade. The reduction reaches about 10% by the sixth decade (Buchthal, Rosenfalck, & Behse, 1975; Mayer, 1963; Norris, Shock, & Wagman, 1953; Wagman & Lesse, 1952).

Remodeling of the motor unit is the result of sprouting of axonal terminals with incorporation of surviving fibers into slow twitch motor units. Terminal axonal sprouting and collateral reinervation with multiple endplates have been documented in aging intramuscular (motor) human nerve endings (Harriman, Taverner, & Woolf, 1970; Woolf, 1965). A similar pattern of terminal axonal sprouting combined with endplate degeneration has been noted in experimental animals (Gutmann & Hanzlikova, 1966, 1972/1973; Tuffery, 1971). Numerous morphological changes have been documented in aging peripheral nerves: stenosis of vasa nervorum, fibrosis, decrease in the number of nerve fibers, variability and multiplication of internodes due to formation of intercalated internodes, axonal loss and degeneration, unmyelinated fiber loss, and segmental demyelinations with remyelination (Arnold & Harriman, 1970; Berg, Wolf, & Simms, 1962; Corbin & Gardner, 1937; Cottrell, 1940; Lascelles & Thomas, 1966; Ochoa & Mair, 1969; Stevens, Lofgren, & Dyck, 1973; Vizoso, 1950).

In addition to other known features of aging of the spinal cord such as myelin pallor, axonal spheroids, and lipofuscin accumulation in anterior horn cells (Bailey, 1953), *lumbosacral* motor neuronal cell loss has been noted to increase dramatically after age 60. This loss may reach 50% of young adult neuronal counts by the ninth decade (Tomlinson & Irving, 1977). Predominance of aging denervational changes in the lower extremities has been attributed to this neuronal loss (Rebeiz, Moore, Holden, & Adams, 1972). However, aging myopathy of experimental animals (rodents) occurs without any spinal neuronal reduction (Gutmann & Hanzlikova, 1972/1973).

In summary, all segments of the lower motor neuron pathway may be implicated in the genesis of the "neurogenic" atrophic changes of the aged muscle, predominantly in the leg. It is likely that all these segments are simultaneously involved, in response to different aging mechanisms. Although spinal changes are of neuronal degenerative nature, those present in the peripheral nerves may be secondary to either entrapment, repeated trauma with elongation, or to ischemic disorders. Ultrastructural findings are very similar in all four conditions, indicating their nonspecific nature (Cooper, 1972). Similar neuromuscular junction abnormalities have been observed in three of the processes (disuse, denervation, and aging): terminal fiber sprouting with enlarged endplates (Brown & Ironton, 1977), development of extrajunctional acetylcholine (ACh) sensitivity (Gilliat, Westgaard, & Williams, 1978; Pestronk & Drachman, 1978), decrease in acetylcholinesterase (AChE) concentration (Butler, Drachman, & Goldberg, 1978), and decrease of the resting membrane potential (Stanley & Drachman, 1979).

Physical Training: Therapeutic Approach to Aging Myopathy

Aging myopathy responds to different training protocols with modification of the histochemical and morphological patterns of muscle, and increases of both isokinetic and isometric strengths. The changes observed suggest a residual capacity to revert disuse and to modify the recruitment pattern of motor units with redeployment of fast twitch units. However, the response to training is *different* from that observed in young adults indicating the irre-

versibility of certain component(s) of the aging muscle process.

Elderly retired subjects (mean age 70.7 ± 0.12) who had participated in three weekly exercise sessions of 45 minutes for 12 weeks were found to increase quadriceps maximum isometric and isokinetic strength from between 9% and 22%. This increase was only significant at low angular velocities and was not associated with MSC improvements (Aniansson & Gustafsson, 1981). An isometric-isokinetic protocol followed by a relatively younger group (mean age 59.2 ± 0.9) resulted in quadriceps strength increase of 7.5% (Larsson, 1982). In elderly persons, no changes either in muscle cell mass (as determined by total body potassium) or in capillary density accompany these improvements in strength (Aniansson, Grimby, Rundgren, Svanborg, & Orlander, 1980; Aniansson & Gustafsson, 1981). However, although the total muscle area remains unchanged and no hypertrophy occurs as in young subjects, the histochemical pattern of aged muscle changes in a similar way as does that of young adult males and females after training (Jansson, Sjodin, & Tesch, 1978; Larsson, 1982; Moritani & DeVries, 1980). A 10% to 19% increase in the Type II (IIA) area, together with either a reduction (Aniansson & Gustafsson, 1981; Orlander & Aniansson, 1980) or an increase (Larsson, 1982) of the Type I area has been noted to occur. In experimental animals (27-month-old BL/6J mice), 10 weeks endurance training was also followed by an increase in the Type II fiber area without a parallel decrease in Type I. The total fiber number remained unchanged and no evidence of hypertrophy was observed (Silbermann, Finkelbrand, Weiss, Gershow, & Reznick, 1983).

Ultrastructural studies have failed to demonstrate any increase in mitochondrial volume in contrast to posttraining young adult findings (Orlander & Aniansson, 1980; Kiessling, Pilstrom, Bylund, Saltin, & Piehl, 1974). After training, the T-system has been noted to multiply and form aggregates (Ludatscher, Silbermann, Gershon, & Reznick, 1983). The histochemical changes primarily suggest a shift to an elevated anaerobic glycolytic capacity with a simultaneous relative improvement of the oxidative pathway. Lactic dehydrogenase (LDH), phosphofructokinase, malate dehydrogenase, and cytochrome oxidase (CO_x) levels have all been seen to significantly increase with training (Kiessling et al., 1974; Orlander & Aniansson, 1980; Suominen, Heikken, & Paarkatti, 1977). CO_x increase is consistent with the increase in mitochondrial function (mitochondrial protein) in spite of the absence of mitochondrial volume changes (Farrar et al., 1981). Kiessling et al. (1974) noted that baseline pretraining total mitochondrial number is already higher in older than in younger subjects; thus, any increase in mitochondrial metabolic activity may not become evident morphologically. However, *the aging process cannot be reversed with exercise.* The fiber number will not increase due to the proliferative incapacity of the decreased satellite cell population of aging muscle (Schultz & Lipton, 1982). Thus, the major cause for functional muscle decline, the *fiber loss,* cannot be corrected with training.

Although elderly muscle is able to sustain exercise with increased endurance and no apparent fatigability (Davies & White, 1983b), is exercise beneficial for the aging muscle? Experimental evidence suggests that training may be deleterious for aging muscle beyond a certain "threshold" (Edington, Cosmas, & McCafferty, 1972; Ludatscher et al., 1983; McCafferty & Edington, 1974). Alterations in muscle ultrastructure, together with a progressive decrease in muscle size and even death, have also been reported. It is evident that exercise will only improve the general cardiorespiratory function of the individual, and will aid in leading to a better metabolical adaptation of the aging muscle to the daily activity functions. No morphological reconstitution can be expected.

AGING OSTEOPENIA

With postmenopausal osteoporosis included in its spectrum, aging osteopenia constitutes the most common human bone disease. Characterized by vertebral fractures, fractures of long bones (forearm and hip), deformities, and chronic postural pain, the syndrome makes its presentation around the fifth decade. Thus, while age-related muscle changes become clinically demonstrable by the seventh and eighth decades, aging osteopenia can be detected much earlier. Bone demineralization initiates and develops at significantly different rates according to race, sex, bone compartment under study, and methods of measurement or detection. For example, bone mass loss begins earlier and progresses at a faster rate in females than in males, in contrast to muscle fiber loss that tends to begin later and to progress at a slower rate in females than in males. Characterized by absolute decrease of its mass, the aging bone may reach structural levels at which it becomes incapable of maintaining its dynamic and static integrity.

Nontraumatic vertebral compression fractures (i.e., crush fractures) are the major cause of acute and chronic pain, leading to activity avoidance and limitation in elderly individuals. These fractures could occur either "spontaneously" or after minor efforts, in contrast to long bone fractures, which are usually associated with guarded or unguarded falls. Such fractures occur more frequently in lower thoracic (8th, 9th, 11th, and 12th vertebrae) and upper lumbar vertebrae (Gallagher et al., 1973; Saville, 1970). Indeed, at the time of their first office visit for spinal symptoms, one-fourth of elderly individuals evidenced at least three fractures. Recurrent vertebral fractures may also be manifested as painless progressive loss of axial height exceeding 2.5 cm per decade. As a consequence, arm span may surpass standing height. Increased kyphosis of the dorsal spine and reduction of lumbar lordosis are also seen. The latter increases resting hip flexion leading to the development of hip flexion contractures and further limitation of activity (Gallagher et al., 1973; Saville & Nilsson, 1966; Saville, 1970).

Decreased skeletal bone strength may be considered the result of a relatively stable, constant rate of bone formation combined with a high (4%–5% per year) rate of bone resorption that practically doubles the former (Heaney, Recker, & Saville, 1977; Nordin, Horsman, Brook, & Williams, 1976; Nordin, Aaron, Speed, & Crilly, 1981). This abnormal turnover occurs simultaneously in both trabecular (20% of skeletal bone mass) and compact (80% of skeletal bone mass) compartments. Compromise of the two compartments is unrelated and not uniform. Bone loss starts earlier in the trabecular (age 30–35 years) than in the compact compartment (age 40–45 years). The progression rate is also clearly different in both compartments as shown by the 6%–8% per decade loss rate of the trabecular bone versus the 3%–5% per decade loss of the compact bone (Mazess, 1979). Thus, compact bone studies are not useful indicators of trabecular bone status.

Peak bone mass is 30% higher in males than in females at the end of the growth period. Thus, critical subsequent reductions in bone mass are achieved faster in females. Reductions of compact bone mass, total body calcium, and bone mineral content are clearly influenced by menopause. Female perimenopausal yearly rates for these compartments may reach 9%–10%, while male loss rates remain constant. By age 80, white women have lost about 40% of their trabecular bone.

Rare in both elderly black men and women, radiographically demonstrable aging osteopenia is present in over 50% of white women by age 50 and in 80% of white women over age 65. Black women have a lower prevalence of postmenopausal osteoporosis than white women (Bollet, Engh, & Parson, 1965, 1968; Engh, Bollet, Hardin, & Parson, 1968; Moldawer, Zimmerman, & Collins, 1965; Smith & Rizek, 1966). The fact that American blacks have a larger peak skeletal mass (about 7% higher) than American whites at the ends of their growth period (Cohn et al., 1977; Garn & Clark, 1975) may allow them to maintain bone integrity longer. Perimenopausal bone loss is also slower in black women than in white women (Garn, 1975), which suggests a different (possibly genetic) response to similar aging mechanisms.

One-third of women after age 75 may suffer hip fracture, the most lethal osteoporotic (compact and trabecular) fracture—resulting in a 21.5% mortality rate within 1 year (Dahl, 1980; Jensen & Tondevold, 1979).

Incidence of clinically documented osteopenia (osteoporosis), manifested by "spontaneous" vertebral fractures, rises from about 30% in white women over age 65 (that is, about 5 million women in the United States) to about 41% in those age 75 and older (Iskrant & Smith, 1969). The cost of hospital treatment for such osteoporotic fractures in the United States approaches $4.0 billion annually.

Methods for Bone Mass Assessment in Aging

Early diagnosis of senile (aging) osteopenia is of great importance, since prevention of its progression is possible, but restoration of the bone loss is not.

A variety of techniques exist that have been developed in order to quantify bone density. They include X-ray methods, radionuclide absorptiometry, computed tomography, neutron activation, and bone histomorphometry. Two or more techniques should be utilized in order to obtain an accurate clinical assessment of the elderly individual. Total body calcium measurements (photon beam absorptiometry, quantitative computed tomography, neutron activation) that reflect the 80% of body cortical bone mass should be always complemented by accurate measurements of the trabecular bone mass, a sensitive indicator of fracture risk (bone histomorphometry, vertebral dual photon beam absorptiometry).

X-Ray Methods Radiographic X-ray techniques and indicators include: radiolucency, vertebral compression fractures, radiographic indices, and radiogrammetry.

Radiolucency A 30–40% decrease of the vertebral trabecular and compact bone mass must occur before the process can be diagnosed by increased radiolucency (Lachman & Whelan, 1936). Therefore, assessment of bone mass loss by this method tends to be unreliable. The initial loss takes place predominantly in horizontal versus vertically oriented trabeculae. The latter, which are structurally more important, may even offer compensation through an increase in thickening (Atkinson, 1967).

Decreased vertebral bone density is associated with an increased risk of fracture estimated at 1.6 per 100 women a year (Smith & Rizek, 1966). Among grade 0 (minimal density) women, the vertebral fracture prevalence rate may reach 7.5 per 100 per annum over age 65 (Iskrant & Smith, 1969; Nordin et al., 1980). Forearm (compact) female fracture rates may double such figures.

Vertebral Compressions Fractures   Lateral X-ray of the thoracolumbar spine should be part of the routine medical examination of all women above age 40. Collapse of the vertebral bodies could occur in *central* (lumbar "codfishing"), *anterior* (dorsal wedge fractures—Dowager's hump), *symmetrical* (waferlike vertebrae), or *combined* fashion. The presence of fractures does not reflect the degree and extent of generalized bone mass loss as demonstrated in studies that included simultaneous measurements of total bone mineral content (BMC) by either absorptiometry or neutron activation. Single crush fractures tend to reflect the degree of local spinal stress and osteopenia rather than the total BMC. Only multiple vertebral fractures are clearly associated with decreased body bone mass (Boyce, Courpron, & Meunier, 1978; Krolner & Pors Nielsen, 1982).

Radiographic Indices   Osteoporosis can be detected by radiographic indices such as the Metacarpal index, Femoral score, Total peripheral score (Barnett & Nordin, 1960, 1961), biconcavity index (Aloia, Vaswani, & Atkins, 1977), and femoral trabecular pattern (Singh index) (Singh, Nagrath, & Maini, 1970; Singh, Riggs, Beabout, & Jowse, 1972). About 50% of vertebral collapses may have a normal Singh index, suggesting that the indices are nonspecific, poorly sensitive indicators of early bone loss. The trabecular index tends to reflect local femoral changes rather than BMC (Kranendonk, Jurist, & Gun Lee, 1972).

Radiographic Morphometry (Radiogrammetry)   Cortical thickness (endosteal bone loss) is determined by radiogrammetry, with the midpoint of the left second metacarpal index as the preferred measuring site (Garn, 1970; Virtama & Helela, 1969). It is simple, but carries several limitations, for example, inability to accurately determine endosteal outline and to evaluate intracortical porosity, as well as the fact that medial and lateral cortical wall measurements may not represent mean true cortical thickness. Like any other appendicular measurement, radiogrammetry fails to accurately estimate total body calcium loss through the determination of focal BMC (Dalen & Lamke, 1974; Manzke, Chestnut, Wergedal, Baylink, & Nelp, 1975). The method is imprecise (5%–10%) and tends to locally overestimate bone loss. According to this method, metacarpal bone loss starts at about age 45 and progresses constantly at about 7%–10% per decade (women) or 3%–5% per decade (men) (Garn, 1970; Virtama & Helela, 1969), that is, at slower rates than the actual body loss. Cortical bone loss has been used to determine vertebral fracture (Meema, Reid, & Meema, 1973; Nordin, 1971) and fracture of long bone risks (Iskrant & Smith, 1969; Nordin, 1971; Smith, Khairi, & Johnston, 1975). The latter amounts to 1 per 100 per year with a risk of a second fracture at 1.3 per 100. The total risk between 30 and 90 years of age has been estimated as 25 per 100 in women and 10 per 100 in men (Allfram, 1964).

Direct Photon Beam Absorptiometry   Radiation transmission measurements of two separate photon energies (153 Gd or 241 Am/137 Cs) passing through a bone and soft tissue medium are the basis of direct photon beam absorptiometry. The anatomical region of interest is scanned and photon transmission (density) data are used to determine BMC in grams per centimeter, bone mineral density (BMD), and total body calcium (TBC). BMC gives an estimate of cortical bone strength.

A single photon (I_{125}) scan of the miradius offers more precision on compact BMC measurements than radiogrammetry (2%–5%). However, it has similar limitations by being restricted to only one-compartment measurements. The single-beam densitometer presents a high error range between 15% and 20% for vertebral/femoral estimations but constitutes a simple means for screening populations at risk. Dual photon absorptiometry (DPA) of the trabecular lumbar spine (Roos, 1975; Roos & Skoldborn, 1974) seems to offer superior diagnostic and follow-up precision on BMC loss to single photon absorptiometry of the distal (25% trabecular bone) or mid-radius (100% cortical bone) (Cameron & Sorenson, 1963; Wahner, Riggs, & Beabout, 1977). DPA simultaneously measures two vertebral compartments, compact and trabecular, allowing for better correlations ($r = .9$) than appendicular measurements for estimation of TBC and early detection of demineralization.

Quantitative Computed Tomography (QCT) QCT readings are the most precise and accurate measurements of vertebral mineral content per compartment. However, QCT does not yet serve as an adequate screening procedure. It carries a precision of 1.6% and is able to quantify decreases of 3%–4% in vertebral trabecular bone content. Vertebral fat increase with aging may bring inaccuracy to QCT measurements. Dual-energy QCT readings of fat, soft tissues, and vertebral bone are compared to standard calibration phantom readings for correction (Cann & Gennant, 1980; Gennant & Boyd, 1977; Weissberger, Samenhof, Aronow, & Neer, 1978).

Whole Body Neutron Activation Analysis The procedure of neutron activation is not used routinely. It is based on the activation of total body calcium with measurements of the short half-life radionuclides produced, for instance, 49 Ca. Despite its complexity and sophistication, the method does not offer better correlation for trabecular measurements than DPA or QCT. Whole body calcium loss is not a good indicator of fracture risk (Nelp et al., 1972).

Bone Histomorphometry Bone biopsy is a useful method to rule out hyperparathyroidism, malignancy (myeloma), and osteomalacia in elderly persons. It may also be a better dynamic indicator of osteoporosis than the above methods that only measure bone density. Osteomalacia of elderly individuals is due to inadequate

sunlight exposure and vitamin D intake. In about 10% of the cases, aging osteopenia may occur in combination with osteomalacia, contributing to an increase in compact bone fragility (Aaron et al., 1974; Nordin et al., 1980). Although the clinical picture of aging osteopenia and osteomalacia in elderly persons may be similar, only bone histopathology is capable of differentiating between those two entities. This is extremely important when considering proper therapeutic measures. In contrast to osteomalacia, which has an excess of osteoid seams per unit area, aging osteopenia shows a ratio of mineral to extracellular organic matrix close to that of normal bone.

Bone aging is characterized by a complex histological picture that reflects the simultaneous, yet different involvement of cortical and trabecular compartments. Decreased cortical thickness and increased cortical porosity (Haversian and Volkmann canals) have been noted to occur predominantly in females (Melsen, Melsen, Mosekilde, & Bergmann, 1978). While cortical width declines 54% between the second and seventh decades (from 1606 μm to 900 μm), that is about 10% per decade, cortical porosity only increases from 3.7% to 7.4%. Porosity increases are not accompanied by any detectable increase in the cortical osteoclastic resorption. As documented by radiogrammetry and single photon absorptiometry, the cortical bone loss amounts to about 10% per decade in females and to 5% per decade in males (Morgan, 1973; Newton-John & Morgan, 1970). Female loss is more significant and rapid during menopause (2% per year) versus premenopausal loss (1% per year) (Garn, 1970; Smith, Khairi, & Johnson, 1975).

Trabecular bone loss in elderly individuals is accompanied by declines in both trabecular width and mean wall thickness. In some cases, mean trabecular width is normal and even increased. The progressive trabecular loss leads to enlargement of the marrow cavity (Eder, 1960; Frost, 1973; Lindahl & Lindgren, 1962; Merz & Schenk, 1970; Meunier et al., 1973; Wakamatsu & Sissons, 1969). A number of parameters are routinely evaluated in iliac bone histomorphometry of aging osteopenia.

One of the most important indices is the trabecular (total) bone volume (TBV), which is the percentage of bone medullary space occupied by mineralized and nonmineralized trabecular tissue. TBV begins to decrease at about age 30 (at the end of the period of bone growth) in both sexes and continues thereafter at a 5%–10% per decade rate. While this decrease averages 5% per decade in males, it may reach 8%–10% per decade in postmenopausal females (Meunier et al., 1973, 1976). In females, TBV decreases from 22%–26% during the third decade to 16% during the ninth decade, whereas in males, the decrease is from 22%–24% in the third decade to 18% in the ninth decade (Melsen et al., 1978; Meunier et al., 1973, 1976; Wakamatsu & Sissons, 1969). These amount to about a 30% loss in males and to a more than 40% loss in females. It should be noted that the so-called "critical TBV or vertebral fracture threshold" beyond which there is high risk of vertebral collapse has been established at 11% ± 3% TBV (Meunier et al., 1973, 1976). Caution should be exercised when using TBV values because the overall error of the method (histomorphometry) amounts to 3%–5%, with a coefficient of variation of 10%–20% (Mazess, 1979).

Aging osteopenia results from a negative imbalance between resorption and formation, in which the former exceeds the latter although both rates could be lower than adult values. To some authors (e.g., Nordin et al., 1981), decline in trabecular width and mean wall thickness are indicators of both increased bone resorption and a nonsignificant but detectable decrease in bone formation. About 50% of the osteoporotic biopsies show normal ratios of osteoid and resorptive surfaces with normal calcification rates (i.e., osteoblastic opposition rates) (Meunier et al., 1978; Whyte, Bergfeld, Avioli, & Teitelbaum, 1982). In contrast, high remodeling and inactive forms are present in the remaining 50% of the cases. The high remodeling form shows an increase in osteoid and osteoclastic surfaces with raised urinary hydroxoproline and normal calcification rates. The inactive form is characterized by increased trabecular wall thickness and depressed osteo-

blastic activity. Osteoid and osteoclastic surfaces are normal (Parfitt, 1981; Whyte et al., 1982). These changes indicate a heterogeneous complex morphological picture in aging osteoporosis, probably reflecting the diverse pathogenetic mechanisms.

Laboratory Findings in Aging Osteopenia (Osteoporosis)

Serum concentrations of calcium, phosphorus, and alkaline phosphatase are usually normal. However, the variability of certain other laboratory parameters confirms the heterogeneity suggested by the above histopathological studies.

About one-fifth of osteoporotic patients have normal or elevated urinary calcium, increased urinary hydroxyproline, and elevated parathyroid hormone (iPTH) serum levels. Levels of iPTH had been found to gradually rise with age and even double by age 60 (Chapuy, Durr, & Chapuy, 1983; Gallagher, Riggs, Jerpbak, & Arnaud, 1980; Wiske et al., 1979). These findings are consistent with increased bone turnover and a mild secondary hyperparathyroidism with osteoclastosis, probably of intestinal or renal origin. Intestinal absorption of calcium decreases with age (Gallagher et al., 1979). This iPTH increase has also been seen to be accompanied by normal serum calcium levels and then interpreted alternatively to represent a primary type of hyperparathyroidism.

Serum levels of vitamin D_3 active metabolites have also been alternatively reported to be either normal or reduced in elderly individuals (Gallagher et al., 1979; Nordin, Peacock, Crilly, & Marshall, 1979; Riggs et al., 1978). Low 25-hydroxycholecalciferol and 1,25 dihydroxycholecalciferol serum levels or their diminished response to PTH injection (Chapuy et al., 1983; Slovik, Adams, Neer, Holick, & Potts, 1981) had been implicated in the reduced intestinal calcium absorption. Decreased renal synthesis of vitamin D may in turn be secondary to the abnormal calcium levels and to the estrogen deficiency, and not a primary event. Vitamin D deficit may also be nutritional (Aaron et al., 1974).

Raised serum alkaline phosphatase and urinary cyclic AMP levels have also been reported (Chapuy et al., 1983). Either secondary hyperparathyroidism or active fracture repair and bone formation may lead to these elevated values. Plasma calcitonin levels have been found to be decreased in elderly women, a factor that may also increase bone turnover (Heath & Sizemore, 1977; Shamonski et al., 1980).

Recently, elevated serum levels of bone j-carboxyglutamic acid, a noncollagenous bone matrix protein, have been cited as valuable indicators of the increased bone turnover (resorption) in aging (Delmas, Stenner, Wahner, Mann, & Riggs, 1983).

Pathogenesis of Aging Osteopenia Different pathomechanisms for osteoporosis have been proposed since Albright, Smith, and Richardson (1941) first suggested that decreased postmenopausal estrogen levels resulted in deficient osteoblastic activity with inadequate bone formation. Current hypotheses place estrogen deficiency in a different context: that it is responsible for accelerated bone resorption and loss. Estrogen deficiency is thought to act through a series of unknown extraskeletal mechanisms since no estrogen receptors have been identified either in osteoclasts or osteoblasts (Chen & Feldman, 1978). But estrogen replacement seems to inhibit preferentially compact bone loss versus trabecular loss, suggesting, however, that an estrogen local action on the remodeling mechanism does take place (Horsman, Gallagher, Simpson, & Nordin, 1977; Nachtigall, Nachtigall, Nachtigall, & Beckman, 1979; Nordin et al., 1976; Nordin et al., 1980; Recker, Saville, & Heaney, 1977).

Other estrogen effects on bone metabolism include: decrease of *in vitro* bone resorption, inhibition of paratohormone-stimulated resorption (Atkins, Zanelli, Peacock, & Nordin, 1972; Heaney, 1965; Jasani, Nordin, Smith, & Swanson, 1965), regulation of intestinal calcium absorption (Thomson & Frame, 1976), stabilization of bone collagen through an effect on macrophage collagenases (Peck, 1978), and elevation of 1,25 (OH) D_3 plasma levels (Crilly, Francis, & Nordin, 1981). Although

low plasma estrogen levels may be linked to the rapid postmenopausal bone loss, bone loss initiates before menopause (remodeling imbalance) and continues beyond it at a constant rate.

Male hypogonadism has been associated with osteoporosis and muscular atrophy. Whether or not low testosterone levels contribute to bone loss directly or through decreased estrogen levels secondarily to androgen deficiency is not known (Crilly et al., 1981). The rate of bone resorption in aging osteopenia is also increased by several *nutritional* mechanisms that act coincidentally with the hormonal deficiency. Such nutritional mechanisms include decreased calcium intake and absorption (Albanese, Edelson, Lorenze, Woodhull, & Wein, 1975; Gallagher et al., 1979; Recker et al., 1977), abnormal dietary calcium-phosphorus ratio (Lutwak, Singer, & Urist, 1974), and decreased vitamin D intake (see discussion under the heading "Laboratory Findings").

The role of *decreased new bone formation* should not be entirely disregarded in aging osteopenia since it has been shown to be present by the documented delays in fracture healing and production of small callus seen in elderly individuals (Tonna, 1965; Tonna & Cronkite, 1962), as well as by the abnormal response of the aging bone matrix to experimental implants (Irving, LeBolt, & Schneider, 1981; Syftestad & Urist, 1982). *Reduction of bone blood flow,* evidence of osteocytic osteolysis and cortical-trabecular bone necrosis in cases of osteoporosis associated with chronic circulatory insufficiency suggest that chronic bone ischemia could play a role in aging osteopenia (Duriez & Cauchoix, 1967; Hruza & Wachtlova, 1969; Rutishauser, Rhoner, & Held, 1960; Sherman & Selakovich, 1957). Repeated microfractures may alter bone microvasculature leading to further bone ischemia (Vignon & Meunier, 1973).

Role of Disuse and Aging Myopathy in Osteoporosis of Aged Individuals

Inactivity or immobilization leads to accelerated bone mass loss (Chantraine, 1971; Minaire et al., 1974; Whedon, 1960). Elderly individuals who remain inactive because of bone fracture, articular, muscular, or neurological disease may also develop osteoporosis through this mechanism. Accelerated bone loss may bring individuals below their bone fracture threshold even though the initial BMC was adequate for age. In long-term immobilization, bone loss is rapid during the first 6 months with stabilization after that time. The bone loss in long bones (30%–50%) is predominantly periosteal (Uthoff & Jaworski, 1978). Trabecular bone loss after immobilization secondary to spinal cord injury amounts to 33% over 6 months before stabilizing (Minaire et al., 1974). In fact, 14 days of bed rest may reduce bone mass by 12% as shown on radiogrammetry (Mack & Lachance, 1967).

A correlation between degree of bone loss and muscle loss has been observed in elderly males (Doyle, Brown, & Lachance, 1970; Meema et al., 1973; Saville & Nilsson, 1966; Smith, Khairi, Norton, & Johnston, 1976). This correlation has been denied by some (Sinaki, Opitz, & Wahner, 1974); however, methods of measurement varied considerably among all the studies. It is likely that muscle atrophy will produce an effect on the muscular load applied on the bone, a phenomenon that may lead to abnormal bone remodeling and resorption (Doyle et al., 1970).

It is unknown which percentage of the aging bone loss is due to the simultaneous aging myopathy and arthropathy, compared to other simultaneous mechanisms (e.g., postmenopausal estrogen changes, testosterone level decrease, bone ischemia, decreased bone formation rate, nutritional changes, etc.). However, it is clear that aging osteopenia is a heterogeneous process and that a variety of factors act simultaneously or successively to affect bone metabolism. This heterogeneity should be considered when deciding about therapeutic and preventive strategies. It also explains the failure to control bone loss and formation after calcium and estrogen therapies.

AGING ARTHROPATHY

A number of articular and perarticular syndromes may result in progressive motor disability in elderly persons. *Osteoarthritis* (osteoar-

throsis) is the most common articular disorder of aging followed by *periarticular rheumatism* (tendonitis, bursitis, fibrositis, polymyalgia rheumatica and nerve entrapment syndromes) and *chondrocalcinosis,* which manifests itself by a progressive arthritis simulating osteoarthritis, gout, or rheumatoid arthritis. Osteoarthritic changes are observed in stress-bearing or weight-bearing joints as early as in the third decade (Gordon, 1968; Lawrence, Bremner, & Bier, 1966). Hand and knee joint prevalence rates of 45% between 55 and 64 years of age rise to 85% in the eighth decade (Gordon, 1968). However, in only 20%–60% of the cases are changes symptomatic and lead to restriction of activities.

Osteoarthritis of aging affects women more commonly, indicating a particular predisposition (Kellgren, Lawrence, & Bier, 1963). Stress-bearing joints are frequently affected, for instance, distal interphalangeal (Heberden nodes) and proximal interphalangeal joints (Bouchard nodes). Weight-bearing joint involvement includes spine, knee, and hip joints. The protrusion and osteophytic reaction of vertebral discs can result in progressive cervical myelopathy and lumbosacral radiculopathy.

Spondylosis is present in 80% of males and 60% of females at 50 years and in all individuals by age 70 (Kellgren & Lawrence, 1958; Schmorl & Junghanns, 1971). Despite its frequency, only 60% of the cases are symptomatic, presenting with chronic recurrent pain and stiffness. Limitations of spinal movement are accompanied by loss of height and nerve root symptoms. Spinal stenosis can lead to cervical myelopathy and to cauda equina compression. The myelopathy develops insidiously with signs of motor neuron involvement in lower extremities and loss of abdominal reflexes. Compromise of cauda equina blood supply may also be manifested by muscular claudication and paresthesias on moderate activity. Chondrocalcinosis (calcium pyrophosphate dihydrate deposition) is associated with similar spinal disc involvement, although this disease predominantly affects knee, pubis, and wrist joints. The incidence of nonvertebral chondrocalcinosis rises with age from 11% before age 74 to 47% over age 85. It predisposes to osteoarthrosis; however, no other relationship is present between the two disorders.

Diagnosis of Osteoarthrosis

Radiographic Features Uneven joint space narrowing, subchondral bone sclerosis, marginal osteophytes (spurs), cyst formation in periarticular bone (late), articular deformity, subluxation, and loose bodies are indicative of osteoarthrosis. These, together with the particular distribution of the lesions (interphalangeal joints of the fingers, first metacarpophalangeal joints, knee and hip joints, etc.), constitute the major features that serve to characterize and grade the arthropathy (Kellgren & Lawrence, 1957). Osteoarthrosis of unusual sites, in particular monoarticular, leads to suspicion of chondrocalcinosis (Zitnan & Sitaj, 1963). In this process, multiple calcification of the superficial layers of the articular cartilage occurs. Large osteophytes and joint space narrowing (uniform) may also be present.

Technetium and Gallium Scans Subchondral bone sclerosis, as well as osteophyte and cyst formation, are visualized as areas of increased focal activity in technetium scans. Gallium scans may be useful to rule out superimposed infectious arthritis (Lisbona & Rosenthall, 1977).

Histopathological Features

Synovium Primary uncomplicated osteoarthritis is frequently accompanied to some degree by synovial hyperplasia and fibrosis. Mild, nonprogressive chronic inflammatory changes are also seen, which are occasionally associated with small fragments of cartilage and necrotic bone.

Articular Cartilage Major findings include: fibrillation, thinning and clefting of the collagenous surface layer, proteoglycan loss, and degenerative or proliferative chondrocyte changes (Weiss, 1978).

Subchondral Bone—Osteochondral Junction Trabeculae are thickened, but otherwise their characteristics are normal. Remodeling leads to osteophyte formation.

Other Laboratory Features Routine laboratory parameters are usually within normal limits. Nonsignificant increases in albumin,

calcium, and 25-hydroxycholecalciferol serum levels have been reported in elderly individuals (mean age 76.6 ± 8.0) with hip osteoarthrosis (Rapin & Lagier, 1982). Fasting growth hormone levels have also been noted to be elevated in osteoarthrosis (Franchimont & Denis, 1968). These findings have been interpreted as indicators of the subchondral as well as generalized increased bone density observed in osteoarthrosis (Dequeker, Brussens, Creytens, & Bouillon, 1977) which is considered an initiating factor of this process by some authors (Radin et al., 1973). If synovial fluid aspiration is conducted, effusions have low cellularity and normal parameters. Complement (CH50) levels in synovial fluid are low compared to rheumatoid arthritis and other inflammatory arthritis.

Pathogenesis

Articular aging involves a series of structural and biochemical processes, some of which may be neither causally nor sequentially related. Some of these changes lead to the development of degenerative joint disease while others are only the consequence. Aging manifests itself first with pigmentation and fibrillation of the surface of the articular cartilage. Remodeling of the articular cartilage and of the osteochondral junction (osteophyte formation) accompanies such alterations.

Fibrillation of the superficial collagenous network has been attributed to progressive age-related fatigue-wear or increased cross-linking of collagen with subsequent breakdown when subject to a normal or abnormal stress. This is considered to be the initiating event of osteoarthrosis, making its appearance at about the third decade of life together with a decrease in tensile strength of the cartilage (Kempson, 1982; Sokoloff, 1978). Mechanisms leading to collagen cross-linking are unknown. Through this phenomenon, articular collagen becomes less soluble and rigid with decreased metabolic turnover (Hall, 1976, 1978; Niedermuller, Skalicky, Hofecker, & Kment, 1977). Total collagen content remains unmodified (Venn, 1978). Alteration of the physical properties of the matrix may make it susceptible to loading stress with subsequent fragmentation. Collagen degradation is followed by degradation and redistribution of matrix proteoglycans due to either the release or the penetration of local or synovial degradative enzymes, respectively. Proteoglycan depletion leads to chondrocyte alteration with release of autolytic enzymes. Osteoarthrotic cartilage demonstrates increased deposition of Type I collagen that replaces normal Type II collagen. This type of collagen is more susceptible to collagenase digestion.

A different pathogenetic sequence has been proposed by Radin et al. (1973): increased rigidity of the subchondral bone (due to microfractures and repair) will lead to diminished elasticity of the articular cartilage with fragmentation under normal impact loading. Apart from the increased subchondral density, patients of osteoarthrosis have higher BMC than osteoporotics, indicating a generalized larger bone mass (Roh et al., 1974). Studies of cartilage proteoglycan metabolism have shown a decrease in glycosaminoglycan content. This decline involves primarily chondroitin sulfate. Other findings include a relative increase in keratin sulfate and a failure to form aggregates (Perricone, Palmoski, & Brandt, 1977; Peyron, 1979). These collagen and proteoglycan changes alter the overall mechanical resistance of the cartilage to impact loading.

PREVENTION AND THERAPEUTIC APPROACHES

Exercise Schedules

The primary intervention both for the prevention and treatment of aging myopathy and osteopenia is exercise schedules. Isometric and isokinetic exercises help to improve strength and reduce disuse/denervational-induced muscle changes. Electrical stimulation (Munsat, McNeal, & Waters, 1976) also will assist in the prevention and/or modification of denervational/disuse changes. A program of daily walking combined with isometric (extension) exercises may help in controlling osteoporosis by increasing mechanical strain on the bone (Aloia, Cohn, Ostani, Cane, & Ellis, 1978).

Preventive measures and physiotherapy are mandatory in order to avoid premature arthropathy. Fixed flexor spasms should be avoided and mobility always encouraged. Local heat applications and exercise protocols are particularly valuable.

Calcium Doses

Large doses of calcium (1,500 mg of elemental calcium a day) can reduce or retard the rate of bone remodeling. This effect has been particularly observed in disuse osteoporosis.

Bisphosphonates

These stable pyrophosphate analogs could inhibit bone resorption in experimental systems. Some have been tried without apparent benefit. An agent that has been noted to be effective in preventing disuse osteoporosis by suppressing bone remodeling is dichloromethanediphosphonate (Schneider & McDonald, 1981).

Estrogen Administration

Administering estrogen will result in a reduction of bone resorption and an increase in bone accumulation. Estrogen effects are more prominent in the compact rather than trabecular bone compartment. However, there are a number of potential risks associated with estrogen therapy; these include endometrial carcinoma, cholelithiasis, and hypertension.

Anabolic Steroids

An approach to decreasing bone resorption by effecting a reduction in bone turnover is the administration of anabolic steroids. In addition, anabolic steroids promote the renal tubular resorption of calcium.

Sodium Fluoride

Supplemented with calcium and vitamin D, sodium fluoride may result in an increase in bone mineral content as demonstrated by reductions in the risk and incidence of spinal fracture (Aloia, Zanzi, Vaswani, Ellis, & Cohn, 1982; Riggs, Seeman, & Hodgson, 1982). Fluoride stimulates bone osteoblastic activity.

Long-term fluoride combined with oral calcium intake results in accumulation of new trabecular bone, with an improvement in the long-term control of vertebral fractures. However, fluoride therapy has unpleasant side effects, including gastric irritation and arthralgia.

Nonsteroidal Anti-inflammatory Drugs

Therapeutic interventions in osteoarthritis are few and limited. Weight loss remains the primary advice in the presence of obesity. Nonsteroidal, anti-inflammatory agents and local heat application constitute the only therapeutic approaches available. Inhibitors of prostaglandin synthesis like propionic acids are some of the safest agents for this aging population (however, skin rashes and interstitial nephritis have been noted to occur as a side effect).

Comment

None of the above therapies could restore collapsed vertebral bodies or articular deformities. This indicates the enormous importance of prophylactic therapy of musculoskeletal aging in developmentally disabled individuals. That approach will allow the preservation of the bone and muscle mass content and a reduction of the overall fracture and complication rates.

REFERENCES

Aaron, J. E., Gallagher, J. C., Anderson, J., Stasiak, L., Longton, E. B., Nordin, B. E. C., & Nicholson, M. (1974). Frequency of osteomalacia and osteoporosis in fractures of the proximal femur. *Lancet, 1,* 229–233.

Adams, R. D., Denny-Brown, D., & Pearson, C. M. (1962). *Diseases of muscle* (2nd ed.). New York: Harper & Row.

Albanese, A. A., Edelson, A. H., Lorenze, E. J., Jr., Woodhull, M. L., & Wein, E. H. (1975). Problems of bone health in elderly. *New York State Journal of Medicine, 75,* 326–336.

Albright, F., Smith, P. H. &, Richardson, A. M. (1941). Postmenopausal osteoporosis: Its clinical features. *Journal of the American Medical Association, 116,* 2465–2474.

Allen, T. H., Anderson, E. C., & Langham, W. H. (1960). Total body potassium and gross body composition in relation to age. *Journal of Gerontology, 15,* 348–357.

Allfram, P. A. (1964). An epidemiologic study of cervical and trochanteric fractures of the femur in an urban population. *Acta Orthopedica Scandinavica Supplementum, 65,* 1–109.

Aloia, J. F., Vaswani, A., & Atkins, H. (1977). Radiographic morphometry and osteopenia in spinal osteoporosis. *Journal of Nuclear Medicine, 18,* 425–431.

Aloia, J. F., Cohn, S. H., Ostani, J. A., Cane, R., & Ellis, K. (1978). Prevention of involutional bone loss exercise. *Annals of Internal Medicine, 89,* 356–358.

Aloia, J. F., Zanzi, I., Vaswani, A., Ellis, K., & Cohn, S. H. (1982). Combination therapy for osteoporosis with estrogen, fluoride and calcium. *Journal of American Geriatric Association, 30,* 13–17.

Aniansson, A., Grimby, G., Hedberg, M., & Krotkiewski, M. (1981). Muscle morphology, enzyme activity and muscle strength in elderly men and women. *Clinical Physiology, 1,* 73–86.

Aniansson, A., Grimby, G., Hedberg, M., Rundgren, A., & Sperling, L. (1978). Muscle fiber function in old age. *Scandinavian Journal of Rehabilitation Medicine Supplement, 6,* 43–49.

Aniansson, A., Grimby, G., & Rundgren, A. (1980). Isometric and isokinetic quadriceps muscle strength in 70-year-old men and women. *Scandinavian Journal of Rehabilitation Medicine, 12,* 161–168.

Aniansson, A., Grimby, G., Rundgren, A., Svanborg, A., & Orlander, J. (1980). Physical training in old men. *Age and Aging, 9,* 186–187.

Aniansson, A., & Gustafsson, E. (1981). Physical training in elderly men with special reference to quadriceps muscle strength and morphology. *Clinical Physiology, 1,* 87–98.

Arnold, N., & Harriman, D. G. F. (1970). The incidence of abnormality in control human peripheral nerves studied by single axon dissection. *Journal of Neurology, Neurosurgery and Psychiatry, 33,* 55–61.

Atkins, D., Zanelli, J. M., Peacock, M., & Nordin, B. E. C. (1972). Effect of estrogens on the response of bone to parathyroid hormone in vitro. *Journal of Endocrinology, 54,* 107–117.

Atkinson, P. (1967). Variation in trabecular structure of vertebrae with age. *Calcific Tissue Research, 1,* 24–37.

Bailey, A. A. (1953). Changes with age in the spinal cord. *AMA Archives of Neurology and Psychiatry, 70,* 299–309.

Barnett, E., & Nordin, B. E. C. (1960). The radiological diagnosis of osteoporosis. A new approach. *Clinical Radiology, 11,* 166–174.

Barnett, E., & Nordin, B. E. C. (1961). The clinical and radiological problem of thin bones. *British Journal of Radiology, 34,* 683–692.

Bass, A., Gutmann, E., & Hanzlikova, J. (1975). Biochemical and histochemical changes in energy supply enzyme pattern of muscles of the rat during old age. *Gerontologia, 21,* 31–45.

Berg, B. N., Wolf, A., & Simms, H. S. (1962). Degenerative lesions of spinal roots and peripheral nerves in aging rats. *Gerontologia, 6,* 72–80.

Bersu, E. T. (1980). Anatomical analysis of the developmental effects of aneuploidy in man: The Down syndrome. *American Journal of Medical Genetics, 5,* 399–420.

Blazejowski, C. A., & Webster, G. C. (1983). Decreased rates of protein synthesis by cell-free preparations from different organs of aging mice. *Mechanisms of Aging and Development, 21,* 345–356.

Bollet, A. J., Engh, G., & Parson, W. (1965). Epidemiology of osteoporosis. Sex and race incidence of hip fractures. *Archives of Internal Medicine, 116,* 191–194.

Bollet, A. J., Engh, G., & Parson, W. (1968). Epidemiology of osteoporosis. *Journal of Bone and Joint Surgery, 50A,* 557–562.

Borkan, G. A., Hults, D. E., Gerzof, S. G., Robbins, A. H., & Silbert, C. K. (1983). Age changes in body composition revealed by computed tomography. *Journal of Gerontology, 38,* 673–677.

Boyce, B. F., Courpron, P., & Meunier, P. J. (1978). Amount of bone in osteoporosis and physiological senile osteopenia. Comparison of two histomorphometry parameters. *Metabolic Bone Diseases and Related Research, 1,* 35–38.

Britton, G. W., & Sherman, F. G. (1975). Altered regulation of protein synthesis during aging as determined by in vitro ribosomal assays. *Experimental Gerontology, 10,* 67–77.

Brooke, M. H., & Engel, W. K. (1969). The histographic analysis of human muscle biopsies with regard to fiber types. *Neurology, 19,* 221–233.

Brooke, M. H., & Kaiser, K. K. (1970). Three "myosin adenosine triphosphatase" systems: The nature of their pH liability and sulphydryl dependence. *Journal of Histochemistry and Cytochemistry, 8,* 670–672.

Brown, W. F. (1972). A method for estimating the number of motor units in thenar muscles and the changes in motor unit count with aging. *Journal of Neurology, Neurosurgery and Psychiatry, 35,* 845–852.

Brown, M. G., & Ironton, R. (1977). Motor neurone sprouting induced by prolonged tetrodotoxin block of nerve action potentials. *Nature, 265,* 459–461.

Bucciante, L., & Luria, S. (1934). Transformazione nella struttura dei muscoli voluntari dell uomo nella senescenza [Changes in human voluntary muscle structure with aging]. *Archivo Italiano di Anattomia e Embriologia [Italian Archives of Anatomy and Embriology], 33,* 110–187.

Buchthal, F., Rosenfalck, A., & Behse, F. (1975). Sensory potentials of normal and diseased nerves. In P. J. Dyck, P. K. Thomas, & E. H. Lambert (Eds.), *Peripheral neuropathy* (pp. 442–464). Philadelphia: W. B. Saunders Co.

Bundschu, H. D., Suchenwirth, R., & D'Avis, W. (1973). Histochemical changes in disuse atrophy of human skeletal muscle. In B. A. Kakulas (Ed.), *Basic research in myology. Part 1, Proceedings of the 2nd International Congress on Muscle Diseases* (pp. 108–112). Amsterdam: Excerpta Medica.

Butler, I. J., Drachman, D. B., & Goldberg, A. M. (1978). The effect of disuse on cholinergic enzymes. *Journal of Physiology, 274,* 593–600.

Caccia, M. C., Harris, J. B., & Johnson, M. A. (1979). Morphology and physiology of skeletal muscle in aging rodents. *Muscle and Nerve, 2,* 202–212.

Cameron, J. R., & Sorenson, J. A. (1963). Measurement of bone mineral in vivo: An improved method. *Science, 142,* 230–232.

Campbell, M. J., McComas, A. J., & Petito, F. (1973). Physiological changes in aging muscles. *Journal of Neurology, Neurosurgery and Psychiatry, 36,* 174–182.

Cann, C. E., & Gennant, H. K. (1980). Precise measurement of vertebral mineral content using computed tomography. *Journal of Computer Assisted Tomography, 4,* 493–500.

Carlsson, K. E., Alston, W., & Feldman, D. J. (1964). Electromyographic study of aging in skeletal muscle. *American Journal of Physiological Medicine, 43,* 141–145.

Chantraine, A. (1971). Clinical investigation of bone metabolism in spinal cord lesions. *Paraplegia, 8,* 253–259.

Chapuy, M. C., Durr, F., & Chapuy, P. (1983). Age-related changes in parathyroid hormone and 25 hydroxycholecalciferol levels. *Journal of Gerontology, 38,* 19–22.

Chen, T. L., & Feldman, D. (1978). Distinction between alpha fetoprotein and intracellular estrogen receptor: Evidence against the presence of estradiol receptors in rat bone. *Endocrinology, 102,* 236–244.

Chetsanga, C. J., & Liskiwskyi, M. (1977). Decrease in specific activity of heart muscle aldolase in old mice. *International Journal of Biochemistry, 8,* 753–756.

Clarkson, P. M., Kroll, W., & Melchionda, A. M. (1981). Age, isometric strength, rate of tension development and fiber type composition. *Journal of Gerontology, 36,* 648–653.

Cohn, S. H., Abesamis, C., Yasumura, S., Aloia, J. F., Zanzi, I., & Ellis, K. J. (1977). Comparative skeletal mass and radial bone mineral content in black and white women. *Metabolism, 26,* 171–178.

Cooper, R. R. (1972). Alterations during immobilization and regeneration of skeletal muscle in cats. *Journal of Bone and Joint Surgery, 54A,* 919–953.

Corbin, K. G., & Gardner, E. D. (1937). Decrease in the number of myelinated fibers in human spinal roots with age. *Anatomical Record, 68,* 63–74.

Cottrell, L. (1940). Histologic variations with age in apparently normal peripheral nerve trunks. *AMA Archives of Neurology and Psychiatry,* (Chicago) *43,* 1138–1150.

Coyle, E. F., Costill, D. L., & Lesmes, Q. R. (1979). Leg extension power and muscle fiber composition. *Medicine and Science in Sports, 11,* 12–15.

Crilly, R. G., Francis, R. M., & Nordin, B. E. C. (1981). Steroid hormones, aging and bone. *Clinical Endocrinological Metabolism, 10,* 115–139.

Curless, R. G., Nelson, M. B., & Brimmer, F. (1978). Histological patterns of muscle in infants with developmental brain abnormalities. *Developmental Medicine and Child Neurology, 20,* 159–166.

Dahl, E. (1980). Mortality and life expectancy after hip fractures. *Acta Orthopedica Scandinavica, 51,* 163–170.

Dalen, N., & Lamke, B. (1974). Grading of osteoporosis by skeletal and bone scanning. *Acta Radiologica* (Diagnosis), *15,* 177–186.

Dastur, D. K., Gagrat, B. M., & Manghani, D. K. (1979). Fine structure of muscle in human disease atrophy: Significance of proximal muscle involvement in muscle disorders. *Neuropathology and Applied Neurobiology, 5,* 85–101.

Davies, C. T. M., & White, M. J. (1983a). Contractile proteins of elderly human triceps sural. *Gerontology, 29,* 19–25.

Davies, C. T. M., & White, M. J. (1983b). Effects of

dynamic exercise on muscle function in elderly men, aged 70 years. *Gerontology, 29,* 26–31.

DeCoster, W. J., DeRenck, J., Sieben, G., & Van Der Eecken, H. (1981). Early ultrastructural changes in aging rat gastrocnemius muscle: A stereologic study. *Muscle and Nerve, 4,* 111–116.

D'Elia, G., & Folse, R. (1978). Medical problems of the elderly in nonmetropolitan Illinois. *Journal of Gerontology, 33,* 681–687.

Delmas, P. D., Stenner, D., Wahner, H. W., Mann, K. G., & Riggs, G. L. (1983). Increase in serum bone j-carboxyglutamic acid protein with aging in women. Implications for the mechanism of age-related bone loss. *Journal of Clinical Investigation, 71,* 1316–1321.

Demchenko, A. P., & Orlovska, N. N. (1980). Age dependent changes of protein structure. II. Conformational differences of aldolase of young and old rabbits. *Experimental Gerontology, 15,* 619–627.

Dequeker, J., Brussens, A., Creytens, G., & Bouillon, R. (1977). Aging of bone: Its relation to osteoporosis and osteoarthrosis in postmenopausal women. *Frontiers in Hormonal Research, 3,* 116–130.

Dobbins, D. A., Garron, R., & Rarick, G. L. (1981). The motor performance of educable mentally retarded and intellectually normal boys after covariate control for differences in body size. *Research Quarterly, 52,* 9–18.

Doyle, F., Brown, J., & Lachance, C. (1970). Relation between bone mass and muscle weight. *Lancet, 1,* 391–393.

Dudley, G. A., & Fleck, S. J. (1983). Metabolite changes in aged muscle during stimulation. *Journal of Gerontology, 39,* 183–186.

Duriez, J., & Cauchoix, J. (1967). Le role des osteocytes dans la resorption du tissu osseux [The role of osteocytes in the resorption of boney tissue]. *Presse Medicale* [Medical Press], *75,* 1297–1302.

Eder, M. (1960). Der Strukturumbau der Wirbelslpongiosa [Trabecular bone remodeling]. *Virchows Archives of Pathology (Anatomy), 333,* 509–522.

Edington, D. W., Cosmas, A. C., & McCafferty, W. B. (1972). Exercise and longevity: Evidence for a threshold age. *Journal of Gerontology, 27,* 341–343.

Edstrom, L. (1970). Selective atrophy of red muscle fibers in the quadriceps in long-standing knee-joint dysjunction. Injuries to the anterior cruciate ligament. *Journal of the Neurological Sciences, 11,* 551–558.

Engel, W. K., Brooke, M. H., & Nelson, P. G. (1966). Histochemical studies of denervated or tenotomized cat muscle. *Annals of the New York Academy of Sciences, 138,* 160.

Engh, G., Bollett, A. J., Hardin, G., & Parson, W. (1968). Epidemiology of osteoporosis. II. Incidence of hip fractures in mental institutions. *Journal of Bone and Joint Surgery, 50A,* 557–562.

Ermini, M. (1976). Aging changes in mammalian skeletal muscle. Biochemical studies. *Gerontology, 22,* 301–316.

Ermini, M., Szelenyi, I., Moser, P., & Verzan, F. (1971). The aging of skeletal (striated) muscle by changes of recovery metabolism. *Gerontologia, 1,* 300–311.

Essen, B., & Henriksson, J. (1980). Metabolic characteristics of human type 2 skeletal muscle fibers. *Muscle and Nerve, 3,* 263–264.

Farrar, R. P., Martin, T. P., & Murray-Ardies, C. (1981). The interaction of aging and endurance exercise upon the mitochondrial function of skeletal muscle. *Journal of Gerontology, 36,* 642–647.

Feller, E. R., & Schumacher, H. R. (1972). Osteoarticular changes in Wilson's disease. *Arthritis and Rheumatism, 15,* 259–266.

Fenichel, G. M. (1967). Abnormalities of skeletal muscle maturation in brain damaged children: A histochemical study. *Developmental Medicine and Child Neurology, 9,* 419–426.

Fitts, R. H., Booth, F. W., Winder, W. W., & Holloszy, J. O. (1975). Skeletal muscle respiratory capacity, endurance and glycogen utilization. *American Journal of Physiology, 228,* 1029–1033.

Foss, M. V. L., & Byers, P. D. (1972). Bone density, osteoarthrosis of the hip and fracture of the upper end of the femur. *Annals of the Rheumatic Diseases, 31,* 259–264.

Franchimont, P., & Denis, F. (1968). Determination du taux de la somatotrophine et des gonadotrophines dans des cas d'arthrose apparaissant lors de la menopause. [Determination of the rate of somatotropin and gonadotrophin in cases of arthritis appearing at the time of menopause]. *Journal Belge de Rhumatologie Medicine Physique* [Belgian Journal of Physical Rheumatology Medicine], *23,* 59–64.

Frolkis, V. V., Martynenko, O. A., & Zamostyan, V. P. (1976). Aging of the neuromuscular apparatus. *Gerontology, 22,* 244–279.

Frost, H. M. (1973). *Bone remodeling and its relationship to metabolic bone diseases.* Springfield, IL: Charles C Thomas.

Fujisawa, K. (1975). Some observations on the skeletal musculature of aged rats. Part 2. Fine morphology of diseased muscle fibers. *Journal of the Neurological Sciences, 24,* 447–469.

Gafni, A. (1981). Location of age-related modifications in rat muscle glyceraldehyde-3-phosphate dehydrogenase. *Journal of Biological Chemistry, 256,* 8875–8877.

Gallagher, J. C., Aaron, J., Horsman, A., Marshall, D. H., Wickinson, R., & Nordin, B. E. C. (1973). The crush fracture syndrome in postmenopausal woman. *Clinical Endocrinological Metabolism, 2,* 293–315.

Gallagher, J. C., Riggs, B. L., Eisman, J., Hamstra, A., Arnaud, S. B., & DeLuca, H. F. (1979). Intestinal calcium absorption and serum vitamin D metabolites in normal subjects and osteoporotic patients: Effect of age and dietary calcium. *Journal of Clinical Investigation, 64,* 729–736.

Gallagher, J. C., Riggs, B. L., Jerpbak, C. M., & Arnaud, D. C. (1980). The effect of age on serum immunoreactive parathyroid hormone in normal and osteoporotic women. *The Journal of Laboratory and Clinical Medicine, 95,* 373–385.

Garn, S. M. (1970). *The earlier gain and the later loss of cortical bone.* Springfield, IL: Charles C Thomas.

Garn, S. M. (1975). Bone loss and aging. In R. Goldman (Ed.), *Physiology and pathology of human aging* (pp. 39–57). New York: Academic Press.

Garn, S. M., & Clark, D. C. (1975). Nutrition, growth, development and maturation: Findings from the ten-state survey of 1968–1970. *Pediatrics, 56,* 306–319.

Gennant, H. K., & Boyd, D. P. (1977). Quantitative bone mineral analysis using dual energy computed tomography. *Investigative Radiology, 12,* 545–551.

Gershow, D. (1979). Current status of age altered

enzymes: Alternative mechanisms. *Mechanisms of Aging and Development, 9,* 189–196.

Gilliat, R. W., Westgaard, R. H., & Williams, I. R. (1978). Extrajunctional acetylcholine sensitivity of inactive muscle fibers in the baboon during prolonged nerve pressure block. *Journal of Physiology, 280,* 499–514.

Goldspink, D. F. (1977). The influence of immobilization and stretch on protein turnover of rat skeletal muscle. *Journal of Physiology, 264,* 267–282.

Gollnick, P. D., Armstrong, R. B., Saubert, C. W., Piehl, K., & Saltin, B. (1972). Enzyme activity and fiber composition in skeletal muscle of untrained and trained men. *Journal of Applied Physiology, 33,* 312–319.

Gordon, T. (1968). Osteoarthrosis in US adults. In P. H. Bennett & P. H. N. Woods (Eds.), *Population studies of rheumatic diseases* (pp. 391–397). Amsterdam: Excerpta Med Foundation.

Gregor, R. J., Edgerton, V. R., Perrine, J. J., Campion, D. S., & DeBus, C. (1979). Torque-velocity relationships and muscle fiber composition in elite female athletes. *Journal of Applied Physiology, 47,* 388–392.

Grimby, G., Aniansson, A., Danneskiold-Samsoe, G., & Saltin, B. (1980). Muscle morphology and function in 67–81 year-old men and women. *Medicine and Science in Sports and Exercise, 12,* 95.

Grimby, G. Danneskiold-Samsoe, G., Hvid, K., & Saltin, B. (1982). Morphology and enzymatic capacity in arm and leg muscles in 78–81 year-old men and women. *Acta Physiologica Scandinavica, 115,* 125–134.

Gutmann, E., & Hanzlikova, V. (1966). Motor unit in old age. *Nature, 209,* 921–922.

Gutmann, E., & Hanzlikova, V. (1972/1973). Basic mechanisms of aging in the neuromuscular system. *Mechanisms of Aging and Development, 1,* 319–326.

Gutmann, E., & Hanzlikova, V. (1976). Fast and slow motor units in aging. *Gerontology, 22,* 280–300.

Hall, D. A. (1976). *Aging of connective tissue.* London: Academic Press.

Hall, D. A. (1978). Why do joints degenerate? *Spectrum, 31,* 33–36.

Hansford, R. G., & Castro, F. (1982). Age-linked changes in the activity of enzymes of the tricarboxylate cycle and lipid oxidation, and of carnitine content in muscles of the rat. *Mechanisms of Aging and Development, 19,* 191–201.

Harriman, D. G. F., Taverner, D., & Woolf, A. L. (1970). Ekbom's syndrome and burning parasthesiae. *Brain, 93,* 393–406.

Heaney, R. P. (1965). A unified concept of osteoporosis. *American Journal of Medicine, 39,* 877–880.

Heaney, R. P., Recker, R. R., & Saville, P. D. (1977). Calcium balance and calcium requirements in middle-aged women. *American Journal of Clinical Nutrition, 30,* 1603–1611.

Heath, H., III, & Sizemore, G. W. (1977). Plasma calcitonin in normal man, differences between men and women. *Journal of Clinical Investigation, 60,* 1133–1140.

Herbison, G. F., Jaweed, M. M., & Di Tunno, J. F. (1979). Muscle atrophy in rats following denervation, casting, inflammation and tenotomy. *Archives of Physical and Medical Rehabilitation, 59,* 301.

Hooper, A. C. B. (1981). Length, diameter and number of aging skeletal muscle fibers. *Gerontology, 27,* 121–126.

Hooper, A. C. B., & Shiel, E. (1978). A study of some muscle and bone parameters in mature mice. *Irish Journal of Medical Sciences, 147,* 323–324.

Horsman, A., Gallagher, J. C., Simpson, M., & Nordin, B. E. C. (1977). Prospective trial of oestrogen and calcium in postmenopausal women. *British Medical Journal, 2,* 789–792.

Hruza, Z., & Wachtlova, M. (1969). Diminution of bond blood flow and capillary network in rats during aging. *Journal of Gerontology, 24,* 315–320.

Hulten, B., Thorstensson, A., Sjodin, B., & Karlsson, J. (1975). Relationship between isometric endurance and fiber types in human leg muscles. *Acta Physiologica Scandinavica, 93,* 135–138.

Imamura, K., Ashida, H., Ishikawa, T., & Fujii, M. (1983). Human major psoas muscle and sacrospinalis muscle in relation to age: A study by computed tomography. *Journal of Gerontology, 38,* 678–681.

Irving, J. T., LeBolt, S. A., & Schneider, E. L. (1981). Ectopic bone formation and aging. *Clinical Orthopedics and Related Research, 154,* 249–253.

Iskrant, A. P., & Smith, R. W. (1969). Osteoporosis in women 45 years and over related to subsequent fractures. *Public Health Reports, 84,* 33–38.

Jaffe, D. M., Terry, R. D., & Spiro, A. J. (1978). Disuse atrophy of skeletal muscle. *Journal of Neurological Sciences, 35,* 189–200.

Jansson, E., Sjodin, B., & Tesch, P. (1978). Changes in muscle fiber type distribution in man after physical training. *Acta Physiologica Scandinavica, 104,* 235–237.

Jasani, C., Nordin, B. E. C., Smith, D. A., & Swanson, I. (1965). Spinal osteoporosis and the menopause. *Proceedings of the Royal Society of Medicine, 58,* 441–444.

Jennekens, F. G. I., Tomlinson, B. E., & Walton, J. N. (1971). Histochemical aspects of five limb muscles in old age. An autopsy study. *Journal of the Neurological Sciences, 14,* 259–278.

Jensen, J. S., & Tondevold, E. (1979). Mortality after hip fractures. *Acta Orthopedica Scandinavica, 50,* 161–167.

Johnson, M. S., Polgar, J., Weithman, D., & Appleton, D. (1973). Data on the distribution of fiber types in thirty-six human muscles. An autopsy study. *Journal of the Neurological Sciences, 18,* 111–229.

Kellgren, J. H., & Lawrence, J. S. (1957). Radiological assessment of osteoarthritis. *Annals of the Rheumatic Diseases, 16,* 494–502.

Kellgren, J. H., & Lawrence, J. S. (1958). Osteoarthrosis and disk degeneration in an urban population. *Annals of the Rheumatic Diseases, 17,* 388–390.

Kellgren, J. H., Lawrence, J. S., & Bier, F. (1963). Genetic factors in generalized osteoarthrosis. *Annals of the Rheumatic Diseases, 22,* 237–254.

Kempson, G. E. (1982). Relationship between the tensile properties of articular cartilage from the human knee and age. *Annals of the Rheumatic Diseases, 41,* 508–511.

Kiessling, K. H., Pilstrom, L., Karlsson, J., & Piehl, K. (1973). Mitochondrial volume in skeletal muscle from young and old physically untrained and trained healthy men and from alcoholics. *Clinical Science, 44,* 547–555.

Kiessling, K. H., Pilstrom, L., Bylund, A. C. H., Saltin, B., & Piehl, K. (1974). Enzyme activities and morphometry in skeletal muscle of middle-aged men after training. *Scandinavian Journal of Clinical Laboratory Investigation, 33,* 63–69.

Kovar, M. (1977). Health of the elderly and use of health services. *Public Health Reports, 92,* 9–19.

Kranendonk, D. H., Jurist, J. M., & Gun Lee, H. (1972). Femoral trabecular pattern and bone mineral content. *Journal of Bone and Joint Surgery, 54,* 1472–1478.

Kroll, W., Clarkson, P. M., Melchionda, A. M., & Wilcox, A. (1981). Isometric knee extension and plantar flexion muscle fatigue and fiber type composition in female distance runners. *Research Quarterly, 52,* 200–207.

Krolner, B., & Pors Nielsen, S. (1982). Bone mineral content of the lumbar spine in normal osteoporotic women: Cross-sectional and longitudinal studies. *Clinical Science, 62,* 329–336.

Lachman, E., & Whelan, M. (1936). Roentgen diagnosis of osteoporosis and its limitations. *Radiology, 26,* 165–177.

Larsson, L. (1982). Physical training effects on muscle morphology in sedentary men at different ages. *Medicine and Science in Sports and Exercise, 14,* 203–206.

Larsson, L. Grimby, G., & Karlsson, J. (1979). Muscle strength and speed of movement in relation to age and muscle morphology. *Journal of Applied Physiology, 46,* 451.

Larsson, L., & Karlsson, J. (1978). Isometric and dynamic endurance as a function of age and skeletal muscle characteristics. *Acta Physiologica Scandinavica, 104,* 129–136.

Lascelles, R. G., & Thomas, P. K. (1966). Changes due to age in internodal length in the sural nerve in man. *Journal of Neurology, Neurosurgery and Psychiatry, 29,* 40–44.

Lawrence, J. S., Bremner, J. M., & Bier, F. (1966). Osteoarthrosis: Prevalence in the population and relationship between symptoms and X-ray changes. *Annals of Rheumatic Diseases, 25,* 1–24.

Lexell, J., Henriksson-Larsen, K., Winblad, B., & Sjostrom, J. (1983). Distribution of different fiber types in human skeletal muscles: Effects of aging studied in whole muscle cross sections. *Muscle and Nerve, 6,* 588–595.

Lindahl, O., & Lindgren, A. G. H. (1962). Grading of osteoporosis in autopsy specimens. *Acta Orthopedica Scandinavica, 32,* 85–100.

Lindboe, C. F., & Platou, C. S. (1982). Disuse atrophy of human skeletal muscle. An enzyme histochemical study. *Acta Neuropathologica, 56,* 241–244.

Lindboe, C. F., & Torvik, A. (1982). The effects of aging, cachexia and neoplasms on striated muscle. Quantitative histological and histochemical observations on an autopsy material. *Acta Neuropathologica, 57,* 85–92.

Lisbona, R., & Rosenthall, L. (1977). Observation on the sequential use of 99 mTc phosphate complex and 67 Ga imaging in osteomyelitis, cellulitis and septic arthritis. *Radiology, 123,* 123–129.

Ludatscher, R., Silbermann, M., Gershon, D., & Reznick, A. (1983). The effects of enforced running on the gastrocnemius muscle in aging mice. *Experimental Gerontology, 18,* 113–123.

Lundholm, K., & Schersten, T. (1975). Leucine incorporation into proteins and cathepsin activity in human skeletal muscles. The influence of the age of the subject. *Experimental Gerontology, 10,* 155–159.

Lutwak, L., Singer, F. R., & Urist, M. R. (1974). Current concepts of bone metabolism. *Annals of Internal Medicine, 80,* 630–644.

Mack, P. B., & Lachance, P. L. (1967). Effects of recumbency and space flight on bone density. *American Journal of Clinical Nutrition, 20,* 1194–1205.

Mair, W. G. P., & Tome, F. M. S. (1972). *Atlas of ultrastructure of diseased human muscle.* Edinburgh: Churchill.

Makitie, J., & Teravainen, H. (1977). Histochemical changes in striated muscle in patients with intermittent claudication. *Archives of Pathology and Laboratory Medicine, 101,* 658–663.

Manzke, E., Chestnut, C. H., III, Wergedal, J. E., Baylink, D. J., & Nelp, W. B. (1975). Relationship between local and total bone mass in osteoporosis. *Metabolism, 24,* 605–615.

Matsuki, H., Tadeda, Y., & Tonomura, Y. (1966). Changes in biochemical properties of isolated human skeletal myofibrils with age and in myasthemia gravis. *Journal of Biochemistry, 59,* 122–125.

Mayer, R. F. (1963). Nerve conduction studies in man. *Neurology, 13,* 1021–1030.

Mayer, M., Amin, R., & Shafrir, R. (1980). Differences in response of proteolytic activity in cardiac, skeletal and diaphragm muscles to hormones and catabolic conditions. *Molecular and Cellular Endocrinology, 18,* 49–58.

Mayer, M., Amin, R., & Shafrir, E. (1981). Effect of age on myofibrillar protease activity and muscle binding of glucocorticoid hormones in the rat. *Mechanisms of Aging and Development, 17,* 1–10.

Mazess, R. B. (1979). Noninvasive measurement of bone. In U. S. Barzel (Ed.), *Osteoporosis II* (pp. 5–26). New York: Grune & Stratton.

McCafferty, W. B., & Edington, D. W. (1974). Skeletal muscle and organ weight of aged and trained male rats. *Gerontologia, 20,* 44–46.

McCarter, R. J. M. (1978). Effects of age on contraction of mammalian skeletal muscle. In G. Kaldor & W. J. DiBattista (Eds.), *Aging, Vol. 6.* New York: Raven Press.

Meema, S., Reid, D. B. W., & Meema, H. E. (1973). Age trends of bone mineral mass, muscle width and subcutaneous fat in normals and osteoporotics. *Calcified Tissue Research, 12,* 101–112.

Melsen, F., Melsen, B., Mosekilde, L., Bergmann, S. (1978). Histomorphometric analysis of normal bone from the iliac crest. *Acta Pathologica Microbiologica Scandinavica Sect A, 86,* 70–71.

Merz, W. A., & Schenk, R. K. (1970). Quantitative structural analysis of human cancellous bone. *Acta Anatomica (Basel), 75,* 54–66.

Meunier, P., Courpon, P., Edouard, C., Bernard, J., Bringuier, J., & Vignon, G. (1973). Physiological senile involution and pathological rarefaction of bone. *Clinics in Endocrinology and Metabolism, 2,* 239–256.

Meunier, P., Courpron, P., Giroux, J. M., Edouard, C., Bernard, J., & Vignon, G. (1976). Bone histomorphometry as applied to research on osteoporosis and to the diagnosis of hyperosteridosis states. In S. Pors/Nielsen, & E. Hjorting-Hansen (Eds.), *Calcified tissues, 1975* (pp. 354–360). Copenhagen: FADL.

Meunier, P. J., Courpron, P., Edouard, C., Alexandre, E. C., Bressot, C., Lips, P., & Boyce, B. F. (1978). Bone histomorphometry in osteoporotic states. In U. S.

Barzel (Ed.), *Osteoporosis II* (pp. 27–48). New York: Grune & Stratton.

Millward, D. J. (1978). The regulation of muscle-protein turnover in growth and development. *Biochemistry and Social Transactions, 6,* 494–499.

Minaire, P., Meunier, P. J., Edouard, C., Bernard, J., Courpron, P., & Bourret, J. (1974). Quantitative histological data on disuse osteoporosis. Comparison with biological data. *Calcified Tissue Research, 17,* 57–73.

Moldawer, M., Zimmerman, S. J., & Collins, L. C. (1965). Incidence of osteoporosis in elderly whites and elderly negroes. *Journal of the American Medical Association, 194,* 117–120.

Moller, P., Alvestrand, A., Bergstrom, J., Furst, P., & Hellstrom, K. (1983). Electrolytes and free amino acids in leg skeletal muscle of young and elderly women. *Gerontology, 29,* 1–8.

Moller, P., Bergstrom, J., Furst, P., & Hellstrom, K. (1980). Effect of aging on energy-rich phosphagens in human skeletal muscles. *Clinical Science, 58,* 553–555.

Montoye, H. J., & Lamphier, D. E. (1977). Grip and arm strength in males and females, age 10 to 69. *Research Quarterly, 48,* 109–120.

Morgan, D. B. (1973). *Osteomalacia, renal osteodystrophy and osteoporosis.* Springfield, IL: Charles C Thomas.

Moritani, T., & DeVries, H. A. (1980). Potential for gross muscle hypertrophy in older men. *Journal of Gerontology, 35,* 672–682.

Munsat, T. L., McNeal, D., & Waters, R. (1976). Effects of nerve stimulation on human muscle. *Archives of Neurology, 33,* 608–617.

Nachtigall, L. E., Nachtigall, R. H., Nachtigall, R. D., & Beckman, E. M. (1979). Estrogen replacement therapy. In: A 10-year prospective study in the relationship to osteoporosis. *Journal of the American College of Obstetrics and Gynecology, 53,* 277–281.

Nelp, W. B., Denney, J. D., Murano, R., Hinn, G. M., Williams, J. L., Rudd, T. G., & Palmer, H. E. (1972). Absolute measurement of total body calcium (bone mass) in vivo. *Journal of Laboratory and Clinical Medicine, 79,* 430–438.

Newton-John, H., & Morgan, D. (1970). The loss of bone with age, osteoporosis and fractures. *Clinical Orthopedics, 71,* 229–252.

Niedermuller, H., Skalicky, M., Hofecker, G., & Kment, A. (1977). Investigation on the kinetics of collagen-metabolism in young and old rats. *Experimental Gerontology, 12,* 159–168.

Nohl, H. (1982). Age-dependent changes in the structure-function correlation of ADP/ATP—translocating mitochondrial membranes. *Gerontology, 28,* 354–359.

Nordin, B. E. C. (1971). Clinical significance and pathogenesis of osteoporosis. *British Medical Journal, 1,* 571–576.

Nordin, B. E. C., Aaron, J., Speed, R., & Crilly, R. G. (1981). Bone formation and resorption as the determinants of trabecular bone volume in postmenopausal osteoporosis. *Lancet, 2,* 277–279.

Nordin, B. E. C., Horsman, A., Brook, R., & Williams, D. A. (1976). The relationship between oestrogen status and bone loss in post-menopausal women. *Clinical Endocrinology Supplement, 5,* 3535–3615.

Nordin, B. E. C., Peacock, M., Aaron, J., Crilly, R. G., Heyburn, P. S., Horsman, A., & Marshall, D. H. (1980). Osteoporosis and osteomalacia. *Clinics in Endocrinology and Metabolism, 9,* 177–205.

Nordin, B. E. C., Peacock, M., Crilly, R. G., & Marshall, D. H. (1979). Calcium absorption and plasma $1,25(OH)_2D_3$ levels in postmenopausal osteoporosis In A. Norman (Ed.), *Vitamin D, basic research and its clinical application.* Berlin: DeGruyter.

Norris, A. H., Shock, N. W., & Wagman, I. H. (1953). Age changes in the maximum conduction velocity of motor fibers of human ulnar nerves. *Journal of Applied Physiology, 5,* 589–593.

Nygaard, E., & Sanchez, J. (1982). Intramuscular variation of fiber types in the brachial biceps and the lateral vastus muscles of elderly men: How representative is a small biopsy sample? *Anatomical Record, 203,* 451–459.

Ochoa, J., & Mair, W. G. P. (1969). The normal sural nerve in man. II. Changes in the axons and schwann cells due to aging. *Acta Neuropathologica, 13,* 217–239.

Orlander, J., & Aniansson, A. (1980). Effects of physical training on skeletal muscle metabolism and ultrastructure in 70 to 75-year-old men. *Acta Physiologica Scandinavica, 108,* 149–154.

Orlander, J., Kiessling, K. H., Larsson, L., Karlsson, J., & Aniansson, A. (1978). Skeletal muscle metabolism and ultrastructure in relation to age in sedentary men. *Acta Physiological Scandinavica, 104,* 249–261.

Orlovska, N. N., Demchenko, A. P., & Veselovska, L. D. (1980). Age-dependent changes of protein structure. I. Tissue-specific, electrophoretic and catalytical properties of muscle aldolase of old rabbits. *Experimental Gerontology, 15,* 611–617.

Parfitt, A. M. (1981). The integration of skeletal and mineral homeostasis. In H. F. DeLuca, H. M. Frost, W. S. S. Jee, C. C. Johnston, Jr., & A. M. Parfitt (Eds.), *Osteoporosis: Recent advances in pathogenesis and treatment* (pp. 115–126). Baltimore: University Park Press.

Patel, A. N., Razzak, Z. A., & Dastur, D. K. (1969). Disuse atrophy of human skeletal muscles. *Archives of Neurology, 20,* 413–421.

Peck, W. A. (1978). What is the local environmental biochemistry of the remodelling process? In R. Heaney (Ed.), *International symposium on osteoporosis* (pp. 24–27). New York: Biomedical Information Corp.

Perricone, E., Palmoski, M. J., & Brandt, K. D. (1977). Failure of proteoglycans to form aggregates in morphologically normal aged human hip cartilage. *Arthritis and Rheumatism, 20,* 1377–1380.

Pestronk, A., & Drachman, D. B. (1978). Motor nerve sprouting and acetylcholine receptors. *Science, 199,* 1223–1225.

Petrofsky, J. S., & Lind, A. R. (1975). Aging, isometric strength and endurance and cardiovascular responses to statis effort. *Journal of Applied Physiology, 38,* 91–95.

Pettersen, J. C., Koltis, G. G., & White, M. J. (1979). An examination of the spectrum of anatomical defects and variations found in eight cases of trisomy 13. *American Journal of Medical Genetics, 3,* 183–210.

Peyron, J. G. (1979). Epidemiologic and etiologic approach to osteoarthritis. *Seminars in Arthritis and Rheumatism, 8,* 288–306.

Radin, E. L., Paul, I. L., & Rose, R. M. (1972). Role of mechanical factors in pathogenesis of primary osteoarthritis. *Lancet, 1,* 519–521.

Radin, E. L., Parker, H. G., Pugh, J. W., Steinberg,

R. S., Paul, I. L., & Rose, S. M. (1973). Response of joints to impact loading. *Journal of Biomechanics, 6,* 51–57.

Ramirez-Castro, J. L., & Bersu, E. T. (1978). Anatomical analysis of the developmental effects of aneuploidy in man—the trisomy 18 syndrome II. Anomalies of the upper and lower limbs. *American Medical Genetics, 2,* 285–306.

Rapin, C. H., & Lagier, R. (1982). Age-related blood changes in hip osteoarthritis patients: A possible indicator of bone quality. *Annals of Rheumatic Diseases, 41,* 215–216.

Rebeiz, J. J., Moore, M. J., Holden, E. M., & Adams, R. D. (1972). Variations in muscle status with age and systemic diseases. *Acta Neuropathologica, 22,* 127–144.

Recker, R. R., Saville, P. D., & Heaney, R. P. (1977). Effect of estrogens and calcium carbonate on bone loss in postmenopausal women. *Annals of Internal Medicine, 87,* 649–655.

Reznick, A. Z., Steinhagen-Thiessen, E., Gellersen, B., & Gershon, D. (1983). The effect of short- and long-term exercise on aldolase activity in muscles of CW-1 and C57/BC mice of various ages. *Mechanisms of Aging and Development, 23,* 253–258.

Riggs, B. L., Gallagher, J. C., DeLuca, H. F., Edis, A. J., Lambert, P. W., & Arnaud, C. D. (1978). A syndrome of osteoporosis, increased serum immunoreactive parathyroid hormone, and inappropriately low serum 1.25 dihydroxyvitamin D. *Mayo Clinic Proceedings, 53,* 701–706.

Riggs, B. C., Wahner, W. W., Dunn, W. L., Mazess, R. G., Offord, K. P., & Melton, L. J. III. (1981). Differential changes in bone mineral density of the appendicular and axial skeleton with aging. Relationship to spinal osteoporosis. *Journal of Clinical Investigation, 67,* 328–335.

Riggs, B. C., Seeman, E., & Hodgson, S. F. (1982). Effect of the fluoride/calcium regimen on vertebral fracture occurrence in postmenopausal osteoporosis. *New England Journal of Medicine, 306,* 446–450.

Roch Nordlund, A. E., & Borrebaek, B. (1978). The decrease with age in the activities of enzymes of human skeletal muscle. *Biochemistry Medicine, 20,* 378–381.

Rockstein, M., & Brandt, K. F. (1961). Changes in phosphorous metabolism of the gastrocnemius muscle in aging white rats. *Proceedings of the Society for Experimental Biology and Medicine, 107,* 377–380.

Roh, Y. S., Dequeker, J., & Mulier, J. C. (1974). Bone mass in osteoarthritis, measured in vivo by photon absorption. *Journal of Bone and Joint Diseases, 56A,* 587–591.

Roos, B. O. (1975). Dual photon absorptiometry in lumbar vertebrae. II. Precision and reproducibility. *Acta Radiologica (Therapeutica), 14,* 290–303.

Roos, B. O., & Skoldborn, H. (1974). Dural photon absorptiometry in lumbar vertebrae. I. Theory and method. *Acta Radiologica (Therapeutica), 13,* 266–280.

Rowe, R. W. D. (1969). The effect of senility on skeletal muscles in the mouse. *Experimental Gerontology, 4,* 119–126.

Rutishauser, E., Rhoner, A., & Held, D. (1960). Experimentelle untersuchungen uber die wirkung der ischamie auf den knochen und das mark [Experimental studies on the effect of ischemia on bone and bone marrow].

Virchows Archiv fur Patologische Anatomie [Virchows Archives of Pathology (Anatomy)], 333, 101–118.

Salminen, A., & Vihko, V. (1981). Effects of age and prolonged running on proteolytic capacity in mouse cardiac and skeletal muscles. *Acta Physiologica Scandinavica, 112,* 89–95.

Sargeant, A. J., Davies, C. T. M., Edwards, R. H. T., Maunder, C., & Young, A. (1977). Functional and structural changes after disuse of human muscle. *Clinical Science and Molecular Medicine, 52,* 337–342.

Saville, P. D. (1970). Observations on 80 women with osteoporotic spine fractures. In U. S. Barzel (Ed.), *Osteoporosis.* New York: Grune & Stratton.

Saville, P. D., & Nilsson, B. E. R. (1966). Height and weight in symptomatic postmenopausal osteoporosis. *Clinical Orthopedics, 45,* 49–54.

Scelsi, R, Marchetti, C., & Poggi, P. (1980). Histochemical and ultrastructural aspects of M. vastus lateralis in sedentary old people (age 65–89 years). *Acta Neuropathologica, 51,* 99–105.

Schmorl, G., & Junghanns, H. (1971). *The human spine in health and disease.* New York: Grune & Stratton.

Schneider, V. S., & McDonald, J. (1981). Prevention of disuse osteoporosis: Clodronate therapy. In H. F. DeLuca, H. M. Frost, W. S. S. Jee, C. C. Johnston, Jr. & A. M. Parfitt (Eds.), *Osteoporosis: Recent advances in pathogenesis and treatment* (p. 491). Baltimore: University Park Press.

Schultz, E., & Lipton, B. H. (1982). Skeletal muscle satellite cells: Changes in proliferation potential as a function of age. *Mechanisms of Aging and Development, 20,* 377–383.

Shafiq, S. A., Lewis, S. G., Dimino, L. C., & Shutta, H. S. (1978). Electron microscopy study of skeletal muscle in elderly subjects. In G. Kaldor & W. J. DiBattista (Eds.), *Aging, Vol. 6.* New York: Raven Press.

Shamonski, I. M., Frumar, A. M., Tataryn, I. V., Meldrum, D. R., Davidson, B. H., Parthemore, J. G., Judd, H. L., & Deftos, L. J. (1980). Age-related changes of calcitonin secretion in females. *Journal of Clinical Endocrinology and Metabolism, 50,* 437–439.

Shannon, A. D., Adams, E. P., & Courtice, F. C. (1974). The lysosomal enzymes acid phosphatase and glucuronidase in muscle following a period of ischemia. *Australian Journal of Experimental Biology and Medical Science, 52,* 157–171.

Sharma, H. K., Prasanna, H. R., & Rothstein, M. (1980). Altered phosphoglycerate kinase in aging rats. *Journal of Biological Chemistry, 255,* 5043–5050.

Sherman, M. S., & Selakovich, W. G. (1957). Bone changes in chronic circulatory insufficiency. *The Journal of Bone and Joint Diseases, 39A,* 892–901.

Sica, R. E. P., Sanz, O. P., & Colombi, A. (1976). The effects of aging upon the human soleus muscle. *Medicina (Buenos Aires), 36,* 443–446.

Silbermann, M., Finkelbrand, S., Weiss, A., Gershow, D., & Reznick, A. (1983). Morphometric analysis of aging skeletal muscle following endurance training. *Muscle and Nerve, 6,* 136–142.

Sinaki, M., Opitz, J. L., & Wahner, H. W. (1974). Bone mineral content: Relationship to muscle strength in normal subjects. *Archives of Physical and Medical Rehabilitation, 55,* 508–512.

Singh, M., Nagrath, A. R., & Maini, P. S. (1970).

Changes in trabecular pattern of the upper end of the femur as an index of osteoporosis. *Journal of Bone and Surgery, 52A*, 457–467.

Singh, M., Riggs, B. L., Beabout, J. W., & Jowse, J. (1972). Femoral trabecular pattern index for evaluation of spinal osteoporosis. *Annals of Internal Medicine, 77*, 63–67.

Sirca, A., & Susec-Michieli, M. (1980). Selective Type II fiber muscular atrophy in patients with osteoarthritis of the hip. *Journal of the Neurological Sciences, 44*, 149–159.

Sjostrom, M., Angquist, K. A., & Rais, O. (1980). Intermittent claudication and muscle fiber fine structure: Correlation between clinical and morphological data. *Ultrastructural Pathology, 1*, 309–326.

Sjostrom, M., Neglen, P., Friden, J., & Eklof, B. (1982). Human skeletal muscle metabolism and morphology after temporary incomplete ischemia. *European Journal of Clinical Investigation, 12*, 69–79.

Slovik, D. M., Adams, J. S., Neer, R. M., Holick, M. F., & Potts, J. T. (1981). Deficient production of 1.25 dihydroxyvitamin D in elderly osteoporotic patients. *New England Journal of Medicine, 305*, 372–374.

Smith, D. M., Khairi, M. R. A., & Johnston, C. C., Jr. (1975). The loss of bone mineral with aging and its relationship to risk of fracture. *Journal of Clinical Investigation, 57*, 773–781.

Smith, D. M., Khairi, M. R. A., Norton, J., & Johnston, C. C., Jr. (1976). Age and activity effects on rate of bone mineral loss. *Journal of Clinical Investigation, 58*, 716–721.

Smith, R. W., & Rizek, J. (1966). Epidemiologic studies of osteoporosis in women of Puerto Rico and southeastern Michigan with special reference to age, race, national origin and other related or associated findings. *Clinical Orthopedics, 45*, 31–48.

Snow, M. H. (1977). The effects of aging on satellite cells in skeletal muscles of mice and rats. *Cell and Tissue Research, 185*, 399–408.

Sokoloff, L. (1978). Osteoarthritis. In W. H. Simon (Ed.), *The human joint in health and disease* (pp. 91–111). Philadelphia: University of Pennsylvania Press.

Solomon, L., Schnitzler, C. M., & Browett, J. P. (1982). Osteoarthritis of the hip: The patient behind the disease. *Annals of Rheumatic Diseases, 41*, 118–125.

Sperling, L. (1980). Evaluation of upper extremity function in 70-year-old men and women. *Scandinavian Journal of Rehabilitative Medicine, 12*, 139–144.

Stalberg, E., & Fawcett, P. R. W. (1982). Macro EMG in healthy subjects of different ages. *Journal of Neurology, Neurosurgery and Psychiatry, 45*, 870–878.

Stanley, E. F., & Drachman, D. B. (1979). Effect of disuse on the resting membrane potential of skeletal muscle. *Experimental Neurology, 64*, 231–234.

Steen, B., Bruce, A., Isaksson, G., Lewin, T., & Svanborg, A. (1977). Body composition in 70-year-old males and females in Gothenberg, Sweden. A population study. *Acta Medica Scandinavica Supplementum, 611*, 87–112.

Steinhagen-Thiessen, E., & Hilz, H. (1976). The age-dependent decrease in creatine kinase and aldolase activities in human striated muscle is not caused by an accumulation of faulty proteins. *Mechanisms of Aging and Development, 5*, 447–457.

Stevens, J. C., Lofgren, E. P., & Dyck, P. J. (1973). Histometric evaluation of branches of peroneal nerve: Technique for combined biopsy of muscle, nerve and cutaneous nerve. *Brain Research, 62*, 37–59.

Suominen, H., Heikken, E., & Paarkatti, T. (1977). Effect of eight weeks physical training on muscle and connective tissue of the M. vastus lateralis in 69-year-old men and women. *Journal of Gerontology, 32*, 33–37.

Syftestad, G. T., & Urist, M. R. (1982). Bone aging. *Clinical Orthopedics, 162*, 288–297.

Thomson, D. L., & Frame, B. (1976). Involutional osteopenia: Current concepts. *Annals of Internal Medicine, 85*, 789–803.

Thorstensson, A., Grimby, G., & Karlsson, J. (1976). Force-velocity relations and fiber composition in human knee extension muscles. *Journal of Applied Physiology, 40*, 12–16.

Thorstensson, A., & Karlsson, J. (1976). Fatigability and fiber composition of human skeletal muscle. *Acta Physiologica Scandinavica, 98*, 318–322.

Tomlinson, B. E., & Irving, D. (1977). The numbers of limb motor neurons in the human lumbosacral cord throughout life. *Journal of the Neurological Sciences, 34*, 213–219.

Tomlinson, B. E., Walton, J. N., & Rebeiz, J. J. (1969). The effects of aging and cachexia upon skeletal muscle: A histopathological study. *Journal of the Neurological Science, 9*, 321–346.

Tomonaga, M. (1977). Histochemical and ultrastructural changes in senile human skeletal muscle. *Journal of the American Geriatric Society, 25*, 125–131.

Tonna, E. A. (1965). Skeletal cell aging and its effects on the osteogenetic potential. *Clinical Orthopedics and Related Research, 40*, 57–81.

Tonna, E. A., & Cronkite, E. P. (1962). Changes in the skeletal cell proliferative response to trauma concomitant with aging. *Journal of Bone and Joint Surgery, 44A*, 1557–1568.

Tuffery, A. R. (1971). Growth and degeneration of motor endplates in normal cat hind limb muscles. *Journal of Anatomy, 110*, 221–247.

Tzankoff, S. P., & Norris, A. H. (1977). Effect of muscle mass decrease on age-related BMR changes. *Journal of Applied Physiology, 43*, 1001–1006.

Uthoff, H. K., & Jaworski, Z. F. G. (1978). Bone loss in response to long term immobilization. *The Journal of Bone and Joint Surgery, 60B*, 420–429.

Vassilopoulos, D., Lumb, E. M., & Emery, A. E. H. (1977). Karyometric changes in human muscle with age. *European Neurology, 16*, 31–34.

Venn, M. P. F. (1978). Variation of chemical composition with age in human femoral head cartilage. *Annals of Rheumatic Diseases, 37*, 168–174.

Vignon, G., & Meunier, P. (1973). Reflexions sur la pathogenie de l'osteonecrose primitive de la tete femorale [Reflexions on the pathogenesis of the primary osteonecrosis of the femoral head]. *Nouvelle Press Medicale [New Medical Press], 2*, 1751–1753.

Virtama, P., & Helela, T. (1969). Radiographic measurement of cortical bone. Variations in a normal population between 1 and 90 years of age. *Acta Radiologica Supplementum, 293*, 1–268.

Vizoso, A. D. (1950). The relationship between internodal length and growth in human nerves. *Journal of Anatomy*

(London), 84, 342–353.

Wagman, I. H., & Lesse, H. (1952). Maximum conduction velocities of motor fibers of ulnar nerve in human subjects of various ages and sizes. *Journal of Neurology and Physiology, 15,* 235–244.

Wahner, H. W., Riggs, B. L., & Beabout, J. W. (1977). Diagnosis of osteoporosis: Usefulness of photon absorptiometry at the radius. *Journal of Nuclear Medicine, 18,* 432–437.

Wakamatsu, E., & Sissons, H. A. (1969). The cancellous bone of the iliac crest. *Calcified Tissue Research, 4,* 147–161.

Weiss, C. (1978). Light and electron microscopic studies of osteoarthritic articular cartilage. In W. H. Simon (Ed.), *The human joint in health and disease* (pp. 112–121). Philadelphia: University of Pennsylvania Press.

Weissberger, M. A., Samenhof, R. G., Aronow, S., & Neer, R. M. (1978). Computed tomography scanning for the measurement of bone mineral in the human spine. *Journal of Computer Assisted Tomography, 2,* 253–262.

Whedon, G. D. (1960). Disuse osteoporosis. In K. Rodahl, J. T. Nicholson, & E. M. Brown (Eds.), *Bone as a tissue.* New York: McGraw-Hill Book Co.

Whedon, G. D., (1968). Osteoporosis. *Clinical Endocrinology, 2,* 349–376.

Whyte, M. P., Bergfeld, M. A., Avioli, L. V., Teitelbaum, S. L. (1982). Postmenopausal osteoporosis. A heterogeneous disorder as assessed by histomorphometry analysis of iliac crest bone from untreated patients. *American Journal of Medicine, 72,* 193–202.

Wiske, P. S., Epstein, S., Bell, N. H., Queener, S. F., Edmondson, J., & Johnston, C. C., Jr. (1979). Increases in immunoreactive parathyroid hormone with age. *New England Journal of Medicine, 300,* 1419–1421.

Woolf, A. L. (1965). The pathology of the intramuscular nerve endings. In F. Luthy & A. Bischoff (Eds.), *Proceedings of the 5th International Congress of Neuropathology* (pp. 641–647). Amsterdam: Elsevier.

Young, A., Stokes, M., & Crowe, M. (1981). The relationship between quadriceps size and strength in elderly women. *Clinical Science, 63,* 35P–36P.

Zitnan, D., & Sitaj, S. (1963). Chondrocalcinosis articularis. Section I. Clinical and radiological studies. *Annals of the Rheumatic Diseases, 22,* 142–152.

chapter

15

Nutrition, Aging, and Developmental Disabilities

Agnes M. Huber

During aging, physiological changes take place in the body that affect nutrient requirements. It is of the utmost importance for health and disease prevention to achieve optimum nutritional status and to make the necessary adjustments.

Elderly individuals need to choose their diets carefully. They must select a variety of foods from each food group. They need to watch calories so as not to become obese, and must include foods of high nutrient density with sufficient fiber in their diets.

If elderly persons are disabled and cannot care for themselves, their caregivers must have sufficient nutritional knowledge to plan appropriate diets for them.

IN PLANNING ADEQUATE nutrition for disabled aging persons, several unique factors must be considered. The aging process in general is associated with changes in metabolism, and while nutrient needs in the elderly are qualitatively the same as in younger persons, there are considerable differences in the quantities of nutrients required. The prevalence of chronic and acute disease states that require specific nutrient intervention therapies is higher in elderly individuals. In addition, elderly persons comprise a heavily medicated population, and only in recent years have the drug-nutrient interactions affecting nutrient needs been appreciated. Disabilities, either lifelong or acquired in later life, may interfere with self-feeding and may even limit food intake. Social and economic factors, such as ignorance of good nutrition or the stresses brought about by ever-increasing isolation and

loss of independence, may have profound effects on food intake and nutrient status of the aging person.

PHYSIOLOGICAL CHANGES DURING AGING

Although the causes of the changes associated with aging are obscure, aging can be described in phenomenological terms. Many of the physiological changes observed affect nutritional considerations either directly or indirectly.

Cell Mass

With advancing age there appears a loss of cell mass. Body composition data indicate a steady decrease of lean body mass once the aging process commences (Forbes, 1976). McGandy et al. (1966) estimated a decline in metabolic rate, which closely relates to lean body mass, of 5.23 kcal/day per year. Loss of active cells occurs in liver, kidney, muscle, brain, and elastic tissues. Accompanying this loss of cell mass are functional changes, changes that may occur gradually over many years or, if accelerated, result in premature aging.

Decreasing lean body mass lowers energy requirements. The basal energy expenditure (BEE), or the energy requirement at rest in the postabsorptive state, steadily decreases. In addition, older persons are also less active, and this too lowers energy needs. It has been estimated that total caloric requirement decreases 2%–5% per decade in the later years. Nutritional surveys for various populations have consistently shown a decrease in actual caloric intake with old age. In the United States National Center for Health Statistics survey (1977), caloric intakes were 2,888 kcal/day for the 20- to 24-year-old male group, while the caloric intake was 1,805 kcal/day for males 65–74 years of age. The corresponding intakes for females were 1,690 kcal/day in the younger age group versus 1,307 kcal/day for the older women. These figures approximate decreases of 200 kcal/decade in males and 80 kcal/decade for females.

Obesity

All calories in excess of energy need are deposited in adipose tissue as fat. Nutrition surveys, summarized by Kart and Metress (1984), have documented a high prevalence of obesity in older adults. In general, obesity in the older age groups is related to decreasing activity, lowered basal energy need, and high caloric diets. Onset of obesity may occur later in life, but more often obesity has been present for a long time. In genetic obesities of the Prader-Willi and Laurence-Moon-Biedl type, tendency toward increased adiposity is manifest early in childhood and, if untreated, may progress to uncontrollable adiposity. Such cases, as well as obesity of unknown origin and of long standing, are almost impossible to treat in later years.

Diagnosis of obesity by measuring adipose tissue content can be carried out by measurement of skinfold thickness (triceps, biceps, subscapular, and suprailiac), as well as by measurements of weight for height. Serial measurements of these parameters may be used as a screening tool throughout the adult years to identify obesity in its early stages. Treatments for obesity in later years are notoriously ineffective because it is more difficult to exercise and to change dietary habits of a lifetime. Prevention of obesity by making the appropriate life-style changes in earlier life is a more effective way to decrease the accompanying risks, such as locomotor disability, osteoarthritis, diabetes, and hypertension.

Gastrointestinal Function

Aging may affect food ingestion because of decreased taste acuity, problems with dentition, mastication, maldigestion, malabsorption, and large bowel disorders.

Taste   It is well documented that the number of taste buds decreases with aging. An elderly person may have only 20% of the number of taste buds of a young adult. Hypogeusia and dysgeusia (decreased or loss of taste) may be present in the wake of virus infections or as a result of drug treatment or due to a nutritional deficiency of zinc or vitamin A. Reversal may occur less readily than in younger adults. The four taste modalities (sweet, salt, sour, and bitter) appear to be affected by aging to differing degrees. Some elderly persons who experience a substantial loss of taste acuity may use excessive amounts of sugar and salt in their diet to compensate. This is an undesirable practice because of the empty calories sugar provides, and because of the relationship of salt to hypertension.

Dentition   When chewing becomes painful or difficult because of missing or painful teeth or ill-fitting dentures, food intake suffers. A mushy, milk-based diet, low in grain and vegetable fiber, cannot provide all essential nutrients. Such a diet also contributes substantially to the chronic constipation so frequently found in elderly and developmentally disabled persons. Low-fiber diets consumed over long periods are also conducive to diverticulosis, hemorrhoids, and colon cancer (Burkitt, 1978).

Mastication   The ability to chew and swallow food in adults between the ages of 25 and 75 years was studied by Feldman, Kapur, Alman, and Chauncey (1980), who observed a significant relationship between age and masticatory ability. Older individuals took much longer to chew food than did younger adults. Oral motor function as assessed by lip closure, masticatory efficiency, tongue function, and swallowing showed characteristic changes with aging. Decreased efficiency of oral function not only impairs the ability of food ingestion but also affects speech, and may lead to a variety of problems such as mouth breathing and traumatic bite injury.

Maldigestion   Problems with digestion may be more common in elderly individuals than previously suspected. Acid production in the stomach declines with aging, resulting in lesser protection from invasive bacteria and viruses. Under normal conditions, the acid produced in the stomach helps to solubilize essential dietary components, such as iron, calcium, and other mineral elements for more efficient absorption in the duodenum. Decreased stomach acidity results in decreased absorption of mineral elements and can lead to iron-deficiency anemia. Vitamin B_{12} absorption may also be reduced due to lack of an intrinsic factor that is produced in the stomach and facilitates its absorption. Although the data on the effect of aging on pancreatic enzyme production are limited, there is some evidence that pancreatic enzymes and bile diminish in later years, adversely affecting fat digestion. Whenever maldigestion states occur, there is the danger of bacterial overgrowth and infection as well as the risk of allergic reactions.

Malabsorption   Efficient nutrient absorption is dependent on the large viable mucosal surface of the small intestine, which even in very old persons has one of the highest growth rates. The lifespan of the mucosal cell is only 1 or 2 days, and new cells have to be generated continually. Subclinical nutrient deficiencies of calories and protein, as well as other nutrients, interfere with this regeneration. In the brush border of the small intestine, enzymes are synthesized that function in the digestion of the disaccharides sucrose and lactose (table

sugar and milk sugar). One of the earliest indications of acquired absorption problems is the maldigestion of lactose. If lactose is not digested, it stays in the gastrointestinal tract, producing bacterial fermentation. Subsequent acid production leads to cramps and diarrhea. That the absorption capacity of the small intestine is less efficient in older individuals has been particularly well demonstrated in women after the menopause (Heaney, Recker, & Saville, 1978).

Large Bowel Disorders   A high proportion of elderly individuals are plagued with chronic constipation, hemorrhoids, and diverticulosis. Epidemiological studies link these disorders to low-fiber diets containing a high proportion of refined foods (Burkitt, 1978). The introduction of some fiber-containing foods may certainly occur later in life, albeit very gradually so as not to irritate the stomach. To be effective, fiber must always be given with sufficient fluid.

Endocrine Changes

A detailed discussion of the endocrine changes accompanying aging is beyond the scope of this text. Brief mention of diabetes mellitus is in order since diet intervention plays a significant role in treatment, and current research implicates nutrition in the prevention of certain types of diabetes.

The characteristic feature of diabetes mellitus is an abnormal clearance of glucose (blood sugar) from the blood after a carbohydrate meal. There are many causes of decreased glucose tolerance, and treatment depends on the type. Formerly it was thought that diabetes was simply an insulin deficiency. It is true that there are diabetics who have an obligatory requirement of insulin, needing daily insulin injections. This type of diabetes, also referred to as Type I (formerly referred to as juvenile onset diabetes) must be distinguished from the much more common Type II (formerly adult onset diabetes) that is predominantly seen in elderly individuals. It is usually associated with obesity. The high blood sugar seen in Type II diabetes is often associated with high insulin levels. Weight reduction to "ideal body weight'' by limiting caloric intake and encouraging energy expenditure has a beneficial effect. While the major thrust of diet intervention (together with insulin injections) of Type I diabetes is timing of balanced meals and consistency of food intake, intervention for Type II stresses weight reduction as the primary objective. Formerly, diabetic diets were high in fat and low in carbohydrates; today, such diets are not recommended because of the implication of high fat diets in the causation of atherosclerosis and heart disease. It is recommended that diabetics obtain approximately 50% of calories from carbohydrates, approximately 15% of calories from protein, and the rest from equal amounts of saturated and unsaturated fat (Nuttall, 1983).

Osteoporosis

The characteristics of osteoporosis are loss of bone matrix (protein) and bone salt (calcium and phosphorus). All through adulthood there is a gradual loss of bone, which greatly accelerates in elderly individuals, particularly among postmenopausal women. The cause of osteoporosis is multifactorial. Among the factors that play a significant role are inactivity, hormonal changes, heredity, and diet. Osteoporosis must be distinguished from osteomalacia, which occurs through a lack of the active form of vitamin D (1,25-dihydroxycholecalciferol), resulting in loss of bone salt with normal bone matrix.

Subclinical osteoporosis is present for a long period before symptoms of osteoporosis become evident. If severe, loss of bone results in diminished height, decreased strength of bones, and, in severe cases, fractures. Osteoporosis is usually more severe in women than in men. It has been estimated that 50% of postmenopausal women in the United States are significantly affected by these changes. Although it is impossible to prevent osteoporosis, various factors can slow the progressive bone loss. One of the most important factors in the development of osteoporosis is the amount of bone present at onset of maturity; this stresses the point that nutrition during growth and development affects health for many years to come.

The negative calcium balances (calcium loss from body in excess of dietary calcium intake) seen in elderly persons, which result in osteoporosis, have been related to reduced efficiency of calcium absorption by the gastrointestinal tract, to stress, to estrogen withdrawals after menopause, to decreased activity, and to immobility.

The suggestion has been made that elderly individuals might benefit from calcium intakes over and above those recommended by the RDA (RDA for calcium in adults is 800 mg/day). Amounts ranging from 1,200 to 1,500 mg of calcium per day have been suggested. While claims have been made that calcium intakes of up to 2,500 mg/day are safe, the long-term intake of such high calcium levels may be questioned (Lee, Lawler, & Johnson, 1981). High dietary calcium may interfere with the gastrointestinal absorption of other minerals such as zinc. It may also contribute to kidney stone formation, especially in individuals who are immobile.

Vascular Changes

Half the people who die in the United States each year do so from heart and blood vessel disease (Siegel, 1976). Atherosclerosis is characterized by lipid deposits in blood vessels resulting in heart disease and a high incidence in cerebral vascular stroke. Conditions that lower serum cholesterol and normalize blood pressure are beneficial in the prevention of vascular events. In a comparatively small number of individuals, atherosclerotic disease is of genetic origin; however, the epidemic of atherosclerotic disease at ever earlier ages relates predominantly to dietary and other environmental factors. Smoking, elevated serum cholesterol levels, and hypertension are the three major risk factors in the precipitation of cardiovascular disease. The dietary goals proposed suggest changes in life-style that decrease the risks for heart disease. Since serum cholesterol is a function of the dietary intake of fat, modification of total fat as well as the type of fat is recommended. In addition to dietary changes, reduction in cigarette smoking and control of blood pressure by medication and/or decrease of sodium intake must occur.

NUTRITIONAL ASSESSMENT

Nutritional surveys have shown that a substantial proportion of the United States population over age 65 is nutritionally vulnerable (Kart & Metress, 1984). Within the elderly population group, it appears that the low-income, sick, and disabled elderly are at particular risk. Nutritional problems in this age group in general relate to decreased food intake or problems of food assimilation, and the presence of disease or disabilities that interfere with optimum nutrient status.

The objective of nutritional assessment is to identify the factors that prevent the elderly person from being well nourished. Based on nutritional evaluation, reasonable recommendations should be made for preventive or therapeutic interventions. For the assessment of nutrient status of individuals, a large number of diagnostic methods are available. Since in most situations resources are limited, it is important to select the most appropriate assessment methods to provide maximum information on an effective cost-benefit basis. Since no two elderly individuals are alike, nutritional assessment and therapies must be individualized for each person. From a practical approach, the diagnostic methods are classified in the categories discussed below.

Food and Nutrient Intake Analysis

The evaluation of food intake is part of every nutritional assessment. Information is obtained regarding what the person is eating, how much of these foods he or she is eating, and whether regular meals are consumed. When suboptimum nutrient intakes are found, it is of utmost importance to identify whether the deficiency is related to economic, medical, or other factors.

To evaluate a diet in terms of adequacy, the 24-hour recall is often used. Problems with this method relate to the failing memory of the elderly person who may not remember what he or she has eaten over the last 24 hours. Posner, Borman, Morgan, Borden, and Ohls (1982)

have successfully taken 24-hour telephone recalls with elderly people using paper models provided in advance for portion estimates. An estimation of the frequency of intake of specific foods, combined with the 24-hour dietary recall, gives information on how representative the 24-hour recall is (e.g., milk or milk products must be consumed on a daily basis to ensure adequate calcium intake, while liver eaten once a week will provide sufficient iron in the diet). Written food records taken over a number of days may be more accurate in describing the type and amount of food eaten. However, disabled individuals may not be able to fill out such detailed records, and the task of recording may have to be carried out by a care provider.

Once the food intake has been determined, either by recall or food diaries, comparisons with recommendations are made. The simplest comparison is with the recommendations of the four food groups (Table 1). Elderly persons who regularly eat foods from the four food groups are at lower risk than those who omit whole nutrient classes (no dairy products, vegetables, meat, or meat substitutes). However, a diet that provides the recommended servings from each food group may not necessarily be a problem-free diet. A variety of different foods from each food group must be chosen to provide all essential nutrients. It is recommended that the vegetable/fruit group should include a food high in vitamin C on a daily basis, and a dark green leafy vegetable for folic acid (spinach or kale) twice a week. Some of the cereal from the grain group should contain fiber on a daily basis.

Nutrient analyses based on 24-hour food intake or food diary data formerly required lengthy manual calculations. With the advent of the computer, these analyses can be carried out with greater speed and efficiency. Many microcomputers have programs for the analysis of nutrients in food. Such programs not only calculate the daily nutrient intake, but also compare the nutrient intake with the recommended dietary allowances (Table 2), taking into account age and sex. Of special interest regarding elderly individuals are intakes of

Table 1.   Eating from the four food groups for variety

Food group	Servings	Strengths	Weaknesses
Milk			
1 cup milk		Protein	Fiber
1 cup yogurt	2	Calcium	Vitamin C
1½ oz cheddar cheese		Riboflavin	Iron
1¾ cup ice cream		Vitamin D (if fortified)	Copper
Meat			
2 oz cooked lean meat		Protein	Fiber
2 oz fish		Iron	Vitamin C
2 oz poultry	2	B vitamins	Calcium
2 eggs			
4 tbs. peanut butter		Zinc	
Grain/cereals			
1 slice bread		Starch	Vitamins C, A, and K
1 cup ready-to-eat cereal	4	Fiber	
½ cup cooked cereal		Some B vitamins	
½ cup pasta		Incomplete protein	
Vegetables/fruit			
½ cup vegetables		Vitamin C, A, and folacin	Protein
1 cup fruit juices	4	Trace minerals	Vitamin B_{12}
1 fresh fruit, apple, banana, pear		Fiber	

calories and protein, saturated and polyunsaturated fat, calcium, iron, vitamin A, vitamin C folic acid, sodium, and fiber.

In elderly persons, especially those who are nonverbal, fluid intake should be monitored as well. While fluid requirement depends on many factors, a high-protein and high-salt diet increases the requirement for fluids.

Anthropometric Assessment

Measurements of body size and proportions are a useful tool to identify potential or actual over- or underweight conditions. Such measurements are also useful for the calculation of calorie and protein intake. If serially taken, these measures may identify problems of obesity or below-normal weight in their early stages, when preventive measures may be more effective than therapies administered at a later date. Height is measured and recorded. If a disability precludes a standing height measurement, height may be computed from sitting height plus length of legs. Such measurements are usually not very accurate, but they may allow approximate calculations of energy requirements. Body weight should be taken in the morning, after emptying the bladder, on a scale that is calibrated (this can be done by weighing a standard weight for constancy). Height and weights

are compared with standards (Table 3). Skin-fold measurements on triceps, biceps, subscapular, and suprailiac locations are taken by skin calipers (Bray, 1975; Frisancho, 1981). Standards for comparisons of skinfold measurements with norms are summarized in Table 4.

Laboratory Values

Special laboratory tests can be useful in the determination of vitamin, protein, and mineral status. Care should be taken when selecting such parameters for nutritional assessment because such methods are invasive and may be costly. During a medical illness or other situation requiring medical intervention, blood tests are routinely ordered by the physician. Red blood cell indices, lymphocyte counts, albumin, or transferrin values, any of which are commonly measured, will give some information on the nutrient status of the patient. In addition, blood vitamin levels or load tests to establish functional levels of certain nutrients may be analyzed. Summarized in Table 5 are selected laboratory tests of value in nutritional assessment.

Assessment of Drug-Nutrient Interactions

Since elderly individuals are a heavily medicated population, the impact of medications on

Table 2.   Recommended dietary allowances for elderly individuals[a]

	Male	Female
Protein (grams)	56.0	44.0
Fat-soluble vitamins		
Vitamin A (μg retinol equivalent)	1,000.0	800.0
Vitamin E (μg tocopherol)	10.0	8.0
Vitamin D (μg cholecalciferol)	5.0	5.0
Water-soluble vitamins		
Ascorbic acid (mg)	60.0	60.0
Folacin (μg)	400.0	400.0
Niacin (mg)	16.0	13.0
Riboflavin (mg)	1.4	1.2
Thiamine (mg)	1.2	1.0
Vitamin B_6 (mg)	2.2	2.0
Vitamin B_{12} (μg)	3.0	3.0
Minerals		
Calcium (mg)	800.0	800.0
Phosphorus (mg)	800.0	800.0
Magnesium (mg)	350.0	300.0
Iron (mg)	10.0	10.0
Zinc (mg)	15.0	15.0
Iodine (μg)	150.0	150.0

[a]From National Academy of Sciences (1980).

nutrient status must be evaluated. Information on drug-nutrient interactions is not easy to come by since the field is still very young and not all drug effects on nutrient status have been evaluated. General information on drug side effects can be obtained from Gilman, Goodman, and Gilman (1980) and Roe (1976). Medications given for a short period of time usually have less effect on nutrient status than do drugs such as seizure medications or hypotensive drugs, which must be taken over long periods of time. In Table 6, the effects of drugs commonly used by elderly individuals on some nutrients are summarized.

Assessment of Self-Feeding

A variety of illnesses as well as chronic feebleness may result in limited self-feeding, which may compromise food intake and eventually lead to malnutrition.

The following may cause major problems with self-feeding:

Lack of mouth, head, and trunk control
Lack of sitting balance
Inability to sit upright to reach and grasp
Inability to bring hand to mouth
Lack of hand-eye coordination

Proper positioning alone can be of great benefit during eating. The goal is to be seated comfortably: the head should be flexed forward (for it is difficult to swallow with head tilted back), arms should be at an angle, and legs should be firmly placed.

Whenever possible, rehabilitation should be encouraged. The ability to self-feed leads not only to greater independence but also to the

Table 3.   Desirable weights for heights for adults[a]

Height		Weight	
Inches	cm	lb	kg
		Females	
58	147	102 (92–119)	46 (42–54)
60	152	107 (96–125)	49 (44–57)
62	158	113 (102–131)	51 (46–59)
64	163	120 (108–138)	55 (49–63)
66	168	128 (114–146)	58 (52–66)
68	173	136 (122–154)	62 (55–70)
70	178	144 (130–163)	65 (59–74)
72	183	152 (138–173)	69 (63–79)
		Males	
62	158	123 (112–141)	56 (51–64)
64	163	130 (118–148)	59 (54–67)
66	168	136 (124–156)	62 (56–71)
68	173	145 (132–166)	66 (60–75)
70	178	154 (140–174)	70 (64–79)
72	183	162 (148–184)	74 (67–84)
74	188	171 (156–194)	78 (71–88)
76	193	181 (164–204)	82 (74–93)

[a]Average weights with weight ranges in parentheses.
From National Academy of Sciences (1980).

Table 4.   Fat folds and body fat

| Body build | Females 50 years and over | | Males 50 years and over | |
	Sum of four fat folds (mm)	Percentage of body fat (%)	Sum of four fat folds (mm)	Percentage of body fat (%)
Thin	25	25	20	12
Average	35	28	25	15
Plump	45	32	40	23
Fat	60+	36+	55	28

Source: Bray (1975).

consumption of more varied and adequate diets. Baltes and Zerbe (1976) and Geiger and Johnson (1974) have pointed out the importance of motivation for rehabilitation, and have suggested the use of positive reinforcement. Adaptive equipment may be used to great advantage. Shinnar (1983) carried out a small-scale study on the use of adaptive equipment in the rehabilitation of elderly persons. Those patients who were motivated to complete a training period reduced the time nurse's aides spent per meal from 30 minutes to 5 minutes per patient, with nominal cost for adaptive equipment. From the limited data available, it appears that the assessment of self-feeding, as well as other self-help skills, by an occupational or physical therapist is extremely valuable. Since not all elderly persons are equally responsive to intervention, further research must identify those who would receive most benefit from such intervention programs.

PLANNING NUTRITIOUS DIETS FOR ELDERLY PERSONS

Good diets include a variety of foods, thereby providing all the essential nutrients. Such diets should also be palatable, for the most nutritious diet is wasted if not consumed. Diet menus must be planned to take into account nutrient content, the specific needs of the person served, and cost, for most elderly individuals have limited means. Knowledge of energy and nutrient needs of elderly persons may serve as a guide in the planning of nutritious diets.

Calculation of Energy Needs

Total energy needs in adults can be approximated by calculating the basal energy expenditure plus the energy expended for activity. The basal energy expenditure (BEE) is the energy need at rest and during the postabsorptive state. It depends on lean body mass and can be calculated from height, body weight, age, and sex. Using the Harris-Benedict equation (Sherman, 1952), the BEE for males is equal to: $(13.76 \times \text{usual weight in kg}) + (5.0 \times \text{height in cm}) - (6.76 \times \text{age in years}) + 66.5$. BEE for females is equal to: $(9.6 \times \text{usual weight in kg}) + (1.85 \times \text{height in cm}) - (4.7 \times \text{age in years}) - 65.5$. (Conversion factors: 2.2 lbs = 1 kg of body weight; 1 inch = 2.54 cm of height.)

BEE is sufficient to cover energy expended lying in bed with no fever, sepsis, stress, or other catabolic states.

Table 5.   Special laboratory tests used in nutritional assessment

Parameter	Acceptable values are equal or greater than (unless stated otherwise)
Serum ascorbic acid (mg/dl)	0.2
Plasma vitamin A (mcg/dl)	20
Plasma carotene (mcg/dl)	40
Plasma vitamin E (mg/dl)	0.6
Serum folacin (mg/ml)	6.0
Serum vitamin B_{12} (pg/ml)	100
Erythrocyte transketolase-TPP-effect (ratio)	up to 15
Erythrocyte glutathione reductase-FAD effect (ratio)	up to 1.2
Urinary pyridoxine (mcg/g creatinine)	20
Urinary thiamine (mcg/g creatinine)	65
Urinary riboflavin (mcg/g creatinine)	80

Table 6. Drug effects on nutrients

Drug	Nutrient depletion	Supplement
Anticonvulsants	Folic acid Vitamin D	Folate (400 µg) Vitamin D (400 IU)
Antacids	Iron Calcium Phosphorus	Iron
Antitubercular	Vitamin B_6 Niacin	Vitamin B_6 (50 mg) Niacin (100 mg)

Broad spectrum
  antibiotics
	Vitamin K
	Biotin
		Vitamin K and biotin from
		  foods or supplements

Aspirin	Iron and zinc if occult bleeding	Iron and zinc equal to RDA
Cholestyramin	Vitamins A, D, and K Fat Calcium Vitamin B_{12}	Vitamins 100% RDA
Mineral oil	Vitamin A, E, D and K Essential fatty acids	Vitamin/mineral 100% RDA (do not give the same time as mineral oil)

Energy needs for activity depend on the type and duration of activity (sitting, walking, climbing stairs, doing housework). The calculation of actual energy expended in activity is cumbersome. The following factors approximate total energy requirement: BEE $\times$ 1.1 = very light activity; BEE $\times$ 1.2 = light activity; BEE $\times$ 1.3 = moderate activity.

The long-term stability of body weight is the single most useful indicator of whether a person is in energy balance. Since energy requirements vary from person to person, the 1980 RDAs for energy recommend a range of intakes for persons age 65 and older (National Academy of Sciences, 1980). For males between the years of 51 and 75, the energy intake range is estimated at 2,000–2,800 kcal/day; for men age 76 and older, the range is extended from 1,650 to 2,450 kcal/day. Females age 51–75 years require 1,400–2,200 kcal/day; this amount decreases to 1,200–2,000 kcal/day for women age 76 years and over.

Stress states such as trauma and injury affect energy needs considerably. Energy needs of the stressed patient (surgery, fractures) have been reported by Kinney (1975).

Protein

The National Academy of Sciences (1980) suggests a protein intake of 0.8 grams/kg of body weight for individuals over the age of 50. Since calorie need gradually decreases with age, Uauy, Scrimshaw, and Young (1978) recommend 12%–14% of calories from protein (as compared to 10%–12% for young adults). The studies of Gersovitz, Munro, Udall, and Young (1980) have shown that diets providing 0.8 grams of protein per kg of body weight to elderly women and men for 30 days were not adequate for the majority of individuals as evaluated by balance studies. These studies suggest that a protein intake of 1–1.5 grams/kg of body weight, which is above the recommended dietary allowances, may be desirable. Protein requirements during stress states, such as surgery or fractures, are increased due to the hormonal changes brought about by these catabolic states. There are wide variations in nitrogen losses depending on the severity and duration of trauma, and therefore, the protein requirement during refeeding must be assessed for each patient. In the presence of liver or kidney disease, protein intake must be adjusted depending on the type of disorder.

Fat and Cholesterol

The American Heart Association recommends in its dietary guidelines that people limit cholesterol intake to less than 300 mg per day. Major cholesterol sources are egg yolk (275 mg/yolk) and organ meats such as liver and crayfish. In addition, fat intake should not exceed approximately 30% of calories divided equally among saturated, monosaturated, and polyunsaturated fats. Diets high in dairy products, beef, pork, and lamb are high in saturated fats. Chicken and fish, soft margarines, and vegetable oils are rich in polyunsaturated fats. These latter foods should be included in diets along with low-fat milk and occasional use of lean meat.

Carbohydrates

Although there are no official recommendations for carbohydrate intake, since calorie-containing foods must be selected with respect to total calorie intake, it is suggested that excess sugar intake (tea, bread, jam diets) should be discouraged. Elderly individuals can ill afford the empty calories, the constipation often associated with such refined diets, and the risk of precipitation of Type II diabetes. Those who have problems with chewing may incorporate grains such as barley and brown rice in vegetable soups that also provide fiber from vegetables.

Vitamins

A balanced diet chosen from the four food groups can provide all required micronutrients. To conserve nutrients, vegetables should be boiled or steamed in a small amount of water or stir fried until just tender. Inclusion of green and yellow vegetables is necessary for vitamin A and folic acid. Daily vitamin C should be derived from citrus fruits or vegetables (broccoli is a good source of vitamin C). To obtain vitamin D, fortified whole, low-fat, or skim milk should be included in the diet.

Highly refined foods, because of their low nutrient density (high in calories and low in nutrients), have no place in the diet of elderly individuals whose total food intake may be reduced in the first place. Any diet containing fewer than 1,200 kcal/day cannot provide all vitamins and minerals required. Foods need to be chosen carefully in terms of their nutrient contents, and a vitamin/mineral supplement is advisable when dieting. See Table 2 for suggested daily vitamin intake for healthy elderly individuals.

Minerals

To evaluate dietary intake of minerals, both low and excess intakes must be considered. Many diets of elderly persons are excessive in salt intake, especially if convenience foods (TV dinners, canned foods, cold cuts) as well as the salt shaker are used heavily. Sodium is also a hidden ingredient of many medications, and is even in toothpaste. High-salt intake serves no benefit and may indeed contribute to the precipitation of hypertension so prevalent in the older age group. Thus, a gradual decrease in salt intake is desirable (omit the salt shaker and substitute low-salt foods for high-salt products). Adequate and safe intakes of sodium, potassium, and chloride, for which no official RDA have been set, are given in Table 7.

To obtain most other essential mineral elements, the diet of elderly individuals must be planned carefully. For instance, while dairy products are good sources of calcium, it is advisable to use one of the many low-fat dairy products on the market because of their high-saturated fat content. The common refined diet of elderly people is low in potassium. This mineral can be easily obtained from vegetable (potato) or fruits (banana) and is conserved by boiling vegetables in little water. Similarly, it is possible to get sufficient iron from food sources. After menopause; women have the same iron requirement as men; however, it may

Table 7. Estimated safe and adequate daily dietary intakes of selected vitamins and minerals for adults[a]

Nutrient	Amount
Vitamin K	70–140 µg
Biotin	100–200 µg
Pantothenic acid	4–7 mg
Copper	2.0–3.0 mg
Manganese	2.5–5.0 mg
Fluoride	1.5–4.0 mg
Chromium	0.05–0.2 mg
Selenium	0.05–0.2 mg
Molybdenum	0.15–0.5 mg
Sodium	1,100–3,300 mg
Potassium	1,875–5,625 mg
Chloride	1,700–5,100 mg

[a]These recommendations are for healthy adults.

take years for them to build up equivalent iron stores in the liver. Another depletion that may occur is chromium. Elderly individuals who throughout life ingested refined diets have experienced this deficiency (Levander, 1975). Certain types of diabetes have been linked to chromium deficiency. Chromium can be obtained from molasses and whole grains. It is found in negligible amounts in sugar and white flour. Zinc is another mineral element important in the nutrition of elderly people because of its role in wound healing and in the immune response (for fighting infections). Good sources of zinc are meats, chicken, and fish. Milk and milk products are lesser sources, and vegetables are poor sources. Zinc together with vitamin C and other nutrients play a significant role in the prevention of decubitus ulcers that are a significant problem in bedridden elderly individuals (Sandstead, Henricksen, Greger, Prasad, & Good, 1982).

Supplements

Nutritional supplements are useful and desirable in various conditions. They may be useful when there is decreased appetite, when elderly persons cannot eat enough, when there are dislikes of whole food classes, and for specific health reasons. Geriatric vitamin and mineral mixtures are sold under many names, in many forms and doses. For most purposes, a one-a-day type of supplement containing vitamins and trace minerals in amounts specified by the RDA is appropriate. Table 7 suggests safe and adequate daily intakes of those vitamins and mineral elements for which no official RDAs have been set. Excessive doses of practically all micronutrients produce side effects if taken over a period of time. Megadose use of vitamins A and E and selenium, as currently may occur in nontraditional medical approaches to

the treatment of cancer, is not recommended. There is no evidence that these nutrients are of any benefit, and the detrimental effects of toxicity have been well documented (Smith & Goodman, 1976).

Energy and protein supplements can be prepared home-style in many ways (e.g., nutritious snacks or milk shake substitute drinks). Such prepared supplements are comparatively inexpensive and need not lack in variety. For debilitated elderly persons, there are a large number of nutritional supplements on the market. These supplements have known nutrient composition, are usually expensive, and should be given only under the supervision of a dietitian.

A supplement that has sometimes been found useful in elderly individuals because of its relaxing effect is a moderate amount of alcohol (as a glass of wine) before bedtime. In some instances, this may be superior to taking sleeping pills. One glass of wine may contain approximately 15 grams of alcohol, equivalent to 105 kcal.

CONCLUSION

Nutrient needs change with aging, and if optimum health is to be achieved, elderly individuals must select diets that address these needs. Basically, the nutritional requirements of elderly mentally retarded persons are the same as for nonretarded individuals; however, since nutrient status is affected by disease, disability, and medications, recommendations must be based on assessment of individuals. In case an elderly person cannot select his or her own food, the caregivers must be made aware of the changing nutrient needs of the individual so that an appropriate diet can be selected.

REFERENCES

Baltes, M. M., & Zerbe, M. B. (1976). Reestablishing self-feeding in a nursing home resident. *Nursing Research, 25,* 24–26.

Bray, G. A. (Ed.). (1975). *Obesity in perspective: Conference sponsored by Fogarty International Center*

(DHEW Publication No. NIH 75-708). Washington, DC: Department of Health, Education, & Welfare.

Burkitt, D. P. (1978). The link between low-fiber diets and disease. *Human Nature, 1,* 34–41.

Feldman, R. S., Kapur, K. K., Alman, J. E., & Chauncey,

H. H. (1980). Aging and mastication: Changes in performance and in swallowing threshold with natural dentition. *Journal of the American Geriatric Society, 28,* 97–103.

Forbes, G. B. (1976). The adult decline in lean body mass. *Human Biology, 48,* 161–173.

Frisancho, A. R. (1981). New norms of upper limb fat and muscle area for assessment of nutritional status. *American Journal of Clinical Nutrition, 34,* 2540–2544.

Geiger, O. G., & Johnson, L. A. (1974). Positive education for elderly persons: Correct eating through reinforcement. *The Gerontologist, 14,* 432–436.

Gersovitz, M., Munro, H. N., Udall, J., & Young, V. R. (1980). Albumin synthesis in young and elderly subjects using a new stable isotope methodology: Response to level of protein intake. *Metabolism, 29,* 1075–1086.

Gilman, A. G., Goodman, L. S., & Gilman A. (1980). *The pharmacological basis of therapeutics* (6th ed.). New York: Macmillan Publishing Co.

Heaney, R. P., Recker, R. R., & Saville, P. D. (1978). Menopausal changes in calcium balance performance. *Journal Laboratory and Clinical Medicine, 92,* 953–963.

Kart, C. S., & Metress, S. P. (1984). *Nutrition, the aged and society.* Englewood Cliffs, NJ: Prentice-Hall.

Kinney, J. M. (1975). Energy requirements of the surgical patient. In W. F. Ballinger, J. A. Collins, W. R. Drucker, S. J. Dudrick, & R. Zeppa (Eds.), *Manual of surgical nutrition.* Philadelphia: W. B. Saunders Co.

Lee, C. J., Lawler, G. S., & Johnson, G. H. (1981). Effects of supplementation of the diets with calcium and calcium-rich foods on bone density of elderly females with osteoporosis. *American Journal of Clinical Nutrition, 34,* 819–823.

Levander, O. A. (1975). Selenium and chromium in human nutrition. *Journal of the American Dietetic Association, 66,* 338–342.

McGandy, R. B., Borrows, C. H., Spanias, A., Meredith, A., Stone, J. L., & Norris, A. H. (1966). Nutrient intakes and energy expenditure in men of different ages. *Journal of Gerontology, 21,* 581–587.

National Academy of Sciences. (1980). *Recommended dietary allowances* (9th ed.). Washington, DC: Author.

Nuttall, F. Q. (1983). Diet and the diabetic patient. *Diabetes Care, 6,* 167–204.

Posner, B. M., Borman, C. L., Morgan, J. L., Borden, W. S., & Ohls, J. C. (1982). The validity of a telephone administered 24-hour dietary recall methodology. *American Journal of Clinical Nutrition, 36,* 546–553.

Roe, D. A. (1976). *Drug-induced nutritional deficiencies.* Westport, CT: Avi Publishing Co.

Sandstead, H. H., Henricksen, L. K., Greger, J. L., Prasad, A. S., & Good, R. A. (1982). Zinc nutriture in the elderly in relation to taste acuity, immune response, and wound healing. *American Journal of Clinical Nutrition, 36,* 1046–1059.

Sherman, H. C. (1952). *Chemistry of food and nutrition.* New York: Macmillan Publishing Co.

Shinnar, S. E. (1983). Use of adaptive equipment in feeding the elderly. *American Journal of Dietetic Association, 83,* 321–322.

Siegel, J. (1976). *Demographic aspects of aging and the older population in the United States* (CPS, Special Studies, Series P-23, No. 59). Washington, DC: U.S. Government Printing Office.

Smith, F. R., & Goodman, D. S. (1976). Vitamin A transport in human vitamin A toxicity. *New England Journal of Medicine, 294,* 805–808.

Uauy, R., Scrimshaw, N. S., & Young, V. R. (1978). Human protein requirements: Nitrogen balance response to graded levels of egg protein in elderly men and women. *American Journal of Clinical Nutritition, 31,* 779–785.

United States National Center for Health Statistics. (1977). *Dietary intake findings* (U.S. 1971-74. Publication DHEW-MRA 77-1647). Washington, DC: Department of Health, Education, and Welfare.

chapter

16

Medication and Drug Considerations in Aging Individuals

Nithiananda Chatterjie

This chapter discusses certain considerations in drug intervention aimed at ameliorating cognitive dysfunctions in elderly individuals and those with senile dementias of the Alzheimer's type (SDAT). It examines the effects of a number of families of drugs that have been chosen for specific application to aging individuals and, where appropriate, to the aging mentally retarded population. The treatment is divided between the research and clinical aspects of the drug therapy. Among the more popular entities such as cerebral vasodilators, CNS stimulants, metabolic enhancers, and so on, agents such as naloxone, hydergine, and neuropeptides are discussed as less conventional drug therapeutic approaches. Additionally, psychological and behavioral approaches to the treatment of elderly and, where applicable, retarded individuals are mentioned.

THE DYSFUNCTIONS DUE TO aging and mental retardation are widespread handicapping conditions; the latter afflict from 1% to 3% of the population according to varying estimates. Many billions of dollars are expended annually for the ongoing care and habilitation of retarded individuals. Some of the more disabling forms of retardation can involve extensive lifetime care costs. There is no doubt that the social and economic impact of research leading to a reversal of conditions associated with mental retardation as well as dysfunctions concomitant with aging could be enormous. For several years, research in mental retardation has centered on either prevention or amelioration. This focus is to a great extent due to the fact that retardation has traditionally been viewed as irreversible. The

problems of senility also must share this view. Problems of aging as well as retardation clearly demonstrate that efforts to ameliorate them require a multidisciplinary research focus.

A devastating infirmity of age is the deterioration of *memory, cognitive function,* and *personality* ensuing from Alzheimer's disease (AD) and senile dementia of the Alzheimer's type (SDAT) (Terry & Davies, 1980; Wisniewski & Iqbal, 1980). It has been estimated that elderly demented individuals make up more than 5% of the population over 65 years of age (Katzman, 1976; Wang, 1977). A further 10% of individuals over 65 show mild to moderate abnormalities in cognitive functions. Approximately 50%–60% of these persons suffer from SDAT (Tomlinson, 1977). In the United States, patients whose chief symptom is dementia presently cost in excess of an estimated $6 billion per year in terms of nursing home care (Johnson et al., 1979). The proper care of this mentally disabled population is likely to cost staggering sums over the next 7–8 decades. It is imperative that in addition to research in areas of pathology and neurology, new therapeutic agents and the pharmacology of these substances be thoroughly investigated such that maladies in aging and concomitant problems are handled effectively by drug intervention.

Individuals with Alzheimer's disease/senile dementia of the Alzheimer's type (AD/SDAT) and adults with Down syndrome (DS) are known to develop progressive abnormalities of behavior and cognitive function (Jervis, 1948; Katzman, 1976; Katzman & Karasu, 1975; Olson & Shaw, 1969; Owens, Dawson, & Lowson, 1971; Wang, 1977; Wisniewski, Howe, Williams, & Wisniewski, 1978). Irrespective of dealing with early manifestations of aging, like failing memory or severe dementias as in Alzheimer's disease, drug interventions should be developed that are suitable to the needs of persons who are aging and who may require ameliorative or compensatory effects of medications. This chapter examines the effects of a number of families of drugs that have been chosen for specific application to aging individuals and, where appropriate, to the aging mentally retarded population.

GENERAL PHARMACOLOGICAL APPROACHES

Several pharmacological approaches to correct cognitive deficits of elderly individuals and those affected by Alzheimer's disease have been tried. The study of agents affecting cholinergic, dopaminergic, GABAergic, and peptidergic neurotransmission, stimulants of the CNS, metabolic enhancers, and cerebral vasodilators are encompassed in such approaches. There are also treatments that are likely to decrease lipofuscin deposition or the attenuation of antibody formation. Currently, treatment of the cortical dementias (Alzheimer's disease, Pick's disease) is entirely supportive and symptomatic. Attempts at amel-

iorating the known acetylcholine deficit in Alzheimer's disease have only produced transient and inconsistent effects, and most studies have shown the cholinergic agents to be of no benefit (Cummings & Benson, 1983; Neshkes & Jarvik, 1983). However, most other dementing illnesses have treatable aspects and in some cases may be entirely reversible. The progression of multi-infarct dementia can be halted by controlling systemic hypertension or by identifying and eliminating the source of cerebral emboli. Dementia associated with systemic illnesses can be reversed by correcting the underlying abnormality; toxic exposure–related dementias can be reversed by limiting the exposure (Cummings, 1984).

Cerebral Vasodilators

Drugs categorized as cerebral vasodilators constitute an important line of therapeutic investigation in the treatment of elderly individuals. The mechanism of action of these agents involves a direct effect on vascular smooth muscle, thus resulting in decreased cerebrovascular resistance and an increased cerebral blood flow (Karlsberg, Elliot, & Adams, 1963), which is important in dementias of vascular origin. The rationale for the use of such agents is based on the observation that cerebral blood flow declines with age and in old age–associated dementia (O'Brien, 1977).

Papaverine One commonly used brand name for papaverine is Pavabid. Papaverine is an alkaloid dervied from the plant papaver somniferum. Because of the antispasmodic action of this agent on blood vessels, it has been used for the relief of arterial spasm associated with acute vascular occlusion. Uncontrolled studies have been reported suggesting a clinical effectiveness for papaverine in the treatment of mood disturbance, cognitive impairment, and social dysfunction in elderly individuals (Dunlop, 1968; LaBrecque, 1966; McQuillen, Lopea, & Vibal, 1974). Pharmacological evidence suggests that papaverine is a dopamine antagonist. It has been reported that this agent interfered with the therapeutic response to levodopa in a patient with Parkinson's disease (Duvoisin, 1975). In addition, papaverine has shown a beneficial effect in tardive dyskinesia (Gardos, Cole, & Sniffin, 1976). These two reports are consistent with a proposed antidopaminergic action in the human.

Cyclandelate A commonly used brand name for cyclandelate is Cyclospasmol. This agent is indicated for use as an adjunct in peripheral vascular disease in which there is vasospasm.

Clinical studies of cyclandelate, uncontrolled and controlled (Aderman, Giardina, & Koreniowski, 1972; Ball & Taylor, 1967; Fine, 1971; Hall, 1976; Judge, Urquhart, & Blakemore, 1973; Young, Hall, & Blakemore, 1974), appear to demonstrate benefits in some groups of geriatric patients. Even though no invariable improvement in ischemic brain damage results when cerebral blood flow is increased (Dysken, Evans, Chan, & Davis, 1976), this drug has been shown to increase cerebral blood flow and cortical perfusion rates (Fremont, 1964; Gardos et al., 1976) by acting predominantly at the arteriolar and capillary levels. Young et al. (1974) showed that placebo-treated patients deteriorated significantly on several psychometric, behavioral, and neurological parameters, whereas the cyclandelate-treated group did not show such a decline. In a study involving 24 demented patients with cerebral atherosclerosis who were subjected to an extensive medical screening battery and other psychometric tests (designed to assess logical thinking, visual spatial perception, memory, and intelligence), no significant differences between drug and placebo were found during the 12-week study that was indicative of the drug improving higher cortical function (Westreich, Alter, & Lundgren, 1975).

Nicotinic Acid Niacin is another name for nicotinic acid. Some commonly used brands are Nicobid, Nico-Span, and Nicolar. One indication is as an adjunct only in patients with primary hyperlipidemia at doses above those given as a vitamin supplement. The drug is also a vasodilator. Flushing symptoms caused by this compound occur in practically all patients, but generally subside when the drug is discontinued. An initial study by Lehmann and Ban (1970) reported apparent improved performance on a number of perceptual and psychomotor tasks that correlated with a beneficial response to carbon dioxide inhalation. The follow-up report was not as optimistic in a larger group of geriatric patients (Lehmann, Ban, & Saxena, 1972). It has not been proved effective for treatment of peripheral vascular disease.

Other Miscellaneous Vasodilators Ban (1978) has reviewed several other vasodilators. Though a number of these seem to have theoretical possibilities, the therapeutic efficacy is essentially undocumented. Carbon dioxide, either by inhalation or by increased blood concentration as a result of administration of carbonic anhydrase inhibitors, alpha tocopherol (vitamin E), and serotonin antagonists such as methysergide are included in this group.

Anticonvulsants

Valproic acid, or dipropylacetic acid (Depakene), is a proven and effective anticonvulsant. The mechanism of action of this substance consists of blocking two enzymes (GABA transaminase and succinic acid semialdehyde dehydrogenase) involved in the catabolism of gamma-aminobutyric acid (GABA). The anticonvulsant effect is the result of elevation of brain GABA levels. Though the role of the GABAergic system is not well understood, it is believed to be interrelated with several other neurotransmitter systems. Some authors have claimed a beneficial cognitive effect in epileptic individuals (Haigh & Forsyth, 1975; Jeavons & Clarke, 1974; Volzke & Doose, 1973). Reisberg, London, Ferris, Anand, and DeLeon (1983) have indicated that in light of the cognitive and behavioral effects, and, since there has been no trial of a GABA agonist in Alzheimer's disease, a trial of sodium valproate in this disease is warranted. This is influenced by the observed effects of naloxone in SDAT patients that may be the result of its blocking of the enkephalin-mediated inhibition of GABA (Roberts, 1982).

Carbamazepine, an anticonvulsant indicated for the treatment of certain types of seizures, is reported to have rapidly improved a patient with Kluver-Bucy Syndrome when administered 1,000 mg per day; the outcome was improved recent and remote memory (Hoosh-mand, Sepdham, & Vries, 1974). It has been suggested by Reisberg, London, Ferris, An-and, and DeLeon (1983) that carbamazepine deserves a trial in patients with Alzheimer's disease for either cognitive improvement or perhaps behavioral management.

In conclusion, one might believe that the magnitude of suffering associated with Alz-heimer's disease and cognitive dysfunction might justify the search for rational therapies that are not necessarily found along entirely conventional pharmacological avenues. It is conceivable that new compounds possessing the pharmacological properties of naloxone and the anticonvulsant, pharmacophore, such as the cyclic ureide system, might well serve in problems of cognitive dysfunction as well (Chatterjie & Alexander, 1983).

Antidepressants

The lifetime risk of depressive illness has been estimated at 10%–20% (Klerman, 1976). In the case of persons age 65 and over, estimates of prevalence range from 2%–3% to a high of 65% (Gurland, 1976). It has been said that until the pathogenesis of depressive disorders is determined, the influence of age changes must remain speculative (Jarvik & Kakkar, 1981); however, certain age differences are clearly apparent. Notably, monoamine oxidase, the enzyme responsible for the intracellular break-down of catecholamines and serotonin, has been reported to increase progressively with age after age 40 in both human brain tissue and platelets (Robinson et al., 1972; Robinson, Levins, Williams, & Statham, 1978). Thus, increased enzymatic degradation of catecho-lamines might contribute to a relative decrease in brain norepinephrine (NE) and dopamine, and a relative deficiency in the biogenic amines (NE, dopamine, and serotonin) at critical syn-aptic sites in the brain. This deficiency has been hypothesized as the major biological etiol-ogy of depression (Prange, 1974; Schildkraut, 1978; VanPraag, 1977).

It is not known which factors account for the differences in symptomatology of depression observed in older versus younger adults. El-derly individuals frequently substitute somatic symptoms for dysphoric mood. This has been termed "masked depression" (Kielholz, 1973), and is particularly difficult to diagnose in this group that also frequently has concurrent phys-ical illnesses. Complaints of failing memory, confusion, impaired intellectual functioning, agitation, and sleep disturbance are common in cases of depression and dementia. A number of psychological tests and rating scales may be helpful in the differential diagnoses (Jarvik, 1980). However, the diagnosis is made after antidepressant medication, unless contraindi-cated by physical illness. As is well known, physical illness and concomitant drug use fre-quently coexist with depression in elderly indi-viduals (Jarvik & Perl, 1981).

Drug-drug interactions are important in common geriatric depressions; cardiac gly-cosides, antihypertensive agents, diuretics, antiarrhythmics, antibiotics, sedatives, hyp-notics, and laxatives are drugs most often used by elderly depressed patients. The tricyclic antidepressants, which are generally consid-ered the drugs of choice for the treatment of depression, are potentially capable of inter-action with a combination of other frequently used drugs in this segment of the population; Table 1 lists some of them. These drug inter-actions are more prevalent in persons age 65 or older than in the younger depressed patients because of the larger number of drugs con-sumed by elderly persons. It may, therefore, be desirable to discontinue as many drugs as pos-sible prior to starting antidepressant medi-cation in elderly individuals; this in itself might eliminate the depressive symptoms associated with drugs such as reserpine, guanethidine, propranolol, cimetidine, or methyldopa.

In the United States, eight tricyclic anti-depressants are currently available (amitripty-line, amoxapine, desipramine, doxepin, imi-pramine, nortriptyline, protriptyline, and trimipramine). The chemical structures of this class of compounds are basically made up of two benzene rings connected by an ethylene bridge and nitrogen atom (in some instances lacking it), appropriately substituted by an amino alkyl group.

Table 1.   Interactions between tricyclic antidepressants and other drugs[a]

Drug	Effect
Antihypertensives	
Guanethidine	Hypotensive effect decreased
Methyldopa	
Reserpine	Hypotensive effect increased
Diuretics	
Thyroid hormones	Increased hormone and tricyclic effects
Amphetamines	Increased hypertensive effects and arrhythmias
Other adrenergic agents	Increased tricyclic effects
Clonidine	Paradoxical increase in blood pressure
Oral anticoagulants	Increased anticoagulant effect
Barbiturates	Decreased tricyclic plasma levels
Levodopa	Possible decrease in levodopa absorption
Narcotics	Increased narcotic and tricyclic effects
Neuroleptics	Increased neuroleptic and tricyclic effects and blood levels
Antipyrine	Possible increase in antipyrine toxicity
Estrogens	Possible increase in tricyclic effects
Quinidine	Increased quinidine effect

[a]Adapted from Gerner (1979).

Amitriptyline (Elavil) and nortriptyline (Pamelor) are related to one another as the dimethylamino derivative and monomethyl-amino derivative (secondary amine), respectively, of the same skeletal structure; imipramine (Tofranil) and desipramine (Norpramin) have the same sort of relationship to one another as the former pair, except that these latter compounds are heterocyclic in nature, having a nitrogen atom in the ring. Protriptyline (Vivactil) has an unsaturated double bond bridging the two benzene rings and no nitrogen in the ring and is a secondary amine. Doxepin (Sinequan) is unique in that it contains an oxygen atom in the tricyclic system. These compounds are presumed to act in the CNS by blocking the reuptake of biogenic amines at the presynaptic neuronal membrane; thus, norepinephrine and serotonin concentrations are increased in the synaptic cleft for neurotransmitter action. A deficiency in functional brain norepinephrine and/or serotonin is believed to play a role in the etiology of depression.

The tricyclic antidepressants mentioned do differ in their sedative and anticholinergic effects, and also in relative noradrenergic and serotonergic activity (Goodwin & Ebert, 1977; Maas, 1975). However, most of these compounds have both noradrenergic and serotonergic activity. Doxepin and amitriptyline are serotonergic. Nortriptyline, which is a metabolite of amitriptyline, has equal noradrenergic and serotonergic activity (Goodwin, 1977). Generally, in a given tricyclic, the greater the serotonergic effect, the greater its sedative effect. Amitriptyline, doxepin, and trimipramine have the most and desipramine, nortriptyline, and protriptyline have the least sedative effect among the currently used drugs.

Since amitriptyline is helpful in controlling daytime agitation and anxiety as well as insomnia at night, it is favored for use with elderly individuals. This drug has been reported to be significantly better than placebo in trials (Davis, 1976). Amitriptyline, with its pronounced cardiovascular and anticholinergic side effects, is somewhat undesirable in elderly persons who have cardiovascular disease and enhanced sensitivity to anticholinergic side effects (Jarvik & Kakkar, 1981).

Doxepin has been reported as being useful in the treatment of depression among geriatric nursing home residents (Chien, Stotsky, &

Cole, 1975). Though Goldberg and colleagues reported significantly better results with doxepin than placebo in elderly persons suffering from memory loss, the study does not seem to have provided diagnostic specification sufficient for the interpretation of the data (Goldberg, Finnerty, & Cole, 1975). Doxepin differs from other tricyclic antidepressants in that it may not decrease rapid eye movement (REM) sleep according to a report on patients between the ages of 23 and 51 years (Karacan, Williams, & Salis, 1977). There is also a prevailing impression that doxepin has fewer cardiovascular side effects than other tricyclics and is preferred for elderly persons; however, data based on carefully controlled clinical trials to substantiate this are not yet available.

Imipramine has, by and large, been the most widely studied tricyclic antidepressant; there have also been favorable results reported for elderly subjects. In a more recently completed study of 60 depressed geriatric outpatients, imipramine was found clearly superior to placebo. In excess of 50% of patients who had completed 4 weeks of treatment on imipramine achieved nearly normal scores on the Hamilton Depression Scale (i.e., scores of 6 or less) in comparison with only 8% of the patients on placebo (Gerner et al., 1980). However, imipramine produces significant cardiovascular side effects that preclude its use in some patients, and anticholinergic effects in other elderly depressed individuals.

There seems to be no data published on the use of desipramine or protriptyline in depressed geriatric individuals.

Nortriptyline is a demethylated metabolite of amitriptyline and is present in the system when amitriptyline is administered. There is an enormous variability in the plasma levels for a given dose. Because of the differences among individuals in rates of metabolism and disposition of amitriptyline and nortriptyline, the so-called "therapeutic window" for nortriptyline shows large variability (Asberg, Chronholm, Sjoquist, & Tuck, 1971).

In conclusion, though plasma levels have been advocated as a guide to treatment of elderly individuals, the value of plasma levels as a guide remains to be demonstrated. Plasma levels have been shown to vary enormously from patient to patient. Generally, higher levels are found in elderly patients (Nies et al., 1977). The elevated levels may reflect decreased hepatic function, which results in slower demethylation and reduced renal excretion. Also, at equal plasma levels, the elderly patient may have more of the free drug as a result of an age-related decrease in plasma protein level and concomitant decrease in the protein binding of the tricyclics.

Central Nervous System Stimulants

Included in the category of compounds known as CNS stimulants are pentylenetetrazol (Metrazol), caffeine, pemoline, methylphenidate (Ritalin), and the amphetamine drugs. The rationale for using CNS in SDAT, or with normal aging patients, is based on the assumption that any drug that stimulates the patient should appear beneficial to physical and cognitive performance.

Metrazol was formerly used by injection for treatment of drug-induced coma and as a convulsant for shock therapy. It has now been replaced by more effective and less hazardous agents. There is extensive literature on the efficacy of CNS stimulants, especially pentylenetetrazol which has been comprehensively reviewed (Lehmann & Ban, 1975). Numerous uncontrolled studies report the benefit of this agent to institutionalized and, therefore, severely affected subjects; however, the controlled studies are for the most part negative. More recently, Cole and Branconnier (1977) reported that administration of 600–800 mg per day for 12 weeks to elderly community volunteers with mild memory difficulties showed a modest advantage over placebo in a neuropsychological battery of tests, although many patients were unimproved.

Pemoline   Pemoline is known by the brand name Cylert. It has been shown that stimulants such as pemoline, amphetamine, and methylphenidate are effective in reducing the behavioral signs of minimal brain dysfunction (Sroufe & Stewart, 1973). It is interesting to note that the oxazolidine structure in this drug is closely related to another class of compounds that are oxazolidinediones, which are effective anticonvulsants. This structural consideration prompts the search for certain anticonvulsants with beneficial properties in old age–associated disorders. Barbiturates may exacerbate the symptoms of minimal brain dysfunction.

The serious side effects accompanying stimulant medication in elderly individuals led some investigators to try pemoline (Jarvik, Gritz, & Schneider, 1972), which was itself used in the treatment of hyperactive children. The optimism prevailing earlier, however, was not borne out by subsequent clinical trials (Droller, Bevans, & Jayaram, 1971; Talland, Hogan, & James, 1967). The mechanism of its central stimulant effect is not known, but studies in rats show an increased rate of dopamine synthesis in the brain. Ferris has indicated clinical trials at higher dosage levels are warranted for this drug (Ferris, 1981).

Amphetamines Amphetamines are potent CNS stimulants. The agents included in this category are amphetamine, dextroamphetamine (Dexedrine), and methamphetamine (Desoxyn). These agents are sympathomimetic amines, and their noted effects on catecholamines with resulting potentiation of psychosis, and their cardiovascular side effects must be taken into consideration. Extensive literature exists on the beneficial effects of amphetamines on human performance, especially following sleep deprivation and fatigue (Weiss & Laties, 1962). The cardiovascular side effects of these substances have discouraged their use in elderly individuals; no controlled geriatric trials have been reported on these agents. Amphetamines are indicated in the treatment of attention deficit disorders in children and narcolepsy.

Methylphenidate A commonly used brand name of methylphenidate is Ritalin. It is also a sympathomimetic amine, with a pharmacological profile similar to amphetamines, but with somewhat weaker peripheral effects. Methylphenidate has been used in the treatment of apathetic or withdrawn senile behavior, with a number of open trials producing positive results (Lehmann & Ban, 1975). A double blind study failed to demonstrate any significant cognitive effects in normal, elderly subjects (Gilbert, Donnelly, Zimmer, & Kubis, 1973). In this study, subjects received a dose of 30 mg per day for 6 weeks. Though the drug produced a slight reduction in fatigue, it did not show a difference in cognitive effects. A study on 24 cognitively impaired outpatients failed to demonstrate any improvement in cognitive function by methylphenidate. Doses of 15–30 mg of this agent wre administered and compared to placebo (Crook, Ferris, Sathananthan, Raskin, & Gershon, 1977). No statistically significant changes were revealed after an extensive cognitive test battery was administered before and after each treatment. Branconnier and Cole (1980) reported that elderly subjects with mild depression, fatigue, and memory impairment treatment with a daily dose of 30 mg of methylphenidate showed no changes in cognitive function; however, mood tended to improve, particularly for those patients with greater levels of initial depression.

Cerebral Metabolic Stimulants

The compounds in the class of cerebral metabolic stimulants are not necessarily direct vasodilators even though they may secondarily enhance cerebral blood flow by increasing cerebral oxidative metabolism. The ergot and vinca alkaloids and purely synthetic compounds such as piracetam, naftidrofuryl, and centrophenoxine should be considered in this group.

Piracetam Piracetam goes by the trade name Nootropil. Although it is already used in Europe for dementia and behavioral disorders, this agent has not been approved by the FDA for use in the United States and is still an investigational drug (White, 1984). The compound is a synthetic one, originally produced in the search for a gamma-aminobutyric acid agonist. This drug and similar compounds belong to a new class of drugs called nootropic agents to describe their stimulant action on neuronal metabolism (Guirgea, 1976). A recent review of the piracetam literature documented its efficacy (Reisberg, Ferris, & Gershon, 1979).

However, a negative report has also been found (Gustafson, Risberg, Johnson, Fransson, & Maximilian, 1978). A study of old age–associated memory impairment in a primate model was documented by Bartus (1979). In these experiments, piracetam was found to be better than two other stimulants of cerebral metabolism (ergot and vinca alkaloids), while in the same model, general CNS stimulants such as pemoline, methylphenidate, pentylenetetrazol, and caffeine showed either negative effects or few positive effects. Claims have been made that piracetam facilitates learning and memory not only in cognitively impaired but also in young and mature healthy normal humans, as well as animal subjects (Dimond, 1976; Guirgea, 1976). In a controlled study (double blind), the effects of piracetam on memory in patients with senile dementia were inconsistent, with no significant differences in other symptoms between piracetam and placebo (Dencker & Lindberg, 1977).

Naftidrofuryl A brand name of naftidrofuryl is Nafronyl. It has been used in Europe for over a decade in the treatment of peripheral vascular diseases and dementias. It would appear to enhance the activities of certain enzymes of the Krebs cycle, as evidenced by histological studies in animals. In clinical trials conducted in Europe with demented elderly individuals, eight double-blind studies have shown positive effects (Judge & Urquhart, 1972; Yesavage, Tinklenberg, Hollister, & Berger, 1979). The results have been replicated in one preliminary study in the United States (Branconnier & Cole, 1977). In another study in the United States, some of the biochemical effects of the naftidrofuryl have been confirmed. For instance, a reduction in the spinal fluid lactic acid levels in demented elderly persons has been noted (Yesavage, Tinklenberg, Hollister, & Berger, 1982). This agent does not have FDA approval for use in the United States.

Centrophenoxine Centrophenoxine is known to reduce the accumulation of the age-related brain pigment lipofuscin in a variety of animal species (Nandy, 1968). It is also known as Meclofenoxate and Lucidril. It apparently enhances glucose metabolism via the glucose shunt pathway (Nandy, 1978).

Animal studies conducted with centrophenoxine have shown a reduction in the effects of anoxia and an enhancement of learning (Dereymaeker, Theeuwissen-Lesuisse, Buu-Hoi, & Lapiere, 1962). In a more recent extensive battery of tests for cognitive performance conducted on normal elderly volunteers with centrophenoxine, the subjects received 1,200 mg per day for a 9-month period (Marcer & Hopkins, 1977); the results showed an enhancement of the ability to consolidate new information into long-term memory and no changes in cognitive functions or other memory. By and large, the limited number of controlled trials are suggestive of some positive effects. Further evaluation of this compound and some new synthetic analogs are merited. It is also used in mentally retarded patients in other countries. It has not been approved by the FDA for use in the United States.

Neuropeptides

The role of neuropeptides in the central nervous system and in cognitive function has been recently reviewed (deWied, 1977; Reisberg et al., 1979). The peptides secreted by the pituitary, namely adrenocorticotropic hormone (ACTH), melanocyte-stimulating hormone (MSH), vasopressin, and the enkephalins have attracted most attention. More emphasis has settled on the ACTH 4-10 fragment that has been tested with mixed results in geriatric populations (Branconnier & Cole, 1979; Will, Abuzzahab, & Zimmerman, 1978).

Several excellent review articles summarize ACTH animal experiments (deWied, 1974, 1976; Sandman & Kastin, 1977). These lead to the conclusion that ACTH analogs enhance attention or motivation or a combination of both. Thus, the behavioral improvement in animals that ACTH analogs brought about has been described as arousal to motivationally relevant stimuli (deWied, 1974) and selective attention (Sandman & Kastin, 1977). In addition to these effects, animal data has led to the hypothesis that ACTH and its analogs may also improve memory consolidation (Flood, Jarvik,

Bennett, & Orme, 1976; Gold & McGaugh, 1977). A very informative review on neuropeptides and senile dementia by Berger and Tinklenberg (1981) may be consulted. Neuropeptides will undoubtedly continue to be studied as potential agents for reversing cognitive deficits in elderly individuals as well as in studies of mentally retarded clients (Sandman, 1983; Tinklenberg & Thornton, 1983).

Ergot Derivatives and Dopaminergic Compounds

It has become more and more evident that aging in both rodents and in humans is associated with an impaired monoaminergic and, in particular, dopaminergic transmission of presynaptic and postsynaptic events (Carlsson & Windblad, 1976; Demerest, Riegle, & Moore, 1980; Finch, 1973).

In the case of parkinsonism in humans, there is a severe depletion of endogenous dopamine levels in the basal ganglia; levodopa and another dopaminergic agonist, bromocriptine, provide a basis for the therapeutic response by dopaminergic stimulation. It is still unclear whether less pronounced impairment in dopaminergic mechanisms found in aging is associated with any change in psychomotor reactivity, mood, cognitive function, or memory, which are known to occur in persons over 65. The testing of drugs that restore or activate dopaminergic transmission in elderly patients can provide clues. Age-related symptoms that improve under such conditions are likely to be due to dopamine deficiency, thus suggesting that dopamine could be a factor related to the process of aging and CNS function.

Ergoloid Mesylates Ergoloid mesylates (Hydergine) is an ergot preparation composed of mesylates of dihydroergocornine, dihydroergocristine, dihydro-α-ergocryptine, and dihydro-β-ergocryptine in the ratio of 3:3:2:1. It has been found to be of particular therapeutic value to elderly individuals with senile mental impairment due to cerebral arteriosclerosis or hypertensive brain disease (Markstein, 1983). This preparation has been reported to exert *in vivo* effects suggesting an interaction with dopaminergic systems.

Hydergine has been found to exert beneficial effects on geriatric patients with mild to moderate stages of SDAT (see reviews by Exton-Smith, Piper, Phillips, & Simpson, 1983; Fanchamps, 1983; Loew & Weil, 1982). In view of the possible role monoaminergic systems play in SDAT, the treatment of such patients with ergoloid mesylates may be based on a pharmacological rationale. It is known that, like most of the ergot compounds, this agent interacts with the central monoaminergic systems.

Ermini and Markstein (1983) conclude that the behavioral effects and biochemical investigations have shown that Hydergine has multiple effects on dopaminergic and serotoninergic systems, acting as a mixed agonist-antagonist and might, therefore, compensate for a transmitter deficit in one brain structure, and at the same time counteract an overactivity of the respective transmitter system in other brain regions.

The effect of ergoloid mesylates in the different monoaminergic synapses is compared with the action of a chemical buffer system and is likened to a synaptic buffer substance (Ermini & Markstein, 1982).

Horowski and McDonald (1983) point out that in the clinical actions of the substance, this agent is influential in alleviating or inhibiting certain symptoms associated with senile dementia as detected by clinicians using behavioral rating scales. They interpret the data as revealing, in the statistical sense, that improvement is mainly in the areas of cognitive dysfunction and mood depression. The work by others supports the possibility that antidepressant activity may be a contributing factor to the efficacy of ergoloid mesylates (Shader, Harmatz, & Salzman, 1974). New ergot derivatives with different pharmacological profiles may help in establishing the effects of chronic administration of these substances on monoamine receptor function and functional changes regulated by them.

Cholinomimetic Drugs

The volume by Davis and Berger (1979) contains reviews of the complex relationships of the cholinergic system to memory and cognition. A basic theoretical argument holds that a relative cholinergic deficiency exists, primarily in the temporal cortex, which leads to impairment of learning in elderly individuals. The elegant animal experiments showing the effect on memory of cholinergic agonists and antagonists has been replicated by work on normal human volunteers (Davis, Mohs, Tinklenberg, Pfefferbaum, Hollister, & Kopell, 1978; Deutsch, 1971). However, it has proved more difficult to document a positive response in elderly persons because of a lack of efficient cholinomimetics and a variety of cerebral abnormalities in demented elderly individuals, of which only some respond to cholinomimetics. The effects of dosage also are important in that the overdosage of cholinomimetics can also result in as much impairment as anticholinergics.

It has been shown that a deficiency of acetylcholinesterase, choline acetyltransferase (ChAT), and degeneration of presynaptic neurons is found in SDAT that correlates with the severity of dementia. This is reflected by decreased acetylcholine and choline in the cerebrospinal fluid (CSF) of SDAT patients in proportion to their degree of cognitive impairment (Johns et al., 1983).

Physostigmine Physostigmine is a competitive inhibitor of acetylcholinesterase when acetylcholine is simultaneously present. Attempts to manipulate the cholinergic system and thereby enhance learning and behavior in SDAT have used this drug both intravenously and orally in small multiple doses. Significant improvements in long-term memory encoding appear after the administration of intravenous physostigmine, and modest improvements in cognition and behavior have resulted following administration of oral physostigmine to some SDAT patients.

The chapter on central cholinergic and adrenergic transmission and memory of Davis (1983) may be profitably consulted for more information on the role of choline and physostigmine in memory. The work by Davis and Mohs (1982) indicated that physostigmine administration (intravenous) enhanced the memory processes in Alzheimer's disease patients.

Other Miscellaneous Agents

Procaine Hydrochloride Jarvik and Milne (1975) have provided a historic review of the elixir, procaine hydrochloride, beginning with the introduction of this agent in Rumania during the late 1950s. The substance is also known in Europe by the trade name Gerovital-H3. The antiarrhythmic effects of procaine hydrochloride were first observed more than 30 years ago. Currently it is approved by the Food and Drug Administration (FDA) in the United States only as a local anesthetic and is known as Novocain. Its intravenous use is limited because of systemic toxicity, especially of the central nervous system, and rapid hydrolysis of the ester functional group by cholinesterases.

Procaine hydrochloride given by intramuscular injection is rapidly absorbed from the injection site. It is hydrolyzed by cholinesterases mainly in the plasma and also to some degree in the liver. The metabolites that are excreted in the urine are para-aminobenzoic acid (PABA) and diethylaminoethanol. It is contraindicated in patients receiving cholinesterase inhibitors (e.g., neostigmine, neuromuscular blocking agents, and some antiglaucoma agents) or in patients with a plasma cholinesterase deficiency.

In terms of its effect, this agent has been reported to improve mood and reduce confusion in senile patients. Gerovital-H3 was found to have a mild euphoric effect in 10 senile patients with depression (Sakalis, Gershon, & Shopsin, 1974). However, in a more extensive trial carried out in senile and arteriosclerotic patients, largely negative results were reported (Kral, Cahn, Deutsch, Meuller, & Solyom, 1962). A renewed interest in this drug has emerged, however, from the observation that it is a reversible monoamine oxidase (MAO) inhibitor (MacFarlane & Besbris, 1974). Since aging has been associated with decreasing MAO activity (Robinson et al., 1972), it has provided a rationale for Gerovital-

H3 use and an explanation for the purported activity of this drug (Aslan, 1974).

Anabolic Substances It has been noted that brain weight and cell number decline with age. None of the agents that have been prescribed are capable of actually restoring brain tissue. However, attempts to reverse the decline with agents capable of producing protein anabolism or improving cellular metabolism have occasionally been reported. A compound called fluoxymesterone, also known as Android F and Halotestin, which has 20 times the anabolic and 10 times the androgenic activity of 17-methyltestosterone, has been given to institutionalized patients; it produces an improved sense of well-being and greater appetite, with mild sedation (Kral & Wigdor, 1961). The drug improved recall of meaningful material, while memory for visually presented arbitrary material declined; in these tests, the drug was given over a 6- to 9-month period. There has been comment that favorable results of increased motivation on the learning of material familiar or relevant to the subject is a factor to be considered. There is evidence that improvement with fluoxymesterone is seen primarily in individuals with mild impairment as gleaned from other tests of cognitive function (Lehmann & Ban, 1970).

OPIOID ANTAGONISTS IN ENHANCEMENT OF MEMORY PROCESSES

A number of investigators have reported that administration of the opiate antagonist naloxone facilitates time-dependent memory processes (Gallagher & Kapp, 1978; Izquierdo, 1979, 1980; Izquierdo & Graudenz, 1980; Messing et al., 1979; Zimmerman, Gorelick, & Colbern, 1980). Several studies have indicated a possible modulating influence on memory storage of endogenous opioid systems (Belluzzi & Stein, 1974; Kastin, Scollan, King, Schally, & Coy, 1976). Recent studies have suggested that the endorphins and endogenous opioid systems may play a role in physiological amnesia (Izquierdo, Paiva, & Elisabetsky, 1980; Rigter, 1978; Rigter et al., 1980).

Naloxone

The studies indicating a possible modulating influence of endogenous opioid systems on memory storage have led some investigators to suggest that naloxone be investigated as a possible treatment for cognitive deficits in patients with SDAT (Kastin, Olson, Sandman, & Ehrensing, 1981; Roberts, 1981). In an open trial, 1 mg of naloxone was administered intravenously to five SDAT patients; it was reported that clinical and psychometric indexes showed notable improvement in three of them (Reisberg, Ferris, Anand, Mir, DeLeon, & Roberts, 1983). This was followed by a double-blind trial that led the authors to conclude that naloxone may have at least temporary positive effects in patients with SDAT, and that the drug merits further investigations (Reisberg, Ferris, Anand, Mir, Geibel, DeLeon, & Roberts, 1983).

Reisberg, London, Ferris, Anand, and DeLeon (1983) point out that evidence from animal studies and more recent physiological and neuroanatomical investigations, and a pilot trial in SDAT patients along with the double-blind trial mentioned above, are all factors indicating that studies of the effects of naloxone, and its oral analogue naltrexone, might prove promising in the search for an effective treatment of a major illness such as SDAT. Further work is required to establish the usefulness of naloxone and similar compounds in cognitive disorders in elderly individuals. It is conceivable that a narcotic antagonist such as naloxone or naltrexone might improve cognitive functioning by reducing the hypothesized attention impairment that endorphins might cause.

GENERAL CONSIDERATIONS

The United States will likely have more than 50 million people who will be growing old by the year 2030. Major changes in life expectancy have contributed to a demographic shift during this century. The result will be an increasing proportion of elderly people. In fact, people over 85 years of age are the fastest growing segment of the nation's elderly population. That segment could triple in the next 50 years. Such an aging population will inevitably demand that medical care be tailored to meet the needs of the elderly patient, even though the specific demands of this population are just beginning to be deciphered.

A clearer picture is beginning to emerge: age-related physiological changes, diseases, and syndromes all contribute to an increase in drug intake among persons age 65 and over. These very factors can also influence an elderly patient's drug tolerance, metabolism, distribution, clearance, and response, but age-associated decrements do not occur at the same rate or to the same degree in all individuals. Geriatric pharmacokinetics will be much better understood as research progresses. However, some tentative findings have emerged.

Renal clearance in the aging patient may be slowed down due to changes in renal tubular function and decreased renal blood flow and glomerular filtration rate. Decreased hepatic flow and possible decreased microsomal enzyme activity may reduce hepatic clearance.

Age-associated changes in body composition can alter drug disposition. In elderly individuals, there is the likelihood of a decreased lean tissue and total body water content and an increase in adipose tissue. This could result in an increased distribution of lipid soluble drugs and a lowered distribution of less lipid soluble agents, especially in women whose adipose tissue exceeds that of men throughout life. Other factors, such as cigarette smoking, alcohol intake, and/or malnutrition may also alter drug response in older patients. Circadian rhythms, which appear to change somewhat in old age, may affect pharmacodynamics or pharmacokinetics.

The problem of drug-drug interactions is serious, particularly in an elderly population that is very likely to receive more prescriptions than young population. Elderly individuals have more adverse reactions, and the number of these reactions increases with the number of drugs taken.

The mechanisms of drug interactions are diverse and complex. For example, it may be risky to mix monoamine oxidase inhibitors with oral hypoglycemic agents, carbamazepine, insulin, meperidine, tricyclic antidepressants, or sympathomimetic amines.

It is known that beta blockers in elderly patients are avoided because of a high rate of chronic pulmonary disease. The combination of cardioglycosides with diuretics that deplete potassium, for instance, can cause severe or fatal digitalis toxicity.

Another consideration in the elderly population is sleep medications. A major nonspecific pharmacological problem relating to nursing home patients in general and to the 60% that are demented (Brody, 1978) is the rational use of medications for sleep. Even though the incidence and prevalance of sleep disorders in elderly persons are not known, according to a recent review it is estimated that up to 35% of the persons over the age of 60 have subjective sleep complaints (Coleman et al., 1981). Also, evaluations in the daytime have indicated that elderly individuals are less likely to stay awake than young persons because older people take more naps.

The daytime sleepiness in elders very likely decreases their alertness and cognitive performance. Compounds such as secobarbital and diazepam are consumed by over 15% of the population that is over 60 years of age (this segment consumes 33% of the prescriptions written for sedative drugs). Such drugs can impair daytime functioning by reducing alertness and inducing sleep. The ability to sleep the following night is impaired as a consequence. These considerations should lead to the evaluation of safe use of sleeping drugs as well as evaluation of nonpharmacological interventions for elderly individuals who use medications for sleep.

PSYCHOLOGICAL AND BEHAVIORAL APPROACHES

Labouvie-Vief (1976) has studied the effect of self-image and the expectations of society on memory and other intellectual functions. She found that some of the decline associated with aging can be modified by social manipulations.

Also, training in which elderly individuals are encouraged to develop strategies of their own for improving performance may be as effective as specific training, such as that proposed by Willis, Blieszner, and Baltes (1981). In a recent study, Yesavage, Rose, and Bower (1983) combined a standard face-name learning mnemonic (organizational device) with a method to increase the elaboration of processing of crucial components of the mnemonic; the results were substantially better than the mnemonic alone. Yesavage and associates (Yesavage, 1984; Yesavage, Rose, & Spiegel, 1982) also showed that combining relaxation training with mnemonic training had facilitative effects. These studies have been expanded to encompass a variety of practical memory problems encountered by elderly persons with difficulties in memory that are associated with the process of normal aging.

There have been positive effects seen in several studies involving cognitive losses associated with normal aging; many of these studies have utilized innovative techniques, based on current theories of cognitive, educational, and social psychology. In the case of elderly individuals with senile dementia, the situation is somewhat different from studies of interventions in elderly persons with memory problems (Reisberg, Ferris, & Gershon, 1981).

REMEDIES FOR ELDERLY PERSONS WITH SENILE DEMENTIAS

Orientation toward Reality

Over the last 20 years of psychological interventions, there have been attempts aimed at improving cognitive deficits in individuals with senile dementias. The most widely studied intervention is "reality orientation," which is a process of primarily repetition and reinforcement of correct responses aimed at orienting demented nursing home residents (Cornbleth & Cornbleth, 1977). According to Yesavage, Rose, and Spiegel (1982) these studies unfortunately suffer from a lack of control medications, small study group size, raters who are nonblind, and a failure to use psychometric measures that are widely accepted to identify the degree of impairment.

The combination of pharmacological and psychological intervention had led to a study that combined a medication for the treatment of senile dementia with an imagery association technique (Yesavage, Westphal, & Rush, 1981). Subjects receiving Hydergine and cognitive psychotherapy improved more on a psychometric test of memory and list learning than subjects receiving the drug and supportive psychotherapy. Some investigators have noted that not much is known about the effect of individual differences between elderly subjects with memory deficits, and that programs do not seem to be tailored to recognize these differences (Perlmuter, Tenney, & Smith, 1980). According to Verwoerdt (1982), psychotherapy of patients who have senile dementia should be an essential part of a comprehensive treatment approach. Yesavage and Karasu (1982) have argued that lack of consideration of individual psychotherapy in even physically normal elderly persons is often due to "gerontophobic" reactions on the part of the physician. It is hoped that future research will explore the role of individual psychotherapy as an adjunct to the treatment of the demented patient.

Furthermore, the role of the family of the patient with senile dementia, with reference to treatment and support, must be considered. Zarit, Zarit, and Reever (1982) found that demented patients receive training programs for improving cognitive deficits that might be perceived at times as having limited value for a given patient. However, it has been found that mutual support derived from viewing other families cope with similar problems resulted in benefit to the family. Thus Zarit's group was led to incorporate the concept of family support groups with an approach to solving problems in his clinical service.

To what extent can medications enhance memory and cognitive powers in mentally retarded individuals? The answer to this question must necessarily be speculative at present. There is reason to believe that neurotransmitters function abnormally in some types of mental retardation. The challenge will be to utilize the same neurochemical techniques and neuropharmacological approaches that have been used to investigate the pathology of Alzheimer's disease, parkinsonism, and Huntington's chorea to study the neurochemical foundations of mental retardation. This would be an effective first step in developing drug therapy for at least some forms of retardation. In several aspects, mentally retarded and dysfunctional elderly individuals share problems that are parallel in terms of treatment and care. Perhaps these similarities need to be recognized more, so that fruitful results will ensue for the individuals concerned.

REFERENCES

Aderman, M., Giardina, W. J., & Koreniowski, S. (1972). Effect of cyclandelate on perception memory and cognition in a group of geriatric subjects. *Journal of the American Geriatrics Society, 20,* 268–271.

Asberg, M., Chronholm, B., Sjoquist, F., & Tuck, D. (1971). Relationships between plasma level and therapeutic effect of nortriptyline. *British Medical Journal, 3,* 331–334.

Aslan, A. (1974). Theoretical and practical aspects of chemotherapeutic techniques in the retardation of the aging process. In M. Rockstein, M. L. Sussman, & J. Chesky (Eds.), *Theoretical aspects of aging* (pp. 177–186). New York: Academic Press.

Ball, J. A., & Taylor, A. R. (1967). Effect of cyclandelate on mental function and cerebral blood flow in elderly patients. *British Medical Journal, 3,* 525–528.

Ban, T. A. (1978). Vasodilators, stimulants and anabolic agents in the treatment of geropsychiatric patients. In M. A. Lipton, A. DiMascio, & K. F. Killam (Eds.), *Psychopharmacology, a generation of progress* (pp. 1525– 1533). New York: Raven Press.

Bartus, R. T. (1979). Four stimulants of the central nervous system: Effects on short-term memory in young versus aged monkeys. *Journal of the American Geriatrics Society, 27,* 289–297.

Belluzzi, J. D., & Stein, I. (1974). Enkephalin and morphine induced facilitation of long term memory. *Society for Neuroscience Abstracts, 3,* 230.

Berger, P. A., & Tinklenberg, J. R. (1981). Neuropeptides and senile dementia. In T. Crook & S. Gershon (Eds.), *Strategies for the development of an effective treatment for senile dementia* (pp. 155–171). New Canaan, CT: Mark Powley Assoc.

Branconnier, R. J., & Cole, J. O. (1977). A memory assessment technique for use in geriatric psychopharmacology: Drug efficacy trial with naftidrofuryl. *Journal of the American Geriatrics Society, 25,* 186–188.

Branconnier, R. J., & Cole, J. O. (1979). ACTH 4-10 in the amelioration of neuropsychological symptomology associated with senile organic brain syndrome. *Psychopharmacology* (Berlin), *61,* 161–165.

Branconnier, R. J., & Cole, J. O. (1980). The therapeutic role of methylphenidate in senile organic brain syndrome. In J. O. Cole & J. E. Barrett (Eds.), *Psychopathology in aged* (pp. 183–203). New York: Raven Press.

Brody, E. M. (1978). The formal support network: Congregate treatment settings for residents with senescent brain dysfunction (1982). In N. E. Miller & G. D. Cohen (Eds.), *Clinical aspects of Alzheimer's disease and senile dementia: Vol. 15. Aging* (pp. 301–331). New York: Raven Press.

Carlsson, A., & Windblad, B. (1976). Influence of age and time interval between death and autopsy in dopamine and 3-methoxytyramine levels in human basal ganglia. *Journal of Neural Transmission, 38,* 271–276.

Chatterjie, N., & Alexander, G. J. (1983). Naloxone-6-spirohydantoin: a new non-toxic compound with anticonvulsive properties. *Neuropharmacology, 22,* 1151–1153.

Chien, C. P., Stotsky, B. A., & Cole, J. O. (1975). Psychiatric treatment for nursing home patients: Drug, alcohol and milieu. *American Journal of Psychiatry, 130,* 543–548.

Cole, J. O., & Branconnier, R. J. (1977). Drugs and senile dementia. *McLean Hospital Journal, 2,* 210–221.

Coleman, R. M., Miles, L. E., Guilleminault, C., Zarcone, V. P., Van den Hoed, J., & Dement, W. C. (1981). Sleep-wake disorders in the elderly: A polysomnographic analysis. *Journal of the American Geriatrics Society, 29,* 289–296.

Cornbleth, T., & Cornbleth, C. (1977). *Reality orientation for the elderly* (MS1539 J. Suppl. Abstr. Serv.). Washington, DC: American Psychological Association.

Crook, T., Ferris, S., Sathananthan, G., Raskin, A., & Gershon, S. (1977). The effect of methylphenidate on test performance in the cognitively impaired aged. *Psychopharmacology, 52,* 251–255.

Cummings, J. L. (1984). Dementia: Definition, classification and differential diagnosis. *Psychiatric Annals, 14*(2), 85–89.

Cummings, J. L., & Benson, D. F. (1983). *Dementia: A clinical approach.* Woburn, MA: Butterworth Publishers.

Davis, J. M. (1976). Overview: Maintenance therapy in psychiatry: II. Affective disorders. *American Journal of Psychiatry, 133,* 1–13.

Davis, K. L. (1983). Central cholinergic and adrenergic transmission and memory. In F. J. Menalascino, R. Neman, & J. A. Stark (Eds.), *Curative aspects of mental retardation: Biomedical and behavioral advances* (pp. 165–179). Baltimore: Paul H. Brookes Publishing Co.

Davis, K. L., & Berger, P. A. (Eds.). (1979). *Brain acetylcholine and neuropsychiatric disease.* New York: Plenum Publishing Corp.

Davis, K. L., & Mohs, R. C. (1982). Enhancement of memory processes in Alzheimer's diseases with multiple dose intravenous physostigmine. *American Journal of Psychiatry, 138,* 1421–1422.

Davis, K. L., Mohs, R. C., Tinklenberg, J. R., Pfeffer-baum, A., Hollister, L. E., & Kopell, B. S. (1978). Physostigmine improvement in long term memory processes in normal humans. *Science, 201,* 272–274.

Demerest, K. T., Riegle, G. D., & Moore, K. E. (1980). Characteristics of dopamine neurons in the aged male rat. *Neuroendocrinology, 31,* 222–227.

Dencker, S. J., & Lindberg, D. (1977). A controlled double-blind study of piracetam in the treatment of senile dementia. *Nordisk Psykiatrisk Tidsskrift, 31,* 48–52.

Dereymaeker, A., Theeuwissen-Lesuisse, F., Buu-Hoi, N. P., & Lapiere, L. (1962). Protective effect of derivatives of p-chlorophenoxyacetic acid. *Medicina Experimentalis* (Basel), *7,* 239–244.

Deutsch, J. A. (1971). The cholinergic synapse and the site of memory. *Science, 175,* 788–794.

deWied, D. (1974). Pituitary-adrenal system hormones and behavior. In F. O. Schmitt & F. G. Worden (Eds.), *The neurosciences, third study program* (pp. 653–666). Cambridge: MIT Press.

deWied, D. (1976). Hormonal influences on motivation, learning and memory processes. *Hospital Practice, 11*(1), 123–131.

deWied, D. (1977). Minireview, peptides and behavior. *Life Sciences, 20,* 195–204.

Dimond, S. J., (1976). Drugs to improve learning in man: Implications in neuropsychological analysis. In R. M. Knights & D. J. Baker (Eds.), *The neuropsychology of learning disorders* (pp. 367–379). Baltimore: University Park Press.

Droller, H., Bevans, H. G., & Jayaram, V. K. (1971). Problems of a drug trial (Pemoline) on geriatric patients. *Gerontologia Clinica, 13,* 269–276.

Dunlop, E. (1968). Cerebrovascular insufficiency treated with papaverine. *Journal of the American Geriatrics Society, 16,* 343–349.

Duvoisin, R. C. (1975). Antagonism of levodopa by papaverine. *Journal of the American Medical Association, 231,* 845–897.

Dysken, M., Evans, H. M., Chan, C. H., & Davis, J. M. (1976). Improvement of depression and Parkinsonism during ECT: A case study. *Neuropsychobiology, 2,* 81–86.

Ermini, M., & Markstein, R. (1982). Hydergine therapy: Mechanism of action. *British Journal of Clinical Practice, Symposium Supplement, 16,* 27–31.

Ermini, M., & Markstein, R. (1983). *Pharmacological rationale for a treatment of senile dementia with co-dergocrine mesylate.* Paper presented at the Internationales Symposium "Senile Dementia in the Next Twenty Years," Lausanne, Switzerland.

Exton-Smith, A. N., Piper, M., Phillips, M., & Simpson, J. (1983). Clinical experiences with ergot alkaloids. In A. Agnoli, G. Crepaldi, P. F. Spano, & M. Trabucchi (Eds.), *Aging brain and ergot alkaloids* (pp. 323–328). New York: Raven Press.

Fanchamps, A. (1983). Dihydroergotoxine in senile cerebral insufficiency. In A. Agnoli, G. Crepaldi, P. F. Spano, & M. Trabucchi (Eds.), *Aging brain and ergot alkaloids* (pp. 311–322). New York: Raven Press.

Ferris, S. H. (1981). Empirical studies in senile dementia with central nervous system stimulants and metabolic enhancers. In T. Crook (Ed.), *Strategies for the development of an effective treatment for senile dementia* (pp. 173–187). New Canaan, CT: Mark Powley Assoc.

Finch, C. E. (1973). Catecholamine metabolism in the brains of aging male mice. *Brain Research, 52,* 261–276.

Fine, E. W. (1971). The use of cyclandelate in chronic brain syndrome with arteriosclerosis. *Current Therapeutic Research, 13,* 568–574.

Fine, E. W., Lewis, D., Villa-Landa, I., & Blackmore, C. B. (1971). The effect of cyclandelate on mental function in patients with arteriosclerotic brain disease. *British Journal of Psychiatry, 117,* 157–161.

Flood, J. F., Jarvik, M. E., Bennett, E. L., & Orme, A. E. (1976). Effects of ACTH peptide fragments on memory formation. *Pharmacology Biochemistry Behavior, 5,* (Suppl. 1), 41–51.

Fremont, R. E. (1964). Clinical and plethysmographic observations on the use of cyclandelate in arteriosclerosis obliterans. *American Journal of the Medical Sciences, 247,* 182–194.

Gallagher, M., & Kapp, B. S. (1978). Manipulation of opiate activity in the Amygdala alters memory processes. *Life Sciences, 23,* 1973–1978.

Gardos, G., Cole, J. O., & Sniffin, C. (1976). An evaluation of papaverine in tardive dyskinesia. *Journal of Clinical Pharmacology, 16,* 304–310.

Gerner, R. H. (1979). Depression in the elderly. In O. Kaplan (Ed.), *Psychopathology of aging* (pp. 97–148). New York: Academic Press.

Gerner, R., Estabrook, W., Steuer, J., Waltuch, L., Kakkar, P., & Jarvik, L. F. (1980). A placebo controlled double-blind study of imipramine and trazadone in geriatric depression. In J. A. Cole & J. E. Barrett (Eds.), *Psychopathology in the aged* (pp. 167–182). New York: Raven Press.

Gilbert, J. G., Donnelly, K. J., Zimmer, L. E., & Kubis, J. F. (1973). Effect of magnesium pemoline and methylphenidate on memory improvement and mood in normal aging subjects. *International Journal of Aging and Human Development, 4,* 35–51.

Gold, P. E., & McGaugh, J. L. (1977). Hormones and memory. In L. H. Miller, C. A. Sandman, & A. J. Kastin (Eds.), *Neuropeptide influences on the brain* (pp. 127–144). New York: Raven Press.

Goldberg, H. L., Finnerty, R. J., & Cole, J. O. (1975). The effect of doxepin in the aged: Interim report on memory changes and electrocardiographic findings. In J. Mendels (Ed.), *Sinequan (Doxepin HCl): A Monograph of Recent Clinical Studies* (pp. 65–69). Princeton: Excerpta Medica.

Goodwin, F. K. (1977). Drug treatment of affective disorders. General principles. In M. E. Jarvik (Ed.), *Psychopharmacology in the practice of medicine* (pp. 241–253). East Norwalk, CT: Appleton-Century-Crofts.

Goodwin, F. K., & Ebert, M. H. (1977). Recent advances in drug treatment of affective disorders. In M. E. Jarvik (Ed.), *Psychopharmacology in the practice of medicine* (pp. 277–287). East Norwalk, CT: Appleton-Century-Crofts.

Guirgea, C. (1976). Piracetam: Nootropic pharmacology of neurointegrative activity. In W. B. Essman & L. Valzelli (Eds.), *Current developments in psychopharmacology* (Vol. 3, pp. 222–273). New York: Spectrum Publications.

Gurland, B. J. (1976). The comparative frequency of depression in various adult age groups. *Journal of Gerontology, 31,* 283–292.

Gustafson, L., Risberg, J., Johnson, M., Fransson, M., & Maximilian, V. A. (1978). Effects of piracetam on regional cerebral blood flow and mental function in patients with organic dementia. *Psychopharmacology, 56,* 115–117.

Haigh, D., & Forsyth, W. I. (1975). The treatment of childhood epilepsy with sodium vaproate. *Developmental Medicine and Child Neurology, 17,* 742–748.

Hall, P. (1976). Cyclandelate in the treatment of cerebral arteriosclerosis. *Journal of the American Geriatrics Society, 24,* 41–45.

Hooshmand, H., Sepdham, T., & Vries, J. K. (1974). Kluver-Bucy Syndrome. Successful treatment with carbamazepine. *Journal of the American Medical Association, 229,* 1782.

Horowski, R., & McDonald, R. J. (1983). Experimental and clinical aspects of ergot derivatives used in the treatment of age-related disorders. In A. Agnoli, G. Crepaldi, P. F. Spano, & M. Trabucchi (Eds.), *Aging brain and ergot alkaloids* (pp. 283–303). New York: Raven Press.

Izquierdo, I. (1979). Effect of naloxone and morphine on various forms of memory in the rat. Possible role of endogenous opiate mechanisms in memory consolidation. *Psychopharmacology, 67,* 265–268.

Izquierdo, I. (1980). Effect of beta-endorphin and naloxone on acquisition, memory and retrieval of shuttle avoidance and habituation in rats. *Psychopharmacology, 66,* 199–203.

Izquierdo, I., & Graudenz, M. (1980). Memory facilitation by naloxone is due to release of dopaminergic and beta-adrenergic systems from tonic inhibition. *Psychopharmacology, 67,* 265–268.

Izquierdo, I., Paiva, A. C. M., & Elisabetsky, E. (1980). Post training intraperitoneal administration of leuenkephalin and beta-endorphin causes retrograde amnesia for two different tasks in rats. *Behavioral and Neural Biology, 28,* 246–250.

Jarvik, L. F. (1980). Diagnosis of dementia in the elderly—a 1980 perspective. In C. Eisdorfer (Ed.), *Annual review of gerontology and geriatrics* (Vol. 1, pp. 180–203). New York: Springer.

Jarvik, M. E., Gritz, E. R., & Schneider, N. G. (1972). Drugs and memory disorders in human aging. *Behavioral Biology, 7,* 643–668.

Jarvik, L. F., & Kakkar, P. R. (1981). Aging and response to antidepressants. In L. F. Jarvik, D. J. Greenblatt, & D. Harman (Eds.), *Clinical pharmacology and the aged patient: Vol. 16. Aging* (pp. 49–77). New York: Raven Press.

Jarvik, L. F., & Milne, J. F. (1975). Gerovital-H₃: A review of the literature. In S. Gershon & A. Raskin (Eds.), *Genesis and treatment of psychologic disorders in the elderly: Vol. 2. Aging* (pp. 203–227). New York: Raven Press.

Jarvik, L. F., & Perl, M. (1981). An overview of physiologic dysfunctions related to psychiatric problems in the elderly. In A. Levenson & R. C. W. Hall (Eds.), *Neuropsychiatric manifestations of physical disease in the elderly* (pp. 1–15). New York: Raven Press.

Jeavons, P. M., & Clarke, J. E. (1974). Sodium valproate in the treatment of epilepsy. *British Medical Journal, 2,* 584–586.

Jervis, G. A. (1948). Early senile dementia in mongoloid idiocy. *American Journal of Psychiatry, 105,* 102–106.

Johns, C. A., Levy, M. I., Greenwald, B. S., Rosen, W. G., Horvath, T. B., Davis, B. M., Mohs, R. C., & Davis, K. L. (1983). Studies of cholinergic mechanisms in Alzheimer's disease. In R. Katzman (Ed.), *Banbury report 15: Biological aspects of Alzheimer's disease* (pp. 435–449). Cold Spring Harbor: Cold Spring Laboratory.

Johnson, R. T., Katzman, R., Shoote, E., McGeer, E., Silberberg, D., & Price, D. (1979). *Report of the panel on inflammatory, demyelinating, and degenerative diseases to the National Advisory, Neurological, Communicative Disorders and Stroke Council* (NIH Publication 79-1916). Washington, DC: U.S. Department of Health, Education, & Welfare.

Judge, T. G., & Urquhart, A. (1972). Naftidrofuryl. A double blind crossover study in the elderly. *Current Medical Research and Opinion, 1,* 166–172.

Judge, T. G., Urquhart, A., & Blakemore, C. B. (1973). Cyclandelate and mental functions. A double-blind crossover trial in normal elderly subjects. *Age and Aging, 2,* 121–124.

Karacan, I., Williams, R. L., & Salis, P. J. (1977). Sleep and sleep abnormalities in depression. In W. E. Fann, I. Karacan, A. D. Pokorny, & R. L. Williams (Eds.), *Phenomenology and treatment of depression* (pp. 167–176). New York: Spectrum Publications.

Karlsberg, P., Elliot, H. W., & Adams, J. E. (1963). Effect of various pharmacologic agents on cerebral arteries. *Neurology, 13,* 772–778.

Kastin, A. J., Olson, G. A., Sandman, C. A., & Ehrensing, R. H. (1981). Possible role of peptides in senile dementia. In T. Crook & S. Gershon (Eds.), *Strategies for the development of an effective treatment for senile dementia* (pp. 139–152). New Canaan, CT: Mark Powley Assoc.

Kastin, A. J., Scollan, E. I., King, M. G., Schally, A., & Coy, D. H. (1976). Enkephalin and a potent analog, facilitates maze performance after intraperitoneal administration in rats. *Pharmacology Biochemistry and Behavior, 5,* 691–695.

Katzman, R. (1976). The prevalence and malignancy of Alzheimer's disease: A major killer. *Archives of Neurology, 33,* 217–218.

Katzman, R., & Karasu, T. B. (1975). Differential diagnoses of dementia. In W. S. Fields (Ed.), *Neurological and sensory disorders in the elderly* (pp. 103–132). New York: Grune & Stratton.

Kielholz, P. (Ed.). (1973). *Masked depression.* Vienna: Hans Huber.

Klerman, G. L. (1976). Age and clinical depression: Today's youth in the 21st century. *Journal of Gerontology, 31,* 318–323.

Kral, V. A., Cahn, C., Deutsch, M., Meuller, H., & Solyom, L. (1962). Senescent forgetfulness benign and malignant. *Canadian Medical Association, 87,* 1109–1113.

Kral, V. A., & Wigdor, B. T. (1961). Further studies on the androgen effect of senescent memory. *Canadian Psychiatric Association Journal, 6,* 345–352.

Labouvie-Vief, G. (1976). Toward optimizing cognitive competence in later life. *Journal of Gerontology, 1,* 75–92.

LaBrecque, D. C. (1966). Papaverine hydrochloride as therapy for mentally confused geriatric patients. *Current Therapeutic Research, 8,* 106–109.

Lehmann, H. E., & Ban, T. A. (1970). Pharmacological lead tests as predictors of pharmacotherapeutic response in geriatric patients. In J. R. Wittenborn, S. C. Goldberg, & P. R. A. May (Eds.), *Psychopharmacology and the individual patient* (pp. 32–54). New York: Raven Press.

Lehmann, H. E., Ban, T. A., & Saxena, B. M. (1972). Nicotinic acid, thioridazine, fluoxymesterone and their combinations in hospitalized geriatric patients: A systematic clinical study. *Canadian Psychiatric Association Journal, 17*, 315–320.

Lehmann, H. E., & Ban, T. A. (1975). Central nervous system stimulants and anabolic substances in geropsychiatric therapy. In S. Gershan & A. Raskin (Eds.), *Aging* (Vol. 2, pp. 179–202). New York: Raven Press.

Loew, D. M., & Weil, C. (1982). Hydergine in senile mental impairment. *Gerontology, 28*, 54–74.

Maas, J. W. (1975). Biogenic amines and depression. *Archives of General Psychiatry, 32*, 1357–1361.

MacFarlane, M. D., & Besbris, H. (1974). Procaine gerovital H₃ therapy: Mechanism of inhibition of monoamine oxidase. *Journal of American Geriatrics Society, 21*, 224–225.

Marcer, D., & Hopkins, S. M. (1977). The differential effects of meclofenoxate on memory loss in the elderly. *Age and Ageing, 6*, 123–131.

Markstein, R. (1983). Dopamine receptor profile of codergocrine (Hydergine) and its components. *European Journal of Pharmacology, 86*, 145–155.

McQuillen, L. M., Lopea, C. A., & Vibal, J. R. (1974). Evaluation of EEG and clinical changes associated with pavabid therapy in chronic brain syndrome. *Current Therapeutic Research, 16*, 49–58.

Messing, R. B., Jensen, R. A., Martinez, J. L., Jr., Spiehler, V. R., Vasquez, B. J., Soumireu-Mourat, B., Liang, K. C., & McGaugh, J. L. (1979). Naloxone enhancement of memory. *Behavioral and Neural Biology, 27*, 266–275.

Nandy, K. (1968). Further studies on the effect of centrophenoxine on the lipofuscin pigments in the neurons of senile guinea pigs. *Journal of Gerontology, 2*, 82–92.

Nandy, K. (1978). Centrophenoxine: Effects on aging mammalian brain. *Journal of the American Geriatrics Society, 26*, 74–81.

Neshkes, R. E., & Jarvik, L. F. (1983). Pharmacologic approach to the treatment of senile dementia. *Psychiatric Annals, 13*(1), 14–30.

Nies, A., Robinson, D. S., Friedman, M. J., Green, R., Cooper, T. B., Ravaris, C. L., & Ives, J. O. (1977). Relationship between age and tricyclic antidepressant plasma levels. *American Journal of Psychiatry, 134*, 790–793.

O'Brien, M. C. (1977). Vascular disease and dementia in the elderly. In L. W. Smith & M. Kinsbourne (Eds.), *Aging and dementia* (pp. 77–90). New York: Spectrum Publications.

Olson, M. I., & Shaw, C. M. (1969). Presenile dementia and Alzheimer's disease in mongolism. *Brain, 92*, 147–156.

Owens, D., Dawson, J. C., & Lowson, S. (1971). Alzheimer's disease in Down's Syndrome. *American Journal of Mental Deficiency, 75*, 606–612.

Perlmuter, L. C., Tenney, Y. J., & Smith, P. A. (1980). *Evaluation and remediation of memory problems in the aged* (Tech. Rep. 80-82). Boston: Geriatric Research Educational and Clinical Center, V. A. Outpatient Clinic.

Prange, A. J., Jr. (1974). L-tryptophan in mania: Contribution to a permissive hypothesis of affective disorders. *Archives General Psychiatry, 30*, 56–62.

Reisberg, B., Ferris, S. H., Anand, R., Mir, P., Geibel, V., DeLeon, M. J., & Roberts, E. (1983). Effects of naloxone in senile dementia: A double-blind trial. *New England Journal of Medicine, 308*, 721–722.

Reisberg, B., Ferris, S. H., Anand, R., Mir, P., DeLeon, M. J., & Roberts, E. (1983). Naloxone effects on primary degenerative dementia (PDD). *Psychopharmacology Bulletin, 19*(1), 44–47.

Reisberg, B., Ferris, S. H., & Gershon, S. (1979). Psychopharmacologic aspects of cognitive research in the elderly: Some current perspectives. *Interdisciplinary Topics in Gerontology, 15*, 132–152.

Reisberg, B., Ferris, S. H., & Gershon, S. (1981). An overview of pharmacologic treatment of cognitive decline in the aged. *American Journal of Psychiatry, 138*, 593–600.

Reisberg, B., London, E., Ferris, S. H., Anand, R., & DeLeon, M. J. (1983). Novel pharmacologic approaches to the treatment of senile dementia of the Alzheimer's type (SDAT). *Psychopharmacology Bulletin, 19*(2), 220–225.

Rigter, H. A. (1978). Attenuation of amnesia in rats by systemically administered enkephalins. *Science, 200*, 83–85.

Rigter, H., Hannan, T. J., Messing, R. B., Martinez, J. L., Jr., Vasquez, B. J., Jensen, R. A., Veliquette, J., & McGaugh, J. L. (1980). Enkephalins interfere with acquisition of an active avoidance response. *Life Sciences, 26*, 337–345.

Roberts, E. (1981). A speculative consideration of the neurobiology and treatment of senile dementia. In T. Crook & S. Gershon (Eds.), *Strategies for the development of an effective treatment for senile dementia* (pp. 267–320). New Canaan, CT: Mark Powley Inc.

Roberts, E. (1982). Potential therapies in aging and senile dementia. *Annals of New York Academy of Sciences, 396*, 165–178.

Robinson, D. S., Davis, J. M., Nies, A., Colburn, R. W., Davis, J. N., Bourne, H. R., Bunney, W. E., Shaw, D. M., & Coppen, A. J. (1972). Aging and monoamine oxidase levels. *Lancet, I*, 290–291.

Robinson, D. S., Levins, R., Williams, A., & Statham, N. S. (1978). Hydroxylase cofactor in human C.S.F. An index of central aminergic function. *Psychopharmacology Bulletin, 14*, 49–51.

Sakalis, G., Gershon, D. O. S., & Shopsin, B. (1974). A trial of gerovital H₃ in depression during senility. *Current Therapeutic Research, 16*, 59–63.

Sandman, C. A. (1983). The effects of neuropeptides on behavior: Implications for mental retardation. In F. J. Menolascino, R. Neman, & J. A. Stark (Eds.), *Curative aspects of mental retardation: Biomedical and behavioral advances* (pp. 181–191). Baltimore: Paul H. Brookes Publishing Co.

Sandman, C. A., & Kastin, A. J. (1977). Pituitary peptide influences on attention and memory. In R. R. Drucker-Colin & J. L. McGaugh (Eds.), *Neurobiology of sleep and memory* (pp. 347–360). New York: Academic Press.

Schildkraut, J. J. (1978). Current status of the catecholamine hypothesis of affective disorders. In M. A.

Lipton, A. DiMascio, & K. F. Killam (Eds.), *Psychopharmacology: A generation of progress* (pp. 1223–1234). New York: Raven Press.

Shader, R. I., Harmatz, J. S., & Salzman, C. (1974). A new scale for clinical assessment in geriatric populations: (SCAG). *Journal of American Geriatrics Society, 22,* 107–113.

Sroufe, L. A., & Stewart, M. A. (1973). Treating problem children with stimulant drugs. *New England Journal of Medicine, 289,* 407–413.

Talland, G. A., Hogan, D. Q., & James, M. (1967). Performance tests of amnesic patients with Cylert. *Journal of Nervous and Mental Disabilities, 144,* 421–429.

Terry, R. D., & Davies, P. (1980). Dementia of the Alzheimer type. *Annual Reviews in Neurosciences, 3,* 77–95.

Tinklenberg, J. R., & Thornton, J. E. (1983). Neuropeptides in geriatric psychopharmacology. *Psychopharmacology Bulletin, 19,* 198–211.

Tomlinson, B. E. (1977). The pathology of dementia. In C. E. Wells (Eds), *Dementia* (2nd ed.) (pp. 113–153). Philadelphia: F. A. Davis.

VanPraag, H. M. (1977). Significance of biochemical parameter in the diagnosis, treatment and prevention of depression disorders. *Biological Psychiatry, 12,* 102–132.

Verwoerdt, A. (1981). Individual psychotherapy in senile dementia. In N. E. Miller & G. D. Cohen (Eds.), *Clinical aspects of Azlheimer's Disease and senile dementia: Vol. 15. Aging* (pp. 187–208). New York: Raven Press.

Volzke, E., & Doose, H. (1973). Dipropylacetate in the treatment of epilepsy. *Epilepsia, 14,* 185–193.

Wang, H. S. (1977). Dementia of old age. In W. L. Smith & M. Kinsbourne (Eds.), *Aging and dementia* (pp. 1–24). New York: Spectrum Publications.

Westreich, G., Alter, M., & Lundgren, S. (1975). Effect of cyclandelate on dementia. *Stroke, 6,* 535–538.

Weiss, B., & Laties, V. G. (1962). Enhancement of human performance by caffeine and amphetamines. *Pharmacology Reviews, 14,* 1–36.

White, J. P. (1984, January). Dementia: New research promises hope. *Drug Topics, 51–54.*

Will, J. C., Abuzzahab, F. S., & Zimmerman, R. L. (1978). The effects of ACTH 4-10 versus placebo in the memory of symptomatic geriatric volunteers. *Psychopharmacology Bulletin, 14,* 25–27.

Willis, S. L., Blieszner, R., & Baltes, P. B. (1981).

Intellectual training research in aging: Modification of performance on the fluid ability of figural relations. *Journal of Educational Psychology, 73,* 41–50.

Wisniewski, H. M., & Iqbal, K. (1980). Aging of the brain and dementia. *Trends in Neurosciences, 3,* 226–228.

Wisniewski, K., Howe, J., Williams, D. G., & Wisniewski, H. M. (1978). Precocious aging and dementia in patients with Down's Syndrome. *Biological Psychiatry, 13,* 619–627.

Yesavage, J. A. (1984). Relaxation and memory training in 39 elderly patients. *American Journal of Psychiatry, 141,* 778–781.

Yesavage, J. A., & Karasu, T. B. (1982). Psychotherapy with elderly patients. *American Journal of Psychotherapy, 36,* 41–55.

Yesavage, J. A., Rose, T. L., & Bower, G. H. (1983). Interactive imagery and affective judgments improve face-name learning in the elderly. *Journal of Gerontology, 38,* 197–203.

Yesavage, J. A., Rose, T. L., & Spiegel, D. (1982). Relaxation, training and memory, improvement in elderly normals: Correlation of anxiety ratings and recall improvement. *Experimental Aging Research, 8,* 195–198.

Yesavage, J. A., Tinklenberg, J. R., Hollister, L. E., & Berger, P. A. (1979). Vasodilators in senile dementia. A review of the literature. *Archives of General Psychiatry, 36,* 220–223.

Yesavage, J. A., Tinklenberg, J. R., Hollister, L. E., & Berger, P. A. (1982). Effect of nafronyl on lactate and pyruvate in the cerebrospinal fluid of patients with senile dementia. *Journal of the American Geriatrics Society, 30,* 105–108.

Yesavage, J. A., Westphal, J., & Rush, L. (1981). Senile dementia: Combined pharmacologic and psychologic treatment. *Journal of American Geriatrics Society, 29,* 164–171.

Young, J., Hall, P., & Blakemore, C. (1974). Treatment of cerebral manifestations of arteriosclerosis with cyclandelate. *British Journal of Psychiatry, 124,* 177–180.

Zarit, S. H., Zarit, J. M., & Reever, K. E. (1982). Memory training for severe memory loss: Effect on senile dementia patients and their families. *Gerontologist, 22,* 373–377.

Zimmerman, E. G., Gorelick, D. A., & Colbern, D. L. (1980). Facilitation of passive avoidance behavior by posttrial administration of naloxone and ethanol in mice. *Society of Neurosciences Abstracts, 6,* 167.

section

V

SERVICE APPROACHES

chapter

17

Service Needs among Older Developmentally Disabled Persons

Matthew P. Janicki, James P. Otis, Paul S. Puccio, Judith H. Rettig, and John W. Jacobson

Older developmentally disabled persons are a heterogeneous population; they are as diverse a group as are non–developmentally disabled older persons. However, there are both similarities and dissimilarities in the nature of service needs of this population. One similarity is that both groups require more attention to health, social, psychological, and various support services; the differences lie in the structure and manner of how some of the services are delivered and the fact that some of the services may be needed earlier in terms of lifespan development. Living arrangements and housing adaptations will vary greatly depending upon individual physical and psychological needs. Day services range from structured full- or partial-day activity services to flexible socialization opportunities. Health services for older developmentally disabled persons include monitoring of health status and routine provision of health, nutrition, and dental services, as well as physical rehabilitative care. Support services include case management and economic assistance, supports to families, transportation, and mental health care. Such services need to be derived from both the generic and specialized services systems. As the older developmentally disabled population continues to grow, special consideration will have to be given to planning for services, to training and allocation of additional personnel, and to provision of adequate budgetary resources.

OLDER PERSONS REPRESENT an ever-growing segment of the population of developed nations (Acheson, 1982; Grundy, 1983; Ikegami, 1982; Siegel & Taeuber, 1982; Wasylenki, 1982). In the United States alone, it has been estimated that the elderly population has doubled since the beginning of the early 1900s and will triple within the next 30 years. As this population increases, and in particular that segment needing special care, the demands upon private and public resources will be enormous (Tobis, 1982). Furthermore, within the

The authors gratefully acknowledge the contribution of the many individuals who, in 1983, as members of the New York State Office of Mental Retardation and Developmental Disabilities Commissioner's Committee on Aging and Developmental Disabilities, spent many hours in meetings studying and discussing the various issues related to aging and developmental disabilities. Many of the ideas and recommendations in this chapter are the product of those discussions. The final product of the committee can be found in the Committee's Report (Office of Mental Retardation and Developmental Disabilities, 1983); copies can be obtained from NYS OMRDD, 44 Holland Avenue, Albany, New York 12229.

older population, persons with mental retardation or other developmental disabilities will continue to represent a significant portion of the demand upon public long-term care and community support systems.

Problems presented by older developmentally disabled persons will offer new challenges to government and service providers (Cotten, Sison, & Starr, 1981; DiGiovanni, 1978; Dybwad, 1962; Janicki & MacEachron, 1984; O'Connor, Justice, & Warren, 1970; Segal, 1977; Snyder & Woolner, 1974; Talkington & Chiovaro, 1969; Tymchuk, 1979; Wieck, 1979). Persons with severe disabling conditions historically have had a relatively short lifespan (Thomae & Fryers, 1982); however, with improved medical services and health care technologies, their life expectancy is lengthening, and an ever-growing developmentally disabled geriatric population will increasingly seek special services. These special services include supports to aging parents, housing, means to maintain existing skills and gain new ones, assistance with obtaining health care, attention to emotional needs, socialization opportunities, transportation, advocacy, and case management (Anglin, 1981; Dickerson, Hamilton, Huber, & Segal, 1979; DiGiovanni, 1978; Fancolly & Clute, 1975; Janicki & MacEachron, 1984; Panitch, 1983; Segal, 1977; Seltzer & Seltzer, in press; Thomae & Fryers, 1982). Most of these needs relate to older developmentally disabled persons already residing in community settings. However, although a large number of older developmentally disabled persons are still in public institutions (Bruininks et al., 1983), their continued stay in these settings may not be warranted (Ballinger, 1978; Janicki & MacEachron, 1984; O'Connor et al., 1970; Talkington & Chiovaro, 1969), adding to the demand for additional community residential care options and related services.

The service needs of older developmentally disabled persons do not appear to be different from those of other older persons; having had a lifelong disability or having been institutionalized for a good portion of one's life, however, may affect the manner in which such needs

should be addressed. The blending of geriatric care practices and the service needs of developmentally disabled persons raises a number of concerns; these include:

Does defining aging developmentally disabled persons aid in determining service needs?

Are service needs of the developmentally disabled population fundamentally different from those of the nondisabled elderly population?

Should services for older developmentally disabled persons be structured differently from other generic aging services?

AGING AND OLD AGE AMONG DEVELOPMENTALLY DISABLED PERSONS

Definitions of aging developmentally disabled persons found in the literature have been for the most part based upon clinical assumptions rather than empirical data (Dickerson et al., 1979; Segal, 1977; Seltzer, Seltzer, & Sherwood, 1982; Thomae & Fryers, 1982). Most of these definitions note that the beginning of aging for developmentally disabled persons occurs during the individual's mid to late 40s or early to mid 50s. Such definitions of entry into "aging" status usually reflect chronological age, clinical observations of changing functional status, and expectations for changes in normative age-related activities. However, several reports have noted such changes more explicitly, in particular, observing that certain mentally retarded persons do show the effects of age sooner. Bell and Zubek (1960) observed decline in intelligence test performance among retarded persons in their 50s. Janicki and Jacobson (1984) noted that age was positively related to diminished skill levels among some 10,000 older developmentally disabled individuals in New York; declines of motoric skills were initially noted among individuals in their mid 50s, while declines in other skill areas did not begin until the individuals were in their early 70s.

The mid 50s mark a period in lifespan development that typically involves the diminution of some physical reserves and the onset of a psychological adjustment to being "older." Consequently, in defining an aging or older developmentally disabled person, the period starting at about age 55 can be seen as a time when life activities are adjusted to reflect normative age patterns, interests, and physical capabilities. There can also be a differentiation between an individual who is "aging" (i.e., between the ages 55 and 75) and "aged" (i.e., over age 75). "Aging" in this sense reflects a period of life when an individual and his or her activities undergo changes that reflect differing orientations and roles as an adult. "Aged" can be characterized by significant changes in physical capacities.

Although these designations can be useful in anticipating changes due to aging in most retarded persons, in some instances certain aging patterns may be observed much earlier. For example, in certain syndromes associated with mental retardation (such as Down syndrome), aging-related changes can occur when such disabled individuals are in their 30s or 40s (Lott & Lai, 1982; Thase, 1982). In these instances, adjustments in program and the provision of geriatric services may have to occur sooner.

Determining whether a developmentally disabled person can be considered to be aging involves, in addition to the person's chronological age, the presence of three factors related to life change. These factors include: a) greater physical debility and lessening of physical reserves attributable to chronological age (rather than trauma or illness); b) diminishing levels of functional skills, particularly in areas of self-care, personal hygiene and toileting, and other basic activities of daily living (again attributable to chronological age rather than to trauma or illness); and c) for less mentally impaired individuals, the self-perception of aging and desire to seek age-appropriate or normative roles and activities.

Just as the character of services tends to change when a disabled individual passes from childhood to adolescence, and from adolescence to adulthood, the character of services should shift when selective aging processes become a factor in the definition of service needs. Concerns regarding the definition of

aging among developmentally disabled persons stem from the need to identify or redefine related service needs and to adjust or develop the appropriate services within the various continua of care. Given that the older developmentally disabled population will increase, and that concerns about how to address this population's needs have been an issue for some time, being able to define what is meant by an aging developmentally disabled person should aid in establishing a responsive public policy and in tailoring individual programs and services.

AGING AND SERVICES

Older developmentally disabled persons do not represent an homogeneous population; they are as diverse as are non–developmentally disabled older persons. Each individual presents service needs that are unique; these needs must be met on an individual basis. There are a number of things that should be considered when addressing these service needs. For example, program policies and practices of service providers need to take into account the physiological and psychological changes that an aging person undergoes. An older developmentally disabled person's habilitation or service plan should not be modified (as that person ages) solely because of that person's chronological age, but because of changes in the person's biological, behavioral, and psychological needs and status. Additionally, when changes are made, they must be tempered by sound clinical judgment.

Changes in routines or living circumstances may frequently be more of a disruption for an older person than for a younger person. Consequently, flexibility is crucial in the adjustment of life routines. Furthermore, changes in residential or activity programs due to aging must not lead to inactivity or signal potentially compound devalued status. When changes occur, they must reflect either alterations in the individual's physical status, or the addressing of age-appropriate and age-related needs. Consequently, professionals dealing with an older developmentally disabled person's aging status must consider:

To what extent diminished physical or functional ability forces change in a program

To what degree modification or departure from active programming is ascribed to chronic conditions rather than the aging process

Whether the program, rather than the individual, can be adapted to changes in the individual

How normative age-related activities can be configured into a meaningful service plan or schedule of activities

Whether the wishes and concerns of the individual have been considered

Services designed to meet the needs of older developmentally disabled persons need to reflect the decreased functional abilities and increased frailty of this population. Such services must be based upon assessments that have noted decline in the development and retention of skills, as well as diminished effectiveness of previously successful programming or services. Decreases in physical strength, stamina, mobility, and fine motor functioning, together with increased likelihood of chronic physical impairment and increased susceptibility to serious acute illness, also represent factors that must be considered when developing or revising an older developmentally disabled person's service plan.

In the broadest sense, the service needs of older developmentally disabled persons are similar to those of younger developmentally disabled persons and other older, but non-disabled persons. All need a balance of health, social, psychological, and support services. However, although the same types of services may be required by younger developmentally disabled persons, or by older non–developmentally disabled persons, it is the *structure and manner* of the services that may differ for older developmentally disabled individuals. Older developmentally disabled persons have special needs that, in many respects, may not have been adequately addressed by the generic services system. These include adequate and normative housing, day programs or socialization activities, clinical and health care services, and a range of social and psychological sup-

ports. Some needs of older developmentally disabled persons may be met by generic social services or aging programs; however, other needs may have to be met by developmental services providers.

Residential Care

The living arrangements and housing adaptations required by older developmentally disabled persons will vary greatly depending upon individual physical and psychological needs. Many older developmentally disabled persons live in institutional care settings (Ballinger, 1978; Bruininks et al., 1983; Cocks & Ng, 1983; DiGiovanni, 1978; Janicki & MacEachron, 1984; Tait, 1983). Many also reside in a variety of community care alternatives or at home (Bruininks, Hill, & Thorsheim, 1982; Janicki & MacEachron, 1984; Sutton, 1983). For those individuals residing in community settings, residential care planning and support services are most crucial.

Older developmentally disabled persons in the community face many problems (Dickerson et al., 1979; Fancolly & Clute, 1975; Segal, 1977; Seltzer et al., 1982; Willer & Intagliata, 1984). Particularly important problems are the loss of parents or a caregiver, difficulties stemming from poor health or diminished capacity to provide for self-care, and the threat of loss of their living situation and having to be institutionalized.

First among these problems is the one faced by disabled persons who live at home with elderly parents. In many instances, the illness or death of an elderly parent will precipitate a move into another setting, sometimes an institution. Instances have been noted where local authorities first discover a disabled older adult upon the hospitalization or death of his or her parent. Special services need to be available that provide for such situations. Several options can be utilized in these circumstances: a) anticipatory planning can permit either the quick provision of short-term inhome supports in the event of parental loss or a placement into a relative's home, foster home situation, or other family-type living situation; b) pre-crisis placement can occur (in this instance the parent knows that a suitable alternative has been arranged and that the older adult son or daughter is content with the new living arrangement); and c) in the event that an ailing parent can be aided, special inhome supports can be provided to assist with basic homemaking tasks and personal care for the parent as well as the developmentally disabled person (in this event, contingency placement planning should also take place).

In most instances, awareness of a potential problem situation will permit interventions that would assist aging parents and/or prepare transitional living arrangements to minimize "transfer trauma" for the developmentally disabled individual, thereby allaying deeply felt fears on the part of the parent and family. Unfortunately, many older parents may be unaware of such options; consequently, the ability to respond to such crises remains a critical problem for service providers.

Those individuals living alone, with friends, or with a spouse pose a second type of problem: declining health along with a decreasing ability to provide self-care. Many, like their nondisabled peers, are vulnerable; loss of function, increasing physical debilitation due to aging, and increased susceptibility to disease are major impediments to continued independent community living (Branch & Jette, 1982). Those individuals who reside in a variety of alternative care options (such as group homes and foster family care) are equally vulnerable due to aging; many are in jeopardy of losing their living situations because their increasing health care needs overwhelm the provider's ability to deal with the problem.

A third type of problem encountered by elderly disabled persons is the threat of institutionalization. At present, most group homes, board and care facilities, or foster family care settings are neither equipped nor staffed to provide services that would preclude the transfer of an increasingly impaired elderly developmentally disabled person to another setting. However, since the group home or the foster family care home is the developmentally disabled person's home, physical adaptations and/or some type of special interventions should be

attempted. To simply shift the individual to an institutional setting (whether a nursing or public retardation facility) is to deny the fact that, just as with any other elderly person, the developmentally disabled person has a right and an expectation to remain at home with his or her friends and possessions.

A potential solution to this problem—with application also to older developmentally disabled individuals living independently with kin, a spouse, or friends—is the use of inhome health or personal care services. These services could be drawn from either the generic health care or social services system, or from the specialized developmental disabilities system. Inhome interventions should be the first, although not the only, response to impairments resulting from aging (Anglin, 1981). Inhome supports, however, are not a long-term solution for the problems faced by most developmentally disabled persons living on their own if these individuals become increasingly more disabled. Research has shown that home-care services, as typically provided, are only applicable to a small group of older people—individuals who are mildly impaired and who have no family supports (Dunlop, 1980).

Other potential solutions, in instances where a group home's residents have progressively grown older and now experience a new set of needs, are the reconstitution (redefinition) of the home's care model (based upon a more intense level of care) or, when applicable, making the dwelling more physically accessible. A redefinition of the care model could include a change in the staffing configuration to include health care and other professionals, selective retraining of existing staff in geriatric care, or an enhancement of the staff complement to allow for more individualized care. Additionally, consideration should be given to whether the dwelling is barrier free and whether simple alterations or adaptations in the physical structure (e.g., ramping, door widening, installing safety rails in bathrooms) would increase the older disabled person's ability to remain in the home.

One difficulty with the use of group homes for older persons is fire safety. There is an increased danger among older persons in the event of fire because most older persons have a reduced tolerance for heat, smoke, or gases and an increased vulnerability to shock; additionally, most fires tend to occur at night when the lowest staff ratios are in effect (Butler, 1979–1980). In the United States, most states that have group homes (and, in particular, those homes funded under Title XIX, i.e., intermediate care facilities for mentally retarded persons [ICFs/MR] with 15-bed or less capacities) have standards concerned with residents' self-preservation capabilities. Self-preservation is the capability of an individual to exit from his or her residence in event of an emergency. An individual is considered to be capable of self-preservation if he or she is ambulatory and capable of following fire drill procedures (whether or not he or she comprehends the reason for such procedures). When serving those individuals who are not considered "self-preserving," group homes are required to meet the institutional building requirements of the National Fire Protection Association's Life Safety Code (National Fire Protection Association, 1981). The number of such homes meeting this restrictive aspect of the code is quite limited, and the conversion of existing homes to meet the code requirements is costly. Older developmentally disabled persons who suffer loss of mobility or mental alertness—and consequently may no longer be self-preserving—are faced with the prospect of having to be moved out of their home if the dwelling does not meet the more restrictive provisions of the code. Providers are frequently faced with the dilemma of either violating the person's right to remain in a home with friends, or permitting that person to remain in a situation where he or she may be exposed to an unacceptable degree of risk. Potential solutions to this problem may be the use of the National Bureau of Standard's Fire Safety Evaluation System (Groner, Levin, & Nelson, 1981; Nelson et al., 1983) that permits the use of compensatory mechanisms (e.g., increased staffing levels) as equivalencies to the code's more stringent requirements, or

physically sectioning the home so that a portion of the dwelling meets more restrictive code requirements.

It has been argued that older developmentally disabled persons who need more intensive health or personal care services should be transferred to a public retardation facility, a health-related or intermediate care facility, or a skilled nursing facility. Although this would appear to be an obvious solution, it does not take into consideration a number of factors: a) that the congregate facility may not have a developmental orientation and not be sensitive to all the needs of the developmentally disabled person, b) that such institutions may not be cost-effective (e.g., more services may be provided than are needed), c) that further deterioration may inadvertently result from being in an institution, and d) that the persons may be subject to transfer trauma (i.e., reactive problems caused by moving out of home and away from friends or family). Preclusion of institutional admissions is now common in the generic aging field (Dunlop, 1980; Seidl, Applebaum, Austin, & Mahoney, 1983). There is no reason why the situation should be handled differently for older developmentally disabled persons.

Another aspect related to this third problem of fear of institutionalization involves anticipatory planning of the need for potential living alternatives for older developmentally disabled persons. The residential care continuum of most developmental disabilities service systems includes a range of long-term and transitional residential options (Glenn, 1976; Janicki, Castellani, & Norris, 1983) that vary in size, intent, and restrictiveness. Private and public institutional options such as nursing facilities, developmental centers or state hospitals, and other structured long-term care facilities are considered the most restrictive settings. Least restrictive are supportive apartment programs or supports in private homes. In between are sheltered care options such as group homes (including the small ICFs/MR in the United States), board and care homes, foster family care homes, and the like. Anticipatory planning would involve the understanding of a geographic area's demographics and potential population shifts, the needs of various dependent populations, and the availability of inhome support services and residential programs both within the specialized developmental disabilities care system and the generic human services system of that area.

Day Services

Day services for adults can be defined as any focused and purposive activity of a full-day duration that involves work or habilitative tasks, or sociorecreational, avocational, and stimulatory activities. There are two major issues related to day services and older developmentally disabled adults. The first involves the concern that older developmentally disabled persons continue their involvement in those day activities or programs that are readily available to other adults—competitive or sheltered work, day activity of a variety of forms, or specialized habilitation services—and the form that those activities or programs take. The second concern is the determination of the point at which an older developmentally disabled person should begin transition from work to retirement activities.

For many older developmentally disabled persons, involvement in some form of day activity or work has been a long-term endeavor, particularly if those persons reside in the community. Many developmentally disabled persons with minimal functional impairments have been competitively employed or involved in a sheltered workshop for a good part of their lives. For persons recently deinstitutionalized, this involvement may have been of a shorter term; for severely disabled persons, the day program may have been more a combination of clinical services and habilitative activities. It is questionable whether developmentally disabled persons who never have been employed or enrolled in a sheltered work situation would need a job or work program (or should be planning for such) at an age when most of their peers are leaving the work force. However, involvement in meaningful and pur-posive activities has been shown among non-disabled persons to be associated with greater longevity.

Certainly a more critical issue is whether older developmentally disabled persons have ready access to programs or services that can act in lieu of lifelong participation in work or work activities. The critical means to ensure continuity in the day services continuum (i.e., from work to avocational or socialization activities) is the design of programs that maintain the "rhythm of the day." Such programs draw the older developmentally disabled person into situations where peer interaction, stimulation, leisure time activities, and some degree of challenge (albeit to a reduced degree) would be present. These programs are intended to enhance the meaningfulness of life and lead to growth even in the later years.

Given the physical and social attributes associated with aging, problems arise from the application of current models of "active treatment" for older developmentally disabled persons. "Active treatment," according to Gardner, Long, Nichols, and Iagulli (1980), is the regular participation, in accordance with an individualized service or program plan, in a program of activities that are designed to attain the optimum physical, intellectual, social, and vocational functioning of which a developmentally disabled person is capable. Normally, such treatment requires the development of an individual written plan of care that sets forth measurable goals and objectives. In many instances, program models may have to be readjusted to shift the emphasis of active treatment toward skill preservation. Furthermore, some extant day program standards in the United States (in accordance with federal guidelines) call for the provision of a minimum number of hours of active treatment. For day services for older developmentally disabled persons, these standards need to be flexible to permit active participation in regular adult programs by an older developmentally disabled person, but at a less intense level of involvement or duration. Additionally, given that a large proportion of older developmentally disabled persons are still engaged in some type of day activity or program—albeit to a lesser degree as age increases (Janicki & MacEachron, 1984)—attention to the programmatic character of the activities is essential.

Select programs and services for older persons are available under the aegis of the locality's area agency for aging; however, persons who are developmentally disabled do experience problems when they try to gain access to these programs and services (Segal, 1977). Because of barriers to service access, there is a need both to improve the accessibility of generic aging services for developmentally disabled persons and to develop and maintain specialized services that address the needs of older developmentally disabled persons. This composite approach may be the most realistic, because no idiosyncratic program model or set of services meets, or can meet, all the needs of older developmentally disabled persons, and because a dedicated services system tends to promote isolation from, rather than integration into, society.

Older persons have a right to continue to be educated, to enhance or reduce their involvement in work, retire, relax, volunteer their time, engage in religious activities, and participate in social and other recreational activities. Older developmentally disabled persons are entitled to the same array of services that is available to other older persons. In this regard, service providers must act both as supplier of the needed services and as advocate within the greater aging and social services systems.

Since many developmentally disabled persons have been stigmatized during their lives, agencies must be careful to provide services or to advocate in a manner that does not place older developmentally disabled individuals in a status of "double jeopardy" (Sweeney & Wilson, 1979); that is, being confronted both with having a developmental disability and being elderly. Providers of services need to be aware of those subtleties in presentation that, when awkwardly handled, provide for further stigmatization (Wolfensberger, Chapter 4, this volume). Such subtleties may include ap-

pearance and dress, or even the manner in which a service provider attempts to integrate its clients into a generic program.

Additionally, as increasingly greater numbers of older persons will be using generic community resources, every effort should be made to provide special training in gerontology and developmental disabilities for agency clientele, care providers, and generic services staff so as to successfully promote social integration.

Developmental disabilities service systems in many areas of North America are models of service coordination and the application of the day continuum of care. Questions can be raised whether service advocacy for older developmentally disabled persons ought not remain within the realm of these systems rather than be directed toward participation in the aging services system. As the demand within society grows for more services for elderly individuals because of a steadily growing older population, the competition for already oversubscribed aging services may preclude access to these services by a population that may be perceived to already have a support system. Developmental disabilities system administrators need to consider whether to use existing program models or to enter a phase of new program and service development. If nonvocational day services for older developmentally disabled persons will be patterned after those already in use in the aging system, then careful studies should be undertaken in order to identify and avoid the problems that may be inherent in these programs. Moving toward dedicated age-specified services for older developmentally disabled persons within the developmental services system may raise another potential problem—that of segregation of older persons in specialized eldercare programs (where age and developmental disability are the sole criteria for entry). There should be opportunities for older developmentally disabled persons to enter age-integrated (i.e., integenerational) programs, as well as age-segregated programs.

Day services for older developmentally disabled persons should range from structured full (or partial) day services to flexible socialization opportunities. Regardless of the strategies used to address day service needs, individualized service plans in day activity programs should include a focus on productive use of leisure time, independent self-care, and/or maintenance of existing skills. Such a focus would also aid in preparing or adapting older individuals for retirement. The character of the day services provided should reflect the needs of the individuals served. Those developmentally disabled persons more at risk of further loss of skills may need to be in programs that stress skill retention. Others, faced with loneliness or lack of challenge, may need to be involved in activities that focus on socialization and engagement. Geography will also dictate the availability and design of such programs and services; those that are readily available in urban areas may be unavailable in rural areas, and program development initiatives should take such variations into account. Finally, retirement, when applicable to individual needs, should always be seen as a legitimate option. However, it should be an option that emphasizes alternative activities that enhance the quality of the person's life and promote skill retention.

Health Services

The single most concrete and readily approachable service for older developmentally disabled persons is health care. Not only does health care cover the special medical needs of this population, but it touches upon a number of related facets, such as dental care, nutrition, and special clinical services. Due to the greater number of developmentally disabled persons now residing at home or in alternative community settings, availability of and access to adequate health care is of critical concern. The movement of the developmentally disabled population from institutions to the community has shifted the dependence of this population from the segregated medical services of institutions to the health care structures of communities (Garrard, 1982).

In the broadest sense, the health care needs of older developmentally disabled persons are similar to those of younger developmentally disabled persons as well as other older persons. As with any at-risk group, demands that the group will make upon the health care system will vary. It has been posited that mentally retarded and developmentally disabled people fall into three groups with regard to their health care needs and use of community health care resources (Garrard, 1982):

A low-consuming group whose requirements for health services are similar to those of people of the same age, sex, and economic status in the general population

An intermediate-consuming group whose increased morbidity necessitates frequent medical encounters and intensified care to maintain health

A high-consuming group whose increased utilization of health services is attributable to chronic medical disorders

Like other people, older developmentally disabled persons are a heterogeneous population; and, like other older persons, they represent an at-risk group that will progressively experience more illness and chronicity of certain conditions. They will also experience, with increasing age, significant increases in the rate of mobility and sensory impairments, medication use, and reliance on special diets, as well as diminished capacities in self-care skills (Janicki & MacEachron, 1984). Therefore, older developmentally disabled persons represent a population at greater risk for the need and use of certain health services. Indeed, it has been noted that among older developmentally disabled persons, the need for a range of health and clinical services (such as routine medical and dental care, nursing services, nutrition assistance, and audiological assessments) tends to increase with advancing age. In contrast, the need for specialized medical care and occupational and physical therapy are constant across all age groups among developmentally disabled persons, while needs for speech therapy decrease with advancing age (Jacobson & Janicki, 1985). Most older developmentally disabled people do appear to be receiving routine medical care and other health-related services. However, more audiological, nursing care, nutritional, physical rehabilitation, and specialized medical care services need to be made available to this group (Janicki & MacEachron, 1984).

Elderly persons in general suffer a variety of illnesses that reflect the wearing out of body organs. Most common are decompensations of the cardiovascular, pulmonary, and renal systems (Jernigan, 1981). Elderly persons are also more prone to infections, particularly pneumonias, and are less able to combat them. For the most part, treatment of disease in elderly individuals is not different in kind from the treatment of the same diseases in the general population (Coulton & Frost, 1982); however, recovery rates following treatment may vary because the capacity of older persons to quickly and/or fully recover may be diminished.

Older persons have more illnesses and hospitalizations than do their younger counterparts (Tobis, 1982). Elderly individuals are additionally subjected to a greater number of tests and procedures as part of their medical care. All these factors are critical to the design of appropriate palliative and ameliorative health care and maintenance services (as well as medical care advocacy and oversight) for older developmentally disabled persons.

Basic health care services must include careful monitoring of an older individual's physical health status, functioning, and interventions. The average number of general drugs taken per person progressively increases with age (Carruthers, 1983). With regard to the use of drugs, older developmentally disabled persons must be carefully observed for their response to medications, particularly for undesirable side effects or interactions, contraindications, cumulative toxic effects, and adverse reactions. Detection and management of disease states necessitates frequent observation of such physical factors as nutritional status, blood pressure, cough, bowel habits, masses, abnormal bleeding, and changes in musculoskeletal and motor function for early signs of disease (particularly for those older developmentally disabled individuals who cannot report symp-

toms). Careful periodic health screenings and assessments are very important.

The need for dental care remains high among developmentally disabled persons of all ages (Callahan, 1983). For older developmentally disabled persons, in particular, poor oral health places such persons at higher medical risk and diminishes the quality of their remaining life. The major emphasis of dentistry for developmentally disabled persons is the promotion of oral hygiene, elimination of pain, and restoration and maintenance of existing dentition, function, and aesthetics (Gotowka, Johnson, & Gotowka, 1982). Indeed, because poor oral hygiene is often found among developmentally disabled persons, they might need multiple prophylaxes and should receive dental care often (at least semiannually, but preferably more frequently). Even edentulous individuals require regular care of oral structures. Dental care in public retardation facilities, though not ample, is usually available. Dental care for developmentally disabled persons residing in the community is not always available; dental care providers are often unwilling to provide the services because of low reimbursement rates or because of inexperience with disabled persons (Gotowka et al., 1982). Special provisions often have to be made to ensure that such services will be available; until fee structures under such programs as Medicaid change, however, this will be an ongoing problem.

Because the onset of old age often brings with it major dietary changes, sound nutritional awareness or advice is very important for older persons (Munro, 1981). Many developmentally disabled individuals, whether they reside in an institutional or a community setting, are on special diets either because they must adjust, limit, or supplement their intake of certain foods or because their edentulous condition requires special preparation of their food (Huber, 1983). In congregate care situations, the control of diet is facilitated by the program. However, in community settings, where many older developmentally disabled persons live on their own or in small groups, they often do their own food preparation, cooking, or diet planning. In these instances, dietary planning or nutritional counseling should be a necessary component of the older individual's overall service plan.

When an older developmentally disabled person is terminally ill, very frail, or approaching death, special arrangements such as hospice care may appropriately supplement the more normal life-easing modalities. Care must also be taken to support the emotional needs of a terminally ill developmentally disabled person; the individual should be given the opportunity to plan for the disposition of valued possessions, means of notification of friends and relatives, and choice of memorial services as well as burial arrangements.

Health services are a crucial element in the provision of care to any older person. With regard to older developmentally disabled persons, special consideration needs to be given to problems they may have in gaining access to basic health and dental care, as well as obtaining the services of specialists such as nutritionists, physical therapists, ophthalmologists, and audiologists. Health and physical status assessments should note potential physical changes due to early biological aging as well as the lessening of physical capabilities. Health care service plans should be integrated into the individual's overall service plan so that other providers of care are aware of limitations and special considerations.

Support Services

A range of support services should be readily available to assist older developmentally disabled persons to carry out their normal activities (Seltzer & Seltzer, in press). Such services should include case management and economic assistance, supports to the families of older developmentally disabled persons, assistance with mobility and transportation, and counseling or mental health services.

Most persons who have been chronically impaired have been, in some form or another, dependent upon some public or charitable agency or organization for their room, board, and/or training/habilitative services for a good part of their lives. The responsibility for their financial support as well as for the management or coordination of the residential, vocational/habilitative, and clinical services they have received has been assumed by one or more of these agencies. In other instances, where impairments resulting from aging have driven an older developmentally disabled person (who at one point was fully independent) back into the care of human services agencies, such responsibility will have to be assumed. In either case, such responsibilities, which would include case management (or follow-along services), client advocacy, and assistance to gain access to entitlement programs, should be undertaken within the context of a well-planned and coordinated interagency framework.

The provision of such primary coordinative services is very important because it will ensure that the individual will have access to services he or she may require, most of which probably have to be obtained from a diverse group of agencies and even possibly from different care systems (e.g., public welfare for financial supports, aging office for nutritional assistance, housing authority for residential assistance). Case management should serve to ensure that there is coordination among the services provided within the dedicated system, whereas case advocacy should be undertaken in instances where the needed services lie outside the dedicated system. Case advocacy also has to contend with issues related to service quality and accessibility. For example, in areas related to health care (and this applies to all elderly persons), special concerns center on physical inaccessibility of some health care settings, as well as problems associated with the geographic maldistribution of medical and allied health care professionals.

In instances where an older developmentally disabled person resides with his or her family, and in particular in situations where the disabled individual's own parents or caregivers are elderly themselves, enhanced home-care and support services will often be necessary. These services, paired with the social services provided by the individual's day program, should serve to assist aging parents in coping with the care and supervision of their developmentally disabled daughter or son. Other social and psychological services should be provided. Such special social services should include emotional supports through counseling and permanency planning, as well as provision of home management assistance (Anglin, 1981; Seltzer & Seltzer, in press). Home management supports teach elderly parents how to deal with the behavioral changes that may accompany aging in their adult son or daughter. Furthermore, parental anxiety related to the burden of care can be reduced once the planning process for placement into a community residential option begins. Such planning allows the parents to know that the transition from home to another residential environment will be neither precipitous nor traumatic.

As an individual ages, getting around is not as easy as it once was. Special assistance to obtain walkers, canes, wheelchairs, or other adaptive or ambulation aids may be necessary for those older developmentally disabled individuals experiencing mobility impairments. Difficulties in getting around may not be limited to mobility impairments; such difficulties may also be related to a lack of local transportation resources. Such barriers to external mobility are all too common for older persons in general. Assistance with transportation, whether to the individual's day activities and to obtain medical or clinical services, or simply to enjoy a fuller, more active life, is a necessity. Provisions to enhance external mobility may include obtaining special senior citizen bus or subway passes (if available in the individual's locality) so that public transportation can be used, or arranging for special transport assistance from the individual's primary program agency or from the local social services agency.

The process of aging brings with it a number of attendant problems related to the mental well-being and quality of life for an older person. Some have estimated that as many as 20% of elderly persons in general are in need of mental health services (Romaniuk, McAuley, & Arling, 1983; Zarit, 1980). Older developmentally disabled persons, like other older persons, also have a need for mental health services. Although there is no indication that developmentally disabled persons will experience a higher rate of psychiatric impairment than their non–developmentally disabled peers, certain persons with mental retardation, particularly those with Down syndrome, appear prone at a younger age to exhibit senile dementia of the Alzheimer's type (Miniszek, 1983; Wisniewski, Howe, Williams, & Wisniewski, 1978). However, as Eisner (1983) has noted, although persons with Down syndrome experience accelerated neurological aging, they do not represent a group with a high incidence of behavioral disorders or overt senile dementia.

Notwithstanding the occurrence of major behavioral changes attributed to organic brain conditions, most older, less mentally impaired, developmentally disabled persons have the same needs for mental health services as do other older persons. Such services range from guidance for minor adjustment difficulties, and focused counseling and therapy addressing significant psychological issues (both related and unrelated to aging), to application and monitoring of psychoactive medications (Schmidt, 1976; Zarit, 1980). With more functionally impaired individuals or in instances where senile dementia is a factor, special attention should be given to such individuals because they may exhibit less control over their behavior due to impaired memory, decreased capacity to attend to their self-care needs, and changes in awareness of immediate surroundings. In these circumstances, greater supervision of older developmentally disabled individuals must be exercised; psychological services should be directed more toward assisting the staff, caregivers, or parents in behavior management techniques.

Supportive psychological services also need to be provided to address problems associated with death and dying. Many older developmentally disabled persons will be confronted with the death of a cherished spouse or friend, as well as having to come to terms with their own impending death (Matse, 1975). Supportive psychological services should provide older developmentally disabled persons with the means and supports that they need to deal with their feelings and concerns in this area. Similar services should be available to staff who work in living arrangements where many older persons reside.

The lack of available mental health professionals who are also trained in gerontology and the treatment of developmental disabilities is an obvious impediment to providing needed services. Mental health services for older developmentally disabled persons may have to be drawn from the dedicated developmental disabilities system, since it is generally acknowledged that the generic mental health system has not been able to meet the demand created by the existing older population (Wasylenki, 1982; Zarit, 1980).

COMMENTARY

The recognition that a new service population is being created as mentally retarded people grow older is not a new one. Early advocates (Dybwad, 1962), administrators (Bair & Leland, 1959), clinicians (Hillman & Libro, 1966), and researchers (Jervis, 1948) all recognized and commented on the fact that aging and increasing longevity were factors with which professionals in the field of developmental disabilities had to contend. It is now generally recognized that the combination of greater longevity among mentally retarded persons and the population trends of developed nations augurs for an ever greater number of mentally retarded and developmentally disabled older adults and a consequent growth in demand for services.

Like the general older population, older developmentally disabled persons are a heterogeneous population, and as with any other population, the adoption of a common definition of this group can be helpful. The use of a definition that combines the presence of mental retardation (and/or another developmental disability) with being in the latter period of one's life can lead to suppositions about needs for services. Much is known about the biological,

psychological, and social aspects of aging; this knowledge is further aided by a general understanding of the concomitant needs for services that emerge within the general older population. Preliminary studies now show that there are common service needs among the older developmentally disabled population. Additionally, there is empirical evidence showing that persons with mental retardation with certain conditions do age earlier. The recognition that some older developmentally disabled persons will begin to show signs of aging some 10 years earlier than the general population should affect the design of services.

The needs of older developmentally disabled persons, in many instances, reflect decreased functional abilities and increased physical frailty. All older persons experience decline in functional skills as well as lessening responsiveness to previously successful treatment regimens, although the magnitude and timing of these declines can vary widely. Physically, decreases in strength, stamina, mobility, and fine motor functioning, together with increased likelihood of chronic physical impairment and increased susceptibility to serious acute illness also represent growing limitations for older persons. These same behavioral and physical declines and limitations are found among older developmentally disabled persons, albeit sometimes at a younger age.

The service needs of older developmentally disabled persons are similar, in many respects, to those of other older persons. Older persons have many needs that are not specific to their age: a comfortable and secure living setting, stimulation and friendship, involvement in activities, good medical care, emotional supports, and a range of other physical and social elements that contribute to the maintenance of a good quality of life. For many older persons, services that address these needs include home health or alternative living arrangements, senior citizen and recreational activities, work, nutrition, nursing and health care, adult protective and social welfare services (such as case management, advocacy, economic assistance, and legal services), and a range of other supports (e.g., transportation).

However, the ways in which the needs of developmentally disabled persons who have been impaired most of their lives are defined or addressed might be quantitatively or qualitatively different from those of other older persons. For example, it has been noted that previously institutionalized older developmentally disabled persons adapt more easily to long-term care environments (such as skilled nursing facilities) than do other older persons (Cotten et al., 1981). Although the need for placement in such settings may be common to both populations, there is a qualitative difference in the expression of that need (e.g., the rationale for placement, or the disabled individual's response to placement); furthermore, this difference defines the manner of addressing that need. In general, service needs of older developmentally disabled persons do not fundamentally differ from those of other older persons although the character and expression of the needs may differ and in some situations the service response will also differ.

There are certain special needs that are particular to an older developmentally disabled population:

Many older developmentally disabled persons reside with their families and relatives; as the parents and guardians themselves age, their capacity to maintain the developmentally disabled member in the family home decreases.

Many older developmentally disabled persons live in a variety of community care settings; with increasing age, they develop chronic medical conditions or functional impairments that will require long-term supportive services.

Many older fragile, severely developmentally disabled persons remain in public facilities for mentally retarded residents, despite the deinstitutionalization efforts of the past decade, and now require increased medical and nursing services.

In many instances, the needs of older developmentally disabled persons can be addressed by the available services provided within a locality's social services or aging services network. However, in other instances, the generic services network may be insufficient to address special needs. In these instances, the developmental disabilities services agencies must develop and accommodate these special needs within their own structures. In many instances, developmental disabilities providers have to come to terms with the "greying" of their service population (Kauppi, 1983) and begin to structure services for older developmentally disabled persons that are consonant with their needs. Current concepts of habilitative and residential care for adults may not be fully consistent with the needs of the growing older developmentally disabled population. A balance of residential, habilitative, medical, social, and recreational, and supportive care services related to the needs of each older developmentally disabled individual appears most appropriate. Some of these services may come from within the dedicated developmental disabilities network; others may come from the generic services sector.

In summary, need and service issues surrounding older developmentally disabled persons will be affected by a number of considerations:

Older developmentally disabled persons represent a growing population.

Some older developmentally disabled persons show signs of aging earlier than the general population.

Older developmentally disabled persons generally have similar needs to those of other older persons.

Older developmentally disabled persons may experience difficulties in gaining access to needed services within the generic services network.

In general, the services most needed by older developmentally disabled persons include housing, including barrier-free accommodations, and assurances of inhome supports on an as-needed basis; health care services to meet medical, dental, and physical care needs; adequate diet and nutritional assistance; leisure time and recreational activities, exercise, and other social and physical activities for mental and physical health maintenance appropriate to disability and aging impairment levels; skill development and skill maintenance opportunities; peer socialization and friendships; and counseling and life planning. As this population grows larger, special consideration will have to be given to adequate planning for special services, training and allocation of personnel, and the dedication of sufficient budgetary resources.

REFERENCES

Acheson, E. D. (1982). The impending crisis of old age: A challenge to ingenuity. *Lancet, 2*, 592–594.

Anglin, B. (1981). *They never asked for help: A study of the needs of elderly retarded people in Metro Toronto*. Maple, Ontario: Belsten Publishing.

Bair, H. V., & Leland, H. (1959). Management of the geriatric mentally retarded patient. *Mental Hospitals, 10*(5), 9–12.

Ballinger, B. R. (1978). The elderly in a mental subnormality hospital: A comparison with the elderly psychiatric patient. *Social Psychiatry, 13*, 37–40.

Bell, A., & Zubek, J. P. (1960). The effect of age on the intellectual performance of mental defectives. *Journal of Gerontology, 15*, 285–295.

Branch, L. G., & Jette, A. M. (1982). A prospective study of long-term care institutionalization among the aged. *American Journal of Public Health, 72*, 1373–1379.

Bruininks, R. H., Hauber, F. A., Hill, B. K., Lakin, C., McGuire, S. P., Rotegard, L. L., Scheerenberger, R. C., & White, C. C. (1983). *1982 National census of residential facilities: Summary report (Brief #21)*. Minneapolis: University of Minnesota, Center for Residential and Community Services.

Bruininks, R. H., Hill, B. K., & Thorsheim, M. J. (1982). Deinstitutionalization and foster care for mentally retarded people. *Health and Social Work, 7*, 198–205.

Butler, R. N. (1979–1980). Public interest report No. 28: Fires in boarding homes for the elderly. *International Journal of Aging and Human Development, 10*, 401–404.

Callahan, W. P. (1983). Dental disease: A continuing education problem for the disabled individual. *Journal of Special Education, 17*, 355–359.

Carruthers, S. G. (1983). Clinical pharmacology of aging. In R. D. T. Cape, R. M. Coe, & I. Rossman (Eds.), *Fundamentals of geriatric medicine* (pp. 187–196). New York: Raven Press.

Cocks, E., & Ng, C. P. (1983). Characteristics of those persons with mental retardation registered with the Mental Retardation Division, Health Commission of Victoria, and some implications for future service development. *Australian and New Zealand Journal of Developmental Disabilities, 9*, 117–127.

Coe, R. M. (1983). Comprehensive care of the elderly. In R. D. T. Cape, R. M. Coe, & I. Rossman (Eds.), *Fundamentals of geriatric medicine* (pp. 3–7). New York: Raven Press.

Cotten, P. D., Sison, G. F. P., & Starr, S. (1981). Comparing elderly mentally retarded and non-mentally retarded individuals: Who are they? What are their needs? *The Gerontologist, 21*, 359–365.

Coulton, C., & Frost, A. K. (1982). Use of social and health services by the elderly. *Journal of Health and Social Behavior, 23*, 330–339.

Dickerson, M., Hamilton, J., Huber, R., & Segal, R.

(1979). The aged mentally retarded: The invisible client, a challenge to the community. In D. P. Sweeney & T. Y. Wilson (Eds.), *Double jeopardy: The plight of aging and aged developmentally disabled persons in Mid-America* (pp. 8–36). Ann Arbor: University of Michigan, Institute for the Study of Mental Retardation and Related Disabilities.

DiGiovanni, L. (1978). The elderly retarded: A little-known group. *The Gerontologist, 18*, 262–266.

Dunlop, B. D. (1980). Expanded home-based care for the impaired elderly: Solution or pipe dream. *American Journal of Public Health, 70*, 514–519.

Dybwad, G. (1962). Administrative and legislative problems in the care of the adult and aged mental retardate. *American Journal of Mental Deficiency, 66*, 716–722.

Eisner, D. (1983). Down's syndrome and aging: Is senile dementia inevitable? *Psychological Reports, 52*, 119–124.

Fancolly, J. K., & Clute, W. T. (1975, October). *The social environment of the aging mentally retarded: Implications for the aging process and service delivery*. Paper presented at the 28th annual meeting of the Gerontological Society of America, Louisville, KY.

Gardner, J. F., Long, L., Nichols, R., & Iagulli, D. M. (1980). *Program issues in developmental disabilities: A resource manual for surveyors and reviewers*. Baltimore: Paul H. Brookes Publishing Co.

Garrard, S. D. (1982). Health services for mentally retarded people in community residences: Problems and questions. *American Journal of Public Health, 72*, 1226–1228.

Glenn, L. (1976). The least restrictive alternative in residential care and the principle of normalization. In M. Kindred, J. Cohen, D. Penrod, & T. Shaffer (Eds.), *The mentally retarded citizen and the law* (pp. 499–514). New York: The Free Press.

Gotowka, T. D., Johnson, E. S., & Gotowka, C. J. (1982). Costs of providing dental services to adult mentally retarded: A preliminary report. *American Journal of Public Health, 72*, 1246–1250.

Groner, N. E., Levin, B. M., & Nelson, H. E. (1981). Measuring evacuation difficulty in board and care homes. *Fire Journal, 75*(5), 44–50.

Grundy, E. (1983). Demography and old age. *Journal of the American Geriatrics Society, 31*, 325–332.

Hillman, W. A., & Libro, A. C. (1966). Aging in retardation. *Journal of Psychiatric Nursing, 4*, 540–545.

Huber, A. M. (1983). Nutrition and mental retardation. In J. L. Matson & J. A. Mulick (Eds.), *Handbook of mental retardation* (pp. 271–287). New York: Pergamon Press.

Ikegami, N. (1982). Institutionalized and the non-institutionalized elderly. *Social Science and Medicine, 16*, 2001–2008.

Jacobson, J. W., & Janicki, M. P. (1985). Needs for

professional and generic services within a mental retardation services system. In J. A. Mulick & R. Antonak (Eds.), *Transitions in mental retardation (Vol. II)*. Norwood, NJ: Ablex Publishing Co.

Janicki, M. P., Castellani, P. J., & Norris, R. G. (1983). Organization and administration of service delivery systems. In J. L. Matson & J. A. Mulick (Eds.), *Handbook of mental retardation* (pp. 3–23). New York: Pergamon Press.

Janicki, M. P., & Jacobson, J. W. (1984, May). *Behavioral abilities of older mentally retarded persons*. Paper presented at the 108th annual convention of the American Association on Mental Deficiency, Minneapolis, MN.

Janicki, M. P., & MacEachron, A. E. (1984). Residential, health and social service needs of elderly developmentally disabled persons. *The Gerontologist, 84*, 128–137.

Jernigan, J. A. (1981). Loss of physical function and disability: Health problems of older people. *Journal of Rehabilitation, 47*(4), 34–37.

Jervis, G. A. (1948). Early senile dementia in mongoloid idiocy. *American Journal of Psychiatry, 105*, 102–106.

Kauppi, D. R. (1983, August). *An agency perspective on community services for aging retarded clients*. Paper presented at the 91st annual convention of the American Psychological Association, Anaheim, CA.

Lott, I. T., & Lai, F. (1982). Dementia in Down's syndrome: Observations from a neurology clinic. *Applied Research in Mental Retardation, 3*, 233–239.

Matse, J. (1975). Reactions to death in residential homes for the aged. *Journal of Death and Dying, 6*(1), 21–32.

Miniszek, N. A. (1983). Development of Alzheimer disease in Down syndrome individuals. *American Journal of Mental Deficiency, 87*, 377–385.

Munro, H. N. (1981). Nutrition and ageing. *British Medical Bulletin, 37*, 83–88.

National Fire Protection Association. (1981) *Life safety code*. Quincy, MA: Author.

Nelson, H. E., Levin, B. M., Shibe, A. J., Groner, N. E., Paulsen, R. L., Alvord, D. M., & Thorne, S. D. (1983). *A fire safety evaluation system for board and care homes*. Washington, DC: U.S. Department of Commerce, National Bureau of Standards.

O'Connor, G., Justice, R. S., & Warren, N. (1970). The aged mentally retarded: Institution or community care? *American Journal of Mental Deficiency, 75*, 354–360.

Office of Mental Retardation and Developmental Disabilities. (1983). *Report of the commissioner's committee on aging and developmental disabilities*. Albany, NY: Author.

Panitch, M. (1983). Mental retardation and aging. *Canada's Mental Health, 31*(3), 6–10.

Romaniuk, M., McAuley, W. J., & Arling, G. (1983). An examination of the prevalence of mental disorders among the elderly in the community. *Journal of Abnormal Psychology, 92*, 458–467.

Schmidt, L. (1976). Issues in counseling older people. *Educational Gerontologist, 1*, 187–192.

Segal, R. (1977). Trends in services for the aged mentally retarded. *Mental Retardation, 15*(2), 25–27.

Seidl, F. W., Applebaum, R., Austin, C., & Mahoney, K. (1983). *Delivering in-home services to the aged and disabled*. Lexington, MA: Lexington Books.

Seltzer, M. M., & Seltzer, G. B. (in press). The elderly mentally retarded: A group in need of service. *Journal of Gerontological Social Work*.

Seltzer, M. M., Seltzer, G. B., & Sherwood, C. C. (1982). Comparison of community adjustment of older vs. younger mentally retarded adults. *American Journal of Mental Deficiency, 87*, 9–13.

Siegel, J. S., & Taeuber, C. M. (1982). The 1980 census and the elderly: New data available to planners and practitioners. *The Gerontologist, 22*, 144–150.

Snyder, B., & Woolner, S. (1974). When the retarded grow old. *Canada's Mental Health, 22*(4), 12–13.

Sutton, M. S. (1983, August). *Treatment issues and the elderly institutionalized developmentally disabled individual*. Paper presented at the 91st annual convention of the American Psychological Association, Anaheim, CA.

Sweeney, D. P., & Wilson, T. Y. (1979). *Double jeopardy: The plight of aging and aged developmentally disabled persons in Mid-America*. Ann Arbor: University of Michigan, Institute for the Study of Mental Retardation and Related Disabilities.

Tait, D. (1983). Mortality and dementia among ageing defectives. *Journal of Mental Deficiency Research, 27*, 133–142.

Talkington, L. W., & Chiovaro, S. J. (1969). An approach to programming for aged MR. *Mental Retardation, 7*(1), 29–30.

Thase, M. E. (1982). Longevity and mortality in Down's syndrome. *Journal of Mental Deficiency Research, 26*, 177–192.

Thomae, I., & Fryers, T. (1982). *Aging and mental handicap*. Brussels, Belgium: International League of Societies for Persons with Mental Handicap.

Tobis, J. S. (1982). The hospitalized elderly. *Journal of the American Medical Association, 248*, 874.

Tymchuk, A. J. (1979). The mentally retarded in later life. In O. J. Kaplan (Ed.), *Psychopathology of aging* (pp. 197–209). New York: Academic Press.

Wasylenki, D. (1982). The psychogeriatric problem. *Canada's Mental Health, 30*(3), 16–19.

Wieck, C. (1979). Programs for older handicapped adults: The graying of services. *Education Unlimited, 1*(5), 21–25.

Willer, B., & Intagliata, J. (1984). *Promises and realities for mentally retarded citizens: Life in the community*. Baltimore: University Park Press.

Wisniewski, K., Howe, J., Williams, D. G., & Wisniewski, H. M. (1978). Precocious aging and dementia in patients with Down's syndrome. *Biological Psychiatry, 13*, 619–627.

Zarit, S. H. (1980). *Aging and mental disorders: Psychological approaches to assessment and treatment*. New York: The Free Press.

chapter

18

Day Activity and Vocational Program Services

Patricia M. Catapano, Joel M. Levy, and Philip H. Levy

Approaches to day program services for persons who are elderly and developmentally disabled are in the embryonic stages of development. The services that do exist share as their primary goals prevention of regression due to inactivity, minimization of mental and physical debilitation, enhancement of the quality of life for participants, and prolongation of community placement. Program location, agency size, and mean client age appear to have a minimal to moderate effect on service implementation when provided in conjunction with services to other developmentally disabled groups. Philosophical, staffing, and regulatory concerns raise questions regarding service approaches that must be carefully analyzed and resolved.

DURING THE PAST 2 decades, there has been a concerted movement away from institutionalization for persons with developmental disabilities toward the provision of care within the community. The principle of normalization (Wolfensberger, 1972) has provided guidance in this transition, and has stressed the importance of integration, use of generic services, and the attainment of a life-style that approximates the daily rhythms and activities of nondisabled persons. As a result, many developmentally disabled individuals now live in a variety of settings in the community and either receive habilitative and vocational training in a day program or sheltered workshop or are competitively employed.

While the growth of community services represents a significant advancement in care to developmentally disabled persons, it has been noted that the major focus of program development has been in the area of services to children and the young adult (DiGiovanni, 1978; Segal, 1977; Talkington & Chiovaro, 1969). Until recently, elderly disabled persons have received little attention from researchers, policymakers, and planners. This limited attention is due in part to the fact that, in the past, retarded persons had a shorter lifespan than did nonretarded persons; thus, few retarded individuals lived until they became elderly (Seltzer, Seltzer, & Sherwood, 1982).

Improved living conditions and advances in medical diagnosis and care have increased life expectancy for most persons in developed countries. The number of persons who are both developmentally disabled and aging is growing rapidly (Bell & Zubek, 1960; DiGiovanni, 1978; Herrara, 1984; Mueller & Porter, 1969; O'Connor, Justice, & Warren, 1970; Wieck, 1979) and represents a significant subgroup of the elderly population (Janicki & MacEachron, 1984). Research has consequently been con-

305

ducted to investigate the characteristics and service requirements of this emerging group (Branch & Jette, 1982; DiGiovanni, 1978; Janicki & Jacobson, 1984; Janicki & Mac-Eachron, 1984; Kalson, 1976; O'Connor et al., 1970; Segal, 1977; Seltzer et al., 1982; Snyder & Wollner, 1974; Sweeney & Wilson, 1979). In addition, service providers have begun to explore and implement alternative program models in an effort to more appropriately address the changing needs of older developmentally disabled individuals.

This chapter discusses the critical issues related to providing day program services to aging and elderly developmentally disabled persons and includes a brief review of research on service needs and program models for day services; an analysis of philosophical, staffing, and regulatory concerns that can impede implementation of these services; an examination of issues regarding integration with services for nondisabled elderly individuals; and a profile of three current day program services.

CHANGING NEEDS OF AGING DEVELOPMENTALLY DISABLED PERSONS

In order to discuss the critical issues related to providing day program services to aging developmentally disabled persons, the characteristics and changing needs of the group must be considered. To begin, how do these individuals compare with their nondisabled peers in terms of health and physical functioning? Researchers have found many similarities and dissimilarities between these two groups. Among nondevelopmentally disabled elderly persons, Butler and Lewis (1977) reported that four basic aspects of a person's life are affected by the aging process, including physical, intellectual, emotional, and social changes. There tends to be an increased incidence of disabilities as people age. Jernigan (1981) noted that limitations in activity due to chronic conditions affect approximately 45% of those in the general population over age 65, and increase to 65% after age 85. He listed the five most prevalent chronic conditions that affect

elderly individuals as being arthritis and rheumatism, heart disease, blindness or visual impairment, hypertension, and diabetes.

Greater debilitation with advancing age was also found with developmentally disabled persons. In a needs assessment of 7,823 developmentally disabled individuals age 53 or above, Janicki and MacEachron (1984) found that while this group experienced limitation due to the same chronic conditions noted by Jernigan (1981), the highest incidence of limitation was due to cardiovascular conditions, especially among individuals who reside in the community. Janicki and MacEachron's (1984) survey also revealed that, for elderly developmentally disabled persons, debilitation was highest in the areas of motor and self-care skills, with the degree of debilitation varying according to residential setting.

In a longitudinal study of visual, auditory, and grip strength changes in nondisabled, mentally retarded, and schizophrenic elderly persons, it was found that all three groups showed deterioration in these areas as they grew older (Callison et al., 1971). As compared to the other groups, the mentally retarded group showed the greatest changes in near vision and hearing, while their rate of deterioration was the lowest in grip strength.

Research has disproved the commonly accepted belief that intellectual functioning automatically declines with age. A longitudinal and cross-sectional study by Bell and Zubek (1960) of the intellectual functioning of groups of institutionalized retarded individuals at 20, 30, 40, and 50 mean years of age, with retesting 5 years later, revealed that all groups showed an increase in intelligence test scores over time. Although the oldest groups had the lowest scores, it is noteworthy that 64% of the 50–69 age group surpassed, and 16% equaled, their original score (Bell & Zubek, 1960). The authors proposed that improved intellectual functioning was positively correlated with expectations of improvement and the stimulatory quality of the program environment.

The concerns and changing needs of elderly developmentally disabled persons are common to the aging process. However, they may become accentuated or compounded when associated with a primary developmental disability. In planning day program services, providers can apply research findings in the development of their program design. Providers should be sensitive to recognizing physical, social, intellectual, and emotional changes in persons who are elderly and developmentally disabled. Activities must take into account increasing cardiovascular, musculoskeletal, and sensory impairments. Habilitative efforts should address reduction of impairments through health monitoring and preventive interventions; modification of program materials, methodologies, and environments to accommodate increasing sensory impairments (especially visual and auditory); and careful assessment and development of treatment plans designed to stem debilitation of motor and self-care skills. Most importantly, program planners should keep in mind the fact that, like the elderly population in general, elderly developmentally disabled persons are a heterogeneous group and thus require program services based on their individual needs. This suggests that more than one model and a wide array of activities will be necessary.

RESEARCH IN DAY PROGRAM MODELS

Day services for adults can be defined as any focused and purposive activity of a full-day duration that involves work or habilitative tasks, or sociorecreational, avocational, and stimulatory activities (Janicki, Otis, Puccio, Rettig, & Jacobson, Chapter 17, this volume). The primary difficulty experienced by those who develop day service programs for the elderly developmentally disabled population is the dearth of literature available on this subject.

A study in Montana by Talkington and Chiovaro (1969) involved 105 institutionalized developmentally disabled individuals whose ages ranged from 50 to 72 years, with a mean age of 58.7, and a core staff of six senior citizens from the community. The project was a four-phase sequential program through which the senior citizens, functioning as activity aides, worked with the targeted clients on a variety of ac-

tivities designed to counter regression. With each phase, the activities progressed from passive to more active and independent client involvement. In Phase I, activities were structured around passive functions (i.e., viewing magazines, refreshment parties, listening to music) and the purchase or distribution of new clothing and grooming articles. The activities in Phase II involved more active recreational projects (i.e., ballroom dancing, painting) and initiation of training in personal grooming, manners, and socialization skills. A formalized program of training for semi-independent living skills was begun in Phase III, utilizing a model apartment. An outgrowth of this training was the development of a sewing center wherein the older clients repaired the clothing of others who lived at the institution. During Phase IV, which focused on the development of responsibility, the elderly clients were trained to accompany and assist 20 younger blind, retarded residents in a talking book program. In addition, a new group of clients began the program during this phase and were assisted by members of the original group.

The most striking result of this project was the return of 25% of the older developmentally disabled participants to their home communities during the final phase of the program (Talkington & Chiovaro, 1969). Of the participants who remained at the institution, a significant and definite transition to assuming responsibility, independence, and new-found direction was noted. Forty individuals were paid small amounts and continued their work in the sewing center and talking book program. An additional project benefit was the employment and integration of senior citizens from the community who, as activity aides, also served as role models for their developmentally disabled peers.

Herrara (1984) reported on a Seniors Habilitation Program that was developed in 1976 to address the specialized service needs of aging and elderly developmentally disabled persons in the Canton, Ohio, area. The program, which served 51 elderly clients with a mean age of 49, concentrated on four service areas: reality orientation (to reinforce ability to distinguish time, place, persons, and things found in the environment), health and nutrition (to counter disease and functional decline), physical fitness (to enhance physical health, social integration, adaptation to sensory loss, and mental well-being), and activities of daily living (to increase functional skill levels, self-worth, and socialization). Herrara (1984) reports that since initiation of the Senior Habilitation Program, participants have gained a "sense of belonging" and appear more motivated, active, and physically fit.

In the late 1970s, Segal (1977) identified 10 programs throughout the United States with services for older developmentally disabled individuals. The services offered ranged from a specialized nursing and religious program, to recreational programs, to specialized employment opportunities. The diversity in the services reflects and reinforces the need for the availability of a wide array of program activities and alternatives.

PHILOSOPHICAL, STAFFING, AND REGULATORY CONCERNS

Philosophical Concerns

The philosophical concerns that are most frequently mentioned in discussions regarding day program services for older developmentally disabled individuals tend to be interrelated and include the issues of normalization, segregation, dual discrimination, retirement, and quality of life. The concept of normalization, referred to in the introduction, is used to argue both for and against the development of self-contained day program services for this population. On the one hand, opponents claim that normalization requires the aging developmentally disabled person's life-style to approximate that of the elderly population at large, utilizing generic services whenever possible. Given the negative attitudes, limited opportunities and segregation experienced by older persons in society, opponents believe that to approximate such conditions would only result in further diminution of the disabled person's social status and result in decreased quality of

care. Proponents, on the other hand, argue that it is more normalized for people to associate and spend time with their age peers, and that the later years in life typically signify a point of retirement from the active work force with greater time spent in social and leisure activities. They believe that it is possible to utilize some generic services to complement day program services that are age-appropriate, enhance the self-esteem and status of participants, and address the special service needs of older developmentally disabled participants.

The issue of normalization highlights many of the other concerns related to the provision of day program services. A very common and real concern centers on the knowledge that this population runs the risk of dual discrimination due to age and developmental disability. This concern is amplified when coupled with the issues of segregation and retirement, and raises a number of important questions:

Will programs designed to specifically serve an elderly developmentally disabled population result in their segregation from younger developmentally disabled and nondisabled persons?

Will enrollment in such a program be expected or required upon attainment of a given age, perhaps 65 years, regardless of the individual's desire and ability to continue in his or her current day activity?

In developing programs specific to this population, are planners unconsciously responding to and reinforcing the stereotypical attitude that elderly persons are no longer productive or active members of society?

How can planners ensure that retirement for persons with developmental disabilities will not result in regression to custodial care?

By removing someone from his or her daily routines and activities, do planners run the risk of diminishing that person's sense of self-worth and decreasing his or her life expectancy?

All of these questions present serious concerns to which there are no simple answers. However, in reflecting upon these questions, it is important to recognize that the alternative for those aging and developmentally disabled persons who no longer desire or are able to maintain their present day activity is in most cases placement in either an institution or a skilled nursing facility (SNF). While the level of care required may for some individuals necessitate this move, in most instances it would result in placement in an environment that is unnecessarily restrictive and where the deleterious effects inherent in some of the questions raised earlier are more likely to prove true.

Reality indicates that there are older developmentally disabled persons for whom the current day activity is no longer appropriate or feasible. The normalization principle and the movement toward deinstitutionalization support the provision of services in the community. It is clear that community-based day program services must be developed and/or modified in order to address the needs of the rapidly growing older developmentally disabled population. It is the task of researchers, planners, regulatory agencies, advocates, consumers, and providers of service to ensure that the questions and concerns raised receive adequate consideration in the development of these services. Evaluation of proposed programs in terms of both their efforts to maintain or improve a person's quality of life, and their ability to provide services that are tailored to the individual (rather than the reverse), will aid in development. Furthermore, programs will more successfully enhance the clients' self-esteem and acceptance in the community if they: 1) emphasize that aging is not an illness, but a natural life process; 2) utilize activities that highlight participants' strengths and abilities; 3) encourage individual choice and decision-making; and 4) promote intergenerational and community integration.

Staffing Concerns

There are two main areas of concern regarding staffing in relation to day program services for the older developmentally disabled person. These involve the appropriation of sufficient funding to support the clinical and direct care staff required to provide adequate levels of service, and a lack of knowledge and training for staff in gerontology and developmental disabilities. Both concerns can impede the implementation of services for this population.

The issue of staff training has been identified by some professionals, and training curricula are beginning to incorporate modules on aging and developmental disabilities. As this population is only now gaining broad recognition in the field, it will be a matter of time before staff training in this area becomes refined or widely implemented. For this reason, it is imperative that newly developed resources and information be widely disseminated. The issue of sufficient funding appropriations may be more difficult to resolve. In program models where clinical staff are currently funded, the prospects for program development are optimistic. However, these models may not be appropriate for all older developmentally disabled persons, especially those who are least disabled. Continuing efforts must be directed at increasing existing funding sources, identifying and tapping new funding sources, and exploring the possibility of conjoint funding from developmental disabilities and aging funding sources.

Regulatory Concerns

Many day program models have regulations that stipulate the provision of "active treatment" services, usually for a minimum number of hours per day. These services can be defined as objectively measurable interventions, based on client need assessment, that have as their goal the promotion of growth and improvements in health, skills, and habits required for independent living. While goal-directed services based on a thorough needs assessment are integral to the assurance of quality individualized programming, there needs to be greater flexibility in the interpretation of what constitutes "active treatment." For some older developmentally disabled persons, an intervention that is directed at minimizing debilitation due to injury or illness will be more critical to their well-being and quality of life than an objective that specifies measurable growth and improvement. Furthermore, given the decreasing abilities and decline of physical functions that typically accompany the aging process, it may be unrealistic to expect all older individuals to participate in a full day of activity. Regulations need to be sensitive to these issues and should allow for models that incorporate flexible program schedules (e.g., 3 days/week, half day), based on clients' abilities and needs, while still ensuring the provision of high quality care.

INTEGRATION WITH SERVICES FOR NONDISABLED ELDERLY PERSONS

The goal of coordinated and integrated services for disabled and nondisabled persons is fundamental to the normalization principle. However, service systems, as they are currently structured, often render this goal not feasible. Each system is invested in its own provision of services, and there is credence in the fact that each is endowed with its own area of expertise. While there are a number of generic programs for which elderly developmentally disabled persons would qualify, barriers can block access to these services. There needs to be an effort on the part of local developmental disabilities agencies and area agencies for the aging to stimulate sharing of resources, coordination of planning, and improved accessibility of generic services to aging developmentally disabled persons.

There are some projects that have integrated disabled and nondisabled elderly persons in the program design. As was mentioned previously, Talkington and Chiovaro (1969) used six senior citizens from the local community in their project. Segal (1977) identified a number of integrated programs in his listing of community services for older developmentally disabled persons. Kalson (1976) reported on a program of social integration between institutionalized elderly and mentally retarded persons. Utilizing a variety of recreational and social activities, the project goal was to develop a bond that would represent a sense of responsibility and mutual care. Project results showed an improvement in morale and social

interaction, as well as a favorable change in attitude toward mentally retarded persons. Although the disabled participants in this project were not elderly (their mean age was 30), there is no indication that such a project could not also be successful with older individuals who are developmentally disabled.

Developmental disabilities practitioners must be sensitive to the resistance shown by some senior citizens to associating with persons who are both elderly and developmentally disabled. Efforts at integration will require patience and perseverance. As the general public receives more exposure to and education regarding persons with developmental disabilities, and as more integrated program models are developed and maintained, increased program and service coordination should occur.

A PROFILE OF THREE DAY PROGRAM SERVICES

The following profile of three day program services is intended to provide more detailed information regarding focal areas for programming and methodologies utilized. These programs present different perspectives on providing day services to older developmentally disabled persons in terms of the location of their services (suburban, small city, and large urban environment), agency size, and mean age of individuals served. Comparisons are drawn to determine the effect of these variables on program implementation, as well as to identify common themes as they emerge.

The Young Adult Institute (YAI) Senior Groups[1]

YAI is a private, not-for-profit organization that was established in 1957. The agency operates 33 programs that are located throughout the New York City metropolitan area and in an adjacent county. Through its clinical, residential, recreation, and respite programs, YAI provides services to more than 1,000 developmentally disabled persons, ranging from 2

[1]Development of the Young Adult Institute Senior Groups was based upon the work of the YAI Task Force on Aging: Patricia Catapano, chairperson, Michael Blankshard, George Goodwin, Mary Ellen Kramer, Betty Lewis, and Jane Lockwood.

months to 72 years of age. The institute currently operates Senior Groups in its Brooklyn and Westchester Day Treatment Programs.

There are two Senior Groups that operate Monday through Friday, 6 hours per day, as part of the YAI Brooklyn Day Treatment Program—one made up of eight persons and the other of 10 persons. The groups were developed to provide program activities that would more appropriately meet the needs of the older developmentally disabled persons enrolled in the program. The clients range from 48 to 72 years of age, with a mean age of 58 years. In addition, many have medical impairments.

The goals of the Senior Groups are:

1. To provide aging and elderly developmentally disabled persons with day program activities that will foster and maintain their maximum possible state of mental and physical well-being and independence so as to enable them to remain in the community

2. To provide an alternative for developmentally disabled elderly persons who do not desire, or are unable, to participate in commonly available adult day program services, where the majority of clients served are between the ages of 25 and 45

3. To provide a program that incorporates a built-in peer group, and in which staff have received training regarding the special needs of this population

The Senior Groups are located on the ground floor of the program facility in two sunny rooms that open out onto a garden area. In an effort to make the rooms more relaxing and comfortable, some of the work tables and chairs have been replaced with living room furniture. Each group room is staffed with a habilitation specialist and a habilitation assistant. The habilitation assistant is a senior citizen, which helps to foster age recognition and role modeling in the group. Direct clinical services are offered in the following disciplines: medicine, nursing, social work, psychology, speech pathology, occupational therapy, physical therapy, and dance therapy. In addition, clinicians frequently co-lead activities with the Senior

Group habilitation specialist. (For example, the social worker runs a weekly group that focuses on the issues of death and dying, and the nurse runs a nutrition and health awareness group.)

Intergenerational and community integration are ensured through the program's location and structure of activities. The Senior Groups invite the younger members of the day program to join them during break time each day. The seniors assume responsibility for preparing the refreshments and ensuring that their guests enjoy the visit. In addition, members of the Senior Groups assist in teaching skills that they have mastered (e.g., cooking, needlepoint, gardening) to younger program clients. These activities prevent age segregation and enable the senior clients to assume roles that are age-appropriate and enhance their self-esteem. The Senior Groups also participate in area activities for the aging and utilize the community for various educational trips as much as possible. The Groups' members have made visits to the local Senior Citizens Center, and efforts are being directed at establishing a system whereby a disabled and a nondisabled senior are paired to assist each other in activities during these visits.

Focal areas for programming emphasize client interests, strengths, decision-making, and expression of mutual support through activities designed to improve and sustain life skills. Activity areas include:

Medical/Physical Awareness—training and counseling in changing physical abilities, nutrition, and sexuality as they relate to aging, physical fitness, movement, and cooking

Self-Care Skills—sustaining and improving hygiene, grooming, eating, and toileting skills

Independent Living Skills—training in mobility and safety, utilizing community resources, domestic skills, shopping skills, budgeting, and socialization

Reality Orientation—utilizing group discussion and planning for activities to orient participants to the day, month, time, environment, and recognition of others (includes oral history group)

Counseling—utilizing group discussions and activities to explore psychological and physical adjustment to decreasing abilities, assertiveness and self-determination, separation, death and dying, self-esteem, decision-making, group and community living, and fantasy validation

Leisure/Recreation Skills—training and exposure to a wide variety of leisure activities that promote social interaction and cooperation that can be carried over and performed independently during unstructured time

Horticulture—providing sensory stimulation, responsibility for a living thing, improving/maintaining fine and gross motor skills, increasing nutritional and environmental awareness, and increasing attention to tasks and helping to alleviate stress

Language/Communication—woven into all activities, designed for improving receptive and expressive language, improving memory and recall, increasing capacity to think and problem-solve, and encouraging expression of feelings and independent peer interactions

Fantasy Validation/Remotivation — through group discussion, teaching the concept of age and life cycle; providing affirmation of participants' thoughts/wishes, abilities and previous experiences; encouraging growth of self-esteem, mutual support, and motivation

Since initiation of the Senior Groups in 1983, program staff have noted significant benefits for the older developmentally disabled clients. Participation in the group has resulted in the development of a sense of group identity and pride. Clients show improvements in attention span, energy level, socialization, communication and self-expression, mutual support, self-esteem, decision-making, and awareness of physical and mental health. Group participants have come to view their age as a source of satisfaction and look toward the future with enthusiasm and a sense of hopefulness.

Columbia County Association for Retarded Citizens (ARC) Seniors Unit[2]

The Columbia County chapter of the New York State Association for Retarded Citizens is a private, not-for-profit organization that was established in 1974. The agency operates six programs throughout Columbia County, and serves approximately 450 developmentally disabled persons. Columbia County ARC currently operates a Seniors Unit in its Promenade Hill Day Treatment Program, which is located in Hudson, New York.

The Seniors Unit was established in 1981 to provide age-appropriate need-based services to developmentally disabled elderly individuals. The program functions as a self-contained unit within the ARC Promenade Hill Day Treatment Program, Monday through Friday, 6 hours a day. The unit serves 30 clients who range from 72 to 89 years of age, with the median client age being 82. All of the clients served in the Seniors Unit reside in family care homes and receive bus transportation to the programs. It should be noted that Columbia County has one of the highest rates of developmentally disabled persons in family care homes in the State of New York.

The goal of the Seniors Unit is to provide aging and elderly developmentally disabled persons with day program services that address their physical, emotional, intellectual, and social needs through activities and interventions that are stimulating and age-appropriate. These services are designed to minimize deterioration due to the aging process and to promote the development and maintenance of skills needed to remain in the community. The program aims to convey to clients recognition of the concept of age and of their station in the life cycle.

The Seniors Unit is located on the ground floor of the program facility in one large room and is staffed by three direct care workers and a supervisor. In addition, gross motor programming is provided daily by the therapeutic recreation specialist, physical therapy aide, and senior aide; speech and communication ser-

---

[2]Information presented on the Columbia County ARC Seniors Unit was provided through personal communication with Phyllis Howard and Lee J. Larson.

vices are provided by the speech pathologist three times per week; and the social service case manager conducts a weekly self-care activity. Nutrition services are provided by the registered nurse each day at mealtime.

Although the unit is self-contained, clients are not totally segregated. Interaction between Seniors Unit members and other day program clients occurs during lunchtime and through social gatherings and parties. The Seniors Unit is located across the hall from the ARC Early Intervention Center, thus affording opportunities for exposure to infants and young children. Community integration is achieved through a number of activities. Seniors Unit clients take community trips, and occasionally attend the Senior Citizens Center Nutrition Site. In addition, the unit has a display at the annual Columbia County Senior Citizens Fair.

Focal areas for programming emphasize client self-awareness, socialization, and the reduction of physical or mental deterioration. Activity areas include:

Nutrition and Health Awareness—activities that impart knowledge regarding health care maintenance and the nutritional values of different foods

Self-Care Skills—practice in and reinforcement of self-care skills such as eating, grooming, toileting, and hygiene

Training and Habilitation—activities designed to improve and maintain independent living skills with attention to minimizing deterioration due to the aging process (training areas can include mobility training, budgeting and money skills, domestic skills, and socialization)

Reality Orientation—involves review of everyday facts to counter memory loss, confusion, and time-place-person disorientation

Remotivation Therapy—structural activity designed to foster group interaction and appreciation of the world, and to stimulate the desire to function in society

Validation/Fantasy Therapy—discussions that tap long-term memory and nonjudgmentally acknowledge the feelings and inner reality of a confused/disoriented person

Despite the fact that older developmentally disabled persons are more prone to illness and injury, the Seniors Unit has the highest attendance levels in the Promenade Hill Day Treatment Program. Enrollment in the Seniors Unit has enabled many of the very elderly (over 80) developmentally disabled persons to maintain their placement in the community. The unit allows for greater flexibility in activities, and has resulted in clients' improved self-esteem, increased interest and motivation, and greater concern for others.

The East Range Developmental Achievement Center (ERDAC) Special Resource Unit[3]

ERDAC is a private, not-for-profit organization that was established in 1966. The center, located in Eveleth, Minnesota, operates two programs: an Adult Achievement Center that serves 95 individuals, and an Early Childhood Center that serves 30 infants and children. Furthermore, the center offers a Special Resource Unit for developmentally disabled individuals who are aging or elderly.

The Special Resource Unit, initiated in 1976 as a program component of ERDAC, was designed to give support and encouragement to aging program participants. There are 9–13 individuals in the unit who range in age from 49 to 72 years of age, with a mean age of 61 years. Staffing for the unit is provided by a resource unit teacher and a resource unit aide who are required to attend a training program in geriatrics at the St. Scholastica School in Deluth, Minnesota.

The primary goal of the Special Resource Unit is threefold:

1. To provide an alternative day program placement in the community, thus preventing the reinstitutionalization of elderly developmentally disabled persons

2. To enable aging individuals with de-

---

[3]Information presented on the East Range Developmental Achievement Center Special Resource Unit was based upon both personal communication with Howard Margulas and the Wieck (1979) article listed in the references.

velopmental disabilities to keep in contact with the world around them and to prevent their deterioration due to inactivity

3. To provide to these individuals the same services afforded to other developmentally disabled persons, although at a slightly reduced program pace

The unit staff avoid program designs for elderly individuals that center on art and craft activities, and instead endorse a program that provides meaningful experiences. Continued participation is encouraged for aging and developmentally disabled persons through a flexible schedule of reduced program time.

The Resource Unit is located on the third floor of the center and occupies two bright rooms and a large area for independent living skills. The building is equipped with an elevator that facilitates participants' access to the unit. In addition, the Resource Unit utilizes a greenhouse located on the fourth floor for program activities.

Community integration and acceptance of the unit are well established. Relationships are maintained with all local agencies that are affiliated with care for elderly persons. Resource Unit participants are all members of the local senior citizens club and two club members serve as program volunteers to work with their developmentally disabled peers in the greenhouse. The program utilizes many community activities and trips to provide stimulation and encourage the development of new interests.

Focal areas for programming emphasize client motivation, the development of mutual support, exposure to new experiences, and improvement in skill levels. Activity areas include:

Independent Living Skills—that focus on grooming, cooking, budgeting, and self-help

Physical Activities—to promote exercise, physical fitness, and body awareness

Reality Orientation—exercises that concentrate on orientation to the here and now (i.e., time, date, weather, location)

Manual Skills—to develop fine and gross motor coordination, perceptual skills, and creative expression

Academics—activities designed to maintain skills in academic areas (e.g., reading, writing, social studies, math)

Work Activity—to provide compensation to participants for work performed in plant and greenhouse care, provision of coffee during breaks, and maintenance of the third floor of the facility (enables individuals to maintain and practice their work skills)

Health care needs are monitored once per week by a registered nurse who reviews medication administration and identifies any conditions that may limit activities. Additional clinical consultant services are provided in the areas of psychology, speech pathology, and occupational therapy. Leisure activities are engaged in for a maximum of 30 minutes each day and are not given high priority in the Resource Unit. Those activities that can be carried over and practiced independently are emphasized.

Implementation of the Special Resource Unit for aging developmentally disabled persons has proved highly successful. Wieck (1979) reports, ''intellectual progress stimulated by discovery, exposure to new experiences, and revitalized confidence in performing routine activities such as shopping and dining,'' for the elderly developmentally disabled participants.

COMPARISON OF APPROACHES

Upon review, the three day program services presented are more similar than dissimilar, despite the variations in program location, agency size, and mean client age. Where variations in program implementation occur as a result of these factors, the difference is more one of degree than design. The location or environment of a program affects implementation in two areas. In more populated and urban locations, there is a greater likelihood that qualified personnel can be recruited. This holds true with all staff positions, but most particularly for clinical personnel. The second area in which program location affects implementation is in community activities. Although all three programs utilize trips in the community as part of their program design, those services located in a large, urban environment have a broader range of community activities within close proximity to their facility from which to choose. In addition, these activities tend to be more accessible in largely populated areas because of the greater availability of transportation.

The size of the agencies that operate the profiled day program services for aging developmentally disabled persons varies greatly. In terms of number of clients served, a small (East Range Developmental Achievement Center–125), a medium (Columbia County ARC–450), and a large (Young Adult Institute–1,000) agency are represented. This variable appears to have minimal effect on implementation of services, partly because all three programs are either part of or located in a facility with other programs, thus enabling them to share resources. In general, larger agencies have a greater pool of available resources and can provide more administrative support services (i.e., personnel, education and training, fiscal, public information/community education, program development, and social services).

The effect of mean client age upon program implementation is again one of degree. In programs where the population can be characterized as primarily older (i.e., above age 75), there is a greater concentration on skill retention, socialization and leisure activities, and interventions designed to prevent or minimize mental confusion, disorientation, and increasing physical disability. Mean client age also appears to be related to residential setting. In the ERDAC and YAI programs (mean client age of 61 and 58 years, respectively), individuals reside predominantly in community residences. However, in the Columbia County ARC program (median client age of 81 years), 100% of the individuals reside in family care homes. This difference may be a function of both client age (residential facilities might not feel adequately equipped to serve such an elderly individual) and program location (historically, Columbia County farm families have taken mentally retarded adults into their homes).

A number of common themes emerged upon review of the ERDAC, Columbia County ARC, and YAI programs that may serve to guide other providers in the development of day services for this group. Each program recognized the unmet needs of elderly developmentally disabled persons enrolled in their adult program, and developed services that are more consonant with the goals and requirements of an aging population. The largest and most common problem encountered in the development of their programs was the dearth of available literature, program models, and curriculum materials regarding day services for this group. As a result, these agencies utilized what little information they could find, extrapolated ideas from literature and program models in gerontology, and relied on common sense, instinct, and trial and error in the initial design of their services. Interestingly, all three agencies arrived at the following similar conclusions:

1. The primary goals of day program services for aging developmentally disabled persons are to prevent regression due to inactivity, to minimize mental and physical debilitation due to the aging process, to enhance the quality of life for participants, and to assist these individuals in developing and sustaining the skills required for continued community placement.

2. There needs to be a wide array of activities offered that reflect the needs and interests of the individuals served and that highlight their strengths and abilities.

3. The program should strive to prevent segregation through the promotion of intergenerational and community integration.

4. For individuals who attend the program, there needs to be a greater opportunity for client choice and decision-making, and the development of communication and socialization skills, as well as the fostering of mutual support.

5. Staff require training and education regarding gerontology and developmental disabilities in order to meet the special needs of this population; curricula must be developed in this area.

In conclusion, the development of day program services for elderly developmentally disabled persons is still in the embryonic stage. A much broader array of service approaches needs to be created, especially for those individuals who are unable to travel to a day program due to medical restrictions. Existing programs provide models and points of departure from which new approaches can be devised and implemented. Ongoing discussion and careful analysis of the philosophical, staffing, and regulatory concerns discussed previously are essential. Accessibility to and integration with the ge-

neric service system must be actively pursued. And, most importantly, the dissemination of newly developed resources, strategies, and information is imperative. The number of persons who are both elderly and developmentally disabled will continue to grow at a rapid pace; professionals face the challenge and responsibility to anticipate and prepare for the service needs of this emerging population with sensitivity, creativity, and respect for the individuality, independence, and dignity of older developmentally disabled persons.

REFERENCES

Bell, A., & Zubek, J. P. (1960). The effect of age on the intellectual performance of mental defectives. *Journal of Gerontology, 15,* 285–295.

Branch, L. G., & Jette, A. M. (1982). A prospective study of long-term care institutionalization among the aged. *American Journal of Public Health, 72,* 1373–1379.

Butler, R. N., & Lewis, M. I. (1977). *Aging and mental health.* St. Louis: C. V. Mosby Co.

Callison, D. A., Armstrong, H. F., Elam, L., Cannon, R. L., Paisley, C. B., & Himwich, H. E. (1971). The effects of aging on schizophrenic and mentally defective patients: Visual, auditory, and grip strength measurements. *Journal of Gerontology, 26,* 137–145.

DiGiovanni, L. (1978). The elderly retarded: A little-known group. *The Gerontologist, 18,* 262–266.

Herrara, P. (1984). Program for aging persons with developmental disabilities is a success in Ohio. *Links, 14*(2), 21.

Janicki, M. P., & Jacobson, J. W. (1984, May). *Behavioral abilities of older mentally retarded persons.* Paper presented at the 108th annual convention of the American Association on Mental Deficiency, Minneapolis, MN.

Janicki, M. P., & MacEachron, A. E. (1984). Residential, health and social service needs of elderly developmentally disabled persons. *The Gerontologist, 24,* 128–137.

Jernigan, J. A. (1981). Loss of physical function and disability: Health problems of older people. *Journal of Rehabilitation, 47*(4), 34–37.

Kalson, L. (1976). M*A*S*H*: A program of social

interaction between institutionalized aged and adult mentally retarded persons. *The Gerontologist, 16*(4), 340–348.

Mueller, B.J., & Porter, R. (1969). Placement of adult retardates from state institutions in community care facilities. *Community Mental Health Journal, 5,* 289–294.

O'Connor, G., Justice, R. S., & Warren, N. (1970). The aged mentally retarded: Institution or community care? *American Journal of Mental Deficiency, 75,* 354–360.

Segal, R. (1977). Trends in services for the aged mentally retarded. *Mental Retardation, 15*(2), 25–27.

Seltzer, M. M., Seltzer, G. B., & Sherwood, C. C. (1982). Comparison of community adjustment of older vs. younger mentally retarded adults. *American Journal of Mental Deficiency, 87,* 9–13.

Snyder, B., & Wollner, S. (1974). When the retarded grow old. *Canada's Mental Health, 22*(4), 12–13.

Sweeney, D. P., & Wilson, T. Y. (1979). *Double jeopardy: The plight of aging and aged developmentally disabled persons in Mid-America.* Ann Arbor: University of Michigan, Institute for the Study of Mental Retardation and Related Disabilities.

Talkington, L. W., & Chiovaro, S. J. (1969). An approach to programming for aged MR. *Mental Retardation, 7*(1), 29–30.

Wieck, C. (1979). Programs for older handicapped adults: The graying of services. *Education Unlimited, 1*(5), 21–25.

Wolfensberger, W. (1972). *The principle of normalization in human services.* Toronto: National Institute on Mental Retardation.

chapter

19

Health Care
and Inhome Environments

Mary Joan Delehanty

Routine health care should be the norm for each individual. For developmentally disabled persons, this has always been a problem. Most developmentally disabled persons have rarely been able to develop strategies for good health maintenance and routine health care. Such strategies should include sound nutrition, structured exercise, and planned lifelong activity programs. Aging has generally less of an impact upon individuals in good health and who maintain sound physical fitness. Many developmentally disabled adults are in poor general physical condition not usually due to the nature of their handicap but to their lifestyle. This chapter reviews the conditions for sound preventive and ameliorative health care planning, and proposes some means for workers to help older developmentally disabled persons residing in community settings cope with aging and maintain optimal physical functioning.

TRADITIONALLY, THE HEALTH CARE system has been geared to individuals who are ill and require episodic and curative care. In the last several decades, attention has been focused on the concept of health as a state of well-being permitting optimum function in everyday life. This concept stresses that health is more than the absence of disease. Maintenance of a good state of health is seen as a means of preventing disease and disorder and most recently has been regarded as a way to defer the effects of aging.

Strategies chosen to maintain a healthy state vary by individual and environment. For the average adult, they may include routine physical examinations, preventive dental care, and other health screening activities. Other more self-directed activities include programs of sound nutrition, structured exercise, and planned lifelong activity programs.

The developmentally disabled adult has rarely been able to develop a strategy for good health. Care in childhood usually followed a medical model with frequent contact with specialists. Upon reaching adulthood, this high-intensity care often vanishes and is replaced by the health care pattern of the family or by the regulations of a residential placement. Individuals with a language deficit may not be able to report symptoms or reactions that are the basis of a good physical examination for adults. They may not report minor health problems to their caregivers, and the discovery of problems is thus deferred until the problem becomes a major one easily observed by others. Developmentally disabled adults may have received little in the way of health education or training and may not see their state of health as their own responsibility. Factors of daily living, such as nutrition, activity, and planned exercise, are often under the control of caregivers rather than of the individual involved. Exercise and activity, especially, may not have made the transition from childhood to adult programs and even if present may not be age appropriate.

The person in good physical condition is often better able to cope with the demands of daily life. Such persons can be more efficient and more effective in conducting the tasks required of them each day. Thus, the healthy person may sustain an illness or an injury but his or her recovery is faster than that of a peer in poorer condition at the onset of the problem. While some popular authorities claim that activity can defer biological aging, others take a less direct view and suggest that the person who is active tends to remain active, enabling fuller participation in work, community activities, and recreational pursuits for a longer time than society usually expects. Physical ability to cope with life seems to facilitate other coping mechanisms, such as those involving cognitive and emotional spheres. A much more normal breadth of experience is available to the active individual.

The following sections discuss the impact of aging on the systems related to normal bodily function.

IMPACT OF AGING
ON THE MOTOR SYSTEM

Aging is referred to as a developmental process and is often compared with infancy and childhood. In contrast to the wealth of knowledge collected and recorded about the normal child, little is known about the normal phases of aging, especially as aging relates to motor behavior. Information is gleaned from the abnormal elderly individual, or the person who is hospitalized, acutely ill, or massively nonfunctional. As the percentage of older persons in society increases, it is becoming evident that the timetable of aging events is largely unknown and that the extraordinary range of individual variation far exceeds that of infancy and childhood. Categories of senior citizens are being established for descriptive purposes,

such as the young old, the frail old, the very old, and the well old. If the knowledge of normal development is to be used to aid in programming for the developmentally disabled elder (as for the developmentally disabled child), it will be important to understand these categories and apply this information appropriately to the chronically disabled population.

Within the motor system, tissue changes occur in older persons, ranging from changes in the composition of cells to the structure and form of bones and joints (see Rudelli, Chapter 14, this volume; Furukawa & Shomaker, 1982; Kart, Metress, & Metress, 1978). These changes affect the way a person performs activities, especially in terms of speed and energy costs; rarely, if ever, are they a valid reason for cessation of an activity. Tissue changes are not directly correlated with chronological age, and the appearance of these biological changes varies as widely as does their impact on function. This timing is felt to be dependent upon genetic endowment, the amount of stress acting upon an individual, the previous (or lifelong) level of physical and mental conditioning, and other factors less easily identified.

Changes occurring in the cardiovascular, nervous, and skeletal systems are responsible for decreased strength and flexibility occurring in most aging persons. These cause the posture and gait changes associated with old age (Lewis, 1984b). Reaction time, an important factor in motor learning, lengthens as the individual ages, and motor responses are slower. This slower reaction increases the difficulty of and time for learning new motor activities. There is no evidence that new tasks cannot be learned, but the pattern of learning may differ from that established earlier in life. Reduced strength requires more effort to perform the same task; the older person works harder than he or she used to even at recreational tasks.

These changes associated with aging do not constitute illness or disability, and aging alone should never be accepted as a reason for the loss of function. Changes in function do occur with older persons and it is sometimes hard to eliminate the negative connotations of the change. Decreases in strength and endurance affect mobility, a critical component of personal independence. The inability to climb stairs may mandate sweeping changes in an individual's living situation, but should not be a reason for placement in a custodial situation.

Although not directly the cause of disability, some changes of aging may make a person more susceptible to accidental injury. Stiff knees may cause a shuffling gait, which makes one vulnerable to tripping on rough ground. The resulting fall may fracture weak or osteoporotic bone.

The level of physical well-being enjoyed by an adult is an important factor in determining when the biological changes of aging will have functional impact. This is particularly evident when an injury occurs since the necessary immobilization or bed rest will cause deconditioning in any age group. After a fracture, for example, the speed and outcome of recovery will be related to the level of physical conditioning present at the time of injury and to the rate of loss of conditioning during treatment. Conditioning lost in the recent past may be regained (with hard work) but a lifetime pattern of low physical activity and poor condition may have a devastating effect upon rehabilitation.

The presence of a physical handicap or chronic health problem does not necessarily mean that a person is in poor physical condition or is "unhealthy." Wheelchair athletes certainly show excellent strength, endurance, and speed of movement. As many as 75% of United States citizens over 65 years of age report having chronic health problems, but the majority of them function at a satisfactory level of physical well-being in their communities (Lewis, 1984a).

IMPACT OF AGING ON DEVELOPMENTALLY DISABLED PERSONS

Aging in the developmentally disabled population is even less well documented than in the general population. Only recently have developmentally disabled persons begun to reach middle age as lifelong community residents.

Most of the data on older developmentally disabled groups have been gathered from populations living in institutions or released from them to community residences. Little longitudinal data are available on persons who have always been in the mainstream. It is difficult to separate the results of long-term institutionalization from those of aging, since the negative impacts are similar. For example, the posture and gait of elderly persons are very similar to so-called institutional postures. At this time, developmentally disabled elders can be assumed to be more like than unlike age cohorts as they approach the later decades.

Some syndromes associated with developmental disabilities, most notably Down syndrome, have premature aging as one of the symptoms, and persons with this condition show tissue changes at an early chronological age. Changes in the neuromuscular system, such as decreased muscle mass, poor posture, and shuffling gait, may occur quite early. The resulting decrease in strength and endurance may prematurely limit the distance or terrain covered with comfort. Leisure activities and community interactions are decreased, further restricting environmental stimulation.

The abnormal muscle tone often seen in developmentally disabled individuals results in stress on the originally normal joints involved. The weight-bearing joints of the lower extremities, especially, may be affected, but the arms and trunk may show stress-related problems in persons with abnormal movement patterns in these areas. This stress may make the individual prone to early aging of those specific joints deformed by poor muscle activity. The pain of arthritis in a long-abused joint may cause a 40-year-old man to "suddenly" refuse to walk. As stated earlier, the energy cost of an activity increases with age, and many developmentally disabled persons have functioned all their lives at higher than usual energy costs. Spastic gaits, for example, may be very functional but are usually inefficient and stressful. The poor gait pattern may, with age, become too difficult to be practical. Unfortunately, this type of slowly increasing stress may be difficult for the individual to verbalize and may lead to another instance of "sudden" cessation of an important functional activity.

Long-standing deficits in motor planning, coordination, and problem-solving ability may directly affect the coping behaviors available to deal with common problems of the aging. The disabled person may find it difficult to express functional problems, resulting in a high rate of crisis intervention instead of orderly programming for management. Vision and hearing problems may be unreported and sensory input may be reduced or badly warped. Rehabilitation activities may require physical coordination and motor planning at a level not previously present in the disabled person.

Many developmentally disabled adults are in poor general physical health because of their life-style rather than their specific handicaps. They may, therefore, show functional impairment very quickly when age-related changes begin. Few have been involved with adult physical activities, especially those fostering endurance. The resulting lack of strength may make crutch-walking after a fracture difficult or even impossible. Such lifelong patterns of reduced physical activity may predispose the disabled person to premature separation from community interaction by reducing mobility and physical independence.

On a more positive note, developmentally disabled individuals do not suffer many of the losses associated with aging that may be emotionally devastating to average persons. The depression associated with changes in living situation and the loss of personal autonomy are felt to be the greatest impediments to function for many persons in the later decades. The developmentally disabled adult is often in an adapted living situation, has long been connected with a support system in the community, and is not faced with the financial and psychosocial crises of other older people.

INTERVENTION FOR HABILITATION

Persons working with programs for the developmentally disabled adolescent and young adult need to become advocates for general conditioning programs. Activity plans need to be evaluated for their relevance to function in adulthood. The focus on competition and the high intensity but low duration games of childhood are inappropriate. As in all conditioning programs, the ability and interests of the person involved need to be considered. For consistency, the logistics of the community are a vital part of planning.

A swimming pool may be an excellent resource but it must be accessible, transportation must be regularly available, and necessary personal assistance must be at hand before a pool program becomes part of a health maintenance program. Both dollars and people need to be organized if activities are to be conducted the two or three times per week year round that fitness experts report to be adequate for maintenance.

An adult need not learn to swim; pools have many other uses. Water offers an excellent setting for jogging or calisthenics. There is no danger of falling, and even those who have discomfort or instability in standing can often participate with the group in the water.

Aerobic exercise does not have to involve running or jumping; activities in chairs or on mats can effectively raise the heart rate and benefit the cardiovascular system when performed at sufficient intensity and duration. Walking without a program-directed goal may be difficult for a person to continue, but activities such as flower collecting or bird watching incorporate the same motor activity and are more likely to be sustained. Walking in a shopping center has the same conditioning benefit as walking out of doors. Keeping records of distances covered or repetitions performed may be a source of continuing motivation and may be combined with a reward system.

Physical and occupational therapists are interested in motor activity but usually do not have training or experience in group activities or in activities for general conditioning. Because they may be helpful in assessing and communicating individual motor capabilities and precautions, therapists involved in leading activity or fitness programs may be valuable resources for ideas.

Senior citizen programs available in the community are in many instances appropriate and oftentimes accessible. Senior citizen participants can be helpful as "buddies" to disabled individuals and may provide some of the manpower that is vital to consistent programming.

Health screening programs are widely available, and, with some preparation by the caregiver, most disabled adults can fully participate. Vision, hearing, blood pressure, and other screening procedures may be the best way to maintain good health by early detection and remediation of disorders known to occur frequently in older persons. Health education available through community programs for elderly individuals may be valuable to caregivers as well as to the disabled individuals themselves in promoting continued physical functioning.

Knowing the baseline of motor performance is vital if the subtle loss of function is to be avoided. Caregivers should be aware of the level of activity and the manner in which daily tasks are accomplished. It is important to know how far people walk at work and at home and the degree of effort involved. How many stairs can they climb? Do they need a railing? What leisure activities do they enjoy? Do they exhibit fatigue or discomfort and under what circumstances? The answers to these and other environmentally appropriate questions can give a good picture of an individual's physical condition, documenting the usual level of function. Deviations from this standard should be explored, as they are not necessarily a part of growing old.

INTERVENTION FOR REHABILITATION

When a developmentally disabled person loses function because of injury or illness, or more simply by a decrease in strength or flexibility, there must be access to a full range of rehabilitation services. Because hospital stays are shorter than they once were, the majority of rehabilitation activities for all older persons are taking place in the home and not in a specialized setting. Most home health teams have on their staffs both physical and occupational therapists who are usually experienced in the treatment of the common disorders of geriatric patients. Nonetheless, few have had much contact with developmentally disabled persons, and what little they have had has been primarily with young children.

A personal history should be the base of a rehabilitation program for any older person. It is important to know what the person used to do and how it was done to establish reasonable goals. A person who has always walked abnormally should resume walking after a hip fracture, but no amount of therapy will produce a normal gait. If such a person has a bedroom available on the first floor, it is probably better to use this resource than to develop an exhaustive therapeutic regime for stair climbing that may be unsuccessful or carry some risk of further injury.

The primary goal is to maintain or restore functioning. Therapists, caregivers, and the individual must work together to define the activity, identify the impairment to functioning, and find alternate ways or educational strategies for relearning an activity. An individual who has been confined to bed for a long period of time may now find it difficult to stand from a sitting position. An exercise program for knee strengthening may be prescribed, but changing the style of chair or increasing the height of the toilet seat may be more immediately helpful. A disabled person may not be able to master walking with a crutch, but the easier-to-handle walker or a wheelchair may accomplish the goal of returning to community work and leisure activities. Whether as a transitional aid or a permanent alternative, wheelchairs are a means of locomotion and should not be allowed to become an anchor for the individual.

In choosing wheelchairs, crutches, and walkers, individual and home characteristics must be considered for successful selection. A wheelchair may be inappropriate in a small home, and a walker may be chosen over crutches to help the patient attain quick success at walking. Some severely mentally retarded persons have learned to use artificial limbs and other complex apparatus, but the training programs have been long and hard. The older person who loses a leg may prefer to be an active and independent wheelchair user rather than go through prosthesis training. Many normal persons make this choice based on their life-style and daily needs; developmentally disabled people need to have these options also.

The use of gadgets or adaptive equipment to improve function is appealing but deceiving. The necessary ability to make the tool work is often the same ability that has made the function difficult to perform. Many items in adaptive equipment catalogues require dexterity, energy use, and persistence that outweigh potential benefits for many older persons. The goal and the process must be reasonable before time and money are invested. Evaluating daily household function with an occupational therapist can be helpful in identifying the task that may need a tool and then measuring the strength and dexterity required to use the tool for comparison with that of the person for whom it is intended. The history of the individual is important in selecting appropriate assistive devices and should be shared with the therapist.

Rehabilitation workers rarely have educational or behavioral practices included in their formal training. Workers in the field of developmental disabilities are invaluable colleagues for therapists setting up programs for rehabilitation. The persons with experience and training in the developmental disabilities field has a knowledge of educational approaches, behavior analysis skills, and modification approaches that can improve the chances for the success of a therapeutic program. The therapeutic techniques used with developmentally disabled individuals are not different, but the method of application may be. By communicating some of the pre-existing deviations in an individual's motor performance, staff can help in remediation of more recent problems. The expected concerns in older persons caused by slower reaction times and fatigue mandate that therapy activities be carried out throughout the day and be geared to the individual's needs rather than be delivered by a therapist in a time-limited session. With all older patients, the therapist will serve best as an educator of both the client and those who interact with him or her throughout the day. As in general conditioning programs, consistency and follow-through will determine long-range success.

SUMMARY

Extending the viable community life of the developmentally disabled person presents the same challenges as those that face the increasing population of older persons. The needs that disabled individuals share with the majority of senior citizens indicate the appropriateness of integration into existing community-based programs for elders. Focus on preventive health practices and maintenance of optimum physical function must begin early in adult life to maximize function in later decades. Developmentally disabled individuals appear to be subject to the usual problems of physiological aging, although their timetable may be somewhat different. Because of the increasing impact of the older person on public policy, more attention is being paid to their concerns and needs. The resulting flow of information and resources will be helpful in continuing planning for individuals and programs that work with the older developmentally disabled population.

REFERENCES

Furukawa, C., & Shomaker, D. (1982). *Community health services for the aged.* Rockville, MD: Aspen Systems Corp.

Kart, C., Metress, E., & Metress, J. (1978). *Aging and health: Biologic and social perspectives.* Reading, MA: Addison-Wesley Publishing Co.

Lewis, C. (1984a). Rehabilitation of the older person: A psychosocial focus. *Physical Therapy, 64,* 517–522.

Lewis, C. (1984b). What's so different about rehabilitating the older person? *Clinical Management, 4*(3), 10–15.

SUGGESTED READINGS

Harris, R., & Frankel, L. (Eds.). (1977). *Guide to fitness after fifty*. New York: Plenum Publishing Corp.

Saxon, S., & Etten, M. J. (1978). *Physical change and aging: A guide for the helping professions*. Tiresias Press.

section

VI

RESIDENTIAL SERVICES

chapter

20

Characteristics
of Residential Services
for Older/Elderly
Mentally Retarded Persons

Florence A. Hauber, Lisa L. Rotegard, and Robert H. Bruininks

A 1982 national census of residential facilities identified approximately 4.9% of nearly 244,000 mentally retarded people as age 63 or older. This chapter discusses characteristics of the facilities where these individuals live and compares them to the living arrangements of three other age cohorts of mentally retarded residents. In addition, an in-depth discussion of facilities whose mentally retarded residents were all age 63 or older is included. Finally, the health and social characteristics of a national sample of mentally retarded people age 40 to 62 and 63 or older are discussed.

RESIDENTIAL SERVICES FOR the elderly mentally retarded person have been influenced by two conflicting philosophies. On the one hand, advocates for mentally retarded individuals emphasize maximum integration of persons into the normal living, training, and working environments in the community, and the right to a least restrictive environment. For this and other reasons, residential housing for older mentally retarded persons has included a somewhat greater range of structured living settings than has generally been found for non–developmentally disabled people. On the other hand, proponents of services for elderly individuals have concluded that age-segregated facilities (nursing homes, congregate care fa-

cilities) that provide all needed services are the most efficient and effective. Professionals who deal with elderly persons have reacted against less restrictive integrated public housing that is located in unsafe neighborhoods, and that require that elderly individuals be mobile and able to coordinate a myriad of often inaccessible services. The development of structured living arrangements that encourage the evolution of informal support networks and encourage use of health and social services while allowing for continued independent living have not been explored to a great extent for either the elderly population or the mentally retarded population. However, the importance of such policy issues increases yearly as certain

Research reported in this chapter was funded by a grant (54-P-71173/5-04) from the Administration on Developmental Disabilities, Office of Human Developmental Services, Department of Health and Human Services, and a grant (18-P-98078/5-01) from the Health Care Financing Administration, Department of Health and Human Services.

327

demographic realities discourage increased family responsibility for aging or disabled parents needing special assistance in later years.

To the extent that elderly mentally retarded individuals have been part of the long-term care system for mentally retarded people for decades (Allardice & Crowthers, 1975; Cotten, Sison, & Starr, 1981), their alternatives to institutionalization in old age may be greater than for the nonretarded person entering the system because of functional limitations associated with aging. In addition, while there is often reluctance on the part of institutionalized persons to move into alternative settings (Seltzer & Seltzer, in press; Sweeny & Wilson, 1979), there is also evidence of increased adaptability of the elderly disabled individual compared to the elderly nondisabled individual whose cumulative life experiences have not prepared him or her for such a transition (Cotten et al., 1981).

Eleven percent of the United States population is over 65 (Bureau of the Census, 1983); at any time, approximately 5.0%–6.2% of this population is living in a long-term care facility, often inappropriately (Blake, 1981; Minnesota State Planning Agency, 1983). Estimates of the prevalence of mental retardation vary greatly with definition, age, and level of severity; commonly cited rates are from 1% to 3% of the general population (Bruininks, Rotegard, & Lakin, 1984). Efforts have been made on the state and local level to assess the overlap of these two populations that form the focus of this report: the mentally retarded and the elderly populations (Carswell & Hartig, 1979; DiGiovanni, 1978; Kriger, 1975; O'Connor, Justice, & Warren, 1970; Scheerenberger, 1983). Though estimates of elderly individuals have ranged from 2.4% to nearly 6.0% of the mentally retarded population, two facts seem certain: 1) the number is increasing, and 2) a large proportion of this population has not been identified because they do not receive needed services within the formal residential services system (Shanas et al., 1968; United States Department of Health and Human Services, 1979).

The available research literature contains very limited information on either the characteristics of elderly mentally retarded people who live in licensed residential facilities, or the characteristics of programs that serve them. With the increasing numbers of older citizens and the dramatic changes in models of residential and other human services programs, it is important for the formulations of improved policies and practices to be supported by more adequate information.

The 1982 national census of residential facilities conducted by the Center for Residential and Community Services at the University of Minnesota identified 243,669 mentally retarded persons living in 15,633 facilities (Bruininks et al., 1983). It is the purpose of this chapter to focus on approximately 4.9% of these individuals who were age 63 years or older. The first section of this chapter discusses characteristics of the facilities where these individuals live and compares them to the living arrangements of three other age cohorts of mentally retarded residents. Comparisons are also made with the living arrangements of these same age groups in 1977. The 1982 national survey also identified 295 facilities whose mentally retarded residents were all age 63 or older. A more in-depth discussion of these facilities is also included in the chapter. Finally, a selection of the health and social characteristics of a national sample of mentally retarded persons age 40 to 62 and 63 or older who were included in a national probability study of residential facilities is discussed.

1982 CENSUS RESULTS— AGE GROUP COMPARISONS

The 1982 national census of residential facilities included all facilities and homes that met the following definition:

Any living quarter(s) which provided 24-hour, 7 days-a-week responsibility for room, board, and supervision of mentally retarded people as of June 30, 1982 with the exception of: (a) single family homes providing services to a relative; (b) nursing homes, boarding homes, and foster homes that are not formally state licensed or contracted as mental retardation service providers; and (c) independent living (apartment) programs which have no staff residing in the same facility (Hauber, Bruininks, Hill, Lakin, & White, 1984, p. 3).

Semi-independent living programs were included only if staff were in the building at all times when residents were home. Apartment units with shared staff in one building were viewed as one program (facility) and covered by a single questionnaire.

The national mailing list of all facilities or homes potentially serving mentally retarded individuals was compiled between January 20, 1982, and August 15, 1982. Major sources for the list included: 1) the 1982 *Directory of Public Residential Facilities for the Mentally Retarded* maintained by the National Association of Superintendents of Public Residential Facilities for the Mentally Retarded, 2) the 1977 *Registry of Community Residential Facilities* maintained by the Center for Residential and Community Services (CRCS), and 3) state agencies (state mental retardation program agencies, state licensing agencies, state offices reimbursing contracted services, and other state offices).

Most of the 1982 questionnaire items were identical to those used in a 1977 national survey of community residential facilities (Bruininks, Hauber, & Kudla, 1980). Information was requested on the general characteristics of facilities (location, size, ownership, type, year of opening, reimbursement rates) and demographic characteristics of residents (age, level of retardation, resident movement, adaptive behaviors).

The census was completed on June 24, 1983. Of the 22,150 facilities contacted, 15,633 met the inclusion criteria. This number included 864 facilities that did not participate but whose state licensing agencies confirmed eligibility for inclusion. Therefore, the overall response rate for the survey was 94.5%, but since state agencies were able to provide data on the licensed bed capacity and number of retarded residents of all nonresponding facilities, statis-

tics reported are based on the total number of licensed facilities (15,633), unless otherwise indicated.

The 1982 census of residential facilities for mentally retarded individuals was largely a replication of the 1977 census conducted by CRCS. In that census, data were reported for 151,972 residents in 263 state institutions (100% facilities reporting). Responses showed that 62,379 retarded residents lived in 4,427 private and small public facilities (87.9% facilities reporting), and 4,999 residents lived in 1,973 specialized foster homes (76% facilities reporting) (Bruininks et al., 1980; Scheerenberger, 1978). It was estimated that these figures represented an overall facility response rate of 87.3% (6,663 of 7,647 facilities) representing 95.6% of the residents (219,368 of 229,516 residents) in all types of eligible facilities combined.

The 1977 results were not directly comparable to those of 1982, however, due to a difference in procedures for classifying types of facilities and also due to a less complete population coverage in 1977 than in 1982. Adjustments for comparability have been made (Hill, Bruininks, & Hauber, 1984), and statistics for 1977 are based on a total number of 11,025 facilities.

Four age groups were selected for comparison: birth–21, 22–39, 40–62, and 63 and older. The distribution of the four age groups in the 1982 and 1977 census of residential facilities is presented in Table 1. Throughout this chapter, residents age 21 or younger are referred to as "children/youth." "Young mentally retarded adults" is used to describe residents age 22 through 39 years; "older adults" refers to mentally retarded persons age 40 through 62 years of age; and "elderly adults" is used to describe residents 63 years or older.

Persons 63 or older represented 4.9% of the mentally retarded population living in the residential service system in 1982 and 3.8% in 1977. An additional 23.3% of residents were between the ages of 40 and 62 in 1982, compared to 19.6% in 1977. The largest age cohort in both 1982 and 1977 included individuals age

Table 1. National summary data on mentally retarded residents: 1977 and 1982

Age groups	1977[a]		1982[b]	
	N	%	N	%
Birth–21	90,380	36.5	60,003	24.6
22–39	99,351	40.1	114,882	47.1
40–62	48,598	19.6	56,832	23.3
63+	9,467	3.8	11,952	4.9
Total	247,796	100.0	243,669	100.0

[a]54.9% facilities reporting age, representing 76.6% of 247,796 residents.

[b]89.1% facilities reporting age, representing 91.8% of 247,796 residents.

22 to 39 (47.1% and 40.1%, respectively). A very dramatic drop in the number of children (birth–21) served in 1982 was indicated. Approximately 30,000 fewer children were served in 1982 than in 1977.

Table 2 presents the proportion of four age groups represented in each of the following six residential alternative types as of June 30, 1982. These residential classifications represent organizational patterns used in most states:

1. *Foster Home*—a home or apartment owned or rented by a family, with one or more retarded persons living as family members
2. *Group Home*—a residence with staff who provide care, supervision, and training of one or more mentally retarded people
3. *Supervised Apartment*—a residence consisting of semi-independent units or apartments with staff living in a separate unit in the same building
4. *Boarding Home*—a residence that provides sleeping rooms and meals but no regular care or supervision of residents
5. *Personal Care Home*—a residence in which staff provide help with dressing, bathing, or other personal care but no formal training of residents
6. *Nursing Home*—usually an intermediate care facility (not an ICF/MR) or a skilled nursing facility

The foster care alternative, for example, served a greater proportion of mentally retarded persons from birth to 21 years of age than any other age group. While 23.1% of foster care residents were age 40 to 62, only 7.6% were over age 63. Proportionately more residents age 40 to 63 and above were living in boarding homes and personal care homes than in other types of facilities in both 1982 and 1977. Over 17% of residents of personal care homes were 63 or older; an additional 41.1% were age 40 to 62 in 1982. Over 13% of the mentally retarded residents of personal care homes were 63 or older in 1977 with an additional 42.3% age 40 to 62. The proportion of boarding home residents who were between ages 40 and 62 or age 63 and above was nearly as high (15.3% and 40.5%, respectively, in 1982; 14.1% and 42.3%, respectively, in 1977). Compared to other age groups, elderly mentally retarded people (63 or older) represented the smallest proportion of residents of semi-independent living in supervised apartments (1.5%). In a comparison of deinstitutionalized retarded adults age 54 and below with those age 55 or older, Seltzer, Seltzer, and Sherwood (1982) also found that semi-independent/independent living alternatives were far more prevalent among younger developmentally disabled persons. In fact, whereas 18% of the younger group in their study lived in their own apartments, not a single one of the older group did so.

Table 3 examines age groups separately by type of facility. The numbers in this table represent the percentage of each age group that lived in each type of residential alternative in 1977 and 1982. The facility type that housed the greatest proportion of each age group was the large group home with 64 or more mentally retarded persons. In 1977, 70% of all persons in the residential service system for mentally retarded individuals were found to live in large group residences (includes institutions); in 1982, 58% of all mentally retarded residents lived in large group residences. This trend was clearly replicated in each of the four age groups. Residents age 63 and older tend to live in older, more institutional facilities.

While the second and third largest placements for age groups as a whole were group residences with 6 to 15 residents (14.1% in

Table 2. Age cohorts in 1982 by type of facility (percentage)

			Type of facility						
	Foster home	Group home (size[a])				Super-vised apartment	Boarding home	Personal care home	Nursing home
		1–5	6–15	16–63	64+				
Age group	(n=17,147)	(n=7,385)	(n=34,283)	(n=19,989)	(n=143,329)	(n=2,870)	(n=1,264)	(n=4,070)	(n=12,982)
Birth–21	37.4	27.2	18.2	32.0	23.4	7.7	5.9	10.2	38.2
22–39	32.0	49.3	54.2	40.6	49.2	65.4	38.3	31.6	33.6
40–62	23.1	21.1	24.4	22.6	22.7	25.5	40.5	41.1	21.8
63+	7.6	2.5	3.1	4.8	4.7	1.5	15.3	17.1	6.4

Note: *n* equals number of residents. 100% facilities report type of facility and 89.1% report age. Percentages may not equal 100 because of rounding.
[a]Size refers to number of residents.

331

Table 3. Residents in facilities by age cohorts (percentage)

	Age cohorts									
	Birth–21		22–39		40–62		63+		U.S. population	
Age groups	1977 (n= 90,380)	1982 (n= 60,003)	1977 (n= 99,351)	1982 (n= 114,882)	1977 (n= 48,598)	1982 (n= 56,832)	1977 (n= 9,467)	1982 (n= 11,952)	1977 (n= 247,796)	1982 (n= 243,669)
Foster home	3.5	9.5	2.1	4.4	4.5	6.3	7.7	9.9	5.8	7.0
Group home (1–5 residents)	1.1	3.6	1.0	3.4	0.7	2.9	0.3	1.6	1.2	3.2
Group home (6–15 residents)	5.7	11.0	9.1	17.1	8.3	15.5	4.5	9.4	7.9	14.1
Group home (16–63 residents)	8.2	11.0	6.1	7.4	5.9	8.3	4.9	8.4	7.3	8.2
Group home (64+ residents)	77.0	55.4	78.0	60.7	73.4	56.8	71.8	55.7	70.2	58.8
Supervised apartment (Semi-independent living)	0.3	0.4	1.0	1.7	0.7	1.4	0.1	0.4	0.8	1.2
Boarding home	0.1	0.1	0.4	0.5	1.0	1.0	1.7	1.7	0.7	0.5
Personal care home	0.6	0.7	1.1	1.2	3.3	3.2	5.0	6.2	1.7	1.7
Nursing home	3.5	8.0	1.3	3.7	2.2	4.8	3.9	6.7	4.6	5.3

Note: 100% facilities reporting type of facility 1977 and 1982. 54.9% reporting age in 1977 and 89.1% in 1982.

332

1982, 7.9% in 1977) and group residences with 16 to 63 residents (8.2% in 1982, 7.3% in 1977), this was not the case for the 63 or older group. Foster care was found to be the second most common placement for this age group (9.9% in 1982, 7.7% in 1977) and was slightly more common a placement in 1982 than group residences with 6 to 15 residents (9.4%). The increasing use of foster care models for the developmentally disabled elderly person has been documented by other studies (Bruininks, Hill, & Thorsheim, 1982; Seltzer et al., 1982). Though 6.7% of residents 63 or older were living in nursing homes in 1982, children were found living in this alternative more often than any other age group.

Table 4 indicates the percentage of residents in each of four age groups by two facility characteristics: 1) type of operator (profit, non-profit, private, public), and 2) ICF/MR status. Both publicly and privately operated facilities served proportionately the same number of retarded residents age 40 or older in 1982, with approximately 5% of both public and private facility residents age 63 or older. Proprietary facilities (includes all foster homes) consistently tended to serve fewer residents age 22 to 39 and more residents age 40 and older. A decrease in the number of children (birth to 21) served across all types of operators and an increase in the number of young adults (22–39) served was a constant and major trend.

In 1982, intermediate care facilities for the mentally retarded (ICFs/MR) accounted for about 12% of all facilities and 62% of all residents. In 1982, only 4.6% of ICF/MR residents were age 63 or older, a slight increase over that age cohort's proportions of 1977 ICF/MR residents. Overall, the proportion of ICF/MR residents in the older/elderly age cohort is increasing while the number of children served is decreasing. Because of the increasing age of first admissions to the residential service system (Lakin, Hill, Hauber, & Bruininks, 1982), it is not surprising to find the greatest proportion of ICF/MR residents to be young adults rather than children.

Though the largest proportion of all mentally retarded residents still dwell in public ICF/MR

facilities (institutions for the most part), increasingly, residents in all age groups are being placed in privately operated alternatives. Looking at the separate age groups as shown in Table 5, it can be seen that the proportion of residents in publicly operated facilities has decreased considerably for all age groups since 1977. It is only among the children (birth to 21), however, that the number placed in privately operated facilities exceeds those placed in publicly operated facilities. In addition, 1982 data show that among residents who were living in privately operated facilities, individuals 40 years and older were more likely than younger residents to be living in proprietary rather than nonprofit facilities. The distribution of residents living in ICF/MR certified facilities compared to non-ICF/MR certified facilities has remained relatively constant since 1977.

Facilities Serving Only Mentally Retarded Residents 63 Years or Older

Research has shown that age-segregated housing is conducive to the survival, residential stability, and improved personal and social well-being of older persons (Carp, 1977; Harel & Harel, 1978; Lawton, 1974; Rosow, 1967). As a result of this research, a recent objective of alternative public housing for elderly individuals has been to congregate elderly persons in environments designed to provide needed social and health services exclusively to that population. While this philosophy currently prevails among professionals who deal with non–developmentally disabled elderly persons, a reverse philosophy has been practiced with regard to the mentally retarded population. The principles of normalization and least restrictive environment have not only dictated against age-segregated settings, but have also shown the utilization of services available in a community rather than a facility to be most desirable in promoting independence and integration.

According to the 1982 national survey of residential facilities for mentally retarded persons, only 4.9% of system residents (11,952) were age 63 or older. Of this small percentage of elderly disabled persons, 603 resided in

Table 4. Age cohorts by type of operator and ICF/MR status (percentage)

| | Type of operator | | | | | | | | ICF/MR status | | | |
| | Profit | | Nonprofit | | Private | | Public | | ICF/MR | | (Non-ICF/MR) | |
Age groups	1977 (n= 51,464)	1982 (n= 58,619)	1977 (n= 196,332)	1982 (n= 185,050)	1977 (n= 89,095)	1982 (n= 115,032)	1977 (n= 158,701)	1982 (n= 128,637)	1977 (n= 130,016)	1982 (n= 151,793)	1977 (n= 117,779)	1982 (n= 91,876)
Birth–21	32.0	27.3	44.7	28.4	38.3	27.8	35.7	21.7	34.6	22.6	39.1	28.1
22–39	34.0	38.5	39.8	49.1	36.9	43.8	41.5	50.1	41.6	49.6	38.0	42.9
40–62	27.2	26.8	14.1	20.2	20.7	23.5	19.2	23.2	20.1	23.2	18.9	23.5
63+	6.9	7.4	1.4	2.4	4.2	4.8	3.7	5.0	3.7	4.6	4.0	5.5
Total	100.1	100.0	100.0	100.1	100.1	99.9	100.1	100.0	100.0	100.0	100.0	100.0

Note: 99.9% of facilities reporting ownership in 1977 and 100% in 1982. 100% of facilities reporting ICF/MR status in 1977 and in 1982. 54.9% reporting age in 1977 and 89.1% in 1982. Percentages may not total to 100 because of rounding.

334

Table 5. Residents in facilities by age cohorts (percentage)

| | Age cohorts | | | | | | | | | U.S. population | |
| | Birth–21 | | 22–39 | | 40–62 | | 63 + | | | | |
Age groups	1977 (n=90,380)	1982 (n=60,003)	1977 (n=99,351)	1982 (n=114,882)	1977 (n=48,598)	1982 (n=56,852)	1977 (n=9,467)	1982 (n=11,952)	1977 (n=247,796)	1982 (n=243,669)
Private	30.6	53.8	26.7	44.3	30.8	47.9	31.6	46.7	29.1	47.3
Proprietary	13.1	26.3	12.7	19.4	20.7	27.2	26.3	35.3	15.0	24.1
Nonprofit	17.5	27.5	13.9	24.9	10.1	20.7	5.3	11.4	14.1	23.2
Public	69.4	46.2	73.3	55.7	69.2	52.1	68.4	53.3	70.9	53.10
ICF/MR	56.5	57.3	60.7	65.8	59.9	62.2	55.2	58.2	58.8	62.3
Non-ICF/MR	43.5	42.7	39.3	34.2	40.1	37.8	44.8	41.8	41.2	37.7

Note: 99.9% of facilities reporting ownership in 1977 and 100% in 1982. 54.9% reporting age in 1977 and 89.1% in 1982. Percentages may not total to 100 because of rounding.

335

facilities whose mentally retarded population was exclusively age 63 or older. It is the intent of this section to describe these individuals and facilities in greater detail.

Two hundred ninety-five of the 15,633 facilities in existence on June 30, 1982, served mentally retarded residents exclusively age 63 years and older. The average number of mentally retarded residents per facility was 2.0 (*SD* = 1.6); however, the average number of residents was 8.7 (*SD* = 20.2). Table 6 shows the distribution of facilities and mentally retarded residents by size of facility (based on the number of total residents) for the sample and for the total 1982 population of mentally retarded residents. There were proportionately more facilities size 1 to 4 and fewer size 5 to 10 for mentally retarded residents age 63 or older than for the United States mentally retarded resident population as a whole. In fact, among residents, the 63 years and older group had proportionately nine times more retarded residents in facilities size 1 to 4 than the United States mentally retarded resident population and no residents in facilities over size 150. One-half of the United States mentally retarded resident population was found to reside in facilities of size 150 or greater.

The average year of opening for facilities serving only mentally retarded residents who were 63 years or older was 1974, compared to 1975 for the entire population. Half of the facilities opened since January 1, 1977. The majority of facilities (*n* = 261, 88.5%) were operated by individuals, partners, or family. Only 22 facilities (7.5%) were operated by profit corporations, 9 (3.1%) were nonprofit, and 3 (0.01%) were publicly operated. Most of

the residents (*n* = 558, 92.5%) lived in 261 proprietary facilities (including foster homes), 26 (6.3%) lived in nonprofit facilities, and 19 (0.03%) lived in publicly operated facilities.

The figures given in Table 7 compare the number of facilities and number of mentally retarded residents in the entire national resident population to the small number of facilities whose mentally retarded population was exclusively age 63 years or older. One-and-a-half times more foster homes were represented by facilities that served mentally retarded residents exclusively age 63 or older than served the United States resident population as a whole. Facilities whose mentally retarded residents were all age 63 or older also included nearly two-and-a-half times more nursing homes and three-and-a-half times more personal care homes than facilities serving the entire resident population. Over 55% of the sample residents lived in foster homes, compared to 7% of the United States mentally retarded resident population. Personal care homes also provided services to proportionately more residents of facilities whose mentally retarded population was age 63 or older than the United States resident population as a whole (13.6% versus 1.7%).

Across all types of facilities, the mean reimbursement per day per resident was consistently lower for facilities serving retarded residents exclusively age 63 years and older. The overall average for the sample facilities was $17.85 (*SD* = $16.15) compared to $63.03 (*SD* = $39.96) for the total population. This large difference in per diem rates is likely related to substantial differences in services, licensing status, and resident characteristics.

Table 6. Distribution of facilities and mentally retarded residents by size

	Number of facilities				Number of retarded residents			
	Selected 63+ residents		1982 population		Selected 63+ residents		1982 population	
Size	*n*	%	*n*	%	*n*	%	*n*	%
1–4	216	73.2	7,444	47.6	375	62.2	16,778	6.9
5–10	34	11.5	5,420	34.7	92	15.3	35,618	14.6
11–20	20	6.8	1,347	8.6	37	6.1	16,228	6.7
21–150	25	8.5	1,334	8.5	99	16.4	48,747	20.0
151+	0	0	288	1.8	0	0	126,298	51.8

Note: 100% of facilities reporting.

Table 7. Mentally retarded resident distribution by type of facility

	Number of facilities				Number of retarded residents			
	Selected 63+ residents		1982 population		Selected 63+ residents		1982 population	
Type of facility	n	%	n	%	n	%	n	%
Foster home	195	66.1	6,587	42.1	336	55.7	17,147	7.0
Group home (1–5 residents)	16	5.4	2,204	14.1	42	7.0	7,735	3.2
Group home (6–15 residents)	16	5.4	4,210	26.9	51	8.5	34,283	14.1
Group home (16–63 residents)	7	2.4	772	4.9	28	4.6	19,989	8.2
Group home (64+ residents)	0	0.0	483	3.1	0	0.0	143,329	58.8
Supervised apartment (Semi-independent living)	1	0.3	306	2.0	1	0.2	2,870	1.2
Boarding home	8	2.7	185	1.2	17	2.8	1,264	0.5
Personal care home	38	12.9	583	3.7	82	13.6	4,070	1.7
Nursing home	14	4.7	303	1.9	46	7.6	12,982	5.3

Note: 100% facilities reporting.

337

Only three facilities whose mentally retarded population was exclusively 63 or older were ICF/MR certified (0.01%). Together, those facilities served only 17 elderly mentally retarded residents (2.8%). This is in sharp contrast to the resident population as a whole where more than 62% of residents were found to live in ICF/MR certified facilities.

Over half ($n = 308$, 51.1%) of residents age 63 and older who lived in facilities that housed mentally retarded persons exclusively age 63 and older were female. This percentage is slightly higher than that found in the general resident population, where 44.5% of residents were female. The 603 residents represented by this sample of facilities serving retarded residents exclusively age 63 or older were less severely retarded than the general resident population as well. Whereas 60% of the general resident population 63 years or older were either severely or profoundly retarded, only 20% of the sample residents were categorized as such. The percentage of mentally retarded residents with selected limitations in adaptive behavior is found in Table 8. A very small percentage of the selected group of residents age 63 or older were reported to have adaptive behavior limitations. Inability to dress without assistance was the most frequently reported problem in both the selected sample and the general resident population.

A larger proportion of the elderly retarded residents living in facilities whose mentally retarded population was exclusively age 63 or older were first admissions to those facilities than was true of the total mentally retarded resident population. A summary of new admissions, readmissions, formal releases, and deaths by type of facility is given in Table 9. Previous placement of new admissions and subsequent placement of formal releases is reported in Table 10. The largest single previous placement for residents who lived in facilities with mentally retarded persons exclusively age 63 or older was foster/family care homes (28.2%), followed by public residential facilities with 64 or more residents (16.2%). Among the first admissions in the total population, the home of parents or relatives was the single most frequent previous placement, with public residential facilities with 64 or more residents following closely (29.2%). Most (28.8%) of released sample residents moved to nursing homes, while most (30%) residents who were formally released in the population moved to group homes with 1 to 15 residents.

SELECTED CHARACTERISTICS OF OLDER MENTALLY RETARDED PERSONS

The current deinstitutionalization policy stresses moving residents of all ages from more-structured living situations in which they are less independent to less-structured situations in which they can achieve greater independence, and from larger segregated facilities to smaller, more socially integrated living arrangements. Planning residential services that support this societal goal requires the systematic use of information about the residents' characteristics in estimating the numbers and types of community programs required to respond to the needs of those entering community facilities. The continued depopulation of institutions will depend on the availability of greater numbers of facilities specialized for work with less independent and more severely handicapped and behaviorally disordered residents, a group that will include a growing number of elderly developmentally disabled persons.

Table 8. Adaptive behavior limitations (percentage)

Behavior	Selected 63+ residents[a]	U.S. population[b]
Cannot walk without assistance	6.6	18.9
Cannot dress without assistance	16.7	39.1
Cannot eat without assistance	5.2	23.8
Cannot understand spoken word	4.2	16.9
Cannot communicate verbally	8.9	35.4
Are not toilet trained	4.6	25.3

[a]98.0% facilities responding representing 98.5% of 603 residents.

[b]Facility response rates ranged from 87.4% to 87.7% representing 83.2% to 83.9% of 243,669 residents.

Table 9. Movement of mentally retarded residents between July 1, 1981 and June 30, 1982

Type of facility	New admissions %	Readmissions %	Formal releases %	Deaths %	Number of residents
U.S. population[a]	12.7	1.7	11.5	1.2	243,669
Selected 63+ residents[b]	20.0	1.0	9.9	2.5	603
Foster home	20.8	0.9	9.8	1.9	336
Group home (1–5 residents)	14.3	0.0	16.7	7.1	42
Group home (6–15 residents)	13.7	0.0	5.9	2.0	51
Group home (16–63 residents)	3.6	0.0	0.0	3.6	28
Supervised apartment (Semi-independent living)	100.0	0.0	100.0	0.0	1
Boarding home	29.4	0.0	5.9	0.0	17
Personal care home	26.8	2.4	18.3	1.2	82
Nursing home	19.6	2.2	0.0	6.5	46

Note: Percentages are based on the total number of mentally retarded residents on June 30, 1982.
[a]Facility response rates ranged from 87.5% to 88.4% representing 91.9% to 94.2% of 243,669 residents.
[b]98.0% of facilities reporting, representing 98.2% to 98.5% of 603 residents.

Selected characteristics were surveyed in 1978–1979 from a sample of 2,271 older mentally retarded residents of 236 residential facilities. Subjects were selected through a two-stage sampling procedure. In the first stage, a sample of facilities was selected so that the probability of inclusion was based on the number of mentally retarded residents; in the second stage, a sample of facility residents was systematically selected from within the facilities chosen. The design and procedures of this study are described in a report by Hauber, Bruininks, Wieck, Sigford, and Hill (1981).

The sample of facilities used in the study contained public residential facilities and community residential facilities. The selection of

Table 10. Previous placement of new admissions and subsequent placement of formal releases

Type of placement	Previous placement Selected 63+ residents[a]	Previous placement U.S. population[b]	Released placement U.S. 63+ residents[c]	Released placement U.S. population[d]
Home of parents or relatives	11.1	31.2	5.1	17.4
Foster/family care home	28.2	7.1	18.6	18.0
Group home with 1–15 residents	10.3	10.1	6.8	30.0
Community residential facility with 16–63 residents	3.4	4.7	1.7	14.1
Private residential facility with 64 or more residents	2.6	3.4	1.7	13.6
Public residential facility with 64 or more residents	16.2	29.2	5.1	14.0
Boarding home	6.0	1.6	8.5	2.8
Nursing home	9.4	2.7	28.8	4.5
Supervised apartment (Semi-independent living)	3.4	0.7	5.1	7.0
Independent living	0.9	0.6	8.5	3.8
Hospital for mentally ill	6.8	4.1	3.4	2.2
Correctional facility	0.0	0.8	0.0	0.4
Don't know	1.7	0.9	0.0	2.6

Note: Percentages are based on the total number of mentally retarded residents on June 30, 1982.
[a]98.3% new admissions reporting.
[b]96.6% new admissions reporting.
[c]100% new admissions reporting.
[d]91.5% new releases reporting.

the public facilities to be included in the sample was based on a listing of all 263 government-operated residential facilities for mentally retarded persons in the United States. The listing was obtained in 1977 from the directory maintained and periodically revised by the National Association of Superintendents of Public Residential Facilities for the Mentally Retarded. Seventy-eight facilities were selected for study through controlled selection procedures that ensured proportional representation of facilities by size and census region. After selection, six facilities declined to participate in the study, but representative substitutions were possible for three, bringing the number of public facilities to 75.

The selection of the community facilities to be included in the sample was based on a registry of 4,427 community facilities developed in 1977 by the Center for Residential and Community Services (Bruininks et al., 1980). Each of the facilities contained in the registry fit the following operational definition: living quarters in which, as of June 30, 1977, responsibility was assumed for providing room, board, and supervision to mentally retarded persons 24 hours a day, 7 days a week. Excluded from this classification were single-family homes in which services are provided to a relative; nursing homes, boarding homes, and foster homes not formally state licensed or contracted as providers of services to mentally retarded individuals; and independent living programs in which residents are housed in apartments and in which staff do not reside in the facility.

By means of a mail/telephone survey conducted in 1977, basic data had been gathered for the study on the size, location, characteristics of the resident population, and administration of each of the community-based facilities (Bruininks et al., 1980). A probability sampling of the facilities, controlling for size and census region, resulted in a representative sample of 180 facilities. Of these, 154 were still operating and were willing to participate in interviews when they were recontacted in 1978. Seven representative substitutions were pos-

sible for nonparticipating facilities, bringing the total number of facilities in the sample to 161. However, because only one out of six facilities with more than 400 residents participated in the interview, facilities of this size were underrepresented.

In the second stage of sampling, the number of residents to be selected from each of the facilities was predetermined so that the total sample size would be approximately 1,000 public facility residents and 1,000 community facility residents. This stage involved creating a list of all current facility residents and a procedure for the systematic selection of subjects. The final sample included 965 current community facility residents and 953 current public facility residents. All interviews and structured data collection were conducted between September, 1978, and April, 1979.

Descriptive information presented here about selected characteristics of the older/elderly mentally retarded person in residential care is based on a sample of 326 residents age 40 to 62 and 77 residents age 63 or older. Though certain limitations with respect to data interpretation exist as a result of the small sample size of the elderly age cohorts (age 63 or older) and small cell size in certain breakdowns, some descriptive information can be examined and trends discerned. The age of this sample by facility type is summarized in Table 11.

Not unexpectedly, females made up an increasingly larger proportion of each age cohort as residents approached old age (see Table 12). In addition, the table shows that only 12.5% of elderly (63 or older) mentally retarded people living in community facilities were severely or profoundly handicapped, while 62.3% of public facility residents age 63 or older were severely/profoundly handicapped. Thirty-one percent of residents age 40 to 62 living in community facilities were severely/profoundly handicapped as compared to 69.7% of public facility residents age 40 to 62. More interesting, perhaps, is the fact that nearly 16% of public facility residents age 63 years or older were considered to have mild or borderline handicaps.

Table 11. Age of resident sample by facility type

Age of resident	Residents of community facilities (n = 965)	Residents of public facilities (n = 953)	Total (n = 1,918)
Birth–21			
Number	391	281	672
Percent	40.5	29.5	35.0
22–39			
Number	381	462	843
Percent	39.5	48.5	44.0
40–62			
Number	161	165	326
Percent	16.7	17.3	17.0
63 or older			
Number	32	45	77
Percent	3.3	4.7	4.0

Previous Residential Placement

Table 12 shows the previous residential placement of this sample of older/elderly mentally retarded people. The largest proportion of previous placements for older/elderly residents of both public and community facilities was in another public institution. Five out of 10 elderly (63 or older) residents living in community facilities previously lived in public institutions, while 4 of 10 elderly public facility residents came from another public facility. The proportion of both public and community facility residents age 40 to 62 who were previously placed in public institutions was nearly the same (46.0% and 44.5%, respect-

Table 12. Selected characteristics of older residents by facility type (percentage)

Characteristics	Residents of community facilities (n = 193)		Residents of public facilities (n = 210)	
	40–62 years	63 or older	40–62 years	63 or older
Sex				
Male	55.3	50.0	52.7	35.6
Female	44.7	50.0	47.3	64.4
Level of retardation				
Borderline (IQ 69–84)	11.2	21.9	1.8	6.7
Mild (IQ 52–68)	27.3	34.4	11.5	8.9
Moderate (IQ 36–51)	30.4	31.3	17.0	22.2
Severe (IQ 20–35)	25.5	12.5	31.5	35.6
Profound (IQ <20)	5.6	0.0	38.2	26.7
Previous placement				
Foster family care	5.0	9.4	3.7	0.0
Group living (Size 1–15)	7.5	0.0	0.6	0.0
Group living (Size 15+)	3.1	3.1	3.0	2.2
Supported apartment	0.6	0.0	0.0	0.0
Natural/adoptive home	23.0	18.8	42.7	40.0
Independent living	1.2	3.1	0.0	6.7
Boarding home	3.1	0.0	1.2	0.0
Nursing home	5.6	15.6	0.6	2.2
Public institution	46.0	46.9	44.5	44.4
Hospital	2.5	0.0	0.6	0.0
Other	2.5	3.1	3.0	4.4

ively). The percentage of elderly (63 or older) mentally retarded people in both public and community residential facilities who previously resided in nursing homes was approximately eight times higher than the percentage of elderly public facility residents age 40 to 62 who were previously placed in such facilities. Natural and adoptive homes accounted for twice the percentage of previous placements of the 63 years or older public facility resident as compared to the 63 years or older community resident sample. Elderly residents of community facilities were far more likely to have previously lived in foster care homes than were older residents of public residential facilities.

Behavioral Characteristics

Behavioral characteristics of older/elderly residents were evaluated by using the Behavioral Characteristics Assessment, a 65-item adaptive behavior questionnaire completed by a staff person readily familiar with the resident. The questionnaire covered 11 behavioral domains, each of which represented an area of functioning related to establishing and maintaining independence, such as eating, preparing meals, and dressing. In 10 of the domains, residents were assessed on their abilities to perform six distinct behaviors; in one domain, they were assessed on their ability to perform five behaviors. The behaviors were structured in such a way that relative behavioral dependence and independence within each domain could be evaluated. Items on the questionnaire were rated as having been "passed" if the subject performed them well on a regular basis, or if the rater was certain the subject could perform the item if not constrained by environmental circumstances. An average score across the 11 domains yielded a score on overall level of independence for each resident. (In field testing, the average interrater percentage of agreement on the questionnaire items was 88%; the interrater percentage of agreement on the individual items of the questionnaire ranged from 67% to 100%.)

Table 13 shows the level of independence displayed by older/elderly residents of both types of residential facilities. On the whole, residents of community facilities performed more independently than did older/elderly residents of public facilities. While 51.5% of residents age 40 to 62 (44.5% of residents age 63 or older) living in public facilities required substantial supervision and/or assistance performing activities of daily living (levels 1 to 3), only 17.9% of 40- to 62-year-olds (9.7% of residents age 63 or older) living in community facilities fell into levels 1 through 3 on the Behavioral Characteristics Assessment. It is interesting to note that older/elderly residents were less dependent than the general population from which they were selected. Among all community residents, 29.6% placed in levels 1 through 3; among all public residents, 61.5% placed in levels 1 through 3. On the other, more independent end of the scale (levels 5 to 7), 28.8% of residents age 40 to 62 (28.9% of residents age 63 or older) living in public facilities demonstrated semi- or complete independence in activities of daily living, while 63.5% of 40- to 62-year-olds (64.6% of residents 63 or older) living in community facilities displayed that level of independence. Again, older/elderly residents were found to be more independent than the general community or public resident population. Approximately half (50.7%) of all community residents and one-fifth (21.5%) of all public residents displayed independent functioning (levels 5 through 7).

While not directly comparable, data from the 1977 National Nursing Home Survey (National Center for Health Statistics, 1979) described 23% of that nursing home resident population as dependent in all assessed areas of daily living (bathing, eating, dressing, toileting, mobility, and continence). Approximately 10% of residents were found to be totally independent in those areas. No breakdowns were given for the level of independence among nursing home residents with a primary diagnosis of mental retardation (3.3% of nursing home residents) or residents with mental retardation as an accompanying diagnosis (6.1% of nursing home residents). Conservative estimates of the number of elderly persons, as a

Table 13. Level of independence displayed by older residents by type of facility (percentage)

| | Type of facility | | | |
| | Residents of community facilities ($n = 193$) | | Residents of public facilities ($n = 210$) | |
Level of independence	40–62 years	63 or older	40–62 years	63 or older
1. Is dependent. Nearly everything must be done for the resident by direct physical manipulation.	1.3	0.0	9.8	6.7
2. Requires manual guidance. Cooperates if prompted physically or by gestures.	5.1	3.2	19.0	15.6
3. Requires verbal guidance. If shown what to do, takes an active role in everyday activities without physical help.	11.5	6.5	22.7	22.2
4. Takes care of some self-help needs independently, often finds things to do or play with, and can be trusted without direct supervision for short periods of time.	18.6	25.8	19.6	26.7
5. Needs only occasional reminders to perform most everyday household and self-help activities independently, but relies on instruction for more complex activities such as the preparation of meals. Can make short routine trips to the nearby community independently, or if accompanied only by peers.	33.3	32.3	18.4	8.9
6. Performs most routine domestic activities independently and finds his or her way around the community, but needs intermittent supervision and access to a responsible adult who is present in the same building.	19.9	32.3	9.8	15.6
7. Demonstrates skills necessary to live independently in the community without direct supervision. Knows where to get assistance from time to time when the need arises.	10.3	0.0	0.6	4.4

whole, with functional disabilities (more than occasional problems with mobility and self-care) are 12%–16% (Heumann, 1978; Heumann & Lareau, 1979–1980; Nagi, 1975; Shanas et al., 1968).

Secondary Handicaps and Chronic Health Problems

Because many contend that only institutions can meet the health care needs of elderly mentally retarded people, the secondary handicaps and chronic health conditions of this group were assessed. Table 14 displays the chronic health disorders of older residents of public and community facilities. Few residents displayed any of the disorders listed. Among older/

elderly residents of community facilities, 74.5% of those age 40 to 62 and 68.8% of those 63 or older had no chronic health disorders. Among residents of public facilities, 69.7% of those age 40 to 62 and 51.1% of those age 63 or older displayed no chronic health disorders. If older/elderly residents of either type of facility were afflicted with a chronic health disorder, it was most commonly a circulatory problem, followed by diseases of the endocrine or metabolic system. Residents of public facilities had a slightly higher percentage of two or more chronic health disorders, particularly when residents age 63 or older were compared between facility types (6.2% of community residents and 22.2% of public residents). Although

Table 14. Chronic health disorders of older residents by type of facility (percentage)

	Type of facility			
	Residents of community facilities ($n = 193$)		Residents of public facilities ($n = 210$)	
Nature of disorder or organ or system affected	40–62 years	63 or older	40–62 years	63 or older
Infective or parasitic	0.0	0.0	0.0	0.0
Endocrine, nutritional, or metabolic	3.7	6.3	9.1	17.8
Blood and blood forming organs	0.0	0.0	0.6	2.2
Nervous system and sense organs	0.6	3.1	0.0	2.2
Circulatory system	13.0	21.9	13.9	26.7
Respiratory system	3.7	0.0	3.0	4.4
Genitourinary system	0.6	0.0	1.2	0.0
Skin and subcutaneous tissue	0.0	0.0	1.2	0.0
Neoplasms (malignant and nonmalignant)	0.0	6.3	1.2	4.4
Teeth and gums	0.0	0.0	0.6	0.0
Other	3.7	0.0	1.2	11.1
Number of above-listed chronic health disorders:				
None	74.5	68.8	69.7	51.1
One	21.7	25.0	25.5	26.7
Two	2.5	3.1	3.6	17.8
Three or more	1.2	3.1	1.2	4.4

health problems are frequently cited as justification for maintaining institutionalization, this study found few significant differences between public and community facility residents in regard to the prevalence of chronic health problems. Additionally, it would appear that this population is more healthy than the nursing home population and not strikingly different from the elderly population in general in terms of kinds of medical problems. This fact now

has been substantiated by others (Cotten, Sison, & Starr, 1981; Seltzer & Seltzer, in press).

Table 15 presents data on secondary handicaps found in addition to mental retardation among older/elderly residents of community and public facilities. The majority of older/elderly residents living in both types of facilities had no secondary handicaps. This included 51.1% and 65.6% of residents 63 or older living in public and community facilities, re-

Table 15. Handicaps found among older residents in addition to mental retardation by type of facility (percentage)

	Type of facility			
	Residents of community facilities ($n = 193$)		Residents of public facilities ($n = 210$)	
Handicap	40–62 years	63 or older	40–62 years	63 or older
Epilepsy[a]	16.8	6.3	22.4	11.1
Cerebral palsy	8.1	3.1	4.2	8.9
Physical handicap	14.3	12.5	15.6	11.5
Vision impairment[b]	5.0	12.5	7.9	6.7
Hearing impairment[c]	3.1	3.1	3.6	15.6
Behavior disorder[d]	3.7	6.3	0.0	0.0
Number of above-listed handicaps:				
None	60.9	65.6	60.0	51.1
One	29.8	28.1	30.0	37.8
Two	7.5	3.1	9.7	11.1
Three or more	1.8	3.1	0.0	0.0

[a]Has recorded history or is medicated for epilepsy or has had a seizure in the last year.
[b]Is severely impaired or blind.
[c]Is severely impaired or deaf.
[d]Category includes autism, mental illness, alcoholism, and dependence on nonprescribed drugs.

spectively, and 60.0% and 60.9% of residents age 40 to 62 living in public and community facilities, respectively. With regard to number and type of secondary handicaps, residents age 40 to 62 of both types of facilities were not significantly different. Epilepsy was the most common secondary handicap of both public and community facility residents age 40 to 62 (22.4% and 16.8%, respectively), followed by physical handicaps (15.6% and 14.3%, respectively). Hearing impairments were the most common secondary handicap among residents age 63 or older living in public facilities (15.6%). Both physical handicaps and vision impairment were the most common secondary handicaps of residents age 63 or older living in community facilities (12.5%). Epilepsy and behavior disorders followed, with each representing 6.3% of residents.

Much research related to the appropriateness of residential care for elderly mentally retarded people has centered on characteristics of the individuals such as health status, adjustment, age, or length of institutionalization. Relatively less emphasis has been placed on examining the quality of life within different types of residential facilities, the quality of interactions among residents and members of the surrounding community, or the level of individually suited activity promoted within the facility. "Social resources" was the dimension by which most people discriminated between community and institutional residency according to the Older Americans Resources and Services Questionnaire (Carswell & Hartig, 1979) used

in a survey of 187 mentally retarded elderly persons as part of the Research Project on Aging in Georgia. Social resources included not only the extent, quality, and availability of social interactions but also the presence, availability, and willingness of someone to provide some kind of ongoing care in case of illness or disability. At least one other study found primary predictors of morale, life satisfaction, and survival to relate to resident relationships with friends and family outside the residential setting (Noelker & Harel, 1978). The following two tables present some indication of these phenomena in this study of public and community residential facilities.

Table 16 indicates that elderly residents (63 or older) of community facilities were far more likely than elderly residents of public facilities to maintain relationships with family members (71.9% to 48.9%), nonhandicapped peers (28.1% to 6.8%), and special friends (43.8% to 31.1%). In addition, elderly residents of both public and community facilities were more likely than 40- to 62-year-olds and mentally retarded residents as a whole to maintain social contact with nonhandicapped peers (Hill, Rotegard, & Bruininks, 1984). This table also points to the fact that, as mentally retarded people grow older, their contact with family members declines.

Table 17 indicates the level of involvement of older/elderly mentally retarded persons in various leisure activities. Staff were asked to indicate whether the resident had participated in the activity in the last 7 days as part of the

Table 16. Contacts or friendships found among older residents (percentage)

	Type of facility			
	Residents of community facilities (n = 193)		Residents of public facilities (n = 210)	
Contacts or friendships	40–62 years	63 or older	40–62 years	63 or older
Social contact with nonhandicapped peers	17.8	28.1	4.3	6.8
Once a month or more	96.2	88.9	83.4	100.0
Less than once a month	3.8	11.1	16.7	0.0
Contact or visits with relatives	78.6	71.9	55.0	48.9
Contact but resident never visits home of relative	32.8	52.2	67.4	72.7
Contact but relative never visits facility	29.0	30.4	23.8	40.9
Special friendships[a]	52.8	43.8	30.9	31.1

[a]Special friends are people who do special things with a resident on their own time (not as part of employment) and whom a resident looks forward to seeing.

Table 17. Older residents' participation in leisure time activities by type of facility (percentage)

| | Type of facility | | | |
| Contact or friendships | Residents of community facilities (n = 193) | | Residents of public facilities (n = 210) | |
	40–62 years	63 or older	40–62 years	63 or older
Radio, TV, records	90.7	90.6	85.5	86.7
Went shopping	46.0	28.1	18.8	11.1
Hobbies, arts and crafts	26.7	28.1	11.5	17.8
Participated in sports	11.8	3.1	9.7	2.2
Watched sporting event	9.3	0.0	1.8	4.4
Movie, concert	28.6	9.4	36.4	24.4
Party, dance	24.8	18.8	38.2	22.2
Went out on a date	8.1	0.0	3.0	0.0
Visited a friend outside of facility	17.4	15.6	3.0	13.3
Attended club or meeting	13.7	0.0	3.6	4.4
Religious service	49.7	43.8	53.3	40.0
Went out to eat	35.4	25.0	15.8	13.3
Went for a walk outside	28.6	18.8	54.5	33.3
Field trip	9.9	6.3	17.6	13.3
Played cards or games	29.8	37.5	35.8	26.7
Sat around doing nothing	77.6	81.3	81.2	88.9

resident's unstructured leisure time. Notably, as is true of many people, almost all older residents had occasion to involve themselves passively in watching television or sitting doing nothing. Community facilities seem slightly more likely to offer older residents the opportunity to involve themselves in individual activities outside of the facility such as shopping, going out to eat, attending meetings or clubs, or visiting a friend (Hill et al., 1984; Rotegard, Hill, & Bruininks, 1983). Older residents of public facilities appeared to enjoy more group activities such as field trips and movies.

Interestingly, facility staff reported that more than one-third of older residents living in both types of facilities would enjoy more or different activities. The overwhelming reason given as to why individual activities were limited was that facilities lacked the staff to accompany or transport residents. This was particularly true for elderly residents (33.3% of community facility residents and 69.2% of public facility residents).

SUMMARY

This chapter has focused on the older (40 through 62 years of age) and elderly (63 years or older) mentally retarded persons in the residential service system for the purpose of de-

scribing their present living arrangements and presenting several selected characteristics showing their health and social status. In 1982, approximately 12,000 individuals living in residential facilities for mentally retarded persons were over 62 years of age. Close to 70,000 were 40 years or older. The proportion of older/elderly retarded adults requiring specialized living arrangements is steadily growing as fewer children are admitted to residential facilities and as older/elderly adults increase in number due to improvements in health care.

Substantial numbers of older/elderly mentally retarded residents were found in nine different types of facilities. Older (40 years and older) mentally retarded residents were more often found in boarding homes and personal care homes than in other types of residences. Persons over 62 years of age were rarely found in supervised apartments (semi-independent living). Less than 2 people in 100 who were 63 years or older lived in such quarters.

The largest proportion of residents in each age group (birth–21, 22–39, 40–62, and 63 or older) lived in facilities serving 64 or more residents in both 1977 and 1982. Although substantially fewer people lived in these large facilities in 1982 than in 1977, a very large proportion (ranging from 55.4% in the youngest age group to 61% of young adults 22 to 39 years of age) still remained in institutional settings. Foster homes were the second most common placement for elderly retarded residents (over 62 years of age), while group residences with 16 to 63 residents were the second most common for older retarded residents (40 through 62 years of age). Elderly retarded residents lived in older facilities more often than any other age group.

Comparing four age cohorts, fewer residents age 22 to 39 years and more residents age 40 and older lived in proprietary facilities (includes all foster homes) than in facilities operated by nonprofit, religious, or government agencies. The proportion of residents in state, region, county, and city-operated facilities has decreased considerably since 1977. It was only among children, however, that the number placed in privately operated facilities exceeded those placed in publicly operated facilities.

Special analyses were conducted of 295 facilities that served mentally retarded residents exclusively age 63 years and older. The majority (73%) of these facilities were very small (one to four residents). Half of them had opened between January 1, 1977, and June 30, 1982. Over 88% ($n = 261$) were operated by individuals, partners, or a family. More foster homes, personal care homes, and nursing homes were represented in this selected subgroup than in the total 1982 population of residential facilities.

Almost all (92.5%) mentally retarded residents who lived in facilities that served mentally retarded persons exclusively age 63 or older lived in proprietary facilities compared to 35.3% of all elderly retarded residents in 1982. Many of them (62.2%) lived in the small facilities serving one to four residents. More of the age-segregated elderly retarded individuals were represented in foster and personal care homes (55.7% and 13.6%, respectively) than were represented in such facilities by the total population of elderly residents (9.9% and 6.2%, respectively).

The 603 residents residing in this sample of facilities serving retarded residents who were all age 63 or older were far less likely to be categorized as severely or profoundly retarded than the general resident population. Whereas 60% of the general resident population were categorized as severely or profoundly retarded, only 20% of the sample residents were categorized as such. On the whole, this selected group had fewer adaptive behavior limitations than the general population of mentally retarded people in residential facilities.

More than one-fourth (28.2%) of newly admitted elderly retarded adults in age-segregated facilities came from foster/family care homes. Nursing homes were the single most frequent (28.8%) subsequent placement for those elderly retarded individuals formally released between July 1, 1981, and June 30, 1982.

Selected characteristics of a 1979 national sample of mentally retarded residents of public and community facilities showed that the elderly (63 or older) mentally retarded person was more likely to be female. If the elderly person lived in a public facility, she was far more likely than a resident of a community facility to be more severely handicapped and perform less independently in activities of daily living. Though nearly one-third of elderly residents of public facilities were semi- or completely independent in activities of daily living, more than two-thirds of elderly residents of community facilities showed that level of independence.

Comparisons of health status showed few differences for older elderly mentally retarded individuals living in public facilities and in community facilities. The majority of all older/elderly persons living in both types of facilities had no chronic health problems or secondary handicaps, although the proportion of a secondary handicap approached one-half for elderly persons living in public facilities. Additionally, the population was more healthy than the nursing home population and not strikingly different from the elderly population in general in terms of medical problems.

Not surprisingly, elderly residents of community facilities were more likely than elderly residents of public facilities to maintain relationships with family members, nonhandicapped peers, and special friends. Less than one-tenth of elderly residents of public facilities maintained such contacts. Participation of elderly/older residents in leisure activities reflected the greater access of community residents to stores, restaurants, friends, and community activities.

CONCLUSIONS

The residental service system for mentally retarded persons can be characterized as somewhat more mature than the one available to elderly non–mentally retarded persons. States seem to hold a fairly consistent view of what a continuum of care for mentally retarded individuals should be and have been developing them since the early 1970s. In general, there is agreement that institutional care is rarely the most appropriate setting for mentally retarded people and that individuals should be provided residential services in the least restrictive environment. Evidence of this view has been shown in the increasing number of mentally retarded individuals placed in other types of residential care. In particular, it has been shown that small family care is increasingly available to all age groups, particularly the elderly mentally retarded person. At this time, there is no generally accepted view that all, or even most, states share about the ''best'' system of care for their elderly clients. Elderly mentally retarded persons may benefit somewhat from their association with both systems. However, in that their numbers are small in both systems, they are not easily found, categorized, assessed, or appropriately served.

While it is known that large numbers (59%–79%) of elderly persons living in nursing homes and state institutions are inappropriately placed because of the paucity of health and social services available to them in their homes and communities (O'Connor et al., 1970; Toff, 1981), the economic capacity to provide alternatives to institutionalization has been severely lacking. Although the cost of caring for mentally retarded persons in communities has been studied somewhat more extensively and is better understood than the cost of providing such service to elderly individuals, there has existed, until recently, almost no funding incentive to develop such alternative care settings.

Until recently, Medicaid (Title XIX), the major public funding mechanism available for developing residential services for elderly disabled individuals, has been a source of strong institutional bias. While reimbursement for inhome and community services to elderly and disabled persons flows from a variety of federal and state sources, Title XIX has been most responsible for supporting and building the available public systems of residential care. A possible alternative to the high costs of institutional care may partially result from the implementation of Section 2176 of the Omnibus Budget Reconciliation Act of 1981 (PL 97-35). This act enabled states to waive existing Title XIX statutory requirements and to finance noninstitutional long-term care services to individuals who would otherwise require residential care in a nursing home (ICF or SNF) or an intermediate care facility for the mentally retarded (ICF/MR). States now have greater flexibility to experiment with the development of community-based delivery systems if such systems would serve as more cost-effective alternatives to nursing homes or ICFs/MR (institutions). The group most often targeted to be served by state waivers has been the elderly and physically disabled population, followed by mentally retarded individuals (Greenberg, Schmitz, & Lakin, 1983). Programs for mentally retarded persons have stressed deinstitutionalization, whereas programs for elderly disabled individuals have stressed diversion of nursing home admissions. Although not specifically targeted, elderly mentally retarded persons are likely to benefit from the funding of community- and home-based living alternatives made possible by this act.

The startling finding that elderly retarded people in residential facilities possess reasonably good adaptive behavior skills and health status, especially in comparison to residents generally, suggests that they could benefit from further deinstitutionalization efforts. It is particularly important to examine the characteristics of this subpopulation for further deinstitutionalization and placement in more appropriate care settings. The data in this chapter suggest that their potential for less restrictive residential placements, perhaps within more generic service programs for older citizens, may be underestimated.

The expansion and development of residential alternatives for this heterogeneous and frequently unidentified group has progressed somewhat indirectly according to an ideology primarily espoused by advocates for mentally retarded individuals, as has been evidenced in the previous discussion. Developing meaningful and lasting support for qualitative living alternatives, however, will undoubtedly depend upon a growing commitment to elderly disabled individuals and to a funding mechanism that ensures the success of such commitment.

REFERENCES

Allardice, M. S., & Crowthers, V. L. (1975). The role of the practitioner in serving the elderly mentally retarded. In J. C. Hamilton & R. M. Segal (Eds.), *Proceedings: A consultation conference on the gerontological aspects of mental retardation* (pp. 33–67). Ann Arbor: University of Michigan.

Blake, R. (1981). Disabled older persons: A demographic analysis. *Journal of Rehabilitation, 47,* 19–34.

Bruininks, R. H., Hauber, F. A., Hill, B. K., Lakin, K. C., McGuire, S. P., Rotegard, L. L., Scheerenberger, R. C., & White, C. C. (1983). *1982 national census of residential facilities: Summary report* (Brief #21). Minneapolis: University of Minnesota, Department of Educational Psychology, Center for Residential and Community Services.

Bruininks, R. H., Hauber, F. A., & Kudla, M. S. (1980). National survey of community residential facilities: A profile of facilities and residents in 1977. *American Journal of Mental Deficiency, 84,* 470–478.

Bruininks, R. H., Hill, B. K., & Thorsheim, M. S. (1982). Deinstitutionalization and foster care for mentally retarded people. *Social Work, 7,* 198–205.

Bruininks, R. H., Rotegard, L. R., & Lakin, K. C. (1984). Epidemiological aspects of mental retardation and trends in residential services in the United States. In: S. Landesman-Dwyer (Ed.), *Social ecology of handicapped people.* Baltimore: University Park Press.

Bureau of the Census. (1983). *America in transition: An aging society* (Series P-23, *128*). Washington, DC: Author.

Carp, F. (1977). Impact of improved living environments on health and life expectancy. *The Gerontologist, 17,* 242–249.

Carswell, A. T., & Hartig, S. A. (1979). *Older developmentally disabled persons: An investigation of needs and social services.* Athens, Georgia: Georgia Retardation Center, Research Project on Aging.

Cotten, P. D., Sison, G. F. P., & Starr, S. (1981). Comparing elderly mentally retarded and nonmentally retarded individuals: Who are they? What are their needs? *The Gerontologist, 21,* 359–365.

DiGiovanni, L. (1978). The elderly retarded: A little known group. *The Gerontologist, 18,* 262–266.

Greenberg, J. N., Schmitz, M. P., & Lakin, K. C. (1983) *An analysis of responses to the medicaid home and community-based long-term care waiver program (Section 2176 of P.L. 97-35).* Washington, DC: National Governors Association, Center for Policy Research.

Harel, Z., & Harel, B. B. (1978). On-site coordinated services in age-segregated and age-integrated public housing. *The Gerontologist, 18,* 153–158.

Hauber, F. A., Bruininks, R. H., Hill, B. K., Lakin, K. C., & White, C. C. (1984). *National census of residential facilities: Fiscal year 1982.* Minneapolis: University of Minnesota, Department of Educational Psychology.

Hauber, F. A., Bruininks, R. H., Wieck, C. A., Sigford, B. B., & Hill, B. K. (1981). *1978–1979 in-depth national interview survey of public and community residential facilities for mentally retarded persons: Methods and procedures.* (Project Report No. 11). Minneapolis: University of Minnesota, Department of Educational Psychology.

Heumann, L. F. (1978). Planning assisted independent living programs for the semi-independent elderly: Development of a descriptive model. *The Gerontologist, 18,* 145–152.

Heumann, L. F., & Lareau, L. S. (1979–1980). Local estimates of the functionally disabled elderly: Toward a planning tool for housing and support service programs. *International Journal on Aging and Human Development, 10,* 77–93.

Hill, B. K., Bruininks, R. H., & Hauber, F. A. (1984). *Trends in residential services for mentally retarded people: 1977–1982* (CRCS No. 20). Minneapolis: University of Minnesota, Department of Educational Psychology.

Hill, B. K., Lakin, K. C., Sigford, B. B., Hauber, F. A., & Bruininks, R. H. (1982). *Programs and services for mentally retarded people in residential facilities* (Project Report No. 16). Minneapolis: University of Minnesota, Department of Educational Psychology.

Hill, B. K., Rotegard, L. R., & Bruininks, R. H. (1984). The quality of life of mentally retarded people in residential care. *Social Work, 29,* 275–281.

Kriger, S. F. (1975). On aging and mental retardation. In J. C. Hamilton & R. M. Segal (Eds.), *Proceedings: A consultation conference on the gerontological aspects of mental retardation* (pp. 20–32). Ann Arbor: University of Michigan.

Lakin, K. C., Hill, B. K., Hauber, F. A., & Bruininks, R. H. (1982). Changes in age of first admission to residential care for mentally retarded people. *Mental Retardation, 20,* 216–219.

Lawton, M. P. (1974). The relative impact of congregate vs. traditional housing on elderly tenants. *Gerontology, 29,* 194–204.

Minnesota State Planning Agency. (1983). *Population*

notes (December). St. Paul: Office of the State Demographer.

Noelker, L., & Harel, Z. (1978). Predictors of well-being and survival among institutionalized aged. *The Gerontologist, 18,* 562–567.

Nagi, S. Z. (1975). *An epidemiology of adulthood disability in the United States.* Columbus: Ohio State University, Mershon Center.

National Center for Health Statistics. (1979). *The national nursing home survey: 1977 summary for the United States* (DHEW Publication Series 13, No. 43). Washington, DC: Office of Health Research, Statistics and Technology.

O'Connor, G., Justice, R. S., & Warren, N. (1970). The aged mentally retarded: Institutions or community care? *American Journal of Mental Deficiency, 75,* 354–360.

Rosow, I. (1967). *Social integration of the aged.* New York: the Free Press.

Rotegard, L. L., Hill, B. K., & Bruininks, R. H. (1983). Environmental characteristics of residential facilities for mentally retarded persons in the United States. *American Journal of Mental Deficiency, 88,* 49–56.

Scheerenberger, R. C. (1978). *Public residential services for the mentally retarded: 1977.* Madison, WI: National Association of Superintendents of Public Residential Facilities for the Mentally Retarded.

Scheerenberger, R. C. (1983). *Public residential services*

for the mentally retarded: 1982. Madison, WI: National Association of Superintendents of Public Residential Facilities for the Mentally Retarded.

Seltzer, M. M., & Seltzer, G. B. (in press). The elderly mentally retarded: A group in need of service. *Journal of Gerontological Social Work.*

Seltzer, M. M., Seltzer, G. B., & Sherwood, C. C. (1982). Comparison of community adjustment of older vs. younger mentally retarded adults. *American Journal of Mental Deficiency, 87,* 9–13.

Shanas, E., Townsend, P., Wedderburn, D., Friis, H., Milhj, P., & Stehouwer, J. (1968). *Old people in three industrial societies.* New York: Atherton Press.

Sweeny, D. P., & Wilson, T. Y. (Eds.). (1979). *Double jeopardy: The plight of aging and aged developmentally disabled persons in Mid-America.* Ann Arbor: University of Michigan, Institute for the Study of Mental Retardation and Related Disabilities.

Toff, G. E. (1981). *Alternatives to institutional care for the elderly: An analysis of state initiatives.* Washington, DC: George Washington University, Intergovernmental Health Policy Project.

United States Department of Health and Human Services, Federal Council on Aging. (1979). *The need for long term care: Information and issues chartbook.* Washington, DC: Author.

chapter

21

Patterns of Congregate Care
Existing Models and Future Directions

Barbara A. Kenefick

This chapter discusses four topics that relate to congregate care. First, it examines the characteristics of elderly and aging developmentally disabled individuals in congregate care facilities and reports on how these individuals are similar to and different from their contemporaries without this handicap. Following a presentation of these demographic data, brief vignettes describe a variety of innovative patterns of congregate care to show that the association of congregate services with the custodial institution is arbitrary—a vestige of past experience that does not have to be carried into the future. A discussion follows of the constraints that interfere with the design and development of patterns of care that are responsive to those who use them. New possibilities for congregate care are suggested, describing those factors that will make these prototypes feasible from fiscal, policy, and consumer perspectives.

IT IS AN OFTEN QUOTED adage that developmentally disabled individuals are most like their nonhandicapped contemporaries at the beginning and end of their lifespans. This similarity suggests that design of generic services would be easiest for these periods, especially as services relate to management of health problems and support for activities of daily living. Congregate care, here defined as residential and/or residential and day programs for groups of unrelated individuals who require assistance and/or supervision in meeting everyday needs, becomes a critical component in the establishment of such services. In this context, congregate care is regarded as one of a variety of treatment settings appropriate as an ameliorative resource for certain developmentally disabled persons. Frequently, congregate care has been regarded as reflective of society's lack of concern for handicapped members, resulting in blindness to actual and potential environmental abuse. However, circumstances now permit a reappraisal of the functions and conditions under which congregate care contributes to the network of human services. While study is necessary to determine the assets of a relatively large group setting, an *ad hoc* observation indicates that this service arrangement has at least three possible advantages. It offers the opportunity for social engagement with a greater variety of peers and care providers than most other treatment alternatives. Congregate care also permits the delivery of intensive services to a group with an economical use of time, space, and personnel. Finally, this option provides a centripetal means of garnering treatment resources in short supply so as to be available to a maximal number of persons.

PRESENT PATTERNS

Congregate care for very young children began and still occurs primarily as the result of pervasive medical needs requiring intensive observation and treatment. In contrast, for the aging and elderly developmentally disabled person, assignment to congregate care often stems from a lack of treatment alternatives.

Elderly individuals, whether or not they are developmentally disabled, move into supportive living arrangements, including congregate care, for three kinds of limitations on their independence: 1) inability to use community resources, 2) inability to maintain a household, and 3) inability to sustain basic life functions. However, for the older person who is not developmentally disabled, the event that is most likely to precipitate admission into congregate care is the inability of a family member who served as a primary care provider to continue in that role. It is estimated that approximately 80% of the elderly population in this country live independently or with relatives, while only 5% of the aging and elderly developmentally disabled group have these same living arrangements (Boudreaux, 1983). In a review of 2,271 developmentally disabled persons housed in 236 residential facilities, 15% of those 51 years of age and above lived in public facilities and 11% in community facilities. Four percent of both new admissions and readmissions to public facilities also occurred within this age group (Hill, Bruininks, & Lakin, 1983).

National estimates list 5% of all persons over age 65 as living in congregate settings (Butler, 1975), but in New York between 50% and 60% of elderly and aging developmentally disabled individuals reside in institutions (Puccio, Janicki, Otis, & Rettig, 1984). In a study completed in Indiana, 96% of older individuals selected by developmental disabilities were reported to be served by public agencies or nursing homes; however, private agencies and college and university affiliated programs offered minimal, if any, services to this group (Sweeney & Wilson, 1979).

Although demographic data indicate that a significantly larger proportion of developmentally disabled elderly persons reside in congregate care settings than do other older persons with more recent handicaps, this information also demonstrates that the level of care received by developmentally disabled individuals, especially those in public residential facilities and nursing homes, may be inappropriate, and their needs may be met in less restrictive and less costly surroundings (Janicki & MacEachron, 1984). In the state of New York alone, there is a need for approximately three times as many community units, especially group homes, as currently exist (Puccio et al., 1984).

At the beginning of the community initiative in the early 1970s, many of the elderly clients in public facilities were bypassed in order to resettle younger people. At a 1974 conference, held in Albany, New York, Wolf Wolfensberger stated that he had deliberately sacrificed older individuals for younger, mildly impaired persons because he believed the latter group could more easily pioneer community integration. At some later point, elderly and more handicapped individuals would follow. Several states continued this pattern, moving elderly residents of large facilities for mentally retarded individuals to nursing homes as part of the effort to reduce the census of these institutions. Results of this policy are varied. In a Nebraska study, 40% of mentally retarded persons in nursing homes were judged as inappropriately located in relation to existing community alternatives (Wood, 1979). The Connecticut Association for Retarded Children, in their litigation, named former residents of a large state training school who had been moved to nursing homes as members of the plaintiff class (*C.A.R.C. v. Thorne et al.*, 1974).

As indicated in the preceding comments, the term "congregate care" as applied to the elderly and aging developmentally disabled population evokes for most people the image of a nursing home or a state facility for mentally retarded individuals. A congregate care setting is often envisioned as a large facility, old buildings, clients dependent on others for total care, barren surroundings devoid of personal belongings, few concessions to individual privacy, and a paucity of employees resulting in very limited staff-client interaction. So potent is this representation of the institution through personal experience or others' descriptions that thinking is restricted to stereotypes rather than extended to innovative variations on the theme of group living. Of course, such institutions still exist, but their perpetuation indicates shortsightedness in continuing to support expensive and inefficient custodial establishments when there are other choices for congregate care that cost less and do more.

In the United States, there is a continued emphasis on the development of small group homes and foster care to produce a better quality of life for developmentally disabled persons than that provided by most existing congregate care establishments. The majority of nursing homes continue to average about 100 beds (Boudreaux, 1983), with pressue to add rehabilitation units. In Europe, there is the view that 100–150 persons constitutes the optimal size for geriatric residential sites, except in Great Britain and Scotland, where the desired census is considered to range between 40 and 60. In his study of six countries (Sweden, Norway, the Netherlands, Israel, Great Britain, and Scotland), Kane (1976) found a pervasive opinion that facilities with less than 20 residents were relatively inefficient in provision of services and not cost effective. However, he also observed that most of the countries he studied had a higher ratio of professional staff to clients than exists in the United States, as well as a lower turnover of personnel, probably attributable in part to fringe benefits, such as employee housing.

Of particular interest to this investigation was the Norwegian planning mechanism for geriatric services. Each county designed its own plan, which required approval before implementation from the central health authority. On a national basis, 2,000 geriatric beds were being added each year, maintaining a ratio of 2:1 for retirement home and nursing home units. Fifteen day care slots were recommended for each 50 nursing home beds. Staffing requirements called for three registered nurses for a home with 25 beds, as well as an occupational and physical therapist. For a home of this size, an assigned physician was mandated to visit residents at least weekly. If the home housed more than 30 individuals, the physician visited the facility twice weekly on a regular schedule (Kane, 1976).

Alternative models of congregate care have their roots both in developmental disabilities and gerontology. It is anticipated that the latter field will produce new patterns of care as the population of elderly individuals, both healthy and infirm, continues its rapid expansion. Indeed, the pressure for the creation of new patterns of care originates not only from the increasing numbers of elderly persons, but from other potential customers as well. Predictions from the use of diagnostically related groups as a control on length of hospital stay show an increase in the demand of convalescents of all ages for utilization of beds in health-related and extended care facilities, simultaneously decreasing availability of beds for elderly individuals, for whom there is already a scarcity of placements. In all probability, those most affected by the increased demand will be elderly persons, with or without developmental disabilities, who require active treatment and continued surveillance for prolonged periods of time.

With these caveats in mind, it appears timely to examine briefly some existing prototypes of congregate care.

Camphill Villages

Designed as largely self-sufficient units, Camphill Villages integrate developmentally disabled individuals with nonhandicapped co-workers who volunteer their services as companions and care providers. Located throughout Europe, and with three communities in the United States, the philosophy of village life represents the thinking of Rudolph Steiner, the Swiss philosopher and educator. Villagers and co-workers live together as families in homes of approximately 9–12 individuals sharing the responsibilities that community living entails. Daily assignments include the farm, the bakery, weaving, and other supportive endeavors. During the past few years, the Camphill Village in upstate New York has operated a factory making a particular type of orthopaedic bed. Factory employees include not only villagers and co-workers, but also developmentally disabled persons from the surrounding area who do not live within the Village. Another recent project of this same community has been the construction of a house to accommodate the family members of villagers as guests. Because both villagers and their relatives are aging, travel in some instances has become burdensome. The pattern of villagers returning to their homes to visit has now been reversed so that the villagers host their families.

Two criticisms have been directed toward the Camphill movement in recent years: 1) its isolation from the larger community, and 2) the impracticality of using volunteers as care providers. In New York, the Village has responded to the first concern by increasing interaction with the community through acquisition of the factory, use of the community for such varied purposes as haircuts and recreation, and by bringing neighbors and friends into the Village to share in its many artistic and cultural events. The second critique regarding the impracticality of using volunteers as care providers is countered by two responses. First, co-workers perceive themselves not as employees but as part of a family group embracing developmentally disabled villagers. Second, since co-workers are supported by the Village, they do not incur expenses as a result of their volunteer efforts and their mission to their developmentally disabled peers. Indeed, the Village provides co-workers with education and opportunities for self-development, health benefits, and assurance of care during illness or retirement. The experience of the Camphill co-worker is not dissimilar to that of the foster grandparent or other volunteer, except that it constitutes a total, rather than a partial commitment of care, time, and energy. Co-workers may become a part of the Village for a limited period or permanently.

On Lok Senior Health Services

On Lok Senior Health Services combines congregate care with a variety of other services for a densely populated and culturally diverse area of San Francisco, which includes Nob Hill, Fishermen's Wharf, and Chinatown (Zawadski & Ansat, 1983). Beginning with a day care center that grew to incorporate a continuum of health-related services and eventually long-term care, the Community Care Organization for Dependent Adults of On Lok links and services needs of elderly individuals through the "consolidated model" of the Community Care Organization for Dependent Adults (CCODA). In this model, program applicants are assessed by an interdisciplinary team for eligibility for intermediate or skilled nursing care. Once admitted into CCODA, the individual may remain in the program regardless of changes in health conditions. Participants are re-evaluated every 90 days and are eligible to receive, directly from On Lok staff or under contract, such assistance as hospitalization, skilled nursing care, hospice care, housing, inhome services, medical services (including diagnostic studies, consultations with physicians, and prescription drugs), rehabilitation therapy, recreation, family counseling, and fiscal management. CCODA manages all aspects of client care, from transportation to the brokering of a congregate housing unit (which is a HUD 202 project) containing a central dining room and health clinic as well as residential space. Most On Lok participants have multiple medical problems together with sensory, mobility, and cognitive impairments. The nursing home and acute hospital days of participation (6.4% and 1.8%, respectively) in 1980 were well below national averages. Almost every participant, even nursing home residents, attended day care center programs at least a few times each month.

Funding for On Lok is supplied by several sources; however, major support comes from a Medicaid waiver from the Health Care Financing Administration with assistance from the

Administration on Aging and a grant from the Office of Human Development Services.

While the On Lok model does appear to have melded all aspects of care required for both the elderly and developmentally disabled elderly population, the project has faced major problems. Eligibility criteria, including age, residence, and certification for institutional care, eliminated more than 80% of referrals. In addition, eligible persons were often so disabled as to have difficulty contacting program staff. Finally, many persons who could have benefited from the variety of offerings of the project were reluctant to ask for assistance until faced with a major crisis.

Peter Buckley Terrace

Located in the renovated headquarters of what was once the school department in Concord, Massachusetts, Peter Buckley Terrace contains living quarters for 36 persons and typifies a congregate living arrangement for older persons who can still maintain some independence in daily life. State regulations require that applicants for residences of this kind be age 65 or older, unless a handicapping condition allows lowering of the age limit, and have a gross income that does not exceed $12,180 and assets of no more than $15,000. Services available to residents include home health care, including assistance from the visiting nurses' association and the local mental health clinic. A not-for-profit agency receives money from the Department of Elder Affairs to operate nutrition programs, homemaker service, legal and financial advice, housing referrals, and transportation. Entry requirements include a referral by a physician and self-assessment of the applicant, with resident evaluation continuing on a regular basis by a team of human service professionals (Pave, 1984).

This project cannot be considered unique, but can be seen as one example of congregate housing bonded to programs and services designed to support individual independence and/or compensate for age-related infirmity. Residential accommodations of this sort may receive full or partial public subsidies. They may also be part of a special congregate setting, the "continuing care" community, directed toward individuals who are able to purchase housing units and pay additional monthly fees. In return for the investment of personal funds, those who become part of the community are usually assured of additional "on-campus" perquisites, such as public dining facilities, and transportation and medical care, which can range from a retirement home to an infirmary and/or intermediate and skilled nursing facilities. Often, communities of this kind are sponsored by church-related groups or philanthropic agencies. Although entry is costly, with the average price in the New England and North Atlantic states hovering around $50,000 for the smallest suites, there are usually waiting lists for the accommodations that may stretch over several years (Pave, 1984).

The Swedish Residential Hotel

In Sweden the "old age house" is rapidly falling from favor as the model of the residential hotel evolves. Usually this residential complex includes from 100 to 300 apartments, offering residences to 100–400 individuals. Some of these hotels have 24-hour nursing coverage; others have nurses on duty during the day. All have physicians on the staff who visit each occupant at least weekly. At present, this alternative is so popular that there were more than 6,000 persons on waiting lists for admission when the program description was written (Kane, 1976).

Summary

In examining the concept of a continuing-care community, it is interesting to note its similarity to the "continuum of care" available to most developmentally disabled individuals in community settings. State and local governments provide an array of backup services common to those available to the non–developmentally disabled person of means who buys his or her way into such a network. Except for veterans of the armed forces or persons fortunate enough to be within the catchment area of a demonstration project like On Lok Health Services, the aging person who is not developmentally disabled does not have these resources to command.

From the preceding examples one finds that congregate care is a theme with a growing repertoire of variations. Even the familiar tunes for nursing homes and public residential facilities for mentally retarded persons are being played in new keys. Lively debates continue on the composition of these programmatic arrangements. Optimal size of the facility and characteristics of consumers remain as topics of dissonance.

Unfortunately, the discussion of the relative merits and drawbacks of congregate care has not been accompanied by research that definitely supports specific congregate confirmations for a particular clientele. Two conflicting voices reiterate their messages. One speaks philosophically of the need for small units approximating family living arrangements, while the other demands a larger population, often 50 or more individuals, for a cost-effective treatment milieu. The more extensive the handicaps of the population in question, the greater becomes the divergence in the expressed points of view. Although there is a paucity of available literature on the topic, the structures that do exist indicate that smallness of living units tends to be primarily an American concern.

PARAMETERS OF A PROCRUSTEAN FIT

In considering the new directions and structures that exist for congregate care, the planner and program designer immediately come face to face with obstacles that shape programs to fit available resources and the body politic rather than client need. Primary among these impediments is the increasing demand for human services from an aging population in a country with a shrinking tax base and an eroding Social Security system.

For the aging and elderly developmentally disabled person, seven additional constraints can be identified that distort program initiatives. These include: 1) competition among elder groups for services, 2) fiscal viability,

3) the regulatory squeeze, 4) structure of the bureaucracy, 5) planning myopia, 6) disengagement among the service providers, and 7) the refusal by their contemporaries to accept aging and elderly developmentally disabled individuals.

Competition among
Elder Groups for Services

With demographics projecting that the percentage of Americans age 65 and older, which has doubled since 1900, will triple by the beginning of the next century (Blake, 1981) it is expected that demands for services from elderly citizens will rapidly increase. At present, approximately 25.5 million persons, or 11% of the population, have reached aged 65 (Siegal & Taeuber, 1982). Since mentally retarded persons comprise only 0.55%–4.3% of the population (Janicki & MacEachron, 1984), they represent a relatively small proportion of the aging citizenry and, by the very nature of their disability, will have few family members or advocates to act on their behalf.

Even when the needs for services are generic, elderly and aging developmentally disabled individuals may be disadvantaged by virtue of the programs and services they are already receiving. If they are recipients of Supplemental Security Income and reside in a publicly or privately operated intermediate care facility for mentally retarded persons, the cost of their care is likely to be two to four times greater than that of their non–developmentally disabled peers in a nursing home. The fact that this relatively small percentage of persons who have not contributed to the mainstream of social life receives benefits unavailable to the elderly citizen who has been a "producer" is likely to evoke public protest, as has happened with deinstitutionalized psychiatric patients. Kuttgen and Haberstein (1984) describe as "reverse serendipity" the displeasure of elderly private patients in nursing homes who are ineligible for the variety of activities offered to those residents who have been discharged from psychiatric facilities with funding following their placement.

Fiscal Viability

For the past decade, results of litigation and the availability of federal funds have made realistic the aspirations of families and advocates of developmentally disabled persons for the generation of community-based services. In many localities, court orders for community placement of heretofore institutionalized persons created a providers' market. Requests for proposals to house and program clients flowed from the state agencies with provider agencies virtually able to name their price if they would adhere to requisite standards and accept individuals who, by nature of their handicaps, were difficult to serve.

In some instances, the constraints issuing from the large numbers of people to be accommodated into the community within a restricted time led to overdevelopment of voluntary agencies. Administrators, unaccustomed to a constricting economy, found that a rapid expansion of services could often be followed by financial problems. For example, one United Cerebral Palsy affiliate in New York grew from an agency serving approximately 250 clients in 1975 to one providing for 850 individuals in 1980. During the past year, this agency has been reorganized because of major funding pressures.

In a sequence of actions certain to escalate service costs, 37 states opted for Title XIX funds to develop intermediate care facilities for the mentally retarded (ICFs/MR). Within these states, agencies structured budgets to take full advantage of combined federal and state entitlements without necessarily attending to cost-efficient models based on client need and outcome studies. For example, a study completed by the Human Resources Research Institute found that at Pennhurst (in Pennsylvania) the average client cost per day during the 1981–82 fiscal year was $122, in contrast to $90 for former clients of this facility who had been relocated to community residential programs (Katz, 1984).

The movement toward intermediate care facilities for the mentally retarded is now offset in many areas by a move in the other direction toward less costly alternatives, such as family care and community residences, as federal allotments decrease and state and local governments must bear a heavier onus for reimbursement.

Since the "fiscal tail wags the program dog," this cycle could well be repeated in service development for the aging and elderly developmentally disabled population. In a period of austerity and competition for funds, the necessity becomes more pressing for a phenomenological approach that meshes client outcomes with the simultaneous setting of standards and rates.

Regulatory Squeeze

Federal and state regulations, which impose standards governing the expenditure of public monies to ensure they meet the purpose for which they were appropriated, may actually produce results counter to this intent. For example, the regulatory requirement for active programming in intermediate care facilities for the mentally retarded provides for no means of programmatic egress for the elderly person in terms of retirement from daily habilitation. To avoid referral to an alternate residential program, usually a skilled nursing facility, which in all probability has no space for this admission, the developmentally disabled individual continues in his or her present program. To do otherwise carries the threat of loss of Medicaid dollars to the state or voluntary agency administering the intermediate care facility.

Regulations may be ill-suited to the goals of certain kinds of programs. As an illustration, the Camphill Village emphasis on family cohesiveness of villagers and co-workers makes the maintenance of individual records for villagers an impediment to the intended social structuring of the Villages. The required treatment planning process, with the mandated individual program, segregates villagers from co-workers.

Afferent-Efferent
Connections in the Bureaucracy

The "neurological" structure, or communicating network, of a state bureaucracy is very different from that of the individual human beings who work within it. Most bureaucracies suffer from an afferent-efferent imbalance. They require constant information from all body parts about events and conditions that take place at these locations, yet these data are not analyzed and processed to provide their extremities with recommendations for efficient responses in completion of assigned functions.

Moreover, the central nervous system of the bureaucracy appears further afflicted with a temporal fault. It is ahistorical in nature, lacking an accurate long-term memory to differentiate between successful and unsuccessful outcomes. Thus, both in planning and in action, the bureaucracy often repeats previously unsuccessful patterns of service delivery without being able to apply refinements of previous experience to aspects of client care. Even in the computer age, the ingestion of facts often looks unrelated to the creation of muscle within the human services or the "know-how" to build connective tissue.

Planning Myopia

Like the world of fashion design, the surroundings of human services exist in a "trendy" atmosphere. Increasingly, planning and appropriations of federal, state, and local governments follow the pointing fingers of the politician and advocate. On the one hand, this responsiveness ensures attention to identified consumer need, but, on the other hand, it may ignore emerging service gaps that have not reached consumer attention or that conflict with a current priority. To illustrate, there are, at present, three groups of developmentally disabled persons receiving special attention: 1) elderly persons, 2) the individual with a second diagnosis of mental illness, and 3) the young adult "aging out" of subsidized educational programs. Of these three clusters, the latter receives particular concentration as assessed over a 2-year period in three states by increasing budget appropriations and the number of conferences devoted to relevant subject matter. Yet, based on demographic data, the problem of the young adult is confined to one generation, while an increase in the number of

elderly retarded persons will continue. Here, strategic planning could focus on development of services for young persons that could be transitioned for elderly individuals with the passing of time. Such projection might satisfy an existing demand for service while bringing to public awareness a concern for future needs.

Disengagement among the Workers

The practice of geriatrics for the elderly and aging developmentally disabled population carries few intrinsic rewards for professionals and direct care staff alike. Habilitation for this population emphasizes maintenance of existing skills or a slowing of regression rather than restoration of abilities. Change, when it does occur, happens slowly and frequently imperceptibly. Unlike the situation with non–developmentally disabled elderly persons, there are usually no family members to offer praise for employee efforts nor will many developmentally disabled individuals be able to tell life stories that bond caregivers to care receivers, enabling the former to perceive the latter as similar to a relative with whom to empathize and identify.

As in other areas of human services, the congregate care field employs people who actively selected the elderly and aging developmentally disabled individual as the focus of their careers. However, many find employment in large congregate care settings to be the only available vocational choice, especially those in direct care positions. These employees soon become aware that they are caught on a one-rung career ladder. Faced with repetitive and routine tasks of personal care for persons who may not recognize those who provide for them, and recognizing that options for advancement in position or pay are limited, it is little wonder that these staff members rarely derive much social or personal satisfaction from their work.

A similar situation exists for professionals. Children and young adults with remedial handicaps remain clients of choice in a milieu where the edifices of business and high technology overshadow the field of human services. Perhaps burnout is too strong a term for those who see themselves as forced to work with groups of aging developmentally disabled persons. Yet, observation of large congregate care settings often indicates the lack of interaction between client and caregiver that signifies the presenting symptom of an occupational disease in which the employee, like the client, has nowhere else to go.

Unacceptable Images

For many elderly persons, confrontation of contemporaries with obvious infirmities constitutes a threat to independence. The frailty of another becomes a mirror of one's self, an image that causes fright and flight. Avoidance of individuals with developmental disabilities by individuals of the same age but without this impairment has been noted by specialists in program development.

In New York, Kenefick (1983) commented on the difficulty of operating residential programs combining a developmentally disabled and non–developmentally disabled elderly population, while, in Hawaii, Matsunami (1984) has noted the slowness with which developmentally disabled persons are accepted into senior centers by nondisabled peers, even with a ratio of one developmentally disabled person to 25–30 nonhandicapped elders. In his study of long-term care in six European countries, Kane (1976) found a general reluctance to accept older individuals with psychiatric and/or behavioral problems into congregate settings accommodating elderly persons without these symptoms. Efficient use of generic services needed by the elderly with or without a developmental disability requires dissolution of psychological boundaries between these groups.

Summary

Seven impediments have been noted that prevent or restrict the construction of innovative models of congregate care to meld the aging and elderly developmentally disabled individuals with contemporaries who require similar services. These constraints relate to competition for scarce resources, bureaucratic complexities, and characteristics of developmen-

tally disabled persons and their peers who are limited primarily by age-related complaints. Solutions to these problems may be elicited in specific instances through careful analysis of gerontological services by planners and providers. However, these obstacles require consideration in all aspects of service delivery to ensure a transformation of the outdated custodial institution into models that enhance the capabilities of those who use them.

NEW DESIGNS FOR CONGREGATE CARE

The greying of the general population, and the increased visibility of elderly and aging developmentally disabled individuals, offer a potent combination for searching out new directions in congregate care while simultaneously addressing some of the obstacles that limit such expansion. Three dimensions of this topic warrant further examination: 1) special populations to be served, 2) program content, and 3) program support.

Special Populations

The design of innovations in congregate care for special populations carries the following prerequisites:

1. Assessment to show that the need for the program or service exists
2. Rationale that demonstrates the appropriateness of this structure for the delivery of the program or service, including the reasons why it would be most effectively delivered in a congregate setting
3. Consideration for combining two or more groups, such as elderly and aging developmentally disabled individuals and elderly infirm individuals, into a single clientele to increase potential sources of funding and advocacy (this strategy also may lessen complaints that aging developmentally disabled individuals receive more than their share of public support as competition for services to elderly persons increases)
4. Description of the parameters of the program or service, including characteristics

of the clientele, staff, and environment with specific outcomes and strategies for their attainment

5. Regulatory standards for the meshing of congregate care with other program/ service alternatives so as to clearly define admission and discharge criteria

As previously stated, from an empirical perspective, the use of congregate care implies consumer dependency on a provider for services, residential arrangement, and/or total life support. This provider employs a group of individuals, usually not related to the consumer, to fulfill its obligations. Examples of a continuum of congregate services, moving from the most delineated and specific to the most encompassing and general, could include the hospital, housing for elderly individuals or the retirement home, and the intermediate and extended care facility. Clients of a provider responsible for a continuum of care are able to move among the various service modalities without having to find a new provider every time their needs change.

In general, it appears that the explicitness of standards governing provision of care, funding to support these standards, and the dependency of the consumer population are the three variables that relate most closely to the employment of congregate care for its intended purposes. For example, the restrictions on length of hospital stay imposed by required use of diagnostically related groups can be expected to significantly increase the demand for both intermediate care and skilled nursing facilities. This will further limit the already restricted availability of these beds for developmentally disabled individuals.

In planning new adaptations of congregate care, the prerequisites and variables that have been described become important factors in the choice of the group or groups to be served. There exist three basic options for this process. Providers may select: 1) persons of similar characteristics and common service needs, 2) persons with diverse characteristics and similar service needs, or 3) persons with diverse characteristics and complementary ser-

vice needs. Until now, the first two of these options have been the most popular, perhaps because they are easier to design and support. Both have as their foundation an identified population with an assessed need. Institutional prototypes, hospitals, and schools epitomize these models. The advantages they offer to the provider include tested models of successful operations, identified consumers, and, usually, available public and private funding. The disadvantages of these prototypes exist as reciprocals to the advantages. The clientele may be limited by number and by social policy, as that policy supports the deinstitutionalization of developmentally disabled persons. Moreover, fiscal backing for such an endeavor may shrink or disappear as governments and foundations face competing social demands. If the need for this service persists or grows, government regulation may increasingly constrain providers.

Elderly and aging developmentally disabled persons constitute one homogeneous group for which in some instances congregate care may comprise the treatment of choice. As previously stated, these individuals now vie with other non–developmentally disabled persons for scarce skilled nursing beds. Moreover, the response of this group to active programming, mandated by standards for intermediate care facilities for the mentally retarded, indicates that, even as the group faces greater infirmity and medical problems, some benefit could be attained from less stringent programming.

Perhaps it is time for the birth of the skilled nursing facility for mentally retarded individuals, which combines health care with certain kinds of habilitation. This model would fall between the nursing and rehabilitative units common to the extended care facility. Indeed, the skilled nursing facility for mentally retarded individuals also could conform to the second option in selection of special populations by providing services to a heterogeneous group with similar service needs. Many non–developmentally disabled elderly persons have impairments that resemble those of their developmentally disabled peers, requiring similar management. Some of these deficits comprise chronic and acute illness, dementia (specifically Alzheimer's disease and its counterpart in the younger developmentally disabled individual with a diagnosis of Down syndrome), and problematic or maladaptive behaviors.

In all probability, it is more difficult to conceptualize and operate a congregate prototype for individuals with diverse backgrounds and handicaps who also require differing but complementary services than to utilize this kind of care for those whose needs are similar. To develop a reciprocity between differing clients with their varying demands may necessitate a prolonged period of exploration and testing with uncertain fiscal support. In this instance, the designer is uncovering rather than responding to a manifest need. The advantage of this approach to the selection of special populations over the two others previously described derives from participants being able to assume a dual role of provider and consumer that, in turn, can result in a bonding of participants to each other, a lessened dependence on the external care given, and consequent cost effectiveness.

Using this model, one could conceptualize a cluster of apartments that elderly and aging developmentally disabled individuals share with non–developmentally disabled contemporaries. If less infirm than their housemates, developmentally disabled individuals could assist in their personal care and assume some responsibility for maintenance of their home. The non–developmentally disabled person would be the planner and link to the community at large.

During the 1981 national meeting of the American Association on Mental Deficiency, a special interest group on geriatrics convened to discuss this and similar proposals. At the meeting, representatives from several states reported resistance from older non–developmentally disabled persons not only to sharing services but to any association with peers who demonstrated impairments differing from their own. Discussants hypothesized that a developmental disability represented to these people a threat of increased and intolerable loss of function. However, given Goodman's (1984) findings,

which differentiate between characteristics of natural helpers and isolates who are neighbors in retirement housing, it appears that a more careful choosing of companions might avoid the previous objections to this and similar proposals. Clearly, the co-location of developmentally disabled and non–developmentally disabled elderly individuals can result in greater independence with a decreased amount of assistance to and supervision of both parties by external care providers.

Program Content

When planning innovative congregate care, the kind of services and the milieu in which delivery takes place are critical areas for consideration. Here, it is relevant to remember the previously discussed similarities between older developmentally disabled persons and their contemporaries (Puccio et al., 1984). Use of a generic prototype appears most applicable in attending to health problems because the developmentally disabled group shares many of the same medical conditions and impairments in function of sensory and motor systems as do their peers. Moreover, developmentally disabled persons who survive past the middle years tend to have fewer associated handicaps than their younger counterparts. This is demonstrated in decreased incidence of seizures and cerebral palsy (Janicki & MacEachron, 1984). In the future, the most likely difference between developmentally disabled persons and other elderly individuals for whom congregate care becomes the therapeutic option will be the older age of the latter group. During the last decade, the mean age of admission to skilled nursing facilities has risen from 70 to 82 (Boudreaux, 1983), while investigators are noting the trend toward premature aging among individuals with diagnosed developmental disabilities (Puccio et al., 1984).

One novel approach to provision of health care already described is the skilled nursing facility with a habilitative, as contrasted to rehabilitative, component. Here the emphasis would be on maintaining existing skills in personal care and activities of daily living, rather than seeking to restore those that have been lost or diminished. Akin to this approach is the adaptation of the Swedish retirement hotel (Kane, 1976), using a blend of developmentally disabled and retired people. Another alternative for individuals requiring medical surveillance consists of connecting housing to an ambulatory health center. Extended nursing coverage from the center could be offered in a cost-effective manner to a cluster of apartments and group homes. Residents of the complex would have access to the varied resources the center offered without the need for additional transportation. Such an arrangement becomes advantageous both for convenience of consumers and when particular professional providers represent a scarce resource. For example, physical therapists might find such a setting attractive because of the presence of a varied clientele that would be of greater interest to them.

As noted previously, another content area likely to expand encompasses the behavioral therapies. Growth of the technology for eliminating maladaptive behaviors and enhancing adaptive ones is only now beginning to extend into geriatric care (MacDonald, 1983). This technology often represents the alternative of choice to decrease or eliminate use of physical and chemical restraints, as well as to engage individuals in ongoing activity and staff interaction. To date, the technology has been employed primarily by practitioners to control the behaviors of clientele rather than as a tool for clients to achieve greater control of themselves and their relationships with significant others. Thus, two potentially fruitful areas for expansion of behavior programs include: 1) the incorporation of these techniques into extended care and health-related programs other than the intermediate care facility for the mentally retarded where they are already in use, and 2) the teaching of behavioral management to aging persons who can make use of these skills. Prospective students would include less intellectually impaired developmentally disabled elderly and aging persons.

Referral to student status also raises the possibility of employing existing educational resources for the elderly and aging develop-

mentally disabled group. This is already occurring in community colleges in several states. Varying course offerings include activities of daily living, basic academic skills, and activities of daily living with such subspecialities as travel training. However, the annexing of dormitory or residential space, even for short periods of time, has yet to take place. To illustrate, one might adopt the Elderhostel model for developmentally disabled persons. Such a program would enable students to spend a week or more with peers at a college for intensive learning of a topic or skill with associated recreational and cultural pursuits. This appears as an age-appropriate alternative to the current use of summer camps. Such ventures also create a new outlook on congregate care in which it is viewed as a short-term program offering rather than as a more permanent residential arrangement.

Program Supports

Three root systems give strength to new patterns of congregate care: 1) the structure of the environment, 2) management of human resources, and 3) fiscal support. Separately and together these systems shape both content and outcomes in congregate care, as in other kinds of service delivery.

Environmental Variation   While it is difficult, if not impossible, to imagine a congregate setting without walls, placement of these walls permits great variation. The "institutional warehouse" of the past need only act as the point of departure for thought. Boundaries between a congregate and small group or individually structured environment may vary from clear demarcation to imperceptibility. This plasticity functions as a strength for a type of care that can range from a large intermediate care facility for the mentally retarded serving multiply handicapped individuals, gathering under one roof a skilled interdisciplinary treatment team of professional specialists, to a cluster of apartments for one or more individuals, blending together developmentally disabled and non–developmentally disabled elderly citizens who exchange services to accommodate demands of community living.

Providers of congregate care to elderly and aging developmentally disabled individuals may expect to become involved in the two environmental battles now being fought in the general field of developmental disabilities. These battles concern the site and size of the treatment setting. The site debate relates to the institution–community dichotomy. Most consumer groups support the community as the location of choice, although this attitude is not universal. It is possible that site distinctions may be more apparent than real. To illustrate, in one study of habilitative living arrangements undertaken pursuant to litigation, no distinctions were found which in all instances differentiated a community program from an institutional one (Kenefick, 1982). This review demonstrated that residential attributes usually linked to community alternatives, such as access to shopping and recreational resources, integration into a neighborhood, and contact with nonhandicapped peers, occurred as frequently in a public residential facility as in its community counterpart.

With regard to size, a popular consumer attitude has been "smaller is better." However, every provider is subject to two applications of the reality principle: reimbursement must exceed the break-even point by a safe margin, while gathering larger numbers of clients in a centralized setting conserves both fiscal and human resources. When professionals, such as physiotherapists, are in short supply, it may be more efficient to have one clinician providing services in a given location than moving among several smaller ones.

At present there exists a large differential in the size of congregate units. The continuum varies from the Camphill Village paradigm, with 10–12 handicapped and nonhandicapped persons in one home to the small intermediate care facility for the mentally retarded of under 15 persons, to the larger intermediate care facility of around 50, to the average skilled nursing facility with 100 patients (Boudreaux, 1983), and to the large institution that, nationwide, has approximately 1,500 clients as a maximal census (Scheerenberger, 1983).

Currently, the active effects of environmen-

tal constellations are not easily distinguishable from changes due to other variables. For example, most state programs, as well as the National Association of Superintendents of Public Residential Facilities for the Mentally Retarded (Scheerenberger, 1983), publish at regular intervals reports on characteristics of clients in congregate settings. However, there are not sufficient data to determine whether these characteristics represent artifacts of placement, reflect intrinsic aspects of programming, or stem directly from environmental attributes. This is an area where applied research is necessary to define parameters associated with client change.

Staff Recognition The alienation and lack of work satisfaction of staff in congregate care settings is a topic that has already been discussed. The lack of control by staff over their working conditions has been correlated with a paucity of staff-client interaction (Raynes, Pratt, & Roses, 1977). Studies (Carsrud, Carsrud, & Standifer, 1980; Risley & Favell, 1979; Wills, 1973) have shown that it is the quality and quantity of this interaction that is often the critical factor in the care and improvement of chronically disabled populations. It appears that enhancement of the therapeutic milieu through the provision of greater control to care providers could increase the response of care receivers.

Solutions to this problem also entail being able to offer an increasing number and variety of reinforcers to employees. Traditionally, rewards for work well done have included praise from supervisors, raises in salary, appointment to groups with ascribed organizational status, and promotions. Since all but the first of these responses carries intrinsic limits, especially in a contracting economy, a search for other forms of recognition often becomes a priority for establishing and maintaining stability in personnel. To be successful, this endeavor requires that management set and follow policy in this area. Another appropriate measure includes the establishment of a group, with heavy representation from direct care staff, to recommend new and meaningful reactions to the accomplishments of employees. Avenues of exploration include the honoring of particular staff members at regular intervals (e.g., employee of the month), provision of special benefits, such as sabbatical or educational leave, and development of expanded methods of positive feedback by supervisors.

Two additional management strategies may also directly address work satisfaction. The first consists of a matrix approach. This includes the development of a committee or task force structure to increase the upward flow of information and decision-making. Other groupings of personnel, such as quality circles, also assist in such an approach. The second technique calls for making selected direct care staff an actual part of the management team. In this role, direct care staff not only supply information to the administration and participate in decision-making, but also help to set policy.

Clearly, this strategy is easier to install in a small not-for-profit setting where there is likely to be greater bonding and less organizational separation among administrative, professional, and "hands-on" employees. This approach has been utilized by the corporate sector in such firms as the airline People Express. In the larger business world, this type of management often requires employees to exchange working roles on a regular basis so they become familiar and competent with the multiple positions and tasks required for the organization's success. In some instances, employees become stockholders so they are actually working for themselves. Clearly, adaptation of this type of management to congregate care for an aging population would require some modifications. The number of roles that an individual employee may successfully assume in this environment depends not only on individual skills but on professional training and accreditation. Especially in the public sector, with the constraints posed by a civil service system, it is probably more difficult to link gains in employee productivity and the learning of new skills to salary increments. Acquisition of ownership in a human services endeavor may be possible only in the private sector. However, the success of profit-making organizations with these strategies may serve

as subject matter for study and a model for emulation.

Funding Tactics   At this point, when fiscal roads to programs in developmental disabilities are often in ill repair and often far from the main thoroughfares in human services, the potential provider of new patterns in congregate care requires considerable ingenuity to pave a way toward sufficient funding. Strategies to secure backing include financial "tailgating," "piggybacking" of services, location of new sponsors, and increased reliance on the pilot project.

Financial "tailgating" takes place when, in order to meet the needs of one group of consumers, the provider also serves another. Most frequently, services for the population that constitutes the primary concern of the provider are difficult to support because these individuals are not the focus of public attention or advocacy. The provider joins this relatively unpopular group directly with one currently receiving fiscal support through creation of a generic bond in program design. This is exemplified in linking elderly developmentally disabled persons to available and funded programs for their contemporaries (such as day care or meals on wheels). The advantage of this strategy is the access it gives to public funding; its disadvantage is perceived when the tie between the two groups results in increasing isolation from the mainstream of social life.

"Piggybacking" occurs when a provider offers several services or programs, each of which has one or more separate funding sources. If one source shrinks or disappears, expenses can be covered through allocations to other offerings. This is not a new practice. However, in the past, providers have generally tried to tap varied sources of support for one specific population. In the field of developmental disabilities, it is relatively common for a single agency to sponsor residential arrangements, day programs, and sheltered workshops. Now, it may be advantageous to expand this practice to encompass a varied service menu for two or more major populations. Thus, a provider might add services for elderly and aging developmentally disabled individuals to programs operated for developmentally disabled or geriatric groups per se, as well as appending them to other delivery systems for children, mentally ill individuals, or other similar clusters of persons with an identified need and assured backing for provision of care.

As a third means of obtaining dollars, the prospective provider may be able to elicit support from new sponsors such as agencies or philanthropic groups already providing geriatric care. At present, primary providers in the field of developmental disabilities tend to be drawn mainly from the public sector or voluntary associations such as the Association for Retarded Citizens and United Cerebral Palsy. In contrast, church-affiliated agencies and fraternal and local groups have traditionally sponsored programs for elderly persons. Another source of backing may come from the private sector if the program appears likely to generate sufficient revenues to warrant an initial investment. With the corporate sector increasingly immersed in provision of human services, this alternative merits exploration.

Finally, providers may be able to draw at least time-limited funds from a foundation or public agency for a pilot project, which entails the linkage of two or more populations to be served. In applying this method, there will be the need to demonstrate fresh routes of delivery that offer a fiscal advantage in cost containment. This may be achieved through setting a lower rate for existent services, providing increased services at a current rate, or through novel program design providing to local and state government units a means of capturing additional monies from state or federal sources.

PATHWAYS TO THE FUTURE

In conceptualizing new directions for congregate care, the familiar question arises, "How do we get there from here?" The task becomes one of moving in a competitive environment from a service system that is either nonexistent or heavily dependent on the custodial institution toward settings that conserve resources while being tailored to preserve the independence of clientele. Clearly, this is a difficult assignment that requires pioneering efforts and scouting of the best routes for travel. The situation becomes more complex because, as previously mentioned, the individuals to be served often lack the advantages of advocacy and social support both in planning and program development. However, pathfinders do exist within government agencies, consumer groups, and professional organizations.

Adaptive responses to the identified needs of elderly and aging developmentally disabled persons include at a governmental level recommendations such as those found in the Report of the Committee on Aging and Developmentally Disabled in New York State (Puccio et al., 1984) and the initiation of guardianship procedures by local Associations for Retarded Citizens for families with a developmentally disabled member, when relatives can no longer represent his or her interests. Within the professional sector, concern is expressed through conference proceedings, research, and demonstration programs. However, closer affiliation among the public servant, advocate, and provider exists as a precursor to the setting of social policy to guarantee service delivery to this newly identified group.

As an increasing proportion of the population grows older, the black-and-white attitudes that separate elderly individuals from young persons will also begin to grey. Only when the social ethic ascribes value to persons regardless of their years and handicaps will the shadow of the custodial facility fade and the possibilities for congregate care come of age.

REFERENCES

Blake, R. (1981). Disabled older persons: A demographic analysis. *Journal of Rehabilitation, 47,* 19–27.

Boudreaux, E. (1983). *Review manual for nursing home administration examiners.* Lafayette, LA: Professional Examination Review Systems.

Butler, R. N. (1975). *Why survive? Being old in America.* New York: Harper & Row.

C.A.R.C. v. Thorne et al. 344 F. Supp. 371.

Carsrud, A. L., Carsrud, K. B., & Standifer, J. (1980). Social variables affecting mental health in geriatric mentally retarded individuals: An exploratory study. *Mental Retardation, 18,* 88–89.

Cliff, P., & Campbell, W. (1975). The social corridor: An environmental and behavioral evaluation. *The Gerontologist, 15,* 15–23.

DiGiovanno, L. (1978). The elderly retarded: A little known group. *The Gerontologist, 18,* 262–266.

Frankfurter, D. (1977). *The aged in the community.* New York: Praegar Publishers.

Fullerton, A., Eng, B., Stowitschek, J., & Strain, P. (1980). *Promoting social interaction with mentally retarded persons through peer confederates* (Tech. Rep. No. 54). Nashville, TN: Special Education Department, George Peabody College, Vanderbilt University.

Goodman, C. (1984). Natural helping among older adults. *The Gerontologist, 24,* 138–143.

Hill, B., Bruininks, R., & Lakin, K. C. (1983). Characteristics of mentally retarded people in residential facilities. *Health and Social Work, 8,* 85–94.

Janicki, M. P., & MacEachron, A. E. (1984). Residential, health, and social service needs of elderly developmentally disabled persons. *The Gerontologist, 24,* 128–136.

Kane, R. (1976). *Long term care in S.A.* Washington, DC: U.S. Department of Health, Education and Welfare.

Katz, R. (1984). Study compares institutional/community costs. *New Directions, 3.*

Kenefick, B. (1982). *Observations of facility and community programs.* Unpublished report from the defendants, Connecticut Association of Retarded Citizens, Inc. v. Mansfield Training School, 1982.

Kenefick, B. (1983). *Constraints in program design for the aging and aged developmentally disabled.* Unpublished paper, Letchworth Developmental Services, Thiells, NY.

Knypers, J., & Bengston, V. (1973). Social breakdown and competence. *Human Development, 16,* 197–199.

Kuttgen, P., & Haberstein, R. (1984). Processes and goals in aftercare program for deinstitutionalized elderly mental patients. *The Gerontologist, 24,* 167–173.

MacDonald, M. L. (1983). Behavioral consultation in geriatric settings. *The Behavioral Therapist, 6,* 172–174.

Manard, B., Kurt, C., & VonGils, R. (1975). *Old age institutions.* Lexington, MA: Lexington Books.

Matsunami, L. (1984, May). *Reintegrating the elderly developmentally disabled: Hawaii's attempt.* Paper presented at the 108th annual meeting of the American Association on Mental Deficiency, Minneapolis, MN.

Pave, M. (1984, June 11). They like sharing wealth and independence. *The Boston Globe.*

Puccio, P., Janicki, M., Otis, J., & Rettig, J. (1984). *Report of the committee on aging and developmentally disabled.* Albany: Office of Mental Retardation and Developmental Disabilities.

Raynes, N. V., Pratt, M. W., & Roses, S. (1977). Aide's involvement in decision-making and the quality of care in institutional settings. *American Journal of Mental Deficiency, 81,* 570–577.

Risley, T. R., & Favell, J. (1979). Constructing a living environment in an institution. In L. A. Hamerlynck (Ed.), *Behavioral systems for the developmentally disabled: II. Institutional, clinic and community environments* (pp. 3–24). New York: Brunner/Mazel.

Scheerenberger, P. C. (1983). *Public residential services for the mentally retarded, 1982.* Madison, WI: National Association of Superintendents of Public Residential Facilities for the Mentally Retarded.

Siegal, J. S., & Taeuber, C. M. (1982). The 1980 census and the elderly: New data available to planners and practitioners. *The Gerontologist, 22,* 144–150.

Sweeney, D., & Wilson, T. (Eds). (1979). *Double jeopardy: The plight of aging and aged developmentally disabled persons in mid-America.* Ann Arbor: University of Michigan, Institute for the Study of Mental Retardation and Related Disabilities.

Ward, R. (1979). *The aging experience: An introduction to social gerontology.* Philadelphia: J. B. Lippincott Co.

Wills, R. H. (1973). *The institutionalized severely retarded: A study of activity and interaction.* Springfield, IL: Charles C Thomas.

Wood, J. (1979). *Residential services for older developmentally disabled persons. Gerontological aspects of developmental disabilities: The state of the art.* Omaha: University of Nebraska.

Zawadski, R., & Ansat, M. (1983). Consolidating community based long-term care: Early returns from the On Lok demonstration. *The Gerontologist, 23,* 364–369.

chapter

22

Foster Family Care
A Residential Alternative for
Mentally Retarded Older Persons

Evelyn S. Newman, Susan R. Sherman, and Eleanor R. Frenkel

In recent years, the philosophy of service for both mentally ill and mentally retarded persons has been placement in community living alternatives rather than institutions. Foster family care provides, within approved private homes, care for older adults who are not capable of functioning adequately in their own homes or in other completely independent living arrangements. A particular strength of foster family care is its ability to serve as a vehicle for the integration of its residents into the life of the community. This chapter presents data regarding two facets of community integration: the *acceptance* of the resident by the community, and the *participation* of the resident in some aspects of community life. Certain predictors of successful community integration are identified; and the important role of the care provider is stressed, as is the role of the state in providing training to monitor the program.

DUE TO IMPROVEMENTS in health care, elderly retarded persons constitute a rapidly growing segment of the mentally retarded population (DiGiovanni, 1978). Although there is growing awareness of their existence and of the fact that older retarded persons have special needs, there is little research on the services most appropriate to meet these needs (Cotten, Sison, & Starr, 1981; DiGiovanni, 1978; Janicki & MacEachron, 1984). In recent years, the philosophy of service for both mentally retarded and mentally ill persons has been normalization through community-based services and placement in alternative community residences rather than institutions. This philosophy has stressed treating people in an environment close to their home through use of individual, familial, and "natural" community resources and supports.

THE FAMILY, THE COMMUNITY, AND COMMUNITY CARE

Although the concept of community care may be a good one, there is frequently no one to whom institutionalized persons can be released. This is true for both the mentally ill and the mentally retarded populations. Lack of family interest may thus be one of the obstacles to community placement. Farber (1968) de-

The project reported in this chapter was funded by a grant from the New York Health Research Council. The authors wish to acknowledge the valuable assistance of Matthew P. Janicki, John W. Jacobson, and Tom O'Brien of the New York State Office of Mental Retardation and Developmental Disabilities, and Larry G. Brown who helped with all phases of the study, particularly the data analysis.

scribes persons entering residential institutions for retarded individuals as characterized by high rates of family instability and the presence of health and emotional problems in the family. Furthermore, middle-class families tend to maintain a low rate of contact with the institutionalized person. This is particularly significant as the amount of contact maintained during institutionalization is considered one of the best measures of family interest (Windle, 1962). According to Morrissey (1966), families are often reluctant to have the handicapped individual home again after institutionalization.

A second drawback to community placement, in addition to lack of primary family, continues to be public misconceptions and lack of community acceptance regarding both mentally ill and mentally handicapped individuals. This is true not only in the residential sphere but on the part of potential employers as well (Sigelman, 1976). O'Connor (1976) found that one-third of 611 community residential facilities reported opposition from neighbors, businessmen, or local officials. Similar findings are reported by Baker, Seltzer, and Seltzer (1974). Indeed, nonacceptance by the community has often been cited as a major cause of failure of community placements (Gollay, 1976; Justice, Bradley, & O'Connor, 1971; Morrissey, 1966; Tinsley, O'Connor, & Halpern, 1973). In many communities, intense public rejection has led to community attempts to isolate and exclude former mental patients and mentally retarded individuals through zoning, municipal ordinances, and other formal and informal mechanisms (Aviram & Segal, 1963; Heal, Sigelman, & Switzky, 1978). In contrast, however, there is a body of evidence indicating that opposition to a facility tends to decline over time after the facility has opened (Lauber & Bangs, 1974; O'Connor, 1976). Thus, based on this conflicting evidence, the degree of acceptance by the community is still largely unknown, particularly with respect to the elderly handicapped individual.

THE CONCEPT OF
FOSTER FAMILY CARE

Foster family care provides, within approved private homes, care for adults who can benefit from living in a community environment but who are not capable of functioning adequately in their own homes or in other completely independent living arrangements. Foster family care programs can be integrated into the continuum of housing alternatives as a major form of residential treatment.

Family care is designed to serve a number of purposes. During a crisis, it may substitute for hospitalization. It can serve as a transitional placement for the development of independent living skills, and can be used as an indefinite placement for severely disabled institutionalized or elderly clients who require long-term supervision and can benefit from a family environment.

The early years of family care emphasized custodial care. Placements were primarily made in rural areas and there was little expectation of community participation. Currently, the intent of family care is that the residents use community resources, including social and recreational programs as well as medical services. The underlying assumption is that a disabled individual has not truly been returned to the community if the rest of his or her days are spent in isolation, whether in a large impersonal hotel, his or her own home, or even in a family care setting. Since the family care provider can be expected to be integrated into the neighborhood—in contrast to "professional" caregivers in other community placements—the foster family can serve more naturally as liaison between the resident and the community.

Family care is widely used in the United States (Bradshaw, Vonderhaar, Kenney, Tyler, & Harris, 1975; Bruininks, Hill, & Thorsheim, 1982). Research on residential alternatives for mentally retarded clients of all ages indicates that elderly individuals are disproportionately found in this mode of community care (Bruininks et al., 1982; Intagliata, Crosby, & Neider, 1981). Seltzer, Seltzer, and Sherwood (1982), in a Massachusetts study, found that 68% of the older retarded persons in their sample lived in foster homes as compared to only 15% of younger persons. The opposite was found with regard to independent living. Not a single older person was found to live independently as contrasted with 18% of the younger people. The state of New York, which has the largest family care program nationally, has a similar high concentration of older persons; 47% of the family care residents are age 45 or above in contrast to 30%–35% of clients in other community residences. Fifteen percent of the family care residents are age 65 and above as contrasted to a range of 3%–14% of the clients in other community residences (Office of Mental Retardation and Developmental Disabilities, 1981). The same disproportionate concentration of elderly persons in family care has been noted with regard to mentally ill individuals as well (Sherman, Newman, & Frenkel, 1982).

HISTORY OF FOSTER
FAMILY CARE FOR ADULTS

Davies and Ecob (1959) have provided a thorough review of the development of the family care program. Early accounts of patients being boarded in private homes date from the 14th century in Gheel, Belgium, where persons with mental problems visited the shrine of Dymphna, the patron saint of lunatics, and then were taken in and cared for by the residents (Handy, 1968). Mentally ill individuals were absorbed into the families of Gheel—and cared for in some cases by the children (Linn, Klett, & Caffey, 1980)—while insane individuals in other parts of Europe were manacled in dungeon-like institutions (Padula, 1964). It was not until 1852, however, that this religious-municipal system became a medically supervised government institute in Belgium. Similar programs in Scotland, France, Germany, and Switzerland soon followed.

Family care was first introduced in the United States by the state of Massachusetts in 1885. According to Davies and Ecob, "family care for the mentally ill, . . . preceded, nearly everywhere, the same service for the retarded. Thus, Massachusetts which had begun family care for the mentally ill in 1885, extended it to mental defectives about 1940" (1959, p. 140).

The state of New York was the site of the first American family care program exclusively for mentally retarded individuals. The program was started by the Newark State School

in 1931 to serve school-age children. As the program grew, other types of disabled persons were placed in homes and, in a reversal of the trend elsewhere, 4 years after the opening of its family care for retarded individuals, the state of New York appropriated funds for a foster care program for mentally ill persons in the community.

By 1974, family care programs operated by New York's Department of Mental Hygiene accounted for 7,220 mentally retarded and mentally ill individuals living in the community. In 1980, 15.3% of persons receiving residential care services for mentally retarded individuals were in family care. Family care at that time represented 36% of those receiving community residential services (Office of Mental Retardation and Developmental Disabilities, 1984).

One of the duties and responsibilities of a family care provider is to furnish a home-like family living environment that integrates the resident into family activities. Furthermore, providers are required to supply recreational and leisure time materials and to arrange and encourage recreational and special activity in the community.

In addition to activities arranged by the care provider, agencies supervising family care programs provide day programs for family care residents. Over two-thirds of family care residents regularly attend some day program with the balance working at sheltered workshops. These activities are considered essential to the success of family care placements, and the unavailability of day programs may prevent the movement of an individual into family care. The emphasis on such programs is consistent with the goals of normalization.

FOSTER CARE AS
A VEHICLE FOR NORMALIZATION

The extent to which family care effectively serves as a vehicle for normalization for mentally retarded persons has been reviewed by Heal et al. (1978) and Intagliata et al. (1981). In reviewing the large number of studies of family care, Intagliata et al. (1981) concluded that the quality of life of mentally retarded persons in family care varies a great deal. They feel that "an important aspect of normalized life in the community is the degree to which mentally retarded persons make use of a variety of community resources frequented by others" (p. 243).

Sternlicht (1978), in a review of variables affecting foster care of institutionalized retarded individuals, found four sources of potential problems: 1) the residents, 2) care providers, 3) community, and 4) the institution. Eagle (1967) and Windle (1962) estimated that more than one-third of failures in foster care were related to environmental rather than client factors.

In describing the complexity of a foster home, Cohen and Kligler (1980) have proposed that

> There is nothing inherently therapeutic about a foster home. The fact that it is located in the community does not guarantee integration for the client if community support systems do not exist. The living arrangements should not be seen as normalization in itself so much as facilitating normalization, literally providing a home base. (p. 43)

Despite the recognition of this complexity, most studies of foster care continue to focus on identifying factors that predict either success or failure within the placement, success being defined as continued residence within the community and failure as return to the institution.

This chapter examines the foster family care model and the extent to which the homes used serve as facilitators of normalization, that is, the extent to which residents are integrated not only into the home but into the community as well. Data regarding one state's family care program are presented as they relate specifically to middle-age and elderly residents, and the data analysis describes and relates predictor variables (client, provider, and home characteristics) to the outcome variable, community integration.

As used here, community integration refers to two facets of community life. The first facet—necessary, although perhaps not sufficient for a full life in the community—is the *acceptance* of the mentally ill or mentally re-

tarded persons by the community. This acceptance has, in fact, been cited to be essential for the success of family care and other community placements (Morrissey, 1966), and can be viewed as a prerequisite for participation.

Beyond mere tolerance by the community, however, integration requires that the resident also participate in the life of the community and interact with its members. Thus, the second aspect of integration entails the active *participation* of the resident in some aspects of community life.

Three levels of community participation were studied: 1) use of community resources, 2) socialization, and 3) sharing in community activities. It was expected that these represented increasingly independent penetration into the community by the resident. Since the residents could in theory receive all the benefits of community resources (physician's care, food delivery, etc.) either through centers or in their homes, actual use of the resources in the community (the first level of participation) is an indicator of an attempt at integration. This type of integration, however, may be limited to a passive, consumptive role (Segal & Aviram, 1978) and may involve only minimal interaction with community members. The next level of integration, socialization, reflects interaction with familiar persons: relatives, friends, and neighbors. Although some might argue that going to restaurants, churches, parks, and so on, might be done in isolation and involve no actual participation with others, it was felt that participation in these activities requires a higher level of independence than socialization with familiar persons. Therefore, the most demanding level of integration is that in which the residents share and participate in the same activities as do other members of the community (the last level of community participation), as occurs in the use of public places or attendance at social events.

The Study

Data were collected from a study of 151 developmentally disabled adults, age 45 and above, residing in family care homes. With the assistance of the staff of the New York State Office of Mental Retardation and Developmental Disabilities, residents were selected to represent each county of the state, and their care providers were interviewed by telephone. The questionnaire was based primarily on the community integration and familism scales employed in the authors' earlier studies of family care (Newman & Sherman, 1979–1980; Sherman et al., 1982). Other data on resident functional abilities, language, disabilities, and programs attended were obtained from the Developmental Disabilities Information Survey (DDIS) (Janicki & Jacobson, 1979) supplied by the New York State Office of Mental Retardation and Developmental Disabilities.

The chief characteristic of a program such as foster family care, in contrast to other group living arrangements, is its ability to provide a family-like environment for its residents. The provision of a family-like environment serves a purpose, however, beyond the traditional intrinsic source of security, comfort, and satisfaction. The family-like environment can serve to pave the way for integration into the life of the community. Steinhauer (1982) has pointed out that geriatric family care should not be a specific service that culminates with the placement of the client in the home. "If family care is to be a community-based program . . . then other community resources must become part of the sustained placement" (p. 297). Not all clients, however, can be expected to "use" the community to the same extent. In order to examine the degree of community integration, therefore, it is first important to examine the context in which this activity takes place.

The Residents The residents in the study ranged in age from 46 to 92 years with a mean age of 62.9. Fifty-eight percent were female. Over 90% of the residents were white and 99% were single. Almost half (48%) had lived in their present home for 5 years or longer and only 10% had lived there 1 year or less. Almost two-thirds had no relative living within 2 hours of their homes.

In terms of intellectual level, 9% were profoundly retarded, 25% were severely retarded, 28% moderately retarded, 29% mildly retarded, and 9% normal or borderline. A large majority of the residents could perform self-care skills such as eating, toileting, and dressing independently. Slightly more than half were able to shop or use the phone either independently or with assistance. In contrast, more than half could not use a stove to prepare a meal or do laundry either independently or with assistance. Most residents were completely dependent on others for use of savings and checking accounts.

The Care Providers The family member responsible for the care of the resident was almost uniformly the "housewife" who had some family members at home (husband and/or children). Care providers were primarily middle-age. Most were high school graduates. Twenty percent had at least some college education.

Care providers were found generally to be long-time residents of their communities. One-third reported having lived at the same address for at least 20 years. Eighty-one percent of the care providers who had lived at the same address for less than 10 years had lived in the neighborhood or area for at least 5 years. The average length of time that the providers had been in the program was 8 years. Ninety-five percent of the care providers spent time with friends at least several times per year, 82% spent time with neighbors, and 93% spent time with relatives. Among the providers, over 80% went to restaurants, meeting places, religious services, and parties at least several times a year. About 40% went to plays, movies, or clubs at least several times a year.

The Homes The family care homes in the study were generally small with a mean number of 3.4 residents per home. Two-thirds of the homes had 2–4 residents, 14% had 5–6 residents, 13% had 1 resident, and only 7% were occupied by 7 or more residents.

Most of the homes with more than one occupant housed residents of the same sex (80%), with the majority being all female. There was a greater diversity with regard to age. Two-thirds of the homes with more than one client were age integrated. That is, there was a difference in age between the youngest and oldest residents of 15 years or more. About one-third of the homes had personal care clients present (requiring a higher level of care, and more training for the providers).

The majority of the homes (70%) were located in neighborhoods consisting mainly of single family dwellings. Nineteen percent were in neighborhoods dominated by farmhouses, and only 8% were in areas dominated by stores and businesses. The neighborhoods were almost evenly divided among suburbs (32%), rural areas (29%), and rural villages (28%), with only 9% in urban locations.

The accessibility of the homes to various community resources was examined. An important consideration was the availability of public transportation; 59% of the homes in the study were in communities with no public transportation system. Another measure of convenience was the proportion of homes within an easy walk of various services such as shopping centers (34%), parks (40%), libraries (42%), movie theaters (13%), community centers (31%), volunteer organizations (29%), restaurants or coffee shops (53%), bars (49%), places of worship (60%), and barber/beauty shops (49%).

Interaction with the Family The level of resident participation in family-like interactions was found to be high. Seventy-six percent of the care providers reported that all rooms (excluding bedrooms) were available for use by both family members and residents. Almost all homes (98%) reported that residents ate at least one meal per day with the family, and 91% reported always eating together.

The extent of family-like relationships was most clearly demonstrated by care provider responses to two questions: 1) How do you view your relationship with your resident, and 2) How do you think your resident views his or her relationship with you? In both cases, the relationship between the resident and the care provider was compared to that of a family by a large majority of the respondents.

COMMUNITY INTEGRATION

In order to measure the extent of community integration, six indicators, based on the au-

thors' earlier research on family care for mentally ill individuals, were developed. These six indicators were labeled *neighbor acceptance, use of community resources, socialization with the provider, socialization without the provider, activities with the provider,* and *activities without the provider*. The first indicator measures community *acceptance;* the remaining five, community *participation*. Varying numbers of individual items comprise each of the six indicators. To develop each of the six indicators used in the analysis, the component items were summed and weighed equally. The indicators are defined below in order of increasing penetration into the community, and results are presented for each item.

The first indicator, *neighbor acceptance,* was based on the following six items: 1) residents had met their neighbors (93%), 2) residents had spent time with neighbors along with the provider (76%), 3) residents had been invited into their neighbors' homes (50%), 4) care providers reported having experienced favorable incidents in their neighborhoods with regard to their residents (48%), 5) residents spent time with neighbors without the provider (45%), and 6) residents had any friends in the neighborhood (40%). Neighbor acceptance, for the most part, appears to reflect only a casual acquaintance with neighbors, albeit an accepting one.

Use of community resources, the second indicator, does not necessarily involve extensive interaction with members of the community, but as explained earlier, is regarded as one level of community orientation. The sum score was based on use of six of these resources. Although only somewhat over one-third of the residents used the post office, over 90% were found to use doctors and hairdressers/barbers in the community, and about 75% used dentists. About two-thirds used a grocery store, and 60% a drugstore.

The indicators of *socialization with the provider, socialization without the provider, activities with the provider* and *activities without the provider* supply information on the extent of resident participation and also reflect the degree to which residents depend on the care providers for integration into the community. In the company of the care provider (*socialization with provider*), 79% of the residents spent time with friends at least several times a year, 76% spent time with neighbors, (this number also appears in the *neighbor acceptance* sum score), and 19% spent time with relatives.

The items comprising *socialization without provider* indicated that 36% of the residents spent time with friends, 45% spent time with neighbors (included in the *neighbor acceptance* sum score), and 19% spent time with relatives at least several times a year.

Activities with and without the provider included items indicating how frequently the resident went to meeting places, restaurants, parties, religious services, plays or concerts, movies, and clubs. The proportion of residents participating in *activities with the provider* at least several times a year ranged from 19% going to clubs to 93% going to meeting places.

Activities without the provider, the sum score indicating the greatest depth of independent community integration, showed much less participation. The range was from 17% of the residents going to clubs to 39% attending religious services at least several times a year.

Neighbor acceptance and use of community resources were positively correlated with each of the other indicators. Thus, acceptance may be necessary for participation. Socialization with the provider was correlated with socialization without the provider and with activities with the provider. Socialization without the provider was correlated with activities without the provider, but activities with the provider was not correlated with activities without the provider. It seems that those who tend to socialize do so with or without the provider, whereas being involved in activities without the provider is independent of whether one participates in activities with the provider.

PREDICTION OF COMMUNITY INTEGRATION

Gollay (1981) has noted that the bulk of the literature, "if predictive" (p. 101) relies primarily on the characteristics (e.g., IQ) of the individual retarded person. Lakin, Bruininks, and Sigford (1981), however, note that "if 'successful' adjustment (of released institutional residents) required a complete, unaided independence, then few released residents would be able to succeed" (p. 46). In this study, therefore, in addition to characteristics of the residents, those of the care provider and of the home were examined for their effects on the integration of the resident into the community. In order to determine which variables were the best predictors of community integration, a number of resident, provider, and home characteristics were related in a multiple regression analysis to the outcome indicators of community integration, that is, the six sum scores described above.

The most powerful predictors were found to be care provider characteristics. As a block, they were significantly related to *neighbor acceptance* ($R^2 = .22$), *use of community resources* ($R^2 = .10$), *socialization with provider* ($R^2 = .24$), and *activities with the provider*, ($R^2 = .47$). Resident characteristics were the most powerful predictors for *activities without the provider* (R^2 for the block $= .17$). Generally, the home characteristics were not strong predictors; however, one home characteristic provided a weak predictor for the remaining outcome indicator—*socialization without the provider*.

Provider Characteristics as Predictors

Interestingly, the provider's own level of socialization and level of activities were predictive of several outcome variables. The provider's level of socialization was related not only to the residents' level of socialization, but also to the residents' acceptance by the neighbors. Similarly, the providers' activity level was related not only to the residents' activity level, but to acceptance by neighbors. In terms of more personal characteristics, the provider's age was negatively related to residents' use of community resources, and the provider's education was related to the residents' level of activities with the provider. (The provider's length of time at the same address and in the program were not related to community integration.)

Resident Characteristics as Predictors

As a group, the resident characteristics were most predictive of activities *without* the provider: the younger the resident, and the higher his or her independence capacity, the greater was activity without the provider. As will be discussed below this has implications for adapting family care to the increasing number of elderly mentally retarded individuals. Residents' independence capacity was also predictive of activities *with* the provider, as was intellectual level. Length of time in the home predicted neighbor acceptance, as expected, as well as socialization with the provider. (The presence of relatives nearby did not predict community integration.)

Home Characteristics as Predictors

Although the home characteristics as a group were not predictive of any one outcome indicator, individual home characteristics did show some relationships. Somewhat reassuringly from a programmatic standpoint, if the home contained personal care clients, the resident was likely to have scored higher on neighbor acceptance, use of community resources, and socialization without the provider. The greater the number of residents, the higher was the level of activities without the provider. Finally, the greater accessibility to services, the greater the activities without the provider. (Type of housing, size of community, and transportation were not predictive of community integration.)

DISCUSSION

Four important aspects of clients in the community have been discussed in this chapter: 1) acceptance, 2) use of resources, 3) socialization, and 4) activities. Perhaps most important, the research has distinguished between activities clients engage in with and without their care providers.

Studies such as the one by Borthwick, Meyers, and Eyman (1981) have found that mentally retarded people currently are being placed

in accordance with their overall functioning levels. Generally, client characteristics determine to some extent what can be expected of individuals placed in the community, that is, how much they will be able to benefit from participation in activities and use of resources. However, further research is necessary to determine how much independence after placement is a function of the characteristics of the individual resident, or whether independence can be developed as a progression beginning with activities with the care provider and later advancing to activities without the care provider. Based on individual characteristics such as age and independence capacity, a determination can be made before placement as to whether any particular client can reasonably be expected to function independently of the care provider. Therefore, at the beginning of placement, care plans can reflect this expectation and this information can be transmitted directly to the care provider.

Since fewer than half of the individuals in this study participated in activities without the care provider, the study has demonstrated both the importance of the care provider's role and the need to assess each client individually in order to determine the proper match between the client and the provider. If the initial determination is that the resident will not be able to function totally or even partially independently and will need to rely heavily on the family care provider, care providers can be selected who not only urge residents to participate in community activities, but who are active participants themselves and who include the residents in their activities.

The findings of this study were in sharp contrast to the observations by Bercovici (1981) of smaller group homes (*not* foster placements) in the Los Angeles area, and particularly of the smaller homes with 10 or fewer residents, in which residents were not shown how to go out into the community and were discouraged from or denied permission to make use of community resources or to establish relationships with other persons. In those facilities, caregivers tended to discourage, even prohibit, residents from maintaining contacts with friends or acquaintances or from inviting them to visit at the facility. Residents were sometimes restricted from using the phone at all and were frequently told that they could not give their telephone number to anyone outside their families. The homes examined in the present study, unlike the group homes that appear to be run in a much more "business-like" manner with a rigid routine, helped demonstrate that family care not only provides the residents with encouragement to use the community but that the care providers actually serve as facilitators of the participation. This is particularly important for elderly residents who tend not to participate as much in activities *without* the provider.

State Level Functions

Steinhauer (1982) has suggested that a structural distinction should be made between functions performed at the state level and those reserved for local projects. Functions reserved for the state are guidelines and training, which are applicable regardless of location. The authors of this study would concur that in order to ensure that family care homes conform to the objectives determined feasible for their residents, training at the state level is an essential component of the family care program. A specific strength of adult family care is in teaching age-appropriate personal and interpersonal skills (Willer & Intagliata, 1982).

This study demonstrated that when the care provider is present, residents engage more actively in community socialization and participation. Care providers would benefit from training that would help them capitalize on the strengths they can provide as facilitators. Training can serve to make care providers sensitive to the issues, raised here, of increasing the normalization of both the clients and their environment. The fact that resident age was related only to activities *without* the provider, but was independent of activities *with* the provider, suggests that use of foster family care can be beneficial even for elderly mentally retarded individuals, *if* the provider is encouraged to participate with the resident in community activities.

Intagliata and Willer (1981) attributed resident adjustment to the care provider's avoiding overprotection and rigid control, and encouraging independent thought and freedom to act and express feelings openly. Training would also help care providers to assess their own needs to be overprotective when residents are able to socialize and participate either alone or with other residents without the presence of the care provider.

Local Level Functions

Steinhauer (1982) has suggested that functions designated to the local level should be those that require harmony with local conditions. These would include linkages to existing community services. At the local level, the location and convenience of the home itself has bearing particularly for those individuals who are in family care to receive aid in increasing their own sense of independence rather than merely to live in a protective environment. The authors' study has shown that it is important that homes be so situated that services are accessible. Bjaanes, Butler, and Kelly (1981) have noted that it is not sufficient to focus only on client normalization; environmental normalization must also be present. If activities are to be encouraged without the care provider, it is important to take into consideration the convenience of the home.

While location and convenience of home are a local determination, the family care program should also be monitored at the state level so that residents can be integrated into the community to the fullest extent of their ability.

SUMMARY

A study of the foster family care program for mentally retarded adults in the state of New York disclosed that, with proper selection of both clients and care providers, foster care does serve to aid in the integration of the older retarded person into the community. Six indicators of community integration were used, and characteristics of residents, care providers, and homes were examined for effects as predictors of integration.

The most powerful predictors were found to be care provider characteristics; the provider's own level of socialization and level of activities were predictive of several outcome variables. The study demonstrated that when the care provider is present, residents engage more actively in community socialization and participation. The client's age was related to activities without the provider.

Based on the research, several recommendations are made. These include matching of client and care provider, and training for care providers that would help them capitalize on their strengths as facilitators; careful attention during provider selection and sensitivity to the accessibility of community resources, and continuation of the state's role as program monitor and provider of training.

REFERENCES

Aviram, V., & Segal, S. (1963). Exclusion of the mentally ill: Reflection of an old problem in a new context. *Archives of General Psychiatry, 29,* 126–133.

Baker, B. L., Seltzer, G. B., & Seltzer, M. M. (1974). *As close as possible: Community residences for retarded adults.* Boston: Little, Brown & Co.

Bercovici, S. (1981). Qualitative methods and cultural perspectives in the study of deinstitutionalization. In R. H. Bruininks, C. E. Meyers, B. B. Sigford, & K. C. Lakin (Eds.), *Deinstitutionalization and community adjustment of mentally retarded people* (Monograph No. 4). Washington, DC: American Association on Mental Deficiency.

Bjaanes, A. T., Butler, E. W., & Kelly, P. (1981). Placement type and client functional level as factors in provision of services aimed at increasing adjustment. In R. H. Bruininks, C. E. Meyers, B. B. Sigford, & K. C. Lakin (Eds.), *Deinstitutionalization and community adjustment of mentally retarded people* (Monograph No. 4). Washington, DC: American Association on Mental Deficiency.

Borthwick, S., Meyers, C. E., & Eyman, R. K. (1981). Comparative adaptive and maladaptive behavior of mentally retarded clients of five residential settings in these western states. In R. H. Bruininks, C. E. Meyers, B. B. Sigford, & K. C. Lakin (Eds.), *Deinstitutionalization and community adjustment of mentally retarded people* (Monograph No. 4). Washington, DC: American Association on Mental Deficiency.

Bradshaw, B. R., Vonderhaar, W., Kenney, V., Tyler, L. S., & Harris, S. (1975, April). *Community based residential care for the minimally impaired elderly: A survey analysis.* Paper presented at annual meeting of American Geriatrics Society, Miami.

Bruininks, R. H., Hill, B. K., & Thorsheim, M. J. (1982). Deinstitutionalization and foster care for mentally retarded people. *Health and Social Work, 7,* 198–20.

Cohen, H. J., & Kligler, D. (Eds.). (1980). *Urban community care for the developmentally disabled.* Springfield, IL: Charles C Thomas.

Cotten, P. D., Sison, G. F. P., & Starr, S. (1981). Comparing elderly retarded and nonretarded individuals. Who are they? What are their needs? *The Gerontologist, 21,* 359–365.

Davies, S. P., & Ecob, K. G. (1959). *The mentally retarded in society.* New York: Columbia University Press.

DiGiovanni, L. (1978). The elderly retarded: A little-known group. *The Gerontologist, 18,* 262–266.

Eagle, E. (1967). Prognosis and outcome of community placement of institutionalized retardates. *American Journal of Mental Deficiency, 72,* 232–243.

Farber, B. (1968). *Mental retardation: Its social context and social consequences.* Boston: Houghton Mifflin Co.

Gollay, E. (1976). *A study of the community adjustment of deinstitutionalized mentally retarded persons: Vol. 5. An analysis of factors associated with community adjustment* (Contract No. OEC-0-74-9183). Cambridge, MA: U.S. Office of Education.

Gollay, E. (1981). Some conceptual and methodological issues in studying the community adjustment of deinstitutionalized mentally retarded people. In R. H. Bruininks, C. E. Meyers, B. B. Sigford, & K. C. Lakin (Eds.), *Deinstitutionalization and community adjustment of mentally retarded people* (Monograph No. 4) (pp. 89–106). Washington, DC: American Association on Mental Deficiency.

Handy, I. A. (1968). Foster care as a therapeutic program for geriatric psychiatric patients. *Journal of the American Geriatric Society, 16,* 350–358.

Heal, L., Sigelman, C., & Switzky, H. (1978). Research on community residential alternatives for the mentally retarded. In N. R. Ellis (Ed.), *International review of research in mental retardation* (Vol. 9). New York: Academic Press.

Intagliata, J., Crosby, N., & Neider, L. (1981). Foster family care for mentally retarded people: A qualitative review. In R. H. Bruininks, C. E. Meyers, B. B. Sigford, & K. C. Lakin (Eds.), *Deinstitutionalization and community adjustment of mentally retarded people* (Monograph No. 4) (pp. 233–259). Washington, DC: American Association on Mental Deficiency.

Intagliata, J., & Willer, B. (1981). A review of training programs for providers of foster family care to mentally retarded persons. In R. H. Bruininks, C. E. Meyers, B. B. Sigford, & K. C. Lakin (Eds.), *Deinstitutionalization and community adjustment of mentally retarded people* (Monograph No. 4) (pp. 282–315). Washington, DC: American Association on Mental Deficiency.

Janicki, M. P., & Jacobson, J. W. (1979). New York's needs assessment and developmental disabilities: Preliminary report (Technical Monograph No. 79-10). Albany: New York State Office of Mental Retardation and Developmental Disabilities.

Janicki, M. P., & MacEachron, A. E. (1984). Residential, health and social service need patterns of elderly developmentally disabled persons. *The Gerontologist, 24,* 128–137.

Justice, R. S., Bradley, J., & O'Connor, G. (1971). Foster family care for the retarded: Management concerns for the caretaker. *Mental Retardation, 9* (4), 12–15.

Lakin, K. C., Bruininks, R. H., & Sigford, B. B. (1981). Early perspectives on the community adjustment of mentally retarded people. In R. H. Bruininks, C. E. Meyers, B. B. Sigford, & K. C. Lakin (Eds.), *Deinstitutionalization and community adjustment of mentally retarded people* (Monograph No. 4) (pp. 28–50). Washington, DC: American Association on Mental Deficiency.

Lauber, D., & Bangs, F. S. (1974). *Zoning for family group care facilities* (Planning Advisory Service Rep. No. 300). Chicago: American Society of Planning Officials.

Linn, M. W., Klett, C. J., & Caffey, Jr., E. M. (1980). Foster home characteristics psychiatric patient outcome. *Archives of General Psychiatry, 37,* 129–132.

Morrissey, J. R. (1966). Status of family care programs. *Mental Retardation, 4* (5), 8–11.

Newman, E. S., & Sherman, S. R. (1979–1980). Foster family care for the elderly: Surrogate family or mini-institution? *Aging and Human Development, 10,* 165–176.

O'Connor, G. (1976). *Home is a good place: A national perspective of community residential facilities for developmentally disabled persons* (Monograph No. 2). Washington, DC: American Association of Mental Deficiency.

Office of Mental Retardation and Developmental Disabilities. (1984). *The 1984–87 comprehensive plan for services to persons with mental retardation and developmental disabilities in New York state.* Albany: Author.

Padula, H. (1964). Foster homes for the mentally ill. *Mental Hygiene, 48,* 366–371.

Segal, S. P., & Aviram, V. (1978). Factors that facilitate and hinder the social integration of the mentally ill in the community. Berkeley: School of Social Welfare, University of California.

Seltzer, M. M., Seltzer, G. B., & Sherwood, C. C. (1982). Comparison of community adjustment to older vs. younger mentally retarded adults. *American Journal of Mental Deficiency, 87,* 9–13.

Sherman, S. R., Newman, E. S., & Frenkel, E. R. (1982). *Community integration of mentally retarded adults in (foster) family care.* Albany: Ringel Institute of Gerontology, State University of New York at Albany.

Sigelman, C. K. (1976). Mentally retarded persons as members of the community. *Information Service, 6,* 17–25.

Steinhauer, M. B. (1982). Geriatric foster care: A prototype design and implementation issues. *The Gerontologist, 22,* 293–300.

Sternlicht, M. (1978). Variables affecting foster care placement of institutionalized retarded residents. *Mental Retardation, 16* (1), 25–28.

Tinsley, D. J., O'Connor, G., & Halpern, A. S. (1973). *The identification of problem areas in the establishment and maintenance of community residential facilities for the developmentally disabled* (Working paper No. 64). Eugene, Oregon: Rehabilitation and Training Center on Mental Retardation.

Willer, B., & Intagliata, J. (1982). Comparison of family care and group homes as alternatives to institutionalization, *American Journal of Mental Deficiency, 86,* 588–595.

Windle, C. Prognosis of mental subnormals. (1962). *American Journal of Mental Deficiency, 66* (5). (Monograph Supplement).

chapter

23

Residential Relocation and Reactions of Elderly Mentally Retarded Persons

Tamar Heller

This chapter examines the impact of residential transfers on elderly mentally retarded persons. It addresses the following questions: Are elderly retarded residents more vulnerable to "transfer trauma" than other residents? How can relocation be managed to minimize stress reactions? What features of receiving facilities affect posttransfer adjustment? Careful study indicates that although elderly retarded people are not at a higher risk for "transfer trauma," they are more likely to suffer greater deterioration in physical health and placement in more restrictive settings than younger residents. The role of preparatory programs and social support during the transfer is emphasized, as is the need for mindful consideration of what constitutes appropriate placement.

RESIDENTIAL RELOCATION HAS become a common phenomenon for elderly mentally retarded individuals. In the past 2 decades, thousands of mentally retarded people have been transferred from large state institutions to smaller community-based facilities. Between 1967 and 1981, the developmentally disabled population in state institutions experienced a 39% decline from about 200,000 to 125,000 (Braddock, 1981). In a 1979 survey of 172 public residential facilities, 9% of the residents had been transferred into other facilities within a year. Of these, 38% had been transferred to similar facilities, and 62% to less restrictive facilities (Scheerenberger, 1981).

Throughout the United States, old institutions for mentally retarded persons have been closed or are undergoing substantial phase-downs. Recent major closings have occurred in

six states (Minnesota, Pennsylvania, Maryland, Illinois, Florida, and Michigan), and many others have indicated impending phase-down of their institutions for developmentally disabled individuals (National Association of State Mental Retardation Program Directors, 1982).

Many transferees from these institutions are elderly residents who have lived or worked at the facilities for most if not all of their adult lives. Recent surveys have indicated that about 20% of the population in both community and public residential facilities are between the ages of 40 and 62, and about 4% are over the age of 63 years (Bruininks, Hill, & Thorsheim, 1982).

This chapter reviews the literature, examines major issues and concerns, and presents guidelines for the residential relocation of el-

379

derly and mentally retarded populations. It discusses transfers from one institution or community facility into another, and from one unit of a facility to another. It does not focus on the effects of initial movement into a residential facility from a family home, or residential relocation from one family home to another. Although there is very little research on elderly mentally retarded individuals per se, much can be gleaned from the findings reported in both the gerontological and mental retardation literature.

The following questions are addressed:

Does relocation result in "transfer trauma" for the elderly mentally retarded person?

Are some people more vulnerable than others to adverse transfer effects?

How can the relocation process be managed to minimize stress reactions for the elderly retarded person?

What features of receiving facilities affect the subsequent adjustment to relocation?

EFFECTS OF RELOCATION

For the older mentally retarded person, residential relocation frequently entails widespread changes in accustomed daily living patterns, habilitation programs, interpersonal relationships, and physical settings. Major readjustments and reorientation to the new environment are required changes that are often accompanied by stress. Many families, client advocates, and staff members have strongly resisted residential transfers, fearing that the residents would suffer "transfer trauma," a severe stress reaction involving physical, mental, or behavioral deterioration. Relocation studies of elderly and mentally retarded persons have sought to assess the impact of relocation stress by studying changes in residents' mortality rates, physical health, affect, and behavior following relocation.

Mortality and Physical Health

Separation from familiar surroundings and individuals has been associated with feelings of helplessness and despair, as well as medical problems (Engel, 1968; Schmale, 1958). A number of gerontological studies have documented increased mortality rates after relocation (e.g., Aldrich & Mendkoff, 1963; Aleksandrowicz, 1961; Bourestom & Tars, 1974). These findings are frequently cited by those opposing institutional transfers of elderly people. More recent studies, however, have found either no increase or even a decrease in mortality after transfers (e.g., Borup, Gallego, & Heffernan, 1979; Coffman, 1981; Kowalski, 1978).

Generally, studies of relocated mentally retarded individuals have not documented increases in mortality rates after transfer. However, an exception is Miller's (1975) account of a twofold increase in mortality following the transfer of profoundly retarded residents from Pacific State Hospital to convalescent hospitals.

Deterioration in physical health following relocation has been noted in several studies. Posttransfer effects for elderly residents have included increases in activity restrictions, hospitalization, and health failure (Miller & Lieberman, 1965), and, for mentally retarded children, posttransfer increases in number of sick days (Heller, 1982).

Affect and Behavior

Stressful reactions to relocation are most commonly manifested in adverse behavioral and emotional changes. Geriatric residents have reportedly exhibited decreased social activity (Bourestom & Tars, 1974), mental health, self-care, and social capacities (Marlowe, 1976), and increased confusion, memory deficits, and bizarre behavior (Miller & Lieberman, 1965). At least short-term decrements in adaptive behavior have been noted in residential transfers of mentally retarded children and adults. In a relocation from Pennhurst State School to Woodhaven Center, the intermediate care residents were rated as lower in language development and more withdrawn 6 to 8 weeks after the move. On the other hand, the skilled nursing group showed a general increase in activity, including both adaptive and maladaptive behavior (Cohen, Conroy, Fraser, Snelbecker, & Spreat, 1977). Other studies of mentally retarded people have found short-term decreases in constructive and social interaction activities (Carsrud, Carsrud, Henderson, Alisch, & Fowler 1979; Heller, 1982; Heller, 1984) and increases in social isolation (Schumacher, Wisland, & Qvammen, 1983), maladaptive behavior, and use of antipsychotic drugs (Hemming, Lavender, & Pill, 1981).

Although relocation has frequently resulted in short-term physical, mental, and behavioral problems for elderly mentally retarded residents, transfer to a new environment can also result in long-term benefits that may outweigh the temporary setbacks. A move can provide residents with an opportunity for better programming and staff, and more pleasant living conditions. Studies of placements from institutions to community-based facilities (e.g., Aanes & Moen, 1976; Close, 1977; Conroy, Efthimiou, & Lemanowicz, 1982) have reported general resident progress in self-help, socialization, and communication.

A further examination of the research indicates that the impact of relocation is considerably varied, depending not only on resident characteristics and vulnerabilities, but also on the management of the relocation process itself and on the suitability of receiving facility environments.

High-Risk Groups

Lazarus (1966) has hypothesized that environmental change would be perceived as more stressful and would have more drastic consequences for people lacking adequate resources, supports, and adaptive coping mechanisms. From this perspective, one would expect more severely physically and mentally handicapped elderly people to be particularly vulnerable to the adverse affects of relocation. Neugarten (1968) has noted that as people age, they have less energy available for maintaining involvement with the outside world and less desire for change. Elderly people are also more likely to suffer from deterioration in vision, hearing, and strength; mental and physical health problems; and loss of long-term friendships (Callison et al., 1971; Cotten, Sison, & Starr, 1981). With retirement or cessation of

employment, they also experience excess leisure time, decreased activities, and physical and social dependency.

Studies of mentally retarded (Heller, 1982) and elderly residents (Goldfarb, Shahinian, & Burr, 1972; Killian, 1970; Marlowe, 1976) have provided some evidence that relocation is indeed more detrimental to those who are already in the poorest health. The move itself may be more traumatic for the ailing person, who often lacks physical strength and whose coping resources may already have been depleted because of the illness.

There has been no clear evidence that elderly mentally retarded people are at a higher risk of traumatic transfer effects in comparison with younger mentally retarded people or with nonretarded elderly people. In an observational study of 147 residents moved from an old institution into remodeled units (Landesman-Dwyer, 1982), older residents did not differ from younger residents in their behavioral reactions to transfer, with the exception of demonstrating a greater increase in sleeping behaviors.

Braddock, Heller, and Zashin (1984) investigated the effect of age on the behavioral adaptation of 185 residents who were transferred from a large facility that was being closed into four smaller institutions. The analysis compared the behavioral changes from 1–3 months prior to the move to 1–3 months after the move in four age groups (20–29, 30–39, 40–49, 50 and over). Surprisingly, the elderly group of 26 residents (age 50 and over) did not significantly differ from the younger residents in any of nine major behavior categories (object interaction, positive affect, negative affect, social interaction, staff attention, abnormal, antisocial, other nonsocial, and inactive) prior to the transfer. However, the older residents did demonstrate somewhat different effects of relocation. While the younger residents exhibited a drop in object interaction behavior, the elderly group actually exhibited an *increase* in such behavior. Although all the age groups experienced a significant drop in positive affect (e.g., smiling, laughing) and in attention from staff, this drop was *greater* for the elderly transferees. One possible explanation for this difference in relocation effects is that the staff at the receiving facilities may have focused more attention on the younger residents, whereas at the old facility staff-resident relationships were well established and not as influenced by the residents' ages.

In a re-examination of data from an earlier closure study (Heller & Berkson, 1982), Heller analyzed age effects in resident adaptation to transfers from a large community facility to 13 other smaller community residences. Of the 116 residents transferred, 56 were elderly (over 50 years old). Prior to the move, the elderly residents were somewhat less likely to be in "competitive" or sheltered employment and were in poorer health than the other residents. The age groups did not differ significantly in IQ, diagnosis, rated sociability, disruptiveness, self-care independence, or psychiatric symptoms. Six months following the transfer, the client records did not indicate any significantly worse transfer effects for the elderly group; in fact, psychiatric symptomatology actually *decreased* more for elderly residents than for the younger ones. Thirty months after the transfer, the elderly residents showed similar behavioral adaptation to community living as the younger ones, with the exception of a greater drop in rated sociability. However, as one would expect, throughout the span of the study, the older residents remained in poorer health and were less likely to be employed. Although they represented 45% of the study sample, elderly residents comprised the majority of the mortalities (5 out of 7) and transfers to nursing homes (5 out of 6). They also were more likely to be initially placed in more restrictive settings during the facility closing than were the younger transferees, as they comprised 65% of the placements in either mentally ill facilities or nursing homes, and none of the independent group home placements.

Two main conclusions can be drawn from the study's findings. First, elderly people did *not* experience any greater transfer "trauma" in the initial 6 months following residential relocation. Elderly people who survived and did not experience physical deterioration over the 30 months were able to function as well as the younger people in the community, with the exception of some decrease in employment and sociability.

Second, older mentally retarded people tended to be placed in more restrictive settings, even when their level of independent functioning and sociability was similar to that of younger people. In these instances, physical health problems may have contributed to the placement decision.

Seltzer, Seltzer, and Sherwood (1982) similarly found that mentally retarded elderly people fare poorer in community residential facilities than do younger people. In a study of 153 people placed from a Massachusetts institution into community residences, the 26 older residents (age 55 and over) functioned lower in terms of the: 1) number of community skills they mastered, 2) the extent to which they regularly performed these skills, 3) their motivation for independent performance, and 4) the number of jobs held. Additionally, as in the previous study, the elderly people were not only initially placed in less independent settings, but they also continued to move to more restrictive settings. Although 18% of the younger people moved to independent settings, *none* of the elderly people did. Also, only 8% of the elderly (versus 41% of the younger) people transferred to group homes. Further evidence of the differential placement of elderly individuals is provided in Baker, Seltzer, and Seltzer's (1977) nationwide study of group homes. They found that group homes housing a majority of elderly people (age 50 and over) tended to be more protective of residents and restrictive of their autonomy.

Overall, there has been little evidence of greater "transfer trauma" among elderly mentally retarded persons in terms of short-term behavioral effects. Rather, differences between older and younger residents appear over the longer term, as older residents not only experience more health problems than do other mentally retarded individuals but also receive different placement and staff attention. Concomitantly, elderly residents exhibit lower levels of community functioning.

Much has been written about the "transplantation shock" and quick deterioration following institutionalization of nonretarded elderly people in nursing homes (reviewed in Schulz & Brenner, 1977). For retarded elderly people, a move to a nursing home may not be as traumatic as it is for elderly nonretarded people, whose move to a nursing home is often precipitated by personal or family problems. These problems include physical or mental illnesses, loss of spouse or other primary family members, other changes in family relationships, and/or financial hardships. The nursing home is usually the nonretarded person's first experience with aggregate, institutionalized living characterized by its lack of privacy, forced togetherness, and little autonomy. Conversely, for many mentally retarded persons admitted to nursing homes, the new environment is not so radically different from their previous residential environments. Also, they are less likely to be placed in nursing homes due to family or health reasons. Although there may be the emotional "grief" associated with leaving a residence that was probably home for many years, elderly retarded residents likely experience fewer feelings of family rejection and annoyance with the nursing home milieu than do other residents. Mueller and Porter (1969) reported that mentally retarded residents who moved from institutions to nursing homes adjusted better to their new environment than did the other nonretarded residents. Similarly, Cotten et al. (1981) noted that retarded residents of nursing homes required less staff time and had fewer physical and behavioral problems than did the other residents.

THE RELOCATION PROCESS

The impact that relocation will have on residents largely depends on the manner in which the relocation is handled, how it is perceived by the resident, and the amount of social support provided.

Preparatory Programs

Lazarus (1966) has emphasized the role of cognitive appraisal in reactions to life events. He has theorized that an event will be stressful to an individual if it is perceived as highly unfamiliar, ambiguous, and unanticipated. Anticipatory coping strategies that increase predictablity of the event can alleviate stressful reactions to it. Preparatory programs have been used successfully with both mentally retarded (Weinstock, Wulkan, Colon, Coleman, & Goncalves, 1979) and elderly individuals (Bourestom, Tars, & Pastalan, 1973; Jasnau, 1967; Novick, 1967; Zweig & Csank, 1975) facing residential transfers. These programs provided supportive services, preparatory counseling, site visits, and realistic information about the new settings prior to the move.

Allowing residents greater choice and decision-making powers during the transfer process may also result in greater predictability, optimistic expectations, and better posttransfer adjustment. In their review of elderly relocation studies, Schulz and Brenner (1977) provide evidence supporting the important role of behavioral control by residents during the transfer process. Comparison of voluntary and involuntary relocations indicated that voluntary moves were more likely to result in positive changes in resident well-being and satisfaction. In one study of a preparatory program for mentally retarded residents (Weinstock et al., 1979), the transfer was voluntary, residents' families were involved in the transfer decision, and higher functioning residents were given voluntary choice and a visit to the new facility. The pre-move preparation also provided residents with notification of the transfer date; new clothes; a physical checkup; explanations of the transfer; and information about their possessions, new staff, and future facility. None of these studies reported significant adverse behavioral or medical effects following resident transfers.

The usefulness of these preparatory programs for elderly mentally retarded individuals may be limited depending on the resident's level of awareness and beliefs about personal control. Some mentally retarded residents with profound retardation and sensory handicaps may not understand or benefit from site visits, explanations, or decision-making during the transfer process. Also, residents who have been institutionalized for many years may have grown accustomed to external controls. Felton and Kahana (1974) found that among institutionalized elderly persons, external locus of control was *more* strongly associated with adjustment than was internal control.

Social Disruption and Support

In addition to preparatory programs, continuity of social networks and support from staff, family, and friends can mitigate stressful reactions to relocation. Cassel (1974) and Cobb (1976) have noted that persons undergoing stressful life events are cushioned from harmful psychological and physiological effects when such events are experienced in the presence of social support. During residential transfers, there is considerable disruption of ongoing social relationships as new resident groupings, new staff, and possible changes in family involvement occur. Wells and McDonald (1981) reported an over 30% reduction in the number of close friendships among elderly residents several months after transfers. Decreases in social interaction with other residents and staff have also been noted among mentally retarded transferees (Carsrud et al., 1979; Heller, 1982). These disruptions in accustomed social networks reduce the predictability and familiarity of new settings, resulting in greater adjustive demands placed on the residents.

Studies of both elderly (Bourestom & Tars, 1974) and mentally retarded (Heller, 1982) transferees have provided some evidence for the importance of minimizing social disruption during the transition period. Bourestom and Tars (1974) compared residents who experienced radical environmental changes entailing a move to a new physical environment with new staff, programs, and patient populations, to those who also experienced a physical move but without any accompanying changes in staff, patient groups, or programs. Following the move, the radical change residents experienced higher mortality, reported more pessimism about their health, and demonstrated a greater increase in inappropriate behavior. In

Heller's (1982) study of recently transferred children with mental retardation, greater social disruption was associated with increased abnormal behavior.

In a meta-analysis conducted to determine what differentiated studies that found post-transfer mortality increases from those that did not, the major difference was degree of social disruption (Coffman, 1981). Mortality rates were lower among relocations involving "intact" populations in which a whole ward population was moved together or in which individuals were moved from one stable population to another, than among "disrupted" populations who underwent facility closure or individual placements.

Social support from various sources (i.e., sending and receiving facility staff, families, and friends) can contribute to the resident's smoother transition into new settings. This may be especially critical for older institutionalized retarded residents who may feel the impact of separation from familiar staff more than younger residents who have not spent as many years at the institution. Additionally, there is some evidence that receiving facility staff who have not yet developed any long-term relationships with new residents initially spend more time with younger residents (Braddock et al., 1984). Such staff members may also be less experienced in working with elderly residents who likely have more serious medical needs.

Families can provide support to residents by visiting the facilities, by getting involved in client habilitation plans, and by actually helping with the physical move. Although one might expect an increase in family visits when residents are moved out of institutions into facilities closer to their families, Conroy and Latib (1982) found no such increase. For elderly retarded people, the primary family may play less of a role in their lives than for younger retarded or nonretarded people since their parents are likely to be infirm or deceased and they are not likely to have children. Unlike many nonretarded people, they are less likely to enter nursing homes with resentment toward other family members for sending them there. The importance of family visits was highlighted by Gottesman (1974), who noted that nursing home residents who were frequently visited received more staff attention.

Friends and co-residents are likely to comprise the major sources of support for relocated elderly retarded residents. There is a growing body of evidence that peer relationships aid in the successful adaptation of mentally retarded adults in community settings (reviewed in Romer & Heller, 1983). Gollay, Freedman, Wyngaarden, and Kurtz (1978) reported that among residents released from institutions, those who remained in the community were much more likely to have friends than those who were returned to the institutions. Also, two-thirds of those who remained in community placements still visited or maintained contacts with some of their institutionalized friends. Heller and Berkson's study (1982) of a community facility closing similarly found that 30 months after the transfer, residents moving with chosen friends were rated as more sociable and more independent in self-care and were more likely to be transferred into less restrictive settings than those who were separated from friends or did not indicate pre-move friendship choices. In both of these studies, friends may have buffered the effect of relocation stress by providing both emotional and physical supports.

One way of maintaining friendship networks is to transfer residents as intact groups. In such moves, residents are more likely to feel that they are "all in the same boat." Stable friendships are probably more critical for elderly people who may have greater difficulty making new friends. In community settings for retarded adults, older age has been associated with lower rates of sociability (Romer & Berkson, 1980). Also, as they age, many retarded residents require more physical aid from their friends. Others, who are able, can find emotional fulfillment in helping younger retarded residents or more physically handicapped residents. In nursing homes where placement of nonretarded people is more likely to be contingent on behavioral, physical, or emotional impairment than it is for retarded people, the mentally retarded residents are often in a better position to be active givers rather than merely recipients of peer support.

SUITABILITY OF PLACEMENTS

Successful adaptation to transfer depends not only on the transfer process and degree of disruption, but also on the suitability of the new residence for the transferees. Major facility environmental considerations include: 1) physical design, 2) social climate and orientation, and 3) programmatic aspects.

In housing for elderly individuals, various physical attributes (low building height, safe neighborhood) and policies advocating resident autonomy, locus of control, and individualization have been associated with enhanced resident functioning (Heller, Byerts, & Drehmer, 1984; Lawton, 1975; Linn, Gurel, & Linn, 1977; Moos, Lemke, & David, in press). For retarded residents, physical features of residences such as facility location and proximity of services, comfort and appearance, and openness and blending with neighborhood have been related to resident progress (Eyman, Demaine, & Lei, 1979). A therapeutic staff orientation emphasizing habilitative programming, community involvement, and staff-resident interaction has resulted in greater client utilization of community services. In a study of family nursing homes, a social climate of autonomy, tolerance, cohesion, and mutual support facilitated positive adaptive behavior (Intagliata & Willer, 1980).

The habilitative programs and services offered at residential facilities also contribute significantly to client growth and development (Bjaanes, Butler, & Kelly, 1981). As mentally retarded residents age, their service needs change. In a 1975 survey, the highest service needs were ranked in order of priority: 1) health-related services, 2) social and emotional need, 3) housing programs, 4) vocational services, and 5) recreational and leisure time activities (Segal, 1977).

Despite a higher level of need, retarded elderly residents tend to receive fewer rather than more services (Baker et al., 1977). Bjaanes et al. (1981) have noted that those "in most need of habilitative services are those for whom services are least likely to be provided" (p. 346). Perhaps old residents are not expected to gain as much from the programming efforts. Bell and Zubeck's (1960) findings of IQ score increases for the majority of elderly residents who were in stimulating programs indicated that, contrary to common beliefs, elderly residents can benefit from such efforts. Bair and Leland (1959) have argued that the earlier aging of mentally retarded residents may be partially due to their institutionalization in non-challenging milieus.

In designing the service components of a residence, it is important to maintain a balance between maximizing motivation for independent functioning and not overstepping residents' tolerance of stress. Lawton and Nahemow's (1973) theory of ecological press hypothesizes that negative outcomes occur when environmental demands are either too high (stress) or too low (deprivation) for the individual. Moderate levels of demand that are slightly higher than the adaptation level are stimulating, resulting in maximum performance, while levels slightly lower are supportive, resulting in the maximum comfort. An individual's adaptation level will largely depend on his or her level of competence, the upper limit capacity. Hence, one would expect highly competent and independent residents to benefit less from service-rich programs than more impaired residents.

A study by Byerts, Drehmer, Heller, and Grau (1983) found that relocation to a service-rich environment benefited low competence transferees more than high competence transferees. The low competence subjects who transferred were less likely to experience negative outcomes (e.g., death, move to nursing home) than were those who remained in regular public housing. There was no such effect for the higher competence subjects. Another example of the importance of the person-environment fit is Marlowe's (1976) study, which found that physically and cognitively impaired elderly residents fared best in nonchallenging environments offering individual attention, care, and encouragement, whereas less impaired res-

idents thrived in supportive and encouraging, as well as challenging, environments.

Hence, for elderly retarded residents, transfers to environments that are physically comfortable and that provide both sufficient challenge and support for the residents' levels of competence will likely facilitate positive adaptation to residential relocation.

CONCLUSION

Residential relocation is often a stressful event that can lead to deterioration in physical health and behavioral functioning of elderly and mentally retarded residents. However, in many cases, the long-term benefits of placements in superior environments outweigh the temporary setbacks during the initial transition period.

This review has indicated that elderly mentally retarded individuals are *not* necessarily at a higher risk for traumatic transfer effects than are younger retarded or elderly nonretarded residents. Rather, differences between older and younger residents appear over a longer period of time, as older residents not only experience greater deterioration in health, but also experience placement in more restrictive settings than do younger residents. Despite their lower levels of adaptive functioning, elderly residents often receive fewer habilitative services and less staff attention. In comparison with nonretarded people entering nursing homes, the mentally retarded nursing home residents seem to adjust better to the institutionalized milieu and group living situation.

Stressful reactions during transfers can be mitigated by the proper planning of the relocation process. Preparatory programs and client participation in decision-making can serve to increase predictability and optimistic expectations about the move. Social supports from staff, family, and peers also contribute to a smoother transition into new environments. Ultimately, successful adaptation to transfer depends on the suitability of the new residence for transferees. Elderly retarded residents are likely to benefit most from residences that offer improved physical surroundings, habilitative services, and sufficient challenge and support for each individual's level of competence.

Since residential relocation is often a stressful event and may have adverse effects on individuals, one needs to be cognizant of the human costs involved in excessive or poorly planned transfers. Proper management of the relocation process can contribute substantially to adequate posttransfer adjustment. Several guidelines are presented that have applicability to elderly retarded residents.

The first suggestion is that caution be used in transferring medically fragile residents who may have difficulty coping with the actual move and with an unfamiliar social and physical environment. As a precaution, close medical monitoring of these residents is advocated throughout the transfer process. Extra physical aid may also be required during the actual move.

In order to help physically or sensorily impaired elderly residents orient to their new environment, it is helpful to include such guides as large calendars, weekly activity schedules, familiar objects in their rooms, and nightlights. Most important, situations can be restructured so that they require usage of modalities other than the residents' affected ones (Stotsky & Dominick, 1969). For example, deaf residents will require visual rather than auditory presentations.

Preparatory programs involving counseling, site visits, and family involvement are recommended. Additionally, resident participation in the transfer decision, the planning process, and the packing of possessions can allay anxieties. However, the degree to which residents benefit from these measures depends on their level of awareness, their physical capabilities, and their desire and expectation for behavioral control.

In order to increase environmental stability and to promote supportive relationships among the residents and their staff, it is advisable to move residents as "intact" units so that facility programs, staff, and population groups are maintained. During the later stages of facility phasedowns, program continuity often ceases at precisely the moment that residents require it most. This can be devastating to clients who have developed dependent relations with staff over many years. When it is not possible to move units "intact," anxiety can be reduced by having sending facility staff accompany residents during the move. Also, friendships among residents can be maintained by moving residents with at least one chosen friend.

At the receiving facilities, it is important for staff to continue previous programming efforts and to only gradually institute modifications and greater demands on residents. This recommendation may be especially applicable to elderly residents who are less likely to embrace change. Staff can encourage resident sociability through planned group activities and social events for interested residents. Some elderly residents, of course, will prefer to be alone and will resist attempts at "forced sociability." Others will enjoy these activities and may discover new social roles in their old age.

Finally, residents will benefit most from placements into environments that best match their level of competence and service needs. Elderly retarded residents are often inappropriately placed in overly restrictive environments such as nursing homes when skilled nursing is not required. Such placements may increase dependency. A balance needs to be maintained between client protection and support and environmental challenge.

REFERENCES

Aanes, D., & Moen, M. (1976). Adaptive behavior changes of group home residents. *Mental Retardation, 14*, 36–40.

Aldrich, C. I., & Mendkoff, E. (1963). Relocation of the aged and disabled: A mortality study. *Journal of the American Geriatrics Society, 11*, 185–194.

Aleksandrowicz, D. (1961). Fire and its after-math on a geriatric ward. *Bulletin of the Meninger Clinic, 25*, 23–32.

Bair, H. V., & Leland, H. (1959). Management of the geriatric mentally retarded patient. *Mental Hospitals, 10*, 9–12.

Baker, B. L., Seltzer, G. B., & Seltzer, N. M. (1977). *As close as possible: Community residences for retarded adults.* Boston: Little, Brown & Co.

Bell, A., & Zubek, J. P. (1960). The effect of age on the intellectual performance of mental defectives. *Journal of Gerontology, 15,* 285–295.

Bjaanes, A. T., Butler, E. W., & Kelly, B. R. (1981). Placement type and client functioning level as factors in provision of services aimed at increasing adjustment. In R. H. Bruininks, C. E. Meyers, B. B. Sigford, & K. C. Lakin (Eds.), *Deinstitutionalization and community adjustment of mentally retarded people* (pp. 337–350). Washington, DC: American Association on Mental Deficiency.

Borup, J. H., Gallego, D. T., & Heffernan, P. G. (1979). Relocation and its effect on mortality. *The Gerontologist, 19,* 135–140.

Bourestom, N. C., & Tars, S. (1974). Alterations in life patterns following nursing home relocation. *The Gerontologist, 14,* 506–510.

Bourestom, N. C., Tars, S., & Pastalan, L. (1973). *Alteration in life patterns following nursing home relocation.* Paper presented at the 26th annual meeting of the Gerontological Society of America, Miami, FL.

Braddock, D. (1981). Deinstitutionalization of the retarded: Trends in public policy. *Hospital and Community Psychiatry, 32,* 607–615.

Braddock, D., Heller, T., & Zashin, E. (1984). *The closure of the Dixon Developmental Center: A study of the implementation and consequences of a public policy.* Chicago: Institute for the Study of Developmental Disabilities, University of Illinois at Chicago.

Bruininks, R. H., Hill, B. K., & Thorsheim, M. J. (1982). Deinstitutionalization and foster care for mentally retarded people. *Health and Social Work, 7,* 198–205.

Byerts, T. O., Drehmer, D. E., Heller, T., & Grau, B. W. (1983). *Viability of a new congregate public housing model.* Paper presented at the 36th annual meeting of the Gerontological Society of America, San Francisco, CA.

Callison, D. A., Armstrong, H. F., Elam, L., Cannon, R. L., Paisley, C. B., & Himwich, H. E. (1971). The effects of aging on schizophrenic and mentally defective patients: Visual, auditory and grip strength measurements. *Journal of Gerontology, 26,* 135–145.

Carsrud, A. L., Carsrud, K. B., Henderson, C. J., Alisch, C. J., & Fowler, A. V. (1979). Effects of social and environmental change on institutionalized mentally retarded persons: The relocation syndrome reconsidered. *American Journal of Mental Deficiency, 84,* 266–272.

Cassel, J. (1974). Psychosocial processes and "stress": Theoretical formulations. *International Journal of Health Services, 4,* 471–482.

Close, D. (1977). Community living for severely and profoundly retarded adults: A group home study. *Education and Training of the Mentally Retarded, 12,* 256–262.

Cobb, S. (1976). Social support as a moderator of life stress. *Psychosomatic Medicine, 38,* 300–310.

Coffman, T. L. (1981). Relocation and survival of institutionalized aged: A reexamination of the evidence. *The Gerontologist, 21,* 483–500.

Cohen, H., Conroy, J. Q., Fraser, D. W., Snelbecker, G. E., & Spreat, S. (1977). Behavioral effects of institutional relocation of mentally retarded residents. *American Journal of Mental Deficiency, 82,* 12–18.

Conroy, J., Efthimiou, J., & Lemanowicz, J. (1982). A matched comparison of the developmental growth of institutionalized and deinstitutionalized mentally retarded clients. *American Journal of Mental Deficiency, 86,* 581–587.

Conroy, J. W., & Latib, A. (1982). *Family impacts: Pre-post attitudes of 65 families of clients deinstitutionalized.* Philadelphia: Temple University Developmental Disabilities Center.

Cotten, P. D., Sison, G. F. P., & Starr, S. (1981). Comparing elderly mentally retarded and non-mentally retarded individuals: Who are they? What are their needs? *The Gerontologist, 21,* 359–365.

Engel, G. L. (1968). A life setting conducive to illness: The giving up and given complex. *Annals of Internal Medicine, 69,* 293.

Eyman, R., Demaine, G., & Lei, T. (1979). Relationship between community environments and resident changes in adaptive behavior: A path model. *American Journal of Mental Deficiency, 83,* 330–337.

Felton, B., & Kahana, E. (1974). Adjustment and situationally bound locus of control among institutionalized aged. *Journal of Gerontology, 29,* 295–301.

Goldfarb, A. I., Shahinian, S. P., & Burr, H. I. (1972). Death rate of relocated residents. In D. P. Kent, R. Kastenbaum, & S. Sherwood (Eds.), *Research planning and action for the elderly* (pp. 525–537). New York: Behavioral Publications.

Gollay, E., Freedman, R., Wyngaarden, M., & Kurtz, N. R. (1978). *Coming back: The community experiences of deinstitutionalized mentally retarded people.* Cambridge, MA: Abt Books.

Gottesman, L. E. (1974). Nursing home performance as related to resident traits, ownership, size and source of payment. *American Journal of Public Health, 64,* 269–276.

Heller, T. (1982). Social disruption and residential relocation of mentally retarded children. *American Journal of Mental Deficiency, 87,* 48–55.

Heller, T., & Berkson, G. (1982). *Friendship and residential relocation.* Paper presented at the Gatlinburg Conference on Research in Mental Retardation, Gatlinburg, TN.

Heller, T., Byerts, T. O., & Drehmer, D. E. (1984). Impact of environment on social and activity behavior in public housing for the elderly. *Journal of Housing for the Elderly, 2,* 17–25.

Hemming, H., Lavender, T., & Pill, R. (1981). "Quality of Life" of mentally retarded adults transferred from large institutions to new small units. *American Journal of Mental Deficiency, 86,* 157–169.

Intagliata, J., & Willer, B. (1980). *Factors associated with success in family care homes and community residential facilities.* Paper presented at the annual meeting of the American Academy on Mental Retardation, San Francisco, CA.

Jasnau, K. F. (1967). Individualized vs. mass transfer of nonpsychotic geriatric patients from mental hospitals to nursing homes with special reference to the death rate. *Journal of the American Geriatrics Society, 15,* 280–284.

Killian, E. C. (1970). Effect of geriatric transfers on mortality rates. *Social Work, 15,* 19–26.

Kowalski, N. C. (1978). A home for the aged: A study of short-term mortality following dislocation of elderly residents. *Journal of Gerontology, 33,* 601–602.

Landesman-Dwyer, S. (1982). *The changing structure and function of institutions: A search for optimal group care environments.* Paper presented at the Lake Wilderness Conference on the Impact of Residential Environments on Retarded Persons and their Care Providers, Seattle, WA.

Lawton, M. P. (1975). *Planning and managing housing for the elderly.* New York: John Wiley & Sons.

Lawton, M. P., & Nahemow, L. (1973). Ecology and the aging process. In C. Eisdorfer & M. P. Lawton (Eds.), *Psychology of adult development and aging* (pp. 619–674). Washington, DC: American Psychological Association.

Lazarus, R. S. (1966). *Psychological stress and the coping process.* New York: McGraw-Hill Book Co.

Linn, M. W., Gurel, L., & Linn, B. S. (1977). Patient outcome as a measure of quality of nursing home care. *American Journal of Public Health, 67,* 337–344.

Marlowe, R. A. (1976). When they closed the doors at Modesto. In P. Ahmed & S. Plog (Eds.), *State mental hospitals: What happens when they close* (pp. 83–96). New York: Plenum Publishing Corp.

Miller, C. (1975). *Deinstitutionalization and mortality trends in profoundly mentally retarded.* Paper presented at the Western Research Conference on Mental Retardation, Carmel, CA.

Miller, D., & Lieberman, M. A. (1965). The relationship of affect state and adaptive capacity to reactions to stress. *Journal of Gerontology, 20,* 492–497.

Moos, R. H., Lemke, S., & David, T. G. (in press). Environmental design and programming in residential settings for the elderly: Practices and preferences. In V. Regnier & J. Pynoos (Eds.), *Housing for the elderly: Satisfactions and preferences.* New York: Elsevier Science Publishing Co.

Mueller, J. B., & Porter, R. (1969). Placement of adult retardates from state institutions in community care facilities. *Community Mental Health Journal, 5,* 289–294.

National Association of State Mental Retardation Program Directors. (1982, July). *New Directions Newsletter.*

Neugarten, B. L. (1968). *Middle age and aging: A reader in social psychology.* Chicago: University of Chicago Press.

Novick, L. J. (1967). Easing the stress of moving day. *Hospitals, 41,* 6–10.

Romer, D., & Berkson, G. (1980). Social ecology of supervised communal facilities for mentally disabled adults: II. Predictors of affiliation. *American Journal of Mental Deficiency, 85,* 229–242.

Romer, D., & Heller, T. (1983). Social adaptation of mentally retarded adults in community setting: A social–ecological approach. *Applied Research in Mental Retardation, 4,* 303–314.

Scheerenberger, R. C. (1981). Deinstitutionalization: Trends and difficulties. In R. H. Bruininks, C. E. Meyers, B. B. Sigford, & K. C. Lakin (Eds.), *Deinstitutionalization and community adjustment of mentally retarded people* (pp. 3–13). Washington, DC: American Association on Mental Deficiency.

Schmale, A. H. (1958). Relationship of separation and depression to disease. *Psychosomatic Medicine, 20,* 259–267.

Schumacher, K., Wisland, M., & Qvammen, B. (1983). *Relocation effects on adaptive and communication behaviors.* Paper presented at the 107th annual meeting of the American Association on Mental Deficiency, Dallas, TX.

Schulz, R., & Brenner, G. (1977). Relocation of the aged: A review and theoretical analysis. *Journal of Gerontology, 32,* 323–333.

Segal, R. (1977). Trends in services for the aged mentally retarded. *Mental Retardation, 15,* 25–27.

Seltzer, M. M., Seltzer, G. B., & Sherwood, C. C. (1982). Comparison of community adjustment of older vs. younger mentally retarded adults. *American Journal of Mental Deficiency, 87,* 9–13.

Stotsky, B. A., & Dominick, J. R. (1969). Mental patients in nursing homes: II. Intellectual impairment and physical illness. *Journal of the American Geriatrics Society, 17,* 45–55.

Weinstock, A., Wulkan, P., Colon, C. J., Coleman, J., & Goncalves, S. (1979). Stress inoculation and interinstitutional transfer of mentally retarded individuals. *American Journal of Mental Deficiency, 83,* 385–390.

Wells, L., & McDonald, G. (1981). Interpersonal networks and post-relocation adjustment of the institutionalized elderly. *The Gerontologist, 21,* 177–183.

Zweig, J., & Csank, I. (1975). Effects of relocation on chronically ill geriatric patients of a medical unit: Mortality rates. *Journal of the American Geriatrics Society, 23,* 132–136.

chapter

24

Architectural Setting and the Housing of Older Developmentally Disabled Persons

Julia Williams Robinson

Physical environment affects behavior at two levels: the symbolic and the functional. The changes associated with aging make the role of the environment for developmentally disabled individuals similar to that for other aging persons. Because of the tendency to institutionalize this group, however, care must be taken not to prematurely remove them from community settings. The difference between traditional institutional settings and private housing settings described in this chapter, affects, at the symbolic level, attitudes of the community and attitudes of direct caregivers. The effect of these differences at the functional level is felt on the motor ability, the orientation, and the identity of the resident. Principles are presented for modifying a residence to accommodate the needs of the aging developmentally disabled person.

THE IMPORTANCE OF social environment to behavior has been well documented. The extent to which physical setting alone, however, affects behavior has been difficult to distinguish from the effects of the broader social environment because there are few reliable ways to rigorously measure the variables of the physical settings in isolation from other environmental variables. Nonetheless, there seem to be two ways in which physical setting affects the behavior of people: indirectly, by previous experience of what is expected (the association of worship behavior, for example, with the building type of church), and directly, by making it more or less difficult to perform certain tasks (e.g., it would be difficult to hold a basketball game among the church pews). The first type of effect could be called symbolic; the second, functional. But, what makes this complicated is that, for both types of effect, the social environment interacts with the effect of the physical settings as is discussed later (pp. 394–397). In the case of housing elderly mentally retarded people, both symbolic and functional effects are important.

This chapter is based upon *Architectural Planning of Residences for Mentally Retarded People,* a research project supported by grants from the University of Minnesota Center for Urban and Regional Affairs and the University of Minnesota Graduate School, and sponsored by the School of Architecture and the Department of Psychology of the University of Minnesota. In addition to the author, participants in the research project include Travis Thompson, Paul Emmons, Myles Graff, Scott Daas, and Evelyn Franklin. The illustrations are by Richard Laffin.

AGING AND MENTALLY RETARDED INDIVIDUALS

As people age, they often lose their ability to move with ease. The loss of feeling in their joints and limbs makes correct placement of feet difficult and impairs use of the hands. Loss of vision and balance increases the likelihood of tripping or falling. The aging process makes orientation in environments more difficult: diminishing vision and hearing, as well as mental acuity, may result in confusion about where one is and where one is headed. The changes in one's body and mind caused by aging make people feel different from the way they felt before. And as they change, they may not recognize themselves in this new body; they may be unhappy and frustrated with the changes; they may experience through these changes a loss of identity.

In the impairment of mobility, orientation, and identity, the mentally retarded person is no different from other elderly people (DiGiovanni, 1978; Thomae & Fryers, 1980). In fact, the difference between mentally retarded people and others may be smaller at this time of the life cycle than at any other. Architecturally, then, the solutions may be identical to that for other groups. (For information on design for elderly individuals, see Hiatt, 1982; Howell, 1980; Lawton, 1980; Zeisel, Epp, & Demos, 1978; Zeisel, Welch, Epp, & Demos, 1983.) But, because society's attitude toward mentally retarded individuals has traditionally supported their institutionalization, there may be a tendency to institutionalize this group of people before this response is appropriate to their condition. It is, therefore, important to understand the role that physical setting may play in assisting developmentally disabled people to remain independent within their dwelling.

THE INSTITUTIONAL SETTING VERSUS THE PRIVATE HOUSE SETTING

The assumptions in this chapter are that people ought to be able to be self-sufficient and in control of their environment to the maximum extent of their abilities, and that this independence is easier to achieve in a setting "as close as possible to the norms and patterns of society's mainstream" (Nirje, 1969, p. 181) than it is in an institutional setting, whether it be a nursing home or a large state hospital (Gunzburg, 1973; Wolfensberger, 1972).

A traditional institutional setting is a public building, a place where the group of people representing society serves others. In this sense, it is in large part a work environment. A school houses teachers and students, a government building houses civil servants and citizens, a library houses librarians and patrons, a hospital houses staff and patients. In each case there is a group that serves and a group that is served. Public buildings are designed to serve the needs of the average person using them. It is only very recently, and after the expenditure of much time and effort, that physically handicapped individuals have received legislative recognition as "average people," and thus, have the right to buildings that are easily accessible. Constructed for heavy use and ease of maintenance, the materials used in public buildings are durable and difficult to modify. Such buildings are designed to accommodate large numbers of people and thus are large in scale and designed for maximum security, especially for fire safety. The monumentality of the public building (see Figure 1) expresses the priority of collective society over the individual. This is in direct contrast to the small scale and particular character of a private dwelling.

In traditional institutional housing, the public building is used for people to dwell in. This creates a contradiction of terms, for, in American society, the dwelling is the domain of the individual or intimate family group and, therefore, the most private of all buildings (Altman, 1975). There are, however, situations for which society accepts public group living situations as appropriate: for temporary housing (dormitories, hospitals, nursing homes), or for groups of people considered antisocial (prisoners, and in the past, mentally ill, physically disabled, or developmentally disabled persons). Except in the case of temporary housing, group living was not selected by the residents, but provided on their behalf by the society. The

Figure 1. Public buildings are monumental; private dwellings are modest. Their facades and structures speak to their purpose.

form of traditional government housing for these groups represents attitudes very different from those expressed in the private dwelling. These public buildings are monumental, having formal grounds arranged like a park, large interior spaces, high ceilings, formal internal layout, and are constructed of enduring materials. Public buildings are designed to serve large numbers of people with efficiency; they have many rooms and correspondingly long corridors. Each space is furnished similarly to allow mass-ordering of furniture. Because the cost of maintenance must be kept low despite heavy use, durable flooring, wall, and ceiling

materials are used, as well as cost-effective fluorescent lighting. Since the entire building is a public place, there is no hierarchy of public to private space as in a dwelling, but rather, offices, bathrooms, and bedrooms may be interspersed. The need for fire safety for such a large group requires the provision of wide corridors and fire stairs. Where residents require supervision, the design must allow for security and administrative control of interior and grounds of the facility. In sum, the public building is designed to be impersonal, efficient, and of an assumed economy of scale (see Figure 2).

Figure 2. The lounge in an institution is different from a living room. It expresses an impersonal and general quality due to uniform and austere furnishings, rigid furniture arrangement, and use of materials selected for their durability.

In contrast, the private dwelling is designed to express and to accommodate the desires and needs of individuals. The primary considerations are comfort, privacy, and control by the residents. Instead of responding to the needs of a large group, the private residence responds to the needs of its few inhabitants. Since its construction materials are less enduring, they are more easily rearranged and modified to suit the inhabitants. Even in multiple family housing, it is expected that the dwellers will arrange their space; rules and regulations do not eliminate this possibility, but only limit it. The total number of individuals housed in various residential units within an individual building may be large, but in private settings, the clear delineation of what is public (outside the unit) and what is private (within the unit) is reinforced by the existence of a lockable front door. Furthermore, within the private space, there is clear separation between the semiprivate areas where social activities occur (the living room, dining room, and kitchen), and the areas for intimate activities (bedrooms and bathrooms). These are set apart by a change in level, by being located off a different corridor, or by some other separation device (see Figure 3). The small size of units permits easy access to all conveniences and requirements for daily tasks, and the small scale of activities allows participation by all in a simple, natural way. Furthermore, each unit is furnished and ar-

ranged to suit the particular tastes, habits, activities, and needs of the people who live there; this way each room will be unique. It is unlikely that many pieces of furniture will match, for each has been bought to serve a need experienced at a different time. The needs were not coordinated, but experienced individually. The private dwelling expresses not planned solutions to envisioned problems, but accumulated responses to experienced needs, each responded to in a piecemeal fashion.

SYMBOLIC EFFECT
OF HOUSING SETTING

It is well known that people are strongly affected by the expectations of others (Jencks, 1970; Mercer, 1971). These expectations may be communicated indirectly using the environment as a medium for symbolic messages (Rapoport, 1982). The various attitudes toward inhabitants of institutional housing, such as the custodial and medical models (Canter & Canter, 1979), as opposed to those toward the healthy independent citizen are associated with, and thus expressed in, the architecture of their built form. People who are healthy do not need to go to a state institution or a nursing home; therefore, these places come to be associated with custodial or medical care. The people who dwell within these residences are thus, by definition, dependent, requiring su-

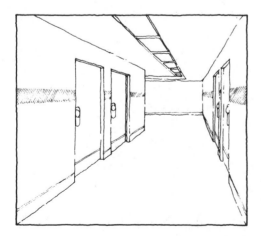

Figure 3.   In an institution the same corridor may serve as access to many different kinds of spaces, whereas in a private dwelling there is a differentiation between public and private spaces, by level change, or other demarcation.

pervision and medical attention. In contrast, people who live in a typical residential area are, by definition, healthy and independent or they would not be living where they are. Thus, the attitudes and expectations of the uneducated outsider toward the developmentally disabled older person may be formulated simply on the basis of where the older person lives. Also, the character of the dwelling, its aesthetic quality and the amenity it provides, influences the public perception of its occupants. For this reason, if disabled people are to become accepted, participating members of society, how and where they live must be taken into account.

In addition to the symbolic effect of setting on society at large, there is another important effect to consider, the effect of the physical environment on direct care staff. Whereas a private residence expresses in its diversity and piecemeal design an attitude of control by the inhabitants, the public institution expresses an attitude of control by the administration. Designed primarily as a workplace, the public institution is a place of control by the caregivers. The lack of a privacy gradient (Chermayeff & Alexander, 1963)—making it necessary for a resident to enter a public corridor on the way from bedroom to bathroom, allowing staff to enter residents' rooms at will, permitting groups of toilet stalls to be located in the bathrooms, and allowing visitors to be entertained in full view of bedrooms and bath-

rooms—clearly distinguishes the institution as a place where the individual resident must be submissive to a force more powerful than the self. The message of the institutional building as primarily a workplace and only secondarily a dwelling makes the challenge of returning to the resident control over self a very difficult one to meet, thus illustrating the complexity of the interaction between physical and social setting.

FUNCTIONAL EFFECTS OF THE HOUSING SETTING

At a functional level, the effect of housing is felt through such variables as proximity to services within the community, or, within the residence, the opportunity for self-sufficiency. For instance, when residents are defined as dependent, food and laundry are brought to the resident, having been prepared by others. Even if the residents were capable of and interested in cooking or washing clothes, the complexity of this disruption to the service of those truly dependent would mediate against such activity. Additionally, in a traditional institutional setting, the facilities for doing either of these tasks are likely to be inconvenient to get to, and the equipment, designed for heavy duty, will probably be difficult to operate (see Figure 4). While the design difficulties that impede the self-reliance of the individual can

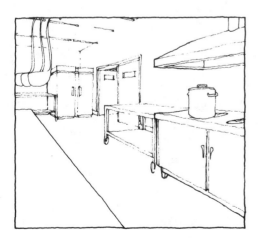

Figure 4. A kitchen in a traditional institution is designed for professional staff to use and does not encourage informal activity by residents. In contrast, the kitchen in a private unit is a natural center of daily affairs.

be overcome by a social pressure encouraging independence, it is easier, obviously, to maintain independence in places where activities are made more convenient by the physical setting.

Among the factors for which the physical environment may play an especially important role for elderly mentally retarded individuals are those of movement, orientation, and identity. One of the many implications of housing setting for elderly mentally disabled persons relates to the issue of the environment's ability to respond to the movement needs of a resident, not as a member of a broad category of people, but as an individual with particular abilities and disabilities. If a grandmother who lives with her son's family has trouble getting out of the bathtub, the family may invest in one grab bar and install it where it will do her the most good. In an institution, however, the four or so grab bars are already provided for and are located according to code, and may actually be inconveniently positioned for those who must rely upon them and a nuisance to others. Because a smaller number of people reside in a normalized setting, the disruption caused by accommodating the needs of one person is minimal. In a place where many people are housed together, deviating from the daily routine or from the established physical setting becomes more of an issue. In many instances, rules and regulations interact with the environment to create a rigid situation. For example, it may be dangerous for an individual to take a bath unsupervised. In a large institution, this problem may be resolved by restricting an individual from bathing; in such instances the only option may be showering under supervision. In an intimate setting, particularly if this is an activity much enjoyed by the person, he or she may be accommodated by arranging for supervision, if not by a staff member, then by a visitor or another resident. This type of flexibility is not always possible in an institutional setting. Accordingly, the ability of the environment to respond to the movement needs of the individual may be greater in a noninstitutional setting (see Figure 5).

The characteristics of institutional settings have implications for the orientation of people within the residence. People who live in institutions are often treated collectively as members of a group. This lack of individuality is reflected in the uniform dimensions, orientation, and furnishings of their bedrooms. In contrast, the bedroom of an occupant of a private dwelling reflects the tastes, abilities, and activities of the individual who spends his or her personal, private time there. Figures 6 and 7 portray these drastic differences. Large institutions have several features that make them confusing: the large number of rooms; the long and often poorly organized corridors; the uniformity of materials, lighting, and furnishing of spaces; and the great separation between

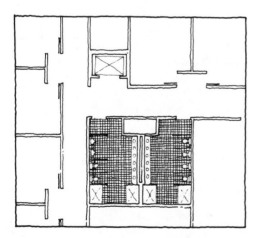 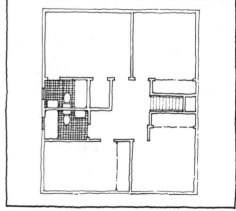

Figure 5.   Bathrooms in institutions are large public rooms. They serve a number of people simultaneously and are located off of a public corridor. In contrast, the bathroom in private housing is located near the bedrooms and is small.

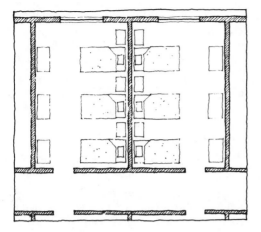
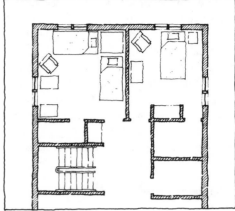

Figure 6.   Unlike inhabitants of private dwellings, residents of institutions are treated like members of a group. This is reflected in the bedrooms by their uniform dimensions, orientation, and furnishings.

activity areas. Whereas in a small residence, the distance between the living room and the dining room is short, and the spaces have distinctly different shapes, as well as varied window placement, wall coverings, lighting fixtures, and furniture, in an institutional setting, there is likely to be a lengthy walk to the dining room past many different rooms and along several corridors. Additionally, the differences between the institutional living and dining rooms may be found only in the use of tables instead of couches. For a person with poor eyesight, some motor disability, and difficulty remembering, a trip between these rooms may become a difficult, even terrifying

event. Where encouragement of self-sufficiency is not forthcoming, the individual might appear to be less able to function independently, and thus prematurely be considered dependent, again illustrating the interaction between social and physical environment.

MODIFICATION FOR ACCESSIBILITY

Accommodation of environments to physical impairment is best done with specific people in mind. What is helpful for one disability may be a hindrance to another, and the options for alteration may vary greatly in cost. Additionally, modification may make a residence look

Figure 7.   In a private dwelling, the bedroom is the territory of the individual who lives there. The room arrangement reflects the tastes, abilities, and activities of its occupants.

more institutional or less so, and selected options should differ depending on individual need. Therefore, in this section, rather than make specific suggestions, some principles are presented that should be considered when making alterations. For more information on these, the reader is referred to a number of excellent sources (e.g., Bednar, 1977; Goldsmith, 1976; North Carolina Department of Insurance, 1980; Raschko, 1982; Veterans Administration, 1977).

Changing Elevation

The act of going up or down can be very difficult for people with particular disabilities. Individuals in wheelchairs cannot negotiate even one step, while people who have limited walking ability, use certain prostheses such as crutches, or have balance problems may be able to use a small number of steps but will have trouble walking down an inclined plane. Elevators are an apparently simple solution to the problem of changing elevation; however, they may imbue a residence with an institutional character if they are located conspicuously, or in many situations, they may be impossible to include without undue expense. It may be possible to house people with such handicaps in a residence that is all on one level, or to simply provide them with a living unit at the same level as nonbedroom activity. If ramps are provided to allow wheelchair access, it is a good idea to keep steps as an alternative method of access. Strong handrails and landings appropriately placed may enable people with limited strengths to use stairs.

Maneuvering

People with wheelchairs, crutches, canes, walkers, or other prostheses need plenty of room to accomplish certain tasks such as opening doors, removing clothing, or even moving along a path or through a door. In certain areas such as entrances or bathrooms, this may require enlarging openings or even rooms to accommodate the need for space. In the bedroom, additional space around the bed may be needed; or in the living room, more area may be needed around furniture. In the bathroom, grab bars may need to be installed. People in wheelchairs or with uncertain footing need a floor or path surface that is neither too slippery nor so textured as to impede movement. For this group of people, area rugs that are not secure may cause tripping.

Reaching

People with limited arm movement, those with a prosthesis that requires the use of the hands, and those who use wheelchairs may have a limited ability to reach. Adjustment of shelves, counter and table heights, and space between counter surface and floor for wheelchair users will enable these individuals to retain their independence. Consideration should also be given to the weight of doors and the type of door hardware, as it is often easier to use a handle than a knob, and sometimes, door closers make opening a door more difficult than necessary.

Seeing and Hearing

People with visual impairments may be assisted simply by ensuring a sufficient light level. This may be especially important in circulation areas that are traditionally not well lit. Glare from a bright light source, such as a poorly shaded lamp or a window located in the direction of movement, may momentarily blind a person with visual problems. The effect of glare can be reduced by screening the light source or by increasing general lighting to reduce contrast. The use of contrasting dark and light tones between architectural elements such as wall and floor will assist discrimination and orientation.

People with hearing disabilities may experience severely reduced ability to distinguish sounds from ambient noise such as television and other appliances, or from the echoing effect of hard surface materials like tile or concrete block, such as occurs frequently in bathrooms. This can be alleviated by isolation of noisy activities from places where conversation or other listening takes place, and with the judicious use of materials.

CONCLUSION

The ability of the small residence to be responsive to the needs of the individual and to provide for orientation has ramifications for a person's sense of dignity and self-worth. In society, people maintain their dignity by being capable of independent action. A smaller scale and more intimate setting fosters such action. Another consideration is that of the individual's ability to control his or her own life. In a large-scale setting, the need for rules and regulations limits this ability. Also, as discussed earlier, the large-scale environment may promote or hinder independent action by merely providing access or removing barriers to certain activities or conveniences. People also gain a sense of their own identity by being able to express themselves through arrangement of their place of dwelling (Cooper, 1974). While this possibility is not necessarily denied in a large-scale institutional setting, more often than not it is severely restricted. Choice of furniture to which one has become accustomed may be impractical in the institutional setting. One may be less able to do nonconforming things that may be tolerated in a more flexible

small-scale residence. And in a small residence, each room is likely to be very different in orientation, in shape, and in location of window and door, thus generating a unique furniture arrangement, and permitting creation of a room that is a distinctive and special place suited to the unique identity of its occupant (Bakos et al., 1981). This physical expression of the person's place in the world is supportive of a sense of self-worth, and fosters independence.

Finally, in considering the role of the architectural setting in housing people, the key concept may be that of adaptation. Adaptation allows for maximum control—thus, comfort and dignity. People vary in their ability to adapt to their environment, and disabled persons are frequently less able to adapt than others. For this reason, the ability of physical environment to be changed may play a more important role in providing independence and dignity to this group than it does for the able-bodied. The physical setting can contribute at both the symbolic and the functional level to the quality of life of the elderly developmentally disabled person, and, for this reason, its potential needs to be understood and used wisely.

REFERENCES

Altman, I. (1975). *The environment and social behavior: Privacy, personal space, territory, crowding.* Monterey, CA: Brooks/Cole Publishing Company.

Bakos, M., Bozic, R., Chapin, D., Gandrus, J., Kahn, S., & Newman, S. (1981). *Group home bedroom booklet.* Cleveland: ARC: Architecture, Research, Construction, Inc.

Bednar, M. J. (1977). *Barrier-free environments.* Stroudsburg, PA: Dowden, Hutchinson & Ross.

Canter, S., & Canter, D. (1979). Building for therapy. In D. Canter & S. Canter (Eds.), *Designing for therapeutic environments: A review of research* (pp. 1–30). New York: John Wiley & Sons.

Chermayeff, S., & Alexander, C. (1963). *Community and privacy: Toward a new architecture of humanism.* Garden City, NY: Doubleday & Company.

Cooper, C. (1974). The house as symbol of the self. In J. Lang, C. Burnette, W. Moleski, & D. Vachon (Eds.), *Designing for human behavior: Architecture and the behavioral sciences* (pp. 130–146). Stroudsburg, PA: Dowden, Hutchinson & Ross.

DiGiovanni, L. (1978). The elderly retarded: A little-known group. *The Gerontologist, 18,* 262–266.

Goldsmith, S. (1976). *Designing for the disabled.* London: Royal Institute of British Architects.

Gunzburg, H. C. (1973). The physical environment of the mentally handicapped: 39 steps toward normalizing living practices in living units for the mentally retarded. *British Journal of Mental Subnormality, 19,* 91–99.

Hiatt, L. G. (1982). Environmental design and the frail older person at home. *PRIDE Institute Journal of Long Term Home Health Care, 2*(1), 13–22.

Howell, S. (1980). *Designing for aging: Patterns of use.* Cambridge, MA: MIT Press.

Jencks, C. (1970). The Coleman report and conventional wisdom. Cambridge, MA: Harvard Center for Educational Policy Research.

Lawton, M. P. (1980). *Environment and aging.* Monterey, CA: Brooks/Cole Publishing Company.

Mercer, J. (1971). Institutionalized Anglocentrism: Labeling mental retardation in the public schools. In P. Orleans & W. Ellis (Eds.), *Race, change, and urban society.* Beverly Hills, CA: Sage Publications.

Nirje, B. (1969). The normalization principle. In R. Kugel & W. Wolfensberger (Eds.), *Changing patterns in residential services for the mentally retarded.* Washington, DC: President's Committee on Mental Retardation.

North Carolina Department of Insurance (1980). *Accessible housing.* Raleigh, NC: Special Office for the Handicapped, North Carolina Department of Insurance.

Rapoport, A. (1982). *The meaning of the building environment: A nonverbal communication approach.* Beverly Hills, CA: Sage Publications.

Raschko, B. B. (1982). *Housing interiors for the disabled and elderly.* New York: Van Nostrand, Reinhold Company.

Thomae, I., & Fryers, T. (1980). *Aging and mental handicap.* Brussels, Belgium: International League of Societies for Persons with Mental Handicap.

Veterans Administration (1977). *Handbook for design: Specially adapted housing.* Washington, DC: Architectural and Transportation Barriers Compliance Board.

Wolfensberger, W. (1972). *The principle of normalization in human services.* Toronto, Canada: National Institute on Mental Retardation.

Zeisel, J., Epp, G., and Demos, S. (1978). *Low-rise housing for older people: Behavioral criteria for design.* Washington, DC: U.S. Government Printing Office.

Zeisel, J., Welch, P., Epp, G., and Demos, S. (1983). *Mid-rise housing for older people: Behavioral criteria for design.* Boston, MA: John Zeisel/Building Diagnostics (Department of Housing and Urban Development Department of Policy Development and Research, H-5037CA).

section
VII

ROLES AND PERSPECTIVES

chapter

25

The Role of the Community Agency in Serving Older Mentally Retarded Persons

Dwight R. Kauppi and Kent C. Jones

Community-based agencies play significant roles in the community adjustment of mentally retarded persons. These roles have become especially important as the deinstitutionalization movement continues to return many mentally retarded persons to the community. This chapter discusses ways in which community agencies can serve aging mentally retarded individuals; problems that are likely to arise; institutional, professional, and personal causes of problems; and possible solutions. Despite problems, the community-based agency is likely to continue to have a vital role in serving aging mentally retarded individuals.

SOCIETY'S TREATMENT OF mentally retarded persons has varied over the years, following shifts in culture, the economy, and public attitudes. At times, some mentally retarded persons have been isolated or allowed to die; at other times, they have been maintained in separate institutions for the purposes of their education or protection, or simply to keep them out of the way. The current trend in the United States and some other countries has been toward a form of integration into society. This trend is exemplified by programs identified as "mainstreaming" or "deinstitutionalization," developed under the model of normalization.

This modern policy of allowing mentally retarded individuals to remain in the community has encouraged an enhanced role for the specialized developmental services community agency to direct and support families and individuals in the care and rehabilitation of

mentally retarded persons. Such agencies may be stimulated and supported by government funds but, in keeping with the trend toward deinstitutionalization, are more likely to be community-based and controlled. These community agencies, with their independent boards and staffs, are reflective generally of the community at large. They can be knowledgeable about and responsive to the needs and characteristics of the community in which they are located. They can be free of the politics, bureaucracy, and regulations that mire many government programs. They can be unrestricted in seeking a broad base of support, and can move quickly to provide programs to fill emerging needs. Such potential advantages are not always realized, but as the deinstitutionalization movement has grown, the role of the community agency in providing services to the person leaving the institution has also grown.

As the community recognizes the inevitable needs of aging mentally retarded persons, the community agency is likely to have a continued role, as long as the force toward deinstitutionalization remains strong. But, special roles and responsibilities of such agencies involve some special problems. This chapter examines some of these problems, offers a historical perspective, and comments on some of the unique issues that are likely to arise. Although the experiences of a particular agency are used to exemplify the problems, what is discussed should apply to any modern community-based agency.

ANTECEDENTS OF COMMUNITY SERVICES

The belief that the community has a responsibility for the welfare of its mentally retarded citizens has both recent and distant origins. Although they may sometimes seem revolutionary, most modern practices and attitudes have antecedents that arose many years ago. There were a number of early efforts at providing community-based services for mentally retarded individuals in the United States. Fernald (1917) reviewed the growth that had occurred in the numbers of mentally retarded persons under state care. He was careful to differentiate the variety of care needs of mentally retarded persons, and he stressed the importance of education and training as well as custodial care. He favorably reviewed the development of "colonies," where mentally retarded adults in good physical condition could be maintained with opportunities for productive activities at a decreased cost to the state. He saw the next step in state care as the development of plans for the placement of some mentally retarded persons in the community, under suitable supervision. He did establish an outpatient clinic in connection with his institution that provided diagnosis, evaluation, and consultation to the families of mentally retarded persons who could not or would not be placed in the institution (Fernald, 1920).

Educational programs for the mentally retarded child also grew, as evidence accumu-

lated that mental retardation was not an unchangeable condition. There was a growth in community services for disabled and retarded individuals and an increase in government involvement, especially following World War II. However, it was not until after the formation in 1950 of the progenitor of the Association for Retarded Citizens of the United States that the greatest growth in community-based programs specifically for mentally retarded persons occurred. Also in the years following World War II, there was a growth in the institutional population for reasons that included the "baby boom," changing medical practices, and public attitudes that increasingly accepted the survival of severely disabled infants. But institutional life was not satisfactory, and increased recognition of the rights of disabled and retarded individuals, plus the knowledge that with better care and help living in the community was possible, led to exposés of institutional horrors, legal battles for improved care, and, ultimately, the deinstitutionalization movement.

PROBLEMS FOR THE COMMUNITY AGENCY

The development of community services has led to a number of problems and issues that now face community agencies serving adult mentally retarded individuals—problems certain to influence future services. Many of the problems are recent, resulting from increasing deinstitutionalization and other societal changes. Other problems have been present since the beginning of the movement, sometimes under a different name or in a different guise. Some of these problems arise out of the nature of the organizations and institutions involved—the inevitable accompaniments of necessary bureaucracies. Some of the problems are professional problems relating to issues of service models and practices. Additional problems come from the psychology of people, the fact that boards and staffs and clients and families are all human beings with the kinds of perceptions, habits, and needs that lead to less-than-perfect societies. Of course, these kinds of problems interact and intermingle so that no problem confronting a community agency has a single source.

Residential Services Problems

Residential services for elderly mentally retarded persons epitomize the problems community agencies face because such services are most often the first sought when an individual enters the jurisdiction of the community agency. When mentally retarded adults living in the community get older, this means that their parents or guardians are also older, and sooner or later will be unable to continue to provide care. As a result, the typical community agency regularly receives calls from other human services agencies, public assistance offices, and families seeking immediate placement of an elderly mentally retarded individual as a result of a parent's death. Usually, there are no beds available in the agency's residential facilities because such placements are considered lifetime and there is little turnover. Even when a bed is available, the agency may be reluctant to accept the crisis referral because there is a list of other community referrals that have been waiting for months. Staff are also reluctant to accept an individual into a group home without complete intake work, including the client's personal history, a physical examination, and the development of program plans.

Sometimes, siblings or other immediate family of the client request temporary emergency placement. Agency staff often suspect that in such cases later alternative residential placement will be difficult, and this may make them hesitant to accept the client. At the same time, the agency staff feel concern when they are unable to provide service. If the community residence does not accept the placement of an elderly mentally retarded person, the individual is likely to be institutionalized, either in a mental retardation facility or other public facility. There is also public and political reaction that must be considered by the agency when rejecting a client for residential placement.

Emergency residential service needs usually arise because parents of aging mentally retarded persons have not provided them with the skills or resources needed to live in an alternative to the parental home. Sometimes the parent's attitude is like that of the father of a 50-year-old day treatment center client who refused to cooperate in obtaining support services for his daughter by saying that he did not care what was done with his daughter after he died, for now he just wanted to be left alone. Such failure to develop any support or alternatives can have potentially serious results. Recently, an elderly male day treatment center client was missing from his program for several days, and all attempts to contact his home by telephone failed. A social worker went to visit the client at home and found that his mother had been dead in the upstairs apartment for several days and that the client had been sitting there, not knowing what to do.

Community agencies must also deal with the problems of aging mentally retarded clients who are already living in their residential facilities. If a client no longer produces sufficient results in a workshop or if the health needs of a client are not met in a day treatment center program, the community agency may seek alternative day programming. Ultimately, if another program is not obtained, the client will be staying home in the community residence. At present, this is occurring in group homes that have been operating for a number of years and that have accepted clients who were middle-age at the time they were accepted. As the health and mobility of these clients deteriorate, their needs become greater and they require more resources from the agency.

Regulatory Problems

A complicating factor is that some state and federal regulations require out-of-home day programming to support client residence in the agency group home. The rationale for this requirement is valid enough when applied to deinstitutionalized young adults who might otherwise be simply spending inactive lives in a community residence. But as mentally retarded residents age and their energy and personal resources make day programming less reasonable, such regulations interfere with sensible planning. In an effort to compromise, agencies sometimes try partial day programming if a day program is willing to accept the arrangement. However, this can lead to problems with transportation because of schedules, and with the level of capability of the individual involved. In addition, the residence must schedule a staff person to be home for that person who is returning from half-day placement.

The application of regulations and procedures developed for younger clientele is troublesome in other services and areas as well. The importance and validity of a developmental model of care for mentally retarded individuals has been stressed for decades, to good effect. As programs have been built on a model assuming development, clients have shown growth. Now, developmental models are so common they are all but assumed by professionals and program evaluators. But what does this mean to programs and professionals working with the aging client? The best result of an exemplary service program may be a slowing of deterioration, not the development of new abilities. It will be difficult to write regulations that will allow programs to develop appropriately and that will assess their results fairly. It will take time for procedures to be developed and codified, and in the meantime the agency serving the aging retarded individual may be penalized.

Service Problems

In a survey of community agencies in the Buffalo, New York area, Jones (1984) found that beyond general concerns with funding and regulations, the problems expressed by agencies in working with aging mentally retarded individuals were related to the nature and scope of services provided by the agency. Vocational agencies were likely to identify clients' physical limitations and their inability to work full days as problems. For agencies serving a broad range of ages and disabilities, problems in relationships between aging mentally retarded persons and other clients were feared. Agencies that had a broad range of services specifically for mentally retarded people were likely to be concerned with the lack of adequate

support services available elsewhere in the system.

One problem that seems to cut across the agencies is the difficulty in articulating a goal for the services provided under the current models. If a normalization model is applied, a normative goal for an aging mentally retarded person might be some kind of retirement. However, current regulations do not allow the kind of reduction in daily activity implied by retirement. Beyond the regulations, the concept of what retirement may involve for individuals who have spent much of their lives in institutions or sheltered work is not yet clearly developed.

Some agencies also express difficulty in individualizing services. The aging process, with its array of problems, is a highly personal and unique one, affecting each person differently, even within a single disability group. Especially for these reasons, elderly mentally retarded persons are difficult to fit into the existing pattern of community services.

Board and Administrative Problems

In addition to the problems felt by the staffs of agencies providing services, there are also some problems that are seen at the agency administration and director's level. One such problem is that of long-range planning, where agencies singly and the community generally must look to the future and plan programs for human problems that will be emerging. A backward look at the success in such planning would suggest that the task of planning is difficult indeed. Although many mentally retarded persons have lived to adulthood, mental retardation literaure as early as 1963 listed only medicine and schooling when discussing services for mentally retarded persons (President's Panel on Mental Retardation, 1963). There was a dearth of materials regarding adult services and vocational adjustment. Now, care providers face the same lack of knowledge and service for an equally predictable population, elderly mentally retarded individuals. When viewed with the knowledge of what has occurred, the failure of earlier leaders to plan adequately seems obvious. Such criticism is unfair, of course, since it is easy to say after the fact what should have been done. But care providers should be aware that planning is difficult, even for what seem to be obvious. Long-range planning is especially difficult for community agencies. Although in many ways their staff and board members are closest to the raw data of service, most agencies lack the resources required to do extensive long-range planning. Once plans are made, the agency must convince an array of individuals and institutions that the directions taken are sensible, cost-effective, and nonpredatory. There should be little wonder that even the obvious seems unexpected.

Another issue of importance to community agency leadership has to do with the degree of integration of elderly mentally retarded individuals with other elderly persons. Integration, consistent with normalization principles, appears as an ideal goal. Integration for elderly mentally retarded people means participation or placement in those activities usually associated with elderly persons, such as senior citizen centers or nursing homes. After a lifetime of special services separated from the mainstream of society, it would seem desirable to have elderly mentally retarded individuals join in these activities. However, many senior citizens do not want mentally retarded persons in their programs. With little prior exposure to the mentally retarded population, many elderly persons experience difficulties in accepting new ideas such as normalization, or in welcoming outsiders into their programs. Senior citizen centers, especially, have expressed reluctance to invite "outsiders" to their programs.

Another dimension of the same issue involves the question of placing mentally retarded individuals in residential services for elderly persons. In many respects, the two groups are seen as similar. Pezzoli (1978) has said, "The two groups (elderly and mentally retarded) show many of the same problems of societal indifference, stinginess, and contempt mixed with equally dehumanizing pity, patronization, and treatment as children" (p. 206). Many nursing homes exemplify society's indifferent treatment of elderly individuals. In contrast, group homes and community intermediate care facilities for the mentally retarded have been found to provide a much more social, supportive environment (Willer & Intagliata, 1984). Should a community agency advocate for integration of their elderly mentally retarded clients into what may be an unfair or inadequate service system?

One of the problems affecting the administrators of community agencies serving an aging mentally retarded population relates to the motivation of board and staff. Many of the staff of community agencies are young people, anxious to interact with clients in growth-producing or facilitative ways. Will such staff remain motivated when their clients are less active, where growth may be less evident, or where the goal of service may be no more than slowed deterioration? Although board members do not have the same personal contact with clients, their motivation to serve may be similarly affected. It is also unlikely that boards will include parents of aging mentally retarded individuals, thus eliminating particular motivation and perspective that parents have brought to the boards of agencies serving children.

There may be related problems at the community or state level. Many programs of active habilitation are sold to legislative and funding bodies on the basis that they will reduce care cost to the community. For example, the cost of establishing community residences is justified because the lifetime expense of supporting a mentally retarded individual in a group home is much less than the cost of maintaining that individual in an institution. The per diem cost differential can range as high as $100 or more. When these costs are projected over a lifespan that may be 50 years or longer, the case for community programs is strong in fiscal as well as in humanistic terms. Although a similar argument might be made for serving elderly mentally retarded individuals, it is unlikely that it can be made as dramatically as was the case for deinstitutionalization of younger persons.

Some of the problems found by the community agency working with aging mentally retarded individuals have been outlined. Many of these problems are organizational, such as the application of inappropriate service regulations. Some of the problems are professional, such as the lack of an adequate service model. Other problems relate to the perceptions and motivation of staff, board, and community. In the process of dealing with these problems, some of their origins should be examined.

PROBLEM ORIGINS

One set of problems discussed was concerned with the apparent blindness of the community to the needs of elderly mentally retarded individuals. It may well be the case that such blindness cannot be avoided. To gain public attention and support for a particular group, advocates need to emphasize the needs of the group members, the similarity of group members to each other, and their dissimilarity to other groups reached by existing services. A dramatic image of the group's needs is also likely to stir the public and their officials to establish the services required. Such advocacy necessarily creates somewhat of a stereotype, as the public cannot be expected to learn the real and potential individual differences of the group members. It also forces community services to be designed as reactions, often overreactions, to dramatic problems, rather than as the routine meeting of individual client needs in day-to-day agency functioning. To avert the problems dramatically publicized by the advocates (such as the problems associated with institutionalization), public agencies write regulations based on yesterday's advocacy; these in turn create problems for today's clients. For example, the mandate of active programming is the result of a strong reaction to the many years of institutional treatment of mentally retarded clients.

It is unlikely that it could be any other way, since very often, services get created only when advocates emerge. Perhaps the greatest problem in meeting the needs of aging mentally retarded individuals is that there is no satisfactory advocate for their needs. With their handicapping conditions and limited power in the service system, the majority of mentally re-

tarded persons have always been dependent on others to voice their concerns and to demand action. Primarily, advocacy for mentally retarded people has been the result of parents organizing chapters of the ARC and similar disability organizations. With the elderly mentally retarded client, however, parents are either deceased or are old themselves and have their own aging needs, so that their impact on the service system is lessened and their own family resources are limited. It is the professionals and agency service providers who are then left to advocate for the needs of the elderly mentally retarded client. This places the staff of the community agency in a compromising position, since advocacy may involve working against the immediate interests of the agency.

Some of the problems associated with the community agencies' service of aging mentally retarded individuals may have personal or psychological causes. One such cause is the tendency to stereotype, to perceive individuals by their group membership, ignoring individual differences. Mentally retarded persons are especially susceptible to being stereotyped, as witnessed by the assumptions often made that they all have short attention spans, enjoy children's activities, and work well at simple repetitive tasks.

Unfortunately, another group very much stereotyped is elderly individuals. There are many assumptions made about the characteristics, needs, and preferences of elderly persons that often get built into programs and services. Although stereotyped perceptions may be correct in many cases, for many individuals they are not. Programs based on stereotyped assumptions are a disservice to many individual clients. Because stereotypes are often unconscious, it is difficult to know when they are influencing programs. Persons who are both mentally retarded and elderly are likely to suffer double stereotyping.

It is often hypothesized that in order to work effectively with elderly persons, individuals must come to terms with their own aging. This psychological phenomenon may influence the ways in which community agencies work with aging mentally retarded people because it affects the behavior of board and staff members. The processes of identification and projection may be more intense with aging mentally retarded clients since aging is something that affects everyone.

POSSIBLE RESOLUTIONS

Several of the problems faced by community agencies serving aging mentally retarded clients have been discussed, with some attention focused on their history and origins. It may be possible to draw some conclusions and make some recommendations regarding the service of aging mentally retarded persons.

One lesson that may be learned from a historical perspective is that problems are unavoidable. Services to mentally retarded individuals have not followed a linear path from a primitive beginning through a progressively better, always more effective series of models. Rather, community services have followed a pendulum path, sometimes more, sometimes less effective, but always making and remaking errors of perception, service, and goal. Progress has not brought care providers any closer to the one true way of serving mentally retarded persons than they were decades, or even centuries, ago.

One reason for this lack of progress may be that there is not "one true way," although service models and regulations often appear to make that assumption. There is strong pressure to stereotype, to design programs and write regulations that obliterate the individual differences among people sharing the same disability. If that pressure can be revised and resisted, the aging mentally retarded person will be better served.

Care providers should also not be too quick to change models in hopes that a new mold will fit better. Developmental models should not be discarded because, at first glance, it is not possible to see how aging mentally retarded persons develop. Normalization concepts should not be dismissed too quickly, nor should they be used to force aging mentally retarded individuals into generic nursing homes.

Increasing the awareness of the influence of psychological processes on the behavior of both board and staff may lead to more effective methods for meeting the needs of elderly mentally retarded persons. While stereotypes and fears that lead to distortions and defenses cannot be avoided, an increase in the awareness of how psychology affects actions brings what happens under conscious control.

Finally, care providers should look to history, and to the organized observation of history that is research, for guidance as to how to proceed. Community agencies must plan and build programs for the future without knowing what the future will hold. Knowing more about the past may make for better plans and decisions. A vigorous and committed community agency can overcome problems and provide worthwhile services to the individual clients it serves and to the community of which it is a part.

Community-based agencies have had a significant role in serving mentally retarded persons, especially as the deinstitutionalization movement has placed more and more mentally retarded persons in the community. Despite continuing problems that will arise from a variety of institutional, professional, and personal sources, community agencies should continue to have an important role in meeting the needs of aging and elderly mentally retarded persons.

REFERENCES

Fernald, W. (1917). The growth of provision for the feebleminded in the United States. *Mental Hygiene, 1,* 34–59.

Fernald, W. (1920). An out-patient clinic in connection with a state institution for the feeble-minded. *Journal of Psycho-Asthenics, 20,* 81–89.

Jones, K. (1984). *Day services for the elderly developmentally disabled in Erie County.* Unpublished masters project, State University of New York at Buffalo, Buffalo, NY.

Pezzoli, J. (1978). National Association for Retarded Citizens and the aged developmentally disabled person.

In R. Segal (Ed.), *Consultation-conference on developmental disabilities and gerontology* (pp. 202–212). Ann Arbor, MI: Institute for the Study of Mental Retardation and Related Disabilities, University of Michigan.

President's Panel on Mental Retardation. (1963). *Bibliography of world literature on mental retardation.* Washington, DC: U.S. Department of Health, Education, and Welfare.

Willer, B., & Intagliata, J. (1984). *Promises and realities for mentally retarded citizens.* Baltimore: University Park Press.

chapter

26

Some Observations from the Field of Aging

Rose Dobrof

The increase in the lifespan of developmentally disabled individuals brings with it new challenges for the professionals working in the field of developmental disabilities. First, on both cognitive and emotive levels, workers in the field now are confronted with the need to examine their own feelings about aging and older persons, and to work on a developmental approach to the later years of intellectually limited people. Second, effective work with older developmentally disabled individuals requires attention also to their elderly parents (not just to the impact of the infirmities and eventual death of the parents on developmentally disabled persons) and to the fact that the parents are older people, facing life's last crisis—their own mortality.

I WRITE FROM a perspective that is somewhat different from the vantage points of the other authors whose writings are included in this volume. I am a social worker by profession whose area of concentration for the last 24 years has been in the field of aging. Prior to my entry into this field, I had worked in settlement houses and community centers, in a large state mental hospital, and in a state-sponsored clinic for the treatment of alcoholics. In none of these settings did I come in direct professional contact with developmentally disabled people or their families. Hence, my lack of knowledge about or direct practice in the field of developmental disabilities requires notation here, although it is not unlikely that the deficits in my knowledge will soon become apparent to the reader.

From the perspective of my location in the field of aging, there are two subject areas that I discuss in this chapter: the first has to do with

the attitudes of professionals who work with older developmentally disabled people, and the second is in the nature of a plea to professionals in this field to attend to the special needs of the elderly parents of adult developmentally disabled children.

ATTITUDES OF PROFESSIONALS WORKING WITH OLDER DEVELOPMENTALLY DISABLED PERSONS

In his brilliant, Pulitzer prize winning book, *Why Survive? Being Old in America,* Robert Butler (1975) writes of "ageism," which he first defined in 1968 as:

a process of systematic stereotyping of and discrimination against people because they are old, just as racism and sexism accomplish this with skin color and gender. Old people are categorized as senile, rigid in thought and manner, old fash-

411

ioned in morality and skills. Ageism allows the younger generations to see older people as different from themselves; thus they subtly cease to identify with their elders as human beings. (p. 12)

Dr. Butler's words will undoubtedly have resonance for workers in the field of developmental disabilities, for surely the people with whom they work have also been subjected to "systematic stereotyping and discrimination," and are often seen as different and not identified as human beings. Indeed, it seems to me that professionals in the fields of developmental disabilities and aging share a common ethos and struggle: both have fought valiantly for public recognition of the humanness of the people with whom they work and for acceptance of them as unique individuals, each with an individual family and life history with personal characteristics and idiosyncrasies that are part of their personhood, making them deserving of understanding and respect.

Professionals in the field of aging are working hard to define a conceptually sound and empirically tested developmental approach to the later years of the life cycle, an approach that can challenge the view that *development,* in the sense of movement toward increasing individuation, complexity of personality, deepening and widening of interests, skills, and knowledge, is a process limited to the early years of the life cycle. "Old people are just like they were when they were young—only more so!" is a familiar statement of one of the stereotypic attitudes that Butler included in his discussion of ageism. Clearly the view of older people as rigidly adhering to the "thoughts and manners" of their youth, "old fashioned in morality and skills" because they cannot accept change or develop new skills is a view of the later years that allows no room for the notion of these years as being anything except a time of steady state, followed by decline and death.

Haven't all professionals who work with developmentally disabled individuals fought a similar battle? They also have had to work on a developmental approach that takes into account the disabilities, but that also focuses on the potentials for growth; they too have searched for evidence to support optimism; and they have had to fight against a public (and unfortunately, often a professional) view of "the retarded" as a homogeneous group of people for whom custodial care is the only humane alternative, and hope is a chimera existing only in the minds and hearts of parents and others who refuse to accept the reality of hopelessness.

Theirs has been a noble struggle and, although it is not over, the evidences of successes are clear. Now, they are confronted with a new challenge. They can believe, and they can provide the evidence that makes other people understand, that the developmentally disabled child or teenager or young adult is educable; can go to school and learn; can develop skills and behaviors that would permit participation in the labor force, independent living, even love and marriage. But now the lifespan of developmentally disabled persons is increasing and professionals are challenged to believe and to provide evidence that the older mentally retarded person is worthy of attention, that maintenance of functional capabilities is a treatment goal at least as important as is the development of those capabilities, that the later years in the lives of developmentally handicapped individuals can be, as they can be for other people, good years.

In "The Reluctant Therapist" in *New Thoughts on Old Age,* Robert Kastenbaum (1964) wrote about the unwillingness of members of the helping professions to engage in therapeutic relationships with older people. Kastenbaum argued that there are "unexamined attitudes which psychotherapists frequently hold in respect to the aged" that he divided into three sets for purposes of his discussion. The first had to do with the low status of older people in society and the therapist's fear that she or he will be tarred with the same brush because of her or his association with the stigmatized old person.

The second set, Kastenbaum wrote, "centers around the satisfactions and anxieties of the clinician" (p. 141). The anxieties and pain that work with older people triggers in clinicians are real. They have to deal first with the "intimations of our own mortality," with the necessity to face what Ernest Becker, in his seminal book, *The Denial of Death* (1973), called the existential dilemma or paradox of the human being, "the condition of individuality within finitude." The paradox is not one that professionals who work in the field of aging can escape, and this is one source of their pain and anxiety.

Finally, Kastenbaum wrote that "The third set of attitudes . . . is concerned with a basic conflict in established values" (p. 142). On the one hand is the seemingly practical question of whether the investment of scarce time and expertise in work with a person who will soon be dead is worth it. Yet the countervailing value, and one that all helping professions subscribe to, has to do with the worth of each person, a worth not measured in terms of the anticipated duration of the individual's life. What I am suggesting is that professionals who have confronted their own and society's negative stereotyping of developmentally disabled individuals must now deal with the complex set of attitudes that everyone has about older people, aging, and death. Professionals in the field of aging have learned that when they fail to deal with these complicated attitudes, they subvert and corrupt their ability to be helpful professionals. They, and the people with whom they work, suffer from this failure.

SPECIAL NEEDS OF
ELDERLY PARENTS OF
DEVELOPMENTALLY DISABLED ADULTS

As professionals in the field of developmental disabilities think about the needs of older developmentally disabled persons, my plea is that they attend also to the needs of their elderly parents. Workers in agencies serving older people have been reporting with increasing frequency that their clientele includes numbers of parents in their 70s and 80s who come to them seeking help in making arrangements for their developmentally disabled children. It is often the case, these workers say, that these are parents who kept their retarded children at home with them, and not infrequently, they are

people who say that they never connected with the services designed for their children. Or if they did, the connection was made years before and not maintained.

From the vantage point of the professional working with the 50- or 60-year-old mentally retarded person, the understandably central concern is for that person. Who will provide the care and love and shelter and food and clothing that the old parents may even now be less able to provide as they face the infirmities and illnesses associated with the aging process? And who will be the responsible people for the developmentally disabled adult child when the parents die? And along with these concrete problems, how is the adult child facing the infirmities of the parent and how will the child cope emotionally with the death of the parent?

That these are among the central issues that workers in the field of developmental disabilities must address cannot be denied. Yet my colleagues and I in the field of aging would ask that the needs of the parent receive attention also. Much can be gained from Erik H. Erikson's (1980) formulation of the life cycle and the "psychosocial crises" that mark the path from birth to death. He conceptualized the crisis of the later years as the polarity of "integrity versus despair and disgust." Integrity in old age, he wrote, means:

> the acceptance of one's own and only life cycle and of the people who have been significant to it as something that had to be and that, by necessity permitted of no substitutions. . . . [T]he lack of or loss of this accrued ego integration is signified by despair and an often unconscious fear of death: the one and only life cycle is not accepted as the ultimate of life. Despair expresses the feeling that the time is short, too short for the attempt to start another life and to try out alternate roads to integrity. (pp. 104–105)

This is a definition of the normative crisis of old age, a conceptualization of the tasks everyone faces as he or she confronts Becker's paradox of individuality within finitude. For no one is this easy, yet most people finally achieve acceptance of their "one and only life cycle," the historical inevitability of what *was*.

But the elderly parents of developmentally disabled children, like their children, face a different kind of crisis. Unlike other parents, their tasks of caring for their children are not yet done. The psychological separation of child from parent may not have been achieved, and the ideal relationships between adult child and parent—the relationship that Margaret Blenkner called "filial maturity" (Blenkner, 1965) may not be possible. The elderly parents may never have come to terms with the reality of the disability of their children, and unresolved feelings of guilt and anger and self-blame (in Erikson's words "the lack or loss of accrued ego integration") may be a blight on the old parents' declining years.

Professionals in the aging network say that these elderly parents who come to the senior centers, nutrition programs, and area aging agencies for help characteristically frame their pleas for help in concrete terms.

An 86-year-old widow, mother of a 48-year-old developmentally disabled son, same to a Catholic Charities office on aging for help. She was facing the possibility of hospitalization, she said, and needed someone to stay with her son while she was in the hospital. As the worker began helping her make these arrangements, her client told her of the recent death of her only living relative other than her son. Her younger brother, in his 70s when he died, had helped her care for her son, and she told the worker she had always thought he would be there for her son after she died. Now there was no one—not just for the time she would be in the hospital, but for the years her son would live after she was gone. When she thought about this, she told the worker, she felt only despair. Why had this happened to her? What was she to do now? The hospitalization that had brought the client to the agency turned out not to be necessary, and the worker was able to help her find out what resources were available in the community.

The worker wrote in her final summary:

But mostly, we talked about her life, and tried to work through her feelings about having had a retarded child–her only one. She couldn't seem to

let go of the questions of why me, and what's to happen when I'm gone. And she was still mourning the loss of her beloved younger brother: there was the grief work she needed to do and it was complicated by the fact that she had relied on him to care for her son after her death. We spent much of our time together sorting this out."

Many of the older people who come to the aging agencies are like the mother in this report; they ask for concrete services, both for now and the future. The provision of these services often becomes the matrix for the struggle to achieve ego integrity, to escape the despair that reflects the inability to accept "one's own and only life cycle and the people who have been significant to it."

CONCLUSIONS

There are two quite specific items that I would like to suggest for consideration. First, professionals in the field of developmental disabilities should give serious attention to the service needs of the elderly parents of their 50- and 60-year-old clients. This means that the parents must be seen not just in terms of what they do for their children, not just as resources or supports that must be shored up and finally compensated for or replaced when they are gone. Rather, they must be seen as individuals, facing life's last great crisis, but with the additional and tragic task of making arrangements for children who are adults, yet still dependent.

Second, systematic efforts should be made, at both the service delivery level in the community and the policy and program planning level of city, state, and federal governments, to achieve communication and linkage mechanisms between the aging and the developmental disabilities service networks. Professionals need to know each other; they need more knowledge about developmental disabilities and about service resources and treatment modalities; and with all due respect, professionals in the developmental disability field need to know about the service network for older people and about the aging process and the situation of older people in the United States today.

REFERENCES

Becker, E. (1973). *The denial of death*. New York: The Free Press.

Blenkner, M. (1965). *Social work and family relationships in later life with some thoughts on filial maturity*. Englewood Cliffs, NJ: Prentice-Hall.

Butler, R. N. (1975). *Why survive? Being old in America*. New York: Harper & Row.

Erikson, E. (1980). *Identity and the life cycle*. New York: W. W. Norton & Company.

Kastenbaum, R. (1964). The reluctant therapist. In: *New thoughts on old age*. New York: Springer Publishing Co.

Index